IBPS RRB PO & Clerk

MOCK TEST PAPERS

EXAM CHAMPION SERIES

IBPS RRB PO & Clerk

MOCK TEST PAPERS

RUPA

Rupa Publications India Pvt. Ltd 2021
7/16, Ansari Road, Daryaganj
New Delhi 110002

Sales centres:
Allahabad Bengaluru Chennai
Hyderabad Jaipur Kathmandu
Kolkata Mumbai

ISBN: 978-93-5333-794-0

First impression 2021

10 9 8 7 6 5 4 3 2 1

The moral right of the author has been asserted.

CONTENTS

PREFACE

Practice can be the one gap you have to close between yourself and your goals. Not practicing efficiently can be that one singular impediment that can hold you back and leave you wondering why others are so much better at something for which you pine. It can make the difference between good and great, mediocre and magnificent. Practicing with mocks will identify your strengths and weaknesses to help you ace the examination. After attempting the tests, you will be well aware of your progress with the topics and the speed and accuracy with which you attempt each different section. That way, in the examination, you will choose to attempt that section first at which you are good.

IBPS RRB Mock Papers for PO & Clerk Book incorporates as many as 20 practice sets: IBPS RRB PO, IBPS RRB Clerk Prelims and 10 memory-based papers of IBPS RRB PO & Clerk Prelims. These papers are prepared under the tactical guidanceof scintillating minds and expert faculties at Adda247 to provide you with the best practice material possible. Practicing with mock papers is important as it helps to familiarize aspirants with the examination pattern. It helps to ascertain how much time they spend on average in solving a particular question and avoid situations where the bottom falls out of all their strategies when they get stuck pondering over a single low-scoring question for too long, thereby overlooking other high-scoring questions. Efficient practice can be your breakaway strategy and your true path to your very own authentic success.

We would like to thank our experienced faculties, subject-matter experts and the expertise of Adda247 without whose cooperation it wouldn't have been possible to come up with this practice book for IBPS RRB PO and Clerk Exams. We hope our readers appreciate the strenuous efforts we have put into this book. Any remarks or suggestions for further refinement are wholeheartedly welcome.

Team Adda247

IBPS RRB PO PRELIMS MOCK PAPERS

REASONING ABILITY

Direction (1-5): Study the following information carefully and answer the questions given below:

Nine persons i.e. P, Q, R, S, T, U, V, W, X were born in different months i.e. January, March, April, May, July, August, September, October and November, but not necessarily in this order.

Four persons were born between P and T. P was born before T. Q was born in the month of 30 days after July. T was born after Q and before R. There were as many persons born before X as after R. One person was born between U and V. S was born before U and after W.

1. How many persons were born between X and V?
   (a) two   (b) three
   (c) one   (d) four
   (e) More than four

2. Who among the following was born in August?
   (a) R   (b) S
   (c) T   (d) P
   (c) None of these

3. In which of the following months S was born?
   (a) March   (b) April
   (c) June   (d) October
   (e) None of these

4. If W is related to April, V is related to July, then P is related to which of the following?
   (a) March   (b) May
   (c) June   (d) August
   (e) October

5. Four of the following five are alike in certain ways based on characteristics of the group. Find the one which does not belong to that group?
   (a) R   (b) S
   (c) T   (d) U
   (e) V

Direction (6-10): In each of the questions below are given some statements followed by two conclusions. You have to take the given statements to be true even if they seem to be at variance with commonly known facts. Read all the conclusions and then decide which of the given conclusions logically follows from the given statements, disregarding commonly known facts.
(a) If only conclusion I follows.
(b) If only conclusion II follows.
(c) If either conclusion I or II follows.
(d) If neither conclusion I nor II follows.

(e) If both conclusions I and II follow.

6. **Statements:**   Only a few Palace is Home. All Home is Office. No Office is Building.
   Conclusion   I. All Palace is Home is a possibility.
   II. Some Palace is Building.

7. **Statements:**   All Men is Women. Some Child is Women. No Men is Boy.
   Conclusion   I. Some Men is Child.
   II. No Men is Child.

8. **Statements:**   No Professor is Student. Only a few Student is Lecturer. All Lecturer is Principal.
   Conclusion   I. All Professor is Principal is a possibility.
   II. All Student is Lecturer is a possibility.

9. **Statements:**   Only a few Palace is Home. All Home is Office. No Office is Building.
   Conclusion   I. Some Home is Building.
   II. No Home is Building.

10. **Statements:**   No Professor is Student. Only a few Student is Lecturer. All Lecturer is Principal.
    Conclusion: I. Some Student is Principal.
    II. Some Lecturer is Professor.

Direction (11-15): Study the following information carefully and answer the questions given below:

Eight persons are sitting around a square table. Four persons are sitting at the middle of the sides of the square and all are facing inside. Remaining four are sitting at the corners and they are facing outside.

Two persons are sitting between P and U. R who is an immediate neighbour of P, sits opposite S. T sits 3rd to the right of V. W sits immediate right of T. Q faces W.

11. Who among the following sits opposite T?
    (a) P   (b) R
    (c) S   (d) W
    (e) None of these

12. How many persons are sitting between P and V when counted from left of P?
    (a) two
    (b) three
    (c) four
    (d) Either (a) or (c)
    (e) None of these

13. What is the position of Q with respect to R?
    (a) Immediate right

(b) Immediate left
(c) 2nd to the right
(d) 2nd to the left
(e) None of these

14. Who among the following persons sits 3rd to the right of Q?
(a) P
(b) U
(c) R
(d) S
(e) None of these

15. Four of the following five being alike in certain ways form a group, find the one which does not belong to that group?
(a) Q
(b) R
(c) S
(d) T
(e) U

Direction (16-17): Study the following information carefully and answer the questions given below:

Eight members are living in a family. Q is the only son of P. T is wife of U. T is sister of Q and R. V is the daughter in law of W. S is the son of T. W is the mother of Q.

16. How is S related to R?
(a) son
(b) daughter
(c) nephew
(d) niece
(e) Can't be determined

17. How many male members are in the family?
(a) four
(b) five
(c) three
(d) six
(e) None of these

18. How many such numerals are there in the number '254136987' which will remain at the same position when arranged in ascending order from left to right?
(a) one
(b) two
(c) three
(d) four
(e) None of these

19. How many pairs of letters are there in the word 'EDUCATION', each of which have as many letters between them in the word as they have between them in the English alphabet?
(a) one
(b) two
(c) three
(d) four
(e) More than four

20. If a four-letter word is formed from the 1st, 3rd, 5th and 6th letter of TRANSLATE, then what is the 3rd letter of the newly-formed word? If more than one meaningful word is formed, then the answer will be Z.
(a) L
(b) T
(c) A
(d) S
(e) Z

Directions (21-25): Read the following information carefully and answer the questions given below:

Twelve people are sitting in two parallel rows containing six people each in such a way that there is an equal distance between adjacent persons. In row 1 – P, Q, R, S, T and U are seated (but not necessarily in the same order) and all of them are facing south. In row 2 – A, B, C, D, E and F are seated (but not necessarily in the same order) and all of them are facing North. Therefore, in the given seating arrangement each member seated in a row faces another member of the other row. P faces D. U does not face A, who sits left to E but not immediate left. R sits at one of the ends and diagonally opposite B. Three persons sit between B and F, who does not face U. C sits immediate left to D but does not face S. Two persons sit between Q and U, none of them sits at the end. The one who faces T sits 2nd right to A.

21. Who among the following faces A?
(a) S
(b) T
(c) Q
(d) R
(e) None of these

22. How many persons sit to the right of R?
(a) No one
(b) one
(c) two
(d) three
(e) four

23. Four of the following five form a group. Who among the following does not belong to that group?
(a) U
(b) T
(c) E
(d) F
(e) A

24. If in a certain way R is related to C, T is related to E, then who among the following is related to D?
(a) U
(b) T
(c) E
(d) F
(e) Q

25. Who among the following sits 3rd right to U?
(a) R
(b) T
(c) P
(d) S
(e) Q

Directions (26-30): Study the following information carefully and answer the questions given below:
In a certain code language
'left right centre' is written as 'yo vo na',
'ahead below behind' is written as 'sa ra la',
'above centre right' is written as 'ha vo na', and
'behind below above' is written as 'ha ra la'.

26. What is the code for 'left'?
(a) sa
(b) ha
(c) yo
(d) na
(e) None of these

27. 'behind' will be written as?
(a) ra
(b) ha
(c) la
(d) Either (a) or (c)
(e) None of these

28. What is the code for 'ahead'?
(a) sa
(b) yo
(c) la
(d) ha
(e) Can't be determined

29. What does 'ha' stand for?
(a) behind
(b) below
(c) ahead
(d) above

(e) None of these
30. What is the code for 'centre'?
    (a) la   (b) yo
    (c) sa   (d) ha
    (e) Can't be determined

Directions (31-35): Study the following information and answer the questions given below:

There are eleven boxes placed one above the other. Five boxes are placed between F and T. Not more than five boxes are kept above T. Two boxes are kept between T and M. Three boxes are kept between M and S and M is kept at one of the positions above S. There are only three boxes kept above the box J. One box is kept between R and S. Two boxes are kept between R and H. Box D is kept at one of the positions below box K and at one of the positions above box C which is not above R. Box E is kept immediately above K.

31. How many boxes are placed between J and R?
    (a) 5   (b) 6
    (c) 3   (d) 4
    (e) None of these
32. Which of the following statements is true regarding C?
    (a) C is placed at one of the positions above D
    (b) C is placed immediately below F.
    (c) R is placed just above C
    (d) C is placed at the bottom most position
    (e) None of these
33. Which of the following is not true regarding J?
    (a) J is immediately below box T
    (b) One of the boxes below J is D

(c) Number of boxes between J and S is four
(d) One of the boxes above J is K
(e) One box is kept between J and M
34. Number of boxes above K is one less than the number of boxes below ______?
    (a) S   (b) R
    (c) F   (d) D
    (e) None of these
35. How many boxes are there between M and H?
    (a) one   (b) two
    (c) three   (d) none
    (e) More than three

Directions (36-40): In each of the questions below, relationships between some elements are shown in the statements. These statements are followed by conclusions numbered I and II. Read the statements and give the answer.
(a) If only conclusion I follows.
(b) If only conclusion II follows.
(c) If either conclusion I or II follows.
(d) If neither conclusion I nor II follows.
(e) If both conclusions I and II follow.
36. **Statements:** $C \leq L = E \leq R \leq K = P \geq O$
    Conclusions: I. $P = C$ II. $C < P$
37. **Statements:** $W > A = S \geq H < I \leq N \leq G$
    Conclusions: I. $H < W$ II. $G > H$
38. **Statements:** $C < O \leq D = S > A \geq P \geq Q$
    Conclusions: I. $Q < D$ II. $C < A$
39. **Statements:** $F \leq B = I \leq C = A \geq S > E$
    Conclusions: I. $S \geq B$ II. $F > E$
40. **Statements:** $I \geq N = T \geq E > L \geq G > M$
    Conclusions: I. $G < N$ II. $I > L$

Quantitative Aptitude

Directions (41-45): Study the table given below and answer the following questions.

Company	Total employee	Employee in HR dept	% of Female in HR dept
A	300	80	75
B	250	50	80
C	400	100	60
D	200	60	60

41. Find the average no. of females in all HR departments?
    (a) 54   (b) 46   (c) 49
    (d) 50   (e) 52
42. Females in the HR dept of company C is what % more than males in HR department of company A?
    (a) 250%   (b) 200%   (c) 100%
    (d) 300%   (e) 150%
43. If the total no. of employees in E is 25% more than D and the no. of employees in the HR dept is same as in company C, then the employees in

other than the HR dept in company E is what % of other dept employees in company B?
    (a) 60%   (b) 80%   (c) 75%
    (d) 50%   (e) 55%

44. Find the difference between males of HR dept in company C and D together and females of HR dept in company B and C together.
    (a) 36   (b) 42   (c) 48
    (d) 40   (e) 30
45. Find the average no. of employees other than the HR dept in A, B and C together.
    (a) 280   (b) 270   (c) 220
    (d) 300   (e) 240
46. If there are total 150 females in company C then how many female employees are there other than the females of the HR dept?
    (a) 90   (b) 100   (c) 80
    (d) 110   (e) 120

Directions (47-51): Find the missing term in the following number series:

47. 1864, 1521, 1305, ? , 1116, 1089
   (a) 1160   (b) 1180   (c) 1095
   (d) 1205   (e) 1220
48. 18, ?, 9, 18, 72, 576
   (a) 12   (b) 9   (c) 18
   (d) 10   (e) 6
49. 12, 6.5, 7.5, 12.75, 27.5, ?
   (a) 66.5   (b) 68.75   (c) 63.75
   (d) 71.25   (e) None of these
50. 5 , 15, 50, ?, 1030, 6185
   (a) 210   (b) 205   (c) 225
   (d) 200   (e) 195
51. 130, 154, 186 , ? , 274, 330
   (a) 216   (b) 220   (c) 240
   (d) 226   (e) 230
52. If a boat travels 18 kms. more in downstream than in upstream in 3 hrs. and if the speed of the boat in still water is 20 kms/hr., find the distance travelled by the boat in downstream in 4 hrs..
   (a) 86   (b) 92   (c) 68
   (d) 96   (e) None of these
53. If A invested Rs. 12000 at some rate of interest of S.I. and B joined him after 3 months investing 16000 at same rate of interest, if A leaves before 2 months of completion, then what will be the share of B's profit after 1 year if total profit is 22000 Rs.?
   (a) 10000   (b) 14000   (c) 12000
   (d) 8000   (e) 11000
54. If the ratio of the ages of P and Q4 years ago was 5:4 and after 12 years the sum of their ages will be 68 years, then what was P's age 2 years ago?

     (a) 24 years   (b) 22 years   (c) 18 years
     (d) 26 years   (e) 20 years
55. If Pipes A and B can fill a tank in 15 mins and 20 mins respectively and Pipe C empties the tank in 12 mins, what will be the time taken by A, B and C together to fill the tank completely?
   (a) 25 min   (b) 30 min   (c) 40 min
   (d) 20 min   (e) 35 min

Directions (56-60): Solve the given quadratic equations and mark the correct option based on your answer—

(a) $x > y$
(b) $x < y$
(c) $x \geq y$
(d) $x \leq y$
(e) $x = y$ or there is no relationship

56. **(i)** $x^2 = 81$ **(ii)** $y^2 - 18y + 81 = 0$
57. **(i)** $4x^2 - 24x + 32 = 0$ **(ii)** $y^2 - 8y + 15 = 0$
58. **(i)** $x^2 - 21x + 108 = 0$ **(ii)** $y^2 - 17y + 72 = 0$
59. **(i)** $x^2 - 11x + 30 = 0$ **(ii)** $y^2 - 15y + 56 = 0$
60. **(i)** $x^3 = 512$ **(ii)** $y^2 = 64$

61. If a shopkeeper marks an item 50% above its CP and if 12% discount is given on the marked price and the shopkeeper makes a profit of 256 Rs, then what will be the actual cost price of the item?
   (a) 1000 Rs.   (b) 800 Rs.   (c) 750 Rs.
   (d) 1200 Rs.   (e) 900 Rs.

Directions (62-67): The line graph shows the data of five sellers selling an item(in units) on Monday and Tuesday.

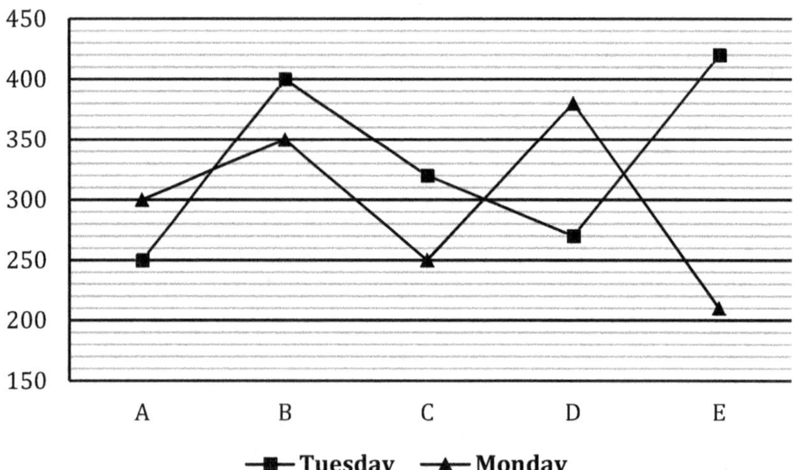

62. The no. of items sold by A and C together is how much more or less then items sold by B and D together on both days?
   (a) 250   (b) 280   (c) 300
   (d) 320   (e) 350

63. What is the average no. of items sold by all five sellers on Monday?
   (a) 298   (b) 305   (c) 280
   (d) 300   (e) 315

64. Items sold by B and C on Tuesday together is what % more than same sellers on Monday together?
(a) 25% (b) 30% (c) 20%
(d) 15% (e) 24%

65. Find the difference between items sold by B, D, E on Monday together from items sold by B and E on Tuesday together?
(a) 150 (b) 180 (c) 160
(d) 120 (e) 200

66. Item sold on Monday by C and E together is approximately what percentage of total items sold by A and B together on Tuesday?
(a) 71% (b) 80% (c) 55%
(d) 85% (e) 65%

67. Find the difference between the average items sold by A and B together on Monday from average items sold by B and C together on Tuesday?
(a) 45 (b) 35 (c) 25
(d) 40 (e) 50

68. If A starts from P with speed 60 km/hr. at 8:00 am and B starts with speed 70 km/hr. at 8:30 am from Q and the total distance between P and Q is 680 km., find out at what time they will cross each other?
(a) 2:30pm (b) 1:30pm
(c) 12:30pm (d) 3:00pm
(e) 4:00pm

69. If a person invested 6000 at T% S.I. for 3 years and the same amount at (T+5)% C.I. for 2 years and the difference between both interest is 60 Rs. then find T.(in %)
(a) 15 (b) 18 (c) 20
(d) 24 (e) 25

Direction (70−74): Read the data carefully and answer the questions.

There are 1800 students in two schools 'A' & 'B' and three streams in each school i.e. art, science and commerce. $18\frac{3}{4}$% of total students in school A are in commerce stream and $28\frac{4}{7}$% of total students in school B are in science stream. Sum of total students in commerce stream in A and science stream in B is 420. $19\frac{1}{21}$% of total students in school B are in commerce stream and 50% of total students in school A are in Art stream.

70. Total students in the art stream in A is what percent more than the total students in the science stream in B?
(a) 75% (b) 70% (c) 90%
(d) 100% (e) 110%

71. Find the ratio of total students in the commerce stream in B to total students in the science stream in A.
(a) 8:15 (b) 8:17 (c) 8:13
(d) 8:11 (e) 8:9

72. If in school C total students are 720 and total students in science stream of school C are 25% more than total students in commerce stream in school B, then find total students of art and commerce stream in school C is how much less than total students in art and commerce stream in school A?
(a) 120 (b) 110 (c) 150
(d) 100 (e) 140

73. Find the average number of students in the science stream in school A & B.
(a) 250 (b) 270 (c) 240
(d) 200 (e) 225

74. If out of total students in arts stream of school A&B, ratio of boys to girls is 5:3 and 7:4 respectively, then find difference between boys and girls in arts stream of school A & B together.
(a) 220 (b) 225 (c) 240
(d) 248 (e) 224

75. P invested 60% more than Q and R invested 20% more than Q. If the ratio of investment time-period (P: Q: R) is 2: 4: 3 and the sum of profit shares of Q and R is Rs. 8550, then find the profit share of P.
(a) Rs. 3200 (b) Rs. 4000 (c) Rs. 2400
(d) Rs. 3600 (e) Rs.3000

76. When a person sold an article, his profit percent was 60% of the selling price. If the cost price is increased by 75% and the selling price remains the same, then find decrement in the profit as percent of the selling price of the article.
(a) 25% (b) 30%
(c) 40% (d) 27.5%
(e) None of these

77. Area of Ist circle and circumference of IInd circle is 1386 cm^2 and 176 cm respectively. There is a square whose side is $35\frac{5}{7}$% of twice of sum of the radius of both the circles. Find the perimeter of the square (in cm).
(a) 132 (b) 136 (c) 140
(d) 116 (e) 124

78. There are 5 red, 6 black and 5 blue balls in a bag. Out of these balls, four balls are picked at random from the bag. Then, what is the probability that one is red, two are black and one is blue?
(a) $\frac{75}{362}$ (b) $\frac{75}{364}$ (c) $\frac{71}{362}$
(d) $\frac{70}{363}$ (e) $\frac{5}{26}$

79. An article is marked $66\frac{2}{3}$% above the cost price and loss incurred on selling that article is 25% of the discount given on it. Then, find the discount % given.
(a) $48\frac{1}{3}$% (b) $53\frac{1}{3}$% (c) $58\frac{1}{3}$%

(d) $63\frac{1}{3}\%$ (e) 60 %

80. A train travelling at 72 km/hr. crosses a platform of 160m. in 18 seconds and another train travelling at 90 km/hr. crosses the same platform in 15 seconds. Find the length of the other train.

(a) 160 m   (b) 180 m   (c) 140 m
(d) 200 m   (e) 215 m

Solutions

REASONING ABILITY

Direction (1-5):

Months	Persons
January	X
March	W
April	P
May	V
July	S
August	U
September	Q
October	T
November	R

1. **(a)**   2. **(e)**   3. **(e)**
4. **(b)**   5. **(a)**

Direction (6-10):

6. **(d)**

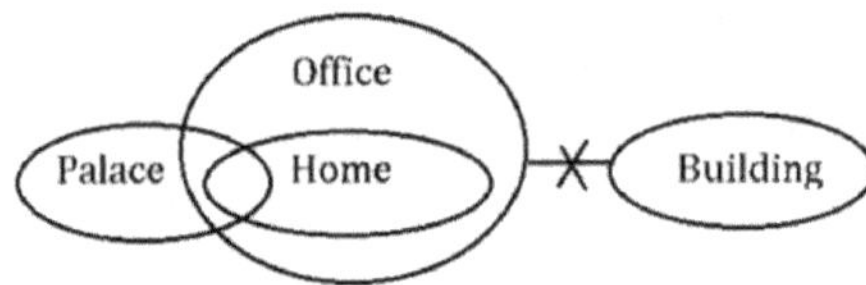

7. **(c)**

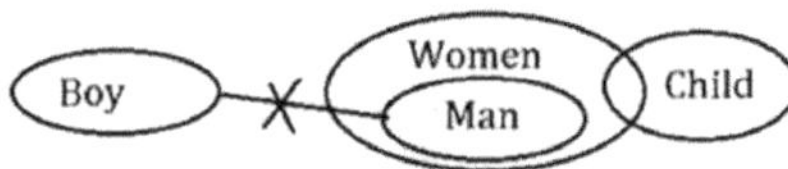

8. **(a)**

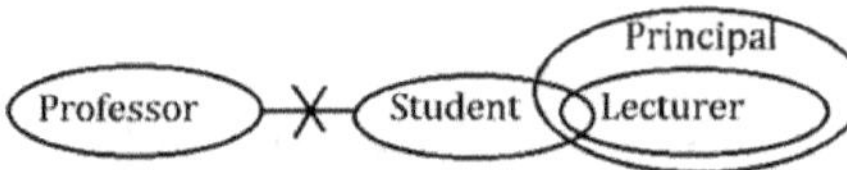

9. **(b)**

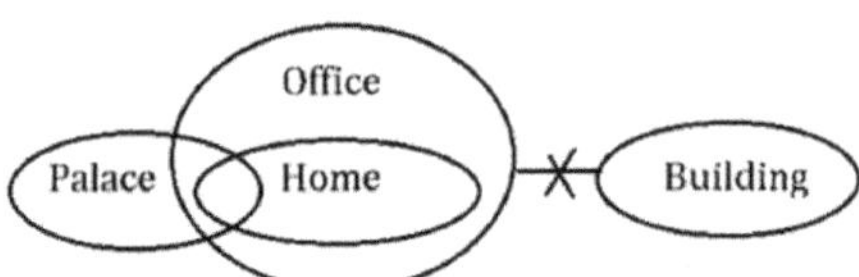

10. **(a)**

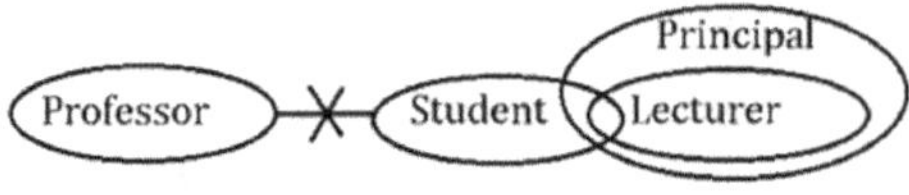

Direction (11-15):

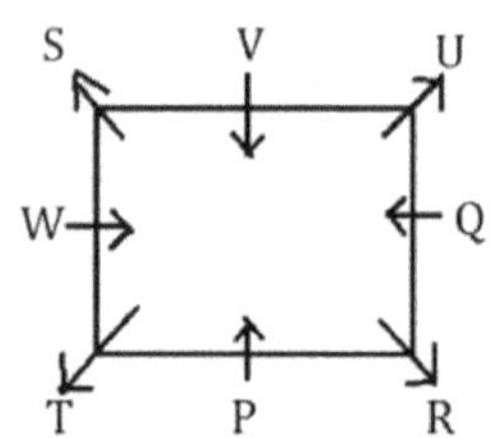

11. **(e)**   12. **(b)**   13. **(b)**
14. **(d)**   15. **(a)**

Direction (16-17):

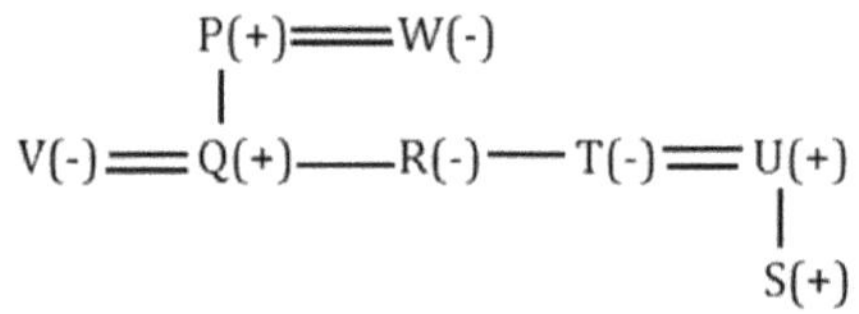

16. **(c)**   17. **(a)**
18. **(b)**

19. **(e)**

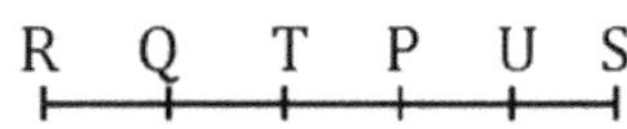

20. **(e)**

Directions (21-25):

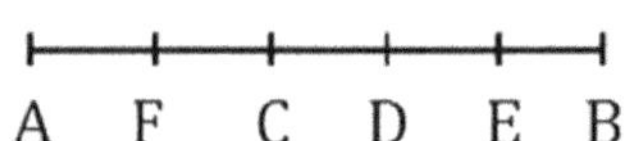

21. **(d)**   22. **(a)**   23. **(e)**
24. **(e)**   25. **(e)**

Directions (26-30):

Word	Code
Right/centre	vo/na
Left	yo
Below/behind	ra/la
Ahead	sa
above	ha

26. (c) **27. (d)** **28. (a)**
29. (d) **30. (e)**

Directions (31-35):

Boxes
E
K
T

J
H
M
D
R
F
S
C

31. (c) **32. (d)** **33. (c)**
34. (c) **35. (d)**

Direction (36-40):
36. (c) I. P = C (False) II. C < P (False)
37. (e) I. H < W (True) II. G > H (True)
38. (a) I. Q < D (True) II. C < A (False)
39. (d) I. S ≥ B (False) II. F > E (False)
40. (a) I. G < N (True) II. I ≥ L (False)

Quantitative Aptitude

41. (c) Average no. of females in HR dept
$$= \frac{80 \times \frac{75}{100} + 50 \times \frac{80}{100} + 100 \times \frac{60}{100} + 60 \times \frac{60}{100}}{4}$$
$$= \frac{60+40+60+36}{4} = \frac{196}{4} = 49$$

42. (b) Females in company C (HR) = $100 \times \frac{60}{100}$ = 60

Males in company A (HR) = $80 \times \frac{25}{100}$ = 20

Difference = 60 – 20 = 40

$\therefore$ % = $\frac{40}{20} \times 100$ = 200% more

43. (c) Total employee in E = $200 \times \frac{125}{100}$ = 250

$\therefore$ employee of HR dept in E = 100

$\therefore$ other employee = 150

$\therefore$% of other employee = $150 \times \frac{100}{200}$ = 75%

44. (a) Males in HR dept in C and D
$$= 100 \times \frac{40}{100} + 60 \times \frac{40}{100} = 40 + 24 = 64$$
Females in HR dept of B and C = $50 \times \frac{80}{100} + 100 \times \frac{60}{100}$ = 100

$\therefore$ Difference = 100 – 64 = 36

45. (e) Average of A, B, C = $\frac{220+200+300}{3} = \frac{720}{3}$ = 240

46. (a) Total females in company C = 150

Females in HR department in company C = $100 \times \frac{60}{100}$ = 60

Therefore, females other than in HR department = 150-60= 90

47. (b)

1864 1521 1305 **1180** 1116 1089

–343 –216 –125 –64 –27

$= -7^3$ $= -6^3$ $= -5^3$ $= -4^3$ $= -3^3$

48. (b) 18, ?, 9, 18, 72, 576

$18 \times 0.5 =$ **9**

$9 \times 1 = 9$

$9 \times 2 = 18$

$18 \times 4 = 72$

$72 \times 8 = 576$

49. (d) $12 \times 0.5 + 0.5 = 6.5$

$6.5 \times 1 + 1 = 7.5$

$7.5 \times 1.5 + 1.5 = 12.75$

$12.75 \times 2 + 2 = 27.5$

$27.5 \times 2.5 + 2.5 =$ **71.25**

50. (b) $5 \times 2 + 5 = 15$

$15 \times 3 + 5 = 50$

$50 \times 4 + 5 =$ **205**

$205 \times 5 + 5 = 1030$

$1030 \times 6 + 5 = 6185$

51. (d)

130 154 186 **226** 274 330

+24 +32 +40 +48 +56

52. (b) (Ds –Du) 3 = 18 km

Different in 1 hr. = 6km

Ds and Du

$\therefore$ Speed of boat in still water = 20 km/hr.

Ds = 23 km/hr., Du = 17 km/hr.

Distance travelled = 4 × 23 = 92 km

53. (c)

A	B
12000	16000
×10	×9
120 :	144
5 :	6

$\therefore$ B's share = $22000 \times \frac{6}{11}$ = 12000

54. (b)

P   Q

–4   5   4

+12   P+Q= 68
Age increased in 16 year = 32 years
Sum of Age of P and Q before 4 years = 36
$\therefore$ 5x + 4x = 36
X = 4
P's age 2 years ago = 5x + 2= 22 years

55. (b)

$$\begin{array}{ccc} A & B & C \\ 15 & 20 & 12 \end{array}$$

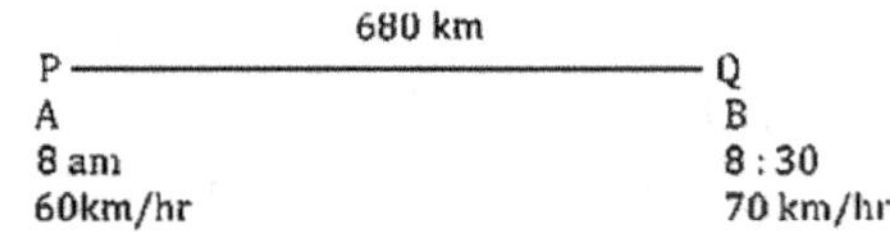

$\therefore$ tank filled in 1 min = 2 units

Total time = $\frac{60}{2}$ = 30 minutes

56. (d) $x^2 = 81$
$x = \pm 9$
$Y^2 - 18y + 81 = 0$
$(y - 9)^2 = 0$
$\therefore y = 9, 9$
$\therefore x \leq y$

57. (e) $4x^2 - 24x + 30 = 0$
$4x^2 - 16x - 8x + 32 = 0$
$4x (x - 4) - 8 (x-4) = 0$
$x = 4, 2$
$y^2 - 8y + 15 = 0$
$y^2 - 5y - 3y + 15 = 0$
$y(y - 5) - 3 (y - 5) = 0$
$\therefore y = 5, 3$
$\therefore$ No relation exists

58. (c) $x^2 - 21x + 108 = 0$
$x^2 - 9x - 12x + 108 = 0$
$x(x - 9) - 12 (x - 9) = 0$
$x = 9, 12$
$y^2 - 17y + 72 = 0$
$\therefore y^2 - 8y - 9y + 72 = 0$
$y (y - 8) - 9 (y - 8) = 0$
$\therefore y = 8, 9$
$\therefore x \geq y$

59. (b) $x^2 - 11x + 30 = 0$
$x^2 - 6x - 5x + 30 = 0$
$\therefore x(x - 6) - 5(x - 6) = 0$
$x = 6, 5$
$y^2 - 15y + 56 = 0$
$y^2 - 7y - 8y + 56 = 0$
$y (y - 7) - 8 (y - 7) = 0$
$\therefore y = 7, 8$
$\therefore x < y$

60. (c) $x^3 = 512$
$x = \sqrt[3]{512} = 8$
$y^2 = 64$
$y = \sqrt{64} = \pm 8$
$\therefore x \geq y$

61. (b) Let CP = 100 x
$\therefore$ marked price = 150x

$\therefore$ selling price after giving discount = 132x
$\therefore$ 32x = 256
x = 8
$\therefore$ CP = Rs 800

62. (b) Item sold by A and C = 550 + 570 = 1120
Item sold by B and D = 750 + 650 = 1400
$\therefore$ diff. =1400 – 1120 = 280

63. (a) Average $= \frac{300+350+250+380+210}{5} = \frac{1490}{5} = 298$

64. (c) Item sold by B and C on Monday
= 350 + 250
= 600
Item sold by B and C on Tuesday
= 400 + 320
= 720
$\therefore$ % increase = $120 \times \frac{100}{600}$ = 20%

65. (d) Items sold on Monday by B, D and E
= 350 + 380 + 210 = 940
Item sold on Tuesday by B and E = 400 + 420
= 820
$\therefore$ diff = 940 – 820 = 120

66. (a) Item sold by C and E on Monday = 250 + 210 = 460
Item sold by A and B together on Tuesday
= 400 + 250 = 650
$\therefore$? = $460 \times \frac{100}{650}$
$\simeq$ 71% (approx)

67. (b) Avg. by A and B on Monday = $\frac{650}{2}$ = 325
Avg. of B and C on Tuesday = $\frac{720}{2}$ = 360
Diff. = 360 – 325 = 35

68. (b)

$$\begin{array}{lcr} & 680 \text{ km} & \\ P & \rule{4cm}{0.4pt} & Q \\ A & & B \\ 8 \text{ am} & & 8:30 \\ 60 \text{km/hr} & & 70 \text{ km/hr} \end{array}$$

Dist travelled by A in $\frac{1}{2}$ hr = 30 km
Remaining distance to be covered = 680 – 30
= 650 km
Relative speed = 60 + 70 = 130
$\therefore$ time taken = $\frac{650}{130}$ = 5 hr
$\therefore$ time = 8 : 30 + 5 hr= 1 : 30 pm

69. (a) By going with the options
Interest received at SI = $\frac{6000 \times 3 \times 15}{100}$ = 2700 Rs
$\therefore$ T + 5 = 20%
Interest received after 2 yrs at CI
$= \frac{6000 \times 44}{100}$
= 2640

∴ Difference = 2700 – 2640 = 60 Rs

T=15%

Direction (70–74):

Let total students in A = x

And, total students in B = y

Total students in school A in commerce stream= $x \times \frac{75}{4} \times \frac{1}{100} = \frac{3x}{16}$

Total students in school B in science stream = $y \times \frac{200}{7} \times \frac{1}{100} = \frac{2y}{7}$

Given, $\frac{3x}{16} + \frac{2y}{7} = 420$ ... (i)

And $x + y = 1800$ ... (ii)

So, from (i) and (ii),

Total students in school A = 960

And total students in school B = 840

Total students in school B in commerce stream $= \frac{400}{21} \times \frac{1}{100} \times 840 = 160$

Total students in school A in art stream $= \frac{1}{2} \times 960 = 480$

Now, total students in school A in science stream $= 960 - \frac{3}{16} \times 960 - 480 = 300$

And total students in school B in art stream

$$= 840 - \frac{2}{7} \times 840 - 160 = 440$$

Streams	A	B
Art	480	440
Commerce	180	160
Science	300	240

70. (d) Required percentage $= \frac{480 - 240}{240} \times 100 = 100\%$

71. (a) Required ratio $= \frac{160}{300} = 8 : 15$

72. (e) Total student art & commerce stream in C $= 720 - 160 \times \frac{125}{100} = 520$

Required difference = (480 + 180) – 520 = 140

73. (b) Required average $= \frac{300+240}{2}$

$= \frac{540}{2} = 270$

74. (c) Total boys in arts stream of school A & B together

$= 480 \times \frac{5}{8} + 440 \times \frac{7}{11} = 300 + 280 = 580$

Total girls in arts stream of school A & B together

$= 480 \times \frac{3}{8} + 440 \times \frac{4}{11} = 180 + 160 = 340$

Required difference = 580 – 340 = 240

75. (d) Let the investment of Q = 100x

Investment of P = 160x

Investment of R = 120x

Ratio of profit:

P	Q	R
160x × 2	100x × 4	120x × 3
8	10	9

ATQ,

19 unit = Rs. 8550

8 unit = 450 × 8 = Rs. 3600

76. (b) Let the selling price be 250x

then, profit = 150x

CP=250x − 150x = 100x

Now, new C.P. $= 100x \times \frac{175}{100} = 175x$

New S.P. = 250x

New profit = 250x – 175x = 75x

Required % $= \frac{150x - 75x}{250x} \times 100 = 30\%$

77. (c) Circumference of any circle = $2\pi \times$ radius

Radius of 1st circle $= \sqrt{\frac{1386}{\pi}} = 21$ cm

Radius of 2nd circle $= \frac{176}{2\pi} = 28$ cm

Side of square $= \frac{5}{14} \times 2 \times (21 + 28) = 35$ cm

Perimeter of square = 4 × 35 = 140 cm

78. (b) Ways to select 4 balls out of 16 balls = 16_{C_4}

Ways to select one red balls = 5_{C_1}

Ways to select two black balls = 6_{C_2}

Ways to select one blue balls = 5_{C_1}

∴ Required probability

$= \frac{5_{C_1} \times 6_{C_2} \times 5_{C_1}}{16_{C_4}} = \frac{75}{364}$

79. (b) Let the cost price be Rs 3x

Then the marked price= Rs 5x

And let the discount given be Rs 4y

Then loss incurred= Rs y

ATQ

$3x − y = 5x − 4y$

$3y = 2x$

Marked price=Rs $\frac{15}{2}y$

Required discount % $= \frac{4y}{\frac{15}{2}y} \times 100 = 53\frac{1}{3}\%$

80. (e) Speed of 1st train $= 72 \times \frac{5}{18} = 20$ m/s

∴ Dist travelled by 1st train = 20 × 18= 360 m

∴ length of train (1st) = 360 – 160 = 200 m

Speed of 2nd train $= 90 \times \frac{5}{18} = 25$ m/s

∴ Distance travelled = 25 × 15= 375 m

∴ length of 2nd train = 375 − 160 = 215 m

REASONING ABILITY

Direction (1-5): Study the following information carefully and answer the given questions:

Eleven boxes A, B, C, D, E, F, G, H, I, J, K are kept one above the other. Box G is kept at fifth position from the top. Two boxes are kept between G and H. Box D is kept just above box H. There are as many boxes above box D as below box B. Five boxes are kept between box F and box K, which is kept at one of the positions below box G. Box A is kept at one of the positions above box F. Only one box is kept between box G and box C. Box I is kept above box E but not just above. Box E is not kept immediately above or immediately below box C.

1. What is the position of box I?
   (a) 8th from the bottom
   (b) 7th from the top
   (c) 3rd from the top
   (d) 6th from the bottom
   (e) None of these

2. How many boxes are kept between box E and box H?
   (a) seven   (b)six   (c) five
   (d) four   (e) eight

3. Which among the following statements is true regarding box J?
   (a) it is 7th from the bottom
   (b) box K is placed above box J
   (c) only two boxes are kept between box B and box J
   (d) it is kept just below box H
   (e) All are true

4. Which of the following represents the boxes kept between boxes A and I?
   (a)C, B   (b) A, K   (c) F, G
   (d) J, D   (e) None of these

5. Which of the following boxes is kept just above box B?
   (a) C   (b) K   (c) F
   (d) D   (e) None of these

Direction (6-8): Study the following information carefully and answer the given questions:

Point B is 14m. east of point A. Point C is 9m. north of point B. Point D is 12m. east of point C. Point E is 15m. south of point D. Point F is 30m. west of point E. Point G is 10m. north of point F. Point H is 18 m. east of point G.

6. If point X is 6m. south of point A, then which point is at the shortest distance from point X?
   (a) E   (b) A   (c) F

   (d) B   (e) G

7. What is the distance of point C from point H?
   (a) 9m   (b) 5m   (c) 4m
   (d) 6m   (e) 7m

8. Point B is in which direction with respect to point F?
   (a) south   (b) south-east   (c) north
   (d) north-east   (e) north-west

Direction (9-13): Study the following information carefully and answer the given questions:

Eight persons A, B, C, D, E, F, G, H are sitting around a circular table such that five of them are facing towards the centre and the rest are facing away from the centre. Three persons who are sitting between F and H, are facing the centre. C is 2nd to the right of F and faces the opposite direction to F. A sits 3rd to the left of C.G is one of the neighbours of E. Two persons sit between G and B, who is not the neighbour of H.G does not face C. G and A face the same direction but opposite to F.

9. What is the position of E with respect to A?
   (a) immediate right   (b) 5th to the left
   (c) 2nd to the right   (d) 2nd to the left
   (e) None of these

10. How many persons are sitting between C and H, when counted from the left of C?
    (a) one   (b) two   (c) three
    (d) four   (e) none

11. Four of the five are alike in a certain way. Which among the following does not belong to that group?
    (a) C   (b) B   (c) F
    (d) D   (e) E

12. Which of the following represents the immediate neighbour of G?
    (a) C   (b) B   (c) F
    (d) D   (e) A

13. Which of the following is not true regarding F?
    (a) It faces towards the centre.
    (b) E is immediate left to F.
    (c) Two persons sit between F and D, when counted from the right to D.
    (d) All are true.
    (e) No one sits between F and B.

Direction (14-18): Study the following information carefully and answer the given questions.

Certain number of persons are sitting in a row facing north. M sits 4th to the right of S. Five persons sit between M and X. T sits at one of the positions left to S. The number of persons sitting between M and U are same as between S and T. Q is 2nd from one of the extreme ends. Four persons sit between S and U. No one sits to the right of N, who is in the immediate right to P. X is 3rd left to P. Not more than two persons sit between Q and U.

14. How many persons are sitting in the row?
    (a) 17   (b) 20   (c) 24
    (d) 26   (e) 27

15. How many persons are sitting between S and T?
    (a) seven   (b) six   (c) five
    (d) four   (e) eight

16. What is the position of U from the left end?
    (a) 6th   (b) 5th   (c) 4th
    (d) 2nd   (e) 3rd

17. How many persons are sitting between Q and M?
    (a) seven   (b) eleven   (c) ten
    (d) nine   (e) eight

18. Which of the following represents the person sitting at an extreme end?
    (a) M   (b) U   (c) X
    (d) P   (e) T

19. If the second, forth, seventh and eighth letter of the word "FRACTION" are combined to form a meaningful word, then what will be the 3rd letter from the left in the so formed word. If more than one meaningful word is formed then the answer is X, if no such word is formed then answer is Z?
    (a) O   (b) X   (c) R
    (d) Z   (e) C

20. How many pairs of digits have the same number of digits between them in the number "573814269" as in the numeric series?
    (a) five   (b) four   (c) six
    (d) three   (e) more than six

Direction (21-25): Study the following information carefully and answer the given questions:

Movies of different durations are released on different days starting from Monday to Friday. Movie A was released on Tuesday. No movie was released between A and the one which was of 75-minutes duration. Only one movie was released between the one which was of 75-minutes duration and the one which was of 100-minutes duration. No movie was released between the one which was of 100 minutes and B. Only one movie released after B. B released immediately after the 100-minutes duration movie. Movie C released immediately after the one which was of 130-minutes duration. More than two movies released in between C and D. The movie which was of 90-minutes duration released before E. One of the movies was of 20 minutes more duration than E.

21. How many movies were released after E?
    (a) one   (b) two

(c) none   (d) three
(e) More than three

22. Which of the following movies was of 150-minute duration?
    (a) E
    (b) A
    (c) There is no such movie.
    (d) C
    (e) D

23. What was the total duration of movie D and E together?
    (a) 135   (b) 225   (c) 165
    (d) 175   (e) 190

24. Which of the following statements is true regarding B?
    (a) The movie released after B was of 120-minutes duration.
    (b) Two movies released between A and B.
    (c) Movie B was of 100-minutes duration.
    (d) Total duration of movie B and A was 225 minutes.
    (e) Movie A was released after B.

25. Which of the following statements is true?
    (a) The movie released before A was of 130-minutes duration.
    (b) Three movies released in between A and E.
    (c) No movie was released between A and E.
    (d) Total duration of movie C and A was230 minutes.
    (e) Movie C released was immediately after E.

Direction (26-28): Study the following information carefully and answer the given questions:

F is the husband of G. K is the mother-in-law of G. H is the Father of F. M is the mother of H, P is the mother of K and B.

26. If Y is the father of H then how is Y related to M?
    (a) mother   (b) father   (c) sister
    (d) brother   (e) husband

27. How is P related to F?
    (a) grandfather   (b) aunt   (c) mother
    (d) grandmother   (e) wife

28. How is B related to H?
    (a) sister
    (b) brother
    (c) husband
    (d) Can't be determined
    (e) wife

Direction (29-31): Study the following information carefully and answer the given questions. There are six persons M, N, O, P, Q, R of different heights. N is shorter than M but taller than Q. Only two persons are taller than M. R is taller than Q and O. Q is not the shortest. The one who is second shortest is 154cm. P is not the shortest person.

29. If M is 19cm. taller than Q, then what is the height of M?
    (a) 190cm.   (b) 181cm.   (c) 175cm.

(d) 130cm.   (e) 173cm.

30. If P is 181cm. than which of the following is true?

  I.   Only one person is taller than P.
  II. The difference between the heights of P and Q is 27cm.
  III. O is the shortest person.

  (a) only I   (b) only II and I
  (c) All are true   (d) only III and II
  (e) only III and I

31. How many persons are shorter than N?

  (a) one   (b) two
  (c) none   (d) three
  (e) More than three

Directions (32-35): Question consists of some statements followed by two conclusions. Consider the given statements to be true even if they seem to be at variance with commonly known facts. Read all the conclusions and then decide which of the given conclusions logically follows from the given statements, using all statements together.

32. Statements: All Grills are Arrow.
  Some Hat are Grills.
  Some Cell are Arrow.

  Conclusions: I. Some Cell are definitely not Grills.
  II. Some Hat can never be Arrow.

  (a) Only I follows
  (b) Only II follows
  (c) Neither I nor II follow
  (d) Both I and II follow
  (e) Either I or II follow

33. Statements: All Grills are Arrow.
  Some Hat are Grills.
  Some Cell are Arrow.

  Conclusions: I. Some Hat are Arrow.
  II. Some Grills are Cell.

  (a) Only II follows
  (b) Only I follows
  (c) Either I nor II follow
  (d) Both I and II follow
  (e) Neither I or II follow

34. Statements: Some Door are Fan.
  No Door is Rose.
  No Fan is Shelf.

  Conclusions: I. Some Fan can never be Rose.
  II. Some Rose are Shelf is a possibility

  (a) Neither I nor II follows
  (b) Only I follows
  (c) Either I or II follows
  (d) Both I and II follow
  (e) Only II follows

35. Statements: Some Door are Fan.
  No Door is Rose.
  No Fan is Shelf.

  Conclusions: I. All Door are Shelf is a possibility.
  II. All Shelf can be Door.

  (a) Either I or II follows
  (b) Only II follows
  (c) Neither I nor II follow
  (d) Both I and II follow
  (e) Only I follows

Direction (36-40): Study the following information carefully and answer the given questions:

Fourteen persons are sitting in two parallel rows such that seven persons are sitting in each row. A, B, C, D, E, F, G are sitting in row-1 facing north while P, Q, R, S, T, U, V are sitting in row-2 facing south. G sits third to the left of A and neither of them sits at an extreme end of the row. The one who faces A sits immediate right to T. Only one person sits between T and Q. The one who faces Q sits third to the right of E. S sits to the immediate left of V. S neither faces G nor E. D is an immediate neighbour of the one who faces S. The one who faces C sits fifth to the left of P. B sits third to the left of F. U sits at one position to the right of R.

36. Four of the following are alike in a certain way and so form a group. Which of the following does not belong to that group?

  (a) U   (b) B   (c) T
  (d) C   (e) P

37. How many persons sit between F and C?

  (a) one   (b) two
  (c) none   (d) three
  (e) More than three

38. Which of the following is not true regarding U?

  (a) No one sits to the right of U.
  (b) U sits third to the right of Q.
  (c) P is an immediate neighbour of U.
  (d) E is an immediate neighbour of the one who faces U.
  (e) Only two persons sit between U and S.

39. What is the position of C with respect to A?

  (a) Second to the left
  (b) Third to the right
  (c) Immediate right
  (d) Immediate left
  (e) Second to the right

40. What is the position of B with respect to D?

  (a) Third to the left
  (b) Second to the left
  (c) Fourth to the left
  (d) Third to the right
  (e) Fifth to the right

Directions (41-45): Find the wrong number in the following number series?

41. $1, 3, 7, 15, 31, 64, 127$
   (a) 1   (b) 3   (c) 15
   (d) 64   (e) 127

42. $1, 15, 119, 475, 949, 947, 473$
   (a) 947   (b) 475   (c) 15
   (d) 473   (e) 1

43. $250, 260, 291, 314, 340, 370, 405$
   (a) 370   (b) 314   (c) 260
   (d) 405   (e) 250

44. $750, 535, 411, 348, 322, 314, 315$
   (a) 315   (b) 750   (c) 411
   (d) 348   (e) 314

45. $2, 7, 27, 107, 427, 1708, 6827$
   (a) 107   (b) 1708   (c) 2
   (d) 6827   (e) 7

Directions (46-50): Study the line-graph carefully & answer the question given below.

The line-graph given below shows the total no. of products (for kids + adults) in two different stores P & Q in five different years.

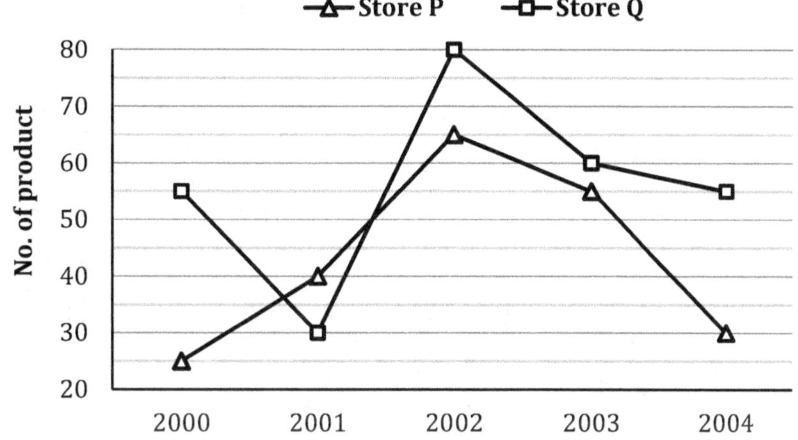

46. What is the difference between the total no. of products in store P in year 2003 &2004and the total no. of products in year 2000?
   (a) None of these   (b) 10   (c) 20
   (d) 15   (e) 5

47. If total products in both the stores in year 2006 is increased by 20% as compared to year 2004, then find the total no. of products in year 2006?
   (a) 102   (b) None of these
   (c) 96   (d) 108
   (e) 92

48. What is the ratio of total products in store Q in year 2002 & 2003 together to total products in store Q in year 2000?
   (a) 23 : 12   (b) 23 : 11   (c) 28 : 11
   (d) None of these   (e) 27 : 13

49. What is the average no. of products in all the years together in store P?
   (a) 48   (b) 43   (c) 57
   (d) None of these   (e) 53

50. Total no. of products in store P in year 2003 and in store Q in year 2004 together is what percent more/less than total no. of products in store Q in year 2000?
   (a) 150%   (b) 40%   (c) 125%
   (d) 100%   (e) 50%

Directions (51-55): Solve the given quadratic equations and mark the correct option based on your answer—

(a) $x \geq y$ (b) $x \leq y$ (c) $x > y$
(d) x = y or no relation can be established between x and y.
(e) $x < y$

51. (i) $x^2 - 20x + 96 = 0$ **(ii)** $y^2 = 64$
52. (i) $4x^2 - 21x + 20 = 0$ **(ii)** $3y^2 - 19y + 30 = 0$
53. (i) $x^2 - 11x + 24 = 0$ **(ii)** $y^2 - 12y + 27 = 0$
54. (i) $x^2 + 12x + 35 = 0$ **(ii)** $5y^2 + 33y + 40 = 0$
55. (i) $4x^2 + 9x + 5 = 0$ **(ii)** $3y^2 + 5y + 2 = 0$

Directions (56-60): Study the following paragraph carefully and answer the questions given below.

There are 1000 students in a college of which some appeared in exams 'X', 'Y' and 'Z', while others did not. Number of students who did not appear in any exam is equal to number of students who appeared in exam 'Z' only. Number of students who appeared in exam 'Y' is 360. Ratio of number of students who appeared in exam 'X' and 'Y' only to the number of students that appeared in exam 'Y' and 'Z' only is 2:3. Number of students that appeared in both exams 'X' and 'Z' is half the number of students that appeared in only exam 'Z'. Number of students that appeared in exam 'X' only is 50% more than number of students who appeared in 'Y' only. Number of students who appeared in all the three exams is 4% of the total number of students in the college. Number of students that appeared in 'Y' exam only is same as the number of students that appeared in 'Y' and 'Z' only.

56. How many students appeared in at least two exams?
(a) 240 (b) 260 (c) 300
(d) 360 (e) 500

57. How many students appeared in two exams only?
(a) 280 (b) 220 (c) 340
(d) 300 (e) 260

58. How many students appeared in at the most two exams?
(a) 240 (b) 260 (c) 300
(d) 500 (e) 960

59. How many students did not appear in exam Y?
(a) 440 (b) 360
(c) 540 (d) 640
(e) None of these

60. How many students appeared in either exam X or exam Z?
(a) 240 (b) 360 (c) 500
(d) 680 (e) 760

Direction (61-65): The bar chart given below shows the no. of tigers in different National Parks i.e. A to D of a country in two different years. Study the data carefully and answer the following questions:

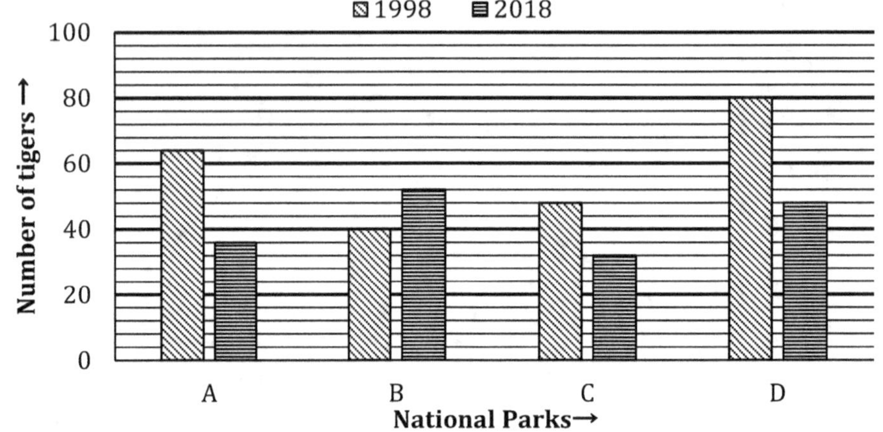

61. No. of tigers in National Park B and C together in 2018 is how much more or less than the no. of tigers in National Park A and D together in 1998?
(a) 40 (b) 44 (c) 52
(d) 60 (e) 72

62. No. of tigers in National Park 'D' in both years together is what percent of the no. of tigers in National Park 'C' in both years together?
(a) 60% (b) 160% (c) 140%
(d) 120% (e) 180%

63. Find the ratio between no. of tigers in National Park 'A' in 2018 to no. of tigers in National Park 'B' in 1998?
(a) 9:10 (b) 10:9 (c) 16:13
(d) 13:16 (e) 3:4

64. No. of tigers in National Park 'E' in 2018 is 40% more than no. of tigers in National Park 'D' in 1998 while no. of tigers in National park 'E' in 1998 is 25% less than no. of tigers in National Park 'C' in 2018. Find the total number of tigers in National park 'E' in 1998 and 2018 together.

(a) 148 (b) 84 (c) 172
(d) 160 (e) 136

65. Average no. of tigers in all National parks in 2018 is how much less/more than average no. of tigers in all National park in 1998?
(a) 14 (b) 16 (c) 18
(d) 20 (e) 22

66. The difference between the downstream speed and the upstream speed of a boat is 6 km/hr. The boat travels 72 kms. from P to Q (downstream) in 4 hours. Find the speed of the boat in still water.
(a) 15 km/hr.
(b) 18 km/hr.
(c) 20km/hr.
(d) 16 km/hr.
(e) 24 km/hr.

67. In a vessel, there are two types of liquids: A and B in the ratio of 5:9. 28 lit. of the mixture is taken out and 2 lit. of type B liquid is poured into it and the new ratio(A:B) thus formed is 1:2. Find the initial quantity of mixture in the vessel.

(a) 84 lit.	(b) 42 lit.	(c) 50 lit.
(d) 56 lit.	(e) 70 lit.

68. The average weight of 5 students in a class is 25.8 kg. When a new student joined them, the average weight increased by 3.9 kg. Find the approximate weight of the new student.
(a) 55 kg.	(b) 49 kg.	(c) 42 kg.
(d) 44 kg.	(e) 58 kg.

69. A person has purchased two adjacent plots, one rectangular in shape and the other in square shape, and combined them to make a single new plot. The breadth of the rectangular plot is equal to the side of the square plot and the cost of fencing the new plot is Rs. 390 (Rs. 5/m). Find the side of square if the length of the rectangular plot is 15 m.
(a) 10 m.	(b) 8 m.	(c) 12 m.
(d) 9 m.	(e) 6 m.

70. A shopkeeper marked his article 50% above the cost price and gave a discount of 20% on it. If he had marked his article 75% above the cost price and gave a discount of 20% on it, then the earlier profit was what percent of the profit he earned later?
(a) 50%	(b) 60%	(c) $33\frac{1}{3}$%
(d) 40%	(e) 75%

71. A person invested two equal amounts in two different schemes. In the first scheme, amount is invested at 8% p.a. on S.I. for T years and S.I. received is Rs. 2000, while in the second scheme, amount is invested at 10% p.a. for 2 years at C.I. and the compound interest received is Rs. 1050. Find the value of T.
(a) 4 yr	(b) 8 yr	(c) 6 yr
(d) 5 yr	(e) 3 yr

72. Satish saves 20% of his monthly salary. Of the remaining salary $\frac{1}{4}$th and $\frac{1}{2}$th he gives to his mother and sister respectively and the remaining salary he submits as his EMI for the payment of his car. If his annual EMI was Rs. 60,000, then find his monthly salary.
(a) Rs. 40,000	(b) Rs. 35,000
(c) Rs. 32,000	(d) Rs. 30,000
(e) Rs. 25,000

73. The sum of four times of an amount 'x' and (x – 9.75) is Rs. 442. Find the approximate value of x.
(a) Rs. 85	(b) Rs.90	(c) Rs. 100
(d) Rs. 1100	(e) Rs. 75

74. A and B entered into a partnership by investing some amounts. The investment of A is twice the investment of B. Another person C joined them after 4 months. At the end of a year, the profit share of A and C is equal. The profit share of B is what percent of the profit share of C?
(a) 50%	(b) $33\frac{1}{3}$%	(c) 40%
(d) 60%	(e) 75%

75. The ratio of the age of Ishu 8 years hence and that of Ahana 6 years hence is 5:6. The age of Ishu 10 years hence is equal to the age of Ahana 6 years hence. Then, find the present age of Ishu.
(a) 1.5 yr	(b) 2 yr	(c) 3 yr
(d) 4 yr	(e) 5 yr

76. What is the difference between 20% of P and 20% of (P + 5000).
(a) 1500	(b) 1200	(c) 1000
(d) 2000	(e) 1600

77. The ratio of the diameter of base and height of a cylinder is 2:3. Find the radius of the cylinder if the approximate volume of the cylinder is 3234.01 cm³.
(a) $\frac{21}{2}$cm.	(b) $\frac{7}{2}$cm.
(c) 21 cm.	(d) 7 cm.
(e) 14 cm.

78. A train of a certain length passes a platform of length 524m. in 55 seconds. Find the length of the train if the speed of the train is 72 km/hr.
(a) 476 m.	(b) None of these
(c) 428 m.	(d) 526 m.
(e) 576 m.

79. Efficiency of B is two times more than efficiency of A. Both started working alternatively, starting with B and completed the work in 37 days. If C alone completes the same work in 50 days then find out in how many days A and C together will complete the work.
(a) 24 days	(b) 30 days	(c) 36 days
(d) 48 days	(e) 18 days

80. 7 men and 6 women together can complete a piece of work in 8 days, while work done by a woman in one day is half the work done by a man in one day. If 8 men and 4 women started working and after 3 days 4 men left the work and 4 new women joined, then in how many more days will the work be completed?
(a) 7 days	(b) 6 days	(c) 5.25 days
(d) 6.25 days	(e) 8.14 days

Solutions

REASONING

Direction (1-5):

BOX
D
H
A
F
G
I
C
J
E
K
B

1. (d)   **2. (b)**   **3. (c)**
4. (c)   **5. (b)**

Direction (6-8):

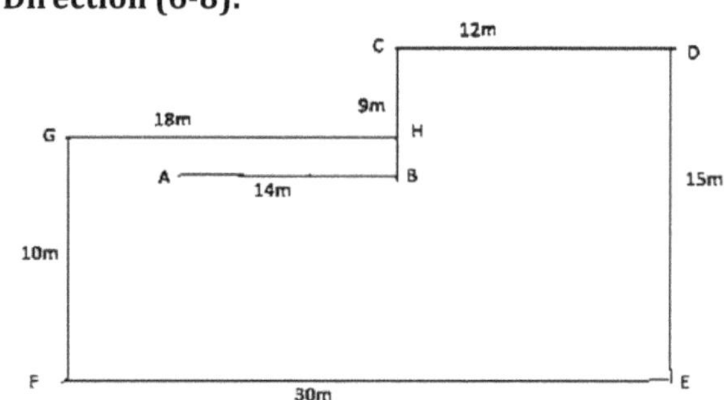

6. (c)   **7. (b)**   **8. (d)**

Direction (9-13):

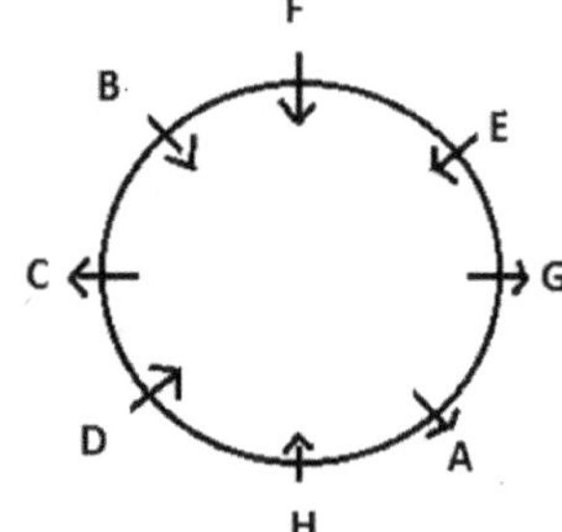

9. (d)   **10. (a)**   **11. (a)**
12. (e)   **13. (c)**

Direction (14-18):

14. (c)   **15. (e)**   **16. (b)**
17. (b)   **18. (e)**
19. (c)   2nd, 4th, 7th and 8th letters are R, C, O, N
The meaningful word formed is CORN

20. (e)

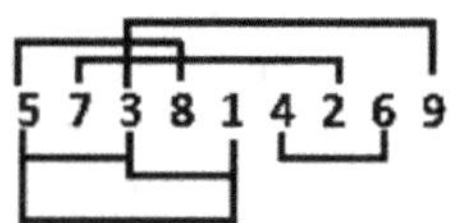

Direction (21-25):

Days	Movies	Duration
Monday	D	75
Tuesday	A	90
Wednesday	E	100
Thursday	B	130
Friday	C	120

21. (b)   **22. (c)**   **23. (d)**
24. (a)   **25. (c)**

Direction (26-28):

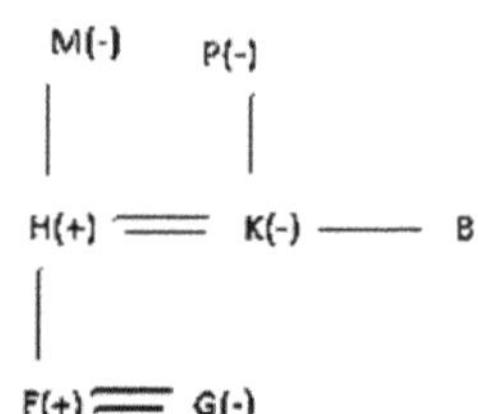

26. (e)   **27. (d)**   **28. (d)**
Direction (29-31): $R/P > R/P > M > N > Q > O$
29. (e)   **30. (d)**   **31. (b)**
Directions (32-35):
32. (c)

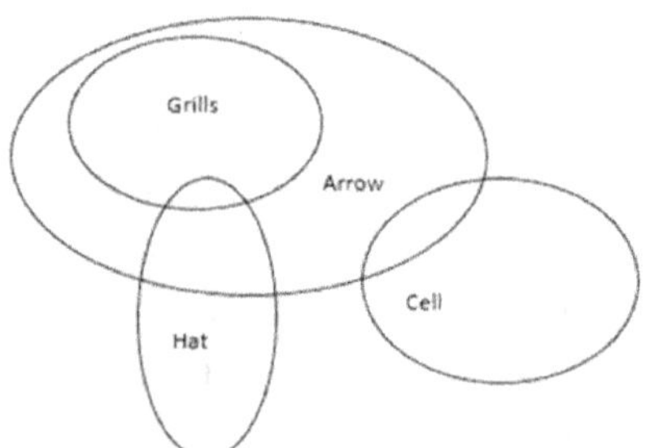

33. (b)

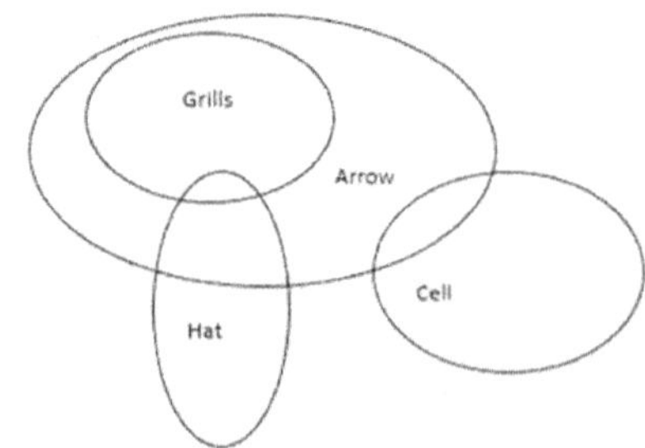

34. (d)

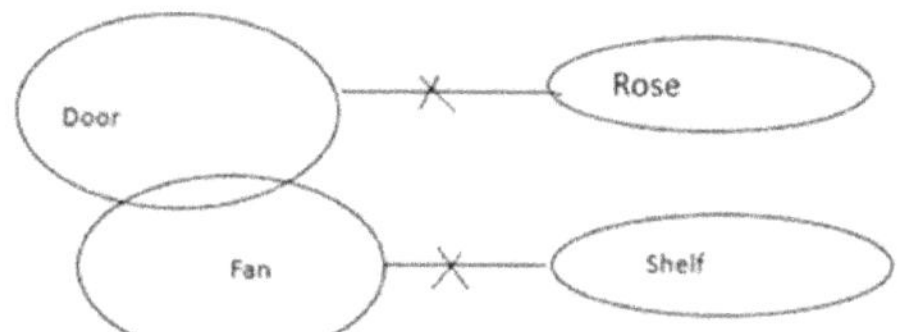

Direction (36-40):

35. (b)

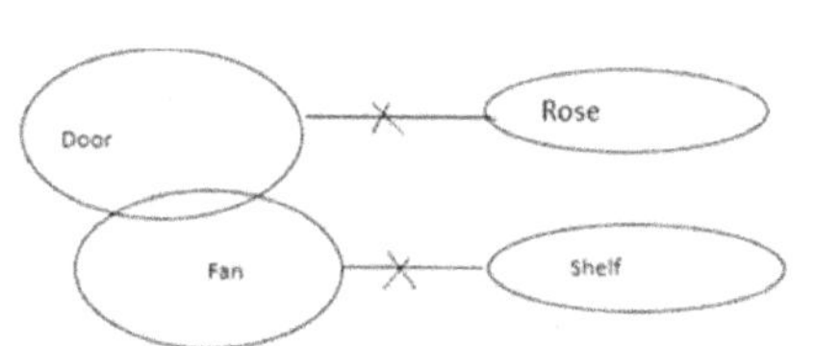

36. (e)	**37. (b)**	**38. (b)**
39. (c)	**40. (c)**	

QUANTITATIVE APTITUDE

41. (d)

$$1 \quad 3 \quad 7 \quad 15 \quad 31 \quad \boxed{64}^{63} \quad 127$$
$$\times 2+1 \quad \times 2+1 \quad \times 2+1 \quad \times 2+1 \quad \times 2+1 \quad \times 2+1$$

42. (a)

$$1 \quad 15 \quad 119 \quad 475 \quad 949 \quad \boxed{947}^{948} \quad 473$$
$$\times 16-1 \quad \times 8-1 \quad \times 4-1 \quad \times 2-1 \quad \times 1-1 \quad \times 0.5-1$$

43. (c)

$$250 \quad \boxed{260}^{270} \quad 291 \quad 314 \quad 340 \quad 370 \quad 405$$
$$+20 \quad +21 \quad +23 \quad +26 \quad +30 \quad +35$$
$$+1 \quad +2 \quad +3 \quad +4 \quad +5$$

44. (e)

$$750 \quad 535 \quad 411 \quad 348 \quad 322 \quad \boxed{314}^{315} \quad 315$$
$$-215 \quad -124 \quad -63 \quad -26 \quad -7 \quad 0$$
$$6^3-1 \quad 5^3-1 \quad 4^3-1 \quad 3^3-1 \quad 2^3-1 \quad 1^3-1$$

45. (b)

$$2 \quad 7 \quad 27 \quad 107 \quad 427 \quad \boxed{1708}^{1707} \quad 6827$$
$$\times 4-1 \quad \times 4-1 \quad \times 4-1 \quad \times 4-1 \quad \times 4-1 \quad \times 4-1$$

Alternate,

$$2 \quad 7 \quad 27 \quad 107 \quad 427 \quad \boxed{1708}^{1707} \quad 6827$$
$$+5 \quad +20 \quad +80 \quad +320 \quad +1280 \quad +5120$$
$$\times 4 \quad \times 4 \quad \times 4 \quad \times 4 \quad \times 4$$

46. (e) Required difference
$= (55 + 30) - (55 + 25) = 5$

47. (a) Total no. of products in year 2006
$= (55 + 30) \times \frac{120}{100} = 102.0$

48. (c) Required ratio
$= \frac{80+60}{55} = \frac{140}{55} = 28 : 11$

49. (b) Required Average
$= \frac{25+40+65+55+30}{5} = \frac{215}{5} = 43$

50. (d) Required percentage
$= \frac{(55 + 55) - 55}{55} \times 100$
$= \frac{55}{55} \times 100 = 100\%$

51. (a) (i) $\quad x^2 - 20x + 96 = 0$

$$x^2 - 12x - 8x + 96 = 0$$
$$x(x - 12) - 8(x - 12)$$
$$= 0$$
$$(x - 12)(x - 8) = 0$$
$$x = 12, 8$$

(ii) $\quad y^2 = 64$
$$y = \pm 8$$
$$\therefore \ x \geq y$$

52. (d) (i) $\quad 4x^2 - 21x + 20 = 0$
$$4x^2 - 16x - 5x + 20 = 0$$
$$4x(x - 4) - 5(x - 4) = 0$$
$$(4x - 5)(x - 4) = 0$$
$$x = \frac{5}{4}, 4$$

(ii) $\quad 3y^2 - 19y + 30 = 0$
$$3y^2 - 9y - 10y + 30$$
$$= 0$$
$$3y(y - 3) - 10(y - 3)$$
$$= 0$$
$$(3y - 10)(y - 3) = 0$$
$$y = \frac{10}{3}, 3$$

$\therefore$ No relation can be established between x and y

53. (d) (i) $\quad x^2 - 11x + 24 = 0$
$$x^2 - 8x - 3x + 24 = 0$$
$$x(x - 8) - 3(x - 8) = 0$$
$$(x - 3)(x - 8) = 0$$
$$x = 3, 8$$

(ii) $\quad y^2 - 12y + 27 = 0$
$$y^2 - 9y - 3y + 27 = 0$$
$$y(y - 9) - 3(y - 9) = 0$$
$$(y - 9)(y - 3) = 0$$
$$y = 9, 3$$

$\therefore$ No relation can be established between x and y

54. (b) (i) $\quad x^2 + 12x + 35 = 0$
$$x^2 + 7x + 5x + 35 = 0$$

$$x(x+7) + 5(x+7) = 0$$
$$(x+7)(x+5) = 0$$
$$x = -7, -5$$

(ii) $5y^2 + 33y + 40 = 0$
$$5y^2 + 25y + 8y + 40$$
$$= 0$$
$$5y(y+5) + 8(y+5) = 0$$
$$(y+5)(5y+8) = 0$$
$$y = -\frac{8}{5}, -5$$
$$\therefore y \geq x$$

55. (b) **(i)** $4x^2 + 9x + 5 = 0$
$$4x^2 + 4x + 5x + 5 = 0$$
$$4x(x+1) + 5(x+1) = 0$$
$$(4x+5)(x+1) = 0$$
$$x = -1, -\frac{5}{4}$$

(ii) $3y^2 + 5y + 2 = 0$
$$3y^2 + 3y + 2y + 2 = 0$$
$$3y(y+1) + 2(y+1) = 0$$
$$(3y+2)(y+1) = 0$$
$$y = -\frac{2}{3}, -1$$
$$\therefore y \geq x$$

Solutions (56-60):

Total students = 1000

Let, students that appeared in exam Z only = a

Total students appeared in exam Y = 360

Ratio of number of students appeared in exam X and Y only to students appeared in exam Y and Z only = 2:3

Students appeared in exam X and Z both = a/2

Number of students appeared in all three exams
$$= \frac{4}{100} \times 1000 = 40$$

Number of students appeared in Y exam only
= No. of students appeared in Y and Z only = 3x

Number of students appeared in exam X and Y only
$$= \frac{2}{3} \times 3x = 2x$$

1000

X   Y (360)

4.5x   2x   3x

40

$\frac{a}{2}$ a   3x

Z

a

Now, 2x + 3x + 3x + 40 = 360
$$\Rightarrow x = 40$$

$$and, 12.5x + a + \frac{a}{2} + a = 1000$$
$$\frac{5a}{2} = 500$$
$$\Rightarrow a = 200$$

1000

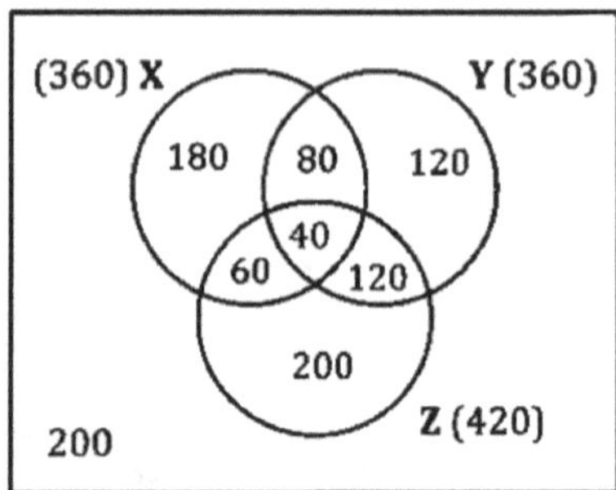

56. (c) Students appeared in at least two exams
= 80 + 60 + 40 + 120 = 300

57. (e) Students appeared in two exams only = 80 + 60 + 120 = 260

58. (e) Students appeared in at most two exams
= 180 + 120 + 200 + 60 + 80 + 120 + 200 = 960

59. (d) Student not appeared in exam Y
= 1000 – 360 = 640

60. (d) Students appeared in exam X or in exam Z
= 180 + 60 + 40 + 80 + 200 + 120 = 680

61. (d) Number of tigers in National Park B and C together in 2018 = 52 + 32 = 84
Number of tigers in National Park A and D together in 1998
= 64 + 80 = 144
Required difference = 144 − 84 = 60

62. (b) Number of tigers in National Park D in 1998 and 2018 together = 80 + 48 = 128
Number of tigers in National Park C in 1998 and 2018 together = 48 + 32 = 80
Required % = $\frac{128}{80} \times 100 = 160\%$

63. (a) Required Ratio = $\frac{36}{40} = \frac{9}{10}$

64. (e) Number of tigers in National Park E in 2018 = $\frac{140}{100} \times 80 = 112$
Number of tigers in National Park E in 1998 = $\frac{75}{100} \times 32 = 24$
Number of tigers in National Park E in 1998 and 2018 together
= 112 + 24 = 136

65. (b) Total number of tigers in 2018
= 36 + 52 + 32 + 48 = 168
Total number of tigers in 1998
= 64 + 40 + 48 + 80 = 232
Required difference = $\frac{232}{4} - \frac{168}{4}$
$$= \frac{64}{4} = 16$$

66. (a) Let the speed of boat in still water be x km/hr

and that of stream be y km/hr

ATQ,

$(x + y) - (x - y) = 6$

$\Rightarrow 2y = 6 \Rightarrow y = 3$ km/hr

Downstream stream = $(x + y) = \frac{72}{4} = 18$ km/hr

$\Rightarrow x = 15$ km/hr

67. (d) Let the initial quantity of mixture in vessel be x lit

ATQ,

$\dfrac{x \times \frac{5}{14} - 10}{x \times \frac{9}{14} - 18 + 2} = \dfrac{1}{2}$

$\Rightarrow \dfrac{5x - 140}{9x - 224} = \dfrac{1}{2}$

$\Rightarrow 10x - 280 = 9x - 224$

$\Rightarrow x = 56$ lit

68. (b) Weight of new student = $6 \times (25.8 + 3.9) - 5 \times 25.8$

≈ 49 kg

69. (c)

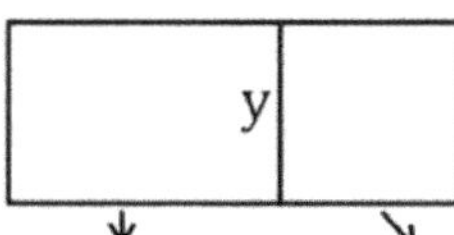

rectangular   square plot

plot

Let the breadth of rectangular plot be y m and length = 15 m

ATQ,

$30 + y + 3y - 390/5$

$\Rightarrow 30 + 4y = 78$

$\Rightarrow 4y = 48 \Rightarrow y = 12$ m

70. (a) Let the CP be Rs. 100x

Then, MP = Rs. 150x

SP = $150x \times \dfrac{80}{100}$ = Rs. 120x

Profits = Rs. 20x

New MP = Rs. 175x

New SP = $175x \times \dfrac{80}{100}$ = Rs. 140x

New Profit = Rs. 40x

Required % = $\dfrac{20x}{40x} \times 100 = 50\%$

71. (d) Let the amount be Rs. x

CI at 10% in 2 years = $10 + 10 + \dfrac{10 \times 10}{100}$

= 21%.

ATQ,

$\dfrac{x \times 21}{100} = 1050 \Rightarrow x = $ Rs. 5000

And,

$\dfrac{5000 \times 8 \times T}{100} = 2000$

$\Rightarrow T = 5$ years.

72. (e) Let the monthly salary be Rs. 100 x.

EMI per month

$= 100x - \left(20x + 80x \times \frac{1}{4} + 80x \times \frac{1}{2}\right) = $ Rs. 20x

ATQ,

$20x \times 12 = 60,000$

$\Rightarrow x = 250$

Monthly Salary = Rs. 25,000

73. (b) ATQ,

$4x + x - 9.75 = 442$

$5x = 451.75$

$x = $ Rs. 90

74. (a) Let the investment of B be Rs. x

$\therefore$ investment of A = Rs 2x

Ratio of profit,

$\quad A \quad : \quad B \quad : \quad C$

$12 \times 2x : 12 \times x : 8 \times y$

ATQ,

$24x = 8y$

$y = 3x$

$\therefore$ Required percentage = $\dfrac{12 \times x}{8 \times 3x} \times 100$

= 50%

75. (b) Let present age of Ishu & Ahana be x year & y year respectively

$\therefore$ ATQ,

$\dfrac{x + 8}{y + 6} = \dfrac{5}{6}$

$6x + 48 = 5y + 30$

$6x - 5y = -18 \qquad \ldots (i)$

$x + 10 = y + 6$

$x - y = -4 \qquad \ldots (ii)$

$\therefore x = 2$ years

$\therefore$ present age of Ishu is 2 years.

76. (c) quired difference = $\dfrac{20}{100}(P + 5000) - \dfrac{20}{100} \times P$

= 1000

77. (d) Let diameter of base be 2x cm & height of cylinder be 3x cm

$\therefore$ radius = $\dfrac{2x}{2} = x$ cm

We know,

Volume of cylinder = $\pi r^2 h \qquad$ (r→radius,

h →height)

ATQ,

$\pi r^2 h = 3234$

$\dfrac{22}{7} \times x^2 \times 3x = 3234$

$x = 7$cm

Radius = 7cm

78. (e) Speed of train in m/s. = $72 \times \dfrac{5}{18} = 20$ m/s

Let length of train be x m

ATQ,

$\dfrac{524 + x}{55} = 20$

$x = 1100 - 524 = 576$m

79. (b) Let efficiency of A be x unit/day and B's
efficiency is 3x unit/day

So, B works for 19 days and A works for 18 days

ATQ—

Total work = 19 × 3x + 18 × x = 75x

$$Efficiency\ of\ C = \frac{75x}{50}$$

$$= 1.5x\ unit/day$$

$$(A + C)\ together = \frac{75x}{(x+1.5x)}$$

$$= 30\ days$$

80. (d) One day work of women = half of work
done by men in one day

Let efficiency of one women = w unit/day

Man's efficiency = 2w unit/day

Total work = (7 × 2w + 6 × w) × 8 =160w unit

8 men and 4 women start work for 3 days

Total work done = (8 × 2w + 4 × w) × 3

= 60w

4 women replace 4 men

= (4 × 2w + 8 × w) =16w

Days required = $\frac{100w}{16w}$= 6.25 days

REASONING ABILITY

1. What should come in place of the question mark (?) in the following series based on the above arrangement?
   ZN   XD   UG   QK   ?
   (a) LK   (b) LO
   (c) LP   (d) KP
   (e) Other than the given options

2. How many pairs of numbers in the given number '46579739'are in the same position (both backward and forward) according to numeric series?
   (a) one
   (b) two
   (c) three
   (d) More than three
   (e) None of these.

3. If it is possible to make only one meaningful word with the 1st, 2nd, 4th and 7th letters of the word **'ECUADOR'** which would be the second letter of the word from the right? If more than one such word can be formed, give 'Y' as the answer. If no such word can be formed, give 'Z' as your answer.
   (a) Y   (b) E   (c) I
   (d) Z   (e) M

4. If 1 is subtracted from each odd number and 2 is added to each even number in the numerical sequence**9436527,**then how many digits will appear twice in the new number thus formed?
   (a) Only 8   (b) Only 8 and 6
   (c) 8, 6 and 4   (d) 2, 4 and 6
   (e) None of these

5. How many letters will remain in the same position in the word **'MONSTER'** when its letters are arranged in the ascending order from left to right?
   (a) one
   (b) two
   (c) three
   (d) More than Three
   (e) none

Directions (6-10): Read the following information carefully and answer the following questions.
Eight boxes A, B, C, D, E, F, G and H are placed one above the other in any particular order. Box no. 1 is at the bottom and box no. 8 is at the top. Three boxes are placed between A and B. Box H is placed immediately below A. There are two boxes between H and G. There are as many boxes between C and D as between H and B. Box C is kept above D. Box E is kept immediately below box D. Three boxes are there between E and F.

6. How many boxes are there above box D?
   (a) 4   (b) 3
   (c) 6   (d) 2
   (e) None of these

7. Which of the following boxes is kept at the top?
   (a) B   (b) A
   (c) D   (d) E
   (e) None of these

8. Choose the odd one out?
   (a) B   (b) G   (c) A
   (d) D   (e) E

9. Which of the following boxes is kept between F and A?
   (a) B   (b) G
   (c) C   (d) H
   (e) None as box F is immediately above box A.

10. How many boxes are there between C and A
   (a) Less than 2   (b) 4
   (c) 5   (d) 6
   (e) None of these

Directions (11-15): In these questions, relationships between different elements are shown in the statements. These statements are followed by two conclusions. Give answer
(a) if only conclusion I follows
(b) if only conclusion II follows
(c) if either conclusion I or conclusion II follows
(d) if neither conclusion I nor conclusion II follows
(e) if both conclusions I and II follow

11. **Statement:** $R \geq S \geq T > U > X; T < V < W$
    Conclusions: I. $R > X$ **II.** $X < W$

12. **Statement:** $E = F < G < H; G \geq I$
    Conclusions: I. $H > I$ **II.** $E > I$

13. **Statement:** $A > B > F > C; D > E > C$
    Conclusions: I. $C < A$ **II.** $B > D$

14. **Statement:** $K \leq L \leq M = N; P \geq O \geq N$
    Conclusions: I. $K < P$ **II.** $K = P$

15. **Statement:** $D < E < F < G; K > F$
    Conclusions: I. $K \leq G$ **II.** $K > D$

Directions (16-20): Read the following information carefully and answer the questions below.

Seven persons A, B, C, D, E, F and G were born in different months viz. January, February, March, April, June, August and October of the same year, but not necessarily in the same order.

Only three persons were born before E and D is not one of them. F was not born immediately after E. B was born after F. A was born immediately before the month in which G was born. Only two persons were born between G and F.

16. How many persons were born between C and E?
    (a) three   (b) two
    (c) four   (d) five
    (e) None of these

17. Who amongst the following is the oldest?
    (a) A   (b) C   (c) E
    (d) B   (e) F

18. Who amongst the following was born between the months in which A and D were born?
    (a) E   (b) G
    (c) C   (d) B
    (e) Both E and G

19. How many persons were born after D?
    (a) one   (b) three
    (c) four   (d) two
    (e) None of these

20. Who amongst the following was born in the month which has less than 30 days?
    (a) F   (b) B   (c) G
    (d) C   (e) A

Directions (21-25): Study the following information carefully and answer the given questions:

In a certain code language

'card win team time' is written as 'la ta ja sa'

'fight game play card' is written as 'ja pa ra da'

'in win team fight' is written as 'da ta fa la'.

21. What is the code for 'time'?
    (a) sa   (b) da
    (c) ja   (d) la
    (e) None of these

22. 'card fight in' can be coded as?
    (a) sa ja ra
    (b) fa ja da
    (c) da ra ta
    (d) Can't be determined
    (e) None of these

23. What is the code for 'game'?
    (a) ra   (b) pa
    (c) Either ra or pa   (d) da
    (e) None of these

24. Which of the following is the code for 'in'?
    (a) ta   (b) da
    (c) la   (d) fa
    (e) None of these

25. If 'game in risk' is coded as 'Pa fa xa' than what will be the code for 'risk card fight'?
    (a) Ja sa da   (b) ja da ra
    (c) sa da fa   (d) xa ja da
    (e) None of these

Directions (26-30): Study the following information to answer the given questions:

Twelve people are sitting in two parallel rows containing six people each in such a way that there is an equal distance between adjacent persons. In row 1—A, B, P, Q, X and Y are seated (but not necessarily in the same order) and all of them are facing south. In row 2—E, F ,R ,Z ,S and U are seated (but not necessarily in the same order) and all of them are facing North. Therefore, in the given seating arrangement each member seated in a row faces another member of the other row. Q sits fourth to the left of A. The one facing A sits third to the left of S. Only one person sits between S and E. E does not sit at any of the extreme ends of the row. The one facing U sits second to the right of B. U does not sit at any of the extreme ends of the row. Only two people sit between B and Y. The one facing B sits second to the left of Z. F is not an immediate neighbour of U. P is not an immediate neighbour of Q.

26. Which of the following groups of people represents the people sitting at extreme ends of both the rows?
    (a) Q, Y, Z, R   (b) F, Y, F, B   (c) S, Y, Z, R
    (d) Q, F, Z, B   (e) Q, Y, Z, S

27. Who amongst the following faces F?
    (a) Q   (b) P   (c) A
    (d) X   (e) B

28. Which of the following is true with respect to the given information?
    (a) B faces one of the immediate neighbours of Z.
    (b) F sits exactly between R and E.
    (c) None of the given options is true.
    (d) A is an immediate neighbour of B.
    (e) A faces U.

29. Which of the following is true regarding X?
    (a) B sits second to the right of X.
    (b) F is an immediate neighbour of the person who faces X.
    (c) Both P and Y are immediate neighbours of X.
    (d) Only one person sits between X and A.
    (e) None of the given options is true.

30. Who amongst the following sits second to the right of the person who faces P?
    (a) F   (b) U   (c) R
    (d) E   (e) S

Directions (31-35): Study the following information carefully and answer the questions given below:

Eight friends M, N, O, P, Q, R, S and T are sitting around a circular table with equal distance between them but not necessarily in the same order. Some of them are facing the centre while some face outside (i.e. opposite to centre).

O sits second to the right of R and R faces the centre. Only two people sit between O and N (either from O's right or O's left). S sits second to the right of O. T sits to the immediate right of N. S and N face opposite directions (i.e. if N faces the centre then S faces outside and vice versa). Immediate neighbours of S face the same direction (i.e. If one neighbour faces the centre then the other also faces the centre and vice-versa). Only three people sit between P and Q. Neither P nor M is an immediate neighbour of R. Q sits second to the right of M. Both T and Q face a direction opposite to that of O (i.e. if O faces the centre then both T and Q faces outside and vice-versa).

31. Who sits exactly between M and P?
(a) N
(b) S
(c) R
(d) Q
(e) None of these

32. How many people in the given arrangement face the centre?
(a) one
(b) three
(c) five
(d) four
(e) None of these

33. Who sits second to the right of T?
(a) O
(b) Q
(c) S
(d) R
(e) Other than the given options

34. Four of the following five are alike in a certain way based on the given seating arrangement and so form a group. Which is the one that does not belong to that group?
(a) P
(b) O
(c) T
(d) M
(e) Q

35. What is P's position with respect to R?
(a) Second to the left
(b) Third to the right
(c) Third to the left
(d) Sixth to the right
(e) Second to the right

Directions (36–40): In each question below are given some statements followed by two conclusions numbered I and II. You have to take the given statements to be true even if they seem to be at variance with commonly known facts. Read all the conclusions and then decide which of the given conclusions logically follows from the given statements, disregarding commonly known facts.
Give answer
(a) If only conclusion I follows.
(b) If only conclusion II follows.
(c) If either conclusion I or II follows.
(d) If neither conclusion I nor II follows.
(e) If both conclusions I and II follow.

36. Statements: All bags are purses.
No purse is black.
All blacks are covers.
Conclusions: I. All bags are covers.
II. Some covers are purses.

37. Statements: Some cats are rats.
Some rats are fishes.
All fishes are birds.
Conclusions: I. Some fishes are rats.
II. All cats being birds is a possibility.

38. Statements: Some flowers are roses.
No rose is red.
All red are leaves.
Conclusions: I. Some flowers are definitely not red.
II. Some leaves are definitely not roses.

39. Statements: All cards are sheets.
All files are cards.
Some sheets are papers.
Conclusions: I. All files being papers is a possibility.
II. All files are not sheets.

40. Statements: Some flowers are roses.
No rose is red.
All red are leaves.
Conclusions: I. Some flowers are not leaves.
II. No leaves are red.

QUANTITATIVE APTITUDE

Directions (41-45): What should come in place of the question mark (?) in following number series problems?

41. 190, 94, 46, 22, ?, 4
(a) 12
(b) 14
(c) 10
(d) 8
(e) None of these

42. 5, 28, 47, 64, 77, ?
(a) 84
(b) 86
(c) 89
(d) 88
(e) None of these

43. 7, 4, 5, 12, 52, ?

(a) 424   (b) 428
(c) 318   (d) 440
(e) None of these

44. 6, 4, 5, 11, 39, ?
(a) 159   (b) 169
(c) 189   (d) 198
(e) None of these

45. 89, 88, 85, 78, 63, ?
(a) 30   (b) 34
(c) 36   (d) 32
(e) None of these

46. There are 3 consecutive odd numbers and 3 consecutive even numbers. The smallest even number is 9 more than the largest odd number. If the square of average of all the 3 given odd numbers is 507 less than the square of the average of all the 3 given even numbers, what is the smallest odd number.
(a) 11   (b) 13   (c) 17
(d) 19   (e) 9

47. A can complete a task in 15 days; B is 50% more efficient than A. Both A and B started working together on the task and after few days B left the task and A finished the remaining $\frac{1}{3}$ of the given work. For how many days A and B worked together.
(a) 3   (b) 5   (c) 4
(d) 6   (e) 2

48. A boat can travel 9.6 km. downstream in 36 min. The speed of the water current is 10% of the speed of the boat in downstream. How much time will boat take to travel 19.2 km. upstream.
(a) 2 hours   (b) 3 hours   (c) 1.25 hours
(d) 1.5 hours   (e) 1 hour

49. A started a business with an initial investment of Rs. 1200. 'X' months after the start of business, B joined A with an initial investment of Rs. 1500. If total profit was 1950 at the end of year and B's share of the profit was 750, find 'X'.
(a) 5 months   (b) 6 months   (c) 7 months
(d) 8 months   (e) 9 months

50. Ratio between the curved surface area and the total surface area of a circular cylinder is 3:5. If the curved surface area is 1848 cm³, then what is the height of the cylinder.
(a) 28   (b) 14   (c) 17
(d) 21   (e) 7

Directions (51-55): Given below is the pie chart which shows the percentage distribution of books by publisher 'XYZ' which are sold in five different stores.

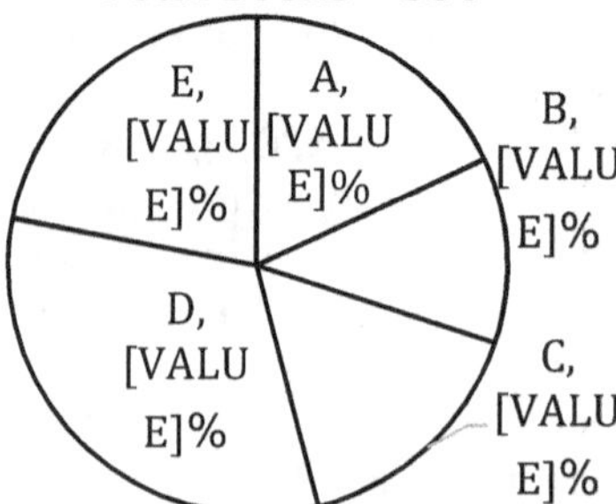

51. If the number of females who bought the books in store E is 21 more than the number of males who bought these books from the same store, find the number of females who bought the books in store E.
(a) 75   (b) 78   (c) 71
(d) 68   (e) 73

52. Find the central angle from the pie-chart for store D.
(a) 117.5°   (b) 115.2°   (c) 112.8°
(d) 108.5°   (e) 118.8°

53. If the total books of another publisher 'MNP' is 20% more than books of 'XYZ' publisher, then what will be the total number of books sold by store A and B together for publisher 'MNP'? Percentage-distribution of books for different stores for MNP remains same as for 'XYZ'.
(a) 200   (b) 178   (c) 181
(d) 186   (e) 198

54. What is the ratio of the total books of publisher XYZ sold by store A and C together to the total books sold by store D and E together?
(a) 17 : 27   (b) 18 : 29   (c) 21 : 28
(d) 22 : 23   (e) 24 : 29

55. What is the difference between the average number of books by XYZ publisher sold by store A and E together and the average books sold by store C and D together?
(a) 33   (b) 11   (c) 22
(d) 44   (e) 20

Directions (56-60): In each of these questions, two equations (I) and (II) are given. You have to solve both the equations and give the answer.
(a) if x>y   (b) if x≥y
(c) if x<y   (d) if x ≤y
(e) if x = y or no relationship can be established.

56. I. $x^2 + 9x + 20 = 0$ II. $y^2 = 16$
57. I. $x^2 - 7x + 12 = 0$ II. $3y^2 - 11y + 10 = 0$
58. I. $x^2 - 8x + 15 = 0$ II. $y^2 - 12y + 36 = 0$
59. I. $2x^2 + 9x + 7 = 0$ II. $y^2 + 4y + 4 = 0$
60. I. $2x^2 + 15x + 28 = 0$ II. $2y^2 + 13y + 21 = 0$

61. Train A completely crosses train B which is 205 m. long in 16 seconds. If they are travelling in opposite directions and the sum of the speed of both trains is 25 m/s. then find the difference (in meters) between the lengths of both trains.

(a) 5   (b) 6   (c) 8
(d) 10   (e) 12

62. A trader mixes 14 kg. rice of variety A which costs Rs. 60/kg. with 18 kg. of quantity of type B rice. He sells the mixture at Rs. 65/kg. and earns a profit of $\frac{100}{3}$%.What was the cost price of type B rice?

(a) 30   (b) 20   (c) 40
(d) 50   (e) 45

63. The present age of A is 3 years less than the present age of B. Ratio of B's age 5 years ago and A's age 4 years hence is 3:4. Find present age (in years) of A.

(a) 20   (b) 17   (c) 23

(d) 26   (e) 29

64. A bag contains 6 Red, 5 Green and 4 Yellow coloured balls. If 2 balls are drawn at random, one after another without replacement, then what is the probability that at least one ball is Green?

(a) $\frac{2}{3}$ (b) $\frac{4}{5}$ (c) $\frac{3}{8}$
(d) $\frac{4}{7}$ (e) $\frac{2}{7}$

65. The cost price of B is Rs. 200 more than the cost price of A. B is sold at 10% profit and A is sold at 40% loss and selling price of A and B are in the ratio 4:11. If A is sold at 20% loss, then what will be the selling price of A.

(a) 320   (b) 400   (c) 240
(d) 160   (e) 360

Directions (66-70): Read the table below carefully and answer the following questions—
No. of students and percentage of students that passed, out of those that appeared are given for two subjects from year 2001 to 2005 in a college XYZ.

Year	Statistics		Economics	
	No. of students appeared	% of students passed	No. of students appeared	% of students passed
2001	2200	45%	4200	40%
2002	2700	55%	3800	45%
2003	2500	35%	2600	60%
2004	3200	65%	4800	55%
2005	4800	60%	2200	50%

66. Find the average number of students who failed in Economics in year 2002 and year 2003 together?

(a) 1435   (b) 1565
(c) 1720   (d) 1590
(e) None of these

67. Number of students that failed in Statistics in the year 2003 is what percentage of the number of students that failed in Economics in the same year?

(a) 145.75%   (b) 150%
(c) 156.25%   (d) 158.25%
(e) None of these

68. Find the ratio between the total number of students who appeared in Economics from 2002 to 2004 together and the total number of students who appeared in Statistics from year 2003 to 2005 together?

(a) 13: 14   (b) 14 : 13
(c) 15 : 16   (d) 16: 15
(e) None of these

69. Find the difference between the total number of students who passed in Statistics from year 2002 and the total number of students who failed in Economics from year 2005.

(a) 690   (b) 385   (c) 485
(d) 550   (e) 610

70. Find the average number of students who appeared in Economics from year 2001 to 2004 together.

(a) 3090   (b) 3015   (c) 3060
(d) 3075   (e) 3850

Direction (71-75): What approximate value should come in place of question mark (?) in the following questions? (Note: You are not expected to calculate the exact value)

71. ? % of $(5284.89 \div 7.08) = 986.01 - 533.06$

(a) 42   (b) 39   (c) 74
(d) 65   (e) 60

72. $(1041.84 + ?) \div 3.02 = 1816.25 \div 4.01$

(a) 442   (b) 337   (c) 385
(d) 268   (e) 320

73. 69.3% of $445.12 \div 14.06 = 623.08 \div ?$

(a) 28   (b) 19   (c) 21
(d) 33   (e) 37

74. $?^2 + 114.09 - 24.06 \times 5.14 = 163.19$

(a) 7   (b) 13   (c) 11
(d) 15   (e) 19

75. $768.16 \div 11.87 \times \sqrt{257} - 58.05 = ?$

(a) 1033 (b) 1175 (c) 966
(d) 880 (e) 975

Directions (76-80): Study the following line graph carefully and answer the following questions.
Number of males and number of females are given. They are visiting a place from Monday to Friday.

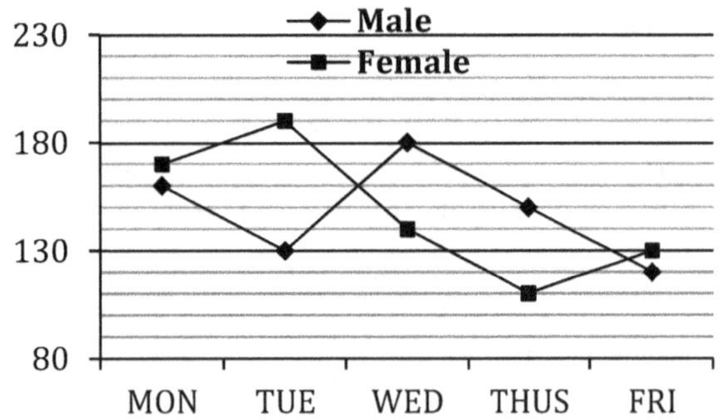

76. Find the ratio of the total number of males who visited the place on Tuesday and Thursday together to the total number of females who visited the place on Monday and Friday together.
(a) 29 : 30 (b) 30 : 29 (c) 25 : 26
(d) 26 : 25 (e) None of these

77. The total number of males and females together who visited the place on Tuesday are what percent more/less than the total number of males and females together who visited the place on Thursday?
(a) $26\frac{12}{13}\%$ (b) $25\frac{3}{13}\%$ (c) $26\frac{3}{13}\%$
(d) $25\frac{7}{13}\%$ (e) None of these

78. Find the difference between the total number of females who visited the place from Monday to Wednesday and the total number of males who visited the place from Wednesday to Friday.
(a) 30 (b) 60 (c) 40
(d) 50 (e) None of these

79. If on Saturday the number of males and the number of females increased by 25% and 20% respectively as compared to that on Friday, then find the total number of males and females together who visited the place on Saturday.
(a) 196 (b) 306 (c) 316
(d) 206 (e) 216

80. The total number of males and females who visited the place on Monday and Tuesday together is how much more than the total number of males and females who visited the place on Thursday and Friday together?
(a) 175 (b) 125 (c) 150
(d) 160 (e) 130

Solutions

REASONING ABILITY

1. **(c)** LP
2. **(d)**

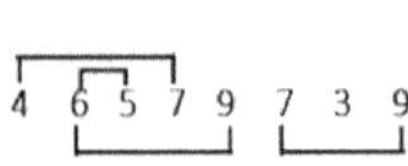

3. **(a)** Race, Care
4. **(c)**

9 4 3 6 5 2 7

8 6 2 8 4 4 6

5. **(a)**

M O N S T E R

E M N O R S T

Directions (6-10):

Number	Box
8	B
7	C
6	G
5	F
4	A
3	H
2	D
1	E

6. **(c)** 7. **(a)** 8. **(e)**
9. **(e)** 10. **(e)**

Directions (11-15):
11. **(e)** Both conclusion I and II follow.
12. **(a)** Only conclusion I follows.
13. **(a)** Only conclusion I follows.
14. **(c)** Either conclusion I or II follows.
15. **(b)** Only conclusion II follows.

Directions (16-20):

Month	Person
January	C
February	A
March	G
April	E
June	D
August	F
October	B

16. **(b)** 17. **(b)** 18. **(e)**
19. **(d)** 20. **(e)**

Directions (21-25):

Word	Code
Card	ja
Time	sa
Win/team	la/ta
Fight	da
Game/Play	pa/ra
In	fa

21. (a)   **22. (b)**   **23. (c)**
24. (d)   **25. (d)**

Direction (26-30):

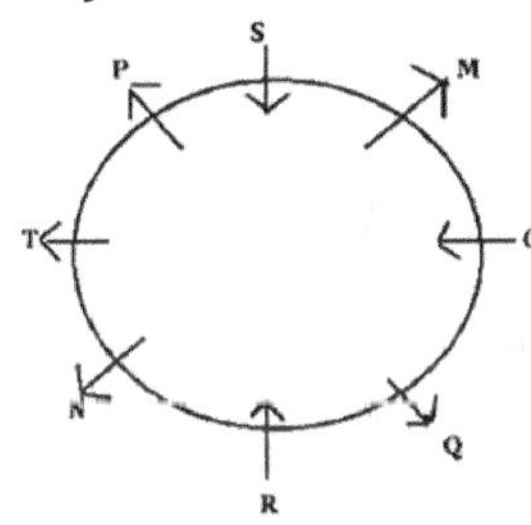

26. (a)   **27. (e)**   **28. (e)**
29. (b)   **30. (e)**

Direction (31-35):

31. (b)   **32. (b)**   **33. (c)**
34. (b)   **35. (c)**

Directions (36–40):

36. (d)

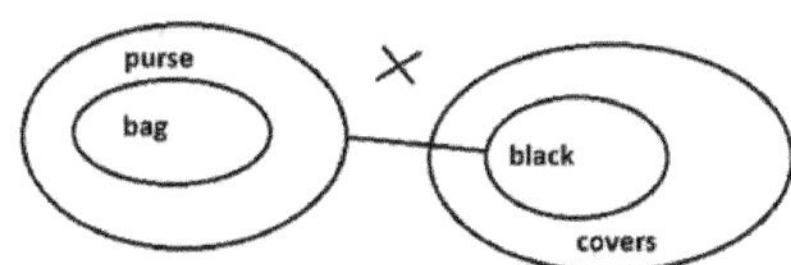

37. (e)

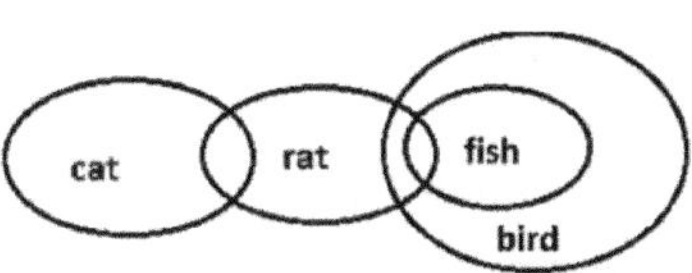

38. (e)

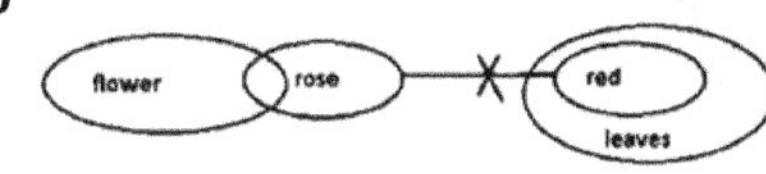

39. (a)

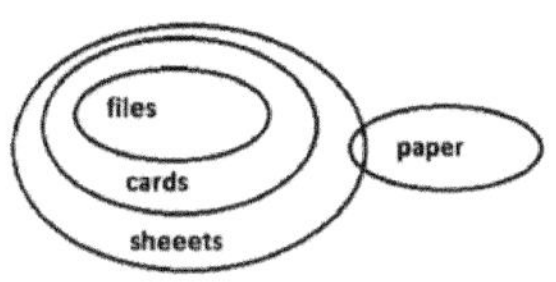

40. (d)

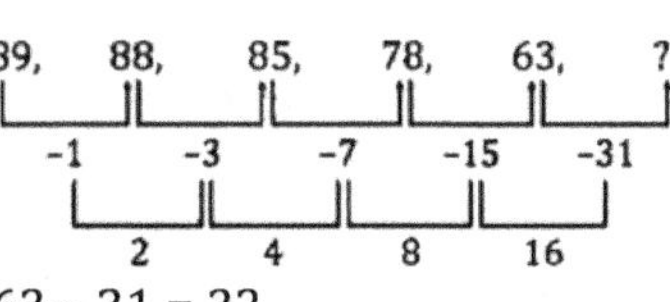

QUANTITATIVE APTITUDE

41. (c) Series is $\div 2 - 1, \div 2 - 1$
$(22 \div 2) - 1 = 10$

42. (d)

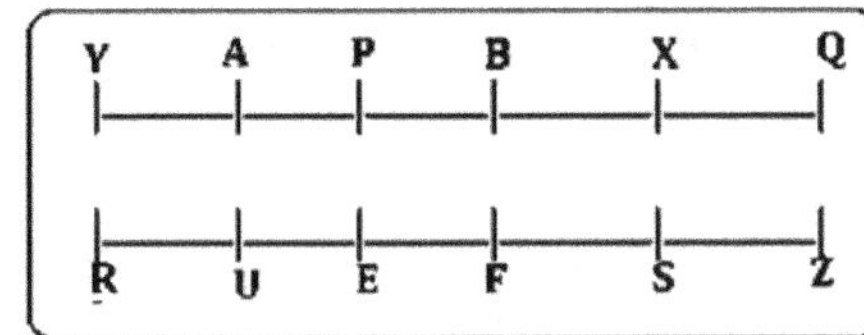

5,   28,   47,   64,   77,   ?
   23   19   17   13   11

Adding prime No.
$77 + 11 = 88$

43. (a) $(7+1) \times 0.5 = 4$
$(4+1) \times 1 = 5$
$(5+1) \times 2 = 12$
$(12+1) \times 4 = 52$
$(52+1) \times 8 = 424$

44. (c) $(6 \times 1) - 2 = 4$
$(4 \times 2) - 3 = 5$
$(5 \times 3) - 4 = 11$
$(11 \times 4) - 5 = 39$
$(39 \times 5) - 6 = 189$

45. (d)

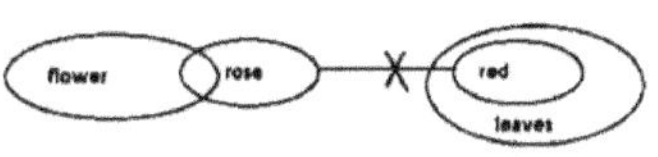

89,   88,   85,   78,   63,   ?
  −1   −3   −7   −15   −31
    2   4   8   16

$63 - 31 = 32$

46. (a) Let a consecutive odd numbers
$= x - 2, \ x$ and $x + 2$
and consecutive even numbers
$= y - 2, \ y, \ y + 2$
So, $y - 2 = 9 + x + 2$
$y - x = 13$ ... (i)
and
$(x)^2 + 507 = (y)^2$
$y^2 - x^2 = 507$
$(x + y)(y - x) = 507$
$(x + y) = \dfrac{507}{13} \Rightarrow x + y = 39$ ... (i)
Solving (i) and (ii) $y = 26$ and $x = 13$
so smallest odd numbers $= x - 2 = 13 - 2 = 11$

47. (c) A complete work in 15 days.
B will complete work in 10 days.
They together will complete whole work
$= \frac{15 \times 10}{25} = 6 \ days$
A and B together worked for $= 6 \times {}^2/_3 = 4$
days

48. (d) $Speed \ of \ downstream = \frac{9.6}{36} km/min$
$= 16 \ km/hr$
Speed of current = 1.6 km/hr
Let speed of man in still water = x
So, x = 16 – 1.6 = 14.4 km/hr
$Required \ time \ in \ upstream = \frac{19.2}{14.4-1.6}$
$= 1.5 \ hours$

49. (b) Ratio of profit of A and B = 1200: 750
= 24: 15 = 8 : 5
So,
$\frac{1200 \times 12}{1500 \times y} = \frac{8}{5}$
$y = 6$ months
$x = 6$ month

50. (d) $\frac{2\pi rh}{2\pi r(r+h)} = \frac{3}{5}$
5h = 3r + 3h
2h = 3r
and
2πrh = 1848
$2 \times \frac{22}{7} \times \frac{2}{3} h \times h = 1848$
$h = 21$

51. (c) Let males who purchased books from Store
E = x
Then
$x + x + 21 = \frac{22}{100} \times 550$
$x = 50$
Number of females = 50 + 21 = 71

52. (b) $\frac{18}{5} = \frac{x}{32}$
$x = \frac{18 \times 32}{5} = 18 \times 6.4 = 115.2$

53. (e) $Total \ books \ of \ Publisher \ MNP = \frac{120}{100} \times$
550
= 660
Total books sold by store A and B
= (18% + 12%) of 660 = 198

54. (a) Required ratio = (18% + 16%): (32% + 22%)
= 34: 54 = 17 : 27

55. (c) Required difference
$= \frac{1}{2}[(32\% + 16\%) - (18\% + 22\%)]550$
$= \frac{1}{2} \times 8\% \ of \ 550 = 4\% \ of \ 550 = 22$

56. (d) I $x^2 + 5x + 4x + 20 = 0$
$x(x + 5) + 4(x + 5) = 0$
$(x + 4)(x + 5) = 0$
$x = -4, -5$
II. $y^2 = 16$
$y = \pm 4$

$\therefore x \leq y$

57. (a) I. $x^2 - 7x + 12 = 0$
$x^2 - 4x - 3x + 12 = 0$
$x(x - 4) - 3(x - 4) = 0$
$(x - 3)(x - 4) = 0$
$x = 3, 4$
II. $3y^2 - 11y + 10 = 0$
$3y^2 - 6y - 5y + 10 = 0$
$3y(y - 2) - 5(y - 2) = 0$
$(3y - 5)(y - 2) = 0$
$y = 2, \frac{5}{3}$
$\therefore x > y$

58. (c) I. $x^2 - 8x + 15 = 0$
$x^2 - 3x - 5x + 15 = 0$
$x(x - 3) - 5(x - 3) = 0$
$(x - 3)(x - 5) = 0$
$x = 3, 5$
II. $y^2 - 12y + 36 = 0$
$y^2 - 6y - 6y + 36 = 0$
$y(y - 6) - 6(y - 6) = 0$
$(y - 6)(y - 6) = 0$
$y = 6$
$\therefore x < y$

59. (e) I. $2x^2 + 9x + 7 = 0$
$2x^2 + 7x + 2x + 7 = 0$
$x(2x + 7) + 1(2x + 7) = 0$
$(x + 1)(2x + 7) = 0$
$x = -1, -\frac{7}{2}$
II. $y^2 + 4y + 4 = 0$
$y^2 + 2y + 2y + 4 = 0$
$y(y + 2) + 2(y + 2) = 0$
$(y + 2)(y + 2) = 0$
$y = -2, -2$
$\therefore$ No relation.

60. (d) I. $2x^2 + 15x + 28 = 0$
$2x^2 + 8x + 7x + 28 = 0$
$2x(x + 4) + 7(x + 4) = 0$
$(2x + 7)(x + 4) = 0$
$x = \left(-\frac{7}{2}\right), -4$
II. $2y^2 + 13y + 21 = 0$
$2y^2 + 7y + 6y + 21 = 0$
$y(2y + 7) + 3(2y + 7) = 0$
$(y + 3)(2y + 7) = 0$
$y = -3, \frac{-7}{2}$
$x \leq y$

61. (d) In 16 second distance covered by both
= 16 × 25 = 400 m
So length of A = 400 – 205 = 195
Required difference = 10 m

62. (c) Let cost price of mixture = y
$So, \frac{4}{3}y = 65$
$y = 48.75$
From mixture and allegation

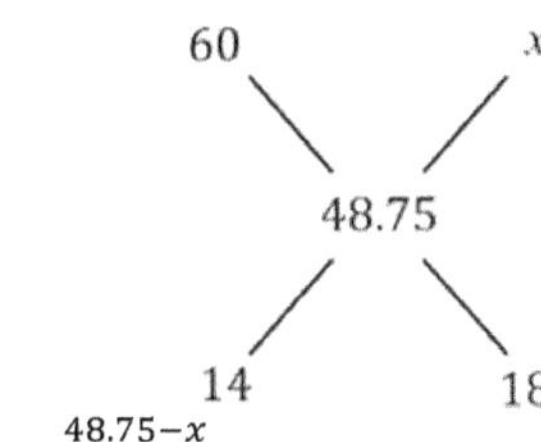

$$\frac{7}{9} = \frac{48.75 - x}{60 - 48.75}$$

$$78.75 = 438.75 - 9x$$

$$360 = 9x$$

$$x = 40 \text{ Rs. /kg}$$

63. (a) Let B's age $= x$

So A's age $= x - 3$

$$\frac{x-5}{x+1} = \frac{3}{4}$$

$$x = 23$$

A's age $= 23 - 3 = 20\ years$

64. (d) Probability that no ball is green

$$\frac{^{10}C_1 \times {}^9C_1}{15 \times 14} = \frac{90}{15 \times 14} = \frac{3}{7}$$

Required probability $= 1 - \frac{3}{7} = \frac{4}{7}$

65. (a) Let C.P. of A $= x$

So C.P. of B $= 200 + x$

According to question

$$\frac{\frac{110}{100}(x+200)}{\frac{60}{100}x} = \frac{11}{4} \Rightarrow \frac{x+200}{6x} = \frac{1}{4}$$

$$x = 400$$

If it is sold at 20% loss, then selling price

$$= \frac{80}{100} \times 400 = 320$$

66. (b) No. of students who failed in Economics in year 2002

$$= \frac{(100-45)}{100} \times 3800 = 2090$$

No. of students failed in Economics in year 2003

$$= \frac{(100-60)}{100} \times 2600 = 1040$$

$Required\ average = \frac{2090+1040}{2} = 1565$

$Short\ trick = \frac{55 \times 38 + 40 \times 26}{2} = 1565$

67. (c) No. of students failed in Statistics in year 2003

$$= \frac{100-35}{100} \times 2500 = 1625$$

No. of students failed in Economics in year 2003

$$= \frac{100-60}{100} \times 2600 = 1040$$

$Required\ \% = \frac{1625}{1040} \times 100 = 156.25\%$

$Short\ trick = \frac{65 \times 25}{40 \times 26} \times 100 = 156.25\%$

68. (d) Total no. of students appeared in Economics from 2002 to 2004

$= 3800 + 2600 + 4800 = 11200$

Total no. of students appeared in Statistics from 2003 to 2005

$= 2500 + 3200 + 4800 = 10500$

Required ratio $= 11,200 : 10,500 = 16 : 15$

69. (b) Total no. of students passed in Statistics in year 2002

$$= \frac{55}{100} \times 2700 = 1485$$

Total no. of students failed in Economics in year 2005

$$= \frac{50}{100} \times 2200 = 1100$$

Required difference $= 1485 - 1100 = 385$

Short trick $= 55 \times 27 - 50 \times 22 = 385$

70. (e) Average no. of students appeared in Economics from year 2001 to 2004 together

$$= \frac{4200+3800+2600+4800}{4} = \frac{15400}{4} = 3850$$

71. (e) $\frac{?}{100} \times 750 = 450 \Rightarrow ? \approx 60$

72. (e) $\frac{(1042+?)}{3.02} = 454 \Rightarrow ? = 320$

73. (a) $\frac{310}{14} = \frac{625}{?} \Rightarrow ? \approx 28$

74. (b) $?^2 = 170 \Rightarrow ? \approx 13$

75. (c) $\approx 64 \times 16 - 58 \approx 966$

76. (a) Total no. of males that visited on Tuesday and Thursday $= 140 + 150 = 290$

Total no. of females that visited on Monday and Friday $= 170 + 130 = 300$

Required ratio $= 290 : 300 = 29 : 30$

77. (a) Total no. of males and females together on Tuesday $= 140 + 190 = 330$

Total no. of males and females together on Thursday $= 150 + 110 = 260$

$Required\ \% = \frac{330-260}{260} \times 100 = 26\frac{12}{13}\%$

78. (d) Total no. of females who visited from Monday to Wednesday $= 170 + 190 + 140 = 500$

Total no. of males who visited from Wednesday to Friday $= 180 + 150 + 120 = 450$

Required difference $= 500 - 450 = 50$

79. (b) On Saturday —

Total no. of males who visited the place

$$= \frac{125}{100} \times 120 = 150$$

Total no. of females visited the place

$$= \frac{120}{100} \times 130 = 156$$

Required males and females

$= 150 + 156 = 306$

80. (c) Total males and females who visited the place on Monday and Tuesday together

$= 160 + 140 + 170 + 190 = 660$

Total males and females that visited the place on Thursday and Friday together

$= 150 + 120 + 110 + 130 = 510$

Required no. of persons $= 660 - 510 = 150$

REASONING ABILITY

Directions: (1–5): In these questions, a relationship between different elements is shown in the statements(s). The statements are followed by two conclusions. Give answer
(a) if only conclusion I is true.
(b) if only conclusion II is true.
(c) if either conclusion I or II is true.
(d) if neither conclusion I nor II is true.
(d) if both conclusions I and II are true.

1. **Statements :** $A > B \geq C < D, C = E > G$
   Conclusions: I. $D > E$ **II.** $B > E$
2. **Statements :** $P \leq Q > M \geq N, Q = S$
   Conclusions: I. $S > P$ **II.** $N < S$
3. **Statements:** $S > M = Z > T < Q > V$
   Conclusions: I. $V = S$ **II.** $Q > M$
4. **Statements :** $T < U = V \leq S > P \geq Q$
   Conclusions: I. $S > T$ **II.** $V \geq Q$
5. **Statements :** $M \geq N > R > W, E = J > L \geq W$
   Conclusions: I. $E > W$ **II.** $M > L$

Directions (6-10): In each of the question-sets below are three statements followed by two conclusions numbered I and II. You have to take the given statements to be true even if they seem to be at variance with commonly known facts and then decide which of the given conclusions logically follows from the given statements, disregarding commonly known facts. Give answer
(a) if only conclusion I follows.
(b) if only conclusion II follows.
(c) if either conclusions I or conclusion II follows.
(d) if neither conclusion I nor conclusion II follows.
(e) if both conclusion I and conclusion II follow.

6. **Statements:** All pencils are Cutters.
   Some Cutters are Scale.
   No Scale is a compass.
   Conclusions: I. All pencils being Scale is a possibility.
   II. No compass is a Cutter.
7. **Statements:** Some circles are triangles.
   All triangles are squares.
   No square is a rectangle.
   Conclusions: I. Some triangles being rectangles is a possibility
   II. All squares being circles is a possibility.
8. **Statements:** All pencils are Cutters.
   Some Cutters are Scale.
   No Scale is a compass.

Conclusions: I. All compass being pencils is a possibility.
II. At least some Cutters are pencils.

9. **Statements:** Some wallets are bags.
   Some bags are leather.
   All purses are leather.
   Conclusions: I. Some purses are bags.
   II. Some purses are wallet.

10. **Statements:** Some circles are triangles.
    All triangles are squares.
    No square is a rectangle.
    Conclusions: I. No rectangle is a triangle.
    II. Some circles are not rectangles.

Directions (11-15): Study the following information to answer the given questions:

Eight students M, N, O, P, U, V, W and X sit around a square table in such a way that four of them are at the four corners while four students sit in the middle of each of the four sides. The ones who sit at the 4 corners face the centre and the others face outside. M who faces the centre sits third to the left of V. U who faces the centre is not an immediate neighbour of V. Only one person sits between V and W. P sits second to the right of N. N faces the centre. O is not an immediate neighbour of M.

11. Which one does not belong to that group out of five?
    (a) N   (b) O   (c) U
    (d) P   (e) M
12. Which will come in the place of ?
    NOU UXM MWP ?
    (a) PVN   (b) PWM
    (c)POW   (d) POV
    (e) None of these
13. What is the position of W with respect to O?
    (a) Third to the right   (b) Second to the left
    (c) Second to the right   (d) Fourth to the right
    (e) None of these
14. Who sits third to the left of N ?
    (a) X   (b) M
    (c) W   (d) V
    (e) None of these
15. Which is true from the given arrangement?
    (a) W faces the centre   (b) N faces outside
    (c) X faces inside   (d) M faces the centre

(e) None of these

Directions (16-18): Study the information carefully and answer the question given below.

M is the father of A and C. R is the brother of C. A is the husband of T and S is the daughter of T. V is the grandmother of S.

16. How is T related to M?
(a) Son in law
(b) daughter
(c) Daughter in law
(d) Can't be determined
(e) None of these

17. If R has only one sister C, then what is the relation of A to S?
(a) mother
(b) father
(c) uncle
(d) Can't be determined
(e) None of these

18. How is M related to S?
(a) father (b) Father in law
(c) grandfather (d) grand daughter
(e) None of these.

Directions (19-23): Study the following information carefully to answer the given questions:

Eight friends P, Q, R, S, T, U, V and W are seated in a straight line facing north, but not necessarily in the same order.

❖ Q sits second to right of U. U sits at one of the extreme ends of the line.
❖ Only three persons sit between Q and T.
❖ R sits third to the left of S. Only two persons sit between S and P.
❖ V is not an immediate neighbour of T.

19. Who among the following represents the person seated at the extreme right of the line?
(a) V (b) W (c) U
(d) R (e) P

20. Who among the following sits exactly between S and P?
(a) U, P (b) Q, U (c) U, V
(d) T, W (e) Q, T

21. What is the position of V with respect to T?
(a) Third to the left (b) Second to the right
(c) Fourth to the right (d) Third to the right
(e) Second to the left

22. Based on the given arrangement, which of the following is true with respect to W?
(a) Only two persons sit between W and R.
(b) Only two persons sit to the right of W.
(c) None of the given options is true.
(d) Both R and P are immediate neighbours of W.
(e) V sits on the immediate right of W.

23. How many persons are seated between V and P?
(a) none (b) one (c) two

(d) four (e) three

24. In a certain code language, SERIES is written as QCGTGU. How is EXPERT written in that code language?
(a) VTGRZG (b) RPCRZG (c) GZRCPR
(d) RPCGZR (e) None of these

25. How many pairs of letters are there in the word COMPOSE, each of which has many letters between them in the word as they have between them in the English alphabetical series (backwards or forwards)?
(a) none
(b) one
(c) two
(d) three
(e) None of these

Directions (26-30): Study the information carefully and answer the question given below.

Nine persons P, Q, R, S, T, U, V, W and X live on separate floors of a multi-storey building but not necessarily in the same order. The ground floor is numbered 1, the first floor is numbered 2 and so on until the topmost floor is numbered nine.

Only two persons live below the floor on which V lives. Only one person lives between V and P.

W lives on an odd-numbered floor but not on floor no. 7.

Only two persons live between W and Q. X does not live on the topmost floor. P does not live on the lowermost floor. S lives immediately below R but R does not sit on the topmost floor. Neither R nor T live on floor no 6. U lives immediately above P.

26. How many persons live between the floors on which P and S live?
(a) three
(b) More than three
(c) none
(d) two
(e) one

27. Who lives on the floor immediately below V?
(a) U (b) T (c) S
(d) Q (e) X

28. On which of the following floor numbers does X live?
(a) four (b) one (c) two
(d) five (e) seven

29. Which of the following is true with respect to U as per the given arrangement?
(a) Only three persons live between U and Q.
(b) Only three persons live above U.
(c) Only one person sits between U and S.
(d) U sits on odd numbered floor.
(e) None of these.

30. Who lives on the floor numbered 5?
(a) U

(b) Q

(c) S

(d) P

(e) None of these

Directions (31-33): Study the information carefully and answer the questions given below.

Mark started from his house and moved in the south direction. After moving 25m., he took a right turn and moved 40 m. to reach his uncle's house. Again, Mark started moving southwards and after travelling 50m. he took a left and travelled80m. to reach his aunt's home.

31. In which direction is his aunt's house located with respect to his house?
    (a) south west
    (b) south east
    (c) north east
    (d) north west
    (e) None of these

32. Hisuncle's house is in which direction with respect to his aunt's house?
    (a) north east
    (b) north west
    (c) south west
    (d) south east
    (e) None of these

33. If Point A is 25m. to the north of his uncle's house then what is the distance between A and Mark's house?
    (a) 40 m.
    (b) 30 m.
    (c) 20 m.
    (d) Can't be determined
    (e) None of these.

Directions (34-38): Study the information carefully and answer the questions given below:

Gaurav joins classes from Monday to Sunday of the same week for different subjects viz. Biology, Chemistry, Physics, Hindi, Mathematics, English and Geography.

❖ Hindi class is taken by him on Wednesday.

❖ There is a one-day gap between Hindi class and Mathematics class.

❖ There is a three-day gap between Mathematics class and English class.

❖ English class is scheduled immediately before Physics class but not on Monday.

❖ Chemistry is scheduled immediately after Mathematics class.

❖ There is a one-day gap between Chemistry class and Geography class. Biology class is scheduled on Sunday.

34. There is a gap of how many days between Mathematics and Chemistry class?
    (a) one   (b) two   (c) three
    (d) four   (e) None

35. Hindi class is scheduled on which day?
    (a) Monday
    (b) Wednesday
    (c) Thursday
    (d) Friday
    (e) None of these

36. Which of the following is the correct combination?
    (a) Hindi= Monday
    (b) Physics= Tuesday
    (c) Chemistry= Thursday
    (d) Mathematics= Monday
    (e) Biology= Friday

37. On which day of the week is Chemistry class scheduled?
    (a) Monday
    (b) Tuesday
    (c) Wednesday
    (d) Thursday
    (e) None of these

38. Four of the following five are alike in certain ways and form a group. Which one does not belong to the group?
    (a) Tuesday=Hindi
    (b) Monday=Chemistry
    (c) Friday=Physics
    (d) Wednesday=Hindi
    (e) Thursday=English

39. If Divyaraj finds that he is fourteenth from the left end of the row and 7th from the right end of the row, then how many boys must be added to the row such that there are 30 boys in the row?
    (a) 8   (b) 10
    (c) 12   (d) 14
    (e) None of these

40. Find odd one out from given series:
    AZD FUI   HSK OLP SHV
    (a) AZD   (b) FUI
    (c) HSK   (d) OLP
    (e) None of these

41. Two pipes can fill a tank in 10 hours and 16 hours respectively. A third pipe can empty the tank in 32 hours. If all the three pipes are opened simultaneously, then in how much time will the tank be full? (in hours)
(a) $7\frac{11}{21}$
(b) $7\frac{13}{21}$
(c) $8\frac{4}{21}$
(d) $6\frac{5}{14}$
(e) $8\frac{9}{14}$

42. a, b, c and d are four consecutive even numbers; if the sum of 'a' and 'c' is 120, what is the product of 'b' and 'd'?
(a) 4030
(b) 3780
(c) 3900
(d) 3900
(e) 3840

43. Three numbers are given. The average of the first and the third numbers is 24 more than the average of the second and the third numbers. Find out the difference between the first and the second numbers.
(a) 36
(b) 40
(c) 42
(d) 48
(e) 46

44. If 3 men or 9 boys can finish a piece of work in 21 days, in how many days can 5 men and 6 boys complete the same piece of work?
(a) 12 days
(b) 8 days
(c) 14 days
(d) 10 days
(e) 9 days

45. A sum of money fetches Rs. 240 as S.I. at the rate of 5 p.c.p.a. after 6 years. What is the principal?
(a) Rs 200
(b) Rs 400
(c) Rs 800
(d) Rs 1,200
(e) Rs 1,000

Directions (46– 50): Study the given table carefully and answer the questions below.
The table shows the total population in five different cities, the ratio of literate to illiterate population and also the percentage of graduate out of literate population in each city.

Cities	Population (in thousand)	Literate: Illiterate	Percentage Graduate out of literate
A	22	5 : 6	20%
B	16	3 : 5	35%
C	96	2 : 1	32%
D	20	2 : 3	25%
E	24	5 : 3	$33\frac{1}{3}\%$

46. The graduate population of city B and D together is approximately what percent more/less than the graduate population of city A and E together?
(a) 54%
(b) 50%
(c) 47%
(d) 42%
(e) 37%

47. The population of city C, who are literate but not graduate, is how much more than the average graduate population of city D and E together?
(a) 40020
(b) 4020
(c) 4200
(d) 4420
(e) 40040

48. If the ratio of illiterate male to female in city B is 3:5 and the ratio of graduate male to female population in city D is 2:3, then find the ratio of the total illiterate males in city B and the graduate females in city D?
(a) 23:7
(b) 8:25
(c) 75:16
(d) 21:8
(e) 25:8

49. The illiterate population of city D is what percent of the illiterate population of city 'C'?
(a) 25%
(b) 37.5%
(c) 40%
(d) 50%
(e) 62.5%

50. The literate population of cities A and B together is approximately what percentage of the population that are not graduates of city D?
(a) 82%
(b) 72%
(c) 93%
(d) 79%
(e) 89%

Directions (51-55): What will come in the place of the question mark (?) in the following number series?

51. 1, 11, 59, 239, 719, ?
(a) 1438
(b) 1439
(c) 1428
(d) 1429
(e) 1419

52. 18, 8, 30, 20, 42, ?
(a) 38
(b) 36
(c) 28
(d) 32
(e) 30

53. 2880, 480, 96, ?, 8, 4
(a) 16
(b) 24
(c) 20
(d) 28
(e) 32

54. 8, 10, 20, 50, ?, 248
(a) 115
(b) 103
(c) 113
(d) 108
(e) 118

55. 8, 6, 8, 14, 30, ?
(a) 75
(b) 76
(c) 77
(d) 78
(e) 79

Directions (56-60):A company produces three different products namely food, drinks and cosmetic products. If the total production of the company was same for all the years and % production of three products in particular years given below, then answer the questions that follow:

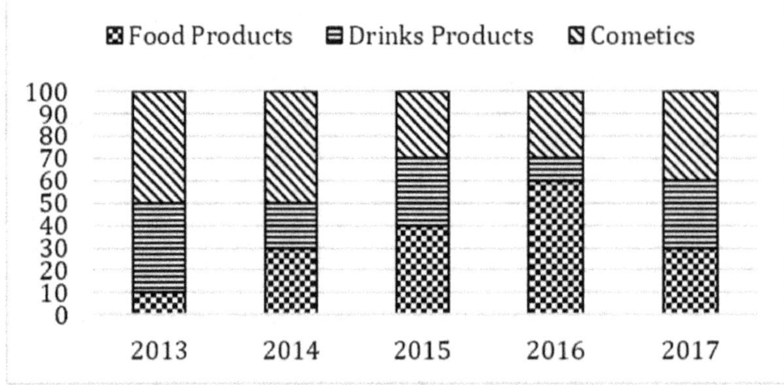

56. In 2013, the number of food products produced by the company is what percent more/less than cosmetic products produced in year 2016?
    (a) $33\frac{1}{3}\%$ (b) 25%   (c) $66\frac{2}{3}\%$
    (d) 20%   (e) 50%
57. If the total production in year 2017 was 1,20,000, find the difference between the number of food products produced in 2017 and drink products produced in 2014.
    (a) 12000   (b) 15000   (c) 12500
    (d) 10000   (e) 11500
58. Find the ratio between the number of cosmetic products produced in 2017 and the number of food products produced in 2013.
    (a) 1: 4   (b) 1 : 2   (c) 2 : 1
    (d) 3: 4   (e) 4 : 1
59. The difference between food products and drink products produced by the company in 2015 is 15000. Find the average of food and cosmetic products produced by the company in 2013.
    (a) 30000   (b) 50000   (c) 40000
    (d) 45000   (e) 25000
60. Find the total production in 2018 if there was an increase of 10% in total production in 2018 as compared to the previous year, given that the number of drink products produced in 2015 was 12000.
    (a) 55000   (b) 44000
    (c) 66000   (d) 33000
    (e) None of these

Directions (61-65): In each of these questions, two equations I and II are given. You have to solve both the equations and give the answer
(a) if $x > y$ (b) if $x \geq y$
(c) if $x < y$ (d) if $x \leq y$
(e) if $x = y$ or no relation can be established between x and y
61. I. $x^2 - 264 = 361$ II. $y^3 - 878 = 453$
62. I. $3x^2 + 14x + 15 = 0$ II. $3y^2 - 13y + 14 = 0$
63. I. $12x^2 - 17x + 6 = 0$ II. $y^2 - 16y + 63 = 0$
64. I. $x^2 - 48x + 575 = 0$ II. $46y^2 - 35y - 11 = 0$
65. I. $15x^2 - 11x - 12 = 0$ II. $20y^2 - 49y + 30 = 0$
66. Three friends Satish, Bhavya and Abhi are able to complete the work in 10 days, 15 days and 12 days respectively. They started to work together but Satish left the work after two days and Abhi left the work one day before the completion of the work. In how many days will the whole work be completed?
    (a) $5\frac{8}{9}$ days   (b) 6 days   (c) $7\frac{7}{8}$ days
    (d) 8 days   (e) 9 days
67. $\frac{2}{3}$rd of first number is equal to the cube of the second number. If the second number is equal to 12% of 100, what is the sum of the first and 2nd number?
    (a) 2408   (b) 2640   (c) 2426
    (d) 2604   (e) 2804
68. A wholesaler sells an item to a retailer at 20% discount, but charges 10% on the discounted price for packaging and delivery. The retailer sells it for 1023 more, thereby earning a profit of 25%. At what price had the wholesaler marked the item?
    (a) Rs. 4620   (b) Rs. 4650   (c) Rs. 4850
    (d) Rs. 5240   (e) Rs. 5445
69. The present age of Bhagat and Abhi is in the ratio of 9:8 respectively. After 10 years the ratio of their ages will be 10:9. What is the difference in their present age?
    (a) 8 years   (b) 6 years   (c) 12 years
    (d) 4 years   (e) 10 years
70. The circumference of two circles is 132 m. and 176m. respectively. What is the difference between the areas of the larger circle and the smaller circle? (in m^2)
    (a) 1052   (b) 1128   (c) 1258
    (d) 1078   (e) 1528

Directions (71-75): Study the given line graph carefully and answer the questions.
The line graph shows the percentage of chairs sold by six shopkeepers.

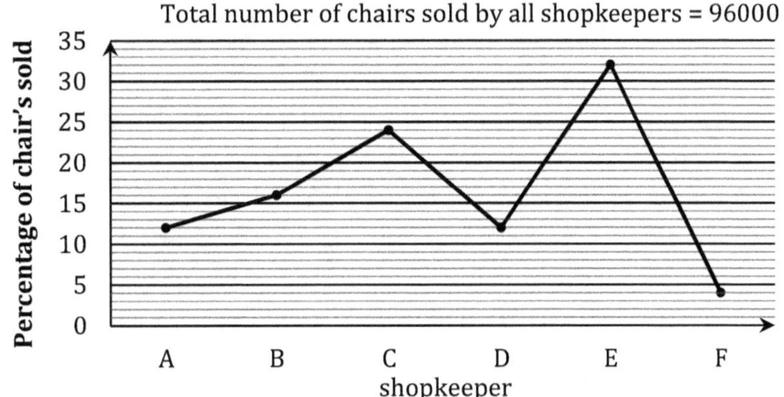

71. Chairs sold by shopkeepers B and D together is how much more than chairs sold by shopkeepers A and F together?
(a) 10420
(b) 11520
(c) 12480
(d) 11740
(e) 15220

72. Chairs sold by shopkeepers A and E together is how much percentage more than chairs sold by shopkeeper B and C together?
(a) 10%   (b) 6%   (c) 8%
(d) 12%   (e) 14%

73. F sold only three types of chairs i.e. K, L and M in the ratio 3:5:4. Find the difference of chairs sold by F of type K and M together and that of type L.
(a) 320   (b) 840   (c) 740
(d) 420   (e) 640

74. There is another shopkeeper P who sells three types of chairs i.e. X, Y and Z. If chairs of type X sold is half of the total chairs sold by shopkeeper F, chairs of type Y sold is 20% of the chairs sold by shopkeeper A and chairs of type Z sold is $\frac{2}{5}$ th of the total chairs sold by shopkeeper B, then find the total number of chairs sold by shopkeeper P?
(a) 12348
(b) 16368
(c) 12244
(d) 10368
(e) 10428

75. What is the ratio of the average number of chairs sold by shopkeepers B, C and D together to the average number of chairs sold by shopkeeper A and E together?
(a) 25:33
(b) 21:11
(c) 26:33
(d) 11:24
(e) 11:26

Directions (76-80): What should come in place of question mark (?) in the following questions?

76. $1528 + 525 \div 25 - 840 = 510 + ?$
(a) 199
(b) 299
(c) 159
(d) 189
(e) 165

77. $\sqrt{1225} \div 7 + 18.5 \times 16 - 18\%$ of $10800 = ? - 1800$
(a) 259   (b) 169   (c) 157
(d) 129   (e) 141

78. 65% of $180 + ?\%$ of $210 = 80\%$ of 225
(a) 45   (b) 30   (c) 40
(d) 50   (e) 25

79. $\sqrt{1500 + ? + 17.5 \times 8 - 5\% \ of \ 20} = 42$
(a) 145   (b) 115   (c) 120
(d) 135   (e) 125

80. $\frac{13}{17}$ of $\frac{8}{156}$ of $153 = ?$
(a) 8   (b) 12   (c) 7
(d) 6   (e) 4

REASONING ABILITY

1. **(a)** $D > C = E\,(True)\ B \geq C = E\,(False)$
2. **(b)** $S = Q \geq P\,(False)\ S = Q > M \geq N\,(True)$
3. **(d)** $V = S\,(False)\ Q > M\,(False)$
4. **(a)** $S \geq V = U > T\,(True)\ V \geq Q\,(False)$
5. **(a)** $E = J > L \geq W\,(True)\ M \geq N > R > W \leq L\,(False)$

6. **(a)**
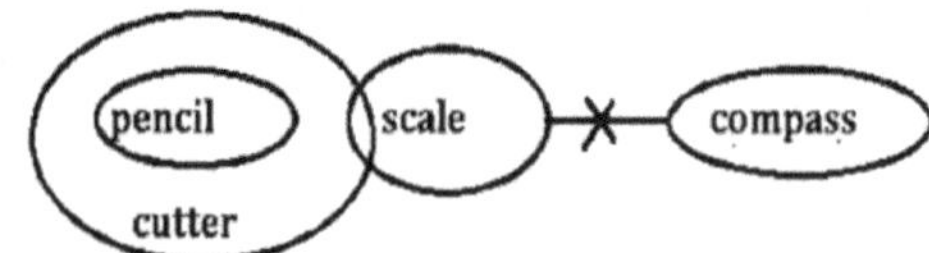

7. **(b)**
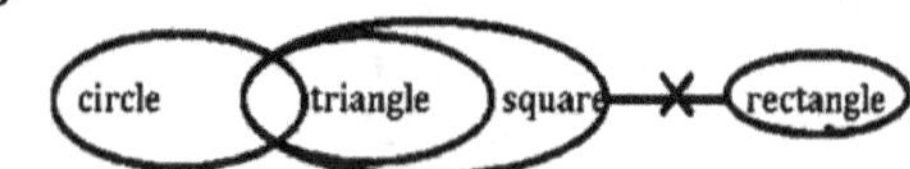

8. **(e)**
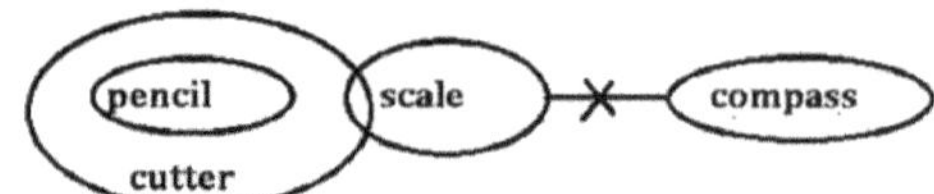

9. **(d)**
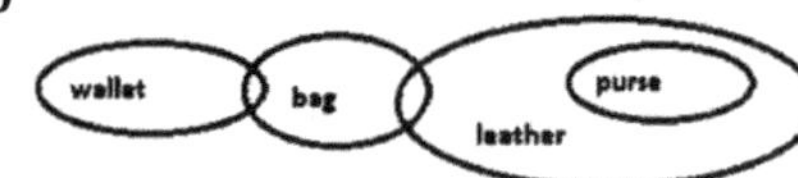

10. **(e)**
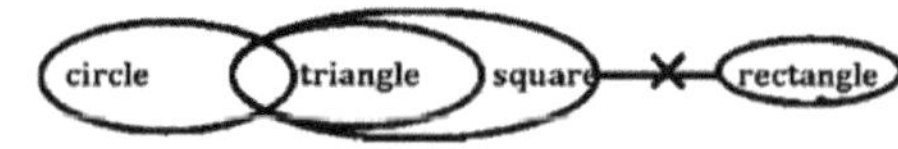

Direction (11-15)
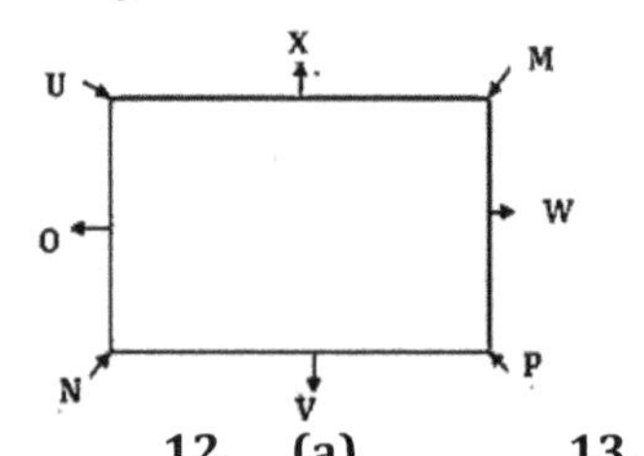

| 11. **(b)** | 12. **(a)** | 13. **(d)** |
| 14. **(a)** | 15. **(d)** | |

Direction (16-18)
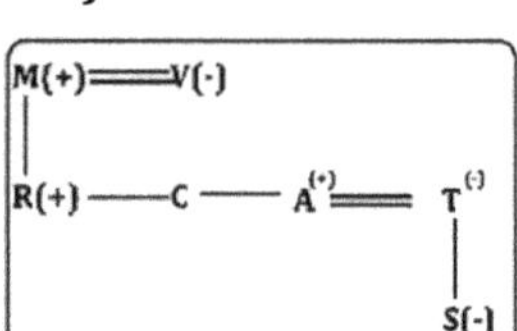

| 16. **(c)** | 17. **(b)** | 18. **(c)** |

Direction (19-23)
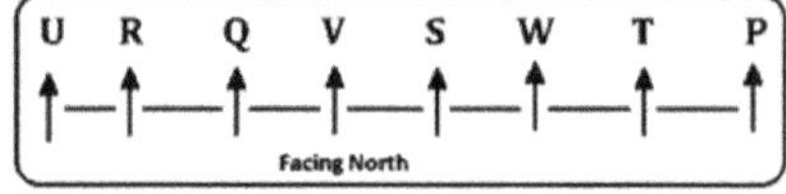

19. **(e)**	20. **(d)**	21. **(a)**
22. **(b)**	23. **(e)**	
24. **(b)**		

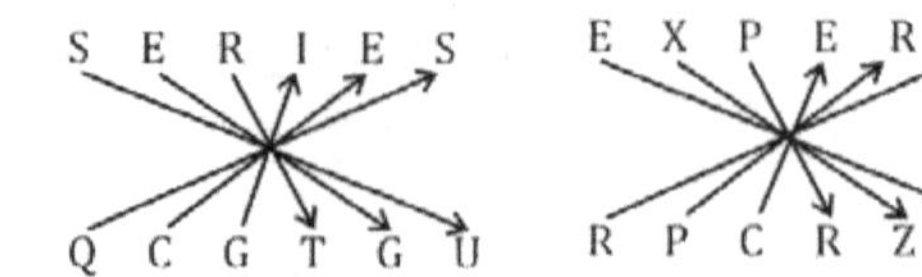

25. **(d)**

Direction (26-30)

Floor	Persons
9	T
8	R
7	S
6	U
5	P
4	Q
3	V
2	X
1	W

| 26. **(e)** | 27. **(e)** | 28. **(c)** |
| 29. **(b)** | 30. **(d)** | |

Direction (31-33)
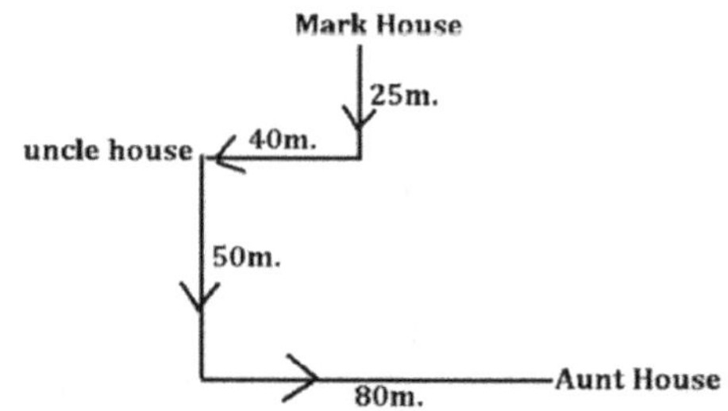

| 31. **(b)** | 32. **(b)** | 33. **(a)** |

Direction (34-38)

Day	Subjects
Monday	Mathematics
Tuesday	Chemistry
Wednesday	Hindi
Thursday	Geography
Friday	English
Saturday	Physics
Sunday	Biology

34. **(e)**	35. **(b)**	36. **(d)**
37. **(b)**	38. **(d)**	39. **(b)**
40. **(d)**		

41. (b) Part of the tank filled in 1 hour

$$= \frac{1}{10} + \frac{1}{16} - \frac{1}{32} = \frac{16+10-5}{160} = \frac{21}{160}$$

$\therefore$ Tank will be filled in $\frac{160}{21} = 7\frac{13}{21}$ hours

42. (e) $\because$ a, b, c and d are four consecutive numbers and a + c = 120

$\therefore$ a +a+4 = 120

$\Rightarrow 2a = 116 \Rightarrow a = 58$

$\therefore$ b = 60 and d= 64

$\therefore$ b × d = 60 × 64 = 3840

43. (d) Let the numbers be a, b, and c respectively.

$\therefore \frac{a+c}{2} - \frac{b+c}{2} = 24$

$\Rightarrow$ (a +c) – (b + c) = 24 × 2 = 48

$\Rightarrow$ a –b = 48

44. (e) $\because$ 3 men = 9 boys

$\therefore$ 1 man = 3 boys

$\therefore$ 5 men + 6 boys

= (5 × 3 + 6) boys = 21 boys

$\therefore M_1 D_1 = M_2 D_2$

= 9 × 21 = 21 × D_2

= $D_2 = \frac{9 \times 21}{21}$ = 9 days

45. (c) Principal $= \frac{SI \times 100}{Time \times Rate}$

$\therefore \frac{240 \times 100}{5 \times 6} = Rs\ 800$

46. (d) Graduate population of city A and E together

$= 22000 \times \frac{5}{11} \times \frac{20}{100} + 24000 \times \frac{5}{8} \times \frac{1}{3}$

= 2000 + 5000 = 7000

Graduate population of city B and D together

$= 16000 \times \frac{3}{8} \times \frac{35}{100} + 20000 \times \frac{2}{5} \times \frac{25}{100}$

= 2100 + 2000 = 4100

Required percentage $= \frac{7000-4100}{7000} \times 100$

$= \frac{2900}{7000} \times 100 \approx 42\%$

47. (a) Population who are literate but not graduate of city C= $96000 \times \frac{2}{3} \times \frac{68}{100}$= 43520

Average graduate population of city D & E together

$= \frac{1}{2}\left[20000 \times \frac{2}{5} \times \frac{25}{100} + 24000 \times \frac{5}{8} \times \frac{1}{3}\right]$

$= \frac{1}{2}$[2000 + 5000] = 3500

$\therefore$ Required difference = 43520 – 3500

= 40020

48. (e) Illiterate male in city B

$= 16000 \times \frac{5}{8} \times \frac{3}{8} = 3750$

Graduate female in city D

$= 20000 \times \frac{2}{5} \times \frac{25}{100} \times \frac{3}{5}$

= 1200

Required ratio $= \frac{3750}{1200} = 25 : 8$

49. (b) Illiterate Population in City D

$= 20,000 \times \frac{3}{5} = 12000$

Illiterate Population in City C

$= 96,000 \times \frac{1}{3} = 32000$

Required % $= \frac{12000}{32000} \times 100 = 37.5\%$

50. (e) *Required percentage*

$$= \frac{22,000 \times \frac{5}{11} + 16,000 \times \frac{3}{8}}{20,000 \times \frac{3}{5} + 20,000 \times \frac{2}{5} \times \frac{75}{100}} \times 100$$

$$= \frac{10,000 + 6,000}{12,000 + 6,000} \times 100 = \frac{1600}{18} \approx 89\%$$

51. (b)

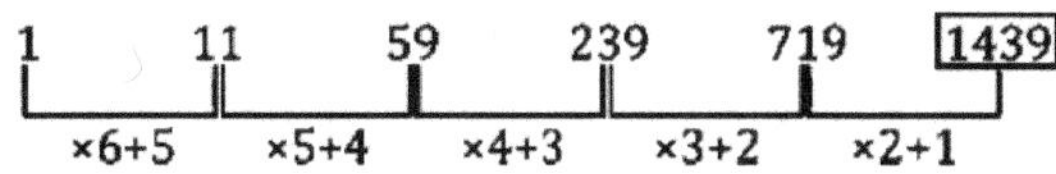

52. (d)

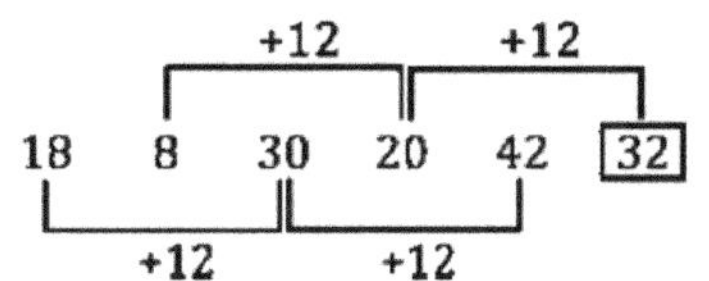

53. (b)

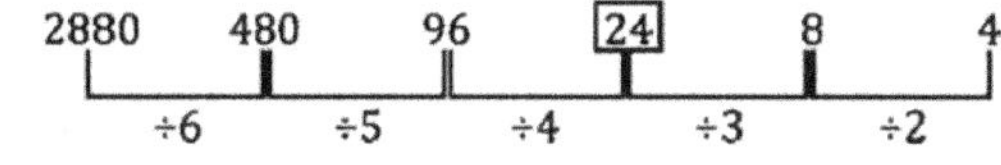

54. (e)

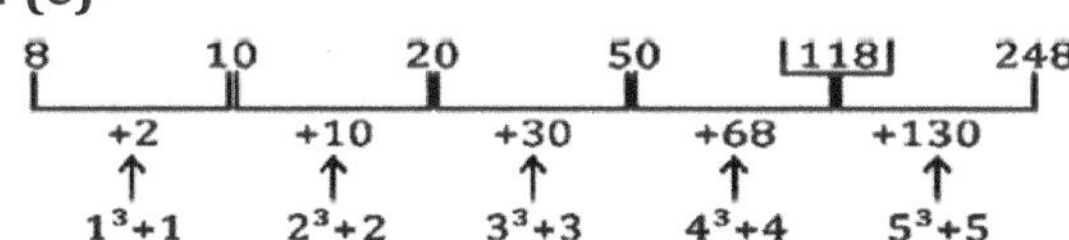

55. (c)

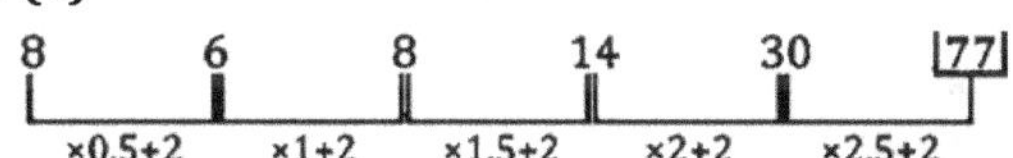

56. (c) Let total production of the company be x

$\therefore$ Required percent $= \frac{(.30x - 0.10x)}{0.30x} \times 100$

$= \frac{2}{3} \times 100 = 66\frac{2}{3}\%$ less

57. (a) Required difference = 30% of 1,20,000 – 20% of 1,20,000= 12000

58. (e) Let total production be x

Required ratio $= \frac{40\% \text{ of } x}{10\% \text{ of } x} = 4 : 1$

59. (d) Let total production be x

ATQ,

10% of x = 15000

$\frac{x}{10} = 15000$

x = 1,50,000

Required average

$= \frac{10\% \text{ of } 1,50,000 + 50\% \text{ of } 1,50,000}{2}$

$= \frac{15000 + 75000}{2} = 45000$

60. (b) Let total production of each previous years

be x

$\therefore \frac{30}{100}x = 12000 \Rightarrow x = 40000$

Total production in 2018 $= \frac{110}{100} \times 40000$

$= 44000.$

61. (e)

I. $x^2 - 264 = 361$	II. $y^3 - 878 = 453$
$or, x^2 = 361 + 264$	$or, y^3 = 453 + 878$
$\therefore x^2 = 625$	$or, y^3 = 1331$
$\therefore x = \sqrt{625} = \pm 25$	$\therefore y = \sqrt[3]{1331} = 11$

Hence no relation can be established.

62. (c)

I. $3x^2 + 14x + 15 = 0$	II. $3y^2 - 13y + 14 = 0$
$or, 3x^2 + 9x + 5x + 15 = 0$	$or, 3y^2 - 6y - 7y + 14 = 0$
$or, 3x(x + 3) + 5(x + 3) = 0$	$or, 3y(y - 2) - 7(y - 2) = 0$
$or, (3x + 5)(x + 3) = 0$	$or, (3y - 7)(y - 2) = 0$
$\therefore x = -\frac{5}{3}, -3$	$\therefore y = \frac{7}{3}, 2$

Hence $x < y$

63. (c)

I. $12x^2 - 17x + 6 = 0$	II. $y^2 - 16y + 63 = 0$
$or, 12x^2 - 9x - 8x + 6 = 0$	$or, y^2 - 9y - 7y + 63 = 0$
$or, 3x(4x - 3) - 2(4x - 3) = 0$	$or, y(y - 9) - 7(y - 9) = 0$
$or, (3x - 2)(4x - 3) = 0$	$or, (y - 7)(y - 9) = 0$
$\therefore x = \frac{2}{3}, \frac{3}{4}$	$\therefore y = 7, 9$

Hence $x < y$

64. (a)

I. $x^2 - 48x + 575 = 0$	II. $46y^2 - 35y - 11 = 0$
$or, x^2 - 23x - 25x + 575 = 0$	$or, 46y^2 - 46y + 11y - 11 = 0$
$or, x(x - 23) - 25(x - 23) = 0$	$or, 46y(y - 1) + 11(y - 1) = 0$
$or, (x - 25)(x - 23) = 0$	$or, (46y + 11)(y - 1) = 0$
$\therefore x = 25, 23$	$\therefore y = -\frac{11}{46}, 1$

Hence $x > y$

65. (e)

I. $15x^2 - 11x - 12 = 0$	II. $20y^2 - 49y + 30 = 0$
$or, 15x^2 - 20x + 9x - 12 = 0$	$or, 20y^2 - 25y - 24y + 30 = 0$
$or, 5x(3x - 4) + 3(3x - 4) = 0$	$or, 5y(4y - 5) - 6(4y - 5)$
$or, (5x + 3)(3x - 4)$	$\therefore y = \frac{6}{5}, \frac{5}{4}$
$\therefore x = -\frac{3}{5}, \frac{4}{3}$	

No relation

66. (a)

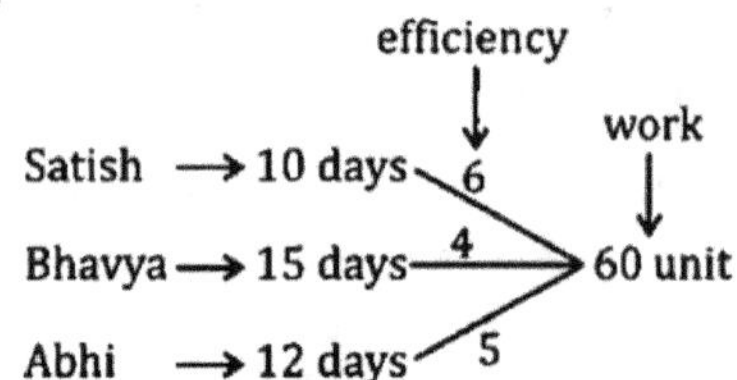

(Satish+ Bhavya+ Abhi) 2 days' work = 15 × 2 = 30 unit

Bhavya 1 day work = 4 unit

$\therefore$ Whole work will be completed

$= 2 + \frac{26}{9} + 1 = 2 + 2\frac{8}{9} + 1$

$= 5\frac{8}{9} days$

67. (d) $Second\ no. = \frac{100 \times 12}{100} = 12$

$\therefore first\ no. = 12^3 \times \frac{3}{2} = 1728 \times \frac{3}{2}$

$= 2592$

$\therefore$ Required sum = 12 + 2592 = 2604

68. (b) Let the price marked by whole seller be Rs. x

$\therefore S.P.\ of\ article\ for\ whole\ seller = x \times \frac{80}{100} \times \frac{110}{100} = \frac{22x}{25} =$

$C.P\ of\ article\ for\ retailer$

$S.P.\ of\ article\ for\ retailer = \frac{22x}{25} \times \frac{125}{100} = \frac{11x}{10}$

ATQ,

$\frac{11x}{10} - \frac{22x}{25} = 1023$

$\frac{55x - 44x}{50} = 1023$

$11x = 1023 \times 50$

$\Rightarrow x = Rs.\ 4650$

69. (e) Let present age of Bhagat and Abhi be 9x and 8x respectively

After 10 years.

$\frac{9x + 10}{8x + 10} = \frac{10}{9}$

$81x + 90 = 80x + 100$

$x = 10$

$\therefore$ required difference = 10 years.

70. (d) Let radius of smaller & larger circles be r_1 & r_2 respectively.

$2\pi r_1 = 132$

$r_1 = 21$ m

$2\pi r_2 = 176 \Rightarrow r_2 = 28$ m.

$\therefore$ Required difference

$= \pi(r_2^2 - r_1^2) = \frac{22}{7} \times 49 \times 7 = 1078$ m^2

71. (b) Required difference

$= \left[(16 + 12)\% - (12 + 4)\%\right] \times 96000$

$= \frac{12}{100} \times 96000 = 11520$

72. (a) Required percentage

$= \frac{(12 + 32) - (16 + 24)}{(16 + 24)} \times 100$

$= \frac{4}{40}$

73. (e) Total chairs sold by shopkeeper F

$= \frac{4}{100} \times 96000 = 3840$

Required difference

$= \frac{(7 - 5)}{12} \times 3840 = 640$

74. (d) Total chairs sold by Shopkeeper P

$= \left[\frac{1}{2} \times 4 + \frac{1}{5} \times 12 + \frac{2}{5} \times 16\right] \times \frac{96000}{100}$

$= 10368$

75. (c) $Required\ ratio = \frac{\frac{16 + 24 + 12}{3}}{\frac{12 + 32}{2}}$

$= \frac{52 \times 2}{3 \times 44} = 26 : 33$

76. (a) $1528 + 21 - 840 - 510 = ?$

$? = 1549 - 1350$

$? = 199$

77. (c) $\frac{35}{7} + 296 - 1944 = ? - 1800$

$301 + 1800 - 1944 = ?$

$? = 157.$

78. (b) $\frac{65}{100} \times 180 + \frac{?}{100} \times 210 = \frac{80}{100} \times 225$

$\frac{?}{100} \times 210 = 180 - 117$

$? = \frac{63 \times 100}{210} = 30$

79. (e) $1500 + 140 - 1 + ? = 1764$

$? = 1764 - 1639$

$? = 125$

80. (d) $\frac{13}{17} \times \frac{8}{156} \times 153 = ? \Rightarrow ? = 6$

REASONING ABILITY

Direction (1-5): In each of the questions below are given some statements followed by some conclusions. You have to take the given statements to be true even if they seem to be at variance with commonly known facts. Read all the conclusions and then decide which of the conclusions given logically follows from the given statements, disregarding commonly known facts.

(a) If only conclusion I follows.

(b) If only conclusion II follows.

(c) If either conclusion I or II follows.

(d) If neither conclusion I nor II follows.

(e) If both conclusions I and II follow.

1. **Statements:** Some Air are Base. Some Club are Base. Only a few Air is Club. Some Gray is Club.

   Conclusions: I. Some Air can be Gray.

   II. No Air is Gray.

2. **Statements:** All Virat are Rohit. Some Hardik are not Rohit.

   Conclusions: I. Some Hardik are Virat.

   II. No Virat is Hardik.

3. **Statements:** Some RRB are SBI. All SBI are RBI. Some NHB are RBI.

   Conclusions: I. All SBI being NHB is a possibility.

   II. Some RRB can never be NHB.

4. **Statements:** Some India are Paris. No Russia is Paris. All Russia are China.

   Conclusions: I. Some Paris can be China.

   II. All India being Russia is a possibility.

5. **Statements:** All New are Bag. Some Bag are Old. Some Old are Paper.

   Conclusions: I. Some New are not Paper.

   II. Some Bag are Paper is a possibility.

Direction (6-10): Study the following information carefully and answer the questions given below:

A certain number of persons are sitting in a row facing north. There are four persons sitting between P and R, who sit at one of the ends. B sits 3rd to the left of Q. There is one person who sits between B and K. L sits 4th to the left of K. M sits immediate left of P. There are two persons sitting between Q and M. At least 15 persons sit between L and R. There is one person who sits between R and T. U sits 2nd from one of the ends. There is one person who sits between U and L.

6. How many persons are seated between U and B?

   (a) six   (b) five   (c) eight

   (d) seven   (e) nine

7. What is the position of K with respect to Q?

   (a) 5th to the left

   (b) 3rd to the left

   (c) 4th to the right

   (d) 2nd to the right

   (e) None of these

8. How many persons are seated to the right of B?

   (a) 19   (b) 11

   (c) 17   (d) 12

   (e) Can't be determined

9. If the position of M and T are interchanged, then how many persons sit between T and B?

   (a) 3   (b) 4   (c) 5

   (d) 6   (e) 8

10. How many persons are sitting in the row?

    (a) 25   (b) 22   (c) 24

    (d) 19   (e) 28

Direction (11-13): Study the following information carefully and answer the questions given below:

Point B is 3kms. east of Point A. Point E is 4kms. north of Point B. Point C is 15kms. east of Point E. Point D is in 9kms. west of Point F. Point C is 10kms. north of Point F.

11. What is the direction of Point E with respect to Point D?

    (a) north-west   (b) north   (c) south

    (d) south-east   (e) north-east

12. What is the shortest distance between Point A and Point E?

    (a) 8km.   (b) 5km.   (c) 6km.

    (d) 9km.   (e) 10km.

13. If Point L is in 6kms. south of Point B, then what is the distance between Point L and Point D?

    (a) 5km.   (b) 16km.   (c) 6km.

    (d) 12km.   (e) 18km.

Direction (14-18): Study the following information carefully and answer the questions given below:

Eight persons H, K, L, M, N, O, P and Q are sitting around a circular table but not necessarily in the same order. Some are facing the centre while some are facing outside.

Both P and H are facing in the same direction. M sits 3rd to the left of L and both are facing in the same direction. O sits 2nd to the right of M. There is one person who sits between O and K who are both facing opposite directions. Both Q and N are facing each other. Q does not sit near to K. P sits 3rd to the right of K. P sits immediate left of H, who faces outside.

14. How many persons are sitting between O and N, when counted to the left of O?
    (a) four   (b) one
    (c) none   (d) five
    (e) None of these

15. What is the position of P with respect to Q?
    (a) 2nd to the right
    (b) 2nd to the left
    (c) 3rd to the left
    (d) 3rd to the right
    (e) None of these

16. Who among the following persons faces K?
    (a) M   (b) H
    (c) O   (d) Q
    (e) None of these

17. Four of the following five are alike in certain ways and hence form a group. Which one of the following does not belong to that group?
    (a) M   (b) K   (c) N
    (d) P   (e) Q

18. If the position of N and L are interchanged, then find who among the following sits 2nd to the right of Q?
    (a) L   (b) N
    (c) K   (d) H
    (e) None of these

Direction (19-22): Each of the questions below consists of a question and two statements numbered I and II given below it. You have to decide whether the data provided in the statements is sufficient to answer the question. Read both the statements and give the answer.

(a) If the data in statement I alone is sufficient to answer the question, while the data in statement II alone is not sufficient to answer the question

(b) If the data in statement II alone is sufficient to answer the question, while the data in statement I alone is not sufficient to answer the question

(c) If the data in either statement I alone or in statement II alone is sufficient to answer the question

(d) If the data given in both statements I and II together is not sufficient to answer the question and

(e) If the data in both statements I and II together is necessary to answer the question.

19. How is 'Can' coded in the code language?
    Statements:
    I. "none of these" is coded as "mnnklp" and "how can these" is coded as "lprtwq".
    II. "each of them" is coded as "nkfdws" and "how could you" is coded as "rt dv bm".

20. If five persons M, N, O, P and Q are sitting around a circular table facing the centre but not in the same order, then who among the following sits 2nd to the left of M?
    Statements:
    I. N sits 2nd to the left of Q. O does not sit near to Q. Both P and N are immediate neighbours.
    II. N sits 3rd to the right of P. O sits 2nd to the left of the one who sits to the immediate left of P.

21. In a five-storey building one person lives on each floor. The ground floor is the 1st floor and the topmost floor is the 5th floor. Who among the following lives on the 2nd floor?
    Statements:
    I. B lives on an odd numbered floor. Two floors gap between B and G.
    II. D lives just above the floor of H. F does not live on the topmost floor.

22. If six persons are sitting in a row facing north, then find who among the following sits at one of the extreme ends?
    Statements:
    I. B sits 2nd to the right of D and both are not sitting at the extreme ends. Both C and F are immediate neighbours.
    II. A sits 2nd to the left of E. Two persons sit between A and C. F does not sit to the immediate left of D.

Directions (23-27): In each of the questions given below, a group of letters is followed by a combination of numbers/symbols. You have to find out which of the given combinations correctly represents the group of letters based on the numbers/symbols codes and the conditions given below. If none of the given combinations represents the group of letters correctly, give (e) i.e. 'None of these' as the answer.

Letter	A	C	R	E	F	B	H	I	J	K	N	U	D	G	M	L
Numbers/ Symbols	1	8	#	$	2	•	5	9	3	&	^	+	@	%	4	6

Condition for coding the group letters:

(i) If the first letter is a vowel and the last letter is consonant, the codes for the first and the last letter are to be interchanged.

(ii) If the first as well as the last letter is a vowel, then both are to be coded by the code for the last letter.

(iii) If the first as well as the last letter is a consonant, then both are to be coded by the code for the first letter.

23. NGCRFL
    (a) ^%82#^   (b) 6%82#6   (c) 62#8%6
    (d) ^%8#2^   (e) None of these
24. BHIDU
    (a) +59@*   (b) *@59*   (c) *59@+
    (d) +95@+   (e) None of these
25. REDKING
    (a) #$@&9^#   (b) %$@&9^%   (c) #59@$*%
    (d) %$@&9^#   (e) None of these
26. UMBRELLA
    (a) +4*#66$+   (b) +4*#$66   (c) 14*#66$+
    (d) 14*#6$61   (e) 14*#$661
27. UNDER
    (a) +^@$#   (b) #^@$+   (c) +^@$+
    (d) #$^@#   (e) None of these

Direction (28-32): Study the following information carefully and answer the questions given below:

Six persons P, Q, R, S, T, and U like different food items i.e. Pizza, Samosa, Biryani, Pettish, Sandwich and Burger and also like different colours viz. Blue, Pink, Red, Yellow, Green and Black, but not necessarily in the same order.

P likes Samosa but does not like Red and Black colours. The one who likes Pettish also likes Yellow colour. T likes Burger but does not like Red colour. U likes Pink colour. Q likes Sandwich but does not like Black colour. R likes neither Pettish nor Green. U does not like Pizza. Q does not like Red. The one who likes Samosa does not like Blue colour.

28. Who among the following persons likes Biryani?
    (a) S   (b) U
    (c) R   (d) Either (a) or (c)
    (e) None of these
29. Who among the following likes Blue colour?
    (a) P   (b) S   (c) Q
    (d) R   (e) T
30. Which of the following is true with regard to R?
    (a) R likes Blue colour
    (b) R likes Biryani
    (c) R likes Red colour
    (d) R likes Yellow colour
    (e) All are true
31. Four of the following five are alike in a certain way and hence they form a group. Which one of the following does not belong to that group?
    (a) P - Black   (b) U - Green   (c) R - Red
    (d) T - Blue   (e) P - Blue
32. Which of the following combinations is true with regard to S?
    (a) Burger-Black   (b) Pettish-Blue
    (c) Biryani-Red   (d) Pettish-Yellow
    (e) None is true

33. How many numerals are there in the number '164824379' which will remain in the same position when arranged in ascending order from left to right?
    (a) one   (b) none   (c) four
    (d) two   (e) None of these
34. How many words can be formed from the 1st, 6th, 8th and 9th letter of the word 'RECEPTION' by using each letter once in the word?
    (a) none   (b) one
    (c) two   (d) three
    (e) More than three

Direction (35-39): Study the following information carefully and answer the questions given below:

Eight boxes L, M, N, O, P, Q, R and S are placed one above the other but not necessarily in the same order.

Box S is not placed above the box P. Box Q is placed just above the box M. Three boxes gap between N and L, which is placed above box N. No box is in between M and N. There are two boxes in the gap between M and P. Box O is placed above the box Q.

35. How many boxes are placed between box O and box N?
    (a) 3   (b) 1   (c) 2
    (d) 5   (e) 4
36. Which of the following boxes is placed just below the box N?
    (a) P   (b) S   (c) R
    (d) L   (e) None of these
37. Which of the following boxes is placed at the topmost position?
    (a) L   (b) O   (c) P
    (d) R   (e) None of these
38. How many boxes are in between box P and box Q?
    (a) none   (b) one   (c) three
    (d) four   (e) five
39. Four of the following five boxes are alike in a certain way and hence form a group. Which one of the following does not belong to that group?
    (a) L and Q   (b) O and M   (c) N and P
    (d) Q and R   (e) R and S
40. Study the following information carefully and answer the question given below:

D is the brother of P. E is the father of P. A is the mother in law of G, who is the mother of P. D does not have any sister. How is P related to A?
    (a) Son   (b) Grand daughter
    (c) Grand son   (d) Daughter
    (e) None of these

41. The cost of paving a circular field at Rs.10/cm² is Rs.3465. If the side of a square field is equal to the diameter of a circular field, then find the perimeter of square field.
(a) 72 cm.　　(b) 96 cm.　　(c) 120 cm.
(d) 84 cm.　　(e) 108 cm.

42. A bag has 6 blue balls, 'x' red balls and 5 green balls. If two balls are picked randomly, then the probability of 1 being red and 1 being green is $\frac{9}{38}$. Find value of x.
(a) 5　　(b) 9　　(c) 4
(d) 7　　(e) 8

43. A and B invested Rs. 2000 and Rs. (2000 +x) respectively. B withdrew from the business after 8 months. If at the end of the year, profit obtained by B is 20% less than the profit obtained by A, then find the value of x.
(a) Rs. 500　　(b) Rs. 400　　(c) Rs. 450

(d) Rs. 600　　(e) Rs. 200

44. The cost price of article A is twice that of article B. If on selling A and B there is a profit of 8.3% and 14.4% respectively and the total profit obtained is Rs. 186, then find the cost price of article A.
(a) 1000　　(b) 1100　　(c) 1200
(d) 1250　　(e) 1050

45. Two vessels A and B of equal capacity contain a mixture of milk and water in the ratio 8:y and 7:6 respectively. If the total quantity of each vessel is 260L and the quantity of milk in A is $14\frac{2}{7}\%$ more than the quantity of milk in B, then find y.
(a) 10　　(b) 4　　(c) 5
(d) 6　　(e) 7

Directions (46-50): Study the charts given below and answer the following questions.

The bar chart below shows the number of employees in 4 different companies (P, Q, R & S) and the following table shows the number of employees whose age is more than 40 years in these companies.

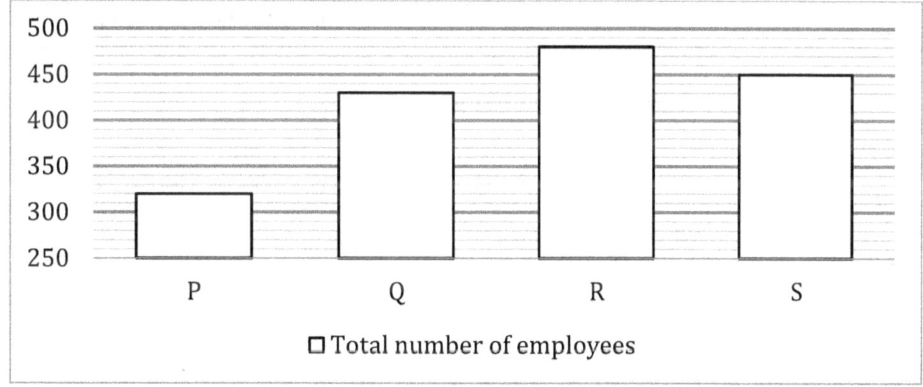

Company	Number of employees whose age is more than 40 years
P	70
Q	130
R	120
S	150

46. Find the ratio of employees whose age is less than or equal to 40 years in Q & R together to the number of employees whose age is more than 40 years in R & S together.
(a) 12:5　　(b) 22:9　　(c) 2:9
(d) 11:16　　(e) 5:8

47. If the ratio of male to female employees whose age is more than 40 years in P and Q is 3:2 and 5:8 respectively, then the female employees whose age is more than 40 years in P & Q together are what percent of the total employees in R?
(a) 17.5%　　(b) 12.5%　　(c) 35.5%
(d) 22.5%　　(e) 31.5%

48. Find the average number of employees whose age is less than or equal to 40 years in Q, R & S.
(a) 370　　(b) 340　　(c) 280
(d) 390　　(e) 320

49. If 80% of employees whose age is less than or equal to 40 years in P are equal to the total male employees in P, then find the total number of female employees in P that is how much more or less than employees whose age is more than 40 years in R & S together?
(a) 120   (b) 150   (c) 110
(d) 130   (e) 140

50. Total employees in P and R together are what percent more than employees whose age is less than or equal to 40 years in Q and S together?
(a) $25\frac{2}{3}\%$ (b) $33\frac{1}{3}\%$
(c) $73\frac{2}{3}\%$ (d) $52\frac{1}{3}\%$
(e) None of the above

Directions (51-55): What will come in place of (?) in the following number series?

51. 1, 11, 99, 693, 3465, ?
(a) 10335   (b) 10285   (c) 10245
(d) 10395   (e) 10375

52. 2, 1, 1, 1.5, 3, ?
(a) 5   (b) 7.5   (c) 8
(d) 6.5   (e) 9.5

53. 28, 40, 60, 90, 132, ?
(a) 188   (b) 190   (c) 174
(d) 212   (e) 182

54. 12, 20, 47, 111, 236, ?
(a) 452   (b) 478   (c) 410
(d) 376   (e) 332

55. 62, 80, 116, 170, 242, ?
(a) 356   (b) 332   (c) 290
(d) 384   (e) 428

Directions (56-60): Study the passage given below and answer the following questions.

A store sells phones of only 3 brands— Samsung, Oppo and Vivo. In a particular week (W1), the store sold 4600 phones of which 1960 phones were of Samsung. Oppo phones sold by the store in W1 were 560 less than the Samsung phones sold by the store in W1.

Ratio of male buyers to female buyers of Samsung phones from the store in W1 was 25:24. Male buyers of Vivo phones from the store in W1 were 40 less than female buyers of Vivo phones from the store in W1. Female buyers of Oppo phones from the store in W1 were equal to male buyers of Vivo phone from the store in W1.

56. Female buyers of Vivo phones from the store in W1 were what percent more or less than male buyers of Samsung phones from the store in W1?
(a) 25%   (b) 42%   (c) 36%
(d) 32%   (e) 30%

57. Find the ratio of the average of male buyers of Samsung and Oppo phones from the store in W1 to female buyers of Oppo and Vivo phones together from the store in W1.
(a) 45:62   (b) 5:9
(c) 16:21   (d) 12:23
(e) None of the above

58. The female buyers of Samsung and Vivo phones together from the store in W1 are what percent of the total Oppo phones sold by the store in W1?
(a) $125\frac{1}{7}\%$ (b) $117\frac{2}{7}\%$ (c) $124\frac{6}{7}\%$
(d) $110\frac{3}{7}\%$ (e) $114\frac{2}{7}\%$

59. Find the total number of Samsung phones sold by the store on each day in W1 (store sold equal number of Samsung phones on each day in W1).
(a) 230   (b) 320   (c) 200
(d) 280   (e) 350

60. The total female buyers of the phones of all brands from the store in W1 are how much more or less than the total Oppo and the total Vivo phones sold by the store in W1 together?
(a) 560   (b) 310   (c) 440
(d) 380   (e) 490

Directions (61-65): In the following questions, two equations **(I)** and **(II)** are given. You have to solve both the equations and mark the appropriate answer.

61. I. $x^2 - 15x + 56 = 0$
II. $y^2 - 12y + 35 = 0$
(a) $x < y$ (b) $x \leq y$
(c) $x > y$ (d) $x \geq y$
(e) $x = y$ or no relation.

62. I. $24x^2 - 38x + 15 = 0$
II. $15y^2 - 46y + 35 = 0$
(a) $x < y$ (b) $x \leq y$
(c) $x > y$ (d) $x \geq y$
(e) $x = y$ or no relation.

63. I. $x^3 = 5832$
II. $(y - 21)^2 = 256$
(a) $x < y$ (b) $x \leq y$
(c) $x > y$ (d) $x \geq y$
(e) $x = y$ or no relation.

64. I. $2x + 3y = 36$
II. $5x + 9y = 102$
(a) $x < y$ (b) $x \leq y$
(c) $x > y$ (d) $x \geq y$
(e) $x = y$ or no relation.

65. I. $35x^2 + 44x + 12 = 0$
II. $28y^2 + 59y + 30 = 0$
(a) $x < y$ (b) $x \leq y$
(c) $x > y$ (d) $x \geq y$
(e) $x = y$ or no relation.

Directions (66-70): Find the approximate value of (?) in the following questions.

66. $24.97\% \ of \ 1799 - (11.012 \times 24.05) = ?$
(a) 138   (b) 164   (c) 157
(d) 186   (e) 123

67. $12.012\% \ of \ (231.989 + 417.91) + 90.98 = (?)^2$
(a) 13   (b) 15   (c) 8
(d) 10   (e) 19

68.
$$(26.99 \times 48.023) \div 54.01 + 57.03\% \ of \ 2500.034 = ?$$
(a) 1485   (b) 1498   (c) 1467
(d) 1454   (e) 1449

69. $\dfrac{55.01\% \ of \ 2199}{67.023 + 54.12} + (2.034 \times 12.01 + 6.02) = ?$
(a) 28   (b) 40   (c) 62
(d) 72   (e) 56

70. $513.89 - 122.11 + 56.987 + 221.123 = ?$
(a) 670   (b) 690   (c) 780
(d) 730   (e) 760

71. A boat takes 9 hours more to travel 65 kms. upstream than to travel 60 kms. downstream. If the speed of the boat in still water is $2\frac{7}{9}$ m/sec., then find speed of the stream in (km/hr.).
(a) 7   (b) 4   (c) 8
(d) 5   (e) 6

72. 4 yrs ago A was four yrs younger than B. 6 yrs hence, the ratio of the ages of A to B will be 16:17. Find the sum of the ages of both, 4 yrs ago.
(a) 108 yrs   (b) 95 yrs   (c) 90 yrs
(d) 80 yrs   (e) 112 yrs

73. A man invested Rs. 6600 on S.I. for two years at the rate of 12 p.c.p.a and Rs. X on C.I. at the rate of 20% p.a. for two years. If the ratio of S.I. to C.I. received by this man after two years is 9:10, then find 'X'.
(a) Rs.4,100   (b) Rs.4,000
(c) Rs.4,900   (d) Rs.4,600
(e) Rs. 4,500

74. The average marks of the students of class XI is 'X'. When the average marks of 15 students reduced by 6, then the average marks of the class reduced by 1.875. If the number of students in class XII is 16 more than in class XI and the total marks of class XII is 5120, then find the average marks of class XII?
(a) 60   (b) 90   (c) 96
(d) 80   (e) 84

75. The perimeter of a triangle is equal to the perimeter of a rectangle. The length of a rectangle is 75% of the side of a square and the ratio of the length to breadth of the rectangle is 3:2. If the difference between the perimeter of the square and that of the rectangle is 36 cm., then find perimeter of the triangle.
(a) 60 cm.   (b) 48 cm.   (c) 72 cm.
(d) 80 cm.   (e) 96 cm.

Directions (76-80): Study the pie chart given below and answer the following questions.

The pie chart shows the percentage distribution of 5000 animals in 5 different forests (A, B, C, D & E).

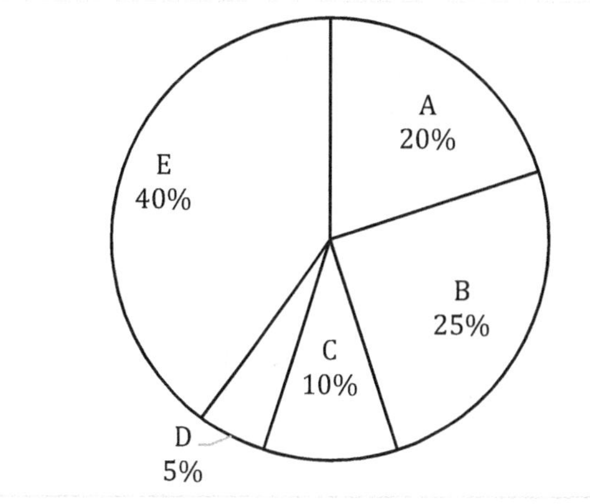

Note Each forest has 3 types of animals — herbivores (grass eating animals), carnivores (flesh eating animals) and omnivores (flesh and grass eating animals).

76. Find the ratio of animals in B and D together to animals in C and E together.
(a) 3 : 5   (b) 1:3   (c) 8:13
(d) 2:5   (e) 7:9

77. If the ratio of Herbivores, Omnivores and Carnivores in the forest B is 9:5:11, then the Herbivore animals in the forest B are what percent of the animals in forest C?
(a) 80%   (b) 65%   (c) 45%
(d) 90%   (e) 30%

78. If the Herbivores animals in forest E are 90% of the total animals in forest C, then find the total number of flesh-eating animals in forest E.
(a) 500   (b) 1550   (c) 550
(d) 800   (e) None of the above.

79. Find the difference between the average number of animals in forests A and B and the average number of animals in forests C and E.
(a) 450   (b) 125   (c) 210
(d) 280   (e) 365

80. Animals in forests B and E together are what percent more or less than animals in forests A and C together?
(a) $116\frac{2}{3}\%$ (b) $111\frac{1}{3}\%$
(c) $118\frac{1}{3}\%$ (d) $114\frac{2}{3}\%$
(e) None of the above

REASONING ABILITY

Direction (1-5):

1. (a)

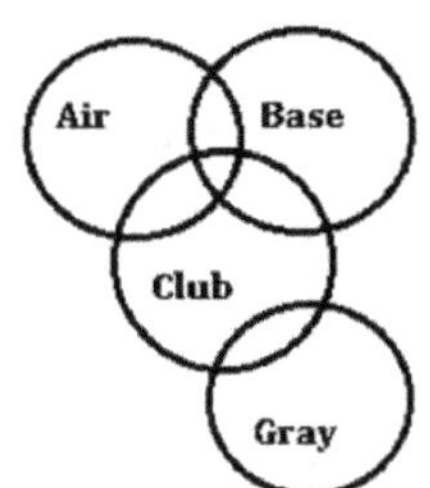

2. (c)

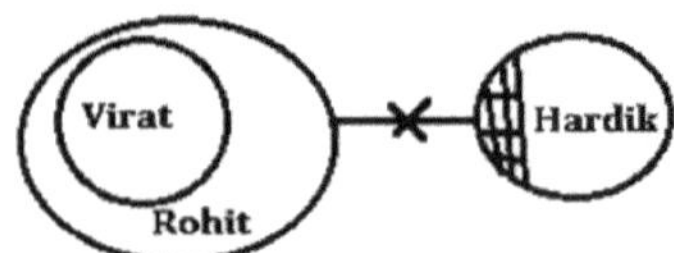

3. (a)

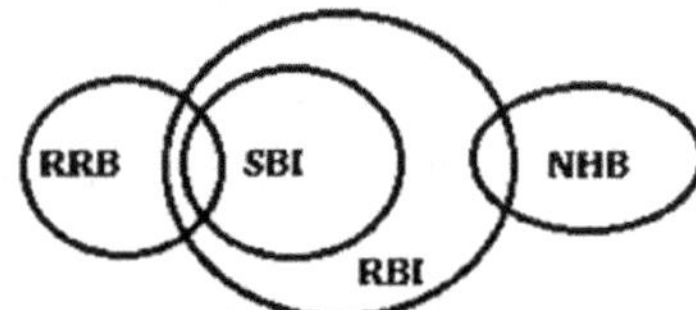

4. (a)

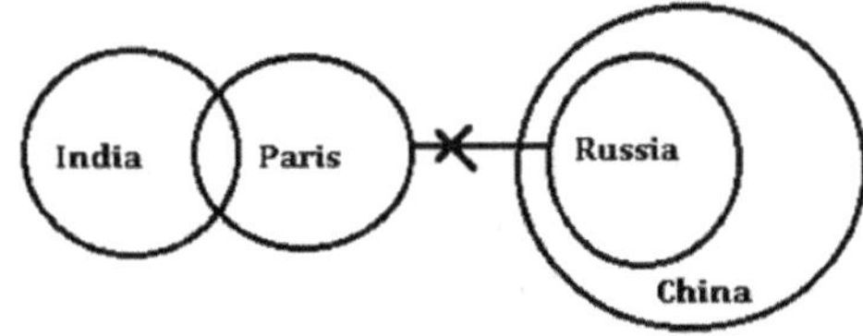

5. (b)

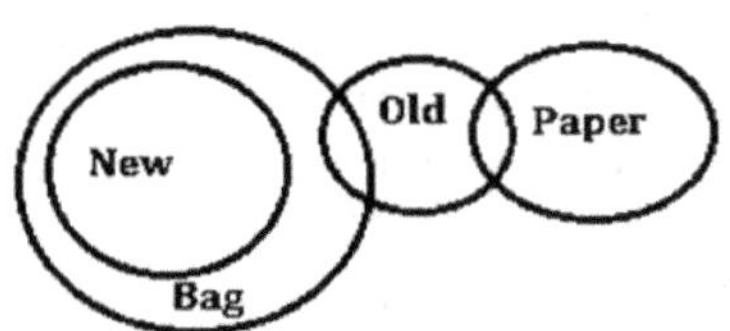

Direction (6-10): From the given statements, B sits 3rd to the left of Q. There is one person who sits between B and K. We get 2 possibilities now – Case 1 and Case 2. L sits 4th to the left of K. There are two persons that sit between Q and M. M sits immediate left of P.

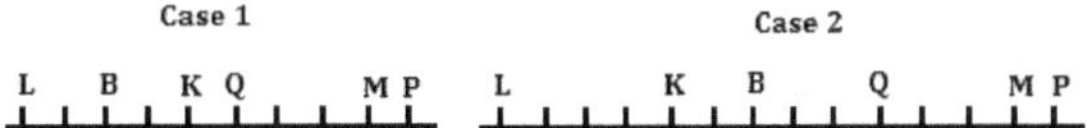

From the given statements, there are four persons that sit between P and R, who sit at one of the ends.

At least 15 persons sit between L and R. Case 1 is ruled out now. There is one person who sits between R and T. U sits 2nd from one of the ends. There is one person who sits between U and L. So, the final arrangement-

U L   K B   Q   M P   T   R

6. (d)   **7. (a)**   **8. (d)**
9. (c)   **10. (b)**

Direction (11-13):

11. (a)

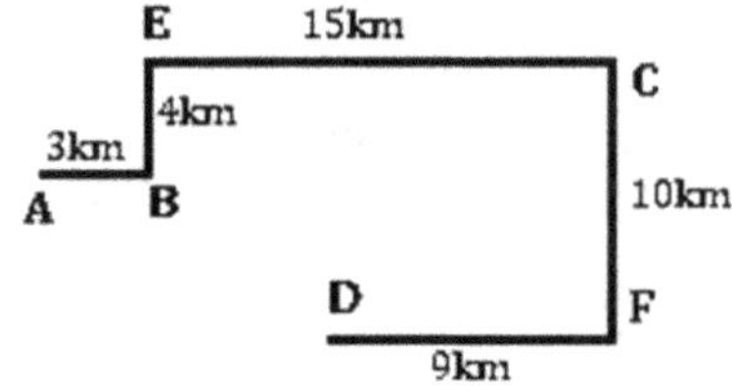

12. (b)

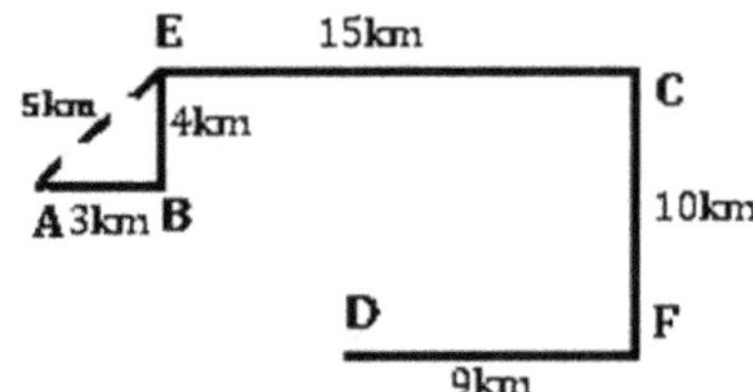

13. (c)

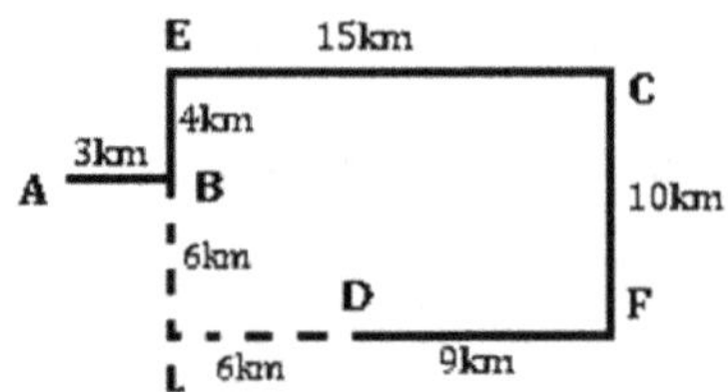

Direction (14-18): From the given statements, M sits 3rd to the left of L and both are facing in the same direction. Here we get two possibilities i.e. Case 1 and Case 2. O sits 2nd to the right of M. There is one person who sits between O and K.

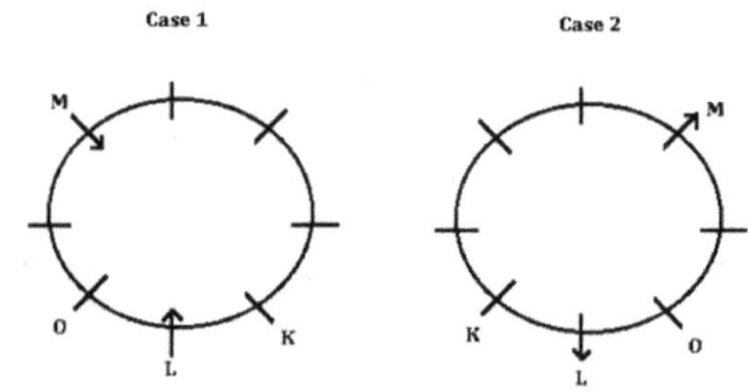

From the given statements, both Q and N are facing each other (It means both are facing inside). Q does not sit near K. P sits 3rd to the right of K. O and K both are facing opposite directions.

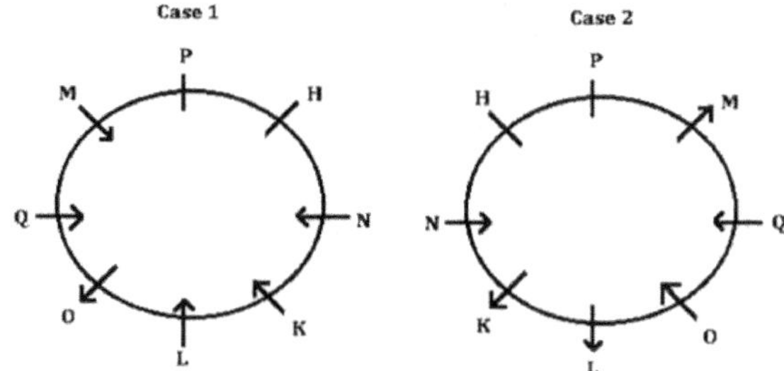

From the given statements, P sits immediate left of H, who faces on the outside. Here Case 2 is ruled out. Both P and H are facing in the same direction.

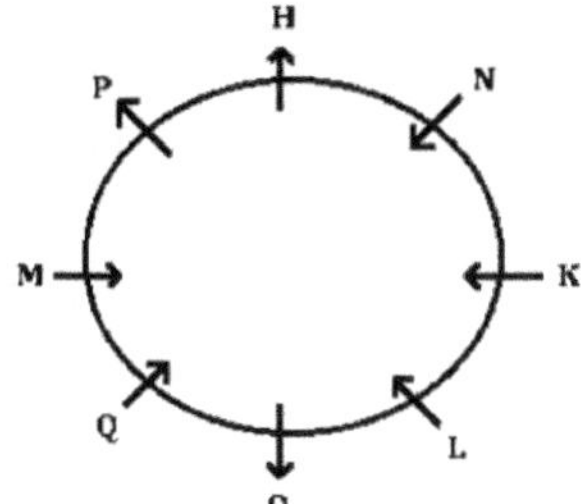

14. (e) Two- L and K

15. (b)   **16. (a)**   **17. (d)**

18. (b)

Direction (19-22):

19. (c) From both I. and II. "Can" is coded as "wq"

Words	Codes
none	mn
of	nk
these	lp
how	rt
can	wq
each/them	fd/ws
could/you	dv/bm

20. (a) Only from I. we know P sits 2nd to the left of M.

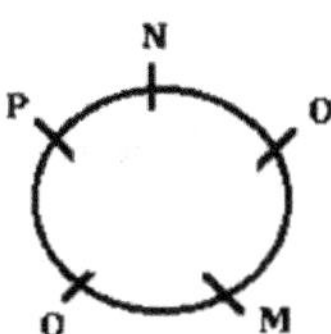

21. (e) From both I. and II. G lives on the 2nd floor.

Floors	Persons
5	B
4	D
3	H
2	G
1	F

22. (d) Sol. From both I. and II. we can't find the person who sits at the extreme ends.

Directions (23-27):

23. (d) Condition III follows.

24. (c) No condition follows.

25. (a) Condition III follows.

26. (e) Condition II follows.

27. (b) Condition I follows.

Direction (28-32): From the given statements, P likes Samosa but not like Red and Black. The one who likes Pettish also likes Yellow. T likes Burger, but not the colourRed. U likes Pink. Q likes Sandwich but does not like Black.

Persons	Food items	Colors
P	Samosa	~~Red/Black~~
	Pettish	Yellow
T	Burger	~~Red~~
U		Pink
Q	Sandwich	~~Black~~

From the given statements, R likes neither Pettish nor Green colour. U does not like Pizza. Q does not like Red colour. The one who likes Samosa does not like Blue colour.

So, the final arrangement –

Persons	Food items	Colours
P	Samosa	Green
S	Pettish	Yellow
T	Burger	Black
U	Biryani	Pink
Q	Sandwich	Blue
R	Pizza	Red

28. (b)   **29. (c)**   **30. (c)**

31. (c)   **32, (d)**

33. (d)

$$\boxed{1}\,6\ 4\ 8\ 2\ 4\ 3\ 7\,\boxed{9}$$
$$\boxed{1}\,2\ 3\ 4\ 4\ 6\ 7\ 8\,\boxed{9}$$

34. (b) Torn

Direction (35-39): From the given statements, Box Q is placed just above the box M. No box is in between M and N. There are two boxes gap between M and P. Here we get two possibilities i.e. Case 1 and Case 2.

Case 1	Case 2
Boxes	Boxes
Q	P
M	
N	Q
	M
P	N

From the given statements, there is a three boxes gap between N and L, which is placed above box N.

This rules out Case 2. Box O is placed above box Q.
Box S is not placed above box P.
So, the final arrangement is: -

Boxes
L
O
Q
M
N
R
P
S

35. (c) **36. (c)** **37. (a)**
38. (c) **39. (d)**
40. (c)

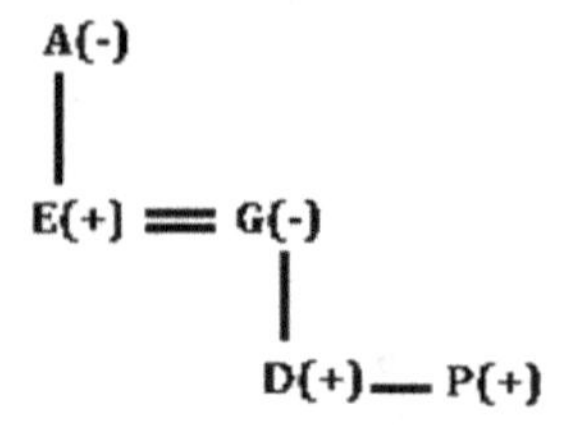

Quantitative Aptitude

41. (d) Sol. Let radius of circular field be 'r cm'

ATQ,

Area of circular field $= \frac{3465}{10}$

$\Rightarrow \pi r^2 = 346.5$

$r^2 = \frac{3465}{10} \times \frac{7}{22}$

$r = \frac{21}{2}$

$r = 10.5$ cm

Hence, side of square field $= 2r$

$= 2 \times 10.5 = 21$ cm

So, required perimeter $= 4 \times 21 = 84$ cm

42. (b) Sol. ATQ,

$\frac{{}^x C_1 \times {}^5 C_1}{{}^{x+11} C_2} = \frac{9}{38}$

$\frac{x \times 5}{(x+11)(x+10)} \times 2 = \frac{9}{38}$

$\Rightarrow \frac{10x}{x^2+21x+110} = \frac{9}{38}$

$\Rightarrow 380x = 9x^2 + 189x + 990$

$\Rightarrow 9x^2 - 191x + 990 = 0$

$9x^2 - 110x - 81x + 990 = 0$

$x(9x - 110) - 9(9x - 110) = 0$

$(9x - 110)(x - 9) = 0$

$x = 9, \frac{110}{9}$

So, x = 9

43. (b) According to question

$\frac{2000 \times 12}{(2000+x)8} = \frac{5}{4}$

$50 \times 48 = 2000 + x$

x = Rs 400

44. (c) Let cp of article A = 4x

And cp of article B = 2x

So,

$4x \times \frac{8.3}{100} + 2x \times \frac{14.4}{100} = 186$

$\frac{2x}{100}[16.6 + 14.4] = 186$

$\frac{2x}{100} \times 31 = 186$

x = 300

Cost price of A = Rs 1200

45. (c) Sol.

Milk in B $= \frac{260}{13} \times 7 = 140$ L

Milk in A $= \frac{8}{7} \times 140$ L

= 160L

So,

$\frac{160}{260-160} = \frac{8}{y}$

$20y = 100$

$y = 5$

46. (b) Sol.

Employees whose age is less than or equal to 40 years in Q & R together = (430 – 130) + (480 – 120) = 300+ 360

= 660

Employees whose age is more than 40 years in R & S together = 120 + 150 = 270

Required ratio $= \frac{660}{270}$

= 22:9

47. (d) Sol.

Female employees whose age is more than 40 years in P & Q together $= 70 \times \frac{2}{5} + 130 \times \frac{8}{13}$

= 28 + 80

= 108

Required % $= \frac{108}{480} \times 100$

= 22.5%

48. (e) Sol.

Total number of employees whose age is less than or equal to 40 years in Q, R & S together = (430 – 130) + (480 – 120) + (450 – 150) = 300 + 360 + 300

= 960

Required average $= \frac{960}{3}$

= 320

49. (b) Sol.

Total female employees in P $= 320 - \frac{80}{100}(320 - 70)$

$= 320 - 200$

$= 120$

Required difference $= (120 + 150) - 120$

$= 150$

50. (b) Employees whose age is less than or equal to 40 years in Q & S together $= (430 - 130) + (450 - 150) = 300 + 300$

$= 600$

Required % $= \frac{(320 + 480) - 600}{600} \times 100$

$= \frac{200}{600} \times 100$

$= 33\frac{1}{3}\%$

51. (d) Pattern of series –

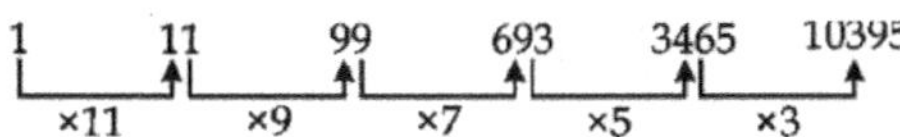

So, missing number is 10395.

52. (b) Pattern of series –

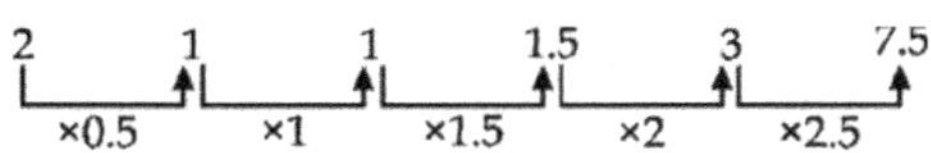

So, missing number is 7.5

53. (a) Pattern of series –

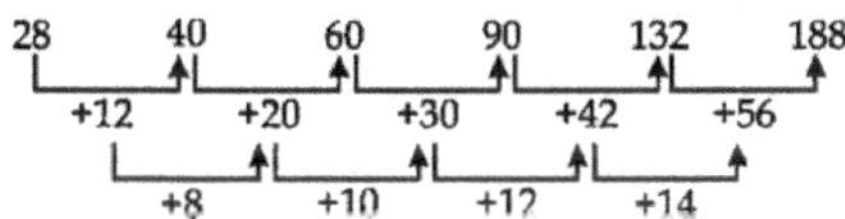

So, missing number is 188.

54. (a) Pattern of series –

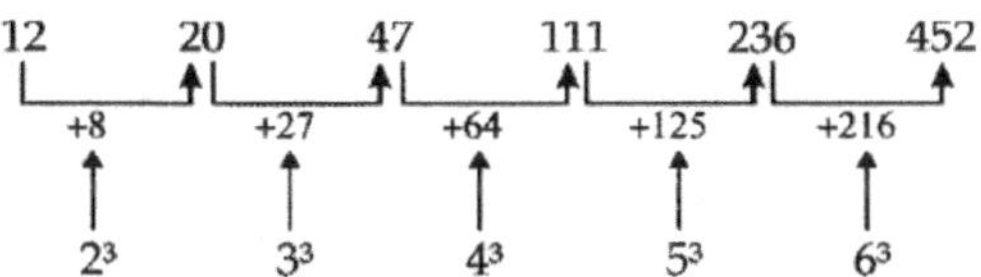

So, missing number is 452.

55. (b) Pattern of series –

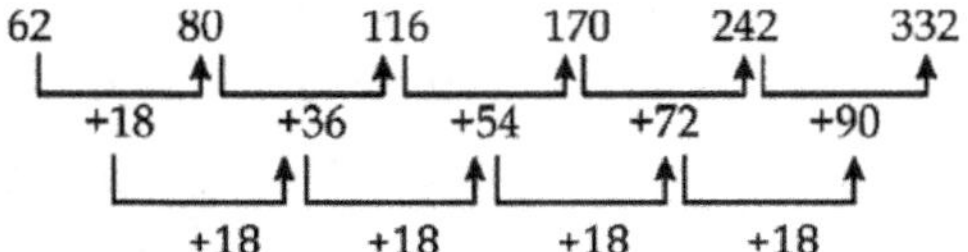

So, missing number is 332.

Solution (56- 60): Samsung phones sold by store in W1 = 1960

Oppo phones sold by store in W1 = 1960 – 560 = 1400

Vivo phones sold by store in W1 = 4600 – 1960 – 1400 = 1240

Male buyers of Samsung phones from the store in W1 $= 1960 \times \frac{25}{49} = 1000$

Female buyers of Samsung phones from the store in W1 = 1960 – 1000 = 960

Let male buyers of Vivo phones from the store in W1 be x.

So, female buyers of Vivo phones from the store in W1 = x + 40

Atq,

x + x + 40 = 1240

x = 600

Female buyers of Oppo phones from the store in W1 = 600

Male buyers of Oppo phones from the store in W1 = 1400 – 600 = 800

Brand	Total phones sold	Male buyers	Female buyers
Samsung	1960	1000	960
Oppo	1400	800	600
Vivo	1240	600	640
Total	4600	2400	2200

56. (c) Required % $= \frac{1000 - 640}{1000} \times 100 = 36\%$

57. (a) Required ratio $= \frac{\left(\frac{1000 + 800}{2}\right)}{(600 + 640)} = \frac{900}{1240} = 45 : 62$

58. (e) Required % $= \frac{(960 + 640)}{1400} \times 100$

$= \frac{800}{7}\% = 114\frac{2}{7}\%$

59. (d) Required number of phones $= \frac{1960}{7} = 280$

60. (c) Required difference $= (1400 + 1240) - 2200$

$= 440$

61. (d) I. $x^2 - 15x + 56 = 0$

$x^2 - 8x - 7x + 56 = 0$

$x(x - 8) - 7(x - 8) = 0$

$(x - 8)(x - 7) = 0$

$x = 7, 8$

II. $y^2 - 12y + 35 = 0$

$y^2 - 7y - 5y + 35 = 0$

$y(y - 7) - 5(y - 7) = 0$

$(y - 7)(y - 5) = 0$

$y = 5, 7$

So, $x \geq y.$

62. (a) I. $24x^2 - 38x + 15 = 0$

$24x^2 - 20x - 18x + 15 = 0$

$4x(6x - 5) - 3(6x - 5) = 0$

$(6x - 5)(4x - 3) = 0$

$x = \frac{5}{6}, \frac{3}{4}$

II. $15y^2 - 46y + 35 = 0$

$15y^2 - 25y - 21y + 35 = 0$

$5y(3y - 5) - 7(3y - 5) = 0$

$(3y - 5)(5y - 7) = 0$

$y = \frac{5}{3}, \frac{7}{5}$

So, $x < y.$

63. (e) I. $x^3 = 5832$

$x = \sqrt[3]{5832}$

$x = 18$

II. $(y - 21)^2 = 256$

$y - 21 = \pm 16$

$y - 21 = 16$

$y = 37$

$y - 21 = -16$

$y = 5$

So, no relation

64. (a) I. $2x + 3y = 36$ ... (i)

II. $5x + 9y = 102$ ... (ii) Multiply (i) by 5 & (ii) by 2:

$10x + 15y = 180$ ... (iii)

$10x + 18y = 204$ ... (iv)

On solving (iii) & (iv), we get:

$y = 8, x = 6$

So, $x < y$.

65. (d) I. $35x^2 + 44x + 12 = 0$

$35x^2 + 30x + 14x + 12 = 0$

$5x (7x + 6) + 2 (7x + 6) = 0$

$(7x + 6) (5x + 2) = 0$

$x = \frac{-6}{7}, \frac{-2}{5}$

II. $28y^2 + 59y + 30 = 0$

$28y^2 + 35y + 24y + 30 = 0$

$7y (4y + 5) + 6 (4y + 5) = 0$

$(4y + 5) (7y + 6) = 0$

$y = \frac{-5}{4}, \frac{-6}{7}$

So, $x \geq y$.

66. (d) $\frac{25}{100} \times 1800 - (11 \times 24) = ?$

$? = 450 - 264$

$? = 186$

67. (a) $\frac{12}{100} \times (232 + 418) + 91 = (?)^2$

$(?)^2 = 78 + 91$

$(?)^2 = 169$

$? = 13$

68. (e) $27 \times 48 \times \frac{1}{54} + \frac{57}{100} \times 2500 = ?$

$24 + 1425 = ?$

$? = 1449$

69. (b) $\frac{\frac{55}{100} \times 2200}{67 + 54} + (2 \times 12 + 6) = ?$

$\frac{1210}{121} + 30 = ?$

$? = 10 + 30$

$? = 40$

70. (a) $514 - 122 + 57 + 221 = ?$

$? = 392 + 278$

$? = 670$

71. (d) Speed of boat in still water $= \frac{25}{9} \times \frac{18}{5} = 10$ km/hr

Let speed of stream be x km/hr

So, $\frac{65}{10-x} - \frac{60}{10+x} = 9$

$65 (10 + x) - 60 (10-x) = 9 (100 - x^2)$ 650

$+ 65x - 600 + 60x = 900 - 9x^2$

$125x + 50 = 900 - 9x^2$

$9x^2 + 125x - 850 = 0$

$9x^2 + 170x - 45x - 850 = 0$

$x(9x + 170) - 5 (9x + 170)$

$\Rightarrow x = 5$ km/h

72. (e) Let age of A and B 6 yrs hence be 16x & 17x respectively.

Difference of age of A & B remains same at any time

So, $17x - 16x = 4$

$x = 4$

Sum of ages of both, 4 yrs ago $= (16 + 17) \times 4 - 10 \times 2 = 132 - 20 = 112$ yrs

73. (b) Simple interest $= 6600 \times \frac{12 \times 2}{100} = 1584$

Compound interest $= 1584 \times \frac{10}{9} = 1760$

$X \times \frac{44}{100} = 1760$

$X = 4000$ Rs.

74. (d) Let total number of students in class XI be 'N'

Total marks of class XI = NX

Total marks of class after reduction in marks of 15 students $= (NX - 15 \times 6) = (NX - 90)$ ATQ –

$(NX - 90) = (X - 1.875)N$

$1.875N = 90$

$N = 48$

Total students in class XII = 48 + 16 = 64

Required average $= \frac{5120}{64} = 80$

75. (a) Let side of square be '4x' cm

So, length of rectangle $= 4x \times \frac{3}{4} = 3x \ cm$

And, breadth of rectangle = 2x cm

ATQ –

$4 \times 4x - 2(3x + 2x) = 36$

$6x = 36$

$x = 6$ cm

Perimeter of triangle = perimeter of rectangle = 2(18 + 12) = 60 cm

76. (a) Required ratio $= \frac{5000 \times \left(\frac{25}{100} + \frac{5}{100}\right)}{5000 \times \left(\frac{10}{100} + \frac{40}{100}\right)} = \frac{30}{100} \times \frac{100}{50} = 3 : 5$

77. (d) Herbivore animals in forest – B $= \frac{9}{25} \times 5000 \times \frac{25}{100} = 450$

Required% $= \frac{450}{\left(5000 \times \frac{10}{100}\right)} \times 100$

$= \frac{450}{500} \times 100 = 90\%$

78. (b) Herbivore animals in forest – E $= \frac{90}{100} \times 5000 \times \frac{10}{100} = 450$

Now, required animals $= 5000 \times \frac{40}{100} - 450$

$= 2000 - 450 = 1550$

79. (b) Average number of animals in forest – A &

$$B = \frac{5000 \times \left(\frac{20+25}{100}\right)}{2} = \frac{2250}{2} = 1125$$

Average number of animals in forest – C &

$$E = \frac{5000 \times \left(\frac{10+40}{100}\right)}{2} = \frac{2500}{2} = 1250$$

Required difference = 1250 – 1125 = 125

80. (a) Animals in forest – B & E together = $5000 \times \left(\frac{25+40}{100}\right) = 3250$

Animals in forest – A & C together = $5000 \times \left(\frac{20+10}{100}\right) = 1500$

$$\text{Required}\% = \frac{3250-1500}{1500} \times 100 = \frac{350}{3}\%$$

$$= 116\frac{2}{3}\%$$

REASONING ABILITY

Directions (1-5): In these questions the symbols @, #, $, & and * are used with different meanings as given below:

'A @ B' means 'A is not smaller than B'

'A # B' means 'A is not greater than B'

'A $ B' means 'A is neither smaller than nor equal to B'

'A & B' means 'A is neither greater than nor equal to B'

'A * B' means 'A is neither smaller nor greater than B'

In each of the following questions, assuming the given statements to be true, find out which of the two conclusions, I and II given below them, is/are definitely true. Give the answer

(a) if only conclusion I is true.

(b) if only conclusion II is true.

(c) if either conclusion I or II is true.

(d) if neither conclusion I nor II is true.

(e) if both conclusions I and II are true.

1. **Statement:** O & N * J # H @ G $ K
   Conclusions: I. G # O **II.** O # H

2. **Statement:** D @ S $ R * X & T # H
   Conclusions: I. X & D **II.** R & H

3. **Statement:** D * C & B $ A * F # E
   Conclusions: I. A # E **II.** B @ D

4. **Statement:** Z @ M * L $ G @ S $ V
   Conclusions: I. V # L **II.** S & M

5. **Statement:** K # E * G @ W @ N & U
   Conclusions: I. U # E **II.** E & U

Direction (6-10): Study the following information carefully and answer the questions given below.

Ten persons are sitting in two parallel rows containing five persons in each row in such a way that there is an equal distance between adjacent persons. In the first row, A, B, C, D and E are seated and all of them are facing south. In the second row, P, Q, R, S and T are seated and all of them are facing north. Therefore, in the given seating arrangement, each member seated in a row, faces another member of the other row.

A faces the one who sits 2nd to the left of R. There are two persons sitting between A and C. B sits 3rd to the left of D. There are three persons sitting between Q and P, who sits near to S. Both S and R are not immediate neighbours.

6. Who among the following faces R?
   (a) A (b) D
   (c) E (d) B

(e) Can't be determined

7. How many persons are seated between P and R?
   (a) No one (b) one
   (c) two (d) three
   (e) Either (b) or (c)

8. What is the position of A with respect to B?
   (a) 3rd to the left
   (b) 2nd to the right
   (c) 3rd to the right
   (d) immediate left
   (e) Can't be determined

9. Four of the following five are alike in a certain way and hence they form a group. Which one of the following does not belong to that group?
   (a) Q (b) A (c) B
   (d) R (e) T

10. Who among the following sits diagonally opposite P?
   (a) D (b) E (c) B
   (d) A (e) C

Directions (11-13): Study the following information carefully and answer the given questions:

There are ten members A, B, C, D, E, F, G, H, J and K in the family. A is married to K. B is son of J. K and J are sisters. E is the brother of B. F is the father-in-law of A. J is the daughter of G. C is the father of E. D is cousin brother of E. H is the mother-in-law of K.

11. How is D related to H?
   (a) son (b) grandson
   (c) father (d) brother
   (e) None of these

12. How is C related to K?
   (a) father-in-law (b) father
   (c) brother-in-law (d) uncle
   (e) None of these

13. How is F related to E?
   (a) mother (b) grandfather
   (c) brother (d) cousin
   (e) None of these

Direction (14-18): Study the following information carefully and answer the questions given below:

Eight persons A, B, C, D, P, Q, R and S are sitting around a rectangular table in such a way that four persons sit on each of the four corners of the table and the other four persons sit on the middle of each side. The one who sits at the middle of the table faces opposite the centre of the table and the one who sits at the corner side of the table faces towards the centre of the table. Persons sitting on opposite sides are exactly opposite to each other.

R sits 3rd to the left of A. There is one person sitting between R and B. Q sits diagonally opposite to B. Both D and S are immediate neighbours. P sits 2nd to the right of S. Both C and Q are immediate neighbours.

14. Who among the following sits 2nd to the left of C?

(a) P   (b) B

(c) A   (d) Q

(e) Can't be determined

15. Who among the following sits opposite to R?

(a) S   (b) D

(c) C   (d) Q

(e) None of these

16. Four of the following five are alike in a certain way and hence they form a group. Which one of the following does not belong to that group?

(a) P   (b) S   (c) A

(d) C   (e) D

17. What is the position of S with respect to R?

(a) 2nd to the left

(b) 3rd to the left

(c) 3rd to the right

(d) Immediate to the left

(e) None of these

18. Which of the following statements is true with respect to C?

(a) S faces C

(b) A sits 2nd to the left of C

(c) Q sits immediate left of C

(d) B sits 3rd to the left of C

(e) None is true

Direction (19-23): Study the following information carefully and answer the questions given below:

In a certain code language:

"poor farmers are helpless" is coded as "lik tik mik bik"

"helpless people are few" is coded as "bik mik pik zxk"

"scheme waiver for farmers" is coded as "qik tik wek sak"

"poor family are helpless" is coded as "lik fik mik bik"

19. What is the code for "farmers" in the given code language?

(a) bik   (b) tik

(c) mik   (d) qik

(e) Can't be determined

20. What is the code for "scheme waiver" in the given code language?

(a) qik wek   (b) fik sak

(c) sak qik   (d) wek sak

(e) Can't be determined

21. Which of the following word is coded as "bik zxk" in the given code language?

(a) few people

(b) helpless people

(c) Either (a) or (b)

(d) few helpless

(e) Either (b) or (d)

22. If "government waiver scheme" is coded as "wek oik sak" then "for you" may be coded as?

(a) qik tik   (b) lik tik

(c) bik fik   (d) Either (a) or (b)

(e) qik jnk

23. What is the code for "few" in the given code language?

(a) pik   (b) fik

(c) qik   (d) zxk

(e) Either (a) or (d)

Direction (24-28): The following questions are based on five three-digit numbers given below:

189 786 434 234 389

24. What is the sum of 2nd digit of highest number and 1st digit of lowest number?

(a) 12   (b) 9

(c) 8   (d) 7

(e) None of these

25. If 1 is added to the first digit of each of the numbers; then all digits are added within the number, how many numbers thus formed will be divisible by three?

(a) none   (b) one

(c) two   (d) three

(e) None of these

26. If all the digits in each of the numbers are arranged in descending order within the number, which of the following will be the highest number in the new arrangement of numbers?

(a) 786   (b) 434   (c) 234

(d) 189   (e) 389

27. If in each number, the second and the third digits are interchanged then which will be the 2nd highest number?

(a) 786   (b) 189   (c) 234

(d) 434   (e) 389

28. What is the difference between the 2nd digit of the lowest number and 3rd digit of the 2nd highest number?

(a) 8   (b) 4   (c) 6

(d) 10   (e) 18

Directions (29-33): Study the following information carefully and answer the questions given below.

Nine persons K, L, M, N, O, P, Q, R and S are living in a nine-floors building in Jaipur, but not necessarily in the same order. Ground floor is as 1st floor, just above is the 2nd floor and so on until the topmost floor as 9th floor.

M lives on an even-numbered floor. There are four persons who live between M and O. P lives below M on an odd-numbered floor, but does not live immediately below M. There are three persons who live between R and N. Only one person lives between N and O. Q lives immediately below S. There are more than three persons who live between K and L, who does not live on one of the floors above S.

29. On which of the following floors does Q live?
    (a) 2nd   (b) 9th
    (c) 5th   (d) 4th
    (e) None of these

30. Who among the following lives on the 8th floor?
    (a) K   (b) S
    (c) O   (d) R
    (e) None of these

31. Who among the following lives immediately below M?
    (a) S   (b) L   (c) K
    (d) N   (e) R

32. How many persons live between O and S?
    (a) No one   (b) two   (c) one
    (d) three   (e) five

33. Four of the following five belong to a group in a certain way, find which one does not belong to that group?
    (a) N   (b) O   (c) Q
    (d) R   (e) K

34. In the word "ASCERTAIN", how many pairs of the letters have the same number of letters between them (backwards or forwards) as in the alphabet series?
    (a) four   (b) one
    (c) two   (d) three
    (e) More than four

Directions (35-39): Study the following information carefully and answer the questions given below.

Five friends B, C, D, E and F are watching different web series viz. Sacred Games, Mirzapur, Breathe, Poison and Smoke on different paid streaming apps viz. Netflix, Amazon Prime, Zee5, Eros Now and Hotstar, but not necessarily in the same order. Each of them likes different colours viz. White, Blue, Black, Yellow and Orange.

E watches Smoke. D watches on Hotstar. B likes Orange colour. The one who watches Smoke likes Yellow colour. The one who watches Sacred Games watches on Netflix. The one who watches Poison watches on Eros Now. Neither D nor F like White colour. B watches Breathe on Amazon Prime. F does not watch Poison. The one who watches Sacred games likes Black colour.

35. Who among the following watches a web series on Zee5?
    (a) F   (b) E
    (c) C   (d) D
    (e) None of these

36. Who among the following watches Mirzapur?
    (a) C   (b) F
    (c) B   (d) D
    (e) None of these

37. Who among the following likes Blue colour?
    (a) D   (b) E
    (c) C   (d) F
    (e) None of these

38. Which of the following colours is liked by the one who watches Poison?
    (a) Blue   (b) Yellow
    (c) Black   (d) White
    (e) None of these

39. Which of the following apps is watched by the one who likes Yellow colour?
    (a) Hotstar   (b) Zee5
    (c) Eros now   (d) Netflix
    (e) None of these

40. In a certain code DRUBBING is written as BURDGNIB. How will EXPEDITE be written in that same code?
    (a) ETIDEPXE
    (b) EPXEETID
    (c) EPXDETIE
    (d) DPXEETIE
    (e) None of these

Directions (41-45): The table given below shows the numbers of five different brands of jeans ordered from Myntra on five different days of the week.

Brands	Monday	Tuesday	Wednesday	Thursday	Friday
Moda Rapido	127	101	83	306	181
Spyker	169	129	203	287	223
Roadster	225	87	189	191	95
Jack & johns	113	93	165	328	85
Here & now	161	123	143	185	126

41. Moda Rapido's jeans ordered on Monday & Thursday together are approximately what percent more than Spyker jeans ordered on Monday & Tuesday together?
(a) 35% (b) 45% (c) 28%
(d) 55% (e) 50%

42. If on Sunday the total number of Here &Now's jeans ordered were $66\frac{2}{3}\%$ more than the total number of Here & now jeans ordered on Tuesday & Friday together, then find how many Here &Now Jeans were ordered on Sunday.
(a) 215 (b) 315 (c) 415
(d) 435 (e) 465

43. Find the ratio between total Roadster's jeans ordered on Tuesday & Thursday together to total Jack & Johns' jeans ordered on Monday, Tuesday & Thursday together.
(a) 137: 267 (b) 267:137
(c) 267:139 (d) 139:267

(e) None of these

44. Find the average number of Here & Now jeans ordered on Monday and Moda Rapido jeans ordered on Tuesday.
(a) 131 (b) 125 (c) 105
(d) 100 (e) 135

45. Find the difference between Spyker's Jeans ordered on Thursday & Friday together and Jack & Johns' Jeans ordered on Thursday & Tuesday together.
(a) 79 (b) 39 (c) 49
(d) 59 (e) 89

Directions (46- 50): What will come at the place of the question (?) mark.

46. 22, ?, 166, 310, 502, 742
(a) 60 (b) 70 (c) 50
(d) 80 (e) 90

47. 28, 18, ?, 37, 78, 199
(a) 20 (b) 16 (c) 22
(d) 24 (e) 28

48. 25, 90, ?, 177, 203, 220
(a) 150 (b) 148 (c) 144
(d) 140 (e) 160

49. 103, ?, 190, 247, 313, 388
(a) 132 (b) 122 (c) 152
(d) 162 (e) 142

50. 21, ?,199, 603, 1817, 5461
(a) 65 (b) 55 (c) 45
(d) 75 (e) 85

Directions (51-55): The line graph shows the quantity of six different items purchased by a person from Myntra.

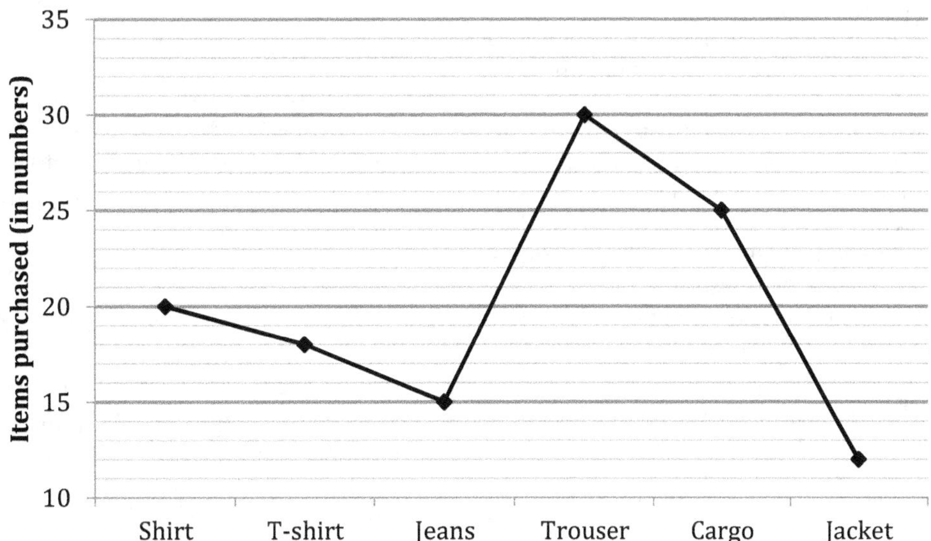

51. If the sum of the price of a shirt and a jeans is Rs.840 and the ratio of the price of a jeans to that of a shirt is 11:10, find the difference in the total price of the shirt and the jeans.
(a) Rs.1200 (b) Rs.1400 (c) Rs.1600
(d) Rs. 2000 (e) Rs.1800

52. If the total price paid for T-shirts is Rs. 9000 and that of trousers is Rs. 15000, then the price of the T-shirts is what percent more or less than the price of the trousers?
(a) 0% (b) 20% (c) 5%
(d) 10% (e) 15%

53. If the price of a jacket and a cargo is Rs. 630 & Rs. 420 respectively, then find the ratio of total price of the jacket to the total price of the cargo.
(a)13:25 (b) 1:2 (c)3:5
(d)18:25 (e)12:13

54. The total number of jeans and shirts purchased is what percent of the total number of trousers and jackets purchased?
(a) $87\frac{1}{3}\%$ (b) $83\frac{1}{3}\%$ (c) 74%
(d)92% (e) $64\frac{1}{3}\%$

55. If the price of a jeans, trouser and cargo is Rs. 560, Rs. 320 & Rs. 400 respectively, then find the sum of the difference of total price of the cargo and that of the trouser and the difference in the total price of the trouser from that of the jeans.
(a) Rs. 2000 (b) Rs.1800 (c) Rs.1200
(d) Rs.800 (e) Rs. 1600

Direction (56 – 60): The following questions are accompanied by two statements I and II. You have to determine which statements(s) is/are sufficient/necessary to answer the questions.

(a) Statement I alone is sufficient to answer the question but statement II alone is not sufficient to answer the questions.
(b) Statement II alone is sufficient to answer the question but statement I alone is not sufficient to answer the question.
(c) Both the statements taken together are necessary to answer the questions, but neither of the statements alone is sufficient to answer the question.
(d) Either statement I or statement II by itself is sufficient to answer the question.
(e) Statements I and II taken together are not sufficient to answer the question.

56. What is the perimeter of a triangle?
  I. Side of triangle is equal to side of square whose area is 196 cm.^{2}.
  II. Side of triangle is equal to length of rectangle whose area is 484 cm.^{2}.

57. What is the speed of train A running in the opposite direction of train B?
  I. Train B crosses a man standing in 10 sec. at the speed of 54 km/hr.
  II. Length of train A is twice the length of train B.

58. What is the age of Veer after two years?
  I. Average of age of Abhimanyu & Kumar is 36 years and the ratio of Kumar & Patel's age is 1:2.
  II. Age of Patel is two years more than the age of Veer &the average age of Patel & Abhimanyu is 48 years.

59. What is the total strength of company A?
  I. The no. of males in company A is 240, which is 20% more than the no. of females in that company.
  II. Ratio of male to female in company A is 6:5.

60. There are some green and some white balls in a bag. Find out how many white balls are there in the bag.
Statement I: The total number of balls in the bag is five. If two balls are selected at random, then the probability of at least one ball being green is $\frac{9}{10}$.
Statement II: The total number of balls in the bag is five. If two balls are selected at random, then the probability of both balls being white is $\frac{1}{10}$.

61. A car travel sat its usual speed of x km/hr. between city A and B, but on return the car loses $\frac{1}{6}$ th of its usual spee. If the distance between these two cities is 144 km. and the car takes total $\frac{33}{10}$ hours for thewhole journey, then find the average speed of the car in the whole journey?
(a) $\frac{840}{11} km/hr$ (b) $\frac{720}{11} km/hr$
(c) $\frac{640}{11} km/hr$ (d) $\frac{960}{11} km/hr$
(e) $\frac{600}{11} km/hr$

62. The marked price of a bat is Rs. 350.A shopkeeper gives a discount of Rs. x and makes a profit of $12\frac{1}{2}\%$. If the manufacturing cost of the bat is Rs. 280, find the discount percent given by shopkeeper on the bat.
(a) 10% (b) 6% (c) 4%
(d) 3% (e) 5%

63. There are total 36 fruits in a basket in which some are bananas and some are apples. If one fruit is taken out at random and the probability of getting an apple is $\frac{1}{6}$, then find the number of bananas in the basket.
(a) 20 (b) 28 (c) 24
(d) 30 (e) 16

64. The ratio between the age of Priya and Swati is 3:4. If Shikha is 6 years younger than Swati and

the average age of all three is 31 years, then find Shikha's age.
(a) 36 yrs   (b) 32 yrs   (c) 20 yrs
(d) 24 yrs   (e) 30 yrs

65. In a vessel, milk and water are in the ratio of 5:2. If 42 litres of this mixture is taken out from the vessel and 32 litres of water is added, then the new ratio of milk and water becomes 7:6. Find the initial quantity of mixture in the vessel.
(a) 84 litres   (b) 98 litres   (c) 126 litres
(d) 154 litres   (e) 140 litres

Directions (66-70): What comes at the place of question (?) Mark:

66. 26% of $250 + ?\%$ of $640 = (15)^2$
(a) 35   (b) 25   (c) 20
(d) 15   (e) 45

67. $23 \times 13 + (11)^2 - ? = (19)^2$
(a) 49   (b) 39   (c) 59
(d) 29   (e) 19

68. $\dfrac{?}{24} + 65\%$ of $260 = 4 \times 49.75$
(a) 640   (b) 840   (c) 960
(d) 720   (e) 800

69. $2.46 \times 15 + 25\%$ of $92.4 = ? \times 15$
(a) 10   (b) 2   (c) 8
(d) 6   (e) 4

70. $460 + 927 - 433 + ? = (31)^2$
(a) 1   (b) 9   (c) 3
(d) 7   (e) 5

71. Manish and Suresh can do task A in 48 days and 60 days respectively. If together they can complete another task B in x days and Manish alone can complete the task B in (x+ 16) days, then find out in how many days Suresh alone can complete task B?
(a) 45 days   (b) 36 days   (c) 28 days
(d) 40 days   (e) 48 days

72. A and B invested Rs. (P + 2400) and (P + 4400) on C.I. at the rate of 10% and 20% respectively for two years and earned a total interest of Rs. 8680. Find the value of P.
(a) Rs. 9200   (b) Rs. 6400   (c) Rs. 8000
(d) Rs. 7200   (e) Rs. 9600

73. Neeraj and Aniket entered into a partnership business. Neeraj invested Rs. x for the first five months and then withdrew $\frac{1}{3}rd$ of his initial capital, while Aniket invested Rs. 1400 for a year. If the ratio of Neeraj and Aniket's profit share after one year becomes29:42,find the amount invested by Neeraj for first five months.
(a) 1400 Rs.   (b) 1600 Rs.   (c) 1800 Rs.
(d) 2000 Rs.   (e) 1200 Rs.

74. A 240 meters long train running at a speed of 80 km/hr. passes a 280 meters long platform in T seconds. If the train passes through a tunnel in (12.6 +T) seconds, then find the length of the tunnel.
(a) 500 meters   (b) 560 meters
(c) 550 meters   (d) 420 meters(e) 540 meters

75. The radius of two circles is in the ratio of 1:3. Sum of the circumference of both the circles is 176 cm., which is equal to the perimeter of a rectangle. If the ratio between the length to breadth of the rectangle is 8:3, then what is the difference between the radius of the bigger circle and the length of the rectangle?
(a) 60 cm.   (b) 65 cm.   (c) 62 cm.
(d) 43 cm.   (e) 59 cm.

Directions (76-80): Two equations I and II are given below in each question. You have to solve these equations and answer accordingly.
(a) if x<y   (b) if x>y
(c) if x≤y   (d) if x≥y
(e) if x=y or no relation can be established

76. I. $3x^2 + 17x + 10 = 0$ II. $10y^2 + 9y + 2 = 0$
77. I. $4x^2 = 49$ II. $9y^2 - 66y + 121 = 0$
78. I. $3x^2 + 5x + 2 = 0$ II. $y^2 + 12y + 27 = 0$
79. I. $x^2 - 7x + 10 = 0$ II. $y^2 - 14y + 45 = 0$
80. I. $6x^2 - 49x + 99 = 0$ II. $5y^2 + 17y + 14 = 0$

Solutions

REASONING ABILITY

Directions (1-5):
1. **(d)** I. G # O (False) II. O # H (False)
2. **(e)** I.X & D (True) II. R & H (True)
3. **(a)** I. A # E (True) II. B @ D (False)
4. **(b)** I. V # L (False) II. S & M (True)
5. **(c)** I. U # E (False) II. E & U (False)

Direction (6-10): From the given statements, A faces the one who sits 2nd to the left of R. There are two persons sitting between A and C. **Here we get** two possibilities i.e. **Case 1 and Case 2.** B sits 3rd to the left of D.

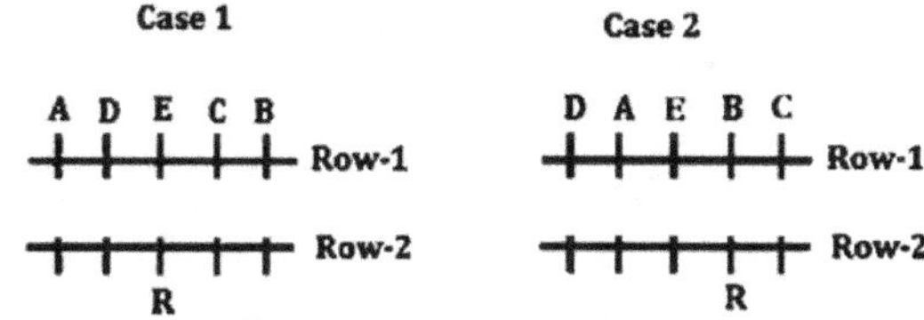

From the given statements, there are three persons sitting between Q and P, who sits near to S. Both S

and R are not immediate neighbours. **Here Case 1 is ruled out.**
So, the final arrangement-

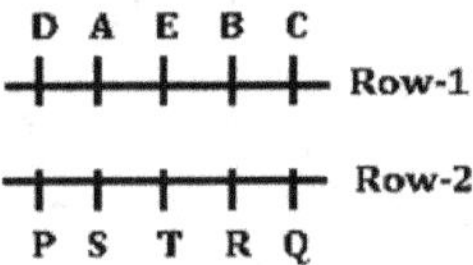

6. **(d)**   7. **(c)**   8. **(b)**
9. **(a)**   10. **(e)**

Directions (11-13):

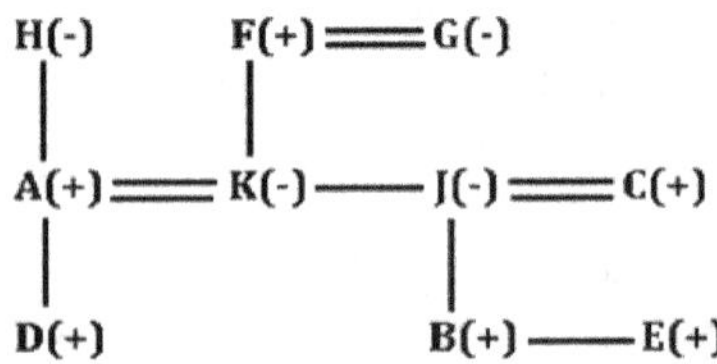

11. **(b)**   12. **(c)**   13. **(b)**

Direction (14-18): From the given statements, R sits 3rd to the left of A. **Here we get 2 possibilities i.e. Case 1 and Case 2.** There is one person who sits between R and B. **Here two more cases were added i.e. Case 1a and Case 2a.**

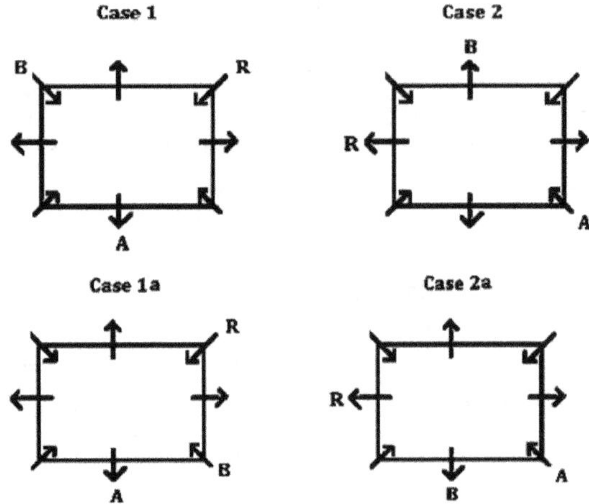

From the given statements, Q sits diagonally opposite to B. **Now Case 2 and Case 2a are eliminated.** Both D and S are immediate neighbours. P sits 2nd to the right of S. Both C and Q are immediate neighbours. **Here Case 1a is ruled out.**
So, the final arrangement-

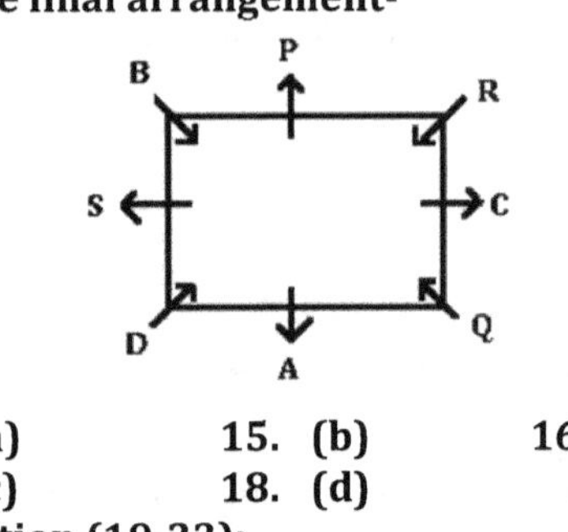

14. **(a)**   15. **(b)**   16. **(e)**
17. **(c)**   18. **(d)**

Direction (19-23):

Words	Codes
poor	lik
farmers	tik
are	mik/bik
helpless	bik/mik
few/people	pik/zxk
scheme/waiver/for	qik/wek/sak
family	fik

19. **(b)**   20. **(e)**   21. **(e)**
22. **(e)**   23. **(e)**

Direction (24-28):

24. **(b)** 2nd digit of highest number = 8, 1st digit of lowest number = 1
: 8 + 1 = 9

25. **(c)**

189 786 **434** 234 **389**
289 886 **534** 334 **489**

26. **(e)**

189 786 434 234 **389**
981 876 443 432 **983**

27. **(d)**

189 786 **434** 234 389
198 768 **443** 243 398

28. **(b)** 2nd digit of the lowest number = 8, 3rd digit of the 2nd highest number = 4
: 8 – 4 = 4

Directions (29-33): M lives on an even numbered floor. There are four persons live between M and O. P lives below M on an odd number floor, but does not live immediate below M. From these conditions we have three possible cases-

Floor	Case- 1 Person	Case- 2 Person	Case- 3 Person
9	O		
8			M
7			
6		M	
5			P/
4	M		
3		P	O
2			
1	P	O	P/

Only one person lives between N and O. By this condition case- 2 is cancelled. There are three persons live between R and N. Q lives immediate below S. So new arrangement will be:

Floor	Case- 1 Person	Case- 3 Person
9	O	R
8		M
7	N	S
6	S	Q
5	Q	N
4	M	
3	R	O
2		
1	P	P

There are more than three persons who live between K and L, who does not live on one of the floor above S. By this condition case-3 is cancelled. So, final arrangement will be:

Floor	Person
9	O
8	K
7	N
6	S
5	Q
4	M
3	R
2	L
1	P

29. (c)   **30. (a)**   **31. (e)**
32. (b)   **33. (e)**
34. (d)

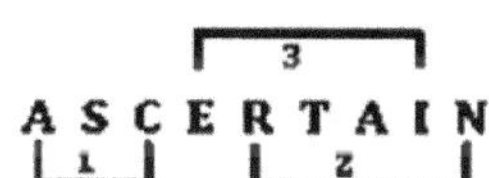

Directions (35-39): E watches Smoke. D watches on Hotstar. B likes Orange colour. Neither D nor F likes White colour. B watches Breathe on Amazon Prime. F does not watch Poison. From these conditions we have the following arrangement -

Friends	Web Series	Apps	Colour
B	Breathe	Amazon prime	Orange
C			
D		Hotstar	~~White~~
E	Smoke		
F	~~Poison~~		~~White~~

The one who watches Smoke likes Yellow colour. The one who watches Poison watches on Eros now. The one who watches Sacred games watches on Netflix. The one who watches Sacred games likes Black colour. So, final arrangement will be:

Friends	Web Series	Apps	Color
B	Breathe	Amazon prime	Orange
C	Poison	Eros now	White
D	Mirzapur	Hotstar	Blue
E	Smoke	Zee5	Yellow
F	Sacred games	Netflix	Black

35. (b)   **36. (d)**   **37. (a)**
38. (d)   **39. (b)**
40. (b)

Quantitative Aptitude

41. (b) Moda Rapido's jeans ordered on Monday & Thursday
$= 127 + 306 = 433$
Spyker's Jeans ordered on Monday & Tuesday $= 169 + 129 = 298$
Required % $= \frac{433-298}{298} \times 100$
$= \frac{135}{298} \times 100 = 45\%$

42. (c) Total number of Here & Now jeans ordered on Tuesday & Friday
$= 123 + 126 = 249$
Total numbered of Here & Now jeans sold on Sunday
$= 249 + 249 \times \frac{2}{3} = 249 + 83 \times 2 = 415$

43. (d) Required ratio $= \frac{(87+191)}{(113+93+328)}$
$= \frac{270}{534} = 139 : 267$

44. (a) Required average $= \frac{(161+101)}{2} = \frac{262}{2} = 131$

45. (e) Required difference $= (223 + 287) - (328 + 93)$
$= 510 - 421 = 89$

46. (b) $\boxed{22 + (48 \times 1) = 70}$
$70 + (48 \times 2) = 166$
$166 + (48 \times 3) = 310$
$310 + (48 \times 4) = 502$
$502 + (48 \times 5) = 742$

47. (c) $28 \times \frac{1}{2} + 4 = 18$
$\boxed{18 \times 1 + 4 = 22}$
$22 \times \frac{3}{2} + 4 = 37$
$37 \times 2 + 4 = 78$
$78 \times \frac{5}{2} + 4 = 199$

48. (d) $25 + 8^2 + 1 = 90$

$$\boxed{90 + 7^2 + 1 = 140}$$
$140 + 6^2 + 1 = 177$
$177 + 5^2 + 1 = 203$
$203 + 4^2 + 1 = 220$

49. (e)

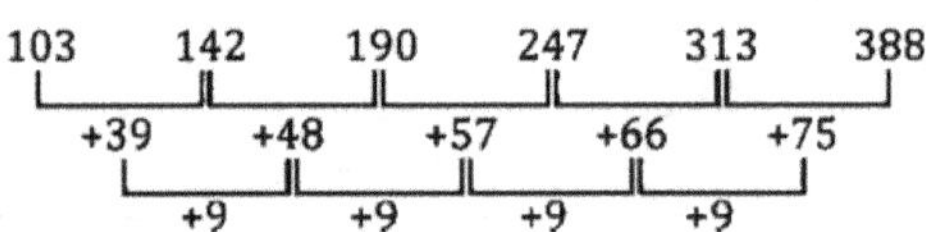

50. (a) Pattern is —
$$\boxed{21 \times 3 + 2 = 65}$$
$65 \times 3 + 4 = 199$
$199 \times 3 + 6 = 603$
$603 \times 3 + 8 = 1817$
$1817 \times 3 + 10 = 5461$

51. (b) Price of a Jeans $= 840 \times \frac{11}{21} = Rs\ 440$

Price of a shirt $= 840 \times \frac{10}{21} = Rs\ 400$

Required difference $= (20 \times 400 - 15 \times 440)$
$= 8000 - 6600 = Rs\ 1400$

52. (a) Price of a T-shirt $= \frac{9000}{18} = Rs\ 500$

Price of a Trouser $= \frac{15000}{30} = Rs\ 500$

Required % $= \frac{500 - 500}{500} \times 100 = 0\%$

53. (d) Required ratio $= \frac{630 \times 12}{420 \times 25} = \frac{18}{25}$

54. (b) Required % $= \frac{20 + 15}{30 + 12} \times 100 = 83\frac{1}{3}\%$

55. (e) Required sum $= (400 \times 25) - (560 \times 15)$
$= 10{,}000 - 8400 = Rs\ 1600$

56. (e) **From I.**

Let side of square be a cm.

Side of triangle $= a = \sqrt{196} = 14\ cm.$

Perimeter of triangle cannot be found out as it is not given which type of triangle it is.

From II.

No information about length/breadth is given. Therefore we cannot find answer from II.

57. (e) **From I & II.**

Speed of train B $= 54 \times \frac{5}{18} = 15\ m/sec.$

Length of train B $= 15 \times 10 = 150$ m.

Length of train A $= 150 \times 2 = 300$ m.

Let speed of train A be x m/sec & time taken to cross train B is t sec.

$$x + 15 = \frac{150 + 300}{t}$$

There are two variables x & t in a single equation.

Therefore, both statements are not sufficient.

58. (c) Let age of Abhimanyu be y years

Age of Abhimanyu & Kumar together $= 36 \times 2 = 72$ years.

Let age of Kumar be x year & Patel be 2x year.

ATQ, From I & II.

$x + y = 72$ ____ (i)

$2x + y = 96$ ____ (ii)

Solving (i) & (ii)

$x = 24$ years.

age of veer after two years $= 24 \times 2 - 2 + 2$
$= 48$ years.

59. (a) **From I.**

No. of males $= 240$

No. of females $= 200$

Total strength $= 200 + 240 = 440$

From statement I can be answered.

60. (d) **From I**

Let number of white balls be x

Green balls $= 5 - x$

Probability of being at least one ball Green

$$\Rightarrow \frac{{}^{x}C_1\ {}^{5-x}C_1 + {}^{5-x}C_2}{{}^{5}C_2} = \frac{9}{10}$$

$$\frac{x(5-x) + \frac{(5-x)(4-x)}{2}}{10} = \frac{9}{10}$$

$x = 2$

From II

Let number of White balls be x

Total $= 5$

Probability of being both balls white is $\frac{1}{10}$

$$\Rightarrow \frac{{}^{x}C_2}{{}^{5}C_2} = \frac{1}{10}$$

$$\frac{x(x-1)}{20} = \frac{1}{10}$$

$x = 2$

So, either statement I or II is sufficient to give the answer of the question.

61. (d) ATQ,

$$\frac{144}{x} + \frac{144}{\frac{5x}{6}} = \frac{33}{10}$$

$$\frac{720 + 864}{5x} = \frac{33}{10}$$

$33x = 1584 \times 2$

$$x = \frac{1584 \times 2}{33}$$

$x = 96$ km/hr

Average speed of car $= \frac{2 \times 96 \times 96 \times \frac{5}{6}}{96 + 96 \times \frac{5}{6}} = \frac{960}{11}\ km/h$

62. (a) Given,

MP of bat $= 350$ Rs

Discount $= x$ Rs

CP of bat $= 280$ Rs

Atq,

$$(350 - x) = 280 \times \frac{9}{8}$$

$x = 35$ Rs

discount percentage $= \frac{35}{350} \times 100 = 10\%$

63. (d) Let total number of apples in basket $= x$

Atq,

$$\frac{^xC_1}{^{36}C_1} = \frac{1}{6} \Rightarrow \frac{x}{36} = \frac{1}{6}$$

x = 6

Total number of banana in basket = 36–6=30

64. (e) Let age of Priya and Swati be 3x and 4x respectively.

Age of Shikha = (4x – 6) years

Atq,

$$\frac{3x+4x+4x-6}{3} = 31$$

11x = 31 × 3 + 6

$$x = \frac{99}{11} = 9$$

Age of Shikha = (4 × 9 -6) = 30 years

65. (e) Let total mixture in vessel be x litres

Atq,

$$\frac{\frac{5x}{7}-42\times\frac{5}{7}}{\frac{2x}{7}-42\times\frac{2}{7}+32} = \frac{7}{6}$$

$$\frac{5x-210}{2x+140} = \frac{7}{6}$$

30x – 1260 = 14x + 980

16x = 2240

x = 140 litres

66. (b) $\frac{26}{100} \times 250 + \frac{?}{100} \times 640 = 225$

65 + 6.4×? = 225

6.4×? = 160

$$? = \frac{160}{6.4}$$

? = 25

67. (c) 299 + 121 - ? = 361

? = 420 – 361

? = 59

68. (d) $\frac{?}{24} + \frac{65}{100} \times 260 = 199$

$$\frac{?}{24} = 199 - 169$$

? = 30 × 24

? = 720

69. (e) $2.46 \times 15 + \frac{25}{100} \times 92.4 = 15 \times ?$

36.9 + 23.1 = 15 × ?

$$? = \frac{60}{15}$$

? = 4

70. (d) 1387 – 433 + ? = 961

? = 961 – 954

? = 7

71. (a) Task A

	Days	Work	Efficiency
Manish	48		5unit/day
Suresh	60	240	4unit/days

ATQ

Task B

One day work of Manish and Suresh = 5+4=9 units

Total work = 9x

Manish alone can do task B in (x + 16) days

So total work = 9x = 5(x+16)

x = 20 days

Total work = 9 × 20

= 180 unit

Suresh alone can do the work = $\frac{180}{4}$ = 45 days

72. (e) After two years CI with 10% = 10 + 10 + $\frac{10\times10}{100}$

= 21%

After two years CI with 20% = 20 + 20+ $\frac{20\times20}{100}$

= 44%

Interest earned

$(P + 2400) \times \frac{21}{100} + (P + 4400) \times \frac{44}{100} = 8680$

21P + 44P = 868000 – (50400 + 193600)

65P = 868000 – 244000

$$P = \frac{624000}{65} = 9600$$

73. (e) Profit share ratio of Neeraj and Aniket

$$= \left(5x + \frac{2x}{3} \times 7\right) : (1400 \times 12)$$

$$= \left(\frac{29x}{3}\right) : (16800)$$

ATQ

$$\frac{\frac{29x}{3}}{16800} = \frac{29}{42}$$

$$x = \frac{16800\times3}{42}$$

x = 1200 Rs

74. (b) Speed of train = $80 \times \frac{5}{18}$

$$= \frac{200}{9} \text{ m/s}$$

Atq,

$$\frac{200}{9} = \frac{240+280}{T}$$

200T = 520 × 9

T = 23.4 sec

Length of tunnel

$$= (12.6 + 23.4) \times \frac{200}{9} - 240$$

= 800 – 240

= 560 meters

75. (d) Let radius of two circles be r cm and 3r cm

Atq,

2πr + 2π(3r) = 176

2π(r+ 3r) = 176

$$4r = \frac{176\times7}{2\times22} \Rightarrow r = 7 \text{ cm}$$

Let, breadth of rectangle is 3x cm and length is 8x cm

Atq,

2(l+b)=176

2(8x + 3x) = 176

11x = 88 ⇒ x = 8

Length of rectangle = 64cm

Required difference = 64 – 7 × 3 = 43 cm

76. (a) I $\quad .3x^2 + 17x + 10 = 0$

$\Rightarrow 3x^2 + 15x + 2x + 10 = 0$

$\Rightarrow 3x(x + 5) + 2(x + 5) = 0$

$\Rightarrow (3x + 2)(x + 5) = 0$

$\Rightarrow x = -5, \left(-\frac{2}{3}\right)$

II. $10y^2 + 9y + 2 = 0$
$\Rightarrow 10y^2 + 5y + 4y + 2 = 0$
$\Rightarrow 5y(2y + 1) + 2(2y + 1) = 0$
$\Rightarrow (5y + 2)(2y + 1) = 0$
$\Rightarrow y = \frac{-2}{5}, -\frac{1}{2}$
$\therefore x < y$

77. (a) I. $4x^2 = 49$
$\therefore x = \pm\frac{7}{2}$

II. $9y^2 - 66y + 121 = 0$
$9y^2 - 33y - 33y + 121 = 0$
$y = \frac{11}{3}, \frac{11}{3}$
$y > x$

78. (b) I. $3x^2 + 3x + 2x + 2 = 0$
$\Rightarrow 3x(x + 1) + 2(x + 1) = 0$
$\Rightarrow x = -1, \frac{-2}{3}$

II. $y^2 + 9y + 3y + 27 = 0$
$\Rightarrow y(y + 9) + 3(y + 9) = 0$
$\Rightarrow y = -3, -9$
$\therefore x > y$

79. (c) I. $x^2 - 5x - 2x + 10 = 0$
$\Rightarrow x(x - 5) - 2(x - 5) = 0$
$\Rightarrow x = 2, 5$

II. $y^2 - 9y - 5y + 45 = 0$
$\Rightarrow y(y - 9) - 5(y - 9) = 0$
$\Rightarrow y = 9, 5$

$\therefore x \leq y$

80. (b) I. $6x^2 - 49x + 99 = 0$
Or, $6x^2 - 27x - 22x + 99 = 0$
Or, $3x(2x - 9) - 11(2x - 9) = 0$
Or, $(3x - 11)(2x - 9) = 0$
$\therefore x = \frac{11}{3}, \frac{9}{2}$

II. $5y^2 + 17y + 14 = 0$
or, $5y^2 + 10y + 7y + 14 = 0$
or, $5y(y + 2) + 7(y + 2) = 0$
or, $(5y + 7)(y + 2) = 0$
$\therefore y = -2, -\frac{7}{5}$
Hence, $x > y$

REASONING ABILITY

Direction (1-5): In each of the questions below are given some statements followed by some conclusions. You have to take the given statements to be true even if they seem to be at variance with commonly known facts. Read all the conclusions and then decide which of the given conclusions logically follows from the given statements disregarding commonly known facts.
(a) If only conclusion I follows.
(b) If only conclusion II follows.
(c) If either conclusion I or II follows.
(d) If neither conclusion I nor II follows.
(e) If both conclusions I and II follow.

1. **Statements:** Only a few Star are Moon. No Moon is Night.
   Conclusions: I. All Star being Moon is a possibility.
   II. Some Star are not Night.

2. **Statements:** All Big are Tiny. All Small are Huge. No Huge is Big.
   Conclusions: I. Some Small are not Big.
   II. No Tiny is small.

3. **Statements:** Some First are Fifth. All Fifth are Ninth. Some Ninth are Third.
   Conclusions: I. Some First are not Third.
   II. Some Ninth can never be First.

4. **Statements:** No Song is Tune. Some Tune are Poet. No Poet is Story.
   Conclusions: I. Some Song can be Story.
   II. Some Tune are not Story.

5. **Statements:** All Big are Tiny. All Small are Huge. No Huge is Big.
   Conclusions: I. All Huge can be Small.
   II. All Small being Tiny is a possibility.

Direction (6-10): Study the following information carefully and answer the questions given below:

There are eight persons i.e. M, O, P, R, S, T, Y and Z sitting around a circular table facing the centre, but not necessarily in the same order.

R sits 3rd to the left of M. Y faces the one who is an immediate neighbour of O. T sits 2nd to the right of O. Z is an immediate neighbour of neither Y nor T. P faces Z. S sits immediate right of P.

6. Who among the following sits 2nd to the left of P?
   (a) T   (b) O   (c) M
   (d) R   (e) Y

7. How many persons are sitting between O and Z, when counted in a clockwise direction from O?
   (a) one   (b) none   (c) two
   (d) three   (e) four

8. Four of the following five are alike in a certain way and hence they form a group. Which one of the following does not belong to that group?
   (a) T - R   (b) O - S   (c) Y - M
   (d) S - T   (e) Z - P

9. Who among the following faces M?
   (a) Y   (b) S
   (c) T   (d) O
   (e) None of these

10. Who among the following sits immediately to the right of Z?
    (a) S   (b) O   (c) M
    (d) T   (e) R

Directions (11-13): Study the following information and answer the questions given below:

Shankar walks 9m. east from point P and reaches point Q. From point Q he takes a left and walks 11m. to reach point R. From point R he takes another left turn and walks 6m. to reach point S. From point S, he takes a right turn and walks 8m. to reach point T. Rakesh walks 10m. west from point J and then he takes a right and walks 12m. and again he takes a right and walks 5m. to reach point K. Point J is 5m. south from point P.

11. What is the shortest distance between point K and T?
    (a) $\sqrt{208}$m.   (b) $4\sqrt{12}$m.   (c) 15m.
    (d) $\sqrt{212}$m.   (e) None of these

12. Point J is in which direction from point R?
    (a) south
    (b) south-east
    (c) south-west
    (d) north-east
    (e) None of these

13. If one more point L is 4m. south of point S, then in which direction is point K, with respect to point L?
    (a) south-west   (b) north-east   (c) north
    (d) west   (e) south

Direction (14-18): Study the following information carefully and answer the questions given below:

Eight persons A, B, C, D, E, F, G and H were born in different months i.e. January, June, November and December on two different dates 15th or 24th but not necessarily in the same order.

B was born on the 15th, just before F and in a month, which has 31 days. Two persons were born between H and F. A was born just after G but not in the same month. More than 3 persons were born between C and D. C was born before E, but not just before E.

14. Who among the following pairs were born on the same date?
(a) G, A (b) D, C (c) B, H
(d) E, B (e) A, F

15. On which of the following dates and months E was born?
(a) 15th , January
(b) 24th , June
(c) 24th, November
(d) 24th, January
(e) None of these

16. How many persons were born between A and F?
(a) none (b) one (c) two
(d) four (e) five

17. Four of the following five are alike in a certain way and hence they form a group. Which one of the following does not belong to that group?
(a) A (b) G (c) C
(d) B (e) H

18. Who among the following persons was born just after the month in which E was born?
(a) H (b) A (c) G
(d) C (e) E

Directions (19-20): Study the following information carefully and answer the question given below.

There are eight friends J, K, L, M, N, O, P and Q each having a different weight. M is heavier than J but lighter than P. N is lighter than Q, but heavier than L. K is heavier than M, but lighter than O. L is heavier than P. P is not as light as O.

19. Who among the following is the third heaviest?
(a) N (b) L
(c) Q (d) O
(e) None of these

20. How many friends are lighter than K?
(a) one (b) two
(c) three (d) four
(e) Can't be determined

Directions (21-25): These questions are based on the following arrangement. Study it carefully and answer the questions below it.
Y 3 V S $ 7 O % 2 R U N 6 ! 9 Z I 4 # & 1 W 5 P * F 8 G C 0 @ K

21. Which element is exactly between sixth from the left end and seventh from the right end?
(a) I (b) 9
(c) Z (d) !
(e) None of these

22. If from the above arrangement all the symbols are deleted, which element will be fifth to the left of ninth from the right end?
(a) 6 (b) 9
(c) G (d) I
(e) None of these

23. How many consonants are there in the above arrangement, each of which is immediately preceded by a number and also immediately followed by a vowel?
(a) none (b) three
(c) two (d) one
(e) More than three

24. How many such symbols are there in the given arrangement, each of which is immediately followed by a number, but not immediately preceded by another symbol?
(a) none (b) one
(c) three (d) two
(e) More than three

25. Four of the following five are alike in a certain way based on their positions in the given arrangement and so form a group. Which is the one that does not belong to the group?
(a) VYS (b) 2OR (c) 8*G
(d) #I1 (e) 6U!

Directions (26-30): Study the following information carefully and answer the questions given below.

Eight friends C, D, G, H, J, K, M and N are sitting on a straight bench in a park, but not necessarily in the same order. Some of them are facing the north and rest are facing the south.

J sits third to the right of K, who sits third to the left of G. N sits at the one of the extreme ends. M sits second to the right of N. M is not an immediate neighbour of J. The ones who sit at the extreme ends, face opposite directions. The immediate neighbours of K face the same direction. H sits immediate left of D, who sits third to the left of C. H does not face the south.

26. How many friends are facing the south?
(a) two (b) three
(c) one (d) four
(e) Can't be determined

27. Who among the following sits to the immediate right of J?
(a) H (b) No one (c) D
(d) C (e) N

28. How many friends sit between C and N?
(a) No one (b) one
(c) two (d) three
(e) More than three

29. What is the position of M with respect to H?
(a) 2nd to the righ

(b) 3rd to the left
(c) 3rd to the right
(d) 2nd to the left
(e) 4th to the right

30. Four of the following five belong to a group in a certain way. Find which one does not belong to that group?
(a) D   (b) H   (c) J
(d) K   (e) C

Directions (31-35): Study the information carefully and answer the questions given below:

Eight employees G, H, J, K, L, M, N and O are going to attend a seminar on two different dates 15th and 30th of four months viz. January, April, May and June, but not necessarily in the same order.

There are four employees who attend the seminar between N and O, who attends the seminar before N. Only one employee attends the seminar between H and K and each of them attends the seminar on an even date. J does not attend the seminar in a month having 30 days. More than one employee attends the seminar between H and O. M attends the seminar immediately after G, but does not attend in the same month. H does not attend the seminar in the month of June.

31. On which of the following dates does L attend the seminar?
(a) 30th January
(b) 15th April
(c) 30th May
(d) 15th June
(c) None of these

32. Who among the following attends the seminar on 30th April?
(a) J   (b) G
(c) M   (d) H
(e) None of these

33. Who among the following attends the seminar immediately before J?
(a) O   (b) L   (c) M
(d) H   (e) No one

34. How many employees attend the seminar between M and N?
(a) No one   (b) two   (c) one
(d) three   (e) four

35. Four of the following five belong to a group in a certain way. Find which one does not belong to that group?
(a) O, J   (b) M, H   (c) K, L
(d) L, G   (e) N, K

Directions (36-40): Study the following information carefully and answer the questions.
In a certain code language,
'carry flag march street' is written as 'be ma xi ke',
'game flag latest bright' is written as 'xi hi ra qi',
'latest street of joke' is written as 'ya gi ra ke',
'march game ultimate flavour' is written as 'ji qi we be'.

36. What is the code for 'bright'?
(a) hi   (b) xi
(c) ra   (d) qi
(e) Can't be determined

37. Which of the following is the code for 'ultimate flag game'?
(a) xi ji qi
(b) gi xi qi
(c) we qi xi
(d) Either (a) or (c)
(e) Either (a) or (b)

38. What is the code for 'March'?
(a) ma   (b) be
(c) xi   (d) ke
(e) None of these

39. What is the code for 'latest'?
(a) xi   (b) hi
(c) ra   (d) qi
(e) None of these

40. Which of the following is the possible code for 'Joke of day'?
(a) ya we gi   (b) ji ra ya
(c) ze we ya   (d) ya ze gi
(e) None of these

Quantitative Aptitude

41. The ratio of the ages of A and B, 6 years ago was 3:4. Sum of the present ages of B and C is 80 years. C is 12 years elder to A. Find the difference of B and C's age, five years later.
(a) 3 years   (b) 7 years   (c) 6 years
(d) 5 years   (e) 4 years

42. A man invested Rs. 40,000 in a mutual fund for 3 years. In the first year, his amount increased by 10%, in the 2nd year his amount decreased by X% and in the 3rd year, his amount again increased by 20% and he got Rs. 4880 more at the end. Find value of X.
(a) 15   (b) 12.5   (c) 20
(d) $13\frac{1}{3}$ (e) $17\frac{1}{2}$

43. A alone takes 20% less time than that of B alone to do a work. When they work together for 8 days, 90% of the work gets completed. Find the difference between their individual time to do the whole work.
(a) $4\frac{1}{2}$ days   (b) 4 days   (c) 5 days

(d) 6 days   (e) 8 days

44. Investment made by A and C is 40% less and 60% more than that of B respectively and the ratio of the period of investment of A, B and C is 3: 2: 1. If their average profit is Rs. 21,600 then find the difference between A's and C's profit share (in Rs.).
    (a) 2400   (b) 2000   (c) 1800
    (d) 2600   (e) 2800

45. The respective ratio of the number of green, red and white balls in a bag is 3:4:5. When two balls are drawn, the probability of drawing exactly one red and one white ball is $\frac{2}{7}$. Find the probability of getting red balls when two balls are drawn.
    (a) $\frac{14}{107}$ (b) $\frac{3}{35}$
    (c) $\frac{11}{105}$ (d) $\frac{3}{34}$
    (e) $\frac{14}{111}$

Directions (46-50): In each of these questions, two equations I and II are given. You have to solve both the equations and give the answer

(a) if $x > y$
(b) if $x \geq y$
(c) if $x < y$
(d) if $x \leq y$
(e) if $x = y$ or no relation can be established between x and y

46. I. $x^2 - 218 = 358$ II. $y^3 - 804 = 1393$
47. I. $3x^2 + 11x + 6 = 0$ II. $6y^2 + 5y + 1 = 0$
48. I. $3x^2 + 10x + 7 = 0$ II. $3y^2 + 4y + 1 = 0$
49. I. $x^2 + 18x + 77 = 0$ II. $y^2 + 18y + 72 = 0$
50. I. $2x^2 + x - 15 = 0$ II. $9y^2 + 9y - 10 = 0$

Directions (51-55): The table given below shows the total number of people and among them the percentage of males who have visited a park on five different days. The table also shows the ratio of females and children who visited the park on five different days.

Note: Total number of people visiting park = male + female + child:

Days	Total no. of people	% of male in total	Female : child
Sunday	2750	40%	1:2
Saturday	3000	$33\frac{1}{3}$%	3:7
Monday	4800	$33\frac{1}{2}$%	2:3
Tuesday	2700	30%	3:4
Friday	1800	25%	1:1

51. Find the ratio of the total number of males who visited the park on Saturday and Monday together to the total number of people who have visited the park on Friday?
    (a) 11:9   (b) 5:3   (c) 14:9
    (d) 8:3   (e) 11:5

52. The total number of females who visited the park on Sunday and Tuesday together is how much more or less than the children who visited the park on Monday?
    (a) 450   (b) 420   (c) 390
    (d) 440   (e) 410

53. The total number of males who visited the park on Sunday and Friday together is what percent more or less than the total number of people who visited the park on Saturday?
    (a) $33\frac{1}{3}$%   (b) None of these
    (c) $48\frac{1}{3}$%   (d) $51\frac{2}{3}$%
    (e) $47\frac{1}{2}$%

54. Find the average number of males who have visited the park on Tuesday, Friday and Monday.
    (a) 1020   (b) 1060
    (c) 1080   (d) 990
    (e) None of these

55. The difference between females and children who visited the park on Saturday is what percent of the difference between males and females who visited the park on Monday?
    (a) $132\frac{1}{7}$%   (b) $133\frac{1}{3}$%   (c) 130%
    (d) 135%   (e) $137\frac{1}{2}$%

Direction (56 – 60): What exact value will come in the place of question marks(?):

56. 42% of 650 + 243 - $\sqrt{?}$ = 2 × $(4)^4$
    (a) 18   (b) 16   (c) 20
    (d) 24   (e) 12

57. ? % of 750 + $(15)^2$ = $(8)^2$ + 356
    (a) 42   (b) 16   (c) 22
    (d) 26   (e) 32

58. $\frac{728}{?}$ × 15 + 24% of 550 – 38 = 484
    (a) 20   (b) 36   (c) 32
    (d) 24   (e) 28

59. 36 × ? + 33 × 4 + $\sqrt{441}$ = $(21)^2$
    (a) 8   (b) 2   (c) 9
    (d) 11   (e) 14

60. 568 + 330 – $(12)^2$ = 8% of ?
    (a) 9255   (b) 9425   (c) 9755
    (d) 9625   (e) 10225

Direction (61-65): Study the given information carefully and answer the following questions.

In Fun Cinema, there are three types of tickets available for the movie Kabir Singh — Silver, Gold and Platinum. Each type of ticket is priced differently. The total number of tickets available is 115. The ratio of the number of Platinum tickets to that of Gold tickets is 4:3. The number of Silver tickets is 50% more than that of Gold. The number of unsold tickets is 5 for each type of ticket. The price of a Gold ticket is 25% less than that of a Platinum ticket, which is priced $71\frac{3}{7}\%$ more than that of a Silver ticket. The price of all unsold tickets is Rs. 3500.

61. What is the difference between the total number of tickets sold and the number of Silver tickets available initially?
(a) 45
(b) 55
(c) 48
(d) 50
(e) None of these

62. If the total tickets sold were Gold tickets, then find how much more or less revenue can be generated.
(a) Rs. 615
(b) None of these
(c) Rs. 605
(d) Rs. 635
(e) Rs. 625

63. Find the average price of a Platinum, a Gold and a Silver ticket?
(a) $Rs\,\dfrac{710}{3}$
(b) $Rs\,\dfrac{740}{3}$
(c) $Rs\,\dfrac{700}{3}$
(d) $Rs\,\dfrac{760}{3}$
(e) $Rs\,\dfrac{770}{3}$

64. If all sold tickets were of the Silver type, then the price of all unsold tickets is what percent of the total revenue generated?
(a) 20%
(b) 25%
(c) 17.5%
(d) 15%
(e) 30%

65. The average price of one ticket of each type is what percent more or less than the price of a Platinum ticket?
(a) $22\frac{2}{9}\%$
(b) None of these
(c) $11\frac{1}{9}\%$
(d) $18\frac{2}{11}\%$
(e) $9\frac{1}{11}\%$

66. The ratio of the radius and height of a cylinder is 7:12. If its volume is 6237 cm.^{3}, then find the difference between its total surface area and curved surface area.
(a) 700 cm.^{2}
(b) 686 cm.^{2}
(c) 679 cm.^{2}
(d) 672 cm.^{2}
(e) 693 cm.^{2}

67. A milkman pays Rs. 12.8 per litre of milk. He adds water to it and sells the mixture at Rs. 16 per litre at a profit of 37.5%. Find the ratio of milk to that of water added to the mixture.
(a) 10: 1
(b) 1: 10
(c) 11: 1
(d) 5: 1
(e) 10: 3

Directions (68 – 72): Study the line graph given below and answer the questions accordingly.

The given graph shows the percentage of students who have passed in Math and Science Olympiad from five different schools. Number of students who have taken Math Olympiad test is same from each of these schools.

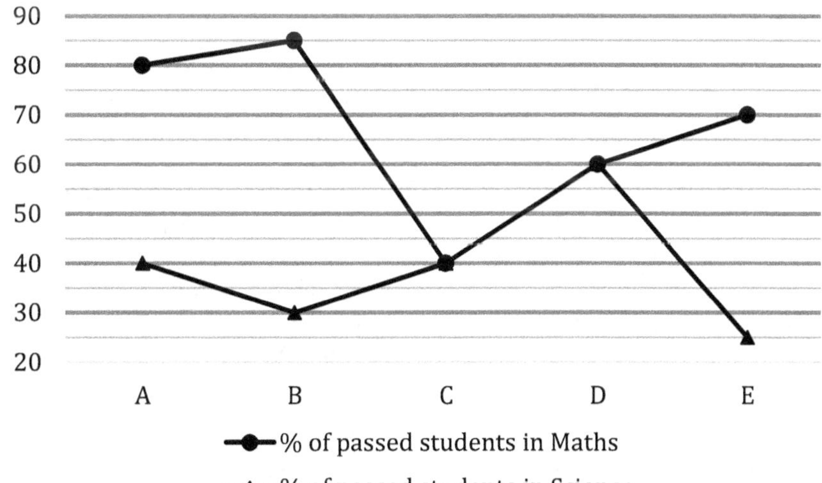

Note: The number of students who have taken the Science Olympiad test is 60% of the students who have taken the Math Olympiad test for each school

68. What is the ratio of the number of students who have passed from school B to that of school E in both the tests?
(a) 104: 85
(b) 103: 85
(c) 101: 84
(d) 105: 83
(e) None of these

69. The difference between the number of students who have failed in science Olympiad from school A and D is 60. Find the total number of students who have appeared in the Olympiad test from school A.
(a) 800
(b) 600
(c) 750
(d) 650
(e) 1000

70. The total students who have passed the Science test from school D and E together is what percent more or less than students who have passed the Maths test from school C?
(a) 22.5%   (b) 25%   (c) 27.5%
(d) 17.5%   (e) 20%

71. If the average number of students who have failed in the Maths test from school B, C and E is 105, then find the average number of students who have appeared in the Maths test from all the schools.
(a) 300   (b) 500   (c) 400
(d) 350   (e) 450

72. If the difference between the number of girls who passed in Science from school A and C is 15, then find the total number of students who have taken the test from these schools, when the girls who passed in Science from school A and C are 50% and 75% respectively of the total students who passed in Science.
(a) 720   (b) 800   (c) 700
(d) 1000   (e) 600

73. A does a work for 5 days and B does the same work for 8 days and the ratio of the work done by B to that of A is 4:5. The efficiency of A is what percent more or less than that of B?
(a) 50 %   (b) 25 %   (c) 60 %
(d) 100 %   (e) 75 %

74. The ratio of the present age of A and B is 3:2 and four years later, age of B will be $56\frac{1}{4}$% of age of C. If the average of the present age of A and C is 54 years, then find the present age of B.
(a) 29 years   (b) 27 years   (c) 25 years
(d) 32 years   (e) 36 years

75. The ratio of upstream speed to that of downstream speed is 3:5. If the speed of the boat in still water is 24 km/hr., then in how much time will the boat cover 36 kms. in upstream and 60 kms. in downstream together?
(a) 4 hours   (b) 5 hours   (c) 3 hours
(d) 6 hours   (e) 4.5 hours

Direction (76-80): The pie chart given below shows the distribution of monthly expenditure of Ayush in six different fields. Study the data carefully and answer the following questions.

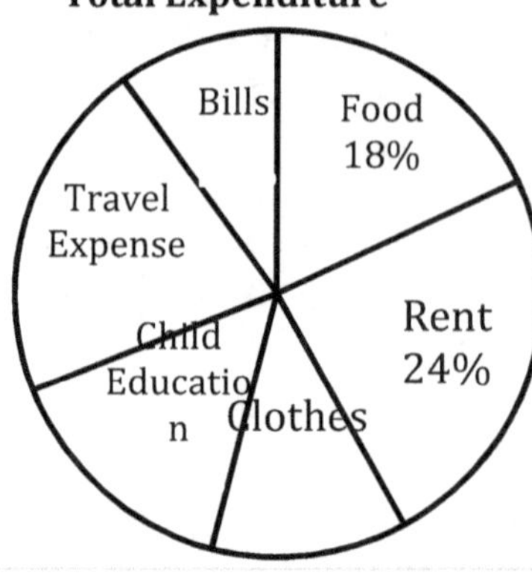

Note: 1. The ratio of monthly expenditure of Ayush to that of Arun is 5:3.
2. Income=Savings + Expenditure
3. The distribution of expenditure is also the same for Arun.

76. If Arun's expenditure on clothes is Rs. 3600, then find the difference between his travel expenses and rent.
(a) Rs. 800   (b) Rs. 1200   (c) Rs. 600
(d) Rs. 720   (e) Rs. 900

77. If the difference in the bills submitted by Arun and Ayush is Rs. 2000, then find the annual income of Ayush, if his monthly saving is Rs 18000.
(a) Rs. 7,96,000
(b) Rs. 7,66,000
(c) Rs. 8,16,000
(d) Rs. 8,06,000
(e) Rs. 8,18,000

78. Find the ratio of Ayush's total expenditure on food, rent and clothes to that of Arun's on child education, travel and bills together.
(a) 9:5   (b) 21:11   (c) 25:12
(d) 45:23   (e) 48:23

79. If Ayush's annual income is Rs. 7.2 lakh, then find the difference between Ayush's monthly expenditure on travel and that of Arun's monthly expenditure on child education and bills together, given that the ratio of income of Ayush and Arun is 5:3.
(a) Rs. 3000   (b) Rs. 3300
(c) Rs. 4500   (d) Rs. 3200
(e) None of these

80. If Rahul's expenditure is 50% more than that of Arun's, then find Rahul's total expenditure on food and bills together is what percent of Ayush's total expenditure on rent (consider the same expenditure distribution for Rahul)?
(a) 85%   (b) 55%   (c) 105%
(d) 150%   (e) 110%

Solutions

REASONING ABILITY

1. (b)

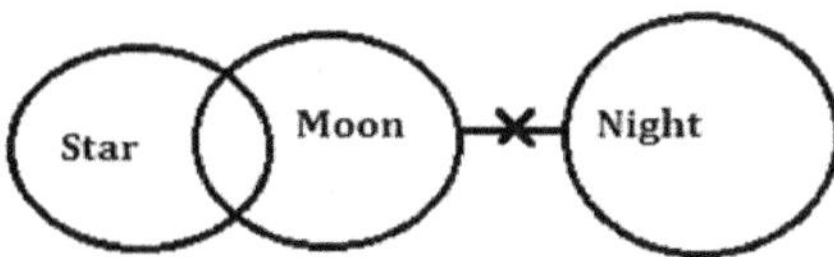

2. (a)

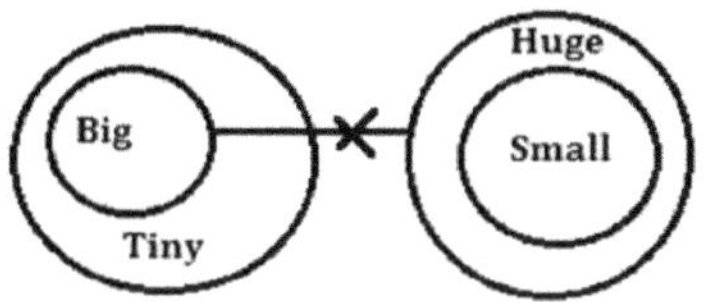

3. (d)

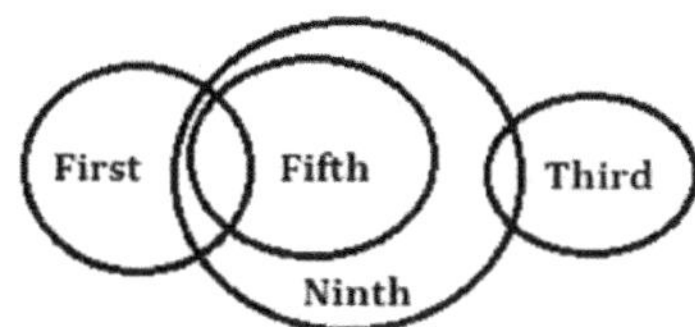

4. (e)

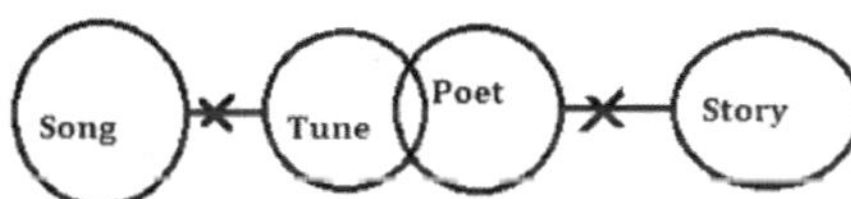

5. (e)

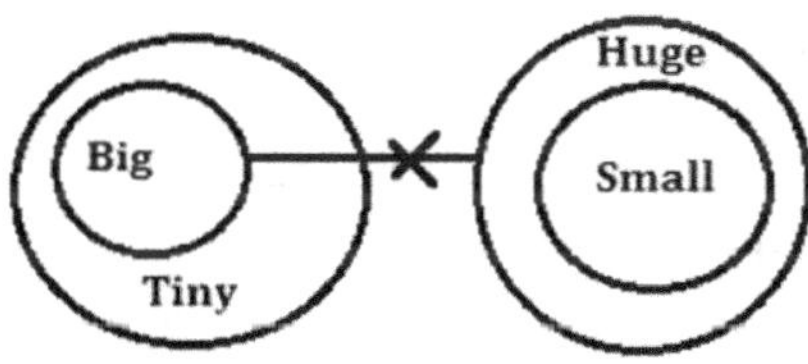

Direction (6-10): From the given statements, Y faces the one who is an immediate neighbour of O. **Here we get 2 possibilities i.e. Case 1 and Case 2.** T sits 2nd to the right of O. Z is an immediate neighbour of neither Y nor T. P faces Z.

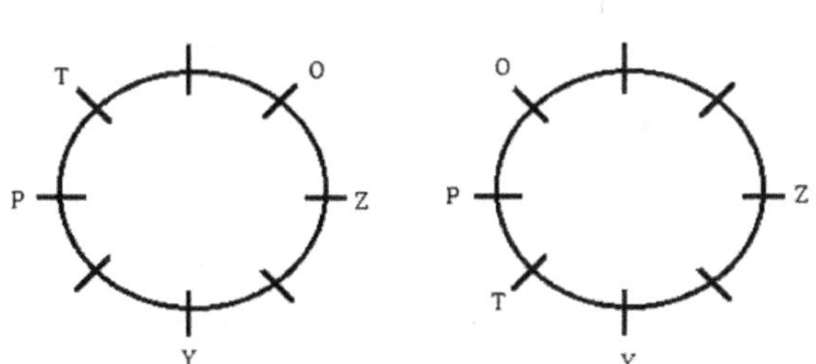

From the given statements, S sits immediate right of P. **Here Case 2 is ruled out.** R sits 3rd to the left of M.

So, **the final arrangement will be like this-**

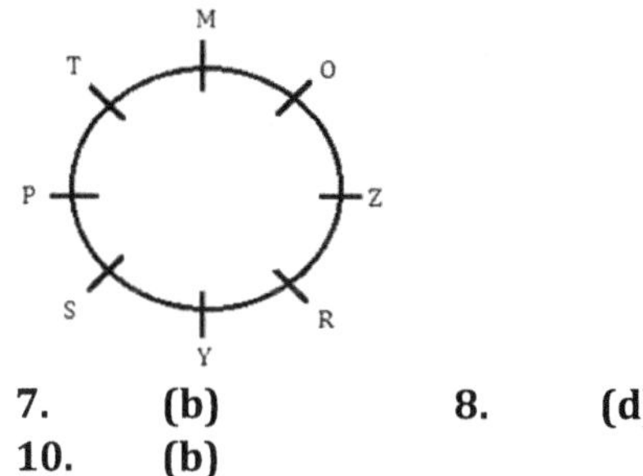

6. (c) **7. (b)** **8. (d)**
9. (a) **10. (b)**

Directions (11-13):

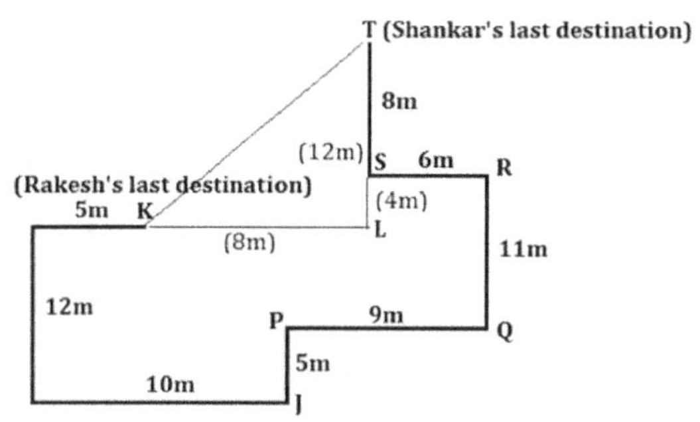

11. (a) $KT^2 = 8^2 + 12^2 = 64 + 144 = 208$
$KT = \sqrt{208}m$

12. (c)

13. (d)

Direction (14-18): From the given statements, B was born on 15th just before F and in the month, which has 31 days. **Here we get 2 possibilities i.e. Case 1 and Case 2.** Two persons were born between H and F. A was born just after G but not in the same month. More than 3 persons were born between C and D.

Month	Date	Case 1 Persons	Case 2 Persons
January	15	B	C/D
January	24	F	G
June	15	C/D	A
June	24	E	E
November	15	H	H
November	24	G	D/C
December	15	A	B
December	24	D/C	F

From the given statements, C was born before E, but not just before E. **Here Case 1 is ruled out.**

So, the final arrangement is such:

71

Month	Date	Persons
January	15	C
	24	G
June	15	A
	24	E
November	15	H
	24	D
December	15	B
	24	F

14. (c) **15. (b)** **16. (d)**

17. (b) **18. (a)**

Directions (19-20):

Q > N > L > P > O > K > M > J

19. (b)

20. (b)

Directions (21-25):

21. (c) Y 3 V S $ 7 0 % 2 R U N 6 ! 9 Z I 4 # & 1 W 5 P * F 8 G C 0 @ K

22. (b) Y 3 V S7 02 R U N 6 9 Z I 4 1 W 5 PF 8 G C 0K

5th (Left) + 9th (right end) = 14th from right end = 9

23. (c) 2 R U,9 Z I

24. (c) S $ 7,0 % 2, 6 ! 9

25. (d)

Directions (26-30): J sits third to the right of K, who sits third to the left of G. From this condition we have four possible cases. N sits at the one of the extreme ends. So, arrangement will be-

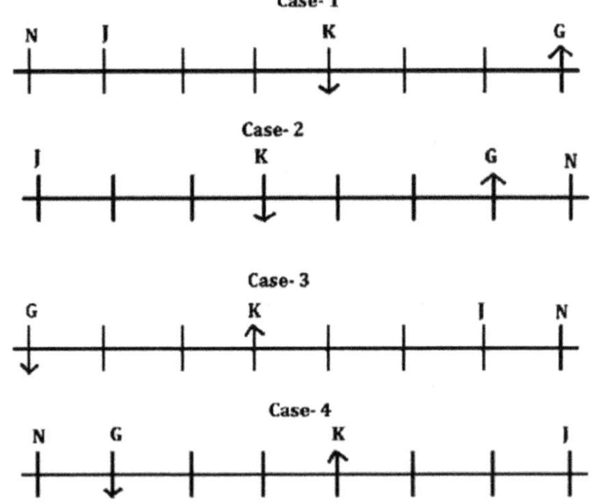

M sits second to the right of N. M is not an immediate neighbour of J. By these conditions case- 1 and case- 3 are cancelled. The ones who sit at the extreme ends face opposite directions to each other. So new arrangement will be:

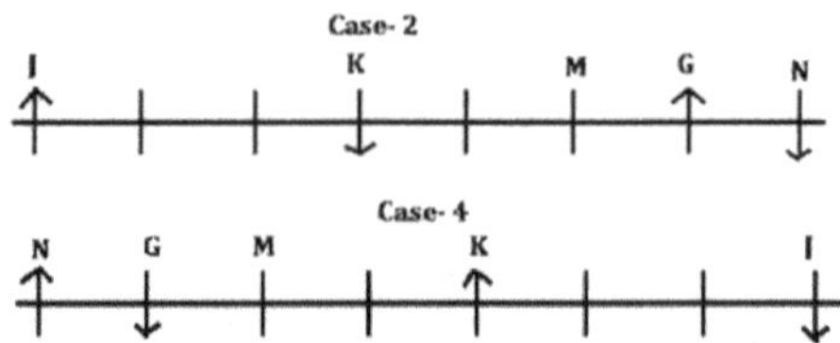

H sits immediate left of D, who sits third to the left of C. The immediate neighbours of K face the same direction. H does not face south direction. By these conditions case- 4 is cancelled. So final arrangement will be:

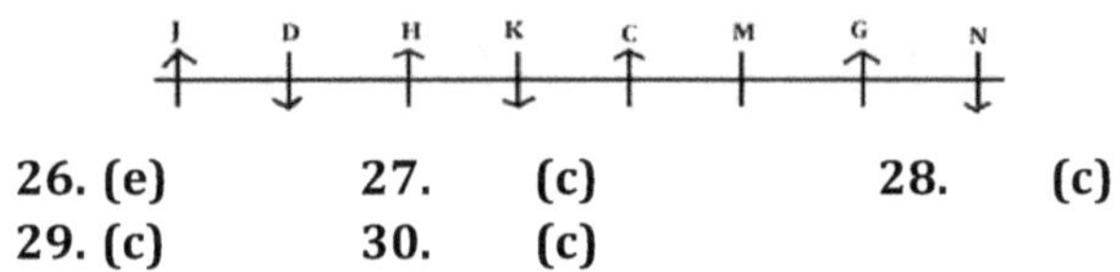

26. (e) **27. (c)** **28. (c)**

29. (c) **30. (c)**

Directions (31-35): There are four employees who attend the seminar between N and O, who attends the seminar before N. More than one employee attends the seminar between H and O. Only one employee attends the seminar between H and K and each of them attends the seminar on an even date. H does not attend the seminar in the month of June. From these conditions we have three possible cases:

Month	Date	Case-1 Employee	Case-2 Employee	Case-3 Employee
January	15	0		
January	30	K	0	
April	15			
April	30	H	K/	K
May	15			
May	30	N	H	H
June	15		N	
June	15		K/	N

M attends the seminar immediately after G but does not attend in the same month. By this condition case- 1 and case-3 are cancelled. J does not attend the seminar in a month having 30 days. So final arrangement will be:

Month	Date	Employee
January	15	J
January	30	O
April	15	L
April	30	G
May	15	M
May	30	H
June	15	N
June	30	K

31. (b)   **32. (b)**   **33. (e)**

34. (c)   **35. (c)**

Directions (36-40):

Word	Code
carry	ma
flag	xi
march	be
street	ke
game	qi

latest	ra
bright	hi
of/joke	ya/gi
ultimate/flavour	ji/we

36. (a)   **37. (d)**   **38. (b)**

39. (c)   **40. (d)**

Quantitative Aptitude

41. (e) Let age of A and B be 3x and 4x years respectively

ATQ,

C's age =(80-(4x+6)) years

And, (74-4x) - (3x+6) =12

$x = 8$

Required difference =4 years

42. (a) ATQ,

$$40{,}000 \times \frac{110}{100} \times \frac{(100-X)}{100} \times \frac{120}{100} = 44880$$

$x = 15$

43. (b) Let time taken by B alone to complete the whole work be $5x$ days

Then, time taken by A alone=4x days

ATQ

$$\frac{8}{4x} + \frac{8}{5x} = \frac{9}{10}$$

$$\frac{40+32}{20x} = \frac{9}{10}$$

$x = 4$

Required difference= 4 days

44. (a) Let the amount invested by B be Rs 5x

Then amount invested by A and C will be Rs 3x and Rs 8x respectively

Ratio of profit

A   B   C

$3x \times 3 : 5x \times 2 : 8x \times 1 = 9 : 10 : 8$

Let profit share of A, B and C be Rs 9y, Rs 10y and Rs 8y respectively.

ATQ

9y=21600

Required difference=y=Rs 2400

45. (c) Let the number of green, red and white balls in the bag be 3x, 4x and 5x respectively.

ATQ

$$\frac{4x c_1 \times 5x c_1}{12x c_2} = \frac{2}{7}$$

$x = 3$

Total number of balls=36

Required probability$=\dfrac{12c_2}{36c_2} = \dfrac{11}{105}$

46. (e) I. $x^2 - 218 = 358$ II. $y^3 - 804 = 1393$

$\therefore x^2 = 576$ or, $y^3 = 2197$

$\therefore x = \pm 24$ $\therefore y = 13$

Hence no relation can be established.

47. (c)

I. $3x^2 + 11x + 6 = 0$

or, $3x^2 + 9x + 2x + 6 = 0$

or, $3x(x + 3) + 2(x + 3) = 0$

or, $(3x + 2)(x + 3) = 0$

$\therefore x = -\dfrac{2}{3}, -3$

II. $6y^2 + 5y + 1 = 0$

or, $6y^2 + 3y + 2y + 1 = 0$

or, $3y(2y + 1) + 1(2y + 1) = 0$

or, $(3y + 1)(2y + 1) = 0$

$\therefore y = -\dfrac{1}{3}, -\dfrac{1}{2}$

Hence $x < y$

48. (d)   I. $3x^2 + 10x + 7 = 0$

$\Rightarrow 3x^2 + 7x + 3x + 7 = 0$

$\Rightarrow (x+ 1)(3x + 7) = 0$

$\Rightarrow x = -1, -\dfrac{7}{3}$

II. $3y^2 + 4y + 1 = 0$

$\Rightarrow 3y^2 + 3y + y + 1 = 0$

$\Rightarrow (y + 1)(3y + 1) = 0$

$\Rightarrow y = -1, -\dfrac{1}{3}$

$y \geq x$

49. (e)   I. $x^2 + 18x + 77 = 0$

$\Rightarrow (x + 11)(x + 7) = 0$

$\Rightarrow x = -11, -7$

II. $y^2 + 18y + 72 = 0$

$\Rightarrow y -12, -6$

No relation can be established

50. (e)   I. $2x^2 + x - 15 = 0$

$2x^2 + 6x - 5x - 15 = 0$

$2x(x + 3) - 5(x + 3) = 0$

$x = -3, \dfrac{5}{2}$

II. $9y^2 + 9y - 10 = 0$

$9y^2 + 15y - 6y - 10 = 0$

$3y(3y + 5) - 2(3y + 5) = 0$

$y = -\dfrac{5}{3}, \dfrac{2}{3}$

$\therefore$ Relation cannot be established.

51. (c) Required ratio$=\dfrac{\frac{1}{3} \times 3000 + \frac{3}{8} \times 4800}{1800} = 14:9$

52. (d) Total number of females who have visited the park on Sunday and Tuesday together

$$=2750 \times \frac{60}{100} \times \frac{1}{3} + 2700 \times \frac{70}{100} \times \frac{3}{7}$$

$$= 1360$$

Number of children who visited the park on Monday$=4800 \times \frac{5}{8} \times \frac{3}{5} = 1800$

Required difference$=440$

53. (c) Total number of males who visited the park on Sunday and Friday together$=2750 \times 0.4 + 1800 \times \frac{1}{4} =1550$

Required %$=\frac{1450}{3000} \times 100 = 48\frac{1}{3}\%$

54. (a) Required

average$=\frac{2700 \times 0.30 + 1800 \times 0.25 + 4800 \times \frac{3}{8}}{3} = 1020$

55. (b) Difference between females and children who visited the park on Saturday$=3000 \times \frac{2}{3} \times \frac{4}{10} = 800$

Difference between males and females who visited the park on Monday$=4800 \times \frac{3}{8} - \left(4800 \times \frac{5}{8} \times \frac{2}{5}\right) = 600$

required %$=\frac{800}{600} \times 100 = 133\frac{1}{3}\%$

56. (b) $\frac{42}{100} \times 650 + 243 - \sqrt{?} = 2 \times (4)^4$

$273 + 243 - \sqrt{?} = 2 \times 256$

$\sqrt{?} = 516 - 512$

$\sqrt{?} = 4$

$? = 16$

57. (d) $\frac{?}{100} \times 750 + (15)^2 = (8)^2 + 356$

$\frac{?}{100} \times 750 + 225 = 64 + 356$

$\frac{?}{100} \times 750 = 195$

$? = \frac{195 \times 100}{750}$

$? = 26$

58. (e) $\frac{728}{?} \times 15 + \frac{24}{100} \times 550 - 38 = 484$

$\frac{728 \times 15}{?} = 484 + 38 - 132$

$? = \frac{728 \times 15}{390}$

$? = 28$

59. (a) $36 \times ? + 33 \times 4 + \sqrt{441} = (21)^2$

$36 \times ? = 441 - 21 - 132$

$? = \frac{288}{36}$

$? = 8$

60. (b) $568 + 330 - (12)^2 = \frac{8}{100} \times ?$

$\frac{8}{100} \times ? = 898 - 144$

$? = \frac{754 \times 100}{8}$

$? = 9425$

Direction (61-65): Let number of Platinum and Gold tickets be 4x and 3x respectively.

Then number of Silver tickets$=4.5x$

ATQ

$4x + 3x + 4.5x = 115$

$x = 10$

Let price of a Platinum tickets be Rs 4y

Then price of a Gold ticket$=$ Rs 3y

And price of a Silver ticket$=4y \times \frac{7}{12} = Rs \frac{7y}{3}$

ATQ

$$5 \times \frac{7y}{3} + 5 \times 3y + 5 \times 4y = 3500$$

$$y = 75$$

Tickets	Number	Price
Silver	45	175
Gold	30	225
Platinum	40	300

61. (b) Required difference$=100 - 45 = 55$

62. (e) Total revenue generated$=175 \times 40 + 225 \times 25 + 300 \times 35 = Rs\ 23,125$

If total sold tickets were Gold tickets, then total revenue generated$=$Rs 22500

Required amount$=$Rs 625

63. (c) Required average$=\frac{175 + 225 + 300}{3} = Rs \frac{700}{3}$

64. (a) Required %$=\frac{3500}{175 \times 100} \times 100 = 20\%$

65. (a) Average price of one ticket of each type$=$ Rs $\frac{700}{3}$

Required %$=\frac{\left(300 - \frac{700}{3}\right)}{300} \times 100 = 22\frac{2}{9}\%$

66. (e) Let radius and height of the cylinder be 7x and 12x cm respectively.

ATQ

$\frac{22}{7} \times 7x \times 7x \times 12x = 6237$

$x = \sqrt[3]{\frac{27}{8}} = \frac{3}{2} = 1.5$

Required difference$=2\pi r^2 = 693$ cm^2

67. (a) S.P. $=$Rs 16

Profit $= 37.5\%$

$\therefore$ CP $= \frac{16 \times 100}{137.5} = Rs\ \frac{128}{11}$

Water		Milk
0		12.8
	$\frac{128}{11}$	
$\frac{64}{55}$		$\frac{128}{11}$
1	:	10

Milk: Water $= 10 : 1$

68. (b) Let the number of students who have taken maths test from each school be 100x

$\therefore$ Required ratio $= \frac{85x + 60x \times \frac{30}{100}}{70x + 60x \times \frac{25}{100}} = 103 : 85$

69. (a) Let the number of students who have taken maths test from each school be 100x

ATQ

$60x \times 0.6 - 60x \times 0.4 = 60$

$x = 5$

Required number of students= 800

70. (c) Let the number of students who have taken maths test from each school be 100x

Required $\% = \frac{(60x \times 0.6 + 60x \times 0.25) - 40x}{40x} \times 100 = 27.5\%$

71. (a) Let the number of students who have taken maths test from each school be 100x

ATQ

$\frac{(15x + 60x + 30x)}{3} = 105$

$x = 3$

Required average=300

72. (b) Let the number of students who have taken maths test from each school be 100x

ATQ

$60x \times 0.4 \times (0.75 - 0.5) = 15$

$x = 2.5$

Required total=800

73. (d) Let efficiency of A and that of B be x unit/day and y unit/day respectively.

ATQ

$\frac{8 \times y}{5 \times x} = \frac{4}{5}$

$\frac{x}{y} = \frac{2}{1}$

Required %=100 %

74. (d) Let the present age of A and B be 3x years and 2x years respectively

Present age of C=$(2x + 4) \times \frac{16}{9} - 4 = \left(\frac{32x}{9} + \frac{28}{9}\right) years$

ATQ

$3x + \left(\frac{32x}{9} + \frac{28}{9}\right) = 108$

$x = 16$

Present age of B=32 years

75. (a) Let upstream speed = 3x km/hr and

Downstream speed = 5x km/hr

ATQ,

Speed of boat = $\frac{5x + 3x}{2} = 4x$

4x=24

x=6

Upstream speed = 3 × 6 = 18 kmph

Downstream speed = 5 × 6 = 30 kmph

Required time = $\frac{36}{18} + \frac{60}{30}$

$= 2 + 2 = 4$ hours

76. (e) Required difference=$3600 \times \frac{3}{12} = Rs\ 900$

77. (c) Let monthly expenditure of Ayush and that of Arun be Rs 500x and Rs 300x respectively.

ATQ

$50x - 30x = 2000$

$x = 100$

Monthly income of Ayush= Rs 68,000

Annual income of Ayush= Rs 8,16,000

78. (d) Let monthly expenditure of Ayush and that of Arun be Rs 500x and Rs 300x respectively.

Required ratio=$\frac{500x \times 0.54}{300x \times 0.46} = 45:23$

79. (e) Monthly income of Ayush= Rs 60,000

Monthly income of Arun=Rs 36,000

Required difference=$60,000 \times 0.21 - 36000 \times (0.25)$ =Rs 3600

80. (c) Let monthly expenditure of Ayush and that of Arun be Rs 500x and Rs 300x respectively.

Monthly expenditure of Rahul=Rs 450x

Required %=$\frac{450x \times 0.28}{500x \times 0.24} \times 100 = 105\%$

REASONING ABILITY

Direction (1-5): Study the following information carefully and answer the questions given below:

Eight persons P, Q, R, S, T, U, V and W are sitting around a rectangular table in such a way that four persons sit on each of the four corners of the table and four persons sit at the middle of each side. The one who sits at the corner of the table faces opposite the centre of the table and the one who sits at the middle side of table faces towards the centre of table. Persons sitting on opposite sides are exactly opposite to each other.

W sits 2nd to the right of V. Three persons sit between S and W. P sits 2nd to the left of S. U sits 2nd to the left of Q and sits at the middle side of the table. Both R and U are facing each other. T is an immediate neighbour of both P and W.

1. Who among the following faces T?
   (a) W   (b) Q   (c) P
   (d) S   (e) V

2. The number of persons sitting between P and U when counted to the left of P is the same as the number of persons sitting between Q and ___ when counted to the left of Q?
   (a) W   (b) T
   (c) S   (d) R
   (e) None of these

3. How many persons sit between P and V?
   (a) one
   (b) two
   (c) four
   (d) Either (b) or (c)
   (e) None of these

4. If all the persons are sitting in alphabetical order in clockwise direction from P, then find how many persons remain in the same position (excluding P)?
   (a) none   (b) one
   (c) two   (d) three
   (e) More than three

5. Four of the following five are alike in a certain way and hence they form a group. Which one of the following does not belong to that group?
   (a) R   (b) W   (c) U
   (d) T   (e) Q

Direction (6-8): In these questions, relationship between different elements is shown in the statements. The statements are followed by conclusions. Study the conclusions based on the given statements and select the appropriate answer:

6. **Statements:** $A > M \geq L < K; Y = T \leq L; D > P$
   Conclusions: I. $A > L$ **II.** $K = Y$
   (a) If only conclusion II follows.
   (b) If only conclusion I follows.
   (c) If either conclusion I or II follows.
   (d) If neither conclusion I nor II follows.
   (e) If both conclusions I and II follow.

7. **Statements:** $R > W \leq Q < P \leq L; W > H \geq V = C$
   Conclusions: I. $Q > C$ **II.** $W < L$
   (a) If only conclusion II follows.
   (b) If only conclusion I follows.
   (c) If either conclusion I or II follows.
   (d) If both conclusions I and II follow.
   (e) If neither conclusion I nor II follows.

8. **Statements:** $D \geq F = K \leq L \leq Q = U \geq S > A$
   Conclusions: I. $F > Q$ **II.** $L < U$
   (a) If only conclusion II follows.
   (b) If neither conclusion I nor II follows.
   (c) If either conclusion I or II follows.
   (d) If both conclusions I and II follow.
   (e) If only conclusion I follows.

9. If it is possible to make only one meaningful word with the first, third, fourth and seventh letters of the word 'MONETARY' which would be the second letter of the word from the right end? If more than one such word can be formed, give 'Y' as the answer. If no such word can be formed, give 'Z' as your answer.
   (a) Y   (b) N   (c) Z
   (d) M   (e) R

10. In the word 'AMNESTY', how many pairs of the letters have the same number of letters between them (backwards or forwards) in the word as in alphabet series?
    (a) four   (b) two
    (c) one   (d) three
    (e) More than four

Ten persons are sitting in two parallel rows containing five persons in each row in such a way that there is an equal distance between adjacent persons. In the first row, D, E, F, G and H are seated and all of them are facing south. In the second row, M, N, O, P and Q are seated and all of them are facing north. Therefore, in the given seating arrangement, each member seated in a row faces another member of the other row.

Two persons sit between G and F. D faces the one who sits 3rd to the left of P. G is an immediate neighbour of D. O faces the one who sits 3rd to the right of E. O does not sit at any of the extreme ends.

Both Q and O are not immediate neighbours. M does not face H.

11. Who among the following faces N?

   (a) E   (b) G   (c) D

   (d) H   (e) F

12. How many persons sit between M and Q?

   (a) two   (b) one

   (c) No one   (d) three

   (e) Can't be determined

13. Who among the following faces the one who sits 2nd to the right of O?

   (a) G   (b) H   (c) F

   (d) E   (e) D

14. Four of the following five are alike in a certain way and hence they form a group. Which one of the following does not belong to that group?

   (a) P   (b) D   (c) Q

   (d) N   (e) F

15. The number of persons who sit between D and E is same as the number of persons sitting between ___ and M?

   (a) O   (b) Q

   (c) P   (d) N

   (e) Can't be determined

Direction (16-20): Study the following information carefully to answer the questions given below.

A word and number arrangement machine when given an input line of words and numbers, rearranges the words and numbersusing a particular rule in each step. The following is an illustration of input and rearrangement.

Input: peak 29 jeep 34 52 around 12 85 the home 21 buy.

Step I.   around 85 peak 29 jeep 34 52 12 the home 21 buy

Step II.   around 85 buy 52 peak 29 jeep 34 12 the home 21

Step III.   around 85 buy 52 home 34 peak 29 jeep 12 the 21

Step IV.   around 85 buy 52 home 34 jeep 29 peak 12 the 21

Step V.   around 85 buy 52 home 34 jeep 29 peak 21 12 the

Step VI.   around 85 buy 52 home 34 jeep 29 peak 21 the 12

And step VI is the last step of this arrangement.

As per the rules followed in the above steps, find out in each of the following questions the appropriate step for the given input.

Input: 19 cherry desert 87 99 team 31 vision from 54.

16. How many steps are required to complete the arrangement?

   (a) three   (b) five   (c) seven

   (d) six   (e) four

17. Which of the following steps is the penultimate step?

   (a) cherry 99 from 54 team 31 19 vision desert 87

   (b) cherry 99 team 31 19 vision desert 87 from 54

   (c) cherry 99 desert 87 19 team 31 vision from 54

   (d) cherry 99 desert 87 from 54 team 31 19 vision

   (e) None of these

18. Which of the following numbers is 3rd from the right end in Step IV?

   (a) 54   (b) 19   (c) 99

   (d) 87   (e) 31

19. What is the sum of the 4th element from left end and 1st element from the right end in the final step?

   (a) 132   (b) 60

   (c) 106   (d) 153

   (e) None of these

20. Which of the following elementsis 3rd to the left of 2nd from the right end in Step III?

   (a) from   (b) 54

   (c) 87   (d) 19

   (e) None of these

Directions (21-25): Study the following arrangement carefully and answer the questions given below:

6 8 4 9 7 2 1 5 2 9 4 5 9 5 2 5 7 1 6 1 8 7 8 9 5 3 8 4 8 6 8 3 6

21. If all the even digits are deleted from the above arrangement, which of the following will be fifth from the left end of the new arrangement?

   (a) 3   (b) 5   (c) 1

   (d) 9   (e) 7

22. How many 5s are there in the above arrangement each of which is immediately preceded by an even digit and immediately followed by an odd digit?

   (a) none   (b) one

   (c) two   (d) three

   (e) More than three

23. How many 8s are there in the above arrangement, each of which is immediately followed by a perfect square?
(a) none   (b) one
(c)two   (d) three
(e) More than three

24. Which of the following digits is eighth to the left of the seventeenth digit from the left end of the above arrangement?
(a) 2   (b) 5
(c) 4   (d) 9
(e) None of these

25. Which of the following digits is seventh to the left of the ninth digit from the right end of the above arrangement?
(a) 3   (b) 5
(c) 1   (d) 7
(e) None of these

Directions (26-30): Study the following information carefully and answer the questions given below.

Nine boxes— B, C, D, E, F, G, H, J and K— are placed one above the other, but not necessarily in the same order.

Four boxes are placed between box E and box C, and one of them is placed either at the top or at the bottom. Only one box is placed between box C and box F, which is placed below box C. Three boxes are placed between box G and box H. Box H is placed neither just above nor just below box C. Only one box is placed between H and K. Not more than two boxes are placed below box K. Only one box is placed between box D and B, which is placed above box J. Box E and box K are not placed adjacent to each other.

26. Which of the following boxes is placed at the top?
(a) B   (b) E
(c) C   (d) G
(e) None of these

27. What is the position of box G from the bottom?
(a) 5th   (b) 1st
(c) 2nd   (d) 8th
(e) None of these

28. How many boxes are placed above the box J?
(a) none   (b) two
(c) three   (d) one
(e) More than three

29. Which of the following boxes is placed just below box D?
(a) C   (b) K
(c) G   (d) H
(e) None of these

30. Four of the following five belong to a group in a certain way, find which one does not belong to that group?
(a) E, J   (b) D, C   (c) J, G
(d) B, G   (e) C, F

Directions (31-35): Each of the questions below consists of a question and two statements marked I and II given below it. You have to decide whether the data provided in the statements is sufficient to answer the question. Read both the statements and give the answer.

(a) If the data in statement I alone is sufficient to answer the question, while the data in statement II alone is not sufficient to answer the question.

(b) If the data in statement I alone is not sufficient to answer the question, while the data in statement II alone is sufficient to answer the question.

(c) If the data either in statement I or in statement II alone is sufficient to answer the question.

(d) If the data even in both the statements I and II together is not sufficient to answer the question.

(e) If the data in both statements I and II together is needed to answer the question.

31. How many brothers does J have?
   I. H and K are brothers of G.
   II. F is the wife of B, who is the father of G. J is the child of F.

32. Among six friends A, B, C, D, E and F, who gets the lowest marks?
   I. A and D get lower marks than B, E and F but none of them gets the lowest marks.
   II. A gets lower marks than D but more marks than C.

33. On which date in March does Rohan celebrate his marriage anniversary, when 1st March is Monday (Week starts from Monday to Sunday)?
   I. Rohan's wife correctly remembers that their anniversary is in the third week of March.
   II. Rohan's brother correctly remembers that Rohan's anniversary is on the last day of the third week of March.

34. How is 'never' written in a code language?
   I. 'just never hurt' is written as 'mi kewr' in that code language.
   II. 'bird hurt just animal' is written as 'mi pbghwr' in that code language.

35. What is D's position from the right end in a row of persons, who are facing north?

    I. There are twelve persons sitting between D and L.

    II. L sits sixth from the right end of the row.

Directions (36-40): Study the following information carefully and answer the questions given below.

Seven students A, B, D, E, G, H and L have practical exams on different days of the same week starting from Monday to Sunday, but not necessarily in the same order. Only one student has a practical exam on each day.

There are more than three students who have a practical exam after A. Only one student has a practical exam between A and H. There are three students who have a practical exam between G and B. G has a practical exam before H but not immediately before H. There are three students who have a practical exam between D and E, who does not have a practical exam on the last day of the week.

36. On which of the following days, L has a practical exam?

    (a) Tuesday   (b) Thursday   (c) Saturday
    (d) Monday   (e) None of these

37. Who among the following has a practical exam on Wednesday?

    (a) A   (b) H
    (c) G   (d) E
    (e) None of these

38. How many students have an exam between E and B?

    (a) No one   (b) one
    (c) two   (d) three
    (e) More than three

39. Who among the following has a practical exam immediately before H?

    (a) E   (b) L
    (c) B   (d) D
    (e) None of these

40. Four of the following five belong to a group in a certain way. Find which one does not belong to that group?

    (a) A, G   (b) H, E   (c) L, B
    (d) E, A   (e) B, D

Quantitative Aptitude

Directions (41-46): Study the bar chart given below and answer the following questions.

The bar chart shows the number of boys in six different schools (A, B, C, D, E & F) in 2017 and 2018.

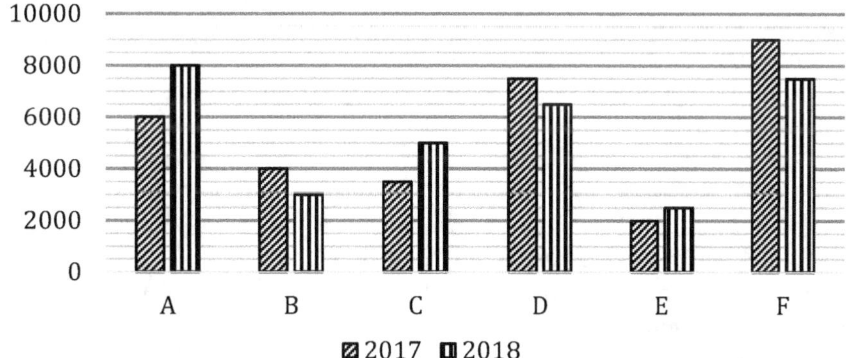

Note Total students in any school in any year = Total (Boys + Girls) in that school in that year.

41. Find the ratio of the total number of boys in A & B in 2017 to the total number of boys in E & F in 2018.

    (a) 5 : 2   (b) 4 : 7   (c) 3 : 8
    (d) 4 : 3   (e) 1 : 1

42. If A & C in 2017 has 40% and 30% girls respectively, then find the girls in A & C together in 2017 as a percentage of the boys in E & F together in 2017?

    (a) 50%   (b) 90%   (c) 70%
    (d) 80%   (e) 60%

43. If total students in C in 2017 are 6000 and total students in C is increased by 80% in 2018 as compared to the previous year, then find girls in C in 2017 & 2018 together are how much more than boys in E in 2017 & 2018 together?

    (a) 3100   (b) 4400   (c) 3800
    (d) 3500   (e) 4000

44. If ratio of boys to girls in B, D & F in 2018 is 5:6, 13:9 and 5:4 respectively, then find average number of girls in B, D & F in 2018 are how much more or less than average number of boys in B, C & D in 2017?

(a) 1500   (b) 900   (c) 300
(d) 1200   (e) 600

45. If total students in A, C & D in 2017 are 11000, 6000 & 12500 respectively, then find the number of girls in A, C & D together in 2017 are what percent of total number of boys in C, E & F together in 2018?

(a) $85\frac{1}{3}\%$ (b) $74\frac{2}{3}\%$
(c) $67\frac{2}{3}\%$ (d) $83\frac{1}{3}\%$
(e) None of the above

46. The number of boys in all schools together in 2018 is how much more than the number of boys in all schools together in 2017?

(a) 500   (b) 1200   (c) 700
(d) 1600   (e) 900

47. An amount is divided among X, Y and Z. The amount of Y is the average of the other two and when the amount of Y is reduced by 20% of that of X, it becomes equal to that of Z. The amount of Z is what percent of the total amount?

(a) 20%   (b) 22.5%   (c) 25%
(d) 27.5%   (e) 30%

48. A retailer marks up an article 35% above its cost price and earns Rs. 96 by giving a 20% discount on the marked price. If he sells the article at 15% discount on the marked price then, find the retailer's profit on selling one article.

(a) 118   (b) 177   (c) 236
(d) 214   (e) 154

49. The present age of Amit is 50% more than Manish's present age, while 5 years ago Amit's age was twice that of Manish's age at that time. If five years hence, the sum of the ages of Manish and Amit is equal to Lalit's age at that time, then find the present age of Lalit.

(a) 35   (b) 40   (c) 20
(d) 25   (e) 30

50. Neha is 50% more efficient than Ritu who takes double the time than Priya to complete a work. Neha can complete a work in 'x' days while Priya can complete the same work in (x – 15) days. In how many days can all three complete the same work together?

(a) 36 days   (b) 30 days   (c) 22.5 days
(d) 20 days   (e) 18 days

Directions (51-55): In the following questions, two equations **(I)** and **(II)** are given. You have to solve both the equations and mark the appropriate answer.

51. I. $(x - 7)^2 = 3x - 23$
II. $y^2 - 21y + 108 = 0$
(a) $x < y$ (b) $x \leq y$
(c) $x > y$ (d) $x \geq y$
(e) $x = y$ or no relation.

52. I. $x^3 = 2744$
II. $(y - 10)^2 = 7y - 80$
(a) $x < y$ (b) $x \leq y$
(c) $x > y$ (d) $x \geq y$
(e) $x = y$ or no relation.

53. I. $(x + 25)^2 = 729$
II. $3y^2 - 20y + 32 = 0$
(a) $x < y$ (b) $x \leq y$
(c) $x > y$ (d) $x \geq y$
(e) $x = y$ or no relation.

54. I. $3x^2 - 26x + 35 = 0$
II. $8y^2 - 26y + 21 = 0$
(a) $x < y$ (b) $x \leq y$
(c) $x > y$ (d) $x \geq y$
(e) $x = y$ or no relation.

55. I. $3x^2 - 17x + 10 = 0$
II. $16y^2 - 14y + 3 = 0$
(a) $x < y$ (b) $x \leq y$
(c) $x > y$ (d) $x \geq y$
(e) $x = y$ or no relation.

Directions (56-60): Study the pie chart given below and answer the following questions.
The pie charts below show the percentage distribution of the total employees of company—X & Y in 5 different departments.

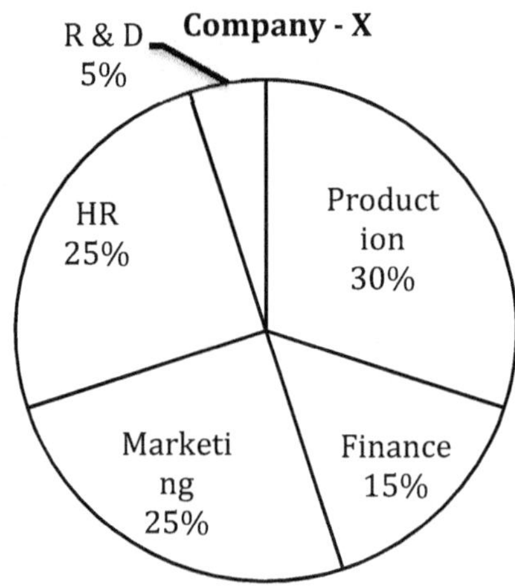

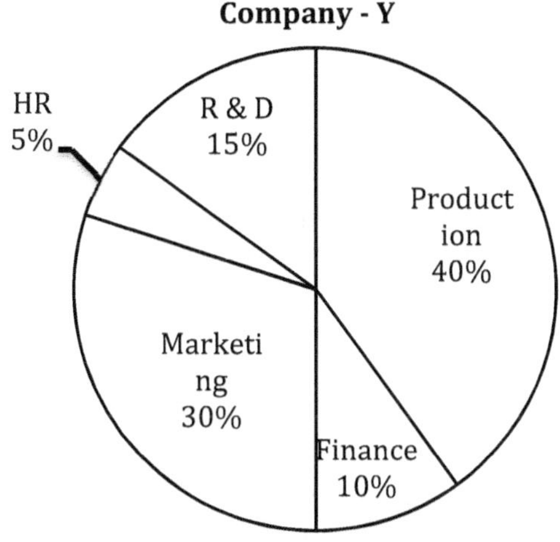

Note: The ratio of the total employees of company X to that of company Y is 3:5.

56. If number of employees in finance department of X & Y together is 11400, then find employees in HR and Marketing department together of X are how much more or less than employees in Production department of Y?
(a) 9000   (b) 6000   (c) 5000
(d) 7000   (e) 8000

57. If employees in HR department of Y are 1500, then find average number of employees in Production, Marketing and R & D department of X are how much more than employees in Finance department of Y?
(a) 800   (b) 1200   (c) 1500
(d) 1600   (e) 600

58. Find the ratio of total number of employees in Finance, Marketing and HR department together of X to total number of employees in Production, HR and R & D department together of Y.
(a) 7:10   (b) 13:20   (c) 13:21
(d) 2:3   (e) 4:7

59. If average number of employees in Production, HR and R & D department of Y are 4000, then find total number of employees in Finance and Marketing departments of both the companies.
(a) 12800   (b) 14400   (c) 17600
(d) 15200   (e) 13400

60. Employees in Marketing & HR department together of X are what percent more or less than employees in Production & Finance department together of Y?
(a) 90%   (b) 30%   (c) 10%
(d) 70%   (e) 40%

Directions (61-65): Study the passage given below and answer the following questions.

The data below gives information about selling price of 6 different articles (A, B, C, D, E & F). Selling price of A is 80% more than that of C and selling price of D is 130% of that of B. Ratio of selling price of A to that of B is 36:25. Selling price of E is equal to the average of selling price of B & C. Selling price of F is Rs.800, which is Rs.150 more than selling price of D.

61. If a shopkeeper sold A at 10% loss and E at 12.5% profit, then find his overall profit/loss on selling A & E is what percent of selling price of C?
(a) 12.5%   (b) 7.5%   (c) 16.5%
(d) 22.5%   (e) 15.5%

62. Find the ratio of the selling price of B & C together to the selling price of E & F together.
(a) 3 : 4   (b) 4 : 5   (c) 18 : 25
(d) 20 : 23   (e) None of the above

63. If a shopkeeper marked C & F, 100% and $33\frac{1}{3}\%$ above their cost price respectively and allowed 20% discount on each of C & F, then find the total profit earned by the shopkeeper on C & F.
(a) Rs.150   (b) Rs.270   (c) Rs.230
(d) Rs.180   (e) Rs.200

64. If a shopkeeper allowed Rs.150 discount on each of D & E and he has marked D & E, 60% and 50% above their cost price respectively, then the cost price of D & E together is what percent of the selling price of A?
(a) 140%   (b) 125%   (c) 195%
(d) 150%   (e) 180%

65. For how many articles, the selling price of that particular article is more than the average of the selling price of all 6 articles?
(a) 3   (b) 2   (c) 5
(d) 4   (e) None of the above

Directions (66-70): What will come in place of (?) in the following questions?

66. $45\% \ of \ 600 \div \{(25 + 15)\% \ of \ 500\} = ? \div 40$
(a) 62   (b) 48   (c) 54
(d) 58   (e) 46

67. $\frac{?-80}{15\times24} \ of \ 432 \times 25 = 4800$
(a) 260   (b) 230   (c) 250
(d) 270   (e) 240

68. $(?)^2 = 210\% \ of \ 800 + (38)^2 + 108 \times 9$
(a) 64   (b) 54   (c) 84
(d) 94   (e) 74

69. $? \times 23 = 24 \times 45 + 820 - 60\% \ of \ 2400$
(a) 20   (b) 50   (c) 40
(d) 80   (e) 60

70. $? \% \ of \ 3500 = 1684 - 488 - 31\% \ of \ 1600$
(a) 40   (b) 30   (c) 25
(d) 20   (e) 35

71. A train covers a certain distance in two parts. Distance covered in the first part is 200% more than the distance covered in the second part, while the speed of the train is in the ratio of 2:1 in the first and second parts respectively. If the average speed of the train is 64 km/hr., then find the speed of the train in the first part (in kmph).

(a) 40   (b) 80   (c) 50

(d) 30   (e) 100

72. Find the probability of forming a 2-digit number by using the starting four prime numbers such that it is divisible by 3.

(a) $\frac{1}{3}$ (b) $\frac{1}{4}$ (c) $\frac{5}{16}$

(d) $\frac{1}{2}$ (e) $\frac{3}{8}$

73. Rahul invested money in scheme 'A' and scheme 'B' in the ratio 2:3. If scheme 'A' offers 10% p.a. at S.I. and scheme 'B' offers 10% at C.I., then the interest earned from Scheme 'B' is what percent more than interest earned from scheme 'A' after 2 years?

(a) 50%   (b) 52.5%   (c) 55%

(d) 57.5%   (e) 60%

74. A boat takes 90 minutes less to travel 36 km. downstream than to travel the same distance upstream. If the speed of the boat in still water is 10 km/h. then speed of the stream is:

(a) 4 km/h.   (b) 3 km/h.   (c) 2.5 km/h.

(d) 2 km/h.   (e) 3.5 km/h.

Directions (75-80): Study the charts given below and answer the following questions.

The line chart shows the number of pens manufactured by 5 different companies (A, B, C, D & E) in 2017 & 2018 and the table shows the number of pens sold by these 5 companies in these 2 years.

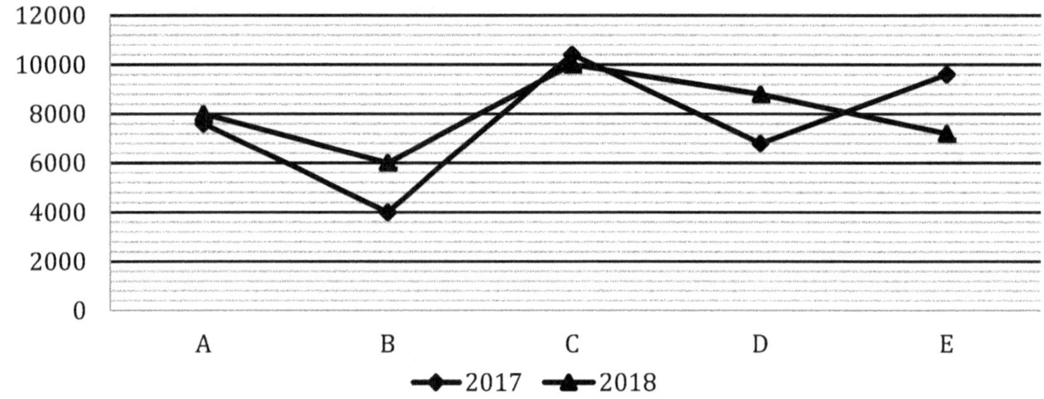

Company	Sold units of pens	
	2017	**2018**
A	6000	7000
B	3600	4500
C	9000	8000
D	6000	8000
E	8000	6500

Note –1) Total pens manufactured by any company in a particular year = Total (sold + unsold) pens of that company in that year.

2) Each company destroys its unsold pens in any year.

75. Find the ratio of unsold pens of A & B together in 2017 to unsold pens of C & E together in 2017.

(a) 5:6   (b) 3:4

(c) 7:12   (d) 2:3

(e) None of the above

76. The average of unsold pens of A, B & D in 2018 is how much less than the average pens sold by all 5 companies in 2017?

(a) 6000   (b) 5760   (c) 5640

(d) 5880   (e) 5420

77. The total unsold pens of A & C together in 2017 & 2018 is what percent more or less than the total pens manufactured by C & E together in 2017?

(a) 90%   (b) 70%   (c) 110%

(d) 50%   (e) 30%

78. The unsold pens of B, D & E together in 2018 is what percent of the total pens manufactured by A, D & E together in 2018?

(a) 22.5%   (b) 16.5%   (c) 12.5%

(d) 18.5%   (e) 10.5%

79. The pens sold by A, B, D & E together in 2018 is what percent of the total pens manufactured by A, B, D & E together in 2018?

(a) $94\frac{1}{3}\%$

(b) $86\frac{2}{3}\%$

(c) $72\frac{1}{3}\%$

(d) $80\frac{2}{3}\%$

(e) $86\frac{1}{3}\%$

80. The total pens manufactured by all 5 companies in 2018 is how much more or less than the total pens manufactured by all 5 companies in 2017?

(a) 2200   (b) 2000   (c) 2500

(d) 1600   (e) 1400

Solutions

REASONING ABILITY

Direction (1-5): From the given statements, W sits 2nd to the right of V. **Here we get 2 possibilities i.e. Case 1 and Case 2.** Three persons sit between S and W. P sits 2nd to the left of S.

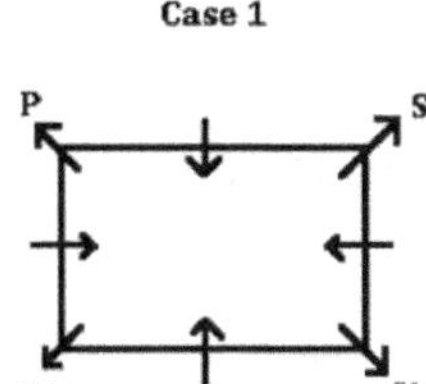
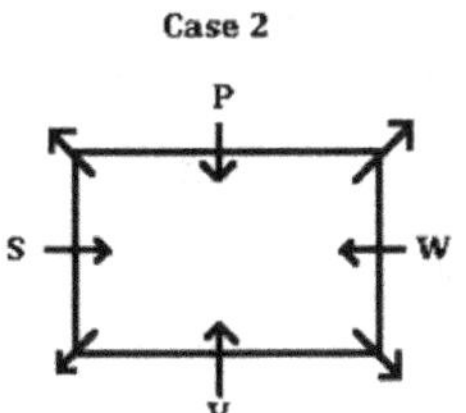

From the given statements, U sits 2nd to the left of Q and sits at the middle side of the table. From this condition, Case 2 is ruled out. T is an immediate neighbour of both P and W. Both R and U are facing each other.

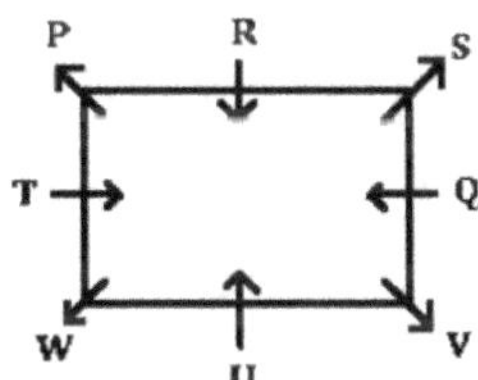

1. (b)   **2. (a)**   **3. (e)**

4. (b)   **5. (b)**

Direction (6-8):

6. (b) I. A > L (True)   II. K = Y (False)

7. (d) I. Q > C (True)   II. W < L (True)

8. (b) I. F > Q (False)   II. L < U (False)

9. (c) first , third, fourth and seventh letters of the word = M, N, E and R

But no meaningful word is made.

10. (b)

⌐ ⌐
A M N E S T Y

Direction (11-15): From the given statements, D faces the one who sits 3rd to the left of P. Here we have 2 possibilities i.e. Case 1 and Case 2. G is an immediate neighbour of D. Two persons sit between G and F.

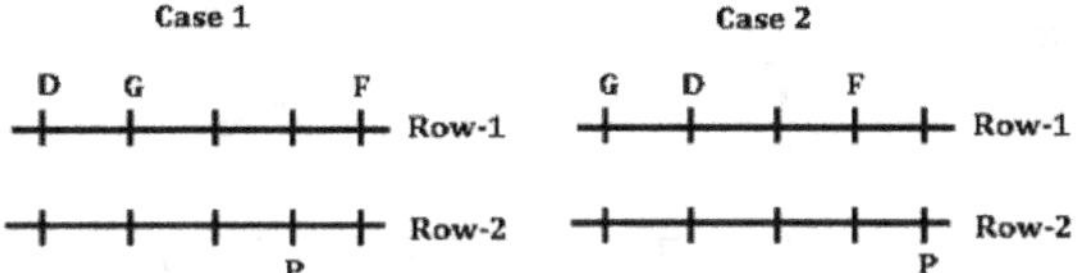

From the given statements, O faces the one who sits 3rd to the right of E. O does not sit at any of the extreme ends. Here Case 1 is ruled out now. Both Q and O are not immediate neighbours. M does not face to H.

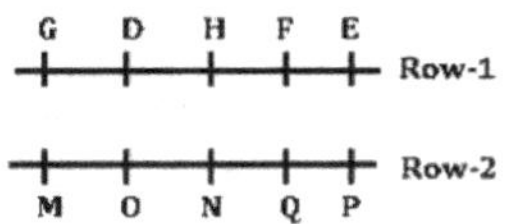

11. (d)   **12. (a)**   **13. (c)**

14. (a)   **15. (b)**

Direction (16-20): In each step, one word and one number are arranged together.

Like – Cherry 99

Logic: Words are arranged in alphabetical order from left to right alternate from the left end.

Numbers are arranged in decreasing order from left to right alternate from the left end.

Input: 19 cherry desert 87 99 team 31 vision from 54.

Step I. cherry 99 19 desert 87 team 31 vision from 54

Step II. cherry 99 desert 87 19 team 31 vision from 54

Step III. cherry 99 desert 87 from 54 19 team 31 vision

Step IV. cherry 99 desert 87 from 54 team 31 19 vision

Step V. cherry 99 desert 87 from 54 team 31 vision 19

16. (b)   **17. (d)**   **18. (a)**

19. (c) 4th element from left end in the final step = 87, 1st element from right end in the final step = 19

: 87 + 19 = 106

20. (b)

Directions (21-25):

21. (d) 9 7 1 5 **9** 5 9 5 5 7 1 1 7 9 5 3 3

22. (c) 4 5 **9** and 2 5 7

23. (d) 6 **8 4** 9 7 2 1 5 2 9 4 5 9 5 2 5 7 1 6
1 8 7 **8 9** 5 3 **8 4** 8 6 8 3 6

24. (a) 17th (left end) – 8th (left) = 9th from left end
= 2

25. (c) 7th (Left) + 9th (right end) = 16th from right
end = 1

Directions (26-30): There are four boxes placed between box E and box C and one of them is placed either at top or at bottom. Only one box is placed between box C and box F, which is placed below box C. From these conditions we have three possible cases:

Case- 1	Case- 2	Case- 3
Box	Box	Box
E	C	
	F	
		C
C	E	F
F		
		E

Three boxes are placed between box G and box H. Box H is placed neither just above nor just below box C. Only one box is placed between H and K. Not more than two boxes are placed below the box K. Box E and Box K are not placed adjacent to each other. By these conditions case-2 and case-3 are cancelled. So new arrangement will be:

Case- 1
Box
E
G
C
K
F
H

Only one box is placed between box D and B, which is placed above box J. So final arrangement will be:

Box
E
B
J
D
G
C
K
F
H

26. (b)   **27. (a)**   **28. (b)**
29. (c)   **30. (d)**

Directions (31-35):

31. (d) From I and II it is not clear how many brotherd J has.

F(-)═══B(+)
|
G(-/+) —— I —— H(+) —— K(+)

32. (a) From I it is clear that C gets the lowest marks.
B/E/F > B/E/F > B/E/F > A/D > A/D > C

33. (b) From II it is clear that Rohan's marriage anniversary is on 21st March.

34. (e) From I and II it is clear that 'never' will be coded as 'ke'.

35. (e) From I and II-
D's position from right end = 6 + 12 + 1 = 19th

Directions (36-40): There are more than three students who have exam after A. Only one student has an exam between A and H. From these conditions we have four possible cases:

Day	Case-1 Student	Case-2 Student	Case-3 Student	Case-4 Student
Monday	H	0		A
Tuesday			A	
Wednesday	A	A		H
Thursday			H	
Friday		H		
Saturday				
Sunday				

G has exam before H but not immediately before H. By this condition case-1 and case-4 are cancelled. There are three students who have an exam between G and B. So new arrangement will be:

Month	Case-2 Student	Case-3 Student
Monday		G
Tuesday	G	A
Wednesday	A	
Thursday		H
Friday	H	B
Saturday	B	
Sunday		

There are three students who have an exam between D and E, who does not have exam on the last day of the week. By this condition case-2 is cancelled. So final arrangement will be:

Day	Student
Monday	G
Tuesday	A
Wednesday	E
Thursday	H
Friday	B
Saturday	L
Sunday	D

36. (c)   **37. (d)**   **38. (b)**
39. (a)   **40. (e)**

41. (e) Boys in A & B together in 2017 = 6000 + 4000 =10000
Boys in E & F together in 2018 = 2500 + 7500 = 10000
Required ratio = $\frac{10000}{10000}$ = 1 : 1

42. (a) Girls in A & C together in 2017 = $\left[\left(6000 \times \frac{40}{60} + 3500 \times \frac{30}{70}\right)\right]$
= 4000 + 1500 = 5500
Boys in E & F together in 2017 = 2000 + 9000 = 11000
Required % = $\frac{11000 - 5500}{11000} \times 100 = 50\%$

43. (c) Total students in C in 2018
= $6000 \times \frac{180}{100}$ = 10800
Girls in C in 2017 & 2018 together = (6000 – 3500) + (10800 – 5000)
= 2500 + 5800 = 8300
Required difference = 8300 – (2000 + 2500) = 3800

44. (c) Total number of girls in B, D & F in 2018 = $\left[\left(3000 \times \frac{6}{5} + 6500 \times \frac{9}{13} + 7500 \times \frac{4}{5}\right)\right]$
= 3600 + 4500 + 6000 = 14100
Total number of boys in B, C & D in 2017 = 4000 + 3500 + 7500 = 15000
Required difference = $\frac{15000}{3} - \frac{14100}{3}$
= 5000 – 4700 = 300

45. (d) Total number of girls in A, C & D together in 2017
= $\left[(11000 - 6000) + (6000 - 3500) + (12500 - 7500)\right]$
= 5000 + 2500 + 5000 = 12500
Boys in C, E & F together in 2018 = 5000 + 2500 + 7500 = 15000
Required % = $\frac{12500}{15000} \times 100 = \frac{250}{3}\%$
= $83\frac{1}{3}\%$

46. (a) Number of boys in all schools together in 2018 =
8000 + 3000 + 5000 + 6500 +2500 + 7500
= 32500
Number of boys in all schools together in 2017
= 6000 + 4000 + 3500 + 7500 + 2000 + 9000 = 32000
Required difference = 32500 – 32000 = 500

47. (c) Let the amount of X and Z be Rs a and b respectively

Amount of Y=$\frac{a+b}{2}$
ATQ
$\frac{a+b}{2} - \frac{a}{5}$ =b
5b=3a
Amount of X=Rs 5p
Amount of Z=Rs 3p
Amount of Y= Rs 4p
Required %=25%

48. (b) Let cost price of an article = 100x
Marked price of an article
= $100x \times \frac{135}{100} = 135x$
ATQ,
$135x \times \frac{80}{100} - 100x = 96$
$\Rightarrow 108x - 100x = 96$
$\Rightarrow x = \frac{96}{8} = 12$
Retailer's profit if he sells article at 15% discount
= $135x \times \frac{85}{100} - 100x$
= 114.75x – 100x
= 14.75x
= 14.75 × 12
= 177

49. (e) Let present age of Manish = x
$\Rightarrow$ Present age of Amit = 1.5x
Manish's age five years ago = x – 5
Amit's age five years ago – 2(x–5)
= 2x – 10
But Amit's age five years ago also equals to (1.5x – 5)
$\Rightarrow$2x – 10 = 1.5x – 5
$\Rightarrow$0.5x = 5
$\Rightarrow$x = 10
Lalit's age five years hence = 10 + 5 + 1.5 × 10 + 5
= 15 + 15 + 5
= 35
Lalit's present age = 35 – 5 = 30

50. (d) Ratio of efficiency of Neha and Ritu = 15 : 10 = 3 : 2
Ratio of time taken by Neha and Ritu alone to complete the work = 2 : 3
Ratio of time taken by Ritu and Priya alone to complete the work = 2 : 1
$\Rightarrow$Ratio of time taken by Neha, Ritu and Priya alone to complete the work = 4 : 6 : 3
ATQ,
$\frac{4}{3} = \frac{x}{x-15}$

$\Rightarrow 4x - 60 = 3x$

$\Rightarrow x = 60$

Neha alone can do the work in 60 days

Priya alone can do the work in (60 – 15 = 45 days)

Ritu alone can do the work $= \frac{60}{4} \times 6 = 90$ days

Work done by Neha, Priya and Ritu together in one day

$= \frac{1}{60} + \frac{1}{45} + \frac{1}{90} = \frac{3+4+2}{180}$

$= \frac{9}{180} = \frac{1}{20}$

Time taken by Neha, Priya & Ritu together to complete the work = 20 days

51. (b) I. $(x - 7)^2 = 3x - 23$

$x^2 + 49 - 14x = 3x - 23$

$x^2 - 17x + 72 = 0$

$x^2 - 9x - 8x + 72 = 0$

$x (x - 9) - 8 (x - 9) = 0$

$(x - 9) (x - 8) = 0$

$x = 8, 9$

II. $y^2 - 21y + 108 = 0$

$y^2 - 12y - 9y + 108 = 0$

$y (y - 12) - 9 (y - 12) = 0$

$(y - 12) (y - 9) = 0$

$y = 9, 12$

So, $x \leq y$.

52. (e) I. $x^3 = 2744$

$x = \sqrt[3]{2744}$

$x = 14$

II. $(y - 10)^2 = 7y - 80$

$y^2 + 100 - 20y = 7y - 80$

$y^2 - 27y + 180 = 0$

$y^2 - 15y - 12y + 180 = 0$

$y (y - 15) - 12 (y - 15) = 0$

$(y - 15) (y - 12) = 0$

$y = 12, 15$

So, no relation.

53. (a) I. $(x + 25)^2 = 729$

$(x + 25)^2 = \pm 27$

$x + 25 = 27$

$x = 2$

$x + 25 = -27$

$x = -52$

II. $3y^2 - 20y + 32 = 0$

$3y^2 - 12y - 8y + 32 = 0$

$3y (y - 4) - 8 (y - 4) = 0$

$(y - 4) (3y - 8) = 0$

$y = 4, \frac{8}{3}$

So, $x < y$.

54. (e) I. $3x^2 - 26x + 35 = 0$

$3x^2 - 21x - 5x + 35 = 0$

$3x (x - 7) - 5 (x - 7) = 0$

$(x - 7) (3x - 5) = 0$

$x = 7, \frac{5}{3}$

II. $8y^2 - 26y + 21 = 0$

$8y^2 - 14y - 12y + 21 = 0$

$2y (4y - 7) - 3 (4y - 7) = 0$

$(4y - 7) (2y - 3) = 0$

$y = \frac{3}{2}, \frac{7}{4}$

So, no relation

55. (c) I. $3x^2 - 17x + 10 = 0$

$3x^2 - 15x - 2x + 10 = 0$

$3x (x - 5) - 2 (x - 5) = 0$

$(x - 5) (3x - 2) = 0$

$x = 5, \frac{2}{3}$

II. $16y^2 - 14y + 3 = 0$

$16y^2 - 8y - 6y + 3 = 0$

$8y (2y - 1) - 3 (2y - 1) = 0$

$(2y - 1) (8y - 3) = 0$

$y = \frac{1}{2}, \frac{3}{8}$

So, $x > y$

56. (b) Let number of employees in X & Y be '300x' & '500x' respectively.

ATQ,

$300x \times \frac{15}{100} + 500x \times \frac{10}{100} = 11400$

$45x + 50x = 11400$

$x = 120$

Number of employees in HR and Marketing department together of X $= 300x \times \left(\frac{25+25}{100}\right)$

$= 150x = 18000$

Employees in production department of Y

$= 500x \times \frac{40}{100} = 200x = 24000$

Required difference = 24000 – 18000

= 6000

57. (e) Let total employees in X & Y be '300x' & '500x' respectively.

ATQ,

$500x \times \frac{5}{100} = 1500$

$x = 60$

Average number of employees in Production, Marketing and R & D department of X

$= 300x \times \frac{1}{3} \times \left(\frac{30+25+5}{100}\right) = 60x$

Employees in Finance department of Y $= 500x \times \frac{10}{100} = 50x$

Required difference $= 60x - 50x = 10x = 600$

58. (b) Let total employees in X & Y be '300x' & '500x' respectively.

Employees in Finance, Marketing and HR department together of X = 300x $\times \left(\frac{15+25+25}{100}\right)$

= 195x

Employees in Production, HR and R & D department together of Y = 500x $\times \left(\frac{40+5+15}{100}\right)$

= 300x

Required ratio = $\frac{195x}{300x}$ = 13 : 20

59. (a) Let total employees in X & Y '300x' and '500x' respectively.

ATQ,

$\frac{1}{3} \times 500x \times \left(\frac{40+5+15}{100}\right) = 4000$

$\Rightarrow 100x = 4000$

x = 40

So, required number of employees = 300x × $\left(\frac{15+25}{100}\right) + 500x \times \left(\frac{10+30}{100}\right)$

= 120x + 200x

= 320x

= 12800

60. (e) Let total employees in X and Y be '300x' and '500x' respectively.

Employees in Marketing & HR department together of X = 300x × $\left(\frac{25+25}{100}\right)$ = 150x

Employees in Production & Finance department together of Y = 500x × $\left(\frac{40+10}{100}\right)$

= 250x

Required % = $\frac{250x - 150x}{250x} \times 100 = 40\%$

Direction (61-65): Selling price of F – Rs. 800

So, selling price of D = 800 – 150 = Rs. 650

Now, selling price of B = 650 × $\frac{100}{130}$ = Rs. 500

Now, selling price of A = 500 × $\frac{36}{25}$ = Rs. 720

And, selling price of C = 720 × $\frac{100}{180}$ = Rs. 400

And, selling price of E = $\frac{500 + 400}{2}$ = Rs. 450

Article	Selling price (in Rs.)
A	720
B	500
C	400
D	650
E	450
F	800

61. (b) Cost price of A = 720 × $\frac{100}{90}$ = Rs. 800

Cost price of E = 450 × $\frac{100}{112.5}$ = Rs. 400

Shopkeeper's overall loss on A & E = (800 + 400) – (720 + 450) = 30

Required % = $\frac{30}{400} \times 100$ = 7.5%

62. (c) Required ratio = $\frac{500 + 400}{450 + 800} = \frac{900}{1250}$ = 18 : 25

63. (e) Marked price of C = 400 × $\frac{100}{80}$

= Rs. 500

Marked price of F = 800 × $\frac{100}{80}$

= Rs. 1000

Cost price of C = 500 × $\frac{100}{200}$ = Rs. 250

Cost price of F = 1000 × $\frac{300}{400}$ = Rs. 750

Required amount = (400–250) + (800 – 750)

= 150 + 50 = Rs. 200

64. (b) Cost price of D = (650 + 150) × $\frac{100}{160}$ = Rs. 500

Cost price of E = (450 + 150) × $\frac{100}{150}$ = Rs. 400

Required % = $\frac{(500 + 400)}{720} \times 100$ = 125%

65. (a) Average of selling price of all 6 articles

$= \frac{(720 + 500 + 400 + 650 + 450 + 800)}{6}$

$= \frac{3520}{6} = \frac{1760}{3}$ = 586.67

Required number of articles = 3

66. (c) $\left(\frac{45}{100} \times 600\right) \div \left(\frac{40}{100} \times 500\right) = ? \times \frac{1}{40}$

$270 \div 200 = ? \times \frac{1}{40}$

$? = 270 \times \frac{1}{200} \times 40$

? = 54

67. (e) $\frac{? - 80}{360} \times 432 \times 25 = 4800$

(? – 80) × 30 = 4800

? – 80 = 160

? = 240

68. (a) $(?)^2 = \frac{210}{100} \times 800 + 1444 + 972$

$(?)^2 = 1680 + 2416$

$(?) = \sqrt{4096}$

? = 64

69. (a) $? \times 23 = 1080 + 820 - \frac{60}{100} \times 2400$

? × 23 = 1900 – 1440

$? = \frac{460}{23}$

? = 20

70. (d) $\frac{?}{100} \times 3500 = 1684 - 488 - \frac{31}{100} \times 1600$

? × 35 = 1196 – 496

$? = \frac{700}{35}$

? = 20

71. (b) Let, total distance = 4x

Let, speed of train in second part = y

$\Rightarrow$ Speed of train in first part = 2y

Distance covered by train in first part = 3x

Distance covered by train in second part = x

ATQ,

$64 = \frac{4x}{\frac{3x}{2y} + \frac{x}{y}}$

$\Rightarrow \dfrac{64}{4} = \dfrac{1}{\frac{3+2}{2y}}$

$\Rightarrow 2y = 16 \times 5$

$\Rightarrow 2y = 80$ kmph

Speed of train in first part = 2y=80 kmph

72. (c) Starting four prime number = 2, 3, 5, 7

Total two-digit numbers can be formed = 4 × 4 = 16

Numbers which are divisible by 3

= {27, 72, 57, 75, 33}

Required probability $= \dfrac{5}{16}$

73. (d) Let sum invested in scheme 'A' = 200x

Let sum invested in scheme 'B' = 300x

Interest earned from scheme 'A' after 2 years $= \dfrac{200x \times 2 \times 10}{100} = 40x$

Interest earned from schemes 'B' after 2 years $= \left[\left(1 + \dfrac{10}{100}\right)^2 - 1\right] \times 300x$

$= 300x \left[\dfrac{21}{100}\right] = 63x$

Required % $= \dfrac{63x - 40x}{40x} \times 100$

$= \dfrac{23}{40} \times 100 = 57.5\%$

74. (d) Suppose speed of the stream = x km/h

Speed of the boat in still water = 10 km/h

∴ Boat will travel with the stream (downstream) at (10 + x) km/h and boat will travel against the stream (upstream) at (10 – x) km/h.

Now, from the question,

$\dfrac{36}{10+x} + \dfrac{90}{60} = \dfrac{36}{10-x}$

$\Rightarrow x = 2$ km/h

75. (d) Unsold pens of A & B together in 2017

= [(7600 − 6000) + (4000 − 3600)]

= 1600 + 400= 2000

Unsold pens of C & E together in 2017 = [(10400 − 9000) + (9600 − 8000)] = 1400 +1600 = 3000

Required ratio $= \dfrac{2000}{3000} = 2 : 3$

76. (e) Average of unsold pens of A, B & D in 2018

$= \dfrac{1}{3}[(8000 - 7000) + (6000 - 4500) + (8800 - 8000)]$

$= \dfrac{1}{3}[1000 + 1500 + 800] = 1100$

Average pens sold by all 5 companies in 2017

$= \dfrac{(6000+3600+9000+6000+8000)}{5} = \dfrac{32600}{5} = 6520$

Required difference = 6520 – 1100 = 5420

77. (b) Total unsold pens of A & C together in 2017 & 2018 =

[(7600 – 6000) + (10400 – 9000) + (8000 – 7000) + (10000 – 8000)]

= 1600 + 1400 + 1000 + 2000 = 6000

Total pens manufactured by C & E together in 2017 = 10400 + 9600 = 20000

Required % $= \dfrac{20000 - 6000}{20000} \times 100 = 70\%$

78. (c) Unsold pens of B, D & E together in 2018

= [(6000 – 4500) + (8800 - 8000) + (7200 – 6500)]

= 1500 + 800 + 700 = 3000

Total pens manufactured by A, D & E together in 2018 = 8000 + 8800 + 7200 = 24000

Required% $= \dfrac{3000}{24000} \times 100 = 12.5\%$

79. (b) Pens sold by A, B, D & E together in 2018

= 7000 + 4500 + 8000 + 6500 = 26000

Total pens manufactured by A, B, D & E together in 2018 = 8000 + 6000 + 8800 + 7200

= 30000

Required% $= \dfrac{26000}{30000} \times 100$

$= \dfrac{260}{3}\% = 86\dfrac{2}{3}\%$

80. (d) Total pens manufactured by all 5 companies in 2018

= 8000+6000+10000+8800 + 7200 = 40000

Total pens manufactured by all 5 companies in 2017 = 7600 + 4000 + 10400 + 6800 + 9600 = 38400

Required difference

= 40000 – 38400 = 1600

REASONING ABILITY

Directions (1-5): Study the following information carefully and answer the questions given below.

There are eight family members A, C, E, G, J, L, N and P who are sitting around a circular table in a café facing outside the centre of the table with equal distance between each other, but not necessarily in the same order. All of them are related to J in some way.

C sits third to the right of J. Only one member sits between J and P. J's brother sits to the immediate left of P. Two members sit between J's brother and J's father. N sits to the immediate left of G. J's sister sits third to the left of N. J's husband sits second to the right of J's sister. J does not sit opposite J's father. Three members sit between J's husband and E. Two members sit between J's mother and J's son. J's daughter sits second to the left of J's mother. L is the male member of the family.

1. How is L related to J?
   (a) husband   (b) brother
   (c) father   (d) son
   (e) None of these
2. Who among the following sits opposite G?
   (a) A   (b) L
   (c) C   (d) P
   (e) None of these
3. Four of the following five belong to a group in a certain way. Find which one does not belong to that group?
   (a) A   (b) J   (c) C
   (d) P   (e) E
4. How is P related to N?
   (a) grand-father
   (b) grand-daughter
   (c) grand-mother
   (d) grand-son
   (e) None of these
5. When counted from the left of E, how many members sit between E and C?
   (a) two   (b) four
   (c) one   (d) More than four
   (e) three

Direction (6-8): In the following questions, the symbols #, @, * , $ and % are used with the following meanings as illustrated below. Study the following information and answer the given questions:
P#Q - P is the father of Q.
P@Q - P is the brother of Q.
P$Q - P is the daughter of Q.
P*Q - P is the husband of Q.
P%Q - P is the wife of Q.

6. If N $ M % L @ J # K then how is J related to N?
   (a) father
   (b) daughter
   (c) grandfather
   (d) uncle
   (e) Can't be determined
7. If A @ B % C # D * E then how is E related to B?
   (a) brother-in-law
   (b) mother-in-law
   (c) son-in-law
   (d) daughter-in-law
   (e) None of these
8. If T # R $ S $ P @ Q then how is P related to T?
   (a) brother   (b) father-in-law
   (c) son   (d) uncle
   (e) Can't be determined

Directions (9-13): Study the following information and answer the given questions:
In a certain code language
'college student have extra enjoy' is written as 'gl tz wr yz mr'
'enjoy student fun college study' is written as 'if gl mr wr ar'
'student fun study exam' is written as 'if ar uz gl'
'game extra college' is written as 'tz mr nl'

9. What does the code 'tz' stand for in the given code language?
   (a) college   (b) student
   (c) have   (d) extra
   (e) None of these
10. What is the code for 'exam' in the given code language?
   (a) if   (b) ar
   (c) uz   (d) gl
   (e) None of these
11. What does the code "wr nl yz" stand for in the given code language?
   (a) exam have enjoy
   (b) game have enjoy
   (c) extra college study
   (d) student have exam
   (e) None of these
12. What will the code 'if gl mr' stand for in the given code language?
   (a) fun college student
   (b) study have fun
   (c) student study college

(d) college study fun
(e) Can't be determined

13. What is the code for 'fun' in the given code language?
(a) mr
(b) ar
(c) if
(d) Either (b) or (c)
(e) Either (a) or (c)

Directions (14-18): Study the following information carefully and answer the questions given below.

There are seven persons A, B, C, G, L, M and O who are living in a seven-floor building, but not necessarily in the same order. The ground floor is numbered as the 1st floor and the floor above it is numbered as the 2nd floor and so on till the topmost floor that is numbered as the 7th floor. Each of them likes different cold drinks viz. Pepsi, Coke, Sprite, Fanta, Maaza, 7up and Slice, but not necessarily in the same order.

The ones who like Fanta and Slice live on the 1st floor and the 7th floor. M lives on the 3rd floor. The ones who like Coke and 7up live on adjacent floors. L likes Maaza. G does not like Slice. C and M live on adjacent floors. Only one person lives between A and B, who likes Coke. The one who likes 7up lives just above C, who likes Sprite. More than one person lives between the ones who like Pepsi and Fanta.

14. On which of the following floors does L live?
(a) 2nd   (b) 4th
(c) 5th   (d) 6th
(e) None of these

15. Which of the following cold drinks does O like?
(a) Fanta   (b) Pepsi
(c) Slice   (d) 7up
(e) None of these

16. The one who likes Pepsi lives on which of the following floors?
(a) 4th   (b) 6th
(c) 3rd   (d) 5th
(e) None of these

17. How many persons live between L and G?
(a) one   (b) No one
(c) two   (d) three
(e) More than three

18. Four of the following five belong to a group in a certain way. Find out which one does not belong to that group.
(a) L   (b) O   (c) M
(d) A   (e) G

Directions (19-20): Study the following information and answer the questions given below:

Dheeraj walks 8m. west from point P to reach point Q. He takes a left turn from point Q and walks 10m. to reach point R. He takes a right turn from point R and walks 12m. to reach point S. He takes another right turn from point S and walks 6m. to reach point T. He takes a left turn from point T and walks 8m. to reach his home.

19. In which direction is point T with respect to point to Q?
(a) north   (b) south   (c) south-east
(d) south-west   (e) north-east

20. What is the shortest distance between point P and Dheeraj's home?
(a) 22m.   (b) $20\sqrt{2}$m.
(c) $\sqrt{794}$m.   (d) 26m.
(e) None of these

Direction (21-25): In each of the questions below are given some statements followed by two conclusions. You have to take the given statements to be true even if they seem to be at variance with commonly known facts. Read all the conclusions and then decide which of the given conclusions logically follows from the given statements, disregarding commonly known facts.
(a) If only conclusion I follows.
(b) If only conclusion II follows.
(c) If either conclusion I or II follows.
(d) If neither conclusion I nor II follows.
(e) If both conclusions I and II follow.

21. Statements: Some Disco are Grand.
    Some Grand are Hotel.
    All Hotel are Pub.
Conclusions: I. Some Hotel can be Disco.
    II. Some Disco are not Pub.

22. Statements: Some Police are Doctor.
    No Doctor is Hall.
    Only a few Hall are Town.
Conclusions: I. All Hall are Town.
    II. Some Police are not Hall.

23. Statements: Only a few Fox are Box.
    Only a few Box are Desk.
    No Desk is Help.
Conclusions: I. All Fox being Desk is a possibility.
    II. Some Box are not Help.

24. Statements: All Child are Born.
    Some Born are Man.
    Some Man are not Old.
Conclusions: I. Some Child are Man.
    II. All Old are Born.

25. Statements: All Kite are Sky. All Sky are Blue.
    Some Sea are Sky.
Conclusions: I. Some Kite can never be Sea.
    II. All Blue can be Kite.

Direction (26-30): Study the following information carefully and answer the questions given below:

Eight persons B, D, F, G, K, M, N and O are sitting in a row facing towards north but not necessarily in the same order. G sits 2nd from one of the ends. There is one person sitting between G and N. B sits 4th to the left of O, who sits near N. K sits 2nd to the right of F. The number of persons who sit to the left of M is one more than the persons sitting to the right of D. M does not sit near F.

26. Who among the following is an immediate neighbour of D?
(a) F
(b) B
(c) K
(d) Either (a) or (c)
(e) Both (a) and (c)

27. Who among the following sits 3rd to the right of M?
(a) D   (b) F   (c) B
(d) G   (e) K

28. Who among the following sits at one of the extreme ends?
(a) F   (b) O
(c) B   (d) M
(e) None of these

29. Four of the following five are alike in a certain way and hence they form a group. Which one of the following does not belong to that group?
(a) G   (b) D   (c) N
(d) M   (e) K

30. If all the persons are sitting in alphabetical order from left to right from B, then find out how many persons remain in the same position (excluding B).
(a) four   (b) five   (c) seven
(d) none   (e) six

Direction (31-35): Study the following information carefully and answer the questions given below:

Seven persons P, Q, R, S, T, U and V like different authors viz. Ernest, Larson, Flynn, Austin, Joan, Bradbury and Martin and also like different colours i.e. Purple, Blue, Green, Black, White, Red and Pink but not necessarily in the same order. S likes Green but does not like Flynn and Joan. U likes Black colour and Austen. The one who likes Pink also likes Joan. P likes Ernest but does not like Red and White. The one who likes Purple also likes Larson. R likes Bradbury. Q likes Pink. T does not like Purple. R does not like White.

31. Who among the following likes Red?
(a) R   (b) V
(c) U   (d) T
(e) None of these

32. Who among the following likes Joan?
(a) T
(b) V
(c) Q
(d) Either (a) or (c)
(e) None of these

33. Which of the following is true with regard to T?
(a) T likes Martin
(b) T likes Red
(c) T likes Blue
(d) T likes Flynn
(e) None is true

34. Four of the following five are alike in a certain way and hence they form a group. Which one of the following does not belong to that group?
(a) P - Martin   (b) S - Green   (c) V - White
(d) T - Larson   (e) V - Pink

35. Which of the following pairs is not true as per the given information?
(a) P - Blue   (b) R - Red   (c) V - Purple
(d) T - White   (e) All are true

Directions (36-40): In each of the questions given below, a group of letters is given followed by some combinations of numbers/symbols. You have to find out which of the given combinations correctly represents the group of letters based on the numbers/symbols codes and the conditions given below. If none of the given combinations represents the group of letters correctly, give (e) i.e. 'None of these' as the answer.

Letter	O	G	K	I	R	S	T	A	E	C	D	N	U	H	M	Y
Numbers/ Symbols	1	@	8	#	$	2	*	5	9	3	&	^	+	!	¥	4

Condition for coding the group letters:
(i) If the first letter is a vowel and the last letter is a consonant, the codes for the first and the last letter are to be interchanged.
(ii) If the first as well as the last letter is a vowel, then both are to be coded by the code for the last letter.
(iii) If the first as well as the last letter is a consonant, then both are to be coded by the code for the first letter.

36. MOTION
(a) ¥#11*¥   (b) ¥1*#1¥   (c) ¥1*#*1
(d) 1*#1¥1   (e) None of these

37. CUSTOM
(a) 3+2*13   (b) 3+2*1¥   (c) ¥+2*1¥
(d) 3+*213   (e) None of these

38. URGENCY
(a) +$@9^34   (b) +$@9^3+   (c) 4$@9^3+
(d) 4$@9^34   (e) None of these

39. RESTING
(a) $92*#^$ (b) $92*#^@   (c) @92*#^@
(d) $92*^#$ (e) None of these

40. GRIST
(a) @$2#@   (b) @$#2*   (c) *$#2@
(d) @$#2@   (e) None of these

41. There are 2 red, 3 black and 3 white coloured balls out of which, three balls are picked at random from the bag. Then, what is the probability that there is one ball of each colour?

    (a) $\frac{7}{50}$ (b) $\frac{9}{56}$ (c) $\frac{7}{52}$

    (d) $\frac{9}{28}$ (e) $\frac{5}{26}$

42. A, B and C can do a piece of work in 20 days, 10 days and 15 days respectively. They all started the work together but after 2 days B left the work and A left the work 1.5 days before the completion of work. Find the time in which work gets completed.

    (a) 7.5 days   (b) $6\frac{2}{3}$ days   (c) 8 days

    (d) 6.5 days   (e) 9 days

43. Veer purchased some pens and 4 pencils. The cost of each pen is 150% more than the cost of each pencil. If the quantity of pens and pencils gets interchanged, then the ratio of the earlier bill to the newer bill will become 19:16. Find the difference between each quantity.

    (a) 3   (b) 1   (c) 2

    (d) 4   (e) 5

44. The profit share of A is Rs.1200 out of the total profit of Rs.1800. He had invested Rs.1600 more than B for 8 months, while B invested his amount for a year. How much amount was invested by A (in Rs)?

    (a) 2800   (b) 1600   (c) 2400

    (d) 1800   (e) 1200

45. The difference between C.I. earned in two years and S.I. received in 3 years on the sum of Rs. 2000 is Rs. 205. Find the rate of simple interest for the 3rd year, if the rate of interest for the first two years is 15% on both C.I. and S.I.. (S.I. of 3 years is more than C.I. of 2 years)

    (a) 12.5%   (b) 10%   (c) 15%

    (d) 5%   (e) $11\frac{1}{9}\%$

Directions (46-50): In the given questions, two quantities are given, one as **'Quantity I'** and another as **'Quantity II'**. You must determine the relationship between these two quantities and choose the appropriate option:

46. **Quantity I, (x):** $4x^2 - 17x + 15 = 0$

    Quantity II, (y): $2y^2 - 17y + 35 = 0$

    (a) Quantity I > Quantity II

    (b) Quantity I < Quantity II

    (c) Quantity I ≥ Quantity II

    (d) Quantity I ≤ Quantity II

    (e) Quantity I = Quantity II or no relation.

47. **Quantity I, (Time taken by A to complete the work alone):** The time taken by A & B together to complete a piece of work is equal to the time taken by C to complete the same work alone. B, by working alone, can complete the same piece of work in 45 days and C is 125% more efficient than B.

    Quantity II: 27 days.

    (a) Quantity I > Quantity II

    (b) Quantity I < Quantity II

    (c) Quantity I ≥ Quantity II

    (d) Quantity I ≤ Quantity II

    (e) Quantity I = Quantity II or no relation.

48. **Quantity I, (Rate of interest):** A man invested an equal amount of money for 2 years in two schemes —A & B. Scheme —A & B offers S.I. and C.I. (compounding annually) respectively. Both schemes offer the same rate of interest. Ratio of the simple interest received to the compound interest received after 2 years is 10:11.

    Quantity II: 16%

    (a) Quantity I > Quantity II

    (b) Quantity I < Quantity II

    (c) Quantity I ≥ Quantity II

    (d) Quantity I ≤ Quantity II

    (e) Quantity I = Quantity II or no relation.

49. Train A crosses a pole in 12.5 seconds. The ratio of the length of train A to that of B is 5:8 and the speed of train A is double that of train B. Length of train B is 800m.

    Quantity I: Time taken by train A to cross train B while running in the same direction.

    Quantity II: 65 seconds.

    (a) Quantity I > Quantity II

    (b) Quantity I < Quantity II

    (c) Quantity I ≥ Quantity II

    (d) Quantity I ≤ Quantity II

    (e) Quantity I = Quantity II or no relation.

50. **Quantity I, (Total surface area of 1 hemispherical bowl):** A spherical ball of radius 42 cm. is melted to form 16 identical hemispherical bowls.

    Quantity II, (Curved surface area of a cylindrical pipe): The volume of each cylindrical pipe is 12320 cm³. The ratio of the radius to that of the height of the cylindrical pipe is 7:10.

    (a) Quantity I > Quantity II

    (b) Quantity I < Quantity II

    (c) Quantity I ≥ Quantity II

    (d) Quantity I ≤ Quantity II

    (e) Quantity I = Quantity II or no relation.

Direction (51-55): The table given below shows the total number of books printed by Adda247 of different subjects and the percentage of books sold out of the total books printed. Read the table carefully to answer the following questions.

Subject	Number of Books printed	Percentage of Books sold
Ace Quant	1800	$55\frac{5}{9}\%$
Ace English	2200	$27\frac{3}{11}\%$
Ace Reasoning	1500	$33\frac{1}{3}\%$
D.I	3300	30%
Puzzle	2800	25%
SSC 100	2300	50%

Note Sold books are not defective.

51. The total number of D.I. and puzzle books sold by Adda247 is what percent more/less than the total number of Ace Quant and Ace Reasoning books sold by Adda247?
(a) $10\frac{1}{3}\%$ (b) $11\frac{1}{3}\%$ (c) $11\frac{2}{3}\%$
(d) $12\frac{1}{3}\%$ (e) $12\frac{2}{3}\%$

52. The unsold books of Ace Reasoning are what percent more/less than the unsold books of Ace English?
(a) 37.5% (b) 60% (c) 25%
(d) 40% (e) 50%

53. Find the average number of 'SSC 100', 'Puzzle' and 'Ace Quant' books sold by Adda247?
(a) 900 (b) 925 (c) 950
(d) 975 (e) 980

54. Find the ratio between unsold books of D.I. and 'SSC 100' together to sold books of Ace Quant and Ace English together?
(a) 7 : 4 (b) 33 : 16 (c) 17 : 8
(d) 173 : 80 (e) 35 : 16

55. If the ratio between defective books to non-defective unsold books of puzzle and SSC 100 is 1:4 and 2:3 respectively, then find the ratio between the total defective books of Puzzle and SSC 100 together to the total sold books of Puzzle and SSC 100 together.
(a) 92:187
(b) 88:185
(c) 83:185
(d) 185:88
(e) 97:191

Directions (56-60): Study the pie chart given below and answer the following questions.

The pie charts show the percentage distribution of total employees of a company in 5 different departments (A, B, C, D & E) and the percentage distribution of the total employees of the company who work in day shifts in these departments.

Total employees = 12000

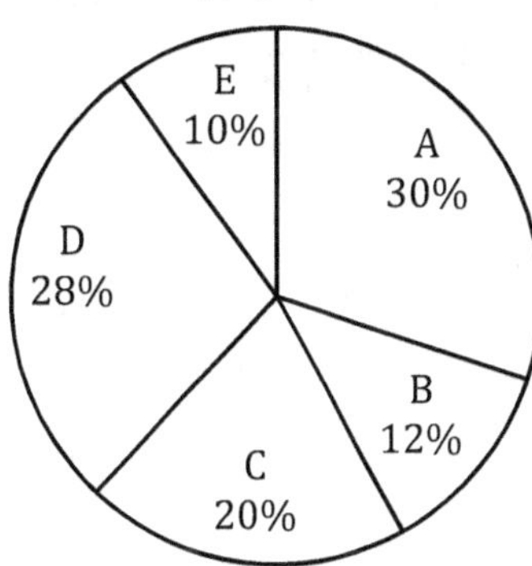

Employees who work in day shifts = 8000

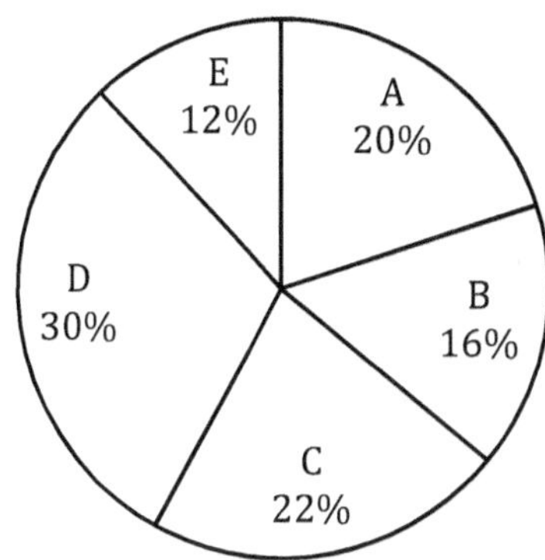

56. What is the difference between the number of employees who work the night shift in B & C departments together and the number of employees who work the day shift in A & D departments together?
(a) 2500 (b) 3200 (c) 2700
(d) 3400 (e) 3000

57. Employees who work the night shift in D & E departments together are what percent lower than the total employees in A & C departments together?
(a) 120% (b) 150% (c) 70%
(d) 90% (e) 80%

58. The average number of employees in C, D & E departments is how much more or less than employees who work the day shift in A & B departments together?
(a) 520 (b) 680 (c) 740
(d) 560 (e) 640

59. Employees working the day shift in C & E departments together are what percent of employees who work the night shift in A department?
(a) 148% (b) 136% (c) 166%
(d) 124% (e) 138%

60. Employees working the night shift in B, D & E departments together are what percent of the total employees in B, D & E department together?
(a) 45% (b) 40% (c) 25%

(d) 35% (e) None of the above.

Directions (61-65): What will come in place of (?) in the following questions?

61. 717, 500, 331, ?, 113, 52
- (a) 216
- (b) 198
- (c) 204
- (d) 156
- (e) None of these

62. 24, 20, 28, 16, ?, 12
- (a) 22
- (b) 18
- (c) 20
- (d) 34
- (e) 32

63. ?, 100, 156, 240, 352, 492
- (a) 64
- (b) 72
- (c) 68
- (d) 60
- (e) 76

64. 68, 140, 220, 327, 498, ?
- (a) 722
- (b) 766
- (c) 568
- (d) 794
- (e) 646

65. 29, 70, 27, 74, 21, ?
- (a) 88
- (b) 85
- (c) 87
- (d) 91
- (e) 80

Directions (66-70): Each of the following questions below consists of a question and two statements numbered I and II. You have to decide whether the data provided in the statements is sufficient to answer the questions.

Give answer

(a) if the data given in statement I alone is sufficient to answer the question while the data in statement II alone is not sufficient to answer the question.

(b) if the data given in statement II alone is sufficient to answer the question while the data in statement I alone is not sufficient to answer the question.

(c) if the data either in statement I alone or in statement II alone is sufficient to answer the question.

(d) If the data in neither statement I nor II is sufficient to answer the question.

(e) If the data in both statements I and II together is necessary to answer the question.

66. Find the cost price of an article sold by a shopkeeper for Rs. 240?
- I. If the article is sold at 25% more, the profit earned will be Rs. 40.
- II. Marked price of the article is Rs. 400 and profit% is equal to discount% and profit% is 40%.

67. Find the volume of right circular cone.
- I. Height of cone is 100% more than radius of cone.
- II. Area of base of cone is 154 cm².

68. Find the value of $2^x \times 3^y$.
- (a) Sum of value of x and y is 8.
- (b) Product of value of x & y is 7.

69. Find the speed of boat in still water.
- I. Time taken by a boat to cover 64 kms. in downstream is half the time taken by the same boat to cover the same distance in still water.
- II. Speed of stream is 5 km/hr.

70. In a box, there are three types of balls, Black, Red and White. If the no. of white balls is given, then find out the probability of getting one white ball.
- I. Probability of getting one Red ball is given.
- II. Probability of getting one black ball is given.

Directions (71-73): Find the approximate value of (?) in the following questions.

71. $\frac{?\% \text{ of } 799}{31.99} \div 34.989 \times (326.03 + 233.97) = 439.98$
- (a) 120
- (b) 110
- (c) 90
- (d) 100
- (e) 80

72. $(?)^2 + 263.052 = 55.97\%$ of $6799 + 40.02\%$ of $5000 - 34.97 \times 72.05$
- (a) 47
- (b) 51
- (c) 45
- (d) 55
- (e) 57

73. $? = (27.02)^2 - (16.91)^2 + (34.03)^2 - (29.99)^2$
- (a) 634
- (b) 696
- (c) 648
- (d) 650
- (e) 682

74. A container of capacity 80 litres is filled with a mixture of milk and water. If a certain quantity of mixture is taken out, then 70% of milk and 30% of water is removed from the mixture and overall 55% of the container will be vacant. Find the initial quantity of water and milk in the container.
- (a) 30l, 50l
- (b) 55l, 25l
- (c) 25l, 55l
- (d) 45l, 35l
- (e) 35l, 45l

75. If 6 years are subtracted from the present age of Veer and the remainder is divided by 18, then the present age of his grand-daughter Sneha is obtained. If Sneha is 2 years younger than her brother whose age is 5 years, then what is the ratio of the age of Veer and Sneha after 6 years?
- (a) 20:3
- (b) 24:5
- (c) 21:4
- (d) 22:3
- (e) 28:3

76. A solid spherical ball of lead 3 cms. in radius is melted and recast into three spherical balls. If the radius of two of these balls is 1.5 cm and 2.5 cm respectively, then find the diameter of the third ball.
- (a) 4 cm.
- (b) 2 cm.
- (c) 5 cm.
- (d) 6 cm.
- (e) 8 cm.

77. The original cost of a TV is three times the cost of the raw material used. The cost of the raw material increases in the ratio of 5:12 and manufacturing expenses in the ratio 4:5. Find the percentage increase in the cost of the TV, if its original cost was Rs 6000.

(Original cost = manufacturing cost + raw material cost)

(a) $55\frac{2}{3}\%$ (b) 65%   (c) $63\frac{1}{3}\%$

(d) 70%   (e) $72\frac{1}{3}\%$

78. Working efficiency of 'A' is twice than that of 'B'. 'A' and 'B' together can complete the work in 60 days, while 'A', 'B' and 'C' together can complete the same work in 45 days. Find in how many days 'B' and 'C' together can complete the work.

(a) 90 days   (b) 45 days   (c) 30 days

(d) 40 days   (e) 75 days

79. The ratio between the speed of a boat in still water to the speed of stream is 5:1. If the boat travels 48 kms. upstream in 3 hours less than 144 km downstream, then find the speed of the boat in still water.

(a) 12 kmph.   (b) 24 kmph.   (c) 20 kmph.

(d) 16 kmph.   (e) 10 kmph.

80. A bag contains 5 black, 7 blue and 4 brown colour balls. 3 balls are drawn at random. Find the probability that all 3 balls are of the same colour.

(a) $\dfrac{29}{280}$ (b) $\dfrac{1}{4}$ (c) $\dfrac{7}{80}$

(d) $\dfrac{13}{80}$ (e) $\dfrac{11}{80}$

Solutions

REASONING ABILITY

Directions (1-5): C sits third to the right of J. Only one member sits between J and P. J's brother sits immediate left of P. Two members sit between J's brother and J's father. From these conditions we have three possible cases-

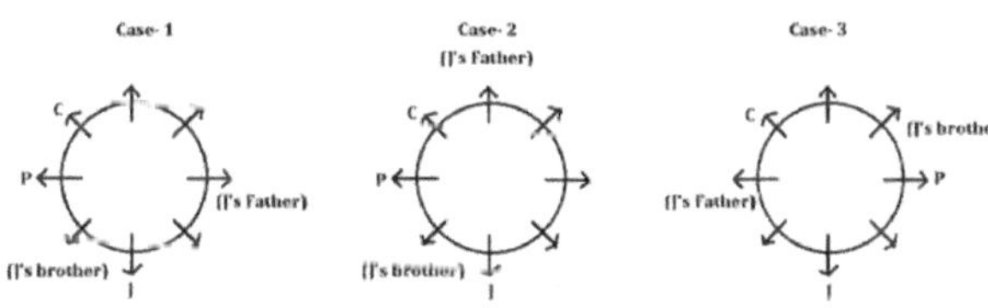

J does not sit opposite to J's father. By this condition case-2 is cancelled. N sits immediate left of G. J's sister sits third to the left of N. J's husband sits second to the right of J's sister. Three members sit between J's husband and E. So the new arrangement will be-

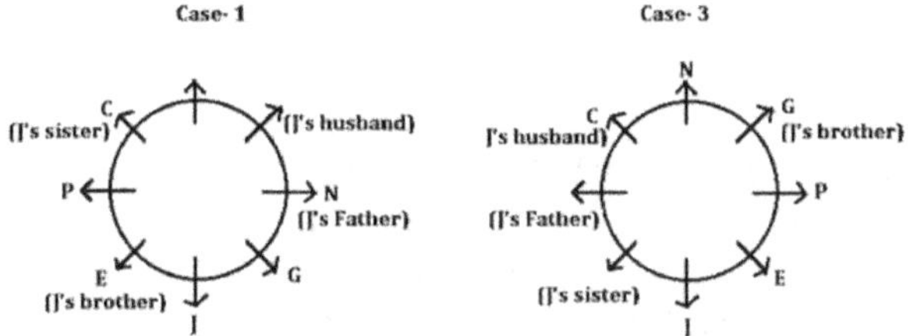

J's daughter sits second to the left of J's mother. Two members sit between J's mother and J's son. By these conditions case-3 is cancelled. L is male member of the family. So, final arrangement will be:

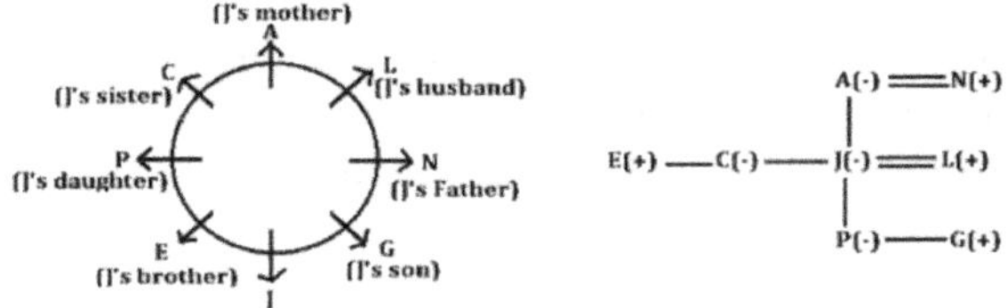

1. (a)   **2.** (c)   **3.** (e)

4. (b)   **5.** (d)

Directions (6-8):

6. (d)

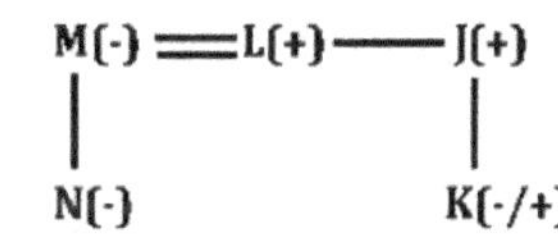

7. (d)

8. (b)

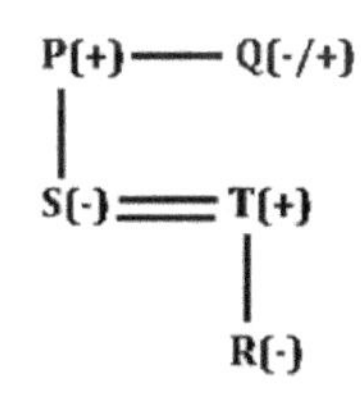

Directions (9-13):

Word	Code
college	mr
student	gl
have	yz
extra	tz
enjoy	wr
fun	if/ar
study	if/ar
game	nl
exam	uz

9. (d)   **10.** (c)   **11.** (b)

12. (e)   **13.** (d)

Directions (14-18): The ones who like Fanta and Slice live on 1st floor and 7th floor. M lives on 3rd floor. C and M live on adjacent floors. From these conditions we have four possible cases:

Floor	Case-1 Person	Case-1 Drink	Case-2 Person	Case-2 Drink	Case-3 Person	Case-3 Drink	Case-4 Person	Case-4 Drink
7		Fanta		Fanta		Slice		Slice
6								
5								
4			C				C	
3	M		M		M		M	
2	C				C			
1		Slice		Slice		Fanta		Fanta

The one who likes 7up lives just above C, who likes Sprite. The ones who like Coke and 7up live on adjacent floors. Only one person lives between A and B, who likes Coke. By these conditions case-2 and case- 4 are cancelled. So new arrangement will be:

Floor	Case-1 Person	Case-1 Drink	Case-3 Person	Case-3 Drink
7		Fanta		Slice
6	A		A	
5				
4	B	Coke	B	Coke
3	M	7up	M	7up
2	C	Sprite	C	Sprite
1		Slice		Fanta

L likes Maaza. G does not like Slice. More than one person lives between the ones who like Pepsi and Fanta. By this condition case-1 is cancelled. So final arrangement will be:

Floor	Person	Drink
7	O	Slice
6	A	Pepsi
5	L	Maaza
4	B	Coke
3	M	7up
2	C	Sprite
1	G	Fanta

14. (c)   **15. (c)**   **16. (b)**
17. (d)   **18. (d)**
Directions (19-20):

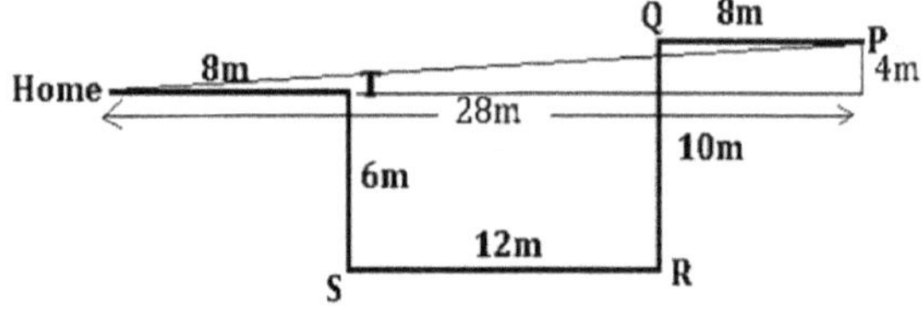

19. (d)
20. (b)
Direction (21-25):
21. (a)

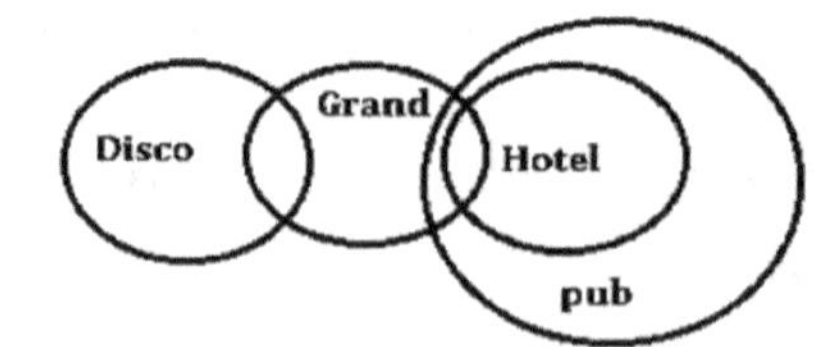

22. (b)

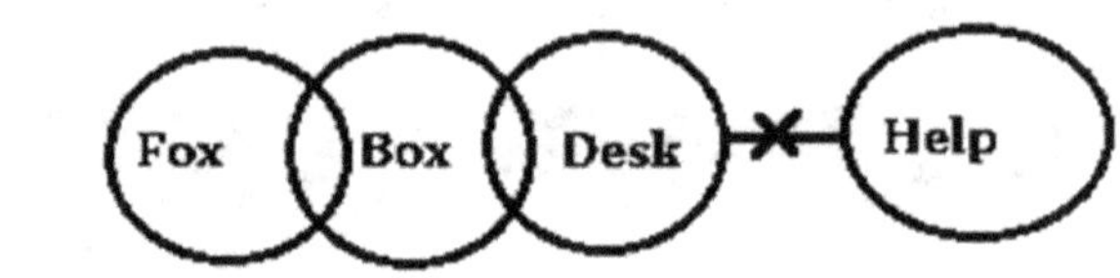

23. (e)

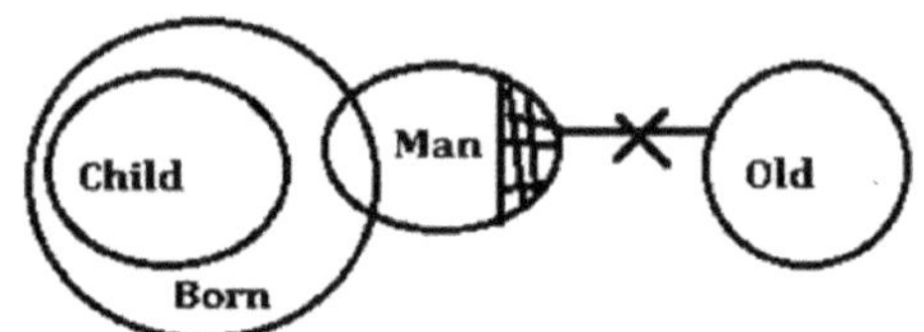

24. (d)

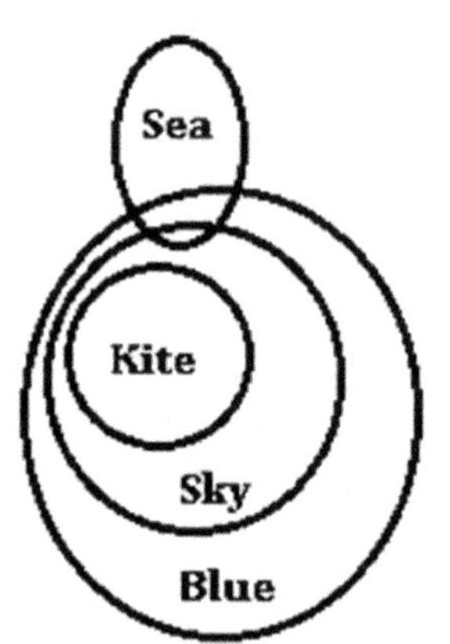

25. (b)

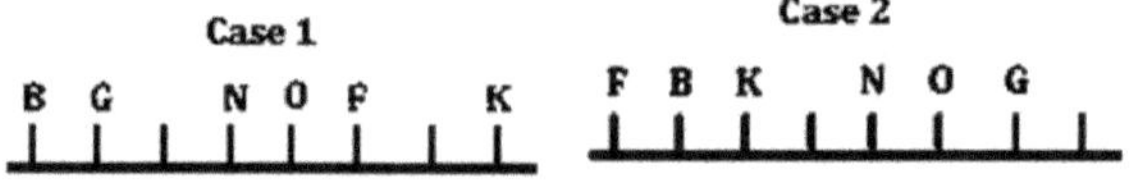

Direction (26-30): From the given statements, G sits 2nd from one of the ends. **Here, we get two possibilities i.e. Case 1 and Case 2.** One person sits between G and N. B sits 4th to the left of O, who sits near N. K sits 2nd to the right of F.

From the given statements, the number of persons who sit to the left of M is one more than the persons sitting to the right of D. **Here Case 2 is ruled out.** M does not sit near F.

So, the final arrangement-

$$\begin{array}{cccccccc} \text{B} & \text{G} & \text{M} & \text{N} & \text{O} & \text{F} & \text{D} & \text{K} \end{array}$$

26. (e) **27. (b)** **28. (c)**
29. (e) **30. (d)**

Direction (31-35): From the given statements, S likes Green but does not like Flynn and Joan. U likes Black colour and Austen. P likes Ernest but does not like Red and White. R likes Bradbury. Q likes Pink. The one who likes Pink also likes Joan.

Persons	Colours	Authors
P	~~Red/White~~	Ernest
Q	Pink	Joan
R		Bradbury
S	Green	~~Joan/Flynn~~
T		
U	Black	Austen
V		

From the given statements, T does not like Purple. The one who likes Purple also likes Larson. R does not like White.

So, the final arrangement:

Persons	Colours	Authors
P	Blue	Ernest
Q	Pink	Joan
R	Red	Bradbury
S	Green	Martin
T	White	Flynn
U	Black	Austen
V	Purple	Larson

31. (a) **32. (c)** **33. (d)**
34. (b) **35. (e)**

Directions (36-40):
36. (b) Condition III is implied.
37. (a) Condition III is implied.
38. (c) Condition I is implied.
39. (a) Condition III is implied.
40. (d) Condition III is implied.

Quantitative Aptitude

41. (d) Ways to select 3 balls out of 8 balls = 8_{C_3}
Ways to select one red ball = 2_{C_1}
Ways to select two black ball = 3_{C_1}
Ways to select one white balls = 3_{C_1}
∴ Required probability
$$= \frac{2_{C_1} \times 3_{C_1} \times 3_{C_1}}{8_{C_3}} = \frac{9}{28}$$

42. (a) Let the total work be 60 units (LCM of 20,10 and 15)
Efficiency of A= 3 units/day
Efficiency of B=6 units/day
Efficiency of C=4 units/day
B's work in 2 days = 2 ×6 = 12 unit.
Total remaining work = 48 unit.
Let C works for x days.
Then, A will work for (x – 1.5) days.
ATQ,
$x \times 4 + (x - 1.5) \times 3 = 48$
$\Rightarrow x = 7.5$ days

43. (c) Let the quantity of pens be x
And let the cost of each pencil be Rs. 2y
Then, the cost of each pen = Rs. 5y
ATQ,
$$\Rightarrow \frac{5x+8}{2x+20} = \frac{19}{16}$$
$\Rightarrow x = 6$
Required difference= 6 – 4 = 2

44. (c) Profit share ratio (A: B) = 1200: 600
= 2:1
ATQ,

Let B invested Rs. X and A invested Rs (X + 1600)
$$\frac{(1600+X)8}{X \times 12} = \frac{2}{1}$$
$12800 + 8X = 24X$
$X = $ Rs 800
Amount of A= 1600 + 800 = Rs 2400

45. (a) Let the rate of simple interest for the 3rd year be x% per annum.
$$\text{Total SI} = \frac{2000 \times 15 \times 2}{100} + \frac{2000 \times x \times 1}{100}$$
$$= \text{Rs. } (600 + 20x)$$
$$\text{CI for 2 years} = P\left(1 + \frac{R}{100}\right)\left(1 + \frac{R}{100}\right) - P$$
$$= 2000\left(1 + \frac{15}{100}\right)\left(1 + \frac{15}{100}\right) - 2000$$
$$= \text{Rs } 645$$
ATQ,
$\Rightarrow 600+20x-645=205$
$\Rightarrow 20x = 250 \Rightarrow x = 12.5\%$

46. (b) Quantity I.
$4x^2 - 17x + 15 = 0$
$4x^2 - 12x - 5x + 15 = 0$
$4x(x - 3) -5(x - 3) = 0$
$(x - 3)(4x - 5) = 0$
$x = 3, \frac{5}{4}$
Quantity II.
$2y^2 - 17y + 35 = 0$
$2y^2 - 10y - 7y + 35 = 0$
$2y(y - 5) -7(y - 5) = 0$
$(y - 5)(2y - 7) = 0$

$y = 5, \dfrac{7}{2}$

So, Quantity I < Quantity II.

47. (a) Quantity I.

Let efficiency of B be '4x units/day'

So, efficiency of C = $4x \times \dfrac{225}{100}$ = 9x units/day

ATQ,

Total work = 45 × 4x = 180x units

Time taken by C alone to complete the work

= $\dfrac{180x}{9x}$ = 20 days

Now, efficiency of A = $\dfrac{180x - 4x \times 20}{20}$ = 5x units/day

Hence, required days = $\dfrac{180x}{5x}$ = 36 days.

Quantity II.

27 days.

So, Quantity I > Quantity II

48. (a) Quantity I.

Let amount invested by man in both schemes be Rs. P. and let rate of interest offered by both schemes is R% p.a.

ATQ,

$\dfrac{\left(\frac{P \times R \times 2}{100}\right)}{\left[P\left\{\left(1+\frac{R}{100}\right)^2 - 1\right\}\right]} = \dfrac{10}{11}$

$\Rightarrow \dfrac{2R}{100} \times \dfrac{10000}{(R^2 + 200R)} = \dfrac{10}{11}$

$\Rightarrow \dfrac{200}{(R+200)} = \dfrac{10}{11}$

$\Rightarrow 10R + 2000 = 2200$

R = 20%

Quantity II.

16%

So, Quantity I > Quantity II.

49. (e) Length of train – A = $800 \times \dfrac{5}{8}$ = 500m

So, Speed of train – A = $\dfrac{500}{12.5}$ = 40 m/sec

Hence, speed of train – B = $\dfrac{40}{2}$ = 20 m/sec

Quantity I.

Required time = $\dfrac{(500+800)}{40-20} = \dfrac{1300}{20}$ = 65 seconds

Quantity II.

65 seconds

So, Quantity I = Quantity II.

50. (a) Quantity I:

Let radius of hemispherical bowl be r cm.

ATQ,

Volume of spherical ball = 16 × Volume of a hemispherical bowl

$\dfrac{4}{3} \times \pi \times (42)^3 = 16 \times \dfrac{2}{3} \times \pi \times r^3$

$\dfrac{(42)^3}{8} = r^3$

$(21)^3 = r^3$

r = 21cm

Hence, total surface area of 1 hemispherical bowl = $3 \times \dfrac{22}{7} \times (21)^2$ = 4158 cm²

Quantity II:

Let radius and height of cylindrical pipe be '7r' cm and '10r' cm respectively.

ATQ,

$\dfrac{22}{7} \times (7r)^2 \times 10r = 12320$

$r^3 = \dfrac{12320 \times 7}{22 \times 7 \times 7 \times 10}$

$r^3 = 8$

r = 2

So, curved surface area of a cylindrical pipe

= $2 \times \dfrac{22}{7} \times 7 \times 2 \times 10 \times 2$ = 1760 cm²

So, Quantity I > Quantity II.

51. (e) DI and Puzzle books sold together

= $3300 \times \dfrac{30}{100} + 2800 \times \dfrac{25}{100}$

= 990 + 700 = 1690

Ace Quant and Ace Reasoning books sold together

= $\dfrac{500}{900} \times 1800 + \dfrac{1}{3} \times 1500$

= 1000 + 500 = 1500

Required percentage = $\dfrac{1690-1500}{1500} \times 100$

= $\dfrac{190}{1500} \times 100 = 12\dfrac{2}{3}\%$

52. (a) Ace Reasoning books which are unsold

= $1500 - \left(1500 \times \dfrac{1}{3}\right) = 1500 - 500 = 1000$

Ace English books which are unsold

= $2200 - \left(2200 \times \dfrac{300}{1100}\right)$

= 2200 – 600 = 1600

Required % = $\dfrac{1600-1000}{1600} \times 100 = \dfrac{600}{1600} \times 100 = 37.5\%$

53. (c) 'SSC 100' books sold = $2300 \times \dfrac{50}{100} = 1150$

'Puzzle' books sold = $2800 \times \dfrac{25}{100} = 700$

'Ace Quant' books sold = $1800 \times \dfrac{500}{900} = 1000$

Required average = $\dfrac{1150+700+1000}{3} = \dfrac{2850}{3} = 950$

54. (d) Unsold books of 'DI' & 'SSC 100' together

= $3300 \times \dfrac{70}{100} + 2300 \times \dfrac{50}{100}$

= 2310 + 1150 = 3460

Ace quant & Ace English books sold together

= $\left[1800 \times \dfrac{500}{900} + 2200 \times \dfrac{3}{11}\right]$

= 1000 + 600 = 1600

Required ratio = $\dfrac{3460}{1600} = 173 : 80$

55. (b) Defective books of puzzle

= $\dfrac{1}{5} \times 2800 \times \dfrac{75}{100} = 420$

Defective books of SSC 100 = $\dfrac{2}{5} \times 2300 \times \dfrac{50}{100} = 460$

Required ratio = $\dfrac{420+460}{2800 \times \frac{25}{100} + 2300 \times \frac{50}{100}}$

$$= \frac{880}{700+1150} = \frac{880}{1850} = 88:185$$

56. (b) Employees who work the night shift in B & C department together

$$= \left[\left(\frac{12}{100} \times 12000\right) - \left(\frac{16}{100} \times 8000\right)\right] +$$
$$\left[\left(\frac{20}{100} \times 12000\right) - \left(\frac{22}{100} \times 8000\right)\right]$$
$$= [1440 - 1280] + [2400 - 1760]$$
$$= 160 + 640 = 800$$

Employees who work the day shift in A & D department together $= 8000 \times \left(\frac{20+30}{100}\right)$

$$= 4000$$

Required difference = 4000 – 800 = 3200

57. (e) Employees who work the night shift in D & E department together

$$= \left[\left(\frac{28}{100} \times 12000\right) - \left(\frac{30}{100} \times 8000\right)\right] +$$
$$\left[\left(\frac{10}{100} \times 12000\right) - \left(\frac{12}{100} \times 8000\right)\right]$$
$$= [3360 - 2400] + [1200 - 960]$$
$$= 960 + 240 = 1200$$

Total employees in A & C department together $= 12000 \times \left(\frac{30+20}{100}\right) = 6000$

Required% $= \frac{6000 - 1200}{6000} \times 100 = 80\%$

58. (d) Average number of employees in C, D & E department $= \frac{1}{3} \times 12000 \times \left(\frac{20+28+10}{100}\right)$

$$= 2320$$

Employees who work in day shifts in A & B department together $= 8000 \times \left(\frac{16+20}{100}\right)$

$$= 2880$$

Required difference = 2880 – 2320 = 560

59. (b) Employees working the day shift in C & E department together $= 8000 \times \left(\frac{22+12}{100}\right)$

$$= 2720$$

Employees who work the night shift in department A $= \left[\left(12000 \times \frac{30}{100}\right) - \left(8000 \times \frac{20}{100}\right)\right]$

$$= 3600 - 1600 = 2000$$

Required % $= \frac{2720}{2000} \times 100 = 136\%$

60. (e) Employees working the night shift in B, D, & E departments together

$$= \left[\left(\frac{12}{100} \times 12000\right) - \left(\frac{16}{100} \times 8000\right)\right] +$$
$$\left[\left(\frac{28}{100} \times 12000\right) - \left(\frac{30}{100} \times 8000\right)\right] +$$
$$\left[\left(\frac{10}{100} \times 12000\right) - \left(\frac{12}{100} \times 8000\right)\right]$$
$$= [1440 - 1280] + [3360 - 2400] + [1200 - 960]$$
$$= 160 + 960 + 240 = 1360$$

Total employees in B, D & E department together $= 12000 \times \left(\frac{12+28+10}{100}\right) = 6000$

Required% $= \frac{1360}{6000} \times 100$

$$= \frac{68}{3}\% = 22\frac{2}{3}\%$$

61. (c) Pattern of series –

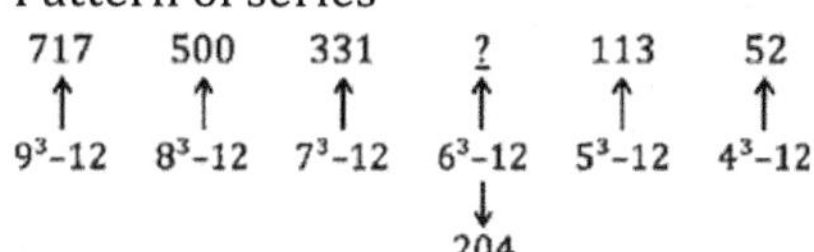

Alternate

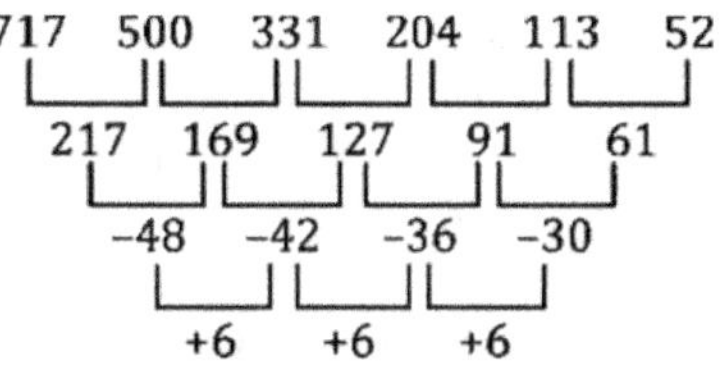

So, missing number is 204.

62. (e) Pattern of series:

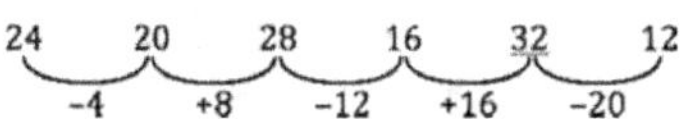

So, missing number is 32.

63. (b) Pattern of series:

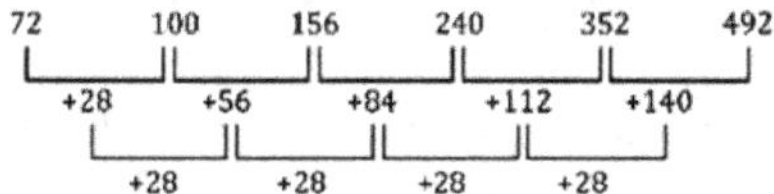

So, missing number is 72.

64. (d) Pattern of series:

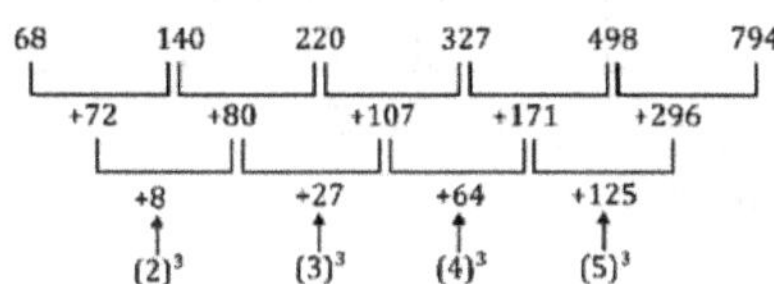

So, missing number is 794.

65. (e) Pattern of series:

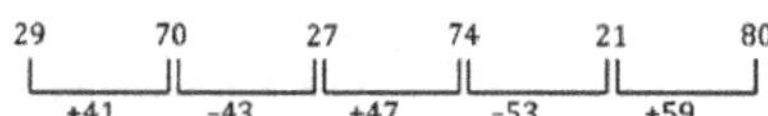

So, missing number is 80.

66. (c) **From I**

Let C.P. of article be Rs. x.

$$\frac{125}{100} \times 240 - x = 40$$
$$x = 300 - 40 = Rs\ 260$$

From II

Since profit% & discount% is given and S.P. & marked price is given.

∴ cost price can be determined.

∴ Either from I or II.

67. (e) **From I & II**

Area of base of cone $(\pi r^2) = 154$

∴$\pi r^2 = 154$

$r^2 = 49$

∴ r = 7 cm

∴ height (h) = 7 × 2 = 14 cm.

Volume $= \frac{1}{3}\pi r^2 h$

$$= \frac{1}{3} \times \frac{22}{7} \times 7 \times 7 \times 14$$

$= \dfrac{2156}{3}$ cm^3

68. (e) **From I & II**

$x + y = 8$ ...(i)

$xy = 7$

$(x - y)^2 = (x + y)^2 - 4xy$

$(x - y)^2 = (8)^2 - 4 \times 7$

$(x - y)^2 = 36$

$x - y = 6$ ...(ii)

$\therefore x = 7$ & $y = 1$

Or $x = 1$ & $y = 7$

69. (e) **From I & II**

Let speed of boat in still water be x km/hr and speed of stream be y km/hr.

$\dfrac{64}{x+y} = \dfrac{1}{2}\dfrac{64}{x}$

$x = y = 5$ km/hr

70. (e) Given no. of white ball

Let $\to a$

From I let probability $\to \dfrac{x}{y}$

Let no. of red ball $\to px$, total balls $\to py$

From II $\to$ Let probability $= \dfrac{s}{t}$

Let no. of black ball = qs, total balls = qt

From I & II

$px + a + qs = qt = py$

we know the values of x, y, s, t and a so we can find the value of p and q

So probability of white ball found $= \dfrac{a}{qt}$ or $\dfrac{a}{py}$

$\therefore$ I & II together are sufficient to answer the question

71. (b) $\dfrac{\frac{?}{100} \times 800}{32} \times \dfrac{1}{35} \times (326 + 234) \approx 440$

$\dfrac{?}{4} \times \dfrac{1}{35} \times 560 \approx 440$

$? \approx \dfrac{440}{4} \Rightarrow ? \approx 110$

72. (d) $(?)^2 + 263 \approx \dfrac{56}{100} \times 6800 + \dfrac{40}{100} \times 5000 -$

35×72

$(?)^2 + 263 \approx 3808 + 2000 - 2520$

$(?)^2 \approx 3288 - 263$

$(?) \approx \sqrt{3025}$

$? \approx 55$

73. (b) $? \approx 27^2 - 17^2 + 34^2 - 30^2$

$? \approx 729 - 289 + 1156 - 900$

$? \approx 1885 - 1189$

$? \approx 696$

74. (a)

Milk	Water
70	30
	55
25	15
5 :	3

Initial quantity of water $= \dfrac{3}{8} \times 80 = 30$ litre.

Initial quantity of milk $= \dfrac{5}{8} \times 80 = 50$ litre.

75. (d) Let the present age of veer be x yr.

Age of Sneha $= \dfrac{x - 6}{18}$ yr.

ATQ,

$\dfrac{x-6}{18} + 2 = 5$

$\Rightarrow x - 6 = 3 \times 18$

$\Rightarrow x = 60$ yrs.

Age of veer after 6 years = 66 years

Age of Sneha after 6 years = 3 + 6 = 9 years

Required ratio = 22 : 3

76. (a) Let the radius of third ball be x cm.

ATQ,

$\Rightarrow \dfrac{4}{3}\pi(3)^3 = \dfrac{4}{3}\pi(1.5)^3 + \dfrac{4}{3}\pi(2.5)^3 + \dfrac{4}{3}\pi(x)^3$

$\Rightarrow (3)^3 = (1.5^3 + 2.5^3 + x^3)$

$\Rightarrow 27 = 3.375 + 15.625 + x^3$

$\Rightarrow x^3 = 8$

$\Rightarrow x = 2$ cm

$\therefore$ the diameter of the third ball = 4 cm

77 (c) The original cost of TV = Rs 6000

Then, original raw material cost = Rs 2000

New cost of raw material

$= 2000 \times \dfrac{12}{5} = Rs\ 4800$

Original manufacturing exp.

= Rs 6000 – 2000 = Rs 4000

New manufacturing exp.

$= 4000 \times \dfrac{5}{4} = Rs\ 5000$

New cost of TV = 4800 + 5000 = 9800

Required %

$= \dfrac{3800}{6000} \times 100 = \dfrac{380}{6} = \dfrac{190}{3} = 63\dfrac{1}{3}\%$

78. (a) Let per day work of A = 2x units

So, per day work of B = x unit

So, total unit of work

$= (2x + x) \times 60 = 180x$ units

Let, per day work of C = y unit

$(2x + x + y) \times 45 = 180x$ units

$y = x$

Time required to complete the work by B & C together

$= \dfrac{180x}{(x+x)} = 90$ days

79. (c) The speed of boat in still water = 5x kmph

Speed of stream = x kmph

ATQ,

$\dfrac{144}{5x+x} - \dfrac{48}{5x-x} = 3$

$\dfrac{144}{6x} - \dfrac{48}{4x} = 3$

$24 - 12 = 3x$

$x = 4$

Speed of boat in still water = 5x = 5×4 = 20 kmph

80. (c) Required Probability $= \dfrac{^5C_3 + {}^7C_3 + {}^4C_3}{^{16}C_3}$

$= \dfrac{10+35+4}{560} = \dfrac{7}{80}$

REASONING ABILITY

Directions (1-5): In each of the questions, relationships between some elements are shown in the statements. These statements are followed by conclusions numbered I and II. Read the statements and give the answer.

(a) If only conclusion I follows.
(b) If only conclusion II follows.
(c) If either conclusion I or II follows.
(d) If neither conclusion I nor II follows.
(e) If both conclusions I and II follow.

1. **Statements:** $M \geq T < V$; $U < V \leq X$; $Z \geq Y \geq X$
    Conclusions: I. $T < Z$ **II.** $U < Y$

2. **Statements:** $W \leq A \leq K = N$; $D \leq A \leq U = L$; $G > L$
    Conclusions: I. $W < G$ **II.** $D \geq N$

3. **Statements:** $N < T \leq O$; $F > N \geq E = I > R$; $R \geq Y$
    Conclusions: I. $Y < O$ **II.** $F > T$

4. **Statements:** $I \geq N \geq O = X$; $D \geq J \geq I = E$
    Conclusions: I. $O < D$ **II.** $X = D$

5. **Statements:** $P > N = L \geq M$; $G = M \leq H \leq S$
    Conclusions: I. $P > S$ **II.** $N \geq G$

Directions (6-8): Study the following information and answer the given questions:

Point K is 12m. to the West of point G. Point M is 4m. to the North of Point K. Point J is 10m. to the South of Point L. Point F is 6m to the West of point J. Point G lies exactly between Point L and Point J.

6. In which direction is Point J with respect to Point M?
    (a) north
    (b) north-west
    (c) south
    (d) south-east
    (e) Cannot be determined

7. What is the shortest distance between Point K and Point L?
    (a) 10m.   (b) 12m.
    (c) 13m.   (d) 17m.
    (e) None of these

8. If Point N is 6m. to the East of Point M, then how far is Point F from Point N?
    (a) 12m.   (b) 10m.
    (c) 9m.   (d) 8m.
    (e) None of these

Directions (9-11): Study the following information to answer the given questions.

In a family of eight members there are four male members. J is the grandfather of L. M is the brother of L. J has only two children and one of them is unmarried. P is the sister-in-law of S. K is the paternal grandmother of M. S is the daughter of K. Q is the son of G and the brother of L.

9. How is G related to K?
    (a) son   (b) daughter
    (c) mother   (d) brother
    (e) Either (a) or (b)

10. How is L related to S?
    (a) aunt
    (b) nephew
    (c) niece
    (d) sister
    (e) Cannot be determined

11. How is P related to M?
    (a) sister   (b) aunt
    (c) grandmother   (d) mother
    (e) None of these

12. If "SOUL" is coded as "5#7$", "FREELS" is coded as "29@@$5", then "OURSELF" will be coded as?
    (a) #759@$2   (b) #795@2$
    (c) #9572$@   (d) #795@$2
    (e) None of these

13. How many pairs of letters are there in the word "**PARTICLE**" which have as many letters between them in the word (backwards or forwards) as in the alphabetical series?
    (a) one   (b) two
    (c) three   (d) four
    (e) None of these

14. If all the alphabets are rearranged within itself as they appear in the English dictionary in the word "**MISUNDERSTANDING**" then which of the following will be fourth to the left of the twelfth from the left end?
    (a) G   (b) N
    (c) M   (d) I
    (e) None of these

15. In a row of students facing North, Piya is 16th from the left end. If nine students sit between Piya and Riya, then a minimum of how many students would fit in the row, if Piya does not sit at any end?

(a) 16   (b) 17
(c) 25   (d) 26
(e) Cannot be determined

Direction (16-20): Study the following information carefully to answer the questions given below.

Seven people viz. A, B, C, D, E, F and G live in a building of seven different floors (but not necessarily in the same order). The ground floor is numbered as 1, the floor just above it is numbered 2 and so on till the top floor, which is numbered as 7. Each of the seven people travel to a different city viz. Delhi, Mumbai, Patna, Chennai, Kolkata, Bengaluru and Lucknow (but not necessarily in the same order).

Only three people live above the floor on which A lives. Only one person lives between A and the one travelling to Bengaluru. F lives immediately below the one travelling to Mumbai. The one travelling to Mumbai lives on an even numbered floor. Only three people live between the ones travelling to Bengaluru and Patna. E lives immediately above C. E does not travel to Patna. Only two people live between B and the one travelling to Kolkata. The one travelling to Kolkata lives below the floor on which B lives. The one travelling to Delhi does not live immediately above or immediately below B. D does not live immediately above or immediately below A. G does not travel to Chennai.

16. Who among the following lives on floor number 3?
    (a) C
    (b) G
    (c) E
    (d) The one travelling to Chennai
    (e) The one travelling to Kolkata

17. D is travelling to which of the following cities?
    (a) Mumbai   (b) Bengaluru   (c) Chennai
    (d) Kolkata   (e) Patna

18. Who among the following lives immediately above E?
    (a) A   (b) B   (c) D
    (d) G   (e) F

19. How many people live between the floors on which D and the one travelling to Mumbai lives?
    (a) none   (b) one
    (c) two   (d) three
    (e) More than three

20. Which among the following statements is true with respect to G?
    (a) G lives on the lowermost floor
    (b) G lives on floor number 7

(c) G lives immediately above E
(d) G is travelling to Bengaluru
(e) None of these

Directions (21-25): Study the information and answer the following questions:

Ten persons are sitting in two parallel rows facing each other. A, B, C, D and E are sitting in row 1 facing north and P, Q, R, S and T are sitting in row 2 facing south (not necessarily in the same order). The persons who are facing each other like the same sports. The sports are Cricket, Football, Hockey, Tennis and Badminton.

B sits third to the right of E and one of them sits at an extreme end of the row. One person sits between S and P and neither of them sits at any end. The pair who likes Badminton sits to the immediate left of B. T sits at one of the ends and does not like Football. C sits second to the right of E. S likes Cricket. D likes football and sits at one of the ends. Q does not like Football. Either of the pair who sits at the extreme ends does not like Hockey. The pair who likes Tennis does not sit to the immediate right of P. Q does not face A.

21. Who among the following sits to the immediate right of the one who faces D?
    (a) S   (b) P
    (c) R   (d) T
    (e) None of these

22. What is the position of C with respect to one who likes Hockey?
    (a) Third to the left
    (b) Third to the right
    (c) Immediate left
    (d) Immediate right
    (e) None of these

23. Who faces R?
    (a) A   (b) B
    (c) C   (d) D
    (e) None of these

24. Who faces the immediate neighbour of E?
    (a) P
    (b) The one who likes Cricket
    (c) The one who likes Football
    (d) The one who likes Tennis
    (e) None of these

25. Four of the following five pairs are alike in a certain way and hence form a group. Who among the following does not belong to that group?
    (a) E, S   (b) B, R   (c) C, P
    (d) A, Q   (e) D, R

Directions (26-30): Study the following information carefully and answer the questions given below:

A word and number arrangement machine when given an input line of words and numbers rearranges them following a particular rule in each step. The following is an illustration of input and rearrangement.

Input: match 8 company 12 better 14 door 16 sequence 10

Step I: better match 8 company 14 door 16 sequence 10 12

Step II: company better match 8 door 16 sequence 10 12 14

Step III: door company better match 16 sequence 10 12 14 8

Step IV: match door company better 16 sequence 12 14 8 10

Step V: sequence match door company better 12 14 8 10 16

Step V: is the last step of the above arrangement. As per the rules followed in the steps given above, find out in each of the following questions the appropriate step for the given input.

Input: roast 14 cricket 16 plug 12 twilight 10 output 8

26. Which of the following element is fifth from the left end in Step II?
    (a) 12 (b) plug
    (c) twilight (d) 10
    (e) None of these

27. Which of the following elements is fourth from the right end in step IV?
    (a) 14 (b) 10 (c) output
    (d) cricket (e) twilight

28. Which of the following is Step III of the given input?
    (a) plug output roast cricket 16 twilight 10 14 12 8
    (b) plug output cricket roast 16 twilight 14 10 12 8
    (c) plug output cricket roast 16 twilight 10 14 12 8
    (d) plug output cricket roast twilight 16 10 14 12 8
    (e) None of these

29. Which element is fifth to the left of '12' in step V?
    (a) twilight (b) plug
    (c) output (d) roast
    (e) None of these

30. Which element is seventh to the right of 'cricket' in step I?
    (a) 8 (b) output (c) 10
    (d) 14 (e) twilight

Directions (31-35): Study the following information carefully and answer the questions given below:

In a certain code language
'study book room rent' is coded as 'dy bk rm rt'
'room rent is high' is coded as 'rm rt si gh'
'pay rent is more ' is coded as 'yp rt si me'
'more study work hard' is coded as 'me dy wk hd'

31. What is the code for 'more room'?
    (a) rm si (b) me gh
    (c) me rm (d) bk rm
    (e) None of these

32. What is the code for 'work is hard'?
    (a) hd gh si (b) wk hd rt
    (c) wk si hd (d) si wk yp
    (e) Cannot be determined

33. 'dy' is denoted as?
    (a) book (b) room
    (c) rent (d) study
    (e) None of these

34. What is the code for 'book'?
    (a) dy (b) bk
    (c) rt (d) rm
    (e) None of these

35. 'wk' is the code for?
    (a) work
    (b) high
    (c) hard
    (d) Either (a) or (b)
    (e) Cannot be determined

Directions (36-40): Study the following information carefully and answer the given questions:

J, K, L, M, N, O and P are seven students studying in three different classes, viz. class IX, class X and class XI. At least two students study in each class. Each one of them likes a different subject viz. English, Hindi, Sanskrit, Mathematics, Computer, Physics and Biology (but not necessarily in the same order).

M likes Mathematics and does not study in class X. K likes Biology and studies in a class only with the one who likes Computer. N studies in Class XI and neither likes Computer nor studies with the one who likes English. P likes Hindi and studies with O. J likes English and does not study in class XI. The one who likes Sanskrit is studying with the one who likes Physics. O does not like Sanskrit

36. Who among the following likes Sanskrit?
    (a) L (b) N
    (c) O (d) J
    (e) None of these

37. Who among the following studies in class X?
    (a) K
    (b) L
    (c) The one who likes Sanskrit
    (d) Either (a) or (b)
    (e) Both (a) or (b)

38. Who among the following studies in class IX?
    (a) O (b) P
    (c) L (d) M
    (e) None of these

39. Which of the following combinations is true?

(a) M – Class XI (b) N – Class X
(c) L – Class IX (d) O – Class XI
(e) None is true

40. Which subject does the one who studies with N like?

(a) Computer (b) Mathematics
(c) Hindi (d) English
(e) Biology

QUANTITATIVE APTITUDE

41. Tap 'P' and tap 'Q' alone can fill a tank in 15 hours and 12 hours respectively. Tap 'R' can empty the same tank in 20 hours. If all the three taps are opened for alternate hours starting with tap 'P' and ending with tap 'R', then in how much time will the tank be filled completely?

(a) 30 hr. (b) 25 hr. (c) $28\frac{2}{5}$ hr.

(d) $26\frac{3}{5}$ hr. (e) $25\frac{2}{5}$ hr.

42. 200 students appeared in an examination containing two subjects, History and Geography. 120 students passed in the history exam and 130 students passed in the Geography exam, while 70 students passed in both the exams. If a student is chosen at random, then what will be the probability that this student failed in both exams?

(a) $\frac{1}{8}$ (b) $\frac{1}{10}$ (c) $\frac{3}{40}$

(d) $\frac{1}{5}$ (e) $\frac{3}{20}$

43. After selling an article, Chiru found that he had made a loss of 15%. If he had sold it for Rs. 62.5 more, he would have made a profit of 10%. Find actual initial loss is what percent of the profit earned, if he had sold the article at 25% profit.

(a) 65% (b) 50% (c) 75%
(d) 60% (e) 80%

44. How many numbers of five digits can be formed by using the digits 0, 1, 2, 3, 4, 5, 6 and 7, if repetition of the digits is not allowed?

(a) 5880 (b) 5180 (c) 5980
(d) 6080 (e) 5780

45. A fraction is such that, if we triple the numerator and double the denominator and again increase the numerator by 20% and decrease the denominator by 10%, we get 62.5% of $1\frac{7}{25}$. Find the original fraction.

(a) $\frac{1}{5}$ (b) $\frac{2}{9}$ (c) $\frac{3}{5}$

(d) $\frac{7}{10}$ (e) $\frac{2}{5}$

Directions (46-50): Find the wrong number in the following number series:

46. 15, 8, 12, 30, 112, 550

(a) 15 (b) 8 (c) 550
(d) 112 (e) 30

47. 1800, 1071, 828, 747, 722, 711

(a) 747 (b) 711 (c) 722

(d) 1071 (e) 1800

48. 35, 68, 108, 161, 227, 306

(a) 306 (b) 35 (c) 68
(d) 161 (e) 227

49. 216, 185, 156, 133, 114, 92

(a) 216 (b) 185 (c) 156
(d) 114 (e) 92

50. 111, 113, 121, 153, 281, 785

(a) 281 (b) 785 (c) 113
(d) 111 (e) 121

Directions (51-55): The following table shows the data related to the employment situation in a city in five different years. It also shows the total population of the city in the given years, percentage of Govt. Employees, Pvt. Employees and out of the remaining, the ratio between the numbers of self-employed persons to unemployed persons. Read the data carefully and answer the questions.

Years	Total Population (in lakh)	% of Govt. employee	% of Pvt. Employee	Self-employed: unemployed
1990	1.25	30%	40%	2:2
1995	2	35%	35%	1:2
2000	1.5	32%	28%	1:1
2005	2.2	48%	32%	2:3
2010	101	40%	45%	3:7

51. Find the ratio between the total number of Govt. employees in year 1995 and 2010 together to the total number of Pvt. Employees in year 2000 and 2005 together.

(a) 95:128 (b) 285:281 (c) 275:271
(d) 517:570 (e) 575:517

52. Find the difference between total number of self-employed persons in year 1990 and 2000 together and the number of unemployed persons in year 2005 and 2010 together.

(a) 7050 (b) 7250 (c) 6850
(d) 7150 (e) 6950

53. Find the average number of Pvt. employees, self-employed and unemployed in year 2015 if the total number of Govt. employees in 2015 is equal to 50% of the total number of Govt. employees in year 1995 and 2000 together and in year 2015, $29\frac{1}{2}$ % of the total employees are Govt. employees.

(a) 94,000 (b) 46,000 (c) 47,500
(d) 46,500 (e) 47,000

54. The total number of Pvt. employees and self-employed in year 2000 is approximately what percent more than the total number of self-employed and unemployed persons in year 2005 and 2010 together?
(a) 15%   (b) 12%   (c) 22%
(d) 19%   (e) 25%

55. Find the average population of the city in the year 1995, 2000 and 2005 together, excluding the number of Pvt. Employees in all these years.
(a) 1,25,800   (b) 1,27,400   (c) 1,29,200
(d) 1,31,200   (e) 1,33,500

Directions (56-60): What approximate value will come in the place of question (?) mark.

56. $\left(\sqrt{120.89}-\sqrt{25.001}\right)+?\%\ of\ 159.993 = 62.011$
(a) 30   (b) 35   (c) 40

57. $(156.002 - 554.93 \div 5.01) \times ? = 989.98$
(a) 15   (b) 12   (c) 30
(d) 22   (e) 32

58. $21.001 + ? = (119.91 \times 38.01) \div 47.953$
(a) 74   (b) 66   (c) 54
(d) 84   (e) 94

59. $\sqrt{(2915.995 \div 81.001) \times 16.992 - ?} = 24$
(a) 46   (b) 26   (c) 22
(d) 52   (e) 36

60. $(24.98\% \ of \ 192.01 \div 15.995) = 59.95\% \ of \ 180.02 - ?$
(a) 95   (b) 105   (c) 115
(d) 125   (e) 85

Direction (61-65): The pie-chart given below shows the percentage distribution of students studying six different courses in a particular college.

Total number of students = 36,000
Boys : Girls (in each course) = 5 : 4

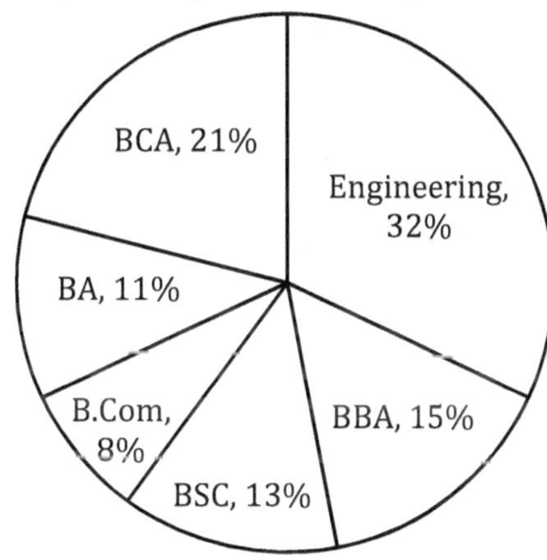

61. What is the ratio between the total number of students studying B.Com to the number of girls studying Engineering?
(a) 7 : 16   (b) 9 : 16   (c) 3 : 8
(d) 1 : 4   (e) 9 : 22

62. The average number of boys studying BSC and BCA is what percent more/less than the number of girls studying BBA.
(a) $41\frac{2}{3}\%$ (b) $83\frac{1}{3}\%$ (c) $141\frac{2}{3}\%$
(d) $183\frac{1}{3}\%$ (e) 37.5%

63. Find the total number of boys studying BA and B.Com together.
(a) 3720   (b) 3600   (c) 4200
(d) 3800   (e) 4150

64. What is the difference between the number of boys studying B.Com and Engineering together and the number of girls studying the same courses together?
(a) 1400   (b) 1600   (c) 1800
(d) 1700   (e) 1200

65. The difference between the number of students studying Engineering and B.com is what percent of the total number of students studying the remaining courses?
(a) $66\frac{2}{3}\%$ (b) 50%   (c) 40%
(d) 48%   (e) 38%

66. A person's present age is 2.5 times his son's present age, whereas the ratio of his wife's present age to his present age is 5:6. 10 years ago, the ratio between the age of this person, his son and his wife was 25:7:20. Find the present average age of all the three.
(a) $44\frac{1}{3}yr.$ (b) $44\frac{2}{3}yr.$ (c) $45\ yr.$
(d) $45\frac{1}{3}yr.$ (e) $46\frac{1}{3}yr.$

67. A sphere of radius 12cm. is melted to form 6 cones of radius 8 cm. Find the slant height of the cone.

(a) 18 cm.   (b) $4\sqrt{47}$ cm.   (c) $3\sqrt{97}$ cm.

(d) $2\sqrt{97}$ cm.   (e) 16 cm.

Directions (68-72): In each question, two equations numbered (I) and (II) are given. You are required to solve both the equations and mark the appropriate answer.

(a) If $x = y$ or no relation can be established

(b) If $x > y$

(c) If $x < y$

(d) If $x \geq y$

(e) If $x \leq y$

68. I. $6x^2 + 13x + 6 = 0$ II. $2y^2 + 7y + 6 = 0$

69. I. $\frac{x}{3} + 1 = \frac{7}{15}$ II. $5(y - 2) + 18 = 0$

70. I. $4x^2 + 16x + 15 = 0$ II. $2y^2 + 5y + 3 = 0$

71. I. $12x^2 - 17x + 6 = 0$ II. $35y^2 - 29y + 6 = 0$

72. I. $x(4x - 9) = 9(16 - x)$ II. $4y^2 + 20y + 25 = 0$

73. The speed of a boat in downstream is equal to the average speed of a boy who went to his school at a speed of 10km/h. from home and returned with a speed of 15 km/hr. Find the ratio between the speed of the boat in still water to the speed of the current if the boat travels $40\frac{1}{2}$ km upstream in 4.5 hours.

(a) $9 : 1$ (b) $14 : 3$ (c) $7 : 1$

(d) $21 : 4$ (e) $15 : 2$

74. A certain amount was loaned at 8% per annum simple interest. After one year, Rs. 10,944 was returned and the remaining amount was repaid at 6% per annum at the end of the second year. If the ratio of the first-year interest to that of the second year is 28:9 then, find the amount that was lent initially.

(a) Rs. 17,400   (b) Rs. 16,800   (c) Rs. 16,600

(d) Rs. 17,200   (e) Rs. 16,400

75. 60% of the revenue of a college came from the post-graduation courses while 40% came from the graduation courses. If the college raises its fees by 30% for the post-graduation courses and by 20% for the graduation courses, then find the percentage increase in the revenues of the college.

(a) 25%   (b) 24%   (c) 28%

(d) 26%   (e) 30%

Directions (76-80): Study the bar graph below and answer the following questions.

The following bar graph gives the percentage of the number of candidates who qualified at an examination out of the total number of candidates who appeared for the examination over a period of six years from 2010 to 2015.

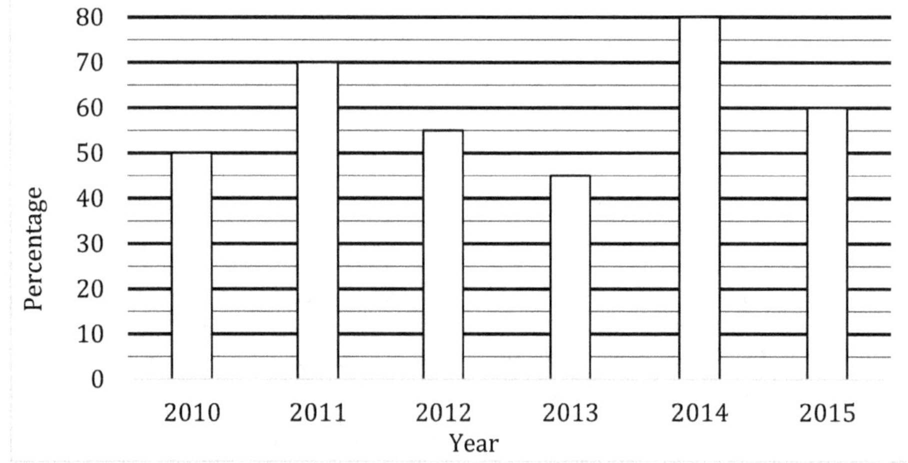

76. If the number of candidates that qualified in 2013 was 6300, then what was the number of girls who appeared in 2013, if the ratio between the number of boys to girls who appeared is 4:3?

(a) 4,500   (b) 5,400   (c) 6,000

(d) 6,300   (e) 6,600

77. If the number of candidates that appeared in the examination in 2014 and 2015 was in the ratio of 2:3, then find the ratio of qualified candidates in the year 2014 to qualified candidates in the year 2015.

(a) $8 : 9$ (b) $2 : 3$ (c) $5 : 9$

(d) $5 : 6$ (e) $10 : 9$

78. If the total number of candidates that appeared in 2010 and 2011 together was 42,400 then, find the average number of qualified candidates in these years if the ratio of qualified candidates in 2010 to that in 2011 was5:7.

(a) 11920   (b) 12420   (c) 11720

(d) 12720   (e) 12920

79. The number of qualified candidates in 2016 is 90% of the total qualified candidates in 2015, whereas the candidates that qualified in 2016 is 63% of the total number of appeared candidates in 2016. Find the ratio of appeared candidates in 2016 to that in 2015.
(a) 5:7   (b) 6:7   (c) 7:6
(d) 8:7   (e) 11:14

80. If the number of candidates not qualified in 2012 and 2014 was 8100 and 4500 respectively then find the number of candidates that qualified in 2012 as a percentage of the candidates that qualified in 2014.
(a) 58.5%   (b) 50%   (c) 66%
(d) 44%   (e) 55%

Solutions

REASONING ABILITY

Directions (1-5):
1. **(e)** I. T < Z (True)   II. U < Y (True)
2. **(a)** I. W < G (True)   II. D ≥ N (False)
3. **(a)** I. Y < O (True)   II. F > T (False)
4. **(c)** I. O < D (False)   II. X = D (False)
5. **(b)** I. P > S (False)   II. N ≥ G (True)

Directions (6-8):
6. **(d)** Southeast

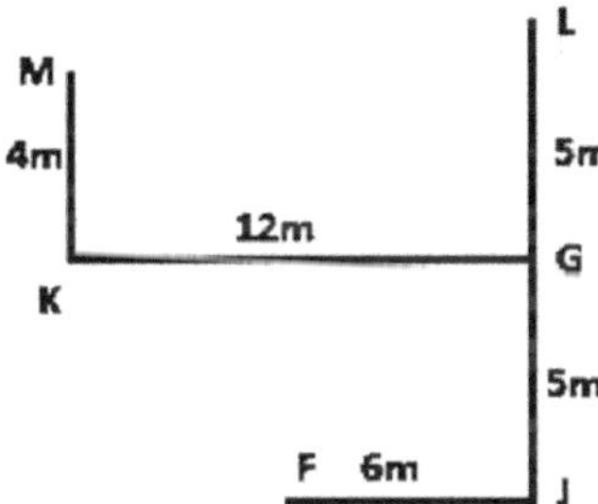

7. **(c)** Distance = $\sqrt{12^2 + 5^2}$ = 13m

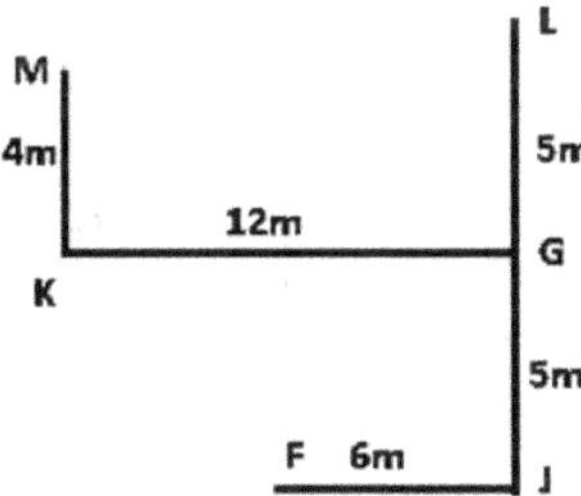

8. **(c)** Distance = 5 + 4 = 9m

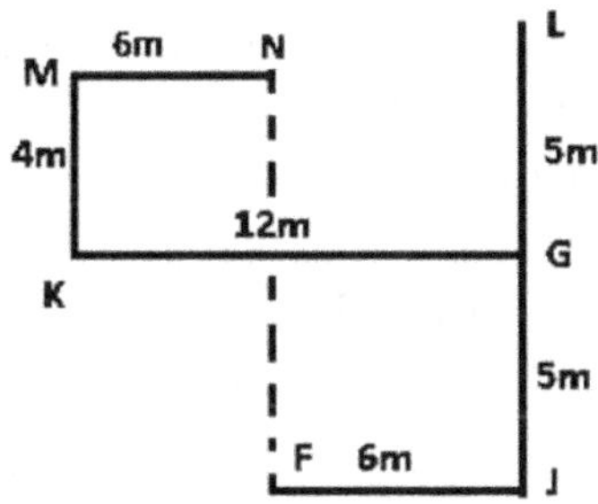

Directions (9-11):

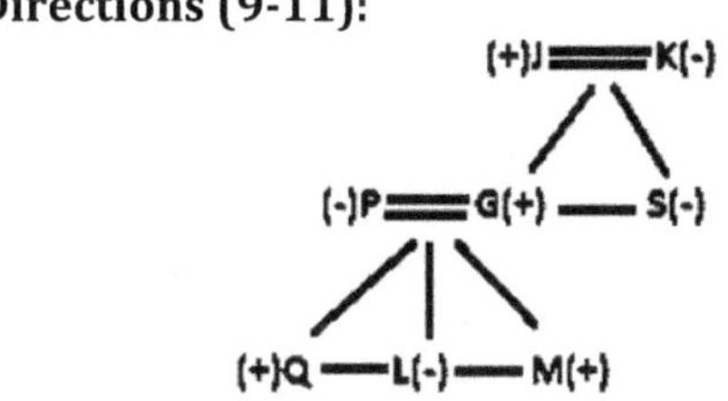

9. **(a)**   10. **(c)**   11. **(d)**

12. **(d)**

O	U	R	S	E	L	F
#	7	9	5	@	$	2

13. **(b)**

14. **(c)**   15. **(b)**

Directions (16-20): Only three people live above the floor on which A lives. Only one person lives between A and the one travelling to Bengaluru. Only three people live between the ones travelling to Bengaluru and Patna. The one travelling to Mumbai lives on an even numbered floor. F lives immediately below the one travelling to Mumbai. Only two people live between B and the one travelling to Kolkata. The one travelling to Kolkata lives below the floor on which B lives. We have two possibilities:

	Case 1			Case 2	
Floor	Person	City	Floor	Person	City
7			7		
6	B	Bengaluru	6	B	Patna
5			5		
4	A	Mumbai	4	A	Mumbai
3	F	Kolkata	3	F	Kolkata
2		Patna	2		Bengaluru
1			1		

E lives immediately above C. E is not travelling to Patna. This will eliminate Case 1. Now, the one travelling to Delhi does not live immediately above or immediately below B. D does not live immediately above or immediately below A. G does not travel to Chennai. So the final arrangement will be:

Floor	Person	City
7	D	Chennai
6	B	Patna
5	G	Lucknow
4	A	Mumbai
3	F	Kolkata
2	E	Bengaluru
1	C	Delhi

16. (e)   **17. (c)**   **18. (e)**
19. (c)   **20. (e)**

Directions (21-25): B sits third to the right of E and one of them sits at an extreme end of the row. One person sit between S and P and neither of them sits at any end. The pair who likes Badminton sits to the immediate left of B. C sits second to the right of E. S likes Cricket. D likes football and sits at one of the ends. T sits at one of the ends and does not like Football. Q does not like Football. We have three possibilities-

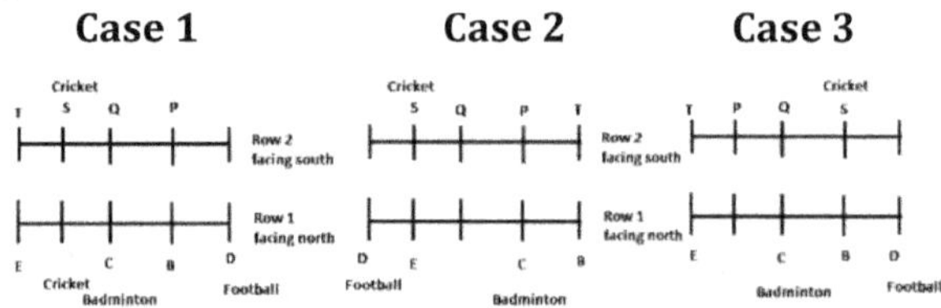

Now, Q does not face A. This will eliminate Case 2. Now, either of the pair who sits at the extreme ends does not like Hockey. The pair who likes Tennis does not sit to the immediate right of P. This will eliminate Case 3. So the final arrangement will be-

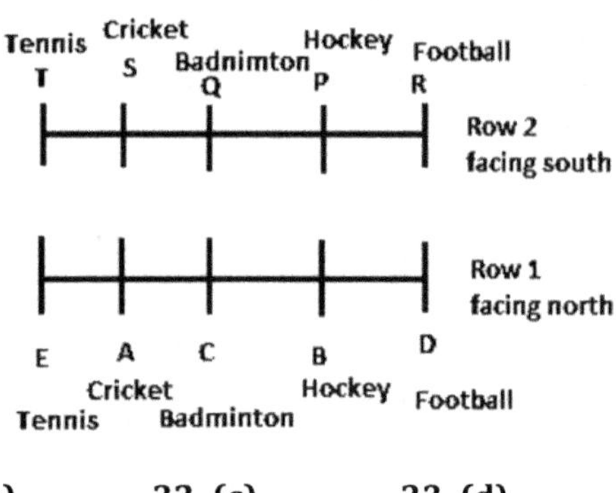

21. (b)   **22. (c)**   **23. (d)**
24. (b)   **25. (e)**

Directions (26-30): The machine rearranges one word and one number in each step. The "words" are arranged in the reverse alphabetical order as they appear in the dictionary from the left end in the last step. Such that "better" will be arranged first in step I, then "company" in step II and so on. "Numbers" are also arranged according to the words as the "numbers" are twice the number of words that appear in the input. So, "better" and "12"will be arranged first, then "company" and "14" will be arranged and so on.

Input: roast 14 cricket 16 plug 12 twilight 10 output 8

Step I: cricket roast 16 plug 12 twilight 10 output 8 14

Step II: output cricket roast 16 plug twilight 10 8 14 12

Step III: plug output cricket roast 16 twilight 10 14 12 8

Step IV: roast plug output cricket 16 twilight 14 12 8 10

Step V: twilight roast plug output cricket 14 12 8 10 16

26. (b)   **27. (a)**   **28. (c)**
29. (d)   **30. (b)**

Directions (31-35): Codes of elements are:

Codes	Elements
study	dy
rent	rt
is	si
room	rm
book	bk
high	gh
more	me
pay	yp
work/hard	wk/hd

31. (c)   **32. (c)**   **33. (d)**
34. (b)   **35. (e)**

Directions (36-40): M likes Mathematics and does not study in class X. K likes Biology. N studies in Class XI and neither likes Computer nor studies with the one who likes English. P likes Hindi and studies with O. J likes English and does not study in class XI. O does not like Sanskrit. According to the given conditions:

Person	Subject	Class
J	English	~~Class XI~~
K	Biology	
L		
M	Mathematics	~~Class X~~
N	~~Computer~~	Class XI
O		
P	Hindi	

Person	Subject	Class
J	English	Class IX
M	Mathematics	Class IX
L	Computer	Class X
K	Biology	Class X
N	Sanskrit	Class XI
O	Physics	Class XI
P	Hindi	Class XI

Now, the one who likes Sanskrit is studying with the one who likes Physics. K studies in a class only with the one who likes Computer. So the given arrangement will be-

36. (b) **37. (e)** **38. (d)**
39. (d) **40. (c)**

QUANTITATIVE APTITUDE

41. (c)

	Time	LCM
P	15 hr.	+4
Q	12 hr.	+5 → 60 (Total capacity of tank)
R	20 hr.	−3

When all three taps are opened for alternate hours:

$$\begin{array}{ccc} P & Q & R \\ +4 & +5 & -3 \end{array}$$

6 units of the tank are filled in 3 hours.

54 units of the tank = $\frac{3}{6} \times 54 = 27$ hours.

Remaining tank is filled by tap P and Q in 1$\frac{2}{5}$ hours

Required time = $27 + 1 + \frac{2}{5} = 28\frac{2}{5}$ hr.

42. (b) Total number of passed students
= 120 + 130 − 70 = 180
Number of failed students = 200 − 180 = 20
Required probability = $\frac{20}{200} = \frac{1}{10}$

43. (d) Let the CP of article be = $100x$ Rs.
SP of article = $85x$ Rs.
ATQ,
$$85x + 62.5 = 110x$$
$$25x = 62.5$$
$\Rightarrow x = 2.5$ Rs.
$\Rightarrow$ CP = 250 Rs.
Required percent = $\frac{\frac{250 \times 15}{100}}{\frac{250 \times 25}{100}} \times 100 = 60\%$

Alternative Solution
Required percent = $\frac{15}{25} \times 100 = 60\%$

44. (a) Required number = 7 × 7 × 6 × 5 × 4 = 5880

45. (e) Let the original fraction be $\frac{x}{y}$

ATQ, $\frac{3x \times \frac{120}{100}}{2y \times \frac{90}{100}} = \frac{5}{8} \times \frac{32}{25}$

$\Rightarrow \frac{3.6x}{1.8y} = \frac{4}{5} \Rightarrow \frac{x}{y} = \frac{2}{5}$

46. (a)

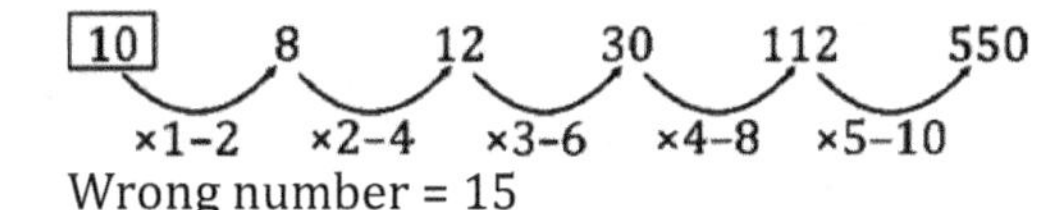

Wrong number = 15

47. (c)

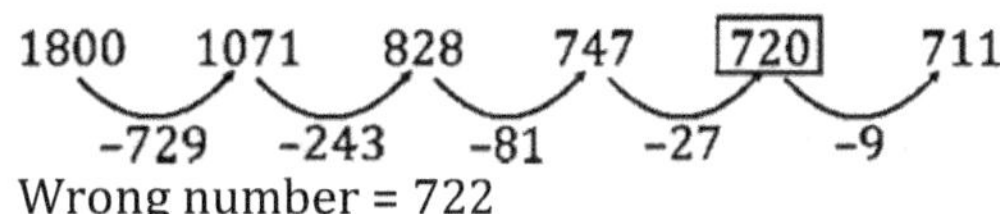

Wrong number = 722

48. (b)

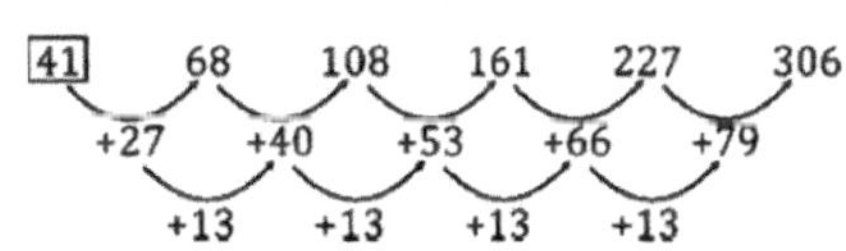

Wrong number = 35

49. (e)

216   185   156   133   114   97
−31 −29 −23 −19 −17 (prime number)
Wrong number = 92

50. (b)

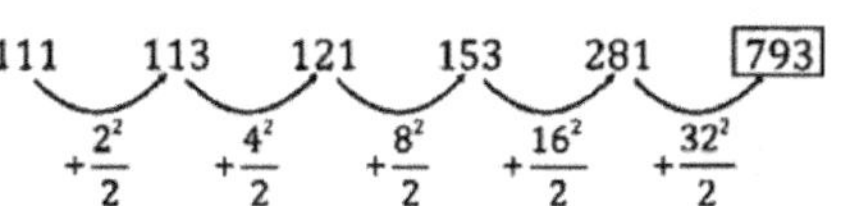

Wrong number = 785
Or

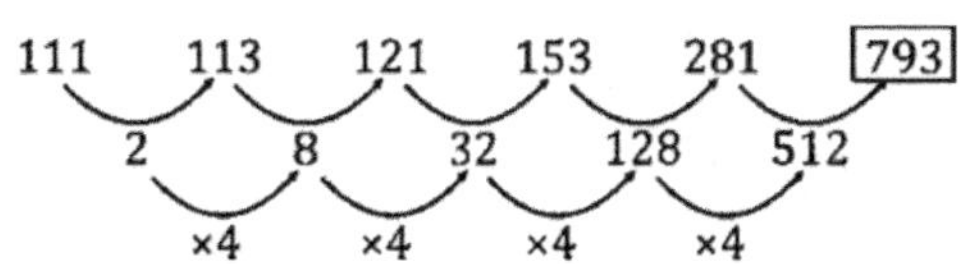

51. (b) Total number of Govt. employees in year 1995 and 2010 together
= $2,00,000 \times \frac{35}{100} + 1,10,000 \times \frac{40}{100}$
= 70,000 + 44,000 = 1,14,000
Total number of Pvt. Employees in year 2000 and 2005 together
= $1,50,000 \times \frac{28}{100} + \frac{2,20,000 \times 32}{100}$

= 42,000 + 70,400

= 1,12,400

Required ratio = $\frac{(1,14,000)}{(1,12,400)} = \frac{285}{281}$

52. (a) The number of self-employed persons in year 1990 and 2000 together

$= 1,25,000 \times \frac{30}{100} \times \frac{2}{5} + 1,50,000 \times \frac{40}{100} \times \frac{1}{2}$

$= 15,000 + 30,000$

$= 45,000$

The number of unemployed persons in year 2005 and 2010 together

$= 2,20,000 \times \frac{20}{100} \times \frac{3}{5} + 1,10,000 \times \frac{15}{100} \times \frac{7}{10}$

$= 26,400 + 11,550$

$= 37,950$

Required difference = 7,050

53. (e) Number of govt. employees in year 2015

$= \frac{50}{100} \times \left(2,00,000 \times \frac{35}{100} + 1,50,000 \times \frac{32}{100}\right)$

$= 59,000$

Total number of Pvt. Employees, self-employed and unemployed in year 2015

$= \frac{59,000}{29.5} \times 70.5$

$= 1,41,000$

Required average = $\frac{1,41,000}{3}$ = 47,000

54. (d) Total number of Pvt. Employees and self-employed in year 2000

$= 1,50,000 \times \frac{28}{100} + 1,50,000 \times \frac{40}{100} \times \frac{1}{2}$

$= 42,000 + 30,000$

$= 72,000$

Total number of self-employed and unemployed in year 2005 and 2010 together

$= 2,20,000 \times \frac{20}{100} + 1,10,000 \times \frac{15}{100}$

$= 44,000 + 16,500$

$= 60,500$

Required% = $\frac{72000-60500}{60500} \times 100 = \frac{2300}{121} \approx$ 19%

55. (c) Required Average

$= \frac{2,00,000 \times \frac{65}{100} + 1,50,000 \times \frac{72}{100} + 2,20,000 \times \frac{68}{100}}{3}$

$= \frac{1,30,000 + 1,08,000 + 1,49,600}{3}$

$= 1,29,200$

56. (b) $\left(\sqrt{121} - \sqrt{25}\right) + \frac{?}{100} \times 160 = 62$

$\Rightarrow \frac{?}{100} \times 160 = 62 - 6 = 56$

$\Rightarrow ? = \frac{56 \times 100}{160} = 35$

57. (d) $(156 - 555 \div 5) \times ? = 990$

$\Rightarrow 45 \times ? = 990$

$\Rightarrow ? = \frac{990}{45} = 22$

58. (a) $21 + ? = (120 \times 38) \div 48$

$\Rightarrow ? = 95 - 21 = 74$

59. (e) $\sqrt{(2916 \div 81) \times 17 - ?} = 24$

$\Rightarrow 612 - ? = (24)^2 = 576$

$\Rightarrow ? = 36$

60. (b) $\left(192 \times \frac{25}{100} \div 16\right) = \frac{60}{100} \times 180 - ?$

$\Rightarrow 3 = 108 - ?$

$\Rightarrow ? = 105$

61. (b) Required ratio $= \frac{8 \times \frac{36000}{100}}{36000 \times \frac{32}{100} \times \frac{4}{9}}$

$= \frac{8 \times 9}{32 \times 4} = \frac{9}{16}$

62. (a) Average number of boys studying in BSC and BCA together

$= \frac{36000\left(\frac{13}{100} \times \frac{5}{9} + \frac{21}{100} \times \frac{5}{9}\right)}{2}$

$= 3400$

Number of girls studying BBA

$= 36000 \times \frac{15}{100} \times \frac{4}{9} = 2400$

Required % $= \frac{3400-2400}{2400} \times 100$

$= 41\frac{2}{3}\%$

63. (d) Total number of boys studying in BA and B.Com together

$= \frac{36000}{100} \times \frac{5}{9} \times (11 + 8) = 200 \times 19 = 3800$

64. (b) Total number of students studying B.com and Engineering together $= 36000 \times \frac{40}{100} = 14,400$

Total number of boys studying B.com and Engineering together $= \frac{5}{9} \times 14400 = 8000.$

Required number of girls = 6400

Required difference = 1600

65. (c) Difference between number of students in Engineering and B.Com $= \frac{24}{100} \times 36000 = 8640$

Total number of students studying BBA, BSC, BA and BCA together

$= \frac{36000}{100} \times 60 = 21600$

Required % $= \frac{8640}{21600} \times 100 = 40\%$

Alternative Sol.

Required % $= \frac{(32-8)}{(21+15+13+11)} \times 100 = 40\%$

66. (b) Let the age of son be x yr.

Then, age of person = 2.5x yr.

Age of his wife $= \frac{25}{12}x.$ yr.

Person: his son: his wife = 30x : 12x : 25x

ATQ,

$\frac{30x - 10}{12x - 10} = \frac{25}{7} \Rightarrow 90x = 180$

$\Rightarrow x = 2.$

Average age of all $= \frac{30x + 12x + 25x}{3} = \frac{67}{3} \times 2 = \frac{134}{3} yr$

$= 44\frac{2}{3} yr.$

67. (d) Let height of the cone be h cm.

ATQ,

$$\frac{4}{3}\pi \times (12)^3 = 6 \times \frac{1}{3}\pi \times (8)^2 \times h$$

$\Rightarrow h = \frac{4 \times 12 \times 12 \times 12}{6 \times 8 \times 8} = 18 cm$

Slant height $= \sqrt{(18)^2 + (8)^2} = \sqrt{388} = 2\sqrt{97}$ cm.

68. (d) I. $6x^2 + 13x + 6 = 0$

$\Rightarrow 6x^2 + 9x + 4x + 6 = 0$

$\Rightarrow 3x(2x + 3) + 2(2x + 3) = 0$

$\Rightarrow x = \frac{-2}{3} \, or \, \frac{-3}{2}$

II. $2y^2 + 7y + 6 = 0$

$\Rightarrow 2y^2 + 4y + 3y + 6 = 0$

$\Rightarrow 2y(y + 2) + 3(y + 2) = 0$

$\Rightarrow (2y + 3)(y + 2) = 0$

$\Rightarrow y = \frac{-3}{2} \, or - 2$

$\therefore x \geq y$

69. (a) I. $\frac{x}{3} + 1 = \frac{7}{15}$

$\Rightarrow \frac{x}{3} = \frac{-8}{15}$

$\Rightarrow x = \frac{-8}{5}$

II. $5(y - 2) + 18 = 0$

$\Rightarrow 5y - 10 = -18$

$\Rightarrow 5y = -8$

$y = \frac{-8}{5}$

$\therefore x = y$

70. (e) I. $4x^2 + 16x + 15 = 0$

$\Rightarrow 4x^2 + 10x + 6x + 15 = 0$

$\Rightarrow 2x(2x + 5) + 3(2x + 5) = 0$

$\Rightarrow x = \frac{-5}{2} \, or \, \frac{-3}{2}$

II. $2y^2 + 5y + 3 = 0$

$\Rightarrow 2y^2 + 3y + 2y + 3 = 0$

$\Rightarrow y(2y + 3) + 1(2y + 3) = 0$

$\Rightarrow y = -1 \, or \, \frac{-3}{2}$

$y \geq x$

71. (b) $12x^2 - 17x + 6 = 0$

$\Rightarrow 12x^2 - 9x - 8x + 6 = 0$

$\Rightarrow 3x(4x - 3) - 2(4x - 3) = 0$

$\Rightarrow x = \frac{3}{4} \, or \, \frac{2}{3}$

II. $35y^2 - 29y + 6 = 0$

$\Rightarrow 35y^2 - 15y - 14y + 6 = 0$

$\Rightarrow 5y(7y - 3) - 2(7y - 3) = 0$

$\Rightarrow y = \frac{3}{7} \, or \, \frac{2}{5}$

$\therefore x > y$

72. (a) I. $x(4x - 9) = 9(16 - x)$

$\Rightarrow 4x^2 - 9x = 144 - 9x$

$\Rightarrow x^2 = \frac{144}{4}$

$\Rightarrow x = \pm 6$

II. $4y^2 + 20y + 25 = 0$

$\Rightarrow 4y^2 + 10y + 10y + 25 = 0$

$\Rightarrow 2y(2y + 5) + 5(2y + 5) = 0$

$\Rightarrow y = \frac{-5}{2}$

$\therefore$ relationship can't be established.

73. (c) Average speed of a boy $= \frac{2 \times 10 \times 15}{10 + 15} = 12 \, km/hr$

(when, distance is same for two different case. Then, average speed $= \frac{2 \times x \times y}{x + y}$)

Speed of boat in downstream = 12 km/hr.

Speed of boat in upstream $= \frac{40.5}{4.5} = 9 km/hr.$

$\therefore$ Required ratio $= \frac{\frac{12+9}{2}}{\frac{12-9}{2}} = 7 : 1$

74. (b) Let the amount be Rs. 100x

1st year interest $= \frac{100x \times 8 \times 1}{100} = 8x$

ATQ,

$$\frac{8x}{\frac{(108x - 10944) \times 6 \times 1}{100}} = \frac{28}{9}$$

$\Rightarrow \frac{8x \times 100}{(108x - 10944) \times 6} = \frac{28}{9}$

$\Rightarrow \frac{100x}{(108x - 10944)} = \frac{7}{3} \Rightarrow 456x$

$= 10944 \times 7$

$\Rightarrow x = 168$ Rs.

$\therefore$ Amount = Rs. 16,800

75. (d) Let the total revenue of the college be 100x Rs.

Revenue from post graduation course = 60x Rs.

Revenue from graduation course = 40x Rs.

New Revenue from post-graduation course

$= 60x \times \frac{130}{100} = 78x$ Rs

New revenue from graduation course

$= 40x \times \frac{120}{100} = 48x$

Total new Revenue = 78x + 48x

= 126x Rs.

$\therefore$ % increase in revenue $= \frac{(126x - 100x)}{100x} \times 100$

$= 26\%$

76. (c) Required number of girls $= \frac{6300}{45} \times 100 \times \frac{3}{7} = 6000$

77. (a) Let the number of candidates that appeared in 2014 and 2015 be $2x$ and $3x$ respectively

Required ratio $= \frac{2x \times 80}{3x \times 60} = \frac{8}{9}$

78. (d) Let the number of candidates that appeared in 2010 be x

Then, in 2011 = $42400 - x$

ATQ,

$$\frac{x \times 50}{(42400 - x) \times 70} = \frac{5}{7} \Rightarrow x = 42400 - x \Rightarrow x = 21200$$

Required average = $\dfrac{21200\left(\frac{50}{100} + \frac{70}{100}\right)}{2} = 12{,}720$

79. (b) Let the total number of candidates that appeared in 2015 and 2016 be x and y respectively

Then, number of qualified candidates in 2016

$$= \frac{90}{100} \times x \times \frac{60}{100}$$

ATQ,

$$y \times \frac{63}{100} = \frac{90}{100} \times x \times \frac{60}{100} \Rightarrow \frac{y}{x} = \frac{54}{63} = \frac{6}{7}$$

80. (e) Number of candidates qualified in 2012

$$= \frac{8100}{45} \times 55 = 9900$$

Number of candidates qualified in 2014

$$= \frac{4500}{20} \times 80 = 18{,}000$$

Required% $= \dfrac{9900}{18000} \times 100 = 55\%$

REASONING ABILITY

Directions (1-5): In each of the questions, relationships between some elements are shown in the statements. These statements are followed by conclusions numbered I and II. Read the statements and give the answer.
(a) If only conclusion I follows.
(b) If only conclusion II follows
(c) If either conclusion I or II follows.
(d) If neither conclusion I nor II follows.
(e) If both conclusions I and II follow.

1. **Statements:** $J \leq K \leq M = L$; $O \geq T \geq M < S$; $P > S$
   Conclusions: I. $M < O$ II. $L = O$

2. **Statements:** $M \leq N = P \leq Q < R$; $Q > T > V \geq W$; $Y < W$
   Conclusions: I. $N > V$ II. $R > Y$

3. **Statements:** $C \geq O \geq D = A \geq L$; $K \leq S \leq A > N$
   Conclusions: I. $S \leq C$ II. $L > N$

4. **Statements:** $F \leq E \leq D \leq X$; $Y = Z \geq X$; $Z < G$
   Conclusions: I. $G > E$ II. $F \leq Y$

5. **Statements:** $W > C > R \geq M$; $P \leq S = T \leq C$
   Conclusions: I. $S > W$ II. $P < R$

Directions (6-10): Study the information and answer the following questions:

Ten persons A, B, C, D, E, F, G, H, I and J are sitting in a row. Some are facing north and some are facing south (but not necessarily in the same manner).

(**Note:** Facing the same direction implies that if one is facing the north then the other also is also facing the north and vice versa. Facing opposite direction implies that if one is facing the north then the other is facing the south and vice versa).

Six persons sit between A and D and none of them sits at any end of the row. Both A and D faces the same direction. Two persons sit between E and D. I sits fourth to the left of E. Only one person sits between H and I. C sits to the immediate left of H. G and B are not the immediate neighbours of A. Persons sitting at the ends face opposite directions. Immediate neighbours of D face the same direction as D. Two persons sit between J and G. F faces north. G and B face the same direction as J. Immediate neighbours of E face the opposite direction. The number of person facing south is not equal to the number of persons facing north.

6. Who among the following sits to the immediate left of B?
   (a) G   (b) E
   (c) I   (d) A
   (e) None of these

7. How many persons sit between F and H?
   (a) none   (b) one
   (c) two   (d) three
   (e) More than three

8. What is the position of A with respect to F?
   (a) Third to the right
   (b) Second to the left
   (c) Immediate right
   (d) Immediate left
   (e) None of these

9. Who among the following sits at the extreme end of the row?
   (a) G   (b) B
   (c) J   (d) F
   (e) None of these

10. How many persons face south?
    (a) one   (b) two
    (c) three   (d) four
    (e) More than four

Directions (11-13): Study the following information and answer the given questions.

Point A is 15 m. to the East of point B. Point D is 18 m. to the South of Point A. Point F is 3 m. to the West of Point C. Point E is 4 m. to the North of Point F. Point C lies exactly between Point A and Point D.

11. In which direction is Point E with respect to Point B?
    (a) north
    (b) northwest
    (c) south
    (d) southeast
    (e) Cannot be determined

12. In which direction is Point A with respect to Point F?
    (a) northwest   (b) northeast
    (c) southwest   (d) southeast
    (e) None of these

13. What is the shortest distance between Point B and Point F?
    (a) 12 m.   (b) 9 m.
    (c) 15 m.   (d) 18 m.
    (e) None of these

Directions (14-17): Study the following information and answer the given questions.

In a family of nine members there are five male members. M is the son of V. V is married to J. L is the daughter-In-law of V. J has three children and two of them are married. U is the mother of B. W is the son-in-law of J. S is the aunt of B and is single. J is the grandfather of A. B doesn't have any siblings.

14. How is L related to A?
(a) mother-in-law   (b) daughter
(c) mother   (d) aunt
(e) None of these

15. How is V related to B?
(a) mother
(b) maternal Grandmother
(c) paternal Grandmother
(d) aunt
(e) Cannot be determined

16. How is A related to M?
(a) son
(b) daughter
(c) nephew
(d) niece
(e) Cannot be determined

17. How is J related to S?
(a) brother   (b) brother-in-law
(c) father   (d) father-in-law
(e) None of these

Directions (18-21): Study the following information carefully and answer the given questions.

A, B, C, D, E and F are six friends sitting around a circle, facing the centre. B sits second to the right of D. A does not face B. F does not face D. B is not an immediate neighbour of A. F does not sit to the immediate right of A. C does not sit second to the right of E.

18. Who among the following faces E?
(a) A
(b) B
(c) C
(d) D
(e) Cannot be determined

19. What is the position of C with respect to F?
(a) Immediate right
(b) Immediate left
(c) Second to the right
(d) Second to the left
(e) Third to the left

20. Who among the following sits to the immediate right of A?
(a) D
(b) F
(c) C
(d) E

(e) Cannot be determined

21. Who among the following faces C?
(a) A
(b) B
(c) D
(d) F
(e) Cannot be determined

22. How many pairs of letters are there in the word "**JOURNEY**" which have as many letters between them (backwards or forwards) in the word as in alphabetical series?
(a) one   (b) two
(c) three   (d) four
(e) None of these

23. If all the alphabets are rearranged as they appear in the English dictionary in the word "**UNDERGRADUATE**", then which of the following will be fifth to the left of the one which is twelfth from the left end?
(a) R
(b) N
(c) E
(d) G
(e) None of these

24. In a row of students facing North, Raj is 12th from the left end. Four students sit between Raj and Rohan. Rohan is sixth from the right end. What is the maximum number of students possible in the row?
(a) 12
(b) 20
(c) 22
(d) 24
(e) Cannot be determined

25. In a certain code 'GROUP' is written as '@2461' and 'PING' is written as '13$@'. How is 'POURING' written in that code?
(a) 14263$@   (b) 14632@$
(c) 14632$@   (d) 14623$@
(e) None of these

Directions (26-30): Study the following information carefully and answer the questions given below:

A word and number arrangement machine when given an input line of words and numbers rearranges them by following a particular rule in each step. The following is an illustration of input and rearrangement.

Input: gained 27 48 our 39 there cost 82 air 14
Step I: there gained 27 48 our 39 cost air 14 82
Step II: our there gained 27 39 cost air 14 82 48
Step III: gained our there 27 cost air 14 82 48 39
Step IV: cost gained our there air 14 82 48 39 27
Step V: air cost gained our there 82 48 39 27 14
Step V: is the last step of the above arrangement.

As per the rules followed in the steps given above, find out the appropriate step for the given input in each of the following questions.

Input: roast 32 59 passion 44 treasure door 79 bill 11

26. Which of the following element is fifth from the right end in Step IV?
    (a) bill (b) 11
    (c) treasure (d) 79
    (e) None of these

27. Which of the following element is fifth from the left end in step II?
    (a) passion (b) door
    (c) 32 (d) 44
    (e) None of these

28. Which of the following is Step III of the given input?
    (a) passion roast treasure door 32 bill 11 79 59 44
    (b) passion roast treasure 32 door bill 79 11 59 44
    (c) passion roast treasure 32 door bill 11 79 59 44
    (d) passion roast treasure door bill 32 11 79 59 44
    (e) None of these

29. Which element is third to the left of 'passion' in step I?
    (a) bill (b) roast
    (c) treasure (d) 32
    (e) None of these

30. Which element is seventh to the right of 'door' in step V?
    (a) 11 (b) 44
    (c) 32 (d) 59
    (e) None of these

Directions (31-35): Study the following information carefully and answer the questions given below:

Eight persons A, B, C, D, E, F, G and H were born in four different months viz. February, April, May and June of the same year. Each of them was born on either of the two dates i.e. 11th or 18th but not necessarily in the same order.

E was born in the month having least number of days. Four persons were born between C and E. G was born in the month having maximum number of days. F was born immediately before G. B was born immediately after A. H is the youngest of them all. D is not older than B.

31. B was born on which of the following days?
    (a) 18th April (b) 18th June
    (c) 11th April (d) 11th Feb
    (e) None of these

32. Who among the following is older than A?
    (a) D (b) E
    (c) C (d) Both (a) and (b)
    (e) Cannot be determined

33. How many persons were born between D and A?
    (a) one (b) two
    (c) three (d) four
    (e) None of these

34. Who among the following was born on 18th May?
    (a) C (b) G
    (c) F (d) A
    (e) Cannot be determined

35. Who among the following was born immediately after C?
    (a) A (b) H
    (c) F (d) D
    (e) Cannot be determined

Directions (36-40): Study the following information and answer the given questions.

Seven students J, K, L, M, N, O and P are preparing for three different exams viz. Banking, SSC and UPSC. At least two students are preparing for one exam. All of them speak different languages viz. English Hindi, Punjabi, Tamil, Telugu, Maithili and Bengali (but not necessarily in the same order).

M speaks Maithili and is preparing for UPSC. P who speaks Punjabi prepares only with the one who speaks Tamil. L speaks English and does not prepare for UPSC. J is preparing with the one who speaks Hindi. The one who speaks Tamil is not preparing for Banking. K is preparing for Banking and neither speaks Hindi nor Telugu. N does not speak Tamil.

36. Who among the following is preparing with P?
    (a) J (b) N
    (c) O (d) K
    (e) None of these

37. Who among the following speaks Bengali?
    (a) N (b) J
    (c) O (d) K
    (e) None of these

38. Who among the following is preparing for UPSC?
    (a) O
    (b) K
    (c) P
    (d) The one who speaks English
    (e) The one who speaks Telugu

39. Which among the following statements is true?
    (a) P is preparing for Banking

(b) L is preparing for SSC
(c) N speaks Telugu
(d) O speaks Hindi
(e) None is true

40. Who among the following speaks Hindi?

(a) The one who is preparing for Banking
(b) The one who is preparing for UPSC
(c) O
(d) K
(e) None of these

Directions (41-45): Study the following pie-chart carefully and answer the following questions.

The pie-chart given below shows the total number of passed candidates in different subjects in a class. Total number of passed students = 12000

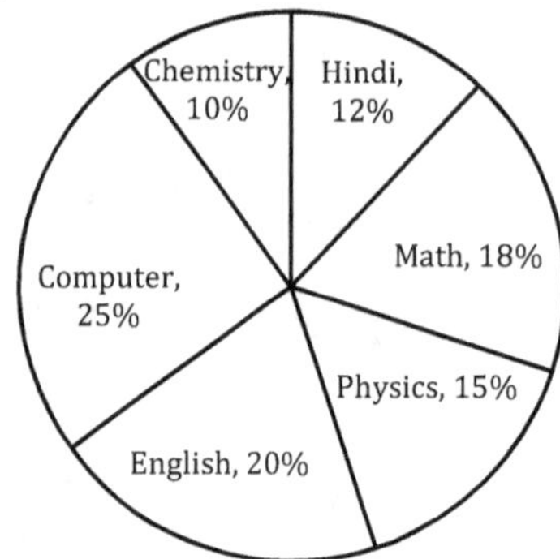

41. The number of failed students in Hindi is 25% more than the number of passed students in Hindi. Find the number of failed students in Hindi as a percentage of the number of passed students in English.
(a) 80%　(b) 75%　(c) 55%
(d) 60%　(e) 70%

42. If the total number of students who had taken the Physics exam is 4000, then find the ratio of the numbers of failed students in Physics to the number of passed students in chemistry.
(a) 11:6　(b) 13:6　(c) 11:5
(d) 3:2　(e) 2:1

43. If the total number of passed students is 25% of the total number of students in the class, then the total number of failed students is how much more/less than the total number of passed students in computer, Math and Hindi together?
(a) 28,800　(b) 27,400　(c) 26,200
(d) 29,400　(e) 29,600

44. The total number of passed students in English and physics together is what per cent more/less than the total number of passed students in chemistry and Hindi together?
(a) $57\frac{1}{11}\%$　(b) $59\frac{1}{11}\%$　(c) $51\frac{2}{3}\%$
(d) $43\frac{2}{5}\%$　(e) $47\frac{1}{9}\%$

45. The ratio of the total number of passed students to the total number of students in class is 2:5. The percentage distribution of failed students is same as that of the passed students in the class. Find the average number of failed students in Chemistry and English.
(a) 2200　(b) 3200　(c) 1500
(d) 1700　(e) 2700

46. Rahul has three children. The first and the second child can complete a work in 12 days and 18 days respectively. Rahul alone can complete the same work in $1\frac{7}{11}$ days. Rahul can do two times the total work done by all his sons together in the same time. In what time can his third child do the same work?
(a) 8 days　(b) 10 days　(c) 5 days
(d) 6 days　(e) 12 days

47. A book bought at Rs. P and sold at Rs. Q, earns a profit of 30%. If the value of P is decreased by 10% and the value of Q is also decreased by Rs. 44, a profit of 20% is earned. Find value of Q.
(a) Rs. 260　(b) Rs. 240　(c) Rs. 320
(d) Rs. 360　(e) Rs. 420

48. Abhi, Rahul and Rola enter into a business. Abhi received $\frac{3}{8}$th of the total profit while the remaining profit is divided equally between Rahul and Rola. If Abhi's income increases by Rs. 420, then the total profit will increase from 8% to 16%. Find the capital invested by Rola.
(a) Rs. 4250　(b) Rs. 3420　(c) Rs. 4375
(d) Rs. 3850　(e) Rs. 5235

49. If a certain sum of money at simple interest amounts to Rs. 5000 in 5 years and Rs. 5400 in 7 years at a certain rate of interest per annum, find the rate of interest at which the sum is invested.

(a) 12%   (b) 10%   (c) 3%
(d) 5%   (e) 8%

50. A fruit seller has three types of fruit in his bucket namely Mango, Orange and Papaya. The probability of selling one mango is $\frac{2}{7}$ and one orange is $\frac{1}{6}$. If the seller has a total of 46 papayas in his bucket, then find the total number of fruits in the seller's bucket.

(a) 78   (b) 84   (c) 96
(d) 80   (e) 72

Directions (51-55): What value should come in place of (?) in the following questions?

51. $(12)^3 \times (6)^4 \div 432 = ?$

(a) 5184   (b) 5060   (c) 5148
(d) 5084   (e) 5220

52. $[(165)^2 \div 75 \times 12] \div 36 = (?)^2$

(a) 13   (b) 169   (c) 21
(d) 11   (e) 21

53. $\left(2\frac{1}{3}\right) + \left(3\frac{2}{5} \times \frac{5}{4}\right) - \frac{8}{3} = ?$

(a) $\frac{37}{12}$ (b) $\frac{17}{12}$ (c) $\frac{9}{2}$
(d) $\frac{47}{12}$ (e) $\frac{2}{5}$

54. $1898 \div 73 \times 72 = (?)^2 \times 13$

(a) −256   (b) 256   (c) 12
(d) 144   (e) −16

55. $(0.81)^2 \div (0.729)^3 \times (0.9)^2 = (0.9)^{?-3}$

(a) 6   (b) 2   (c) 4
(d) 0   (e) 5

Direction (56 - 60): Read the data carefully and answer the following questions:

There are **2800** voters in three villages, i.e. **Vasantpur, Govindpur** and **Vilashpur.**
The ratio of the total voters in Vasantpur, Govindpur and Vilashpur is 27:18:25 respectively. The ratio of male voters in Vasantpur and Govindpur is 10:7 and the total number of female voters in Vasantpur is 60% more than the total female voters in Govindpur. The total male voters in Vilashpur is $42\frac{6}{7}\%$ more than the total male voters in Govindpur.

56. The total male voters in Vasantpur is what per cent more than the total female voters in Vilashpur?

(a) 50%   (b) 60%   (c) 55%
(d) 45%   (e) 40%

57. Find the average number of female voters in Vasantpur and Vilashpur.

(a) 420   (b) 440   (c) 480
(d) 640   (e) 400

58. If 65% and 60% of the total male and female voters respectively are literate in Govindpur, then the total illiterate voters in Govindpur is

what per cent less than the total female voters in Vilaspur?

(a) 33.25%   (b) 31.25%   (c) 35.25%
(d) 30.25%   (e) 29.25%

59. Find the ratio of male voters in Govindpur to female voters Vasantpur.

(a) 6 : 7   (b) 7 : 9   (c) 7 : 10
(d) 7 : 12   (e) 7 : 8

60. Find the difference between the total male voters and the total female voters in all the three villages?

(a) 400   (b) 480   (c) 440
(d) 420   (e) 500

Directions (61-65): Study the following table carefully and answer the following questions.
The table given below shows the distribution of the number of bikes sold by five different shopkeepers in the year 2016 and the ratio of two types of bikes out of the total bikes sold by each shopkeeper.

Shopkeeper	Total bikes sold	Bajaj Bike: Hero Bike
A	18%	3 : 2
B	22%	7 : 3
C	20%	5 : 9
D	15%	3 : 7
E	1250	2 : 3

61. What is the difference between the total number of Bajaj bikes sold by A and E together and the total number of Hero bikes sold by A and B together?

(a) 350   (b) 250   (c) 375
(d) 400   (e) 450

62. The number of Hero bikes sold by D is what per cent more/less than the number of Bajaj bikes sold by B?

(a) $43\frac{2}{3}\%$ (b) $31\frac{1}{9}\%$ (c) $31\frac{9}{11}\%$
(d) $41\frac{9}{11}\%$ (e) $33\frac{1}{11}\%$

63. If the total number of bikes sold by C in 2017 is increased by 20% compared with that of the previous year and the total number of bikes sold by D is also increased by 40% in 2017 as compared with that of the previous year, then find the total number of bikes sold by D in 2017 as a percentage of the total number of bikes sold by C in 2017.

(a) 72%   (b) 92.2%   (c) 87.5%
(d) 78.5%   (e) 83.5%

64. Find the ratio of the number of Bajaj bikes sold by A to the number of Hero bikes sold by C.

(a) 23:31   (b) 21:25   (c) 23:27
(d) 21:31   (e) 23:25

65. Find the total number of Bajaj bikes sold by B and Hero bikes sold by E and D together.

(a) 2045   (b) 1850   (c) 2470
(d) 2255   (e) 2350

Directions (66-70): In the given questions, two quantities are given, one as Quantity I and another as Quantity II. You have to determine the relationship between these two quantities and choose the appropriate option:

66. What is area of the rectangle.
    I. Length is 50% more than breadth.
    II. Perimeter of square is 48 cm. and breadth of rectangle is equal to side of square.
    (a) Only statement I
    (b) Only statement II
    (c) Both I and II together
    (d) Either I or II alone
    (e) Both statement together is not sufficient

67. What is the age of Rahul after 2 years.
    I. Average age of Arun and Neeraj is 24 years and ratio of age of Rahul to Arun is 2:3.
    II. Neeraj is 4 years elder than Satish and ratio of age of Satish to Rahul is 1:2
    (a) Only statement I
    (b) Only statement II
    (c) Both I and II together
    (d) Both statements together are not sufficient
    (e) Either I or II alone

68. What is the speed of a boat in still water when the upstream speed of the boat is equal to the speed of the stream?
    I. Time required to cover certain distance upstream is 24 secs.
    II. Time required to cover certain distance downstream is 8 secs.
    (a) Only statement I
    (b) Only statement II
    (c) Both I and II together
    (d) Both together are not sufficient
    (e) Either I or II

69. Find out the length of train X given that speed of train X is 20 m/sec.
    I. Train X crosses another train Y moving in the opposite direction in 6 secs and the speed of train Y is 50% more than the speed of
       train X.
    II. Length of train Y is 50% less than length of train X.
    (a) Both I and II together
    (b) Only statement I
    (c) Only statement II
    (d) Both I and II together are not sufficient
    (e) Either I or II alone

70. What is the total strength of company Adda247.
    I. Ratio of male to female employees is 1:2
    II. Total number of females is 280 and males are 50% of females.
    (a) Only I and II together
    (b) Only statement I
    (c) Only statement II
    (d) Both I and II together are not sufficient
    (e) Either I or II alone

71. Time taken to cover (A +4) kms. in upstream is three times the time taken to cover (A - 2) kms. in downstream. If the ratio of the speed of a boat in upstream to that of downstream is 1:2 and the time taken to cover (A + 6) kms. in downstream is two hours, then find the speed of the boat in still water.
    (a) 4.5 km/hr.   (b) 5.5 km/hr.   (c) 7.5 km/hr.
    (d) 4 km/hr.   (e) 6 km/hr.

72. Sandy has a vessel of capacity 16 litres full of a mixture of wine and water and the percentage of wine in this mixture is 75%. If Sandy replaced some quantities of this mixture with pure wine, then the vessel would contain only 10% of water. Quantity of water removed from the vessel is what per cent of the capacity of the vessel?
    (a) 22%   (b) 15%   (c) 25%
    (d) 18%   (e) 20%

73. A solid cone of radius 13 cms. and height 16 cms. is recast into n hemispherical bowls of outer diameter 16 cms and inner diameter 14 cms. Find n.
    (a) 14   (b) 12   (c) 10
    (d) 6   (e) 8

74. Balls numbered 1 to 120 are kept in a basket. What is the probability that the drawn ball has a number which is a multiple of 3 or 5?
    (a) $\frac{11}{15}$ (b) $\frac{4}{13}$ (c) $\frac{7}{15}$
    (d) $\frac{3}{5}$ (e) $\frac{8}{15}$

75. How many different words can be formed from the letters of the word 'EVOLUTION' such that the word always ends with a vowel?
    (a) $2 \times \lfloor 9$ (b) $\lfloor 9$ (c) $2 \times \lfloor 7$
    (d) $2 \times \lfloor 8$ (e) $\lfloor 8$

Directions (76-80): What should come in place of the question mark (?) in the following number series?

76. 8000, 3200, 1280, 512, 204.8 , ?
    (a) 80.25   (b) 81.92   (c) 86.75
    (d) 90.00   (e) 76.34

77. 33, 321, 465, 537, 573, ?, 600
    (a) 321   (b) 465   (c) 573
    (d) 537   (e) 591

78. 374, 355, 317, ?, 184, 89
    (a) 248   (b) 255   (c) 265
    (d) 278   (e) 260

79. 30, 45, 90, 225, 675, ?

(a) 1685 (b) 1791.5 (c) 2250
(d) 2362.5 (e) 2476.75

80. 3, 8, 16, 33, 57, ?

(a) 83 (b) 88 (c) 94
(d) 97 (e) 100

Solutions

REASONING ABILITY

Direction (1-5):

1. **(c)** I. M < O (False)   II. L = O (False)
2. **(b)** I. N > V (False)   II. R > Y (True)
3. **(a)** I. S ≤ C (True)   II. L > N (False)
4. **(e)** I. G > E (True)   II. F ≤ Y (True)
5. **(d)** I. S > W (False)   II. P ≤ R (False)

Directions (6-10): Six persons sit between A and D and none of them sits at either end of the row. Both A and D face the same direction. Two persons sit between E and D. I sits fourth to the left of E. Only one person sits between H and I. Immediate neighbours of D face the same direction as D. C sits to the immediate left of H. Two persons sit between J and G. G and B are not the immediate neighbours of A. We have two possibilities:

Case 1   **Case 2**

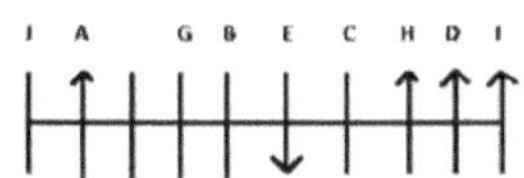

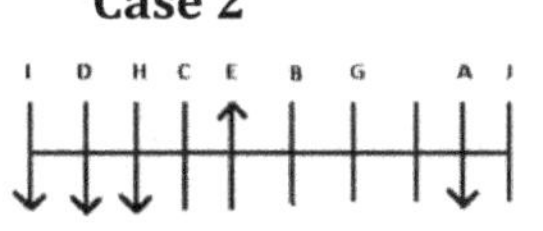

Persons sitting at the end face opposite directions. G and B face the same direction as J. F faces north. Immediate neighbours of E face opposite directions. As the number of persons facing south is not equal to the number of persons facing north, this will eliminate case 2. So the final arrangement will be-

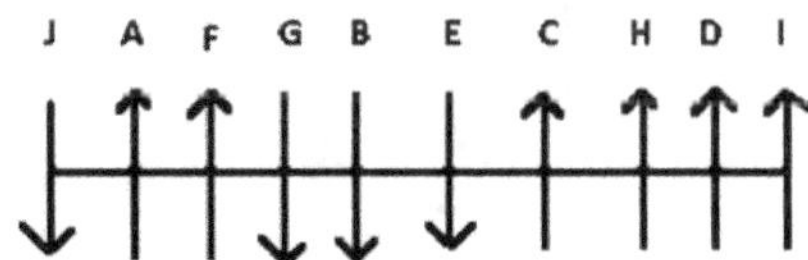

6. **(b)**   7. **(e)**   8. **(d)**
9. **(c)**   10. **(d)**

Directions (11-13):

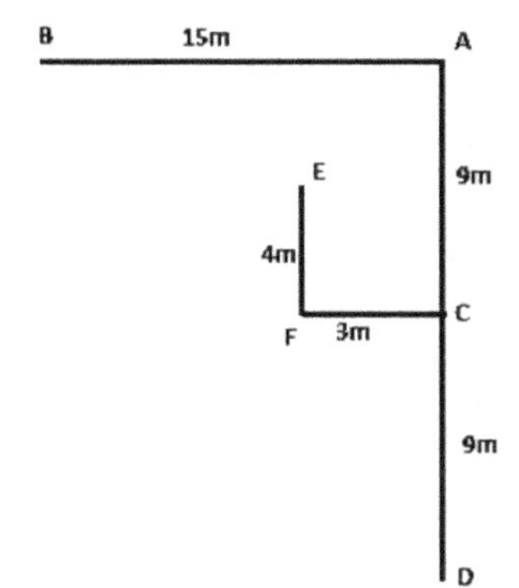

11. **(d)** southeast
12. **(b)** northeast
13. **(c)** Distance = $\sqrt{9^2 + 12^2}$ = 15m

Directions (14-17):

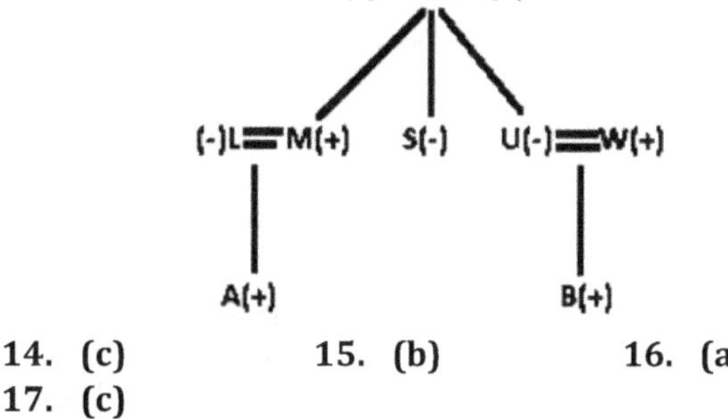

14. **(c)**   15. **(b)**   16. **(a)**
17. **(c)**

Directions (18-21): B sits second to the right of D. A does not face B. B is not an immediate neighbour of A. This will fix position of A to the second left of D. F does not face D. F does not sit to the immediate right of A. This will fix F to the immediate right of D. Now, C does not sit second to the right of E. So the final arrangement will be:

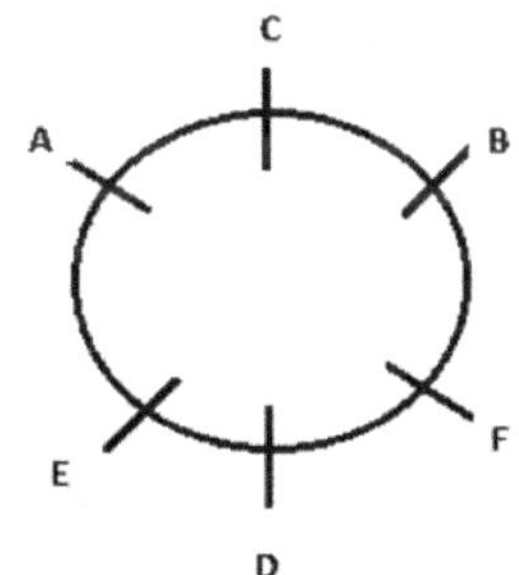

18. **(b)**   19. **(c)**   20. **(d)**
21. **(c)**
22. **(c)** Three

23. **(d)**   24. **(c)**
25. **(d)**

P	O	U	R	I	N	G
1	4	6	2	3	$	@

Directions (26-30): Let us understand the logic behind it- In each step one word and one number is arranged simultaneously, the numbers are arranged from right end and the words are arranged from the left.

For words- One word will be arranged in each step. The word which comes last according to alphabetical series is arranged first from left and then all other words are arranged in the same manner.

For numbers- The numbers are arranged in decreasing order. The highest number is arranged first on right end and then the 2nd highest is arranged at the right most end in the next step and so on.

Input: roast 32 59 passion 44 treasure door 79 bill 11

Step I: treasure roast 32 59 passion 44 door bill 11 79

Step II: roast treasure 32 passion 44 door bill 11 79 59

Step III: passion roast treasure 32 door bill 11 79 59 44

Step IV: door passion roast treasure bill 11 79 59 44 32

Step V: bill door passion roast treasure 79 59 44 32 11

26. (b)   **27. (d)**   **28. (c)**
29. (b)   **30. (c)**

Directions (31-35): E was born in the month having least number of days. Four persons were born between C and E. . H is the youngest of them all. G was born in the month having maximum number of days. F was born immediately before G. B was born immediately after A. We will have two possibilities:

	Case 1			Case 2		
Month	**11th**	**18th**	**Month**	**11th**	**18th**
Feb	E	A	Feb		E
April	B	F	April	A	B
May	G	C	May	F	G
June		H	June	C	H

Now, D is not older than B. This will eliminate case 2. So the final arrangement will be-

Month	11th	18th
Feb	E	A
April	B	F
May	G	C
June	D	H

31. (c)   **32. (b)**   **33. (d)**
34. (a)   **35. (d)**

Directions (36-40): M speaks Maithili and is preparing for UPSC. P speaks Punjabi. L speaks English and does not prepare for UPSC. K is preparing for Banking and speaks neither Hindi nor Telugu. N does not speak Tamil. We will have following conditions-

Students	Exams	Language
J		
K	Banking	~~Hindi, Telugu~~
L	~~UPSC~~	English
M	UPSC	Maithili
N		~~Tamil~~
O		
P		Punjabi

P prepares only with the one who speaks Tamil. J is preparing with the one who speaks Hindi. The one who speaks Tamil is not preparing for Banking. So the final arrangement will be:

Students	Exams	Language
J	UPSC	Telugu
K	Banking	Bengali
L	Banking	English
M	UPSC	Maithili
N	UPSC	Hindi
O	SSC	Tamil
P	SSC	Punjabi

36. (c)   **37. (d)**   **38. (e)**
39. (e)   **40. (b)**

QUANTITATIVE APTITUDE

41. (b) Passed students in Hindi

$$= \frac{12}{100} \times 12{,}000 = 1440$$

Failed student in Hindi $= 1440 \times \frac{125}{100} = 1800$

Passed student in English

$$= 12{,}000 \times \frac{20}{100} = 2400$$

Required percentage $= \frac{1800}{2400} \times 100 = 75\%$

42. (a) Total passed student in Physics $= \frac{15}{100} \times 12{,}000 = 1800$

Passed students in Chemistry $= \frac{10}{100} \times 12{,}000 = 1200$

Required Ratio $= \frac{4000-1800}{1200} = \frac{2200}{1200} = 11 : 6$

43. (d) 25% of total students = 12,000

total students = 48,000

Total failed students = 48,000 – 12,000 = 36,000

Total passed students in Computer, Math and Hindi together $= \frac{55}{100} \times 12{,}000 = 6{,}600$

Required difference = 36,000 – 6,600 = 29,400

44. (b) Required percentage $= \frac{(20+15)-(10+12)}{(10+12)} \times 100$

$= \frac{35-22}{22} \times 100 = 59\frac{1}{11}\%$

45. (e) Total failed students $= \frac{12000}{2} \times 3 = 18{,}000$

Required average $= \frac{1}{2}\left[\frac{10+20}{100}\right] \times 18{,}000 = 2{,}700$

46. (d)

Says efficiency   Work

Rahul $\rightarrow \frac{18}{11}$ 22

1st son $\rightarrow$ 12 — 3 — 36

2nd son $\rightarrow$ 18   2

Rahul's efficiency is twice more than all his son together

$\therefore$ Rahul efficiency $\rightarrow$ 22

All 3 son efficiency $\rightarrow$ 11

$\therefore$ efficiency of 3rd child = 11 – 3 – 2 = 6

$\therefore$ 3rd child can complete work alone

$= \frac{36}{6} = 6$ days

47. (a) $P \times \frac{130}{100} = Q$

$= 1.3P = Q$ ...(i)

$P \times \frac{90}{100} \times \frac{120}{100} = Q - 44$

$1.08P = Q - 44$ ...(ii)

Solving (i) and (ii)

P = 200

Q = 200 × 1.3 = Rs 260

48. (c) Let total capital be Rs 100

When

Profit = 8%

Abhi $= 8 \times \frac{3}{8} = 3 \, unit$

When profit = 16%

Abhi $= 16 \times \frac{3}{8} = 6$ unit

Difference = 3 unit $\rightarrow$ 420

1 unit $= \frac{420}{3} = Rs \, 140$

$\therefore$ Total capital = 100 × 140 = Rs 14,000

<u>Abhi</u> : <u>Rahul + Rola</u>

3 : 5

8 units = 14,000

1 unit = Rs 1750

$\therefore$ Capital invested by Rola $= \frac{1750 \times 5}{2} = Rs \, 4375$

49. (d) Let principal be Rs P

P + SI (for 5 years) = 5,000

P + SI (for 7 years) = 5,400

$\therefore$ SI for 2 years = 400

I for 1 years = Rs 200

$\therefore$ P = 5000 – 200 × 5

= Rs 4000

$\therefore$ Rate $= \frac{200 \times 100}{4000 \times 1}$

= 5%

50. (b) Let the total number of fruits the seller has in his bucket = 42x

Total number of mangoes in the bucket

$= 42x \times \frac{2}{7} = 12x$

Total number of oranges in the bucket

$= 42x \times \frac{1}{6} = 7x$

ATQ,

$12x + 7x + 46 = 42x$

$23x = 46$

$x = 2$

Total number of fruits the seller has

$= 12 \times 2 + 7 \times 2 + 46 = 84$

51. (a) $? = \frac{144 \times 12 \times 36 \times 36}{432} = 5184$

52. (d) $(?)^2 = 121$

$? = 11$

53. (d) $? = \frac{7}{3} + \frac{17}{5} \times \frac{5}{4} - \frac{8}{3}$

$= \frac{7}{3} + \frac{17}{4} - \frac{8}{3}$

$= \frac{17}{4} - \frac{1}{3}$

$= \frac{51-4}{12} = \frac{47}{12}$

54. (c) $\frac{1898}{73} \times 72 = (?)^2 \times 13$

$\Rightarrow 26 \times 72 = (?)^2 \times 13$

$\Rightarrow (?)^2 = \frac{26 \times 72}{13} = 144$

$\therefore ? = \sqrt{144} = 12$

55. (d)

$\{(0.9)^2\}^2 \div \{(0.9)^3\}^3 \times (0.9)^2 = (0.9)^{?-3}$

$\Rightarrow (0.9)^4 \div (0.9)^9 \times (0.9)^2 = (0.9)^{?-3}$

$\Rightarrow (0.9)^{4-9+2} = (0.9)^{?-3}$

$\Rightarrow ? = 3 - 3 = 0$

(56 – 60):

Total voters in Vasantpur $= 2800 \times \frac{27}{70} = 1080$

Total voters in Govindpur $= 2800 \times \frac{18}{70} = 720$

Total voters in Vilaspur $= 2800 \times \frac{25}{70} = 1000$

Let total male voters in Vasantpur and Govindpur be 10x and 7x respectively

And total female voters in Govindpur = 5y

Total female voters in Vasantpur = 8y

ATQ –

$10x + 8y = 1080$ -------------- (i)

also, $7x + 5y = 720$ ------------------------- (ii)

From (i) and (ii) we get ------

$x = 60, y = 60$

Total male voters in Vilashpur

$= 7 \times 60 \times \left(100 + \frac{300}{7}\right) \times 1/100 = 600$

	Vasantpur	Govindpur	Vilaspur
Male voters	600	420	600
Female voters	480	300	400

56. (a) Required percentage

$= \frac{600 - 400}{400} \times 100 = 50\%$

57. (b) Required average $= \frac{480+400}{2} = 440$

58. (a) Total illiterate voters in Govindpur $= 420$

$\times \frac{35}{100} + 300 \times \frac{40}{100} = 267$

Required per cent $= \frac{400-267}{400} \times 100$

$= \frac{133}{400} \times 100 = 33.25\%$

59. (e) Required ratio $= \frac{420}{480} = 7 : 8$

60. (c) Required difference $= (600 + 420 + 600)$
$-(480 + 300 + 400) = 440$

61. (a) Total bikes sold by all shopkeepers

$= \frac{1250}{25} \times 100 = 5000$

Total Bajaj bikes sold by A and E together

$= 5000 \times \frac{18}{100} \times \frac{3}{5} + 1250 \times \frac{2}{5}$

$= 540 + 500 = 1040$

Total Hero bikes sold by A and B together

$= 5000 \times \frac{18}{100} \times \frac{2}{5} + 5000 \times \frac{22}{100} \times \frac{3}{10}$

$= 360 + 330 = 690$

Required difference $= 1040 - 690 = 350$

62. (c) Required percentage

$= \frac{5000 \times \frac{22}{100} \times \frac{7}{10} - 5000 \times \frac{15}{100} \times \frac{7}{10}}{5000 \times \frac{22}{100} \times \frac{7}{10}} \times 100$

$= \frac{770-525}{770} \times 100 = \frac{24500}{770} = \frac{350}{11} = 31\frac{9}{11}\%$

63. (c) Total bikes sold by C in 2017

$= \frac{1250}{25} \times 20 \times \frac{120}{100} = 1200$

Total bikes sold by D in 2017

$= \frac{1250}{25} \times 15 \times \frac{140}{100} = 1050$

Required percentage $= \frac{1050}{1200} \times 100 = 87.5\%$

64. (b) Required ratio $= \frac{18 \times \frac{3}{5}}{20 \times \frac{9}{14}} = 21 : 25$

65. (a) Required total

$= \frac{1250}{25} \times 22 \times \frac{7}{10} + \frac{1250}{25} \times 15 \times \frac{7}{10} + 1250 \times \frac{3}{5}$

$= 770 + 525 + 750 = 2045$

66. (c) From I

Let breadth (b) be x cm

$\therefore$ length $(\ell) = \frac{150}{100} \times x = 1.5x$ cm

From II

Perimeter of square (4a) = 48 cm

$\therefore$ side of square (a) = 12 cm

$\ell = 12 \times 1.5 = 18$ cm

$\therefore$ Area of rectangle $= \ell \times b = 18 \times 12$

$= 216$ cm^2

Can be answered from I and II both

67. (c) From I

Total age of Arun and Neeraj

$= 48$ years

From II

Let age of Satish be x years

age of Neeraj = $(x + 4)$ years

age of Rahul = $2x$ years

then, age of Arun = $3x$ years

ATQ,

$\frac{3x + x + 4}{2} = 24 \, years$

$x = 11$ years

age of Rahul 2 years later $= 2 \times 11 + 2 = 24$ years

Can be answered from I and II together

68. (d) Let speed of boat in still water be x m/s

and speed of stream = y m/s

Atq,

$x - y = y \Rightarrow x = 2y$

From I and II

Let, distance be d m

$(x - y) \times 24 = (x + y) \times 8$

$24y = 24y$

$\therefore$ cannot be answered from I and II together

69. (a) Speed of train X = 20 m/sec

Let length of train X be x m

From II

length of train Y = 0.5 x m

From I

Speed of train Y = 20 × 1.5 = 30 m/sec

From I and II

$\frac{x + 0.5x}{6} = 30 + 20$

$x = 200$ m

70. (c) From II

Females = 280

Males $= 280 \times \frac{50}{100} = 140$

$\therefore$ total strength = 420

Can be answered from II only

71. (c) Let upstream speed be x km/hr and downstream speed be y km/hr

Atq,

$x = \frac{1}{2}y$ ...(i)

$\left(\frac{A+4}{x}\right) = 3\left(\frac{A-2}{y}\right)$ ...(ii)

Solving (i) and (ii)

A = 14 km

$y = \frac{14+6}{2} = 10$ km/hr

x = 5 km/hr

Speed of boat in still water $= \frac{10+5}{2} = 7.5$ km/hr

72. **(b)** Quantity of water in mixture

$= 16 \times \frac{25}{100} = 4$ litre

Quantity of water in new mixture

$= 16 \times \frac{10}{100} = 1.6$ litre

Quantity of water removed = 4 – 1.6 = 2.4 litre

Required percentage $= \frac{2.4}{16} \times 100 = 15\%$

73. **(e)** Volume of cone $= \frac{1}{3}\pi r^2 h$

$\begin{bmatrix} r \to \text{radius} \\ r \to \text{height} \end{bmatrix}$

Volume of hemispherical bowl

$= \frac{2}{3}\pi[a^3 - b^3]$ $\begin{bmatrix} a \to \text{outer radius} \\ b \to \text{inner radius} \end{bmatrix}$

Atq,

$\frac{1}{3}\pi r^2 h = n \times \frac{2}{3}\pi\left[\left(\frac{16}{2}\right)^3 - \left(\frac{14}{2}\right)^3\right]$

$\frac{1}{3}\pi(13)^2 \times 16 = \frac{2}{3}\pi[169] \times n$

$n = \frac{16}{2} = 8$

74. **(c)** Multiple of 3 in 120 balls $= \frac{120}{3} = 40$

Multiple of 5 in 120 balls $= \frac{120}{5} = 24$

Multiple of 15 in 120 balls $= \frac{120}{15} = 8$

Therefore, required no. of balls

= 40 + 24 – 8 = 56

$\therefore$ required probability $= \frac{56}{120} = \frac{7}{15}$

75. **(a)** Total words = 9

O is two times

$\therefore$ total vowels $= E, O, U, I$

Total words $= 4 \times \frac{\lfloor 9}{\lfloor 2} = 2\lfloor 9$

76. **(b)** Series is

$8000 \times \frac{2}{5} = 3200,$

$3200 \times \frac{2}{5} = 1280,$

$1280 \times \frac{2}{5} = 512,$

$512 \times \frac{2}{5} = 204.8,$

$204.8 \times \frac{2}{5} = 81.92$

So, $? = 204.8 \times \frac{2}{5} = 81.92$

77. **(e)** The pattern is-

33 + 288 = 321

321 + 144 = 465

465 + 72 = 537

537 + 36 = 573

573 + 18 = 591

591 + 9 = 600

78. **(e)** Series is

374 – 19 = 355,

355 – 38 = 317,

317 – 57 = 260,

260 – 76 = 184,

184 – 95 = 89

So,

? = 317 – 57

= 260

79. **(d)** Series is

30×1.5 = 45,

45 ×2 = 90,

90 ×2.5 = 225,

225 ×3 = 675,

675 ×3.5 = 2362.5,

So,

? = 675 × 3.5 = 2362.5

80. **(c)** Series is $3 + (2^2 + 1) = 8,$

$8 + (3^2 - 1) = 16,$

$16 + (4^2 + 1) = 33,$

$33 + (5^2 - 1) = 57,$

$57 + (6^2 + 1) = 94$

So,

$? = 57 + (6^2 + 1)$

= 57 + 37

= 94

REASONING ABILITY

Directions (1-5): Study the following information carefully and answer the given questions:

Eight friends A, B, C, D, E, F, G and H are sitting around a square table in such a way that four of them sit at the four corners of the square while the other four sit at the middle of each side. All of them have different professions viz. Athlete, Singer, Dancer, Writer, Anchor, Actor, Businessman and Banker. The ones who sit at the four corners do not face outside (they face the centre), while those who sit in the middle of the sides do not face inside.

Two persons sit between H who is a Businessman and F. The one who is a Dancer sits third to the right of F. The Singer is neither an immediate neighbour of the Businessman nor F. G sits to the immediate right of the Dancer. Two persons sit between G and C. A and D are immediate neighbours. The one who is an Actor sits opposite the one who is an Anchor. F is not an Anchor. The one who is a Writer sits to the immediate right of the Athlete. C is not an Athlete. B is a Banker and faces inside. D does not sit third to the left of the Banker.

1. Who sits exactly between B and the Businessman when counted from the right of B?
   (a) D
   (b) A
   (c) The one who is a Writer
   (d) The one who is an Actor
   (e) None of these

2. What is the position of D with respect to E?
   (a) Second to the left
   (b) Third to the right
   (c) Second to the right
   (d) Third to the left
   (e) None of these

3. Four of the following five are alike in a certain way and so form a group. Who among the following does not belong to that group?
   (a) The one who is a Writer
   (b) The one who is an Athlete
   (c) The one who is a Singer
   (d) The one who is an Actor
   (e) The one who is an Anchor

4. What is the position of A with respect to the one who is a Dancer?
   (a) Second to the left
   (b) Second to the right
   (c) Immediate right
   (d) Immediate left
   (e) None of these

5. How many persons sit between the one who is a Banker and the one who is an Athlete?
   (a) one
   (b) two
   (c) three
   (d) four
   (e) Cannot be determined

Directions (6-10): In each of the questions, relationships between some elements are shown in the statements. These statements are followed by conclusions numbered I and II. Read the statements and give the answer.
(a) If only conclusion I follows.
(b) If only conclusion II follows.
(c) If either conclusion I or II follows.
(d) If neither conclusion I nor II follows.
(e) If both conclusions I and II follow.

6. **Statements:** $P \geq F \geq O; J \leq K = F; Y \geq K$
   Conclusions: I. $J \leq P$ II. $Y \geq O$

7. **Statements:** $D \geq E = F \geq O; G \leq H < F; T < O$
   Conclusions: I. $T < F$ II. $H > D$

8. **Statements:** $A \leq B \leq C = D; E = F \geq G \geq D; H > F$
   Conclusions: I. $F > A$ II. $E = A$

9. **Statements:** $Z < Y = X \leq W; U \geq V > W \leq S < T$
   Conclusions: I. $V < Z$ II. $T > Y$

10. **Statements:** $L \leq N = O < P; J \geq B > P < Q; K > J$
    Conclusions: I. $K < L$ II. $Q < K$

Directions (11-13): Study the following information and answer the given questions:

Point Y is 12m. to the North of Point X. Point Z is 8m. to the East of Point W. Point M is 3m. to the South of Point W. Point M is 4m. to the West of Point N. Point Z lies exactly between Point X and Point Y.

11. In which direction is Point X with respect to Point N?
    (a) north   (b) northeast
    (c) south   (d) southwest
    (e) None of these

12. If Point V lies 6m. to the North of Point W then how far is Point V from Point Y?

(a) 6m.   (b) 8m.
(c) 10m.   (d) 12m.
(e) Cannot be determined

13. What is the shortest distance between Point Z and Point N?
(a) 3m.   (b) 4m.
(c) 5m.   (d) 6m.
(e) None of these

Directions (14-16): Study the following information and answer the given questions:

In a family of nine members, there are five male members. P is the father of M. M is married to N. N is the father of J. J is the brother of O. R is the mother of T. T is married to S. S is the daughter-in-law of P. K is the grandson of P and has no siblings.

14. How is N related to R?
(a) son   (b) son-in-law
(c) nephew   (d) grandson
(e) None of these

15. How is O related to S?
(a) nephew   (b) son
(c) daughter   (d) niece
(e) Either (a) or (d)

16. How is T related to M?
(a) son   (b) husband
(c) brother   (d) brother-in-law
(e) Cannot be determined

17. How many pairs of letters are there in the word "**CONNECT**" which have as many letters between them (backwards or forwards) in the word as in the alphabetical series?
(a) one   (b) two
(c) three   (d) four
(e) None of these

18. If all the alphabets are rearranged within itself as they appear in the English dictionary in the word "**POSTGRADUATE**" then which of the following will be third to the right of the one which is ninth from the right end?
(a) A   (b) O
(c) P   (d) R
(e) None of these

19. In a row of students facing North, Sam is 15th from the right end. Fourteen students sit between Raj and Sam. What is the minimum number of students possible in the row?
(a) 15   (b) 20
(c) 25   (d) 30
(e) Cannot be determined

20. In a certain code 'OFTEN' is written as '7@2$5' and 'MORE' is written as '37#$'. How is 'MENTOR' written in that code?

(a) 3$572#   (b) 35$27#
(c) 3$257#   (d) 3$527#
(e) None of these

Directions (21-25): Study the following information carefully to answer the given questions:

Eight different lectures viz. History, Geography, Mathematics, Physics, Chemistry, English, Hindi and Biology are to be organized on four different days of the week viz. Monday, Tuesday, Friday and Saturday, starting from Monday in two sessions i.e. Morning and Evening (but not necessarily in the same order).

The lecture of languages was organized on Friday. Geography was organized in the morning session but not on Monday. One lecture was organized between Physics and Geography. No lecture was organized after Chemistry. Mathematics was not organized immediately after English. History was organized on Tuesday. Mathematics and Chemistry were not organized on the same day.

21. Which of the following subjects was organized in the morning session of Friday?
(a) Mathematics
(b) English
(c) Hindi
(d) Either (b) or (c)
(e) None of these

22. How many lectures were organized between Biology and Hindi?
(a) two   (b) three
(c) four   (d) five
(e) Cannot be determined

23. Physics was organized on which among the following days and sessions?
(a) Tuesday—Morning Session
(b) Monday—Evening Session
(c) Saturday—Morning Session
(d) Monday—Morning Session
(e) Saturday—Evening Session

24. Which among the following lectures was organized immediately before Chemistry?
(a) Mathematics
(b) Hindi
(c) Biology
(d) Physics
(e) Cannot be determined

25. Biology was organized on?
(a) Monday —Morning Session
(b) Saturday —Morning Session
(c) Tuesday —Evening Session
(d) Tuesday —Morning Session
(e) Monday —Evening Session

Directions (26-30): In each question below are given four statements followed by two conclusions which are numbered as I and II. You have to take the given statements to be true even if they seem to be at variance with commonly known facts. Read all the conclusions and then decide which of the given conclusions logically follows from the given statements, disregarding commonly known facts.

Mark your answer as:

(a) If only conclusion I follows.

(b) If only conclusion II follows.

(c) If either conclusion I or conclusion II follows.

(d) If neither conclusion I nor conclusion II follows.

(e) If both conclusion I and conclusion II follow.

26. **Statements:** Some H is P.
    No H is L.
    Some L is T.
    All T is S.
    Conclusions: I. Some S is not H.
    II. Some P is T.

27. **Statements:** All O is M.
    All M is N.
    Some N is S.
    No S is W.
    Conclusions: I. Some O can be S.
    II. Some N can be W.

28. **Statements:** No K is R.
    All R is Z.
    Some Z is Y.
    No Y is X.
    Conclusions: I. Some X is not R.
    II. Some Z is not K.

29. **Statements:** Some B is D.
    All D is F.
    Some F is not J.
    All J is C.
    Conclusions: I. Some J is not B.
    II. Some B is J.

30. **Statements:** All F is E.
    Some C is not E.
    Some G is F.
    All H is G.
    Conclusions: I. Some H can never be E.
    II. Some G is E.

Directions (31-35): Study the following information carefully and answer the questions given below:

A word and number arrangement machine when given an input line of words and numbers rearranges the words and numbersfollowing a particular rule in each step. The following is an illustration of input and rearrangement.

Input: season 27 often 42 perfect 12 enjoy 55 help 39

Step I: enjoy season 27 often perfect 12 55 help 39 42

Step II: often enjoy season 27 perfect 55 help 39 42 12

Step III: help often enjoy season 27 perfect 39 42 12 55

Step IV: perfect help often enjoy season 27 42 12 55 39

Step V: season perfect help often enjoy 42 12 55 39 27

Step V is the last step of the above arrangement.

As per the rules followed in the steps given above, find out in each of the following questions the appropriate step for the given input.

Input: courage 22 old 29 basket 54 enter 33 rescue 61

31. Which of the following elements is eighth from the left end in Step III?
    (a) enter   (b) rescue   (c) 54
    (d) 61   (e) 22

32. Which of the following is Step II of the given input?
    (a) old enter courage 29 basket 33 rescue 61 54 22
    (b) old enter courage basket 29 33 rescue 61 54 22
    (c) old enter courage 29 basket 33 rescue 54 61 22
    (d) old enter courage 29 basket rescue 33 61 54 22
    (e) None of these

33. Which element is sixth to the right of 'courage' in step V?
    (a) 54   (b) 22
    (c) 61   (d) 33
    (e) None of these

34. Which element is fifth to the left of 'rescue' in step I?
    (a) courage   (b) old
    (c) 29   (d) 22
    (e) None of these

35. Which of the following elements is seventh from the right end in step IV?
    (a) old   (b) enter
    (c) rescue   (d) 54
    (e) None of these

Directions (36-40): Study the following information carefully and answer the questions given below:

In a certain code language

'iron rusting black' is coded as 'ru ku bu'

'black is brown' is coded as 'ni bu su'

'rusting colour brown ' is coded as 'lu ni ru'

'red colour iron suit' is coded as 'dr st ku lu'

36. What is the code for 'red rusting'?
    (a) ru ni
    (b) dr ru

(c) st ru

(d) Cannot be determined

(e) Either (b) or (c)

37. What is the code for 'iron'?

(a) bu   (b) su

(c) ku   (d) lu

(e) None of these

38. 'ni' is denoted as?

(a) is   (b) rusting

(c) black   (d) brown

(e) None of these

39. What is the code for 'iron suit'?

(a) ku dr

(b) ku st

(c) dr st

(d) Either (a) or (b)

(e) Cannot be determined

40. If 'white suit' is coded as 'st wr', then 'red dawn' can be coded as?

(a) bu dr   (b) dr su   (c) dw dr

(d) ru dr   (e) dr lu

QUANTITATIVE APTITUDE

Directions (41-46): Theline graph shows the quantity of five different products purchased by a person.

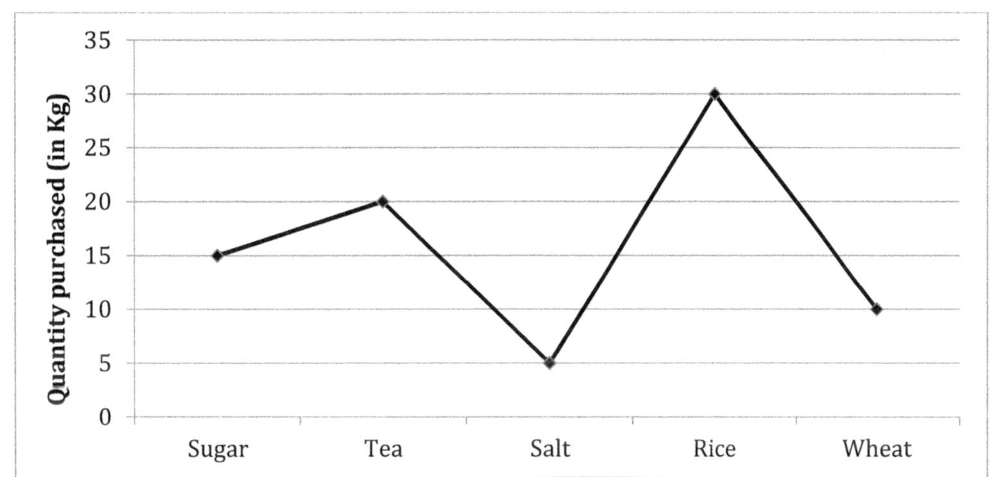

41. If sum of per kg. cost of sugar and that of salt is Rs.90 and the ratio between per kg. cost of sugar and that of salt is 3:2, then, find the difference betweenthe total cost of sugar and the total cost of salt.

(a) Rs. 530   (b) Rs. 630   (c) Rs. 670

(d) Rs. 750   (e) Rs. 720

42. The total cost of Tea is Rs. 5000 and that of wheat is Rs. 450. Findthe cost per kg. of wheat as a percentage more or less than the cost per kg. of Tea?

(a) 72%   (b) 86%   (c) 82%

(d) 78%   (e) 92%

43. One kg. of rice and one kg. of sugar is purchased forRs. 450. If the cost per kg. of rice decreases by $33\frac{1}{3}\%$ andthe cost per kg. of sugar increases by $33\frac{1}{3}\%$, then the total cost per kg. of rice and sugar will becomeRs. 500. Find the per kg. cost of sugar.

(a) Rs. 300   (b) Rs. 350   (c) Rs. 200

(d) Rs. 250   (e) Rs. 450

44. If the cost per kg. of tea and the cost per kg. of rice is Rs. 220 and Rs. 50 respectively, then find the ratio of total cost of tea to total cost of rice.

(a) 53 : 15   (b) 44 : 17   (c) 41 : 17

(d) 47 : 15   (e) 44 : 15

45. Total quantity of sugar and salt purchased together is what percent more/less than the total quantity of tea and wheat purchased together?

(a) $48\frac{2}{3}\%$ (b) $37\frac{1}{3}\%$ (c) $66\frac{2}{3}\%$

(d) $33\frac{1}{3}\%$ (e) $42\frac{2}{3}\%$

46. If the cost per kg. of sugar, salt and rice is Rs. 10, Rs. 30 and Rs. 20 respectively, then find the sum of the difference between thetotal cost of sugar and salt and the difference in thetotal cost of sugar and rice.

(a) Rs. 500   (b) Rs. 475   (c) Rs. 400

(d) Rs. 450   (e) Rs. 435

47. Abhi does a work for four days and leaves; the remaining work is completed by Satish in 18 days. If Abhi does that work for 6 days, then the remaining work will be completed by Satish in 12 days. Find in how many days Abhi alone can complete the whole work.
(a) 10 days　　　　(b) 12 days
(c) 16 days　　　　(d) 20 days
(e) 24 days

48. If a train crosses a tunnel which is half of its length with a speed of 144 km/hr. in ½ min, then find the time in which it will cross another train which is double its length and stands ata platform in the opposite direction, with 60% of its initial speed?
(a) 120 sec.　　(b) 90 sec.　　(c) 150 sec.
(d) 100 sec.　　(e) 180 sec.

49. Arun sells his watch at a profit of $33\frac{1}{3}\%$ and his purse at a loss of $16\frac{2}{3}\%$, but on the whole he gains Rs. 50. If he sells his watch at a loss of $16\frac{2}{3}\%$, purse at a profit of $33\frac{1}{3}\%$, then there will be no profit and no loss. Find the cost price of the watch.
(a) Rs. 300　　(b) Rs. 100　　(c) Rs. 250
(d) Rs. 200　　(e) Rs. 150

50. Neeraj spent 22% of his monthly salary on food and 20% of the remaining monthly salary in F.D. If his savings is Rs. 3120, then find the expenses made by Neeraj on food ?
(a) Rs. 1150　　(b) Rs. 900　　(c) Rs. 1000
(d) Rs. 1100　　(e) Rs. 1200

Direction (51-55): Study the given passage carefully to answer the following questions:

In a sports Academy 'XY', there are some students who can play three games i.e. tennis, cricket and chess. The total number of players who play tennis is 160. All three games are played by 10% of the total tennis players. The ratio of cricket to chess players is 3:5 and the total of cricket and chess players is 100% more than tennis players. The players who play both tennis and chess are $12\frac{1}{2}\%$ of the total tennis players. The ratio of players who play both tennis and cricket to players who play both chess and cricket is 2:3, while the total of players who play both tennis and cricket and players who play both chess and cricket is equal to one-fourth of the chess players.

51. What is the average no. of players who play only one game?
(a) $139\frac{2}{3}$　　　　(b) $129\frac{1}{3}$
(c) 135　　　　(d) None of these
(e) $129\frac{2}{3}$

52. Players who play chess, but not cricket is approximately what percent of the total players?
(a) 35%　　　　(b) 45%
(c) None of these　　(d) 40%
(e) 50%

53. What is the ratio of players who play both tennis and chess to players who play only cricket?
(a) 7 : 13　　　　(b) 9 : 41
(c) 10 : 43　　　　(d) None of these
(e) 2 : 5

54. The players who play at least two games is approximately what percent of players who play utmost two games?
(a) 4%　　(b) 6%　　(c) 15%
(d) 12%　　(e) 9%

55. What is the difference between the number of players who can play tennis andthe players who play only cricket?
(a) 74　　　　(b) 64
(c) 68　　　　(d) None of these
(e) 72

Directions (56-61): Study the table carefully and answer the following questions:The table given below shows the total number of students in five different classes in which some students take part in drama and some in painting, while some students do not take part in any event.

Class	Total number of students	Number of students who o not take part	Ratio of number of students who take part in (Drama: Painting)
6th	320	103	3:4
7th	480	220	5:8
8th	240	105	2:1
9th	510	210	3:2
10th	250	120	8:5

56. What is the difference between the number of students who participate in Drama from class 7th and 8th together and the number of students who participate in painting from class 9th and 10th together ?
(a) 20　　　　(b) 30　　　　(c) 35
(d) 25　　　　(e) 40

57. The total number of students who do not take part from class 7thand 10th together is what percent more or less than the total number of students who take part in painting from class 6thand 7th together?(approx.)
(a) 15%　　　　(b) 30%　　　　(c) 20%
(d) 40%　　　　(e) 25%

58. What is the average of total number of students who take part in drama from class 6th, 8th and 9th?
(a) 169　　　　(b) 121　　　　(c) 127
(d) 138　　　　(e) 148

59. What is the ratio of total number of students who take part in Drama from class 8th and 9th together to the total students who take part in painting from class 6th and 10th together ?
(a) 8 : 5   (b) 5 : 3   (c) 127 : 87
(d) 133 : 87   (e) 45 : 29

60. If the number of students who do not take part in any activity from class 9th is increased by 50% then the number of students taking part in Drama is decreased by what percent if the ratio(Drama : Painting) remains the same?
(a) 40%   (b) 45%   (c) 35%
(d) 30%   (e) 55%

61. Find the sum of the number of students taking part in painting from class 7th, in Drama from class 9th and 10th together.
(a) 540   (b) 320   (c) 360
(d) 420   (e) 480

Directions (62-67): What should come in place of the question mark (?) in the following series?

62. ?, 13.5, 27, 9, 36, 7.2
(a) None of these   (b) 7.25   (c) 10
(d) 13.5   (e) 8.5

63. 102, 114 , 129 , 153 , 204, ?
(a) 292   (b) 282   (c) 309
(d) 2275   (e) 336

64. 813, ? , 818, 782, 998, –298
(a) 812
(b) 810
(c) None of these
(d) 816
(e) 814

65. 12 , 129 , 242 , 346 , 434, ?
(a) None of these   (b) 497
(c) 517   (d) 493
(e) 513

66. 48 , 216 , 756 , 1890, ? , 1417.5
(a) 2345   (b) 2735
(c) None of these   (d) 2745
(e) 2835

67. 9, 5, 7, 22, 120, ?
(a) 1100   (b) 1088   (c) 890
(d) 1050   (e) 1000

68. A fraction when subtracted from its reverse gives $\frac{7}{12}$ as a result and when added with the reverse gives $\frac{25}{12}$ as a result. Find the fraction.
(a) $\frac{4}{3}$ (b) $\frac{3}{4}$ (c) $\frac{5}{6}$
(d) $\frac{3}{7}$ (e) $\frac{1}{2}$

69. Mona and Sunny together can complete a work in 18 days whereas Sunny and Bhavya together can complete the same work in 15 days. If Bhavya is 50% more efficient than Mona then find the time taken by Mona alone to complete the whole work.
(a) 36 days   (b) 42 days
(c) 45 days   (d) 24 days
(e) 48 days

70. A boat can cover an equal distance upstream and downstream in 6 hours. If the speed of the boat in still water is 200% more than the speed of the stream, then find the time taken to cover the same distance upstream.
(a) 5 hours   (b) 3 hours   (c) 4.5 hours
(d) 3.5 hours   (e) 4 hours

71. A rectangular sheet is folded along its length to make a right circular cylinder. If the ratio between magnitude of area of the rectangular sheet to the magnitude of volume of the cylinder is 1:7, then find the radius of the cylinder.
(a) 7   (b) 3.5   (c) 10.5
(d) 21   (e) 14

72. Prabhat invested Rs. 15600 on S.I. at rate of R% p.a. for 3 years, and the interest obtained is Rs. 7020. If he invested the same amount at rate of (R+5)% p.a. for two years on C.I., then find the interest obtained by Prabhat.
(a) Rs. 6864   (b) Rs. 6250
(c) Rs. 6748   (d) Rs. 6468
(e) Rs. 6648

73. The average age of father, mother and their two sons is 41 years. Five years ago, the ratio of ages of father, mother and the two sons (elder and younger) was 7:4:3:2. Find the sum of ages of their two sons after six years.
(a) 59 years.   (b) 62 years   (c) 57 years
(d) 47 years   (e) 67 years

74. A bag contains four red, five yellow and six green balls. Three balls are drawn randomly. What is the probability that the balls drawn contain no yellow ball?
(a) $\frac{24}{91}$
(b) $\frac{33}{91}$
(c) $\frac{12}{65}$
(d) Data inadequate
(e) None of these

Directions (75-80): What should come in place of the question mark (?) in the following questions. Find the approximate value?

75. $6561.01 \div (8.98 \times 3.01) \div 2.98 = ?$
(a) 27   (b) 54   (c) 72
(d) 81   (e) 78

76. $7364.99 + (5.01)^2 + \sqrt{?} = 7433.11$
(a) 1894   (b) 1681   (c) 1764
(d) 2025   (e) 1849

77. $127.001 \times 7.998 + 6.05 \times 4.001 = ?$

(a) 1440   (b) 1400   (c) 1000
(d) 1040   (e) 1140

78. $(215.9\% \ of \ 999.8 \div 9.99)^{1/3} + (42.01\% \ of \ 599.97) = ?$

(a) 252   (b) 258   (c) 268
(d) 278   (e) 248

79. $39.05 \times 14.95 - 27.99 \times 10.12 = (36.01 + ?) \times 4.98$

(a) 20   (b) 30   (c) 40
(d) 35   (e) 25

80. $335.01 \times 244.99 \div 35.001 = ?$

(a) 2345   (b) 2350   (c) 2320
(d) 2410   (e) 2335

Solutions

REASONING ABILITY

Directions (1-5):

The one who is a Dancer sits third to the right of F. Two persons sit between H who is a Businessman and F. Singer is neither an immediate neighbour of Businessman nor F. G sits to the immediate right of the Dancer. Two persons sit between G and C. The one who is an Actor sits opposite the one who is an Anchor. F is not an Anchor. B is a Banker and faces inside. A and D are immediate neighbours. D does not sit third to the left of the Banker. We have two possibilities:

Case 1

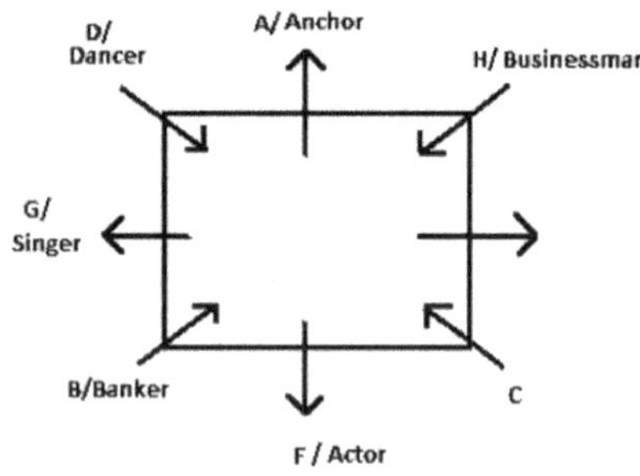

Case 2

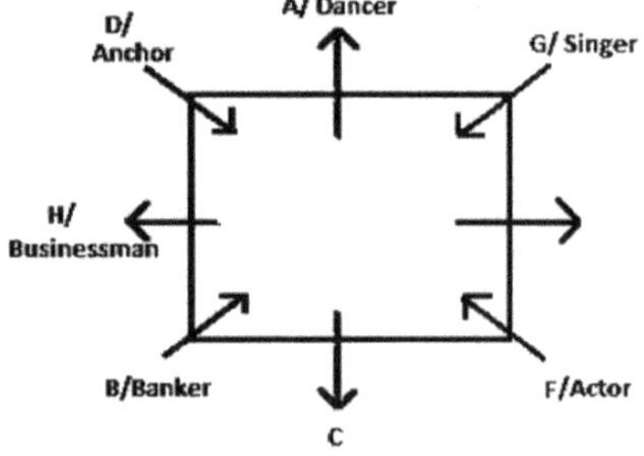

The one who is a Writer sits to the immediate right of the Athlete. C is not an Athlete. This will eliminate Case 2. So the final arrangement will be:

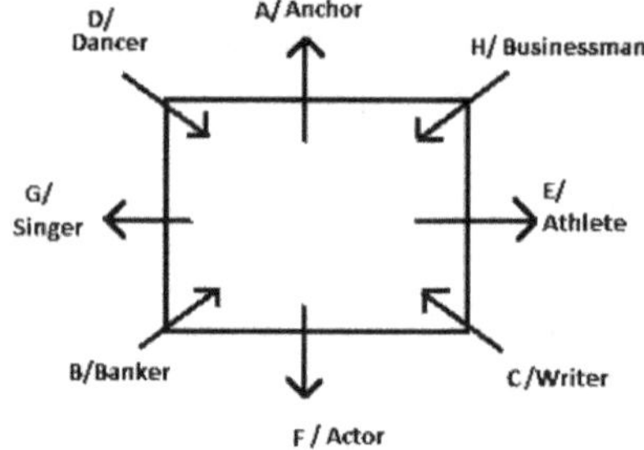

1. **(c)**   2. **(d)**   3. **(a)**
4. **(d)**   5. **(e)**

Directions (6-10):

6. **(e)** I. $J \leq P$ (True)   II. $Y \geq O$ (True)
7. **(a)** I. $T < F$ (True)   II. $H > D$ (False)
8. **(c)** I. $F > A$ (False)   II. $E = A$ (False)
9. **(b)** I. $V < Z$ (False)   II. $T > Y$ (True)
10. **(d)** I. $K < L$ (False)   II. $Q < K$ (False)

Directions (11-13):

11. **(e)** Southeast

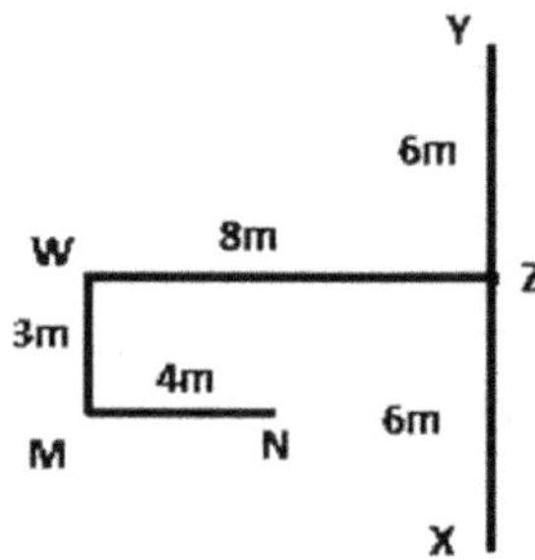

12. **(b)** 8m

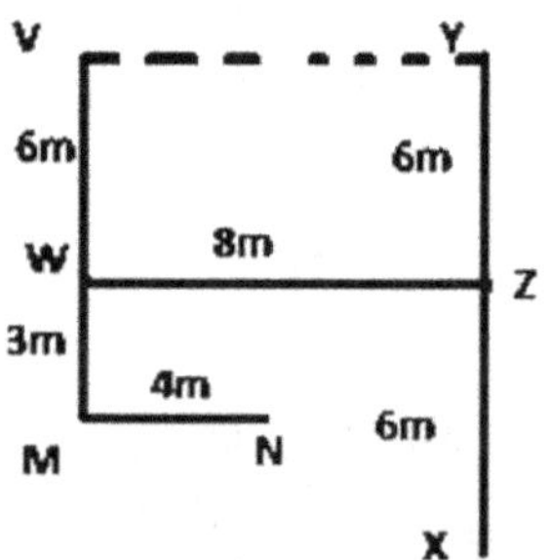

13. (c) Distance = $\sqrt{3^2 + 4^2}$ = 5m

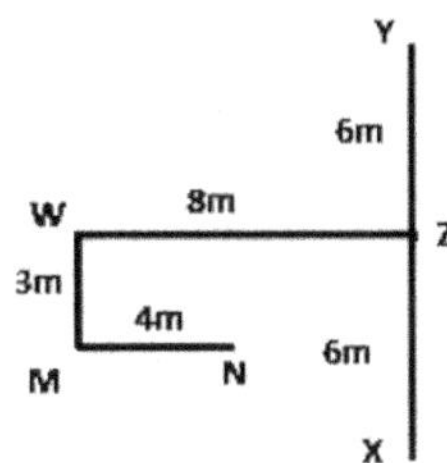

Directions (14-16):

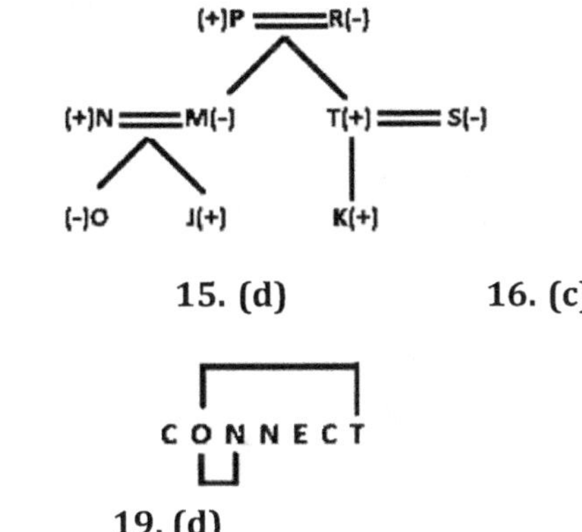

14. (b)   **15. (d)**   **16. (c)**

17. (b)

18. (c)   **19. (d)**

20. (d)

M	E	N	T	O	R
3	$	5	2	7	#

Directions (21-25):
The lecture of languages was organized on Friday. No lecture was organized after Chemistry. Geography was organized in the morning session but not on Monday. One lecture was organized between Physics and Geography. History was organized on Tuesday. We will have two possibilities:

Case 1

Days	Morning Session	Evening Session
Monday	Physics	
Tuesday	Geography	History
Friday	English	Hindi
Saturday		Chemistry

Case 2

Days	Morning Session	Evening Session
Monday	Physics	
Tuesday	Geography	History
Friday	Hindi	English
Saturday		Chemistry

Mathematics was not organized immediately after English. Mathematics and Chemistry was not organized on the same day. This will eliminate Case 2. So the final arrangement will be:

Days	Morning Session	Evening Session
Monday	Physics	Biology
Tuesday	Geography	History
Friday	English	Hindi
Saturday	Mathematics	Chemistry

21. (b)   **22. (b)**   **23. (d)**
24. (a)   **25. (e)**
Directions (26-30):
26. (a)

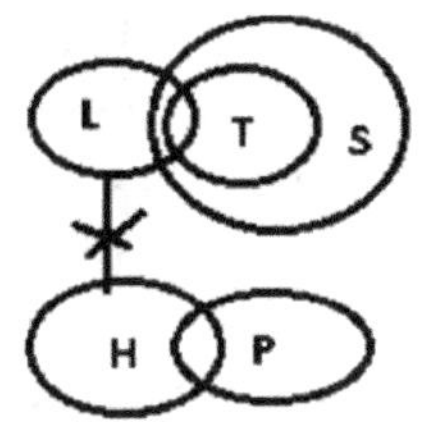

For I – From Venn diagram it is clear that all L which are S cannot be H. Hence, Conclusion I will be true.
For II – As there is no direct relation between P and T, Conclusion II will not hold true.

27. (c)

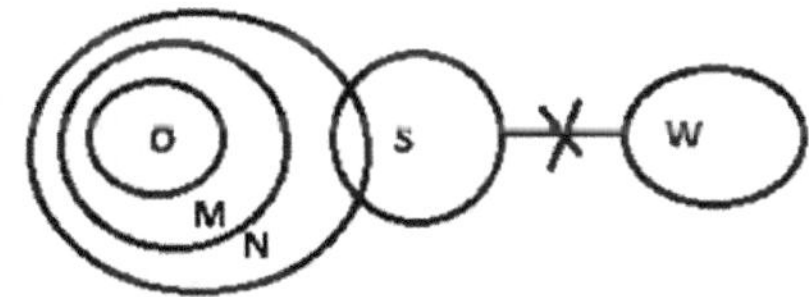

For I – There is no direct relation between O and S, therefore possibility case will hold true. Hence, Conclusion I can be concluded.
For II – Asthere is no direct relation between N and W, possibility case will hold true. Hence, Conclusion II can be concluded.

28. (b)

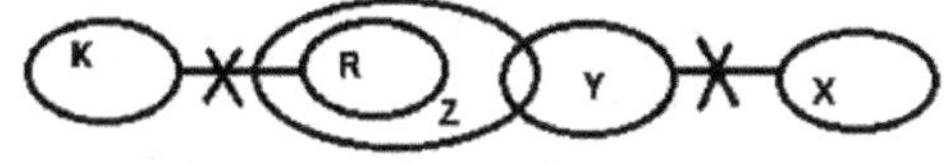

For I –Asthere is no direct relation between X and R, conclusion I will not hold true.
For II – All Z which are R cannot be K, so conclusion II will hold true.

29. (c)

For I – As there is no direct relation between J and B, Conclusion I will not hold true.

For II – As there is a no direct relation between J and B, Conclusion II will not hold true.

Both conclusions are false having the same elements and it is a case of 'some' and 'some not'. Therefore, "Either or" will follow.

30. (b)

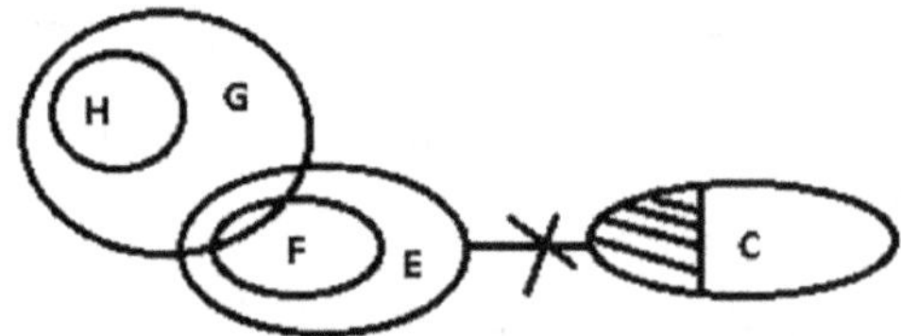

For I – Asthere is no direct relation between H and E conclusion I will not hold true. For II – From Venn diagram it is clear that some G are E. Hence, Conclusion II will hold true.

Directions (31-35):

Let us understand the logic behind it- In each step one word and one number is arranged simultaneously. The numbers are arranged from right end and the words are arranged from left.

For words- One word will be arranged in each step. The words which start with vowels are arranged first in an alphabetical order. Then the words which start with a consonant are arranged.

For numbers- Firstly even numbers are arranged in decreasing order, than odd numbers are arranged in decreasing order.

Input: **courage 22 old 29 basket 54 enter 33 rescue 61**

Step I: enter courage 22 old 29 basket 33 rescue 61 54

Step II: old enter courage 29 basket 33 rescue 61 54 22

Step III: basket old enter courage 29 33 rescue 54 22 61

Step IV: courage basket old enter 29 rescue 54 22 61 33

Step V: rescue courage basket old enter 54 22 61 33 29

31. (c)	**32. (a)**	**33. (c)**
34. (d)	**35. (b)**	

Directions (36-40):

Codes of elements are:

Codes	Elements
iron	ku
black	bu
is	su
brown	ni
rusting	ru
colour	lu
red/suit	dr/st

36. (e)	**37. (c)**	**38. (d)**
39. (d)	**40. (c)**	

QUANTITATIVE APTITUDE

41. (b) Cost per kg of sugar $= 90 \times \frac{3}{5} =$ Rs. 54

Cost per kg of salt $= 90 \times \frac{2}{5} =$ Rs. 36

Required difference $= 15 \times 54 - 5 \times 36$

$= 810 - 180 =$ Rs. 630

42. (c) Cost per kg of tea $= \frac{5000}{20} =$ Rs. 250

Cost per kg of wheat $= \frac{450}{10} =$ Rs. 45

Required percentage

$= \frac{250-45}{250} \times 100 = 82\%$

43. (a) Let cost per kg of rice be Rs. x and cost per kg of sugar be Rs. y

ATQ,

$x + y = 450$ ...(i)

After change

$x \times \frac{2}{3} + y \times \frac{4}{3} = 500$

$2x + 4y = 1500$

$x + 2y = 750$ ...(ii)

From (i) and (ii)

$y =$ Rs. 300

44. (e) Required ratio $= \frac{20 \times 220}{30 \times 50} = 44 : 15$

45. (d) Required percentage $= \frac{(20+10)-(15+5)}{(20+10)} \times 100$

$= 33\frac{1}{3}\%$

46. (d) Required sum $= (15 \times 10 - 5 \times 30) + (30 \times 20 - 15 \times 10) =$ Rs. 450

47. (a) Let efficiency of Abhi and Satish be a and b respectively

Total work $= 4a + 18b$ ...(i)

2nd condition

Total work $= 6a + 12b$ ...(ii)

From (i) and (ii)

$$4a + 18b = 6a + 12b$$

$$a = 3b$$

So, total work $= 4(3b) + 18b = 30b$

Abhi alone can complete the whole work in

$= \frac{30b}{3b} = 10$ days.

48. (d) Let length of train $= 2L$ m

Length of tunnel $= L$ m

ATQ,

$$3L = 144 \times \frac{5}{18} \times 30$$

L = 400 m

Length of train = 800 m

∴ Length of other train = 2 × 800 = 1600 m

60% of speed = $144 \times \frac{5}{18} \times \frac{60}{100} = 24$ m/sec.

∴ (1600 + 800) = 24 × time

∴ time = 100 sec.

49. (d) Using Alligation,

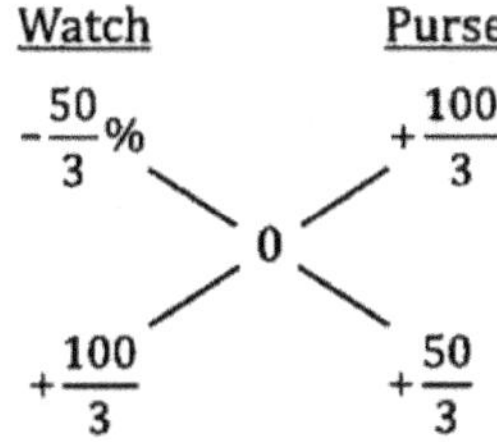

Watch : Purse = 2 : 1

Let cost price of watch be Rs. 2x

Purse be Rs. x

ATQ,

$$\frac{100}{300} \times 2x - \frac{50}{300} \times x = 50$$

$$x = Rs. 100$$

∴ cost price of watch = 2 × 100 = Rs. 200

50. (d) Let total monthly salary of Neeraj be Rs. 100x

ATQ,

His saving = 100x – 22x – 15.6x = 62.4x

∴ 62.4x = 3120

x = 50

∴ monthly salary = Rs. 5000

∴ expense of Neeraj on Food = $\frac{22}{100} \times 5000$

= Rs. 1100

Sol. (51-55):

Players who play tennis = 160

Players who play all three games = $160 \times \frac{10}{100} = 16$

Let players who play cricket and chess be 3x and 5x respectively.

ATQ,

8x=160×2=320

x=40

∴ Cricket players=120

And chess players=200

Players who play both tennis and chess $= \frac{1}{8} \times 160 = 20$

Let players who play both tennis and cricket and players who play both chess and cricket be 2y and 3y respectively.

ATQ,

5y=50 ⇒ y=10

Total no. of players

= 136+166+86+4+4+14+16 = 426

Tennis=160   cricket=120

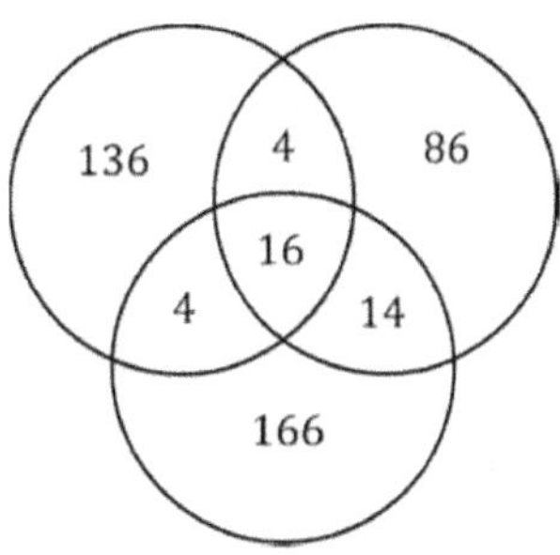

Chess = 200

51. (b) Required average = $\frac{136+166+86}{3}$

$= \frac{388}{3} = 129\frac{1}{3}$

52. (d) Required percentage = $\frac{170}{426} \times 100$

≃40%

53. (c) Required ratio = $\frac{20}{86} = 10:43$

54. (e) Required percentage $= \frac{(4+4+16+14)}{426-16} \times 100$

$= \frac{3800}{410} = 9\%$

55. (a) Required difference =160–86=74

56. (a) Number of Students who participate in Drama from class 7th and 8th together

$= (480-220) \times \frac{5}{13} + (240-105) \times \frac{2}{3}$

$= 100 + 90 = 190$

Number of Students who take part in Painting from class 9th and 10th together

$= (510-210) \times \frac{2}{5} + (250-120) \times \frac{5}{13}$

$- 120 + 50 = 170$

Required difference = 190 – 170 = 20

57. (c) Total number of students who do not take part from class 7th and 10th together=220+120=340

Total students who take part in painting from class 6th and 7th together

$= (320-103) \times \frac{4}{7} + (480-220) \times \frac{8}{13}$

$= 124 + 160 = 284$

Required percentage

$= \frac{340-284}{284} \times 100 \simeq 20\%$

58. (b) Required average $= \frac{1}{3}\left[(320-103) \times \frac{3}{7} + (240-105) \times \frac{2}{3} + (510-210) \times \frac{3}{5}\right]$

$= \frac{1}{3}[93 + 90 + 180] = 121$

59. (e) Required ratio $= \frac{(240-105) \times \frac{2}{3} + (510-210) \times \frac{3}{5}}{(320-103) \times \frac{4}{7} + (250-120) \times \frac{5}{13}}$

$= \frac{90+180}{124+50} = \frac{270}{174} = 45:29$

60. (c) Total new students from class 9th who do not take part in any activity $= 210 \times \frac{150}{100} = 315.$

Total students taking part in Drama previously

$= (510-210) \times \frac{3}{5} = 180$

Total student taking part in Drama now

$= (510 - 315) \times \frac{3}{5} = 117$

Required percentage

$= \frac{180 - 117}{180} \times 100 = 35\%$

61. (d) Required sum $= (480 - 220) \times \frac{8}{13} +$

$(510 - 210) \times \frac{3}{5} + (250 - 120) \times \frac{8}{13}$

$= 160 + 180 + 80 = 420$

62. (d)

| 13.5 | 13.5 | 27 | 9 | 36 | 7.2 |

$\div 1 \quad \times 2 \quad \div 3 \quad \times 4 \quad \div 5$

63. (e)

102   114   129   153   204   336

$+12 \quad +15 \quad +24 \quad +51 \quad +132$

$+3 \quad +9 \quad +27 \quad +81$

$3^1 \quad 3^2 \quad 3^3 \quad 3^4$

64. (a)

813   812   818   782   998   −298

$-6^0 \quad +6^1 \quad -6^2 \quad +6^3 \quad -6^4$

65. (b)

12   129   242   346   434   497

$+117 \quad +113 \quad +104 \quad +88 \quad +63$

$-4 \quad -9 \quad -16 \quad -25$

66. (e)

48   216   756   1890   2835   1417.5

$\times 4.5 \quad \times 3.5 \quad \times 2.5 \quad \times 1.5 \quad \times 0.5$

67. (b) Series is

$\times \frac{1}{2} + 0.5, \quad \times 1 + 2, \quad \times 2 + 8, \quad \times 4 + 32,$

$\times 8 + 128$

$\Rightarrow 120 \times 8 + 128 = 1088$

68. (b) Let fraction is $\frac{x}{y}$

And reverse $= \frac{y}{x}$

$\rightarrow \frac{y}{x} - \frac{x}{y} = \frac{7}{12}$ ...(i)

$\rightarrow \frac{y}{x} + \frac{x}{y} = \frac{25}{12}$ ...(ii)

Solving (i) and (ii)

$\frac{x}{y} = \frac{3}{4}$

69. (c) Let efficiency of Mona and Sunny is a and b respectively.

So, Bhavya's efficiency = 1.5a

ATQ,

$(a + b) \times 18 = (1.5a + b)15 \Rightarrow \frac{a}{b} = \frac{2}{3}$

Time taken by Mona $\Rightarrow \frac{\left(a + \frac{3}{2}a\right) \times 18}{a} = 45$ days

70. (e) Let speed of stream be x km/h

So, speed of boat = 3x km/h

Speed of boat in upstream = 2x km/h

Speed of boat in downstream = 4x km/h

Ratio of speed of boat in downstream and upstream is 2 : 1

So ratio of time taken = 1 : 2

So time taken in upstream $= \frac{2}{(1+2)} \times 6 = 4$ hour

71. (e) Let radius of cylinder = r

and height = h

So area of rectangle = C.S.A. of cylinder

$\Rightarrow 2\pi rh$

Now given ratio $= \frac{2\pi rh}{\pi r^2 h} = \frac{1}{7}$

$r = 14$

72. (a) We know,

$\text{S.I.} = \frac{P \times R \times \text{time}}{100} \quad \begin{bmatrix} P \rightarrow \text{Principal} \\ R \rightarrow \text{Rate} \end{bmatrix}$

$7020 = \frac{15600 \times R \times 3}{100}$

$R = 15\%$

$R + 5 = 20\%$

$\text{C.I.} = 15600\left[\left(1 + \frac{20}{100}\right)^2 - 1\right]$

$\text{C.I.} = 15600\left[\frac{36}{25} - 1\right]$

$= 15600 \times \frac{11}{25} = \text{Rs. } 6864$

73. (e) Let total present age of father, mother and two sons $= 41 \times 4 = 164$ years

Let total ages, 5 years before be 16x

ATQ,

$16x = 164 - 20 = 144$

$x = 9$ years

∴ Total age of both sons after 6 years $= 9 \times 3 + 9 \times 2 + 10 + 12 = 67$ years

74. (a) There are four cases → 3R, (1R, 2G), (2R, 1G), 3G

∴ Required probability

$= \frac{{}^4C_3 + {}^4C_1 \times {}^6C_2 + {}^4C_2 \times {}^6C_1 + {}^6C_3}{{}^{15}C_3}$

$= \frac{4 + 4 \times 15 + 6 \times 6 + 20}{91 \times 5}$

$= \frac{4 + 60 + 36 + 20}{91 \times 5}$

$= \frac{120}{91 \times 5} = \frac{24}{91}$

75. (d) $? = \frac{6561}{9 \times 3 \times 3} = 81$

76. (e) $7365 + 25 + \sqrt{?} = 7433$

$\sqrt{?} = 7433 - 7390$

$\sqrt{?} = 43$

or, $? = 1849$

77. (d) $? \approx 127 \times 8 + 6 \times 4$

$? = 1016 + 24$

$? = 1040$

78. (b) $? \approx \left(\frac{216 \times 1000}{100 \times 10}\right)^{\frac{1}{3}} + \left(\frac{42 \times 600}{100}\right)$

$= 6 + 252$

$? = 258$

79. (e) $\frac{39 \times 15 - 28 \times 10}{5} = 36 + ?$

$\Rightarrow 61 = 36 + ?$

∴ $? = 25$

80. (a) $? = 335 \times 245 \div 35$

$= 335 \times \frac{245}{35} \approx 2345$

IBPS RRB PO Prelims

REASONING ABILITY

Directions (1-3): Study the following information carefully and answer the questions given below:

Five persons P, Q, R, S and T gavepresentations on different dates—12th, 15th, 17th, 26th and 28th —of the same month, but not necessarily in the same order. Each date represents different events i.e. Kargil Vijay Diwas, International Malala Day, World Hepatitis Day, World Youth Skill Day, and World Justice Day, but not necessarily in the same order. More than two persons gave presentations between the date representing International Malala Day and World Hepatitis Day. World Youth Skill Day is not represented on 12th. Only one person made a presentation after Q, who does not give a presentation on World Youth Skill Day. S gave a presentation at last and on World Hepatitis Day. R gave a representation on 12th. T gave a presentation on the date, which represents World Justice Day. P did not make apresentation on 17th and 26th.

1. T gives a presentation on which date?
   (a) 12th   (b) 15th   (c) 17th
   (d) 26th   (e) 28th

2. Kargil Vijay Diwas is on which day and who gives a presentation on it?
   (a) 15th ,R   (b) 17th , Q   (c) 26th , Q
   (d) 17th , R   (e) 15th , P

3. Who among the following gives a presentation on World Youth Skill Day?
   (a) P   (b) Q   (c) R
   (d) S   (e) T

Directions (4-5): Study the following information carefully and answer the questions given below:

There are eight members in a family in which two are married couples. S is the grandmother of K. B is the father-in-law of A. C is the mother of D. J is the brother of K and his mother is D. J and K are unmarried.

4. How is S related to D?
   (a) mother
   (b) sister
   (c) mother-in-law
   (d) grandmother
   (e) None of these

5. How is C related to K?
   (a) mother
   (b) mother-in-law
   (c) paternal grandmother
   (d) maternal grandmother
   (e) Cannot be determined

Directions (6-10): In each of the questions below,some statements are given followed by conclusions numbered I and II. You have to assume all the statements to be true even if they seem to be at variance withcommonly known facts and then decide which of the given two conclusions logically follows from the information given in the statements.
(a) If only conclusion I follows
(b) If only conclusion II follows
(c) If either I or II follows
(d) If neither I nor II follows
(e) If both I and II follow

6. **Statements:** Some Tea are coffee.
   All coffee are milk.
   All tea are water.
   Conclusions:
   I. Some tea are milk is a possibility.
   II. Some milk are water .

7. **Statements:** Some red are brown.
   All brown are green.
   No blue is brown.
   Conclusions:
   I. Some green are not blue.
   II. All red can be blue.

8. **Statements:**
   All key are row.
   No row is table.
   All row are column.
   Conclusions:
   I. No key is table.
   II. Some column are not table.

9. **Statements:**
   Some chair are cross.
   All cross are line.
   Some table are cross.
   Conclusions:
   I. Some chair are line.
   II. Some table are chair.

10. **Statements:** Some paint are brush.
    All colour are brush.
    No colour is canvas.
    Conclusions: I. Some paint are canvas.
    II. All brush are canvas.

Directions (11-15): Study the following arrangement carefully and answer the following questions given below:

    7 ^ L U $ W T 4 B % R # F H * I 2 D 1 M P 5 @ Q 8 E 3 O 6

11. Four of the following five are alike in a certain way based on their positions in the above arrangement and so form a group. Which is the one that does not belong to that group?
    (a) 7U$ (b) T%R   (c) FI2
    (d) M@Q   (e) QE3

12. How many such alphabets are there in the above arrangement each of which is immediately preceded by a symbol and immediately followed by a number?
    (a) none   (b) one   (c) two
    (d) three   (e) More than three

13. Which of the following elements is the fifth to the right of the eighteenth from the right end of the above arrangement?
    (a) ^   (b) I   (c) O
    (d) M   (e) 2

14. Which of the following is exactly between the element which is tenth from the right end and the one which is eight from the left end of the above arrangement?
    (a) *   (b) H   (c) I
    (d) 2   (e) #

15. If all the symbols are dropped from the above arrangement, which of the following will be the ninth to the left of M?
    (a) U   (b) W   (c) 4
    (d) T   (e) B

Directions (16-20): Study the information and answer the following questions:

Ten people are sitting in two parallel rows containing five people each in such a way that there is an equal distance between adjacent persons. In row—1, E, K, C, G and I are seated and all of them are facing north. In row—2, J, H, D, F and B are seated and all of them are facing south. Therefore, in the given seating arrangement, members of each row sit opposite each other. C sits opposite B and 3rd right to K. Two people sit between F and H. I is to the left of G, but not to the immediate left. G neither sits opposite D nor faces H. J sits 2nd to the right of H. D does not sit at either end.

16. Who sits second to the right of E?
    (a) K   (b) G
    (c) C   (d) I
    (e) Cannot be determined

17. Which pair among the following sits in the middle of both rows?
    (a) K, G   (b) F, E   (c) G, D
    (d) E, D   (e) B, C

18. Who among the following sits third to the left of J?
    (a) F
    (b) D
    (c) H
    (d) B
    (e) Cannot be determined

19. Four of the following five belong to a group. Who does not belong to the group?
    (a) H   (b) F   (c) I
    (d) C   (e) B

20. Who among the following sits at eitherof the extreme ends?
    (a) C   (b) G   (c) H
    (d) J   (e) K

Directions (21-25): Study the information and answer the following questions:
In a certain code language
"Bus travel road miles" is coded as "ro mj un lk"
"train miles seat transport" is coded as " mo nj ka ro"
"Train travel track road"is coded as " sa un ka lk"
"bus seat track platform" is coded as"mo sa mj wl"

21. What is the code for "track platform"?
    (a) sa nj   (b) wl un   (c) sa wl
    (d) ka lk   (e) None of these

22. Which of the following is denoted as "un"?
    (a) travel
    (b) track
    (c)road
    (d) either (a) or (c)
    (e) either (b) or (c)

23. What is the code for "miles seat"?
    (a) ro mo   (b) mo ka   (c) un ro
    (d) lk nj   (e) ro wl

24. If "distance travel" is coded as "jy un" then what can be the code for "distance train road"
    (a) jy lk nj   (b) jy ka un   (c) lk jy ka
    (d) wl jy sa   (e) lk wl sa

25. Which of the following is denoted as "wl mj"?
    (a) travel seat
    (b) bus miles
    (c) platform road
    (d) track seat
    (e) platform bus

Directions (26-30): Study the following information carefully and answer the questions given below:

Five persons S1, S2, S3, S4 and S5 live on different floors of the same building i.e. Ground floor is numbered 1, the floor above that is 2 and so on till the top floor which is numbered 5. Each of them studies different subjects viz. Maths, English, Phy, Bio and Chem. One person, who lives between S3 and S4, does not live on an odd-numbered floor.

S1 does not study Chem. One person lives between the person who studies Maths and the one who studies Chem. S5 lives below S4, but not immediately below and he does not study Chem. The person who studies Maths lives just above the floor of S3.Two persons live between S2 and the one who studies English. The one who studies Phy does not live on an even-numbered floor.

26. Who among the following studies Maths?
    (a) S1   (b) S2   (c) S3
    (d) S4   (e) S5

27. Which subject is studied by the one who lives just above the floor of S1?
    (a) Maths   (b) Bio   (c) Chem
    (d) Phy   (e) English

28. The person who studies English lives on which floor?
    (a) 1st (b) 2nd (c) 3rd
    (d) 4th (e) 5th

29. How many persons live between S5 and the one who studies Bio?
    (a) one   (b) two   (c) three
    (d) four   (e) five

30. Who among the following lives on the topmost floor?
    (a) S5   (b) S4   (c) S3
    (d) S2   (e) S1

Directions (31-35): Each of the following questions below consists of a question and two statements numbered I and II given below it. You have to decide whether the data provided in the statements issufficient to answer the question. Read both the statements and answer.

(a) if the data in statement I alone is sufficient to answer the question, while the data in statement II alone is not sufficient in answer the question.

(b) if the data in statement II alone issufficient to answer the question, while the data in statement I alone is not sufficient to answer the question.

(c) if the data in either statement I alone or in statement II alone is sufficient to answer the question.

(d) if the data in both the statements I and II together is not sufficient to answer the question.

(e) if the data in both the statements I and II istogether necessary to answer the question.

31. How is S related to E?
    I.   W is the father of X and P is the grandson of E, who is the wife of W.
    II.   G is the mother of S, who is the sister of P. G is the daughter-in-law of W.

32. Among five friends P, Q, R, S and T having different heights, who is the tallest?
    I.   R is taller than only one friend. Only one friend is taller than T. P is not the shortest.
    II.   R is shorter than only three persons. Only one person is taller than T. P is neither the tallest nor the shortest in the group. Q is the shortest in the group.

33. What is code of 'sum'?
    I.   'sum of two number' is coded as' sa mn ta cq' and ' two third of number' is coded as ' cq ca mn sa' .
    II.   'sum are wind up' is coded as'la za ta cm'.

34. Point 'P' is in which direction with respect to point 'Q'?
    I.   Point P is north west of point A, which is west of point B. Point Q is north of point B.
    II.   Point Q is north east of point A, which is north of point B. Point P is west of point B.

35. Four friends viz. M, N, O and P are sitting around a circular table. Are they facing the centre of the table? If
    I.   N is sitting second to the right of P. P is facing the centre. O is sitting immediately to the right of N and P.
    II.   M is sitting immediate left of N. O is not sitting immediate left of M. O is sitting immediate right of P.

36. If in a certain code "ROUND" is coded as "54739", "TRUE" is coded as "1572",how will"RUDE" be coded?
    (a) 9731   (b) 5712   (c) 7432
    (d) 5792   (e) 4325

Directions (37-38): Study the following information carefully and answer the questions given below:

In a row of 29 persons all facing North, Sumit is at 19th position from the left end. Shivani is at 17th position from the right end.

37. Naveen sits between Sumit and Shivani. What is his position from the right end?
    (a) 16th (b) 12th (c) 15th
    (d) 13th (e) 14th

38. If few more persons join the row and one of the new members, Harsh, is at the extreme right end now and twelfth to the right of Sumit, then how many persons joined the row afterwards?
    (a) one
    (b) two
    (c) three
    (d) four
    (e) Cannot be determined

39. Each consonant in the word "ELEPHANT" is changed to the previous letter in the English alphabetical series and each vowel is changed

to the next letter in the English alphabetical seriesand then the alphabets so formed are arranged in an alphabetical order from left to right.Which alphabet will be the third from the right?

(a) F   (b) O   (c) S
(d) G   (e) M

40. How many such pairs of letters are there in the word MODERN, each of which has as many letters between them in the word (both forward and backward directions) as they have between them in the English alphabetical series?

(a) none
(b) one
(c) two
(d) three
(e) More than three

QUANTITATIVE APTITUDE

Direction (41-45) : Find the wrong number in the following number series.

41. 120, 143, 189, 258, 348, 465
     (a) 120   (b) 143   (c) 258
     (d) 348   (e) 465

42. 255, 216, 175, 132, 85, 32
     (a) 255   (b) 216   (c) 175
     (d) 85   (e) 32

43. 27, 48, 80, 134, 221, 355
     (a) 221   (b) 27   (c) 355
     (d) 48   (e) 134

44. 11, 10, 19, 56, 223, 1115
     (a) 1115   (b) 6   (c) 11
     (d) 223   (e) 56

45. 292, 291, 295, 268, 284, 161
     (a) 292   (b) 284   (c) 291
     (d) 268   (e) 161

Direction (46-50) : The pie chart given below shows the percentage distribution of daily consumption of quantity of water by five different families in a building. Read the pie-chart carefully and answer the following questions:

Total quantity of water consumed in a day =7,000 litres.

Note: Total quantity of water available = Total quantity of water consumed + total quantity of unused water

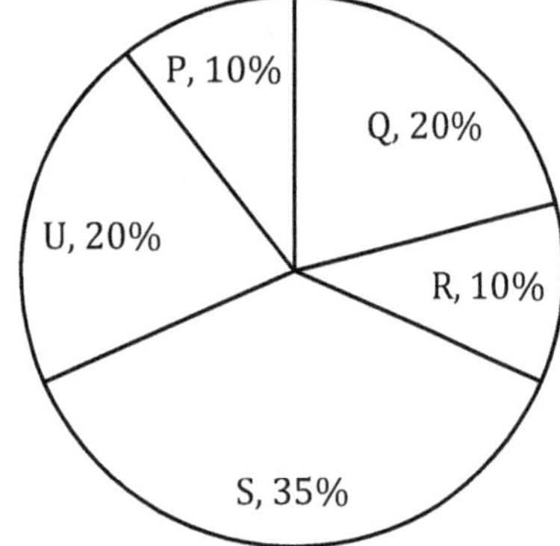

46. The average quantity of water consumed by families P and S is what percent more/less than the average quantity of water consumed by families R and U?

     (a) 25%   (b) 50%   (c) $33\frac{1}{3}$%
     (d) 60%   (e) 75%

47. If 87.5% of the quantity of water available is consumed by all families, then, find the ratio of the quantity of unused water to the difference of the quantity of water consumed by families S and Q?

     (a) 6 : 7   (b) 44 : 45   (c) 62 : 63
     (d) 20 : 21   (e) 14 : 15

48. Find the ratio of the quantity of water consumed by familes S and U together to the quantity of water consumed by families P and R together?

     (a) 11 : 4   (b) 5 : 4   (c) 3 : 2
     (d) 13 : 8   (e) 15 : 8

49. $3\frac{1}{7}$% of the quantity of water consumed by family S is what percent of the quantity of water consumed by R.

     (a) $7\frac{1}{2}$%   (b) $8\frac{1}{2}$%   (c) 10%
     (d) 12.5%   (e) 11%

50. The difference in the quantity of water consumed by families U and S is how much more than the difference in the quantity of water consumed by families Q and R?

     (a) 350 litres   (b) 320 litres
     (c) 330 litres   (d) 360 litres
     (e) 340 litres

51. Shalini's present age is five times her daughter's present age and the ratio between Shalini's present age to her father's present age is 2 : 5. If the average age of all the three,six years hence will be 43 years, then find the ratio of the present ages of her daughter to the difference of the ages of Shalini and her father.

     (a) 1 : 12   (b) 2 : 13   (c) 1 : 7
     (d) 2 :15   (e) 1 : 8

52. Kishan and Bhavya appear in an interview for a vacancy. The probability of Kishan's selection

is $\frac{1}{7}$ and that of Bhavya's selection is $\frac{1}{5}$. What is the probability that one of the them will be selected?

(a) $\frac{5}{7}$ (b) $\frac{4}{5}$ (c) $\frac{2}{7}$

(d) $\frac{3}{7}$ (e) $\frac{1}{7}$

53. A circular road runs around a circular ground. If the radius of the ground is 3.5m. and the difference between the circumference of the outer circle and that of the inner circle is 88 m., then the area of the road is

(a) 920 m.^{2} (b) 918 m.^{2} (c) 924 m.^{2}

(d) 926 m.^{2} (e) 824 m.^{2}

54. How many different five digits numbers can be made from the first seven whole numbers, using each digit only once?

(a) 2160   (b) 2520   (c) 7776

(d) 3360   (e) 5040

55. Chiru goes to a shop to buy some bananas but somehow he managed to save Rs. 3 per 4 bananas and thus purchased eight dozen bananas instead of fivedozen bananas. Find the amount he initially had with him.

(a) Rs. 100   (b) Rs. 160   (c) Rs. 80

(d) Rs. 200   (e) Rs. 120

Direction (56-60): In each question two equations numbered (I) and (II) are given. Students should solve both the equations and mark the appropriate answer.

(a) If x=y or no relation can be established

(b) If x>y

(c) If x<y

(d) If x≥y

(e) If x≤y

56. I. $35x^2 - 12x + 1 = 0$ II. $20y^2 - 14y + 2 = 0$

57. I. $4x^2 + 19x + 22 = 0$ II. $6y^2 + 20y + 16 = 0$

58. I. $3x^2 - 7x + 2 = 0$ II. $4y^2 - 29y + 45 = 0$

59. I. $2x^2 - 17x + 36 = 0$ II. $y\,(y - 2) = 2(2 - y)$

60. I. $5x^2 - 10 = 7x + 3x^2 + 5$

    II. $6y^2 + 10y = 27y - 7$

Direction (61-65): Study the following graph carefully and answer the questions which follow. Profit (in percent) for Reliance and Airtel companies is given, which is calculated on income.

Profit = Income – Expenditure

Profit % = $\dfrac{\text{Income – Expenditure}}{\text{Income}} \times 100$

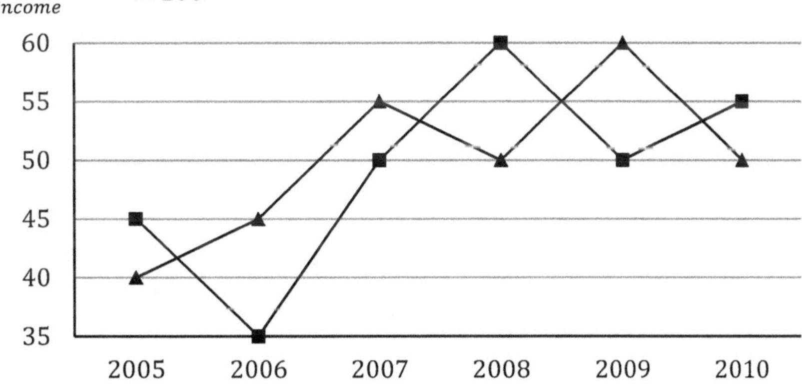

61. If expenditure of Airtel in the year 2007 was Rs. 2.25 lakh, then find the income of Airtel in the same year.

(a) 4 L   (b) 5 L   (c) 4.5 L

(d) 6 L   (e) 5.5 L

62. If the profit of company Reliance in year 2006 was Rs. 1,05,000, then what was its expenditure in that year?

(a) Rs. 2.10 L   (b) Rs. 2.60 L   (c) Rs. 2 L

(d) Rs. 1.75 L   (e) Rs. 1.95 L

63. If the expenditure of companies Airtel and Reliance in the year 2009 was equal, then what was the ratio of the income of Airtel to the income of Reliance in the same year?

(a) 7 : 6   (b) 5 : 4   (c) 6 : 5

(d) 5 : 3   (e) 3 : 5

64. If the income of Airtel in year 2005 and the income of Reliance in year 2010 was Rs. 5.5 lakh and Rs. 7 lakh respectively, then the expenditure of Reliance in year 2010 is what percent of the expenditure of Airtel in year 2005?

(a) 90%   (b) $92\frac{5}{11}$%   (c) $96\frac{5}{11}$%

(d) $95\frac{5}{11}$%   (e) $94\frac{2}{11}$%

65. Find the average of the profit percent of Reliance in all the given years?

(a) $49\frac{1}{6}\%$ (b) $49\frac{2}{3}\%$ (c) $45\frac{2}{3}\%$

(d) $45\frac{1}{6}\%$ (e) $48\frac{1}{3}\%$

66. Two articles P and Q were sold at 20% profit and 12.5% loss respectively. If total profit is Rs. 25.5 in the whole transaction, then find the cost price of P when the cost price of Q is Rs. 60 less than the cost price of P.

(a) Rs. 180   (b) Rs. 250   (c) Rs. 240

(d) Rs. 220   (e) Rs. 260

67. If 10 girls and 11 boys together can do a work in five days and four girls and fourteen boys together can do the same work in $8\frac{1}{2}$ days, find the ratio of efficiency of a boy to a girl.

(a) $7:2$ (b) $2:7$ (c) $4:1$

(d) $1:4$ (e) $3:11$

Direction (68 – 72): The table given below shows the total number of visitors who have visited Taj Mahal on five different days of a week and the percentage of the total visitors who are Indians.

Days	Total number of visitors	percentage of visitors who are Indians
Monday	15,000	75%
Tuesday	17,800	82%
Friday	16,800	82%
Saturday	15,400	77%
Sunday	18,000	85%

Total number of visitors = Indians + Foreigners.

68. If the ratio of male to female foreigners visiting Taj Mahal on Sunday is 4:5, then find the difference between male and female foreigners visiting Taj Mahal on Sunday.

(a) 250   (b) 275   (c) 300

(d) 320   (e) 350

69. Find the average number of Indian visitors on Monday and Tuesday?

(a) 12923   (b) 12833   (c) 12963

(d) 12933   (e) 12833

70. The difference between the number of Indian and foreign visitors on Saturday is what percent of the total number of visitors on Friday?

(a) 50%   (b) 55%   (c) 45%

(d) $49\frac{1}{2}\%$ (e) $46\frac{1}{2}\%$

71. Out of the total number of visitors on Monday, 32% are Indian females. Find the ratio of number of Indian male visitors to the total number of foreign visitors on the same day.

(a) $43:44$ (b) $43:25$ (c) $12:25$

(d) $25:33$ (e) $17:21$

72. Find the difference between the total number of visitors on Sunday and the total number of foreign visitors on Tuesday and Saturday together

(a) 11,154   (b) 11,754   (c) 11,644

(d) 12,254   (e) 11,254

73. A sum is compounded annually for two years at the rate of 10% per annum for the first year and 12% per annum for the second year. If, at the end of two years, the difference between the amount and the sum is Rs. 2,320, then find the sum.

(a) Rs. 8,500   (b) Rs. 10,000   (c) Rs. 11,000

(d) Rs. 12,000   (e) Rs. 10,500

74. A goldsmith has an alloy of gold and copper in the ratio of 11:5 by weight. He sold $12\frac{1}{2}\%$ of the alloy to a person and added some copper to it so that the ratio becomes $7:5$ (gold : copper). Find the new quantity of copper added, if initial weight of the alloy was 16 gm. (in gm)

(a) 2.5 gm.   (b) 1.5 gm.   (c) 2.0 gm.

(d) 3.0 gm.   (e) 1.6 gm.

75. Train A crosses a standing man with a speed of 86.4 km/hr. in some time. Another train B crosses a platform of length 60m. in twice the time in which train A crossed the man, with a speed of 108 km/hr. If the length of train A is half that of train B, then find the length of train B.

(a) 180 m.   (b) 300 m.   (c) 360 m.

(d) 240 m.   (e) 120 m.

Direction (76 – 80): The following questions are accompanied by two statements I and II. You have to determine which statements(s) is/are sufficient to answer the questions.

(a) Statement I alone is sufficient to answer the question but statement II alone is not sufficient to answer the questions.

(b) Statement II alone is sufficient to answer the question, but statement I alone is not sufficient to answer the question.

(c) Both the statements taken together are necessary to answer the questions, but neither of the statements alone is sufficient to answer the question.

(d) Either statement I or statement II by itself is sufficient to answer the question.

(e) Statements I and II taken together are not sufficient to answer the question.

76. There are some Green and some White balls in a bag. Find how many white balls are in the bag.

Statement I: The total number of balls in the bag is five. If two balls are selected at random, the probability of at least one ball being Green is $\frac{9}{10}$.

Statement II: The total number of balls in the bag is five. Iftwo balls are selected from out of the total balls at random, the probability of both ballsbeing white is $\frac{1}{10}$.

77. How many marks did Veer obtain in English?

Statement I: Veer secured on an average 55% marks in English, Physics and Chemistry together.

Statement II: Veer secured 10% marks more in English than the average of English, Physics and Chemistry

78. Find the speed of train A if the length of two trains A and B is 70m. and 80m. respectively.

Statement I: They take 25 seconds to cross each other when they are running in the same direction.

Statement II: They take 15 seconds to cross each other when they are running in the opposite direction.

79. If the number of boys attending school in year 2009 was $33\frac{1}{3}\%$ that of girls, then what was the ratio of boys to girls attending school in 2010?

Statement I: 100 more boys were attending school in 2010 than in 2009 and the average in 2010 was450. Thenumber of girls in 2010 wasequal to the number of girls in 2009.

Statement II: 150 more girls than boys were attending school in 2010 than in 2009.

80. 'P' started a business and Q joined him after three months and R joined them after four months. Find the share of 'R' out of the total profit.

Statement I : 'P' invested Rs. 600 more than 'Q' while 'Q' invested Rs. 300 more than 'R'.

Statement II: P's profit is Rs 18,000 out of total profit.

Solutions

REASONING ABILITY

Directions (1-3):

S made a presentation at last and on World Hepatitis Day. R gave representation on 12th. P did not give presentation on 17th and 26th, So P gave presentation on 15th. Only one person gave presentation after Q. World Youth Skill Day is not represented on 12th.

Date	Person	Event
12th	R	~~World Youth skill day~~
15th	P	
17th		
26th	Q	~~World Youth skill day~~
28th	S	World hepatitis day

More than two persons gave presentations between the date representing international Malala Day and Hepatitis Day. T gave presentation on the date which represents World Justice Day.

Date	Person	Event
12th	R	International Malala Day
15th	P	World Youth Skill Day
17th	T	World Justice Day
26th	Q	Kargil Vijay Diwas
28th	S	World Hepatitis Day

1. (c)   **2.** (c):   **3.** (a)

Directions (4-5):

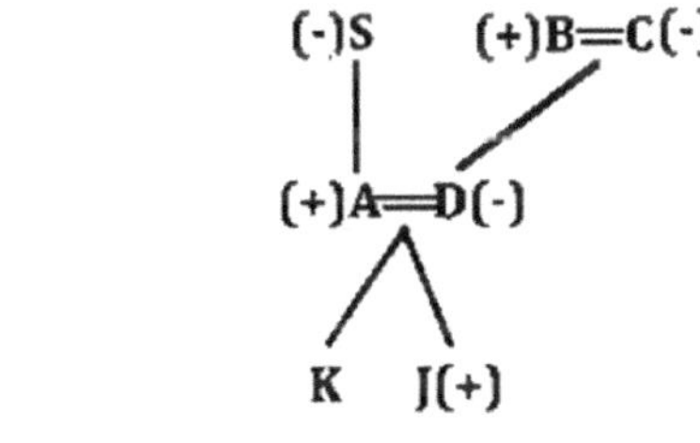

4. (c)   **5.** (d)

Directions (6-10):

6. (b)

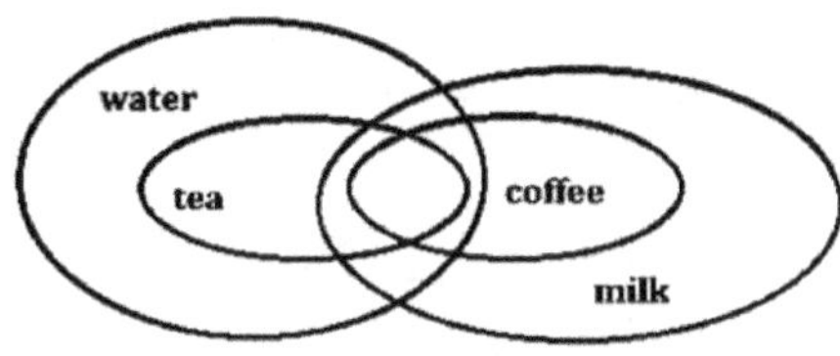

For-I Since it is a definite case so possibility case will not hold true.

For-II From Venn diagram it is clear that some milk are water. Hence conclusion I is true.

7. **(a)**

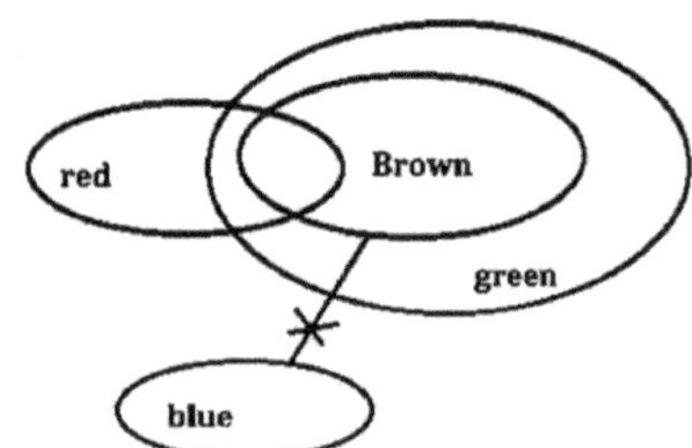

For-I True because All those green which are brown cannot be blue.

For-II False because Some red which are Brown can never be blue therefore, all red cannot be blue.

8. **(e)**

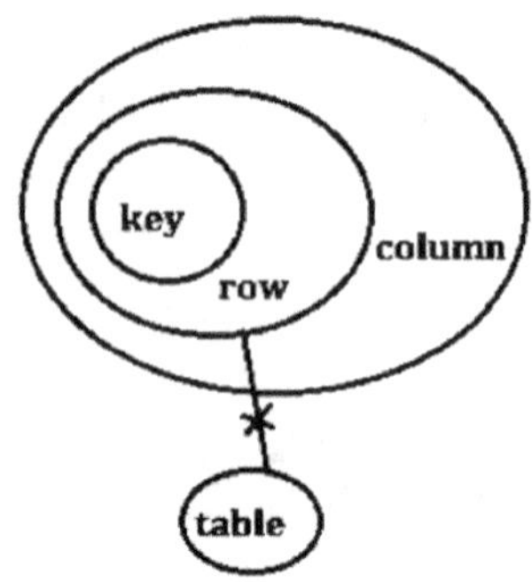

For-I True because All key are row and No row is table. Therefore, No key is table is True.

For-II False because All those columns which are row cannot be table.

9. **(a)**

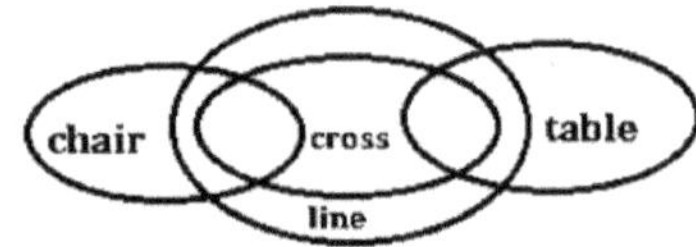

For-I From Venn diagram it is clear that Some Cross are line. Hence conclusion I can be concluded.

For-II False, because there is no direct relation between Chair and table.

10. **(d)**

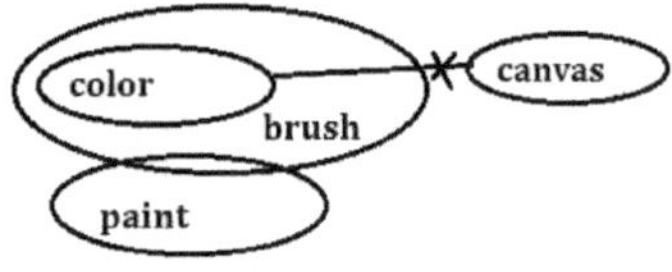

For-I False as there is no direct relation between paint and canvas.

For-II From Venn diagram All those brush which are colour cannot be canvas. Hence conclusion II cannot be concluded.

Directions (11-15):

11. **(e)** 1

12. **(c)** * I 2 @ Q 8

13. **(e)**   14. **(b)**   15. **(c)**

Directions (16-20):

In the given seating arrangement, members of each row sit opposite each other, which means either they can face each other or not. C sits opposite B and 3rd right to K. I is to the left of G but not immediate left. So we get 4 possible cases:

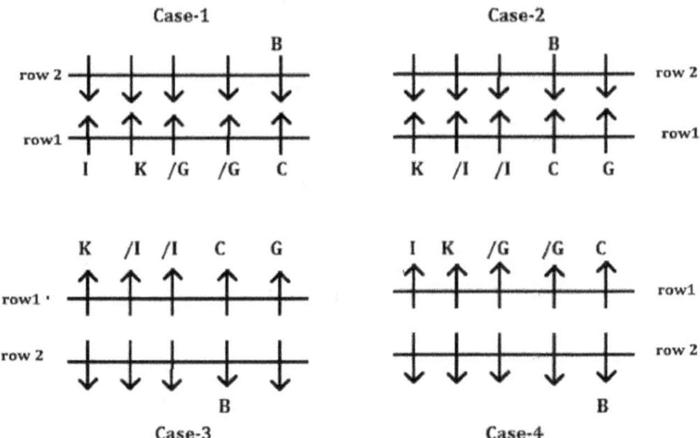

Two people sit between F and H. G neither sits opposite D nor faces H. J sits 2nd to the right of H. By this condition case 1and 2 get cancelled. Also D does not sit at any of the ends. Therefore, case 3 also gets cancelled and we get the final arrangement:

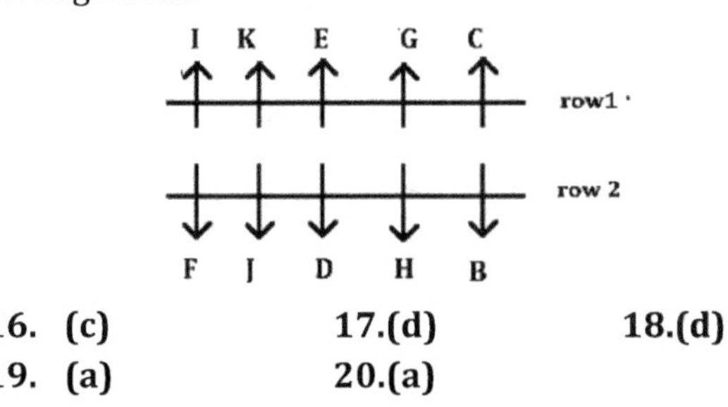

16. **(c)**   17.**(d)**   18.**(d)**

19. **(a)**   20.**(a)**

Directions (21-25):

Element	Code
Bus	mj
Travel/road	un/lk
train	ka
miles	ro
track	sa
platform	wl
seat	mo
transport	nj

21. **(c)**   22.**(d)**   23.**(a)**

24. **(c)**   25.**(e)**

Directions (26-30):

One person lives between S3 and S4, who does not live on an odd numbered floor. The person who studies Maths lives just above the floor of S3. One person lives between the person who studies Maths and the one who studies Chem. So, there will be three possible cases:

Floor	Person	Subject		Floor	Person	Subject		Floor	Person	Subject
5		Chem		5		Maths		5		
4	S4			4	S3			4	S4	
3		Maths		3		Chem		3		Maths
2	S3			2	S4			2	S3	
1				1				1		Chem

Case-1   Case-2   Case-3

S5 lives below S4 but not immediately below. This will eliminate Case 2. S5 does not study chem. So this will eliminate Case 3. Two persons live between S2 and the one who studies English. The one who studies Phy does not live on an even numbered floor. S1 does not studies Chem. So the final arrangement is:

Floor	Person	Subject
5	S2	Chem
4	S4	Bio
3	S1	Maths
2	S3	English
1	S5	Phy

26. (a)   **27.(b)**   **28.(b)**

29. (b)   **30.(d)**

Directions (31-35):

31. (e) From I and II S is granddaughter of E

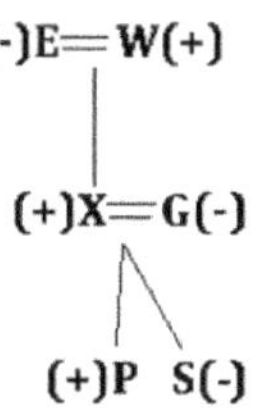

32. (b) From II S is tallest.

$S > T > P > R > Q$

33. (a) From I Sum is coded as 'ta'

34. (b) From II P is in South-west of Q

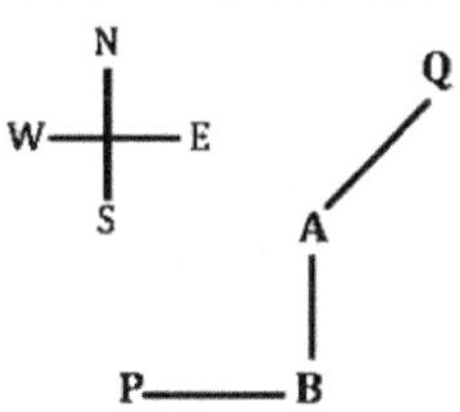

35. (d) From I and II we cannot determine the directions of all four persons.

36. (d)

Directions (37-38):

37. (e)   **38.(b)**

39. (e)

ELEPHANT
FKFOGBMS
BFFGKMOS

40. (c)

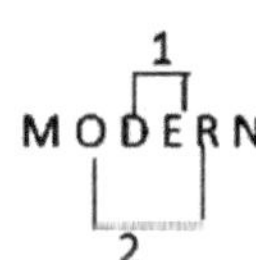

QUANTITATIVE APTITUDE

41. (d)

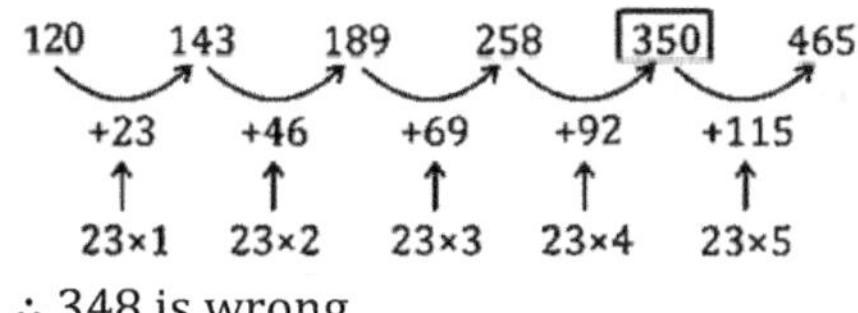

∴ 348 is wrong

42. (a)

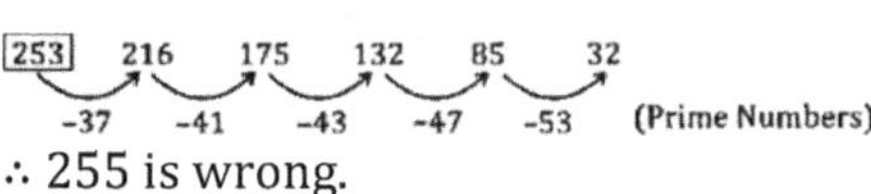

∴ 255 is wrong.

43. (c)

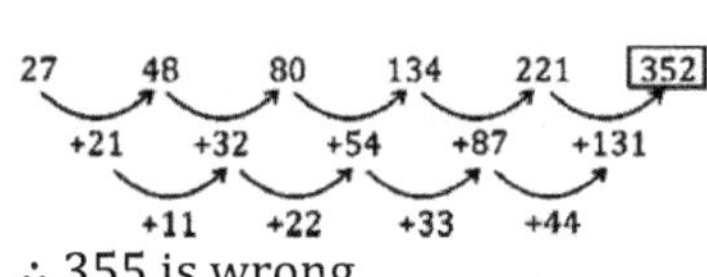

∴ 355 is wrong

44. (a)

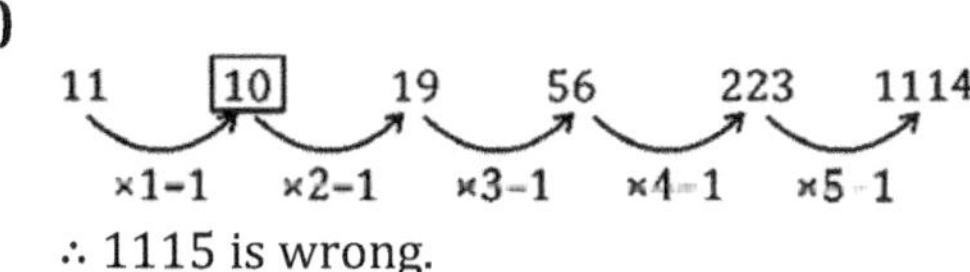

∴ 1115 is wrong.

45. (e)

292   291   295   268   284   159

-1^3 $+2^2$ -3^3 $+4^2$ -5^3

∴ 161 is wrong.

46. (b) Required % = $\dfrac{\left(\frac{10+35}{2}\right)-\left(\frac{10+20}{2}\right)}{\left(\frac{10+20}{2}\right)} \times 100 = 50\%$

47. (d) Total quantity of water available = $7000 \times \dfrac{8}{7}$ liter = 8000 litre

Required ratio = $\dfrac{1000}{(35-20)\times\frac{7000}{100}} = \dfrac{1000}{1050} = \dfrac{20}{21}$

48. (a) Required ratio = $\dfrac{(35+20)}{(10+10)} = \dfrac{55}{20} = \dfrac{11}{4}$

49. (e) $3\frac{1}{7}\%$ of Quantity of water consumed by S

$= \dfrac{22}{7\times100} \times \dfrac{35}{100} \times 7000 = 77$ liter

Required percentage $= \dfrac{77}{\frac{10\times7000}{100}} \times 100 = 11\%$

50. (a) Required quantity

$= \dfrac{(35-20)\times7000}{100} - \dfrac{(20-10)}{100} \times 7000$

$= \dfrac{5}{100} \times 7000 = 350$ liter

51. **(d)** Let daughter's present age be x years.
Then, Shalini's present age = 5x years
Ratio of present age of
Daughter : Shalini : Father
2x 10x25x
ATQ,
$2x + 10x + 25x = 43 \times 3 - 18$
$\Rightarrow x = 3$
Required ratio = $\frac{2x}{25x-10x} = \frac{2\times3}{15\times3} = 2 : 15$

52. **(c)** Required probability = $\frac{1}{7} \times \frac{4}{5} + \frac{6}{7} \times \frac{1}{5}$
$= \frac{4+6}{35} = \frac{10}{35} = \frac{2}{7}$

53. **(c)** let the radius of the outer circle be R m.
And the radius of the inner circle be r m.
Then, according to the question
$2\pi r - 2\pi r = 88$
or, $R - r = \frac{88\times7}{2\times22} = 14$
Or, R = 14 + r = 14 + 3.5 = 17.5 m
Now, area of the road = π (17.5² - 3.5²)
$= \frac{22}{7} \times 21 \times 14 = 924 \ m^2$

54. **(a)** Required number of 5 digit numbers
= −   −   −   −   −
  ↑   ↑   ↑   ↑   ↑
6 × 6 × 5 × 4 × 3
= 2160

55. **(e)** Let initially Chiru have Rs. x with him.
ATQ,
$\frac{x}{8} + 9 = \frac{x}{5}$ (he saves Rs. 9 per dozen)
$\Rightarrow \frac{x}{5} - \frac{x}{8} = 9 \Rightarrow \frac{3x}{40} = 9 \Rightarrow$ x = Rs. 120

56. **(e)** **I.** $35x^2 - 12x + 1 = 0$
$\Rightarrow 35x^2 - 7x - 5x + 1 = 0$
$\Rightarrow 7x(5x - 1) - 1(5x - 1) = 0$
$\Rightarrow x = \frac{1}{5} \ or \ \frac{1}{7}.$
II. $20 \ y^2 - 14y + 2 = 0$
$\Rightarrow 20y^2 - 10y - 4y + 2 = 0$
$\Rightarrow 10y(2y - 1) - 2(2y - 1) = 0$
$\Rightarrow y = \frac{1}{5} \ or \ \frac{1}{2}$
$y \geq x$

57. **(e)** **I.** $4x^2 + 19x + 22 = 0$
$\Rightarrow 4x^2 + 8x + 11x + 22 = 0$
$\Rightarrow 4x(x + 2) + 11(x + 2) = 0$
$\Rightarrow x = -2 \ or \ \frac{-11}{4}$
II. $6y^2 + 20y + 16 = 0$
$\Rightarrow 6y^2 + 12y + 8y + 16 = 0$
$\Rightarrow 6y(y + 2) + 8(y + 2) = 0$
$\Rightarrow y = -2 \ or \ \frac{-4}{3}$
$y \geq x$

58. **(c)** **I.** $3x^2 - 7x + 2 = 0$
$\Rightarrow 3x^2 - 6x - x + 2 = 0$
$\Rightarrow 3x(x - 2) - 1(x - 2) = 0$
$\Rightarrow x = 2 \ or \ \frac{1}{3}$
II. $4y^2 - 29y + 45 = 0$
$\Rightarrow 4y^2 - 20y - 9y + 45 = 0$

$\Rightarrow 4y \ (y - 5) - 9 \ (y - 5) = 0$
$y = 5 \ or \ \frac{9}{4}$
$y > x$

59. **(b)** **I.** $2x^2 - 17x + 36 = 0$
$\Rightarrow 2x^2 - 8x - 9x + 36 = 0$
$\Rightarrow 2x(x - 4) - 9(x - 4) = 0$
$\Rightarrow x = 4 \ or \ \frac{9}{2}$
II. $y(y - 2) = 2(2 - y)$
$\Rightarrow y^2 - 2y = 4 - 2y$
$\Rightarrow y = \pm \ 2.$
$x > y$

60. **(a)** **I.** $5x^2 - 10 = 7x + 3x^2 + 5$
$\Rightarrow 2x^2 - 7x - 15 = 0$
$\Rightarrow 2x^2 - 10x + 3x - 15 = 0$
$\Rightarrow 2x(x - 5) + 3(x - 5) = 0$
$\Rightarrow x = 5 \ or \ \frac{-3}{2}$
II. $6y^2 + 10y = 27y - 7$
$\Rightarrow 6y^2 - 17y + 7 = 0$
$\Rightarrow 6y^2 - 3y - 14y + 7 = 0$
$\Rightarrow 3y(2y - 1) - 7(2y - 1) = 0$
$\Rightarrow y = \frac{1}{2} \ or \ \frac{+7}{3}$
$\therefore$ no relation can be established

61. **(b)** Let the income of Airtel in year 2007 be
Rs x.
ATQ,
$55 = \frac{x-225000}{x} \times 100$
$\Rightarrow 55x = 100x - 225000 \times 100$
$\Rightarrow x = \frac{2,25,000\times100}{45} = 5,00,000 = Rs. \ 5 \ lac$

62. **(e)** Let the total income of Reliance in 2006
be Rs. 100 x
Then, profit = Rs. 35x
$\Rightarrow 35x = 1,05,000 \Rightarrow x = 3000$
$\therefore$ expenditure = $(100 - 35) \times 3000$
= Rs. 1,95,000

63. **(b)** Let the expenditure of both the companies
be Rs. 100x
Required ratio = $\frac{100x\times\frac{100}{40}}{100x\times\frac{100}{50}} = \frac{250}{200} = 5 : 4$

64. **(d)** Required percentage= $\frac{7\times\frac{45}{100}}{5.5\times\frac{60}{100}} \times 100 =$
$\frac{315}{330} \times 100$
$= \frac{1050}{11} \% \ = 95\frac{5}{11} \%$

65. **(a)** Required Average = $\frac{45+35+50+60+50+55}{6}\%$
$= \frac{295}{6} \% = 49\frac{1}{6} \%$

66. **(c)** Let the CP of Q be Rs. x
Then, CP of P = Rs. (x + 60)
ATQ,
$\frac{-x\times12.5}{100} + \frac{(x+60)\times20}{100} = Rs. 25.5$
$\Rightarrow 7.5x + 1200 = 25.5 \times 100$
$\Rightarrow x = Rs. 180$

CP of P = Rs. 180 + 60 = Rs. 240

67. (d) Let the efficiency of girl be G and that of boy be B.

ATQ,

$(10G + 11B) \times 5 = (4G + 14B) \times \frac{17}{2}$

$\Rightarrow 100G + 110B = 68G + 238B$

$\Rightarrow 32G = 128B \Rightarrow \frac{G}{B} = \frac{4}{1} = 4 : 1$

$\frac{B}{G} = \frac{1}{4}$

68. (c) Required difference $= 18000 \times \frac{15}{100} \times \frac{1}{9} = 300$

69. (a) Required average $= \dfrac{\frac{15000 \times 75}{100} + \frac{17800 \times 82}{100}}{2}$

$= \frac{11250 + 14596}{2} = 12{,}923$

70. (d) Required % $= \dfrac{(77 - 23) \times \frac{15400}{100}}{16800} \times 100$

$= \frac{8316}{16800} \times 100 = \frac{99}{2}\% = 49\frac{1}{2}\%$

71. (b) Number of Indian visitors on Monday

$= 15000 \times \frac{75}{100} = 11{,}250$

Number of Indian male visitors on Monday

$= 11{,}250 - 15{,}000 \times \frac{32}{100} = 6450$

Required ratio $= \dfrac{6450}{15000 \times \frac{25}{100}} = 43 : 25$

72. (e) Required difference

$= 18000 - \left(\frac{17800 \times 18}{100} + \frac{15400 \times 23}{100}\right)$

$= 18000 - (3204 + 3542) = 11{,}254$

73. (b) Let the sum be Rs. 100 x.

Amount at the end of two years

$= 100x \times \frac{110}{100} \times \frac{112}{100} = Rs. \frac{616x}{5}$

ATQ,

$\Rightarrow \frac{616x}{5} - 100x = 2{,}320 \Rightarrow \frac{116x}{5} = 2320$

$\Rightarrow x = 100$

$\therefore$ sum = Rs. 10,000

74. (a) Let the initial weight of alloy be 16 gm.

Initial weight of gold = 11 gm

And, initial weight of copper = 5 gm

Let y gm of copper is added

ATQ,

$\dfrac{11 - \frac{11}{8}}{\left(5 - \frac{5}{8}\right) + y} = \frac{7}{5}$

$\Rightarrow \dfrac{77}{35 + 8y} = \frac{7}{5} \Rightarrow 385 = 245 + 56y$

$\Rightarrow 140 = 56y \Rightarrow y = 2.5$ gm

75. (d) Let the length of train A be x m

Then, length of train B = 2x m

ATQ,

$2 \times \left(\dfrac{x}{\frac{86.4 \times 5}{18}}\right) = \dfrac{2x + 60}{\frac{108 \times 5}{18}}$

$\Rightarrow \frac{2x}{24} = \frac{2x + 60}{30} \Rightarrow 30x = 24x + 720$

$\Rightarrow 6x = 720$

$\Rightarrow x = 120\,m$

Length of train B = $120 \times 2 = 240$ m

76. (d) From I

Let number of white balls be x

Green balls = 5 – x

Probability of being at least one ball Green

$\Rightarrow \dfrac{{}^{x}C_1\,{}^{5-x}C_1 + {}^{5-x}C_2}{{}^{5}C_2} = \frac{9}{10}$

$\dfrac{x(5-x) + \frac{(5-x)(4-x)}{2}}{10} = \frac{9}{10}$

x = 2

From II

Let number of White balls be x

Total = 5

Probability of being both balls white is $\frac{1}{10}$

$\Rightarrow \dfrac{{}^{x}C_2}{{}^{5}C_2} = \frac{1}{10} \Rightarrow \dfrac{x(x-1)}{20} = \frac{1}{10} \Rightarrow x = 2$

So, either statement I or II is sufficient to give the answer of the question.

77. (e) In none of the statement given marks have been given in terms of numbers, hence we can't find the mars obtained in English.

78. (e) Using Statement I:

Relative speed in same direction

$= \frac{150}{25} = 6m/s.$ ... (i)

Using statement II:

Relative speed in opposite direction $= \frac{150}{15}$

$= 10\,m/s$ ... (ii)

On solving (i) & (ii), we get the value, but we cannot say which value is speed of train A.

79. (a) Let the number of boys in 2009 be x.

Then girls = 3x

Using statement I:

$\frac{3x + x + 100}{2} = 450 \Rightarrow 4x = 800 \Rightarrow x = 200$

Number of boys in 2010 = 300

Number of girls in 2010 = 600

So, ratio = 1 : 2

Statement II: we can't find the ratio.

ATQ,

Ratio $= \dfrac{x}{3x + 150}$

So, Statement I is alone sufficient.

80. (c) From Statement I,

Let P invested Rs. x, then investment of Q = x – 600 and that of R = x – 900

From Statement II,

P's profit is Rs. 18000

Using both,

Ratio of investment

PQR

$x \times 12 : (x - 600) \times 9 : (x - 900) \times 8$

$12x = 18000$

$\Rightarrow x = \dfrac{18000}{12} = Rs.\, 1500.$

Then, Profit of R $= (x - 900) \times 8 =$ Rs. 4800

REASONING ABILITY

Directions (1-5): Study the information and answer the following questions:

There are eight family members F, G, H, I, J, K, L and M. They all have different professions viz. Athlete, Boxer, Cricketer, Lawyer, Engineer, Coordinator, Doctor and Event Manager (not necessarily in the same order).

H is the father of the Cricketer. L is the daughter of the Event manager. The one who is a Doctor is the grandmother of K, who has two brothers. K is a coordinator. I who is an Event manager is married to F. H is a Boxer who is married to the Lawyer. G is the mother of J and K. There are two married couples in the family. The one who is a Coordinator is a female while the one who is an Engineer is a male. The Athlete is the sister of the Boxer, who is married to G. J is not a Cricketer.

1. How many male members are there in the family?
   (a) two   (b) three
   (c) four   (d) five
   (e) None of these

2. How is L related to G?
   (a) daughter   (b) mother
   (c) sister   (d) sister-in-law
   (e) None of these

3. What is the profession of M?
   (a) Engineer
   (b) Doctor
   (c) Cricketer
   (d) Athlete
   (e) Cannot be determined

4. Who among the following is a Doctor?
   (a) F   (b) G
   (c) J   (d) M
   (e) None of these

5. Which of the following statements is definitely true?
   (a) G is married to the Athlete
   (b) The Event manager is the grandfather of the Athlete
   (c) M is the son of G and is a Cricketer
   (d) All are true
   (e) None is true

Directions (6-8): Study the following information and answer the given questions.

In a family of seven members there are four female members. T is the mother of M. P is the brother of M. G is the grandfather of P. H is the mother-in-law of T. If V is the brother of S, who is the sister-in-law of T?

6. How is H related to P?
   (a) mother   (b) grandmother
   (c) sister   (d) sister-in-law
   (e) None of these

7. How is M related to S?
   (a) niece   (b) nephew
   (c) brother   (d) Either (a) or (b)
   (e)None of these

8. How is V related to G?
   (a) son   (b) father
   (c) brother   (d) father-in-law
   (e) None of these

Directions (9-10): Study the following information and answer the given questions:

In a park J, K, L, M and N are playing a game. All are facing north. K is 50m. to the right of M. J is 70m. to the south of K. L is 50m. to the west of M. N is 95m. to the north of J.

9. Who among the following is to the southeast of the person who is to the left of M?
   (a) J
   (b) K
   (c) L
   (d) N
   (e) Cannot be determined

10. If a kid walks from L, meets K followed by J and then N, how many metres does he walk if he travels the distance in a straight line all through?
    (a) 195m.   (b) 235m.   (c) 210m.
    (d) 265m.   (e) 170m.

Directions (11-15): Study the information and answer the following questions:

Eight boxes M, N, O, P, Q, R, S and T are placed one above the other, but not necessarily in the same order. All boxes contain a different number of coins viz. 5, 18, 25, 30, 35, 48, 50 and 60 (not necessarily in the same order).

Three boxes are placed between box O and box M, which contains 48 coins. N contains 50 coins and is placed immediately above O. There is only one box which is placed between box N and box Q, which contains 60 coins. Box P contains 5 coins and it is placed somewhere below box S. Only two boxes are placed between box S and box T, which contains 25 coins. The box which contains 50 coins is not placed below the box, which contains 48 coins. Box S is not placed at an odd-numbered position when counted from bottom to top. Box S has less coins than box T. The box which contains the highest number of coins is not placed on top. The box which contains least number of coins will not be placed at the bottom. Box R contains more coins than box O. The box which contains 35 coins will not be placed on top.

11. How many boxes are placed between box P and box S?
    (a) none   (b) one
    (c) two   (d) three
    (e) More than three
12. Box which is placed at the bottom contains how many coins?
    (a) 30   (b) 35
    (c) 18   (d) 25
    (e) None of these
13. Which among the following boxes is placed at the top?
    (a) Box R   (b) Box N
    (c) Box O   (d) Box P
    (e) None of these
14. Which box is placed immediately above the box, which contains 35 coins?
    (a) Box O
    (b) Box S
    (c) The box which contains 50 coins
    (d) The box which contains 60 coins
    (e) None of these
15. How many coins does box O contain?
    (a) 18
    (b) 30
    (c) 35
    (d) 25
    (e) Cannot be determined

Directions (16-20): Study the following information carefully and answer the given questions:

Eight friends P, Q, R, S, T, U, V and W are sitting around a square table in such a way that four of them sit at four corners of the square while the other four sit in the middle of each side. All of them like different colours viz. green, blue, red, black, white, pink, yellow and orange. The ones who sit at the four corners do not face towards the centre while those who sit in the middle of the sides do not face outside.

R likes red colour and sits third to the right of T. Only two persons sit between T and the one who likes green colour. S likes black colour and is an immediate neighbour of R. P likes pink colour. Q sits second to the right of the one who likes orange colour. The one who likes red colour faces the one who likes white colour. U is not an immediate neighbour of the one who likes white colour. U likes blue colour. Neither V nor W likes orange colour.

16. Who sits exactly between P and T when counted from the right of P?
    (a) Q
    (b) U
    (c) The one who likes green colour
    (d) The one who likes white colour

(e) Cannot be determined
17. What is the position of V with respect to R?
    (a) Second to the left
    (b) Third to the right
    (c) Fourth to the left
    (d) Third to the left
    (e) Cannot be determined
18. Four of the following five are alike in a certain way and so form a group. Who among the following does not belong to that group?
    (a) R
    (b) U
    (c) The one who likes green colour
    (d) The one who likes white colour
    (e) The one who likes yellow colour
19. What is the position of S with respect to the one who likes yellow colour?
    (a) Second to the left
    (b) Second to the right
    (c) Third to the right
    (d) Fourth to the right
    (e) Cannot be determined
20. How many persons sit between the one who likes yellow colour and the one who likes pink colour?
    (a) one
    (b) two
    (c) three
    (d) four
    (e) Cannot be determined

Directions (21-25): In each of the questions, relationships between some elements are shown in the statements. These statements are followed by conclusions numbered I and II. Read the statements and give the answer.
(a) If only conclusion I follows.
(b) If only conclusion II follows.
(c) If either conclusion I or II follows.
(d) If neither conclusion I nor II follows.
(e) If both conclusions I and II follow.

21. **Statements:** $U > S = P; N < M \leq P; Z \geq M \geq X$
    Conclusions: I. $X > U$ II. $Z > N$
22. **Statements:** $A \leq B = C \leq D; F \geq G \geq D; F < K$
    Conclusions: I. $K > B$ II. $G \leq A$
23. **Statements:** $Z < Y \geq X; W > V \geq Y = U; W \geq T$
    Conclusions: I. $T > Z$ II. $X \geq V$
24. **Statements:** $P \geq V \geq O = M; K \leq L \leq O = E$
    Conclusions: I. $K \leq V$ II. $E = M$
25. **Statements:** $Q \geq N = S \geq P; R \leq C \leq P \leq D$
    Conclusions: I. $R < S$ II. $N = R$

Directions (26-30): Each of the questions below consists of a question and two statements numbered I and II, given below it. You have to decide whether the data provided in the statements is sufficient to answer the question. Read all the two statements and give the answer:

(a) If the data in Statement I is sufficient to answer the question, while the data in Statement II is not required to answer the question.

(b) If the data in Statement II is sufficient to answer the question, while the data in Statement I is not required to answer the question.

(c) If the data in either Statement I alone or Statement II alone is sufficient to answer the question.

(d) If the data neither in Statement I nor in Statement II together is sufficient to answer the question.

(e) If the data in Statements I and II together is necessary to answer the question.

26. How many brothers does G have?
I. S is the only son of V, who is the father of T.
II. S is the brother of T, who is the only sister of G.

27. Among five friends L, M, N, O and P who is the heaviest, if all are having different weights?
I. L is heavier than O. P is heavier than L.
II. N is lighter than only M.

28. What is the code for 'human' in the given language?
I. 'Human have brains' is coded as 'tuvoni'.
II. 'Brains have been working' is coded as 'wkni ne tu'.

29. What is the rank of J (from the top) in a class of 25 students?
I. J is four ranks above V, who is ninth from the bottom.
II. J is five ranks below M, who is eighteenth from the bottom.

30. Five friends A, B, C, D and E are sitting around a circular table facing the centre. What is the exact position of D with respect to B?
I. A sits second to the right of C. D is not an immediate neighbour of A. E does not sit to the immediate right of A.
II. B sits second to the right of E. A is an immediate neighbour of B. C sits to the immediate left of E.

31. How many pairs of letters are there in the word "**SCHEDULE**" which have as many letters between them in the word as in the alphabetical series?
(a) one (b) two
(c) three (d) four
(e) None of these

32. If all the alphabets are rearranged within itself as they appear in the English dictionary in the word "DEFAULTER" then which of the following will be seventh from the left end?
(a) F (b) L
(c) T (d) R
(e) None of these

33. In a row of students facing North, Rahul is 14th from the left end. Five students sit between Rahul and Sam. What is the position of Sam from the left end, if Sam does not sit to the right of Rahul?
(a) Sixth from the left end
(b) Seventh from the left end
(c) Eight from the left end
(d) Twentieth from the left end
(e) Cannot be determined

34. Pointing at a lady, Sameer said, "She is the only sister of my father's only grandson". How is this lady related to Sameer?
(a) daughter
(b) niece
(c) sister
(d) mother
(e) Cannot be determined

35. In a certain code 'CLASS' is written as '47#99' and 'SHAPE' is written as '93#65'. How is 'PALACE' written in that code?
(a) 6#74#5 (b) 6#7#54
(c) 6##745 (d) 6#7#45
(e) None of these

Directions (36-40): Study the following information carefully and answer the questions given below:

In a certain code language
'sweets are tasty food' is coded as 'sara fa ta'
'food are good nutrients' is coded as 'na fa gara'
'nutrients are healthy' is coded as 'ha rana'
'healthy sweets good business' is coded as 'sa ha baga'

36. What is the code for 'healthy food'?
(a) na fa (b) ra ha
(c) ha fa (d) fa ga
(e) None of these

37. What is the code for 'tasty' in the given language?
(a) na
(b) ta
(c) fa
(d) ra
(e) Cannot be determined

38. 'ba' is the code for?
(a) healthy (b) are
(c) tasty (d) business
(e) None of these

39. What is the code for 'are' in the given language?
(a) na (b) ha
(c) ra (d) ga

(e) None of these

40. What is the code for 'good nutrients'?
    (a) sa na
    (b) ga ra
    (c) ga na
    (d) fa na
    (e) Cannot be determined

QUANTITATIVE APTITUDE

41. PNB bank has rolled out a new plan according to which the rate of simple interest on a sum of money is 5% per annum for the first $2\frac{1}{2}$ yrs, 6% per annum for the next $3\frac{1}{2}$ yrs and 9% per annum for the period beyond the firstsix years. Total simple interest received on a sum for a period of 10 years is Rs. 6950. Find the sum.
    (a) Rs. 12,000   (b) Rs. 13,500
    (c) Rs 14,000   (d) Rs 10,000
    (e) Rs 15,000

42. Three friends Veer, Abhi and Ayush donates 9%, 7% and 8% of their respective monthly salary. The monthly salary of Abhi and Ayush are equal and the difference between their donations is Rs. 66. The donation of veer is Rs. 342 less than the total donations made by Abhi and Ayush together. Find the average of their monthly salary?
    (a) Rs. 6840   (b) Rs. 6800   (c) Rs. 6700
    (d) Rs. 6920   (e) Rs. 6900

43. Adda 247 is an education based company which doubled its turnover in 2015 from Rs. 12 crore in 2014. Then, it tripled its turnover in 2016 over its previous year and again increased its turnover by $37\frac{1}{2}$% in 2017 overthe previous year. Its current turnover (2017) is what percent of its turnover in 2014?
    (a) 875%   (b) 925%   (c) 825%
    (d) 850%   (e) 950%

44. If 13 years are subtracted from the present age of Honey and the remainder is divided by 8, it gives the age of his grand-daughter Hardeep. If Hardeep is 27 years younger than her father then find the average age of all three, given that the present age of Honey's only son is 34 years. Honey has no daughter.
    (a) $36\frac{2}{3}$yr
    (b) 35 yr
    (c) $35\frac{2}{3}$yr
    (d) $36\frac{1}{3}$ yr
    (e) $37\frac{1}{3}$ yr

45. Sandeep rolled two dice at the same time. Find the probability of getting the sum 9 or more on both the dice together.
    (a) $\frac{1}{4}$ (b) $\frac{11}{36}$ (c) $\frac{7}{18}$
    (d) $\frac{5}{18}$ (e) $\frac{1}{3}$

Directions (46-50): In each question two equations numbered (I) and (II) are given. You should solve both the equations and mark the appropriate answer.
(a) If x = y or no relation can be established
(b) If $x > y$
(c) If $x < y$
(d) If $x \geq y$
(e) If $x \leq y$

46. I. $15x^2 + 38x + 16 = 0$
    II. $8y^2 + 20y + 12 = 0$

47. I. $8x^2 + 19x + 11 = 0$
    II. $8y^2 + 27y + 22 = 0$

48. I. $6x^2 - 9x + 3 = 0$
    II. $8y^2 - 11y + 3 = 0$

49. I. $5x^2 + 6x - 11 = 0$
    II. $20y^2 + 23y - 43 = 0$

50. I. $3x + 7y = 28$
    II. $5x + 3y = 38$

Directions (51-55): What will come in the place of the question (?) mark in the following number series:

51. 82, 111, 147, 191, ?, 307
    (a) 240   (b) 236   (c) 244
    (d) 252   (e) 232

52. ?, 48, 72, 180, 630, 2835
    (a) 24   (b) 72   (c) 60
    (d) 80   (e) 96

53. 6, ?, 568, 3414, 13660, 27322
    (a) 70   (b) 66   (c) 60
    (d) 72   (e) 84

54. 589, 468, 387, 338, 313, ?
    (a) 306   (b) 303   (c) 312
    (d) 304   (e) 305

55. 12, 12, 15, 23, 38,?
    (a) 63   (b) 61   (c) 62
    (d) 58   (e) 38

56. Ritu and Anu together can do a work in 16 days whereas Anu alone can do it in 24 days. If Neha

alone can do the same work in 30 days, then find the ratio of efficiency of Neha to that of Ritu?
(a) 5:8   (b) 8:5   (c) 5:3
(d) 2:3   (e) 7:8

57. How many integers from 5000 to 5999 have at least one of its digits repeated?
(a) 498   (b) 496   (c) 504
(d) 508   (e) 512

Directions (58-62): Find the exact value of the question mark (?) in the following questions?

58. 35% of 48% of $\frac{2}{5}$ of 15000 = ?
(a) 1004   (b) 996   (c) 1020
(d) 1008   (e) 1012

59. $\sqrt{24 \times 435 \div ? + \sqrt{256} + 45\% \text{ of } 40} = 18$
(a) 30   (b) 24   (c) 36
(d) 48   (e) 18

60. $[(238 \div 4) + 36.5] \div 12 = ?$ % of 64
(a) $12\frac{1}{2}\%$ (b) 15%   (c) 16%
(d) 8%   (e) 10%

61. $\left(\sqrt{11664} + \sqrt[3]{74088}\right) \times ? = 125 \times 12$
(a) 12   (b) 13   (c) 12.5
(d) 15   (e) 10

62. $4\frac{2}{3} - 3\frac{1}{6} + 5\frac{5}{9} - 2\frac{7}{12} = ?$
(a) $4\frac{17}{36}$ (b) $4\frac{19}{36}$ (c) $4\frac{7}{12}$
(d) $4\frac{1}{2}$ (e) $4\frac{4}{9}$

63. Distance between the Delhi Junction and Patna junction is 1200 km. A train P starts from Patna at a speed of x km/h. towards the Delhi junction. Another train Q starts from Patna at a speed of (x + 30) km/hr. in the same direction, 7hours later than the start of train P. If train Q crosses train P in 5 hours after its start, then find the speed of train P.
(a) $\frac{135}{7}$ km/h.   (b) 70 km/h.   (c) 130 km/h.
(d) $\frac{130}{7}$ km/h.   (e) $\frac{150}{7}$ km/h.

64. A shopkeeper purchased an article at some discount on marked price and raised the marked price of an article by 80%. Then he allowed two successive discounts of $37\frac{1}{2}\%$ and $44\frac{4}{9}\%$ on it. On selling the article, he still made a profit of $4\frac{1}{6}\%$. Find at what discount percent the shopkeeper bought the article.
(a) 50%   (b) 40%   (c) 30%
(d) 36%   (e) 42%

65. A is an alloy of two types of metals x and y and B is an alloy of two types of metals y and z. Some quantity of B is mixed with 30 gms. of A to form another alloy, which has 55% of y metal concentration. Find the quantity of B taken if an alloy A has 60% of y concentration and B has 40% of y concentration.
(a) 15 gm.   (b) 12.5 gm.   (c) 10 gm.
(d) 20 gm.   (e) $7\frac{1}{2}$ gm.

Directions (66-70): The line graph given below shows the number of students (in hundreds) who have been selected in Banking exam and in SSC exam from a reputed coaching institute in six different years.

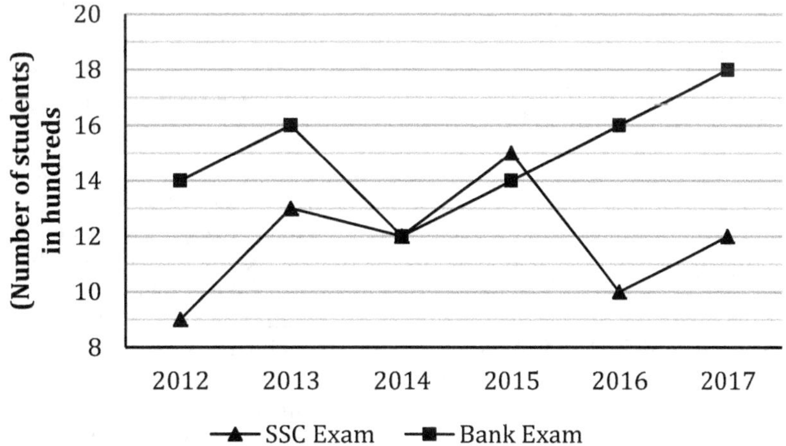

66. Find the ratio of the total number of students selected in Banking exam from 2015 to 2017 together to the total number of students selected in SSC exam from 2012 to 2014 together.
(a) 24:17   (b) 20:17   (c) 22:17
(d) 17 : 24   (e) 17 : 22

67. The average number of students selected in both exams in 2016 is what percent more/less than the average number of students selected in both the exams in year 2017?
(a) $12\frac{1}{2}\%$ (b) $12\frac{3}{5}\%$ (c) $12\frac{1}{3}\%$

(d) $13\frac{1}{3}\%$ (e) $13\frac{2}{3}\%$

68. What is the ratio of total students selected in Banking exam from 2013 to 2015 to total students selected in SSC exam from 2013 to 2015?
(a) 115:91   (b) 21:20   (c) 125:91
(d) 91:125   (e) 10:7

69. If every year 20% of the students who passed the Banking exam also passed the SSC exam, then find the average of number of students who passed both the exams from 2014 to 2016.
(a) 260   (b) 275   (c) 300
(d) 320   (e) 280

70. Find the difference between the total number of students who passed the Banking exam from 2013 to 2015 and the total number of students who passed the SSC exam from 2014 to 2016?
(a) 400   (b) 450   (c) 500
(d) 520   (e) 550

Directions (71-75): The table given below shows the total number of books available in five different college libraries and the number of books for medical study as a percentage of the total number of available books in the library. Study the given table and answer the following questions carefully.

College	Total Number of books	Books for medical study (as a percentage)
A	425	40%
B	350	30%
C	325	20%
D	450	32%
E	480	35%

Total number of books = Books for medical study + Engineering books + Books for management study

71. Find the ratio of the total number of non-medical books available in colleges B and C to the total number of medical books available in colleges A, B and C together?
(a) 103:68   (b) 68:103   (c) 68:101
(d) 101:68   (e) 3:2

72. The ratio of the number of engineering books to the number of management books in college D is 5:4. Find the difference between the number of engineering books and the number of management books?
(a) 32   (b) 34   (c) 30
(d) 28   (e) 36

73. Find the difference between the total number of medical books available in college C and D together and the number of books available in college B.
(a) 140   (b) 142   (c) 141
(d) 144   (e) 143

74. Find the average number of non-medical books available in college C and E and the number of medical books available in college B?
(a) $225\frac{2}{3}$ (b) $225\frac{1}{3}$ (c) $224\frac{1}{3}$
(d) 225   (e) $226\frac{2}{3}$

75. The ratio of engineering to management books in college B and college E are in the ratio of 17:18 and 5:3 respectively. Find the difference between the total number of engineering books and management books in both the colleges.
(a) 61   (b) 51   (c) 71
(d) 59   (e) 81

Directions (76-80): In the following questions, two quantities are given for each question. Compare the numeric value of both the quantities and answer accordingly.

76. Quantity I : The price of wheat falls by 20%. How much wheat can be bought now with the money that was sufficient to buy 20 kg. of wheat previously?

Quantity II : The average weight of 14 students in a school is 13 kg. When a new student is included in this group, the average weight decreases by 0.2 kg. Find the age of the new student.

(a) Quantity I > Quantity II
(b) Quantity II > Quantity I
(c) Quantity I ≥ Quantity II
(d) Quantity II ≥ Quantity I
(e) Quantity I = Quantity II or relation can't be established.

77. Quantity I : Find the probability of getting two heads when three coins are tossed simultaneously.

Quantity II : When the numerator of a fraction is increased by 50% and the denominator is decreased by 10%, the fraction thus obtained is $\frac{5}{8}$. Find the original fraction.

(a) Quantity I > Quantity II
(b) Quantity II > Quantity I
(c) Quantity I >= Quantity II
(d) Quantity II >= Quantity I
(e) Quantity I = Quantity II or relation can't be established.

78. Quantity I : If by selling two items for Rs. 150 each, the shopkeeper gains 20% on one and loses 20% on the other, find the value of gain/loss.

Quantity II : An article is sold for Rs. 805 at a profit of 15%. What would have been the actual profit or loss on it, if it had been sold for Rs. 717?

(a) Quantity I > Quantity II
(b) Quantity II > Quantity I
(c) Quantity I >= Quantity II
(d) Quantity II >= Quantity I

(e) Quantity I = Quantity II or relation can't be established.

79. Quantity I : Find the principal if compound interest is charged on principal at the rate of $16\frac{2}{3}\%$ per annum for two years and the sum becomes Rs. 245.

Quantity II : A sum of Rs. 500 amounts to Rs. 620 in four years at simple interest. What will Rs. 150 amount to if the rate of interest remains same and time period is $2\frac{1}{2}$ yrs.

(a) Quantity I > Quantity II
(b) Quantity II > Quantity I
(c) Quantity I >= Quantity II
(d) Quantity II >= Quantity I

(e) Quantity I = Quantity II or relation can't be established.

80. Quantity I: A metallic spherical ball of radius 3.5 cm. is melted and re-cast into eight identical cones of radius $1\frac{3}{4}$ cm. and height 'x' cm. Find the value of x.

Quantity II: A rectangle has length 4 cm. more than its breadth. Its area is 4 cm.^{2} lesser than the area of a square, with a perimeter of 36 cm. Find the breadth of the rectangle.

(a) Quantity I > Quantity II
(b) Quantity II > Quantity I
(c) Quantity I >= Quantity II
(d) Quantity II >= Quantity I
(e) Quantity I = Quantity II or relation can't be established.

Solutions

REASONING ABILITY

Directions (1-5):

L is the daughter of Event manager. I who is an Event manager is married to F. H is a Boxer who is married to G who is a lawyer. G is the mother of J and K. There are two married couples in the family. Doctor is grandmother of K, who has two brothers. K is a coordinator. Coordinator is a female while the one who is an Engineer is a male. The Athlete is the sister of the Boxer. J is not a Cricketer. So we get the final arrangement as:

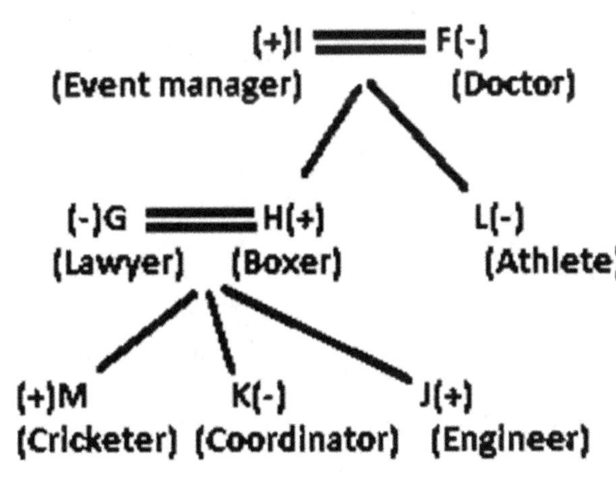

1. (c)   2.(d)   3.(c)
4. (a)   5.(c)

Directions (6-8):

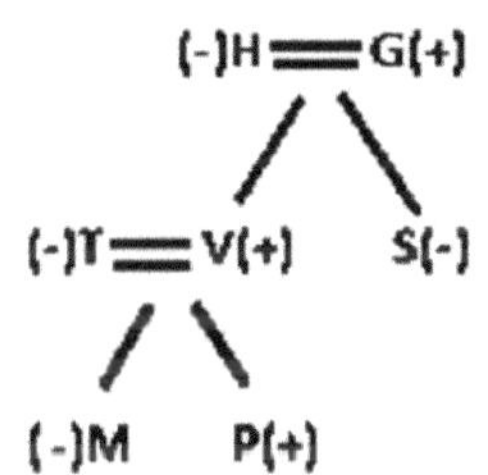

6. (b)   7.(a)   8.(a)

Directions (9-10):

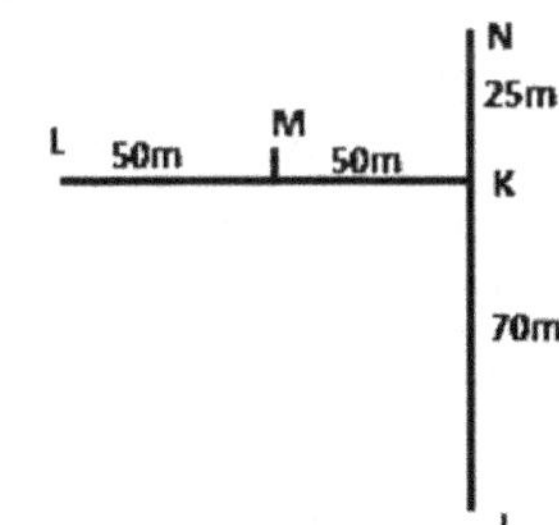

9. (a)   10.(d)

Directions (11-15):

Three boxes are placed between box O and box M, which contains 48 coins. N contains 50 coins and is placed immediately above O. The box which contains 50 coins is not placed below the box which contains 48 coins. There is only one box which is placed between box N and box Q, which contains 60 coins. The box which contains highest number of coins is not placed on top. Only two boxes are placed between box S and box T, which contains 25 coins. Box S has less coins than box T. Box S is not placed at an odd numbered position when counted from bottom to top. Box P contains 5 coins. We have following possibilities:

	Case 1			Case 2	
Box No.	Box	No. of coins	Box No.	Box	No. of coins
8			8	N	50
7	N	50	7	O	
5	Q	60	5		
4	S	18	4	S	18
3			3	M	48
2	M	48	2		
1	T	25	1	T	25

Now, box P is placed somewhere below box S. Box R contains more coins than box O. The box which contains 35 coins will not be placed on top. So the final arrangement will be:

Box No.	Box	No. of coins
8	N	50
7	O	30
6	Q	60
5	R	35
4	S	18
3	M	48
2	P	5
1	T	25

11. (b)   **12. (d)**   **13. (b)**
14. (d)   **15. (b)**

Directions (16-20):

R likes red colour and sits third to the right of T. Only two persons sit between T and the one who likes green colour. The one who likes red colour faces the one who likes white colour. S likes black colour and is an immediate neighbor of R. P likes pink colour. U likes blue colour. Q sits second to the right of the one who likes orange colour. U is not an immediate neighbor of the one who likes white colour. We have following possibilities-

Case 1

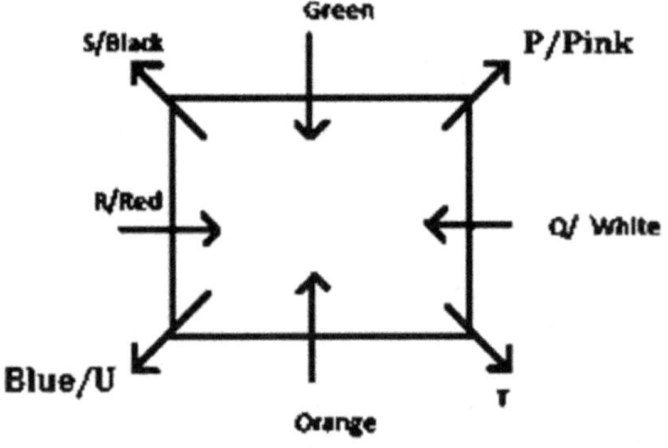

Case 2

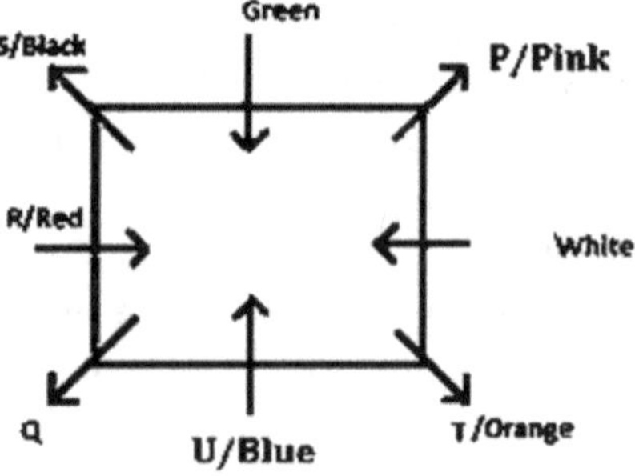

Now, Neither V nor W likes orange colour. This will eliminate Case 1. So the final arrangement will be-

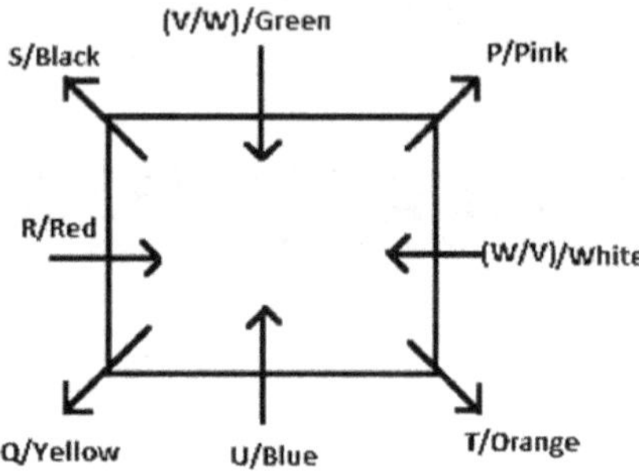

16. (d)   **17. (e)**   **18. (e)**
19. (b)   **20. (c)**

Direction (21-25):

21. (b)	I. X > U (False)	II. Z > N (True)
22. (a)	I. K > B (True)	II. G ≤ A (False)
23. (d)	I. T > Z (False)	II. X ≥ V (False)
24. (e)	I. K ≤ V (True)	II. E = M (True)
25. (c)	I. R < S (False)	II. N = R (False)

Directions (26-30):

26. (e) From both I and II, G has only one brother.

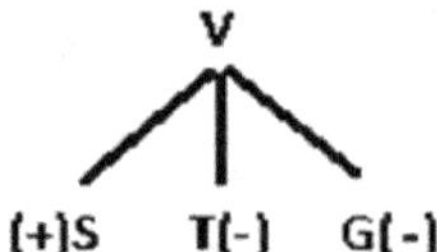

27. (b) From I, P > L > O

From II, M > N > __ > __ > __

Hence only II is sufficient to answer the question

28. (e) From I and II both it is clear that 'Human' is coded as 'vo'

29. (c) From I, Position of V from top = 25 – 9 + 1 = 17th

Thus position of J from top = 17 – 4 = 13th

From II, Position of M from top = 25 -18 +1 = 8th

Thus position of J from top = 8 + 5 = 13th

30. (a) From I, D is to the immediate right of B

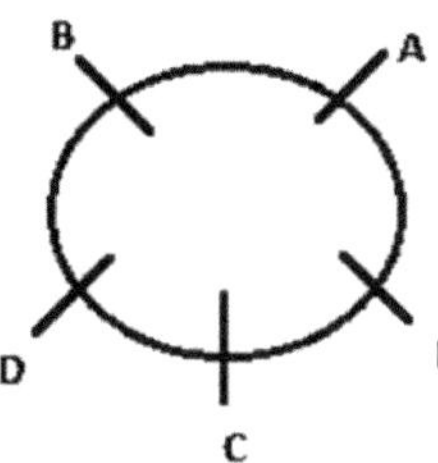

From II, Position of D is not confirmed.

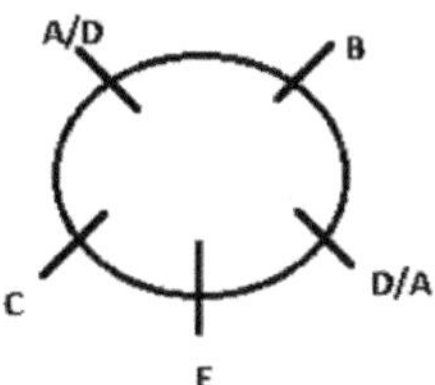

31. (c)

32. (d)   **33.(c)**

34.(e)   She can be Sameer's niece or daughter.

35. (d)

Directions (36-40):

Elements	Codes
sweets	sa
are	ra
food	fa
tasty	ta
good	ga
nutrients	na
healthy	ha
business	ba

36. (c)   **37. (b)**   **38. (d)**

39. (c)   **40. (c)**

QUANTITATIVE APTITUDE

41. (d) Let the sum be Rs x

Atq,

$$\frac{x \times 5 \times \frac{5}{2}}{100} + \frac{x \times \frac{7}{2} \times 6}{100} + \frac{x \times 9 \times 4}{100} = 6950$$

$$\Rightarrow \frac{x}{8} + \frac{21x}{100} + \frac{9x}{25} = 6950$$

$$\Rightarrow \frac{139x}{200} = 6950 \Rightarrow x = Rs\ 10,000$$

42. (b) Let the monthly salary of Abhi and Ayush be Rs x

Atq,

$$\frac{x \times 8}{100} - \frac{x \times 7}{100} = 66 \Rightarrow x = Rs\ 6600$$

Total donations made by Abhi and Ayush = 15% of 6600= Rs 990

Let the monthly salary of Veer beRs y.

Donations made by Veer $= \frac{y \times 9}{100} = 990 - 342$

$$\Rightarrow y = \frac{648 \times 100}{9} = Rs\ 7200$$

Average monthly salary $= \frac{6600 + 6600 + 7200}{3}$

= Rs 6800

43. (c) Turnover in 2015 = Rs 24 crore

Turnover in 2016 = Rs 72 crore

Turnover in 2017 $= 72 \times \frac{11}{8} = 99$ crores

Required % $= \frac{99}{12} \times 100 = 825\%$

44. (a) Let the present age of Honey be x yrs

Age of his Grand-daughter Hardeep$= \frac{(x-13)}{8}$yr

Atq,

$$\frac{x-13}{8} + 27 = 34 \Rightarrow x - 13 = 56 \Rightarrow x = 69$$

Age of Hardeep = 7 yrs

$\therefore$ Average age $= \frac{69+7+34}{3} = \frac{110}{3} = 36\frac{2}{3}$ yr

45. (d) Favourable cases : (3, 6,), (4, 5), (4, 6), (5, 4), (5, 5), (5, 6), (6, 3), (6, 4), (6, 5), (6, 6)

Required probability $= \frac{10}{36} = \frac{5}{18}$

46. (a) **I.** $15x^2 + 38x + 16 = 0$

$\Rightarrow 15x^2 + 30x + 8x + 16 = 0$

$\Rightarrow 15x (x + 2) + 8 (x + 2) = 0$

$\Rightarrow x = -2 \text{ or} \frac{-8}{15}$

II. $8y^2 + 20y + 12 = 0$

$\Rightarrow 8y^2 + 8y + 12y + 12 = 0$

$\Rightarrow 8y(y + 1) + 12 (y + 1) = 0$

$\Rightarrow y = -1 \text{ or} \frac{-12}{8}$

$\therefore$relationship can't be established

47. (d) **I.** $8x^2 + 19x + 11 = 0$

$8x^2 + 8x + 11x + 11 = 0$

$\Rightarrow 8x (x + 1) + 11(x + 1) = 0$

$\Rightarrow x = \frac{-11}{8} \text{ or} - 1$

II. $8y^2 + 27y + 22 = 0$

$\Rightarrow 8y^2 + 16y + 11y + 22 = 0$

$\Rightarrow 8y (y + 2) + 11(y + 2) = 0$

$\Rightarrow y = \frac{-11}{8} \text{ or} - 2 = x \geq y$

48. (a) **I.** $6x^2 - 9x + 3 = 0$

$\Rightarrow 6x^2 - 6x - 3x + 3 = 0$

$\Rightarrow 6x\,(x-1)-3(x-1)=0$

$\Rightarrow x=1 \text{ or } \dfrac{1}{2}$

II. $8y^2 - 11y + 3 = 0$

$\Rightarrow 8y^2 - 8y - 3y + 3 = 0$

$\Rightarrow 8y\,(y-1)-3\,(y-1)=0 \Rightarrow y=1 \text{ or } \dfrac{3}{8}$

= no relation

49. (a) I. $5x^2 + 6x - 11 = 0$

$\Rightarrow 5x^2 + 11x - 5x - 11 = 0$

$\Rightarrow x\,(5x+11)-1\,(5x+11)=0$

$\Rightarrow x=1 \text{ or } \dfrac{-11}{5}$

II. $20y^2 + 23y - 43 = 0$

$\Rightarrow 20y^2 - 20y + 43y - 43 = 0$

$\Rightarrow 20y\,(y-1)+43(y-1)=0$

$\Rightarrow y=1 \text{ or } \dfrac{-43}{20}$

Relationship can't be established

50. (b) **(i)** $3x + 7y = 28$

(ii) $5x + 3y = 38$

Multiple (i) by 5 and multiple (ii) by 3 and subtract

So, $y = 1$

$x = 7$

$\therefore x > y$

51. (c)

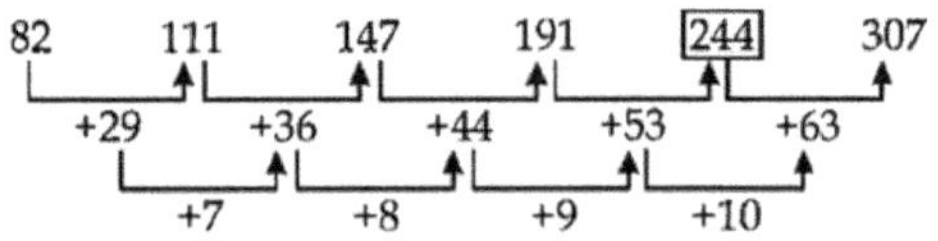

```
82      111     147     191     [244]    307
   +29     +36     +44     +53      +63
      +7      +8      +9      +10
```

52. (e)

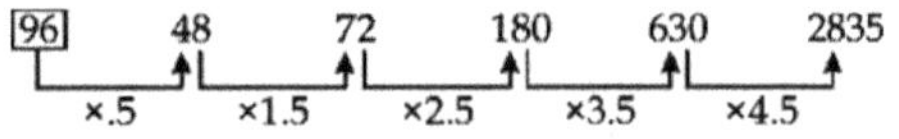

```
[96]    48      72      180     630     2835
   ×.5     ×1.5    ×2.5    ×3.5    ×4.5
```

53. (a)

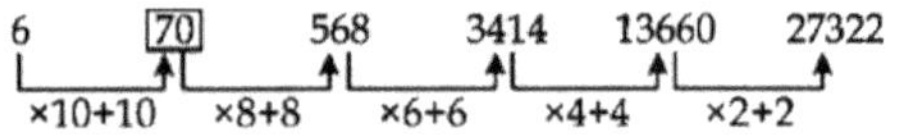

```
6      [70]    568     3414    13660    27322
  ×10+10   ×8+8    ×6+6    ×4+4     ×2+2
```

54. (d)

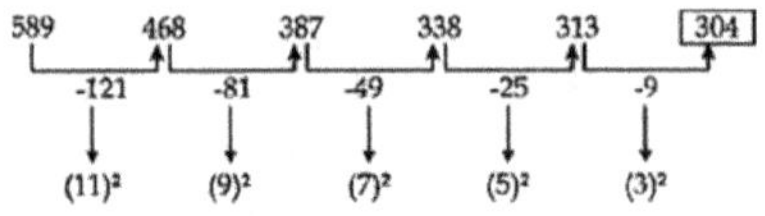

```
589    468     387     338     313     [304]
   -121    -81     -49     -25     -9
   (11)²   (9)²    (7)²    (5)²    (3)²
```

55. (c) Series is

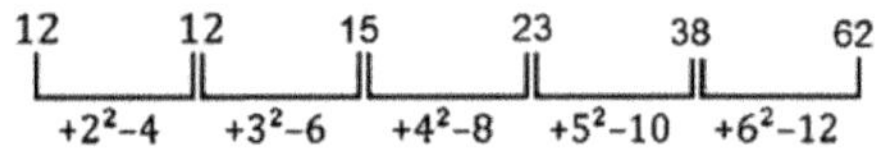

```
12     12     15     23     38     62
  +2²-4   +3²-6   +4²-8   +5²-10   +6²-12
```

Alternate,

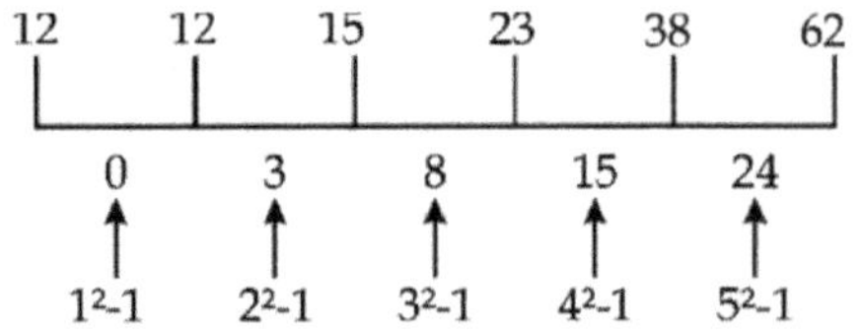

```
12     12     15     23     38     62
     0      3      8      15     24
   1²-1    2²-1    3²-1    4²-1    5²-1
```

56. (b) Ritu and Anu's one day work $= \dfrac{1}{16}$

Anu's one day work $= \dfrac{1}{24}$

Ritu's one day work $= \dfrac{1}{16} - \dfrac{1}{24} = \dfrac{1}{48}$

Neha's one day work $= \dfrac{1}{30}$

Ratio of Efficiency of Neha and Ritu is

$= \dfrac{1}{30} : \dfrac{1}{48}$

$= 8 : 5$

57. (b) Total required number of numbers = All numbers -numbers with none of its digits repeated

Total numbers with none of its digits repeated

$= 1 \times 9 \times 8 \times 7 = 504$

So, the required number $= 1000 - 504 = 496$

58. (d) $? = \dfrac{35}{100} \times \dfrac{48}{100} \times \dfrac{2}{5} \times 15000 = 1008$

59. (c) $\sqrt{24 \times 435 \div ? + 16 + 18} = 18$

$\Rightarrow 24 \times 435 \div ? + 34 = (18)^2 = 324$

$\Rightarrow \dfrac{24 \times 435}{?} = 290 \quad \Rightarrow \quad ? = \dfrac{24 \times 435}{290} = 36$

60. (a) $[(238 \div 4) + 36.5] \div 12 = \dfrac{? \times 64}{100}$

$\Rightarrow (59.5 + 36.5) \div 12 = \dfrac{? \times 64}{100}$

$\Rightarrow 8 = \dfrac{? \times 64}{100} \Rightarrow ? = 12\dfrac{1}{2}\%$

61. (e) $(108 + 42) \times ? = 1500$

$\Rightarrow ? = \dfrac{1500}{150} = 10$

62. (a) $? = (4 - 3 + 5 - 2) + \left(\dfrac{2}{3} - \dfrac{1}{6} + \dfrac{5}{9} - \dfrac{7}{12}\right)$

$? = 4 + \left(\dfrac{24 - 6 + 20 - 21}{36}\right) = 4\dfrac{17}{36}$

63. (e) Distance covered by train P in 7 hours= 7x

$5 = \dfrac{7x}{(x+30)-x} \Rightarrow x = 150/7 \text{ km/hr}$

64. (b) Let the initial MP for shopkeeper be Rs 100x

New MP $= 100x \times \dfrac{180}{100} = $ Rs 180x

SP (on which article is sold by Shopkeeper)

$= 180x \times \dfrac{5}{8} \times \dfrac{5}{9} = $ Rs 62.5x

CP for the shopkeeper $= \dfrac{62.5x \times 24}{25} = $ Rs 60x

$\therefore$ Required discount $= \dfrac{(100x - 60x)}{100x} \times 100 = 40\%$

65. (c) Using allegations on y concentration;

```
     A              B
    60%            40%
          55%

    15      :      5
     3      :      1
```

3 units= 30gm

So,1 unit=10gm

66. **(a)** Required ratio $= \frac{(1400+1600+1800)}{(900+1300+1200)} = \frac{24}{17}$

67. **(d)** Required % $= \frac{\left(\frac{1800+1200}{2}\right)-\left(\frac{1600+1000}{2}\right)}{\left(\frac{1800+1200}{2}\right)} \times 100$

$= \frac{200}{1500} \times 100 = 13\frac{1}{3}\%$

68. **(b)** Required ratio $= \frac{1600+1200+1400}{1300+1200+1500} = 21:20$

69. **(e)** Required average $= \frac{\frac{1200\times20}{100}+\frac{1400\times20}{100}+\frac{1600\times20}{100}}{3}$

$= \frac{240+280+320}{3} = 280$

70. **(c)** Required difference $= (1600 + 1200 + 1400) - (1200 + 1500 + 1000)$
$= 4200 - 3700 = 500$

71. **(d)** Required ratio $= \frac{\frac{350\times70}{100}+\frac{325\times80}{100}}{\frac{425\times40}{100}+\frac{350\times30}{100}+\frac{325\times20}{100}}$

$= \frac{245+260}{170+105+65} = \frac{505}{340} = \frac{101}{68}$

72. **(b)** Number of engineering books in college D
$= \frac{450\times68}{100} \times \frac{5}{9} = 170$

Number of management books in college D
$= \frac{450\times68}{100} \times \frac{4}{9} = 136$

Required difference $= 170 - 136 = 34$

73. **(c)** Required difference $= 350 - \left(\frac{325\times20}{100} + \frac{450\times32}{100}\right)$
$= 350 - (65 + 144) = 141$

74. **(a)** Required average
$= \frac{325\times\frac{80}{100}+480\times\frac{65}{100}+350\times\frac{30}{100}}{3}$

$= \frac{260+312+105}{3} = \frac{677}{3} = 225\frac{2}{3}$

75. **(c)** Number of engg. books in college B
$= \frac{350\times70}{100} \times \frac{17}{35} = 119$

Number of management books in college B
$= 350 \times \frac{70}{100} \times \frac{18}{35} = 126$

Number of engg. books in college E
$= 480 \times \frac{65}{100} \times \frac{5}{8} = 195$

Number of management books in college E
$= 480 \times \frac{65}{100} \times \frac{3}{8} = 117$

Required difference $= (195 + 119) - (126 + 117)$
$= 71$

76. **(a)** **Quantity I**
Let the previous price be Rs 100 per kg
total cost of 20 kg wheat = Rs 2000
New price = Rs 80 per kg
New quantity $= Rs\frac{2000}{80} = 25$ kg
Quantity II

Weight of new student $= (15 \times 12.8) - (14 \times 13)$
$= 192 - 182 = 10$ kg
Quantity I > Quantity II

77. **(e)** **Quantity I**
Favourable cases : HHT, HTH, THH
Total cases $= 2^3 = 8$
∴ Required probability $= \frac{3}{8}$

Quantity II
Let the fraction be $\frac{x}{y}$

Then,
$\frac{x\times1.5}{y\times0.9} = \frac{5}{8} \Rightarrow \frac{x}{y} = \frac{5\times0.9}{8\times1.5} = \frac{3}{8}$
Quantity I = Quantity II

78. **(b)** **Quantity I**
Total SP = Rs 150 ×2 = Rs 300
Total CP $= \frac{150\times100}{120} + \frac{150\times100}{80} = $ Rs 312.5
Loss = Rs 12.5
Quantity II
CP $= \frac{805}{115} \times 100 = $ Rs 700
Profit = Rs 717 – Rs 700 = Rs 17
Quantity II > Quantity I

79. **(a)** **Quantity I**
$A = P\left(1+\frac{R}{100}\right)^n$

$\Rightarrow 245 = P\left(1+\frac{1}{6}\right)^2 \Rightarrow 245 = P\left(\frac{7}{6}\right)^2$

$\Rightarrow \frac{245\times36}{49} = P = $ Rs 180

Quantity II
$R = \frac{120\times100}{500\times4} = 6\%$

Amounts $= 150 + \frac{150\times6\times5}{2\times100} = 22.5 + 150$
$= Rs\ 172.5$

Quantity I > Quantity II

80. **(e)** **Quantity I**
Volume of spherical ball = Volume of 8 identical cones
$\Rightarrow \frac{4}{3} \times \pi \times (3.5)^3 = 8 \times \frac{1}{3} \times \pi \times \left(\frac{7}{4}\right)^2 \times (x)$
$\Rightarrow x = 7$ cm
Quantity II
Let the breadth of rectangle be x cm
Then, length = x + 4 cm
Side of square = 9 cm
Area of square = 81 cm^2
Atq,
$x \times (x+4) = 81 - 4$ cm^2
$\Rightarrow x^2 + 4x - 77 = 0$
$\Rightarrow x = -11$ or 7
$\Rightarrow$ breadth = 7 cm
Quantity I = Quantity II

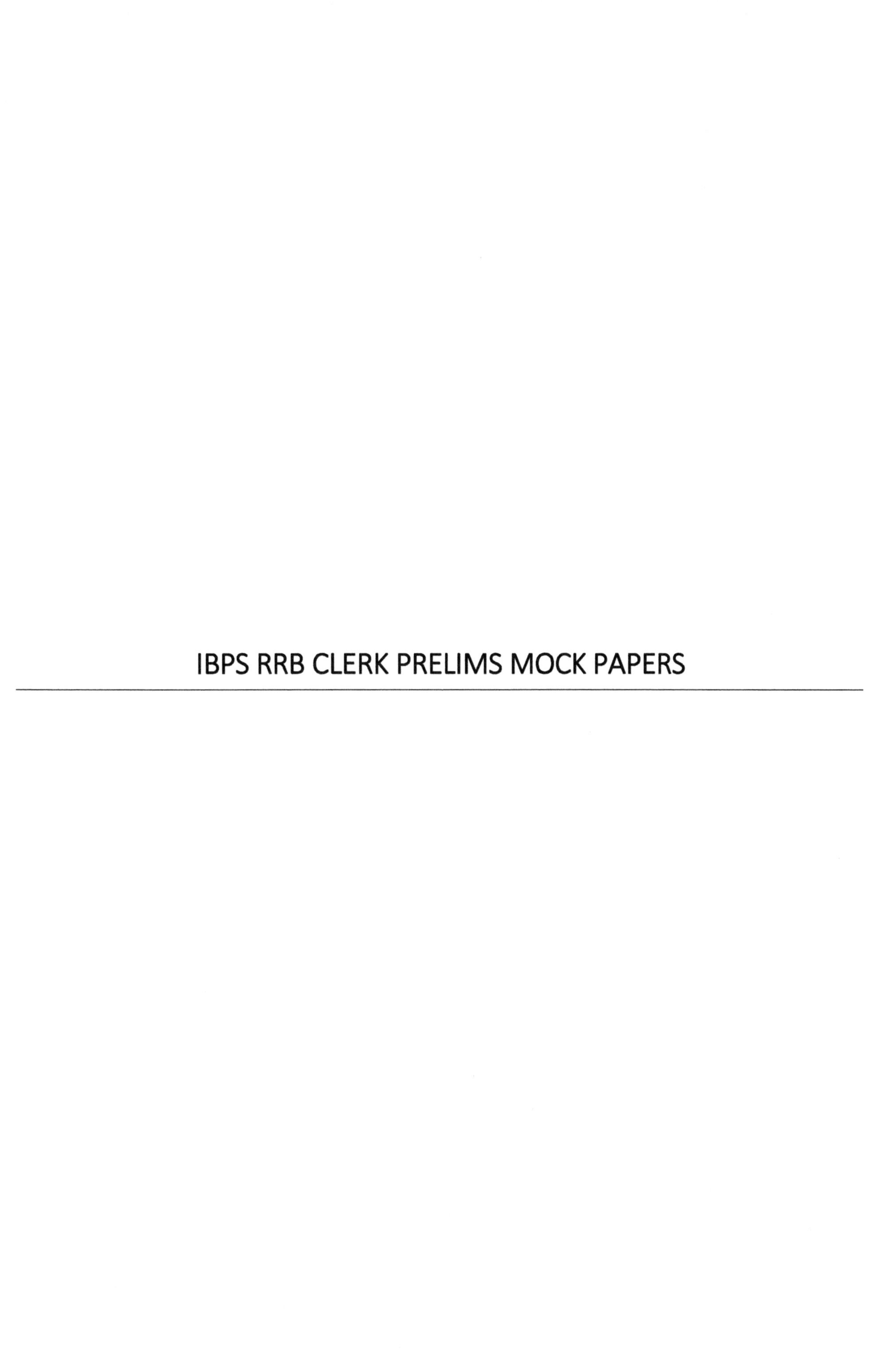

IBPS RRB CLERK PRELIMS MOCK PAPERS

REASONING ABILITY

Directions (1-4): In each of the questions, relationships between some elements are shown in the statements. These statements are followed by conclusions numbered I and II. Read the statements and give the answer.
(a) If only conclusion I follows.
(b) If only conclusion II follows.
(c) If either conclusion I or II follows.
(d) If neither conclusion I nor II follows.
(e) If both conclusions I and II follow.

1. **Statements:** $P < R \leq M = L > O \leq V > Y$
   Conclusions: I. $L > P$ **II.** $O > R$
2. **Statements:** $A \geq B > D = F < E \leq C$
   Conclusions: I. $B > E$ **II.** $D < C$
3. **Statements:** $A = E \geq D \geq C < F \leq B$
   Conclusions: I. $C < A$ **II.** $A = C$
4. **Statements:** $F \geq N = O > P \leq K > T$
   Conclusions: I. $K < F$ **II.** $N < K$

Direction (5-9): Study the following information carefully and answer the questions given below.

Seven people viz. A, B, C, D, E, F and G live in a building on seven different floors such that the ground floor is numbered 1, the floor just above is numbered 2 and so on till the top floor which is numbered as seven, but not necessarily in the same order.

There are less than three floors above A. Only one person lives between C and A. G lives immediately below D. D lives on an even-numbered floor. B lives immediately above A. F lives above E. F does not live on the 5th floor. F does not live on an even-numbered floor.

5. Four of the following five belong to a group. Find the one that does not belong to that group.
   (a) CD   (b) EC   (c) FB
   (d) AB   (e) GC
6. Who among the following lives on the top floor?
   (a) E   (b) B
   (c) F   (d) D
   (e) None of these
7. Number of persons who live above F is same as the number of persons below __ ?
   (a) B   (b) D
   (c) C   (d) G
   (e) None of these
8. How many floors are there above the floor on which G lives?

(a) one
(b) two
(c) three
(d) More than Four
(e) four

9. Who lives immediately below A?
   (a) D   (b) E
   (c) F   (d) C
   (e) None of these

Directions (10-14): Study the following sequence and answer the given questions.

A @ 3 % 4 E N M $ 8 & 6 L D S ♠ 9 8 6 Q Y Z 1 7 %
R O G ⌊ 2 I B 2 U &

10. Which of the following elements is twelfth to the left of the twentieth element from the left end of the given arrangement?
    (a) 6   (b) &
    (c) M   (d) $
    (e) None of these
11. If all the symbols are dropped from the series, which element will be fourth to the right of the one which is twelfth from the right end?
    (a) 9   (b) O
    (c) R   (d) 7
    (e) None of these
12. How many such numbers are there in the given series, which are immediately preceded by a symbol and followed by a letter?
    (a) none   (b) one   (c) two
    (d) three   (e) four
13. Four of the following five are alike in a certain way and form a group. Find the one that does not belong to that group.
    (a) 3E%   (b) R⌊2   (c) M&$
    (d) D9S   (e) Y7Z
14. What should come in place of the question mark (?) in the following series based on the above arrangement?
    34% N$M 6DL 8Q6 ?
    (a) %OR   (b) 7Z%   (c) O%R
    (d) R%O   (e) R%7

Direction (15-19): Study the following information carefully and answer the questions given below.

Seven people viz. P, Q, R, S, T, U and V are sitting around a circular table with an equal distance between them. All of them are facing inside.

P sits to the immediate right of Q. Only one person sits between P and S (either from left or right). U sits third to the right of S. T is an immediate neighbour of U. R sits second to the left of V.

15. If all the persons are arranged to sit in an alphabetical order in anti-clockwise direction starting from P, then the position of how many persons will remain unchanged (except P)?
    (a) three   (b) one
    (c) two   (d) none
    (e) None of these

16. How many persons sit between Q and U, if counted from the left of Q?
    (a) one   (b) two
    (c) three   (d) none
    (e) None of these

17. Who sits second to the right of T?
    (a) P   (b) Q
    (c) R   (d) S
    (e) None of these

18. Four of the following five belong to a group. Find the one that does not belong to that group?
    (a) VQ   (b) PV   (c) RT
    (d) SU   (e) TQ

19. Who among the following sits second to the left of the one who sits 4th to the right of V?
    (a) U   (b) T
    (c) R   (d) S
    (e) None of these

Directions (20-22): In each of the questions below are given some statements followed by two conclusions. You have to take the given statements to be true even if they seem to be at variance with commonly known facts. Read all the conclusions and then decide which of the given conclusions logically follow from the given statements, disregarding commonly known facts to give the answer.

20. **Statements:** Only a few lamps are bottles.
    No bottle is ship.
    Conclusions I. Some ships are definitely not lamps.
    II. All lamps can never be ships.
    (a) Both I and II follow.
    (b) Either I or II follows.
    (c) Only II follows.
    (d) Only I follows.
    (e) Neither I nor II follows.

21. **Statements:** All bamboos are sticks
    No bamboos is a fish.
    Conclusions: I. Some sticks are fish.
    II. No sticks are fish.
    (a) Both I and II follow.
    (b) Either I or II follows.
    (c) Only II follows.
    (d) Only I follows.

    (e) Neither I nor II follows.

22. **Statements:** Only a few wells are mats.
    All pillows are mats.
    Conclusions: I. At least some pillows are wells.
    II. All wells can never be pillow.
    (a) Both I and II follow.
    (b) Either I or II follows.
    (c) Only II follows.
    (d) Only I follows.
    (e) Neither I nor II follows

Direction (23-27): Study the following information carefully and answer the questions given below.

There are ten persons sitting in two parallel rows such that five persons are sitting in each row. A, B, C, D and E are sitting in row 1, facing north and M, N, O, P and Rare sitting in row 2 facing south such that persons sitting in row 1 face the persons sitting in row 2.

B sits to the immediate right of A. Neither A nor B sit at the extreme ends. Two persons sit between P and N. B faces the one who sits on the immediate left of P. M sits on the immediate right of R. C sits at the end of the row. D sits on the left of E. D does not face R.

23. Four of the following five belong to a group. Find the one that does not belong to that group.
    (a) O   (b) C   (c) D
    (d) P   (e) N

24. Who among the following sits second to the left of the one who faces B?
    (a) R   (b) N
    (c) O   (d) M
    (e) None of these

25. How many persons sit on the left of N?
    (a) one   (b) two
    (c) No one   (d) three
    (e) None of these

26. How many persons sits between D and C?
    (a) one
    (b) two
    (c) three
    (d) No One
    (e) Can't be determined

27. Who among the following faces A?
    (a) M   (b) N
    (c) O   (d) R
    (e) None of these

28. IF 'He will Say' is coded as '1 3 9' and 'Say To Him' is coded as '3 5 2' and 'He May Do' is coded as '8 7 9' then what will be the code of '**will**'?
    (a) 3   (b) 1
    (c) 9   (d) 8
    (e) Can't be determined

29. How many pairs of letters are there in the word "MINUTE" each of which have as many letters

(backwards or forwards) between them in the word as they have between them in the English alphabetical series?

(a) three   (b) one
(c) two   (d) More than three
(e) none

Direction (30-33): Study the following information carefully and answer the questions given below.

Six persons, A, B, C, D, E and F are of different weights. No two persons have the same weight. Only two persons are lighter than A. B is heavier than A but lighter than C and D. F is heavier than E but lighter than D. D is not the heaviest. The weight of the 2nd heaviest person is 115 kgs and the weight of the lightest is 56 kgs.

30. How many persons are heavier than F?

(a) one   (b) two
(c) three   (d) four
(e) None of these

31. If the sum of the weight of E and A is 131 and the sum of the weight of D and B is 213, then what is the sum of the weight of A and B?

(a) 172   (b) 173
(c) 174   (d) 175
(e) None of these

32. Who among the following persons is the second heaviest?

(a) A   (b) B
(c) C   (d) D
(e) None of these

33. Which of the following statements is true?

I.   Only two persons are heavier than B.
II. Sum of the weight of D and E is 171 Kg.
III. Weight of E is 58 Kg.

(a) Only II
(b) Both I and II
(c) Both III and II
(d) All are True
(e) Only III

Direction (34-36): Study the following information carefully and answer the questions given below.

A certain number of persons are sitting in a linear row facing north. B sits fifth to the left of E. Two persons sits between B and D. D sits in the second position from one of the extreme ends. Five persons sit between S and E. S is not an immediate neighbour of B. As many as five persons sit between E and S as between S and C. As many as two persons sit between D and B as between B and F. C sits third position from the extreme end.

34. How many persons are sitting in the row?

(a) 21   (b) 23
(c) 24   (d) 26
(e) Can't be determined

35. If G sits second to the right of S, then what is the position of G from the right end?

(a) 7   (b) 9
(c) 8   (d) 6
(e) None of these

36. What is the position of F with respect to E?

(a) Second to the right
(b) Second to the left
(c) Third to the left
(d) Fifth to the Right
(e) None of these

Direction (37-39): Study the following information carefully and answer the questions given below.

Point C is 12m. west of point A. Point B is 18m. north of point A. Point E is 9m. south of point D. Point F is 14m. west of point E. Point D is 28m. east of point B. F is 13m. south of point G.

37. Four of the following five belong to a group. Find the one that does not belong to that group.

(a) CB   (b) AD   (c) AE
(d) BG   (e) FB

38. In which direction is point A with respect to point G?

(a) North-west   (b) South-east
(c) South-west   (d) North
(e) North-east

39. If point S is 4m. south of point G, then what is the distance between point B and point S?

(a) 28m.   (b) 9m.
(c) 8m.   (d) 14m.
(e) None of these

40. Find the odd one out.

(a) PSRQ   (b) MONL   (c) ADCB
(d) VYXW   (e) ILKJ

Quantitative Aptitude

41. 1, 2, 5, 16, 65, 328, 1957

(a) 5   (b) 328   (c) 16
(d) 1957   (e) 65

42. 4, 11, 25, 46, 74, 129, 151

(a) 129   (b) 11   (c) 151
(d) 4   (e) 46

43. 84, 96, 83, 95, 80, 94, 81

(a) 95   (b) 81   (c) 83
(d) 80   (e) 84

44. 3, 5, 8, 17, 33, 58, 94

(a) 8   (b) 94   (c) 58
(d) 3   (e) 5

45. A boat covers 36 kms. in upstream in 2 hours and 66 kms. in downstream in 3 hours. Find the speed of boat in still water.

(a) 21km/h.   (b) 19 km/h.

(c) 20.5 km/h.   (d) 20 km/h.

(e) 19.5 km/h.

46. Two inlet taps A and B can fill a tank in 36 minutes and 60 minutes respectively. Find the time taken by both the taps together to fill $\frac{1}{6}th$ of the tank.

(a) 3 minutes   (b) $3\frac{3}{4}$ minutes

(c) $3\frac{1}{2}$ minutes   (d) $3\frac{1}{3}$ minutes

(e) $2\frac{1}{3}$ minutes

47. If circumference of the first circle is 132 cms. and circumference of the second circle is 110 cms., then find the difference between the area of both the circles.

(a) 423.5 cm.²   (b) 412.5 cm.²

(c) 420 cm.²   (d) 422.4 cm.²

(e) 419.8 cm.²

48. In 64 litres of pure milk, 20 litres of water is mixed and then $\frac{1}{4}$th of the mixture is taken out. When x litres of water is added to the mixture again, then the ratio of water to milk becomes 1:2. Find the value of x.

(a) 10 litres   (b) 8 litres

(c) 12 litres   (d) 6 litres

(e) 9 litres

49. Total cost of x pens and (x-2) pencils is Rs. 424. If one pencil and one pen costs Rs. 4 and Rs. 20 respectively then find x.

(a) 16   (b) 18   (c) 15

(d) 20   (e) 21

50. A is 6 years younger than B and the ratio of the present age of B to C is 12:5. If ratio of the present age of A to C is 2:1, then find present age of B.

(a) 20 years   (b) 30 years

(c) 24 years   (d) 18 years

(e) None of these

Directions (51-55): The given bar graph shows the data of two types of school buses X and Y for three schools A, B and C. Study the chart carefully and answer the following questions.

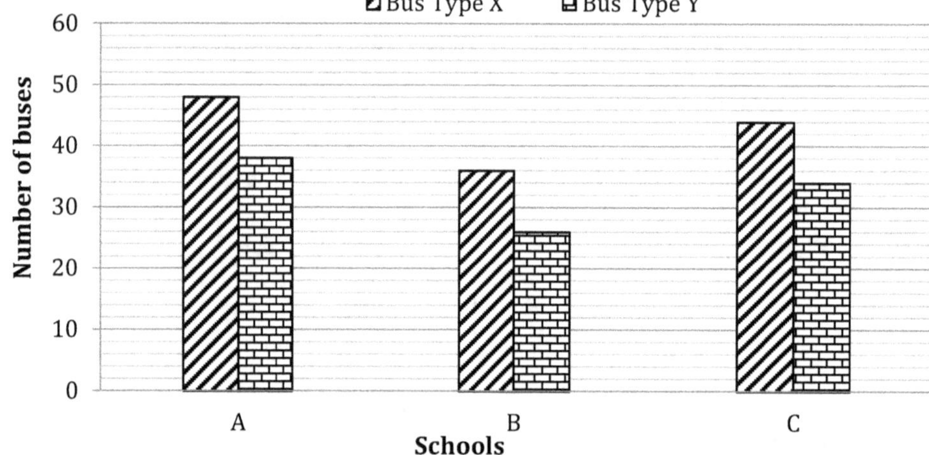

51. What is the average number of X type buses from school B and school C together?

(a) 40   (b) 70   (c) 30

(d) 59   (e) 54

52. X type buses from school A are how many more than X type buses from school B in terms of percentage?

(a) $55^5/_{19}\%$ (b) 25%   (c) $5^5/_9\%$

(d) $45^5/_6\%$ (e) $33^1/_3\%$

53. What is the average number of all the buses from school B?

(a) 43   (b) 39   (c) 31

(d) 54   (e) 59

54. What is the difference of average number of all buses from school A and the average number of all buses from school C?

(a) 16   (b) 4   (c) 8

(d) 24   (e) 12

55. Which school has the maximum number of buses?

(a) School B

(b) School C

(c) School A & School C

(d) School A & School B

(e) School A

Directions (56-60): Given below are two equations in each question, which you have to solve to give the answer.

(a) if $x > y$
(b) if $x \geq y$
(c) if $y > x$
(d) if $y \geq x$
(e) if $x = y$ or no relation can be established

56. I. $2x^2 - 5x + 2 = 0$ II. $2y^2 - 9y + 7 = 0$
57. I. $3x^2 + 7x + 4 = 0$ II. $y^2 + 9y + 20 = 0$
58. I. $x^2 - 7x + 10 = 0$ II. $y^2 - 14y + 45 = 0$
59. I. $x^2 - 3x = 4$ II. $y^2 + 6y + 8 = 0$
60. I. $x^2 - 3x = 10$ II. $y^2 + 7y + 10 = 0$

Directions (61-65): Following are the details of three shopkeepers and the number of items sold by them on three different days:

Shopkeepers	Monday	Tuesday	Wednesday
A	160	240	210
B	200	180	320
C	150	330	280

61. Find the ratio of items sold by A and B on Monday to items sold by B and C on Wednesday?
(a) 5:3   (b) 3:5   (c) 3:4
(d) 4:7   (e) 5:8

62. Find the average number of items sold by all three shopkeepers on Wednesday.
(a) 280   (b) 290   (c) 270
(d) 250   (e) 260

63. Items sold by A and B together on Tuesday is what percentage of items sold by B and C on Wednesday?
(a) 70%   (b) 75%   (c) 60%
(d) 65%   (e) 80%

64. Find the difference in the number of items sold by B on Monday and Tuesday together and the items sold by A on Tuesday and Wednesday.
(a) 80   (b) 60   (c) 50
(d) 70   (e) 100

65. Find the ratio of items sold by B on all three days together to the items sold by C on all three days.
(a) 35:38   (b) 38:35   (c) 30:34
(d) 30:38   (e) 35:41

66. Marked price of an article is Rs. 250 more than the cost price of that article and it is sold at a discount of 15% on the marked price. Find the cost price of the article, if the profit percent earned is 27.5%.
(a) Rs. 600   (b) Rs. 550   (c) Rs. 500
(d) Rs. 750   (e) Rs. 900

67. In year 2016, the ratio of boys to girls in a school is 36:19. And in year 2017, the number of boys is increased by 1440 and the number of girls is increased by 15%. If in 2017, the total increase in the number of students is 1725, then find the increased number of boys in the school.
(a) 7240   (b) 5440   (c) 6040
(d) 4440   (e) 5040

68. The ratio of salary of A to that of B is 1:3 and each spends 15% of his salary on house rent. Find the house rent paid by A, if the amount remaining with A and B together is Rs. 42,500.
(a) Rs. 1800
(b) Rs. 1845
(c) Rs. 1785
(d) Rs. 1760
(e) Rs. 1875

69. A started a business by investing Rs. 50,000. After six months, B joined him by investing Rs. 75,000. After another six months, C joined with Rs. 1,25,000. What is the ratio of profit shared after two years among A, B and C?
(a) 4:5:6   (b) 8:9:10
(c) 8:9:12   (d) 4:5:8
(e) None of these.

70. At what rate will a sum of Rs. 1000 amount to Rs. 1102.50 in two years at compound interest?
(a) 6.5%   (b) 6%
(c) 5%   (d) 5.5%
(e) None of these

Directions (71-80): What should come in place of the question mark (?) in the following questions?

71. $?^2 = 40\%$ of $\dfrac{5}{11}$ of 352
(a) 12   (b) 16   (c) 6
(d) 4   (e) 8

72. $?^2 = \left(\sqrt{1444} + \sqrt{676}\right) \div 4$
(a) 6   (b) 16   (c) 8
(d) 2   (e) 4

73. $\left(\dfrac{?-0.5}{0.2}\right) = \dfrac{120}{2}$
(a) 30   (b) 12.5   (c) 25
(d) 17.5   (e) 22.5

74. 60% of $? - \sqrt{324} = 222$
(a) 600   (b) 250   (c) 200
(d) 400   (e) 350

75. $\dfrac{2^3 \times 3^2}{(90 \div ?)} = \sqrt{64}$
(a) 15   (b) 12   (c) 10
(d) 11   (e) 16

76. $\sqrt{4 \times ?} = \dfrac{160}{10}$
(a) 64   (b) 60   (c) 68
(d) 56   (e) 72

77. $\sqrt{5929} + \sqrt{8464} = (?)^2$
(a) 17   (b) 21   (c) 15
(d) 13   (e) 11

78. $7\dfrac{1}{2} - 2\dfrac{1}{2} = \dfrac{50}{?}$
(a) 8   (b) 5   (c) 15
(d) 12   (e) 10

79. $\left[\left(2 \times \dfrac{1}{4}\right) + 4\right] \times 8 = ? \times 10$

(a) 4.8   (b) 3.6   (c) 2.4

(d) 3.2   (e) 4.2

80. 80% of $(1.5 \times 4 + ?) = 24$

(a) 30   (b) 36   (c) 24

(d) 28   (e) 42

Solutions

REASONING ABILITY

Directions (1-4):

1. **(a)**   2. **(b)**   3. **(c)**

4. **(d)**

Direction (5-9):

Floors	Person
7	F
6	B
5	A
4	E
3	C
2	D
1	G

5. **(e)**   6. **(c)**   7. **(d)**

8. **(d)**   9. **(b)**

Directions (10-14):

10. **(c)**   11. **(c)**   12. **(d)**

13. **(b)**   14. **(a)**

Direction (15-19):

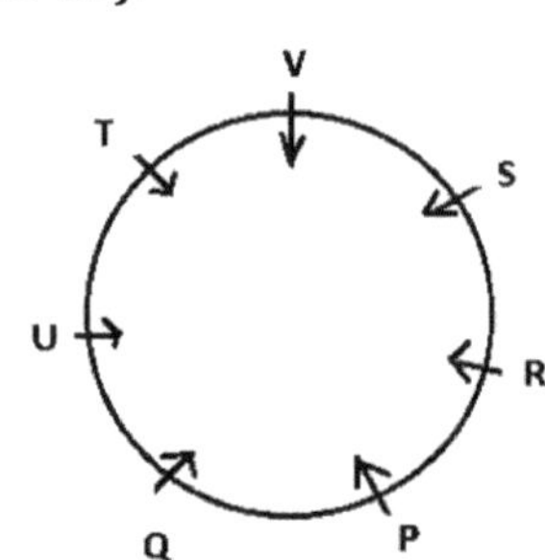

15. **(c)**   16. **(d)**   17. **(b)**

18. **(e)**   19. **(a)**

Directions (20-22):

20. **(c)**

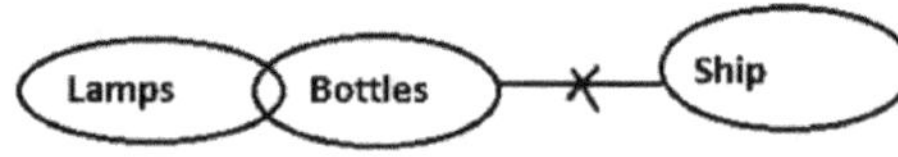

21. **(b)**

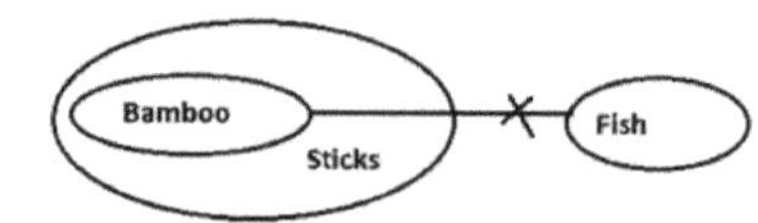

22. **(c)**

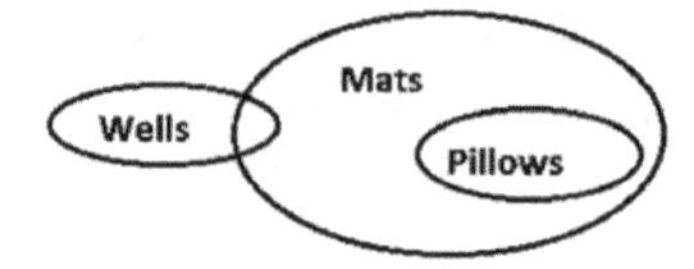

Direction (23-27):

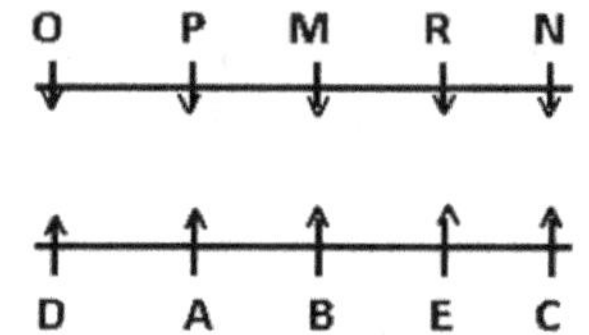

23. **(d)**   24. **(b)**   25. **(c)**

26. **(c)**   27. **(e)**   28. **(b)**

29. **(c)**

Direction (30-33):

C > D (115kg) > B > A > F > E (56kg)

30. **(d)**   31. **(b)**   32. **(d)**

33. **(b)**

Direction (34-36):

34. **(c)**   35. **(a)**   36. **(b)**

Direction (37-39):

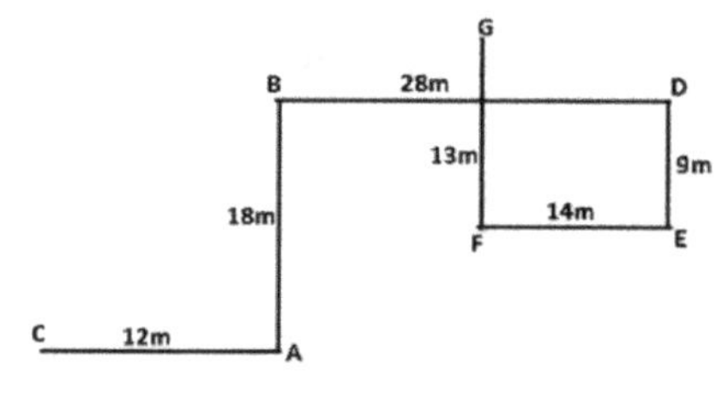

37. **(e)**   38. **(c)**   39. **(d)**

40. **(b)**

41. (b) The wrong no. is 328
$1 \times 1 + 1 = 2$
$2 \times 2 + 1 = 5$
$5 \times 3 + 1 = 16$
$16 \times 4 + 1 = 65$
$65 \times 5 + 1 = 326$
$326 \times 6 + 1 = 1957$
So, there should be 326 instead of 328

42. (a) The wrong no is 129

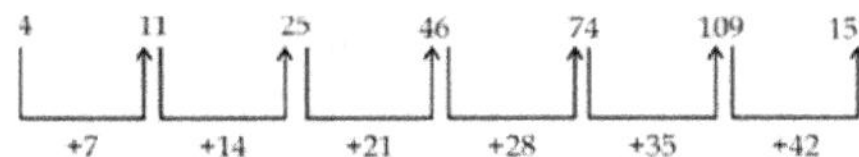

So, there should be 109 instead of 129

43. (d) The wrong no. is 80

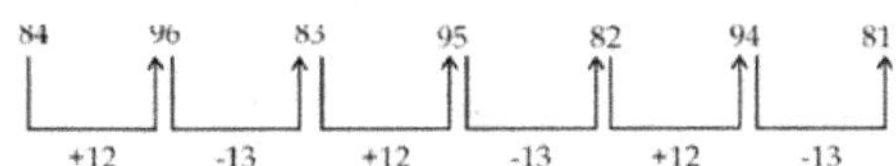

So, there should be 82 instead of 80

44. (e) The wrong no. is 5

3   [4]   8   17   33   58   94
+1   +4   +9   +16   +25   +36
1^2 2^2 3^2 4^2 5^2 6^2

So, there should be 4 instead of 5.

45. (d) Upstream speed of boat=18 km/hr
Downstream speed of boat=22 km/hr
Speed of boat in still water=$\frac{18+22}{2} =$
$20\ km/h$

46. (b) Let the capacity of the tank be 180 units
(LCM of 36 and 60)
Efficiency of tap A=5 units/ minute
Efficiency of tap B=3 units/minute
$\frac{1}{6}$th of the tank= 30 units
Required time=$\frac{30}{5+3} = 3\frac{3}{4}$ minutes

47. (a) Radius of first circle=$\frac{132 \times 7}{2 \times 22} = 21\ cm$
Area of first circle=$\frac{22}{7} \times 21 \times 21 = 1386$
cm^2
Radius of second circle=$\frac{110 \times 7}{2 \times 22} = 17.5$ cm
Area of second circle=$\frac{22}{7} \times 17.5 \times 17.5 =$
962.5 cm^2
Required difference=423.5 cm^2

48. (e) Ratio of milk to water in the initial
mixture=16:5
$\frac{1}{4}th$ of the mixture=21 liter
$$\frac{64 - 21 \times \frac{16}{21}}{20 - 21 \times \frac{5}{21} + x} = \frac{2}{1}$$

$x = 9$ liter

49. (b) ATQ
$20x + 4 \times (x - 2) = 424$
$24x = 432$
$x = 18$

50. (e) Let present age of B and C be 12x years
and 5x years respectively.
Then present age of A=10x years
ATQ
$$12x - 10x = 6$$
$$x = 3$$
Present age of B=36 years

51. (a) Average number of X type buses from
school B and school C together
$= \frac{36+44}{2} = 40$

52. (e) X type buses of school A = 48
X type buses of school B = 36
Required value = $\frac{48-36}{36}$ X 100 = $33\frac{1}{3}$%

53. (c) Average number of all the buses from
school B = $\frac{36+26}{2} = 31$

54. (b) Average number of all the buses from
school A = $\frac{48+38}{2} = 43$
Average number of all the buses from
school C = $\frac{44+34}{2} = 39$
Required difference = 43 – 39 = 4

55. (e) Total buses from school A = 48 + 38 = 86
Total buses from school B = 36 + 26 = 62
Total buses from school C = 44 + 34 = 78
Clearly, School A has maximum number of
buses.

56. (e)

I. $2x^2 - 4x - x + 2 = 0$
$\Rightarrow 2x(x - 2) - 1(x - 2) = 0$
$\Rightarrow (2x - 1)(x - 2) = 0$
$\Rightarrow x = \frac{1}{2}, 2$

II. $2y^2 - 9y + 7 = 0$
$\Rightarrow 2y^2 - 7y - 2y + 7 = 0$
$\Rightarrow y(2y - 7) - 1(2y - 7) = 0$
$\Rightarrow y = \frac{7}{2}, 1$

∴ No relation

57. (a)

I. $3x^2 + 3x + 4x + 4 = 0$
$\Rightarrow 3x(x + 1) + 4(x + 1) = 0$
$\Rightarrow x = -1, \frac{-4}{3}$

II. $y^2 + 5y + 4y + 20 = 0$
$\Rightarrow y(y + 5) + 4(y + 5) = 0$
$\Rightarrow y = -4, -5$

∴ $x > y$

58. (d)

I. $x^2 - 5x - 2x + 10 = 0$
$\Rightarrow x(x - 5) - 2(x - 5) = 0$
$\Rightarrow x = 2, 5$

II. $y^2 - 9y - 5y + 45 = 0$
$\Rightarrow y(y - 9) - 5(y - 9) = 0$
$\Rightarrow y = 9, 5$

∴ $x \leq y$

59. (a) I. $x^2 - 3x - 4 = 0$
$x^2 - 4x + x - 4 = 0$
$(x - 4)(x + 1) = 0$

$x = 4, -1$

II. $y^2 + 6y + 8 = 0$
$y^2 + 2y + 4y + 8 = 0$
$(y + 2)\,(y + 4) = 0$
$y = -2, -4$
$\Rightarrow x > y$

60. (b) I. $x^2 - 3x = 10$
$x^2 - 3x - 10 = 0$
$x^2 - 5x + 2x - 10 = 0$
$(x - 5)\,(x + 2) = 0$
$x = -2, 5$

II. $y^2 + 7y + 10 = 0$
$y^2 + 5y + 2y + 10 = 0$
$(y + 5)\,(y + 2) = 0$
$y = -2, -5$
$\Rightarrow x \geq y$

61. (b) items sold by A and B on Monday
$= 200 + 160 = 360$
Items sold by B and C on Wednesday
$= 320 + 280 = 600$
$\therefore$ Required ratio $= \dfrac{360}{600} = \dfrac{6}{10} = \dfrac{3}{5}$

62. (c) Average of items sold by A, B, C on Wednesday
$= \dfrac{210+320+280}{3} = \dfrac{810}{3} = 270$

63. (a) items sold by A and B on Tuesday $= 240 + 180 = 420$
Items sold by B and C on Wednesday $= 320 + 280 = 600$
$\therefore$ Required percentage $= \dfrac{420\times100}{600}$
$= 70\%$

64. (d) items sold by B on Monday and Tuesday $= 200 + 180 = 380$
Items sold by A on Tuesday and Wednesday $= 240 + 210 = 450$
$\therefore$ Required difference $= 450 - 380 = 70$

65 (a) Items sold by B on all 3 days
$= 200 + 180 + 320 = 700$
Items sold by C on all three days
$= 150 + 330 + 280 = 760$
Required ratio $= \dfrac{700}{760} = \dfrac{35}{38}$

66. (c) Let the marked price be Rs 100x
Then selling price $=$ Rs 85x
Cost price $= Rs\,\dfrac{200}{3}x$
ATQ
$100x - \dfrac{200}{3}x = 250$
$x = 7.5$
Cost price $=$ Rs 500

67. (e) Let the number of students in the exam be 55x

Then number of boys $= 36x$
Number of girls $= 19x$
ATQ
$55x + 1725 = (36x + 1440) + 19x \times 1.15$
$x = 100$
Increased number of boys $= 3600 + 1440 = 5040$

68. (e) Let the salary of A and B be Rs 100x and Rs 300x respectively
ATQ
$$85x + 255x = 42500$$
$$x = 125$$
House rent paid by A $=$ Rs 1875

69. (b)

	A	:	B	:	C
Capital $\rightarrow$	50000	:	75000	:	1,25,000
Time $\rightarrow$	2		$\frac{3}{2}$		1
Profit $\rightarrow$	100000	:	112500	:	125000

Required ratio $= 8{:}9{:}10$

70. (c) ATQ, $\dfrac{1102.50}{1000} = \left(1 + \dfrac{r}{100}\right)^2$
or, $\left(1 + \dfrac{r}{100}\right)^2 = \left(\dfrac{105}{100}\right)^2$
or, $\left(1 + \dfrac{r}{100}\right)^2 = \left(1 + \dfrac{5}{100}\right)^2$
Thus, on comparing, $r = 5\%$

71. (e) $?^2 = 40\%$ of $\dfrac{5}{11} \times 352$
$?^2 = \dfrac{2}{5} \times \dfrac{5}{11} \times 352 = 64 \Rightarrow ? = 8$

72. (e) $?^2 = \dfrac{(\sqrt{1444}+\sqrt{676})}{4} = \dfrac{38+26}{4} = \dfrac{64}{4} = 16 \Rightarrow ? = 4$

73. (b) $(? - 0.5) = 60 \times 0.2$
$? = 12 + 0.5 = 12.5$

74. (d) $\dfrac{60}{100} \times ? - 18 = 222$
$$\dfrac{60}{100} \times ? = 240$$
$? = \dfrac{240\times100}{60} \Rightarrow ? = 400$

75. (c) $\dfrac{8\times9\times?}{90} = 8$
$? = \dfrac{90\times8}{8\times9} = 10 \Rightarrow ? = 10$

76. (a) $\sqrt{4 \times ?} = 16$
$$4 \times ? = 256$$
$$? = 64$$

77. (d) $77 + 92 = ?^2$
$169 = ?^2 \Rightarrow ? = 13$

78. (e) $5 = \dfrac{50}{?} \Rightarrow ? = 10$

79. (b) $\dfrac{9}{2} \times 8 = ? \times 10 \Rightarrow ? = 3.6$

80. (c) $\dfrac{80}{100} \times (6 + ?) = 24$
$6 + ? = 30 \Rightarrow ? = 2$

REASONING ABILITY

Directions (1-5): Read the following information carefully and answer the questions given below.

Six persons J, P, Q, R, V and Z are sitting in a row. Some of them are facing north while some of them are facing south. J sits second from one of the extreme ends of the row. P sits third to the right of J. R is not an immediate neighbour of P and Z. Both the immediate neighbours of V face opposite directions. Both the immediate neighbours of Z face the same direction. V sits second to the left of P. Q sits to the right of R. R faces north. Q faces the same direction as Z.

1. Four of the following five are alike in a certain way, and so form a group. Which of the following does not belong to that group?
   (a) R, V   (b) V, P   (c) J, P
   (d) V, Q   (e) J, R

2. What is the position of Q with respect to Z?
   (a) Second to the left   (b) Third to the right
   (c) Third to the left   (d) Fifth to the right
   (e) Second to the right

3. Who amongst the following sits exactly between Z and J?
   (a) R
   (b) P
   (c) Q
   (d) Both V and Q   (e) V

4. How many persons in the given arrangement are facing north?
   (a) More than four   (b) four
   (c) one   (d) three   (e) two

5. Who is sitting 4th to the right of Q?
   (a) R   (b) Z
   (c) P   (d) J
   (e) None of these

Directions (6-8): The statements given below are followed by two conclusions. You have to consider the statements to be true even if they seem to be at variance from commonly known facts. You have to decide which of the conclusions follows from the given statements:

6. **Statements**: No symbol is letter.
   All expression are letter.
   Some symbols are word.
   Conclusions: I. No word is letter.
   II. Some symbols being expression is possibility.
   (a) Only I follows.
   (b) Only II follows.
   (c) Either I or II follows.
   (d) Neither I nor II follows.
   (e) Both I and II follow.

7. **Statements:** Some logic are answers.
   All keys are answers.
   Conclusions: I. All keys are logic.
   II. No keys are logic.
   (a) Only I follows.
   (b) Only II follows.
   (c) Either I or II follows.
   (d) Neither I nor II follows.
   (e) Both I and II follow.

8. **Statement:** All numbers are digits.
   Some numbers are points.
   Some points are marks.
   Conclusions: I. Some points are digits.
   II. All marks being numbers is a possibility.
   (a) Only I follows.
   (b) Only II follows.
   (c) Either I or II follows.
   (d) Neither I nor II follows.
   (e) Both I and II follow.

Directions (9-13): Read the following information carefully and answer the questions given below:

Seven boxes M, N, O, P, Q, R, S are arranged one above the other. Only two boxes are placed above box P. Only one box is placed between box S and P. Between boxes S and Q there are same number of boxes as between boxes Q and M. Three boxes are placed between boxes N and O. N is placed above O.

9. What is the total number of boxes placed in between boxes S and Q?
   (a) two
   (b) one
   (c) three
   (d) More than three
   (e) none

10. Which of the following is true regarding box N?
   (a) Three boxes are placed between box Q and N.
   (b) Box N is placed below Q.
   (c) Box N is placed at the top.

(d) Only one box is placed above box N.

(e) No box is placed between box N and R.

11. Which box is placed at the top?

(a) S   (b) N   (c) Q

(d) R   (e) M

12. Which box is placed immediately above box Q?

(a) M   (b) P   (c) S

(d) N   (e) R

13. How many boxes are placed in between R and M?

(a) two

(b) one

(c) three

(d) More than three

(e) none

Directions (14-18): Answer the questions below based on the following information:

In a certain code:

"arrange things in order" is coded as - "po gb ik mn"

"order for new things" is coded as "po gb fc bv"

"new places to order" is coded as "gb cq bv ra"

"places in unknown country" is coded as " de ra lf ik"

14. What will be the code for "order"?

(a) gb

(b) fc

(c) cq

(d) ik

(e) Can't be determined

15. What willbe the code for "things to vanish"?

(a) po cq hx   (b) po vm ik

(c) cq fc ik   (d) either (a) or (b)

(e) None of these

16. What will be the code for "arrange"?

(a) gb

(b) mn

(c) cq

(d) ik

(e) Can't be determined

17. What will be the code for "in country"?

(a) lf ik

(b) de ik

(c) po gb

(d) either (a) or (b)

(e) None of these

18. "bv" is the code for?

(a) things   (b) new

(c) arrange   (d) places

(e) None of these

Directions (19-23): Read the following information carefully and answer the questions given below.

Six persons A, C, Q, R, T, Y were born in six different months of a year: January, April, May, August, September and December. Three persons were born in between A and Y. A was born before Y. No one was born in between C and A. Two persons were born in between C and R. T was born before Q.

19. Who among the following was born in May?

(a) C   (b) A   (c) Q

(d) T   (e) Y

20. How many persons were born between A and Q?

(a) one   (b) three

(c) four   (d) two

(e) None of these

21. How many persons were born before R?

(a) one   (b) three

(c) four   (d) two

(e) None of these

22. Who amongst the following is the oldest?

(a) C   (b) A   (c) Q

(d) T   (e) Y

23. Which of the following is not true regarding Y?

(a) Four persons born between C and Y

(b) R was born before Y

(c) Q was born immediately after Y

(d) Only Q was born between Y and R

(e) No one was born after Y

24. A family consists of five members A, P, R, T and H. P is the wife of A. R is the daughter of A. R has only one brother T. H is the daughter-in-law of P. How is H related to R?

(a) mother   (b) sister-in-law

(c) daughter   (d) daughter-in-law

(e) None of these

25. If all the digits of the number "46752983" are arranged in increasing order from left to right, then how many digits will remain in the same position after the applied operation?

(a) two   (b) one

(c) three   (d) four

(e) None of these

26. How many meaningful words can be made by using the letters 'A', 'E', 'L' and 'T', keeping L as the first letter of the word?

(a) one   (b) two

(c) three   (d) four

(e) None of these

Directions (27-31): Read the following information carefully and answer the questions given below.

Point E is 15m. east of point B. Point G is 20m. north of point E. Point K is 10m. east of point G. Point M is 30m. south of point K. Point P is 20m. west of point M. Point L is 10m. north of point P.

27. If point V is 10m east of point S and point S is 10m. north of point L, then what will be the distance between point E and V?

(a) 10m.   (b) 15m.   (c) 20m.

(d) 5m.   (e) 25m.

28. What is the total distance between point B and L?

(a) 10m.   (b) 15m.   (c) 20m.

(d) 5m. (e) 30m.

29. If point Z is 10m. north of point M, then what is the distance between point E and Z?
    (a) 10m. (b) 15m. (c) 20m.
    (d) 25m. (e) 30m.
30. Point K is in which direction from point P?
    (a) south (b) south-east
    (c) north (d) north-east
    (e) north-west
31. Four of the following five are alike in a certain way, and so form a group. Which of the following does not belong to the group?
    (a) P, L (b) P, M (c) G, E
    (d) L, E (e) G, B

Directions (32-36): These questions are based on the following arrangement. Study it carefully and answer the questions below it.

1 3 5 3 4 5 9 2 8 7 2 3 6 5 2 7 3 8 1 2 1 8 4 9 8 1 2 4 7 3 5 2 4 8 9 8 2 4

32. Which element is exactly midway between the seventh element from the left end and sixteenth from the right end?
    (a) 8 (b) 2 (c) 5
    (d) 6 (e) 7
33. How many perfect squares are there to the right of the fourteenth element from the right end?
    (a) two (b) one
    (c) three (d) four
    (e) More than four
34. How many perfect cubes are there in the above arrangement, each of which is immediately preceded by an odd number and immediately followed by an even number?
    (a) none
    (b) three
    (c) two
    (d) one
    (e) More than three

35. How many odd digits are there in the given arrangement, each of which is immediately followed and preceded by an odd number?
    (a) none (b) one
    (c) two (d) three
    (e) More than three
36. Which of the following elements is 5th to the right of 10th from the right end?
    (a) 9 (b) 8 (c) 2
    (d) 1 (e) 4

Directions (37-40): Read the following information carefully and answer the questions given below.

There are six wallets A, B, C, P, Q and R, each containing different amounts of money. Wallet B has more money than wallet Q, but less than wallet P. Only wallet R has more money than wallet C. Wallet Q does not have the least amount of money. The wallet containing the third highest amount of money has Rs. 3000, which is Rs.1000 more than the wallet which has second lowest amount money.

37. Which of the following wallets has the least amount of money?
    (a) A (b) B (c) C
    (d) Q (e) P
38. What is be the amount of money in wallet C?
    (a) Rs. 2500 (b) Rs. 2000 (c) Rs. 3500
    (d) Rs. 2250 (e) Rs. 2100
39. What is be the amount of money in wallet B, if it has Rs. 250 less than the wallet P?
    (a) Rs. 2500 (b) Rs. 2750 (c) Rs. 3500
    (d) Rs. 3250 (e) Rs. 2200
40. Which of the following is true regarding wallet P?
    (a) Only wallet A has less money than wallet P
    (b) Wallet B has more money than wallet P
    (c) Wallet P has the third highest amount of money
    (d) Wallet Q has more money than P
    (e) None of these

QUANTITATIVE APTITUDE

41. The upstream speed of a boat is 18 km/hr. which is 500% more than the speed of the stream. Find out how much distance the boat will cover in three hours while travelling downstream.
    (a) 66 km. (b) 63 km. (c) 72 km.
    (d) 75 km. (e) 78 km.
42. If $A^2 - B^2 = 252$ and $A + B = 42$ then find the value of 'B'?
    (a) 18 (b) 16 (c) 14
    (d) 20 (e) 22

43. A alone can do a work in 40 days. The ratio of time taken by A and B to do the same work is 5:3. Find in how many days both will they complete the work together.
    (a) 18 days (b) 12 days (c) 20 days
    (d) 15 days (e) 10 days
44. A train moving at a speed of 72 km/hr. crosses a pole in 18 seconds and a platform in 33 seconds. Find the length of the platform.
    (a) 320 m. (b) 300 m. (c) 330 m.
    (d) 360 m. (e) 350 m.

45. The circumference of a circle is 66 cm. Find the approximate area of a square, if the radius of the circle is two times the side of a square.
   (a) 18 cm²   (b) 32 cm²   (c) 25 cm²
   (d) 36 cm²   (e) 28 cm²

Directions (46-50): What approximate value should come in place of the question mark (?) in the following questions?

46. $\sqrt{1443.98} \div 18.98 + 328.1 = ? \times 22.01$
   (a) 10   (b) 12   (c) 18
   (d) 15   (e) 22

47. 29.98% of 880.001 = ? + 110.9
   (a) 144   (b) 153   (c) 158
   (d) 160   (e) 163

48. $(?)^2 + 255.93 = 49.932\%$ of 800.112
   (a) 12   (b) 8   (c) 15
   (d) 18   (e) 6

49. $\sqrt[3]{1728.01} + ? = 256.01$
   (a) 230   (b) 235   (c) 238
   (d) 241   (e) 244

50. 74.91% of ? = $(17.932)^2$
   (a) 420   (b) 425   (c) 408
   (d) 432   (e) 444

Directions (51-55): Find the wrong number in the given number series:

51. 100, 118, 136, 149, 160, 167, 172
   (a) 172   (b) 160   (c) 100
   (d) 118   (e) 136

52. 1.5, 2.5, 6, 24, 100, 505, 3036
   (a) 1.5   (b) 6   (c) 100
   (d) 3036   (e) 2.5

53. 160, 80, 80, 120, 240, 600, 900
   (a) 240   (b) 120   (c) 160
   (d) 900   (e) 600

54. 5040, 2520, 840, 210, 42, 8, 1
   (a) 8   (b) 5040   (c) 840
   (d) 1   (e) 42

55. 15, 17, 26, 151, 200, 929, 1050
   (a) 17   (b) 1050   (c) 15
   (d) 929   (e) 26

Direction (56-60): There are five departments in a company. There are 90 employees in the Finance department, which is 25% of the total employees in the company. 2/9 of the total employees of the company are working in the HR department. The number of employees working in the Sales department is 25% more than that in the HR department. The ratio between employees working in the Security and Housing department is 4:5.

56. The number of employees working in the HR department is what percent more than the number of employees working in the Security department?
   (a) 250%   (b) 200%   (c) 150%
   (d) 100%   (e) 50%

57. Find the average number of employees working in the Sales, Finance and Housing departments?
   (a) 60   (b) 70   (c) 80
   (d) 90   (e) 100

58. The number of employees in the Housing department is how much more than the number of employees in the Security department?
   (a) 10   (b) 20   (c) 30
   (d) 40   (e) 50

59. In the Security department, 40% are female employees. Find the total number of male employees working in Security department.
   (a) 16   (b) 40   (c) 32
   (d) 8   (e) 24

60. The ratio between the total number of male and female employees in the HR department is 2:3. Find the total number of female employees working in the HR department.
   (a) 32   (b) 48   (c) 64
   (d) 40   (e) 56

Directions (61-70): What value should come in place of the question mark (?) in the following questions?

61. $?^2 = 4^2 + 8^2 - 31$
   (a) 6   (b) 7   (c) 8
   (d) 9   (e) 10

62. $13 \times 6 + ? \times 4 = 18 \times 7$
   (a) 6   (b) 8   (c) 10
   (d) 12   (e) 14

63. 40% of ? = 25% of 320 + 75% of 160
   (a) 500   (b) 400   (c) 300
   (d) 200   (e) 100

64. $11^2 + 6^2 = ? + 37$
   (a) 130   (b) 110   (c) 120
   (d) 140   (e) 150

65. $\dfrac{360}{?} = 12 \times 6 - 3^3$
   (a) 9   (b) 5   (c) 6
   (d) 7   (e) 8

66. $\sqrt{225} + \sqrt{441} = ?^2$
   (a) 3   (b) 4   (c) 5
   (d) 6   (e) 8

67. $16 \times 8 - ? = 2^6$
   (a) 64   (b) 32   (c) 128
   (d) 192   (e) 96

68. $16 \times 54 \div 36 + 6 = ?$
   (a) $\dfrac{144}{7}$ (b) 30   (c) 20
   (d) 24   (e) 16

69. $? = \sqrt{6 \times 3 \times 5 + 50\% \text{ of } 620}$
   (a) 14   (b) 16   (c) 18
   (d) 10   (e) 20

70. $6^2 = \dfrac{18 \times 8 - ? \times 2}{3}$
   (a) 36   (b) 27   (c) 18
   (d) 9   (e) 54

Direction (71-75): The table given below shows the marks obtained by four students in four different subjects in an exam. Study the data carefully and answer the following questions:

Subjects / Students	English	Hindi	Science	Maths
Paul	65	60	80	65
Aditya	75	75	60	75
Neeraj	85	55	95	85
Sandy	60	60	65	60

71. Marks scored by Sandy in English and Maths together is what percent of the marks scored by Aditya and Neeraj in English together?
(a) 25%   (b) 50%   (c) 75%
(d) 100%   (e) 125%

72. Find the ratio of the total marks scored by all four students together in Hindi to the total marks scored by all four students together in Science?
(a) 5:6   (b) 57:50   (c) 1:1
(d) 20:19   (e) 6:5

73. The total marks scored by Paul is how much more/less than the total marks scored by Neeraj?
(a) 70   (b) 60   (c) 40
(d) 50   (e) 80

74. Find the average of the marks scored by Aditya in English, Hindi and Science together.
(a) 65   (b) 85   (c) 80
(d) 75   (e) 70

75. If maximum marks for each subject is 100 then find the percentage of total marks obtained by Sandy.

(a) 64.25%   (b) 61.25%   (c) 67.25%
(d) 70.25%   (e) 73.25%

76. An article was sold at a discount of 20% at Rs. 1020. If the article was sold at a discount of Rs. 199 in place of 20% discount, then find the selling price.
(a) Rs. 1066   (b) Rs. 1076   (c) Rs. 1086
(d) Rs. 1096   (e) Rs. 1094

77. The sum total of the age of A, B and C four years hence will be 98 years. Find the age of C four years hence, if the present age of A and B is 32 years and 23 years respectively.
(a) 31 yr.   (b) 32 yr.   (c) 35 yr.
(d) 37 yr.   (e) 33 yr.

78. A invests Rs. 12,000 for X months while B invests Rs. 16,000 for 9 months in a scheme. If the profit share of B is Rs. 12,000 out of the total profit Rs. 21,000, then find the value of X?
(a) 6 months   (b) 9 months   (c) 8 months
(d) 7 months   (e) 10 months

79. A mixture of milk and water contains 60% milk and the remaining is water. How much water should be added (in percentage) into the mixture to reverse the proportion of milk and water?
(a) 25%   (b) 37.5%   (c) 62.5%
(d) 75%   (e) 50%

80. The simple interest on a certain sum for 2 years at 8% per annum is Rs. 225 less than the compound interest on the same sum for 2 years at 10% per annum. The sum is:
(a) Rs. 3200   (b) Rs. 4200   (c) Rs. 4000
(d) Rs. 3600   (e) Rs. 4500

Solutions

REASONING ABILITY

Direction (1-5):

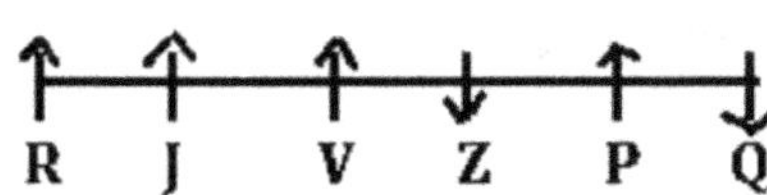

1. (d)   2. (a)   3. (e)
4. (b)   5. (d)

Directions (6-8):
6. (d)

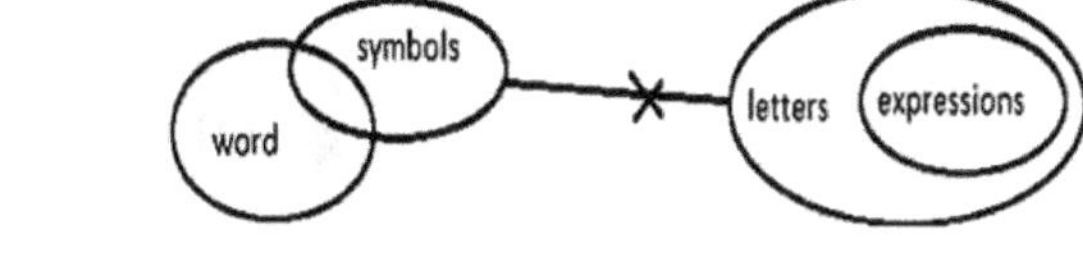

7. (d)

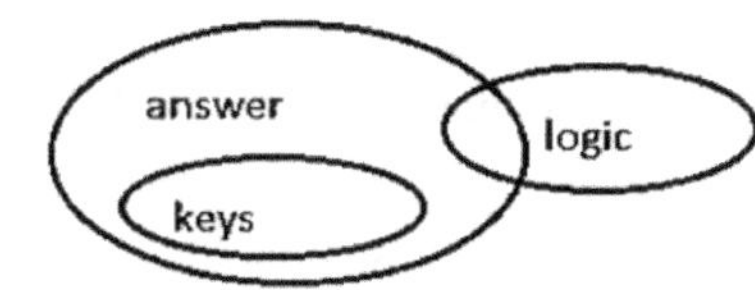

8. (€)

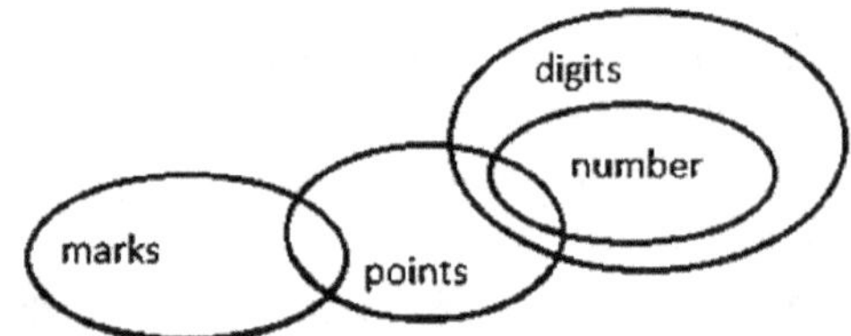

Direction (9-13):

Boxes
S
N
P
Q
R
O
M

9. (a)   10. (d)   11. (a)

12. (b)   13. (b)

Directions (14-18):

Word	Code
Places	ra
Order	gb
New	bv
To	cq
Things	po
For	fc
In	ik
Arrange	mn
Unknown/country	de/lf

14. (a)   15. (a)   16. (b)

17. (d)   18. (b)

Direction (19-23):

Months	Persons
January	C
April	A
May	T
August	R
September	Q
December	Y

19. (d)   20. (d)   21. (b)

22. (a)   23. (c)

24. (b)

$$A(+) = P(-)$$
$$|$$
$$R(-) —— T(+) = H(-)$$

25. (a)

$$4\ 6\ 7\ 5\ 2\ 9\ 8\ 3$$
$$|\ \ \ \ \ \ \ \ \ |$$
$$2\ 3\ 4\ 5\ 6\ 7\ 8\ 9$$

26. (b) LATE, LEAT

Direction (27-31):

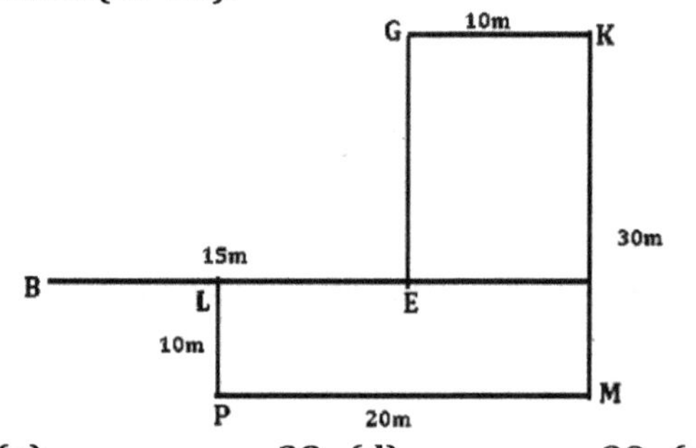

27. (a)   28. (d)   29. (a)

30. (d)   31. (e)   32.(b)

33.(e)

34. (c) 184,982

35. (d)735,135,353

36. (b)

Directions (37-40):

R > C > P (Rs. 3000) > B > Q (Rs.2000) > A

37. (a)   38. (c)   39. (b)

40. (c)

QUANTITATIVE APTITUDE

41. (c) Let the speed of stream be x km/hr
Then,
Speed of upstream = $x \times \frac{600}{100} = 18$
$\Rightarrow x = 3$km/hr
Speed of boat in still water = 18 + 3 = 21 km/hr
Distance covered in 3 hours in downstream
= (21 + 3) × 3 = 72 km

42. (a) $(A + B)(A - B) = 252$
$\Rightarrow 42 \times (A - B) = 252\ [A + B = 42\ given]$
$\Rightarrow (A - B) = 6$ ...(i)
And $A + B = 42$ ...(ii)
Solve (i) and (ii), we get
$B = 18$

43. (d) Let the time taken by A and B be $5x$ days and $3x$ days respectively.

⇒$5x$ = 40 days

⇒x = 8 days

B's time = 3 × 8 = 24 days

Time taken by both together to complete the work

$= \frac{40 \times 24}{40 + 24}$ $\left[use\ \frac{a \times b}{a+b}\ for\ two\ persons\right]$ = 15 days.

44. (b) Speed of train = 72 km/hr

$= 72 \times \frac{5}{18} = 20$ m/s

Length of train = 18 × 20 = 360 m

Length of (train + platform)

= 20 × 33 = 660 m

∴ Length of platform = 660 m – 360 m

= 300 m

45. (e) ATQ,

$2\pi r = 66$ cm

$\Rightarrow 2 \times \frac{22}{7} \times r = 66$ cm

$\Rightarrow r = \frac{66 \times 7}{44} = \frac{21}{2}$ cm

Side of a square $= \frac{21}{2 \times 2} = \frac{21}{4}$ cm

∴ Area of square $= (side)^2 = \left(\frac{21}{4}\right)^2$

$= \frac{441}{16} \approx 28\ cm^2$

46. (d) $\sqrt{1444} \div 19 + 328 = ? \times 22$

$\Rightarrow 2 + 328 = ? \times 22$

$\Rightarrow ? = \frac{330}{22} = 15$

47. (b) 30% of 880 = ? + 111

$\Rightarrow \frac{30 \times 880}{100} = ? + 111$

$\Rightarrow ? = 264 - 111 = 153.$

48. (a) $(?)^2 + 256 = \frac{50 \times 800}{100}$

$(?)^2 + 256 = 400$

$\Rightarrow (?)^2 = 144$

$\Rightarrow ? = 12$

49. (e) $12 + ? = 256$

$\Rightarrow ? = 244$

50. (d) $\frac{75 \times ?}{100} = (18)^2$

$\Rightarrow \frac{75 \times ?}{100} = 324$

$\Rightarrow ? = \frac{324 \times 100}{75} = 432.$

51. (d)

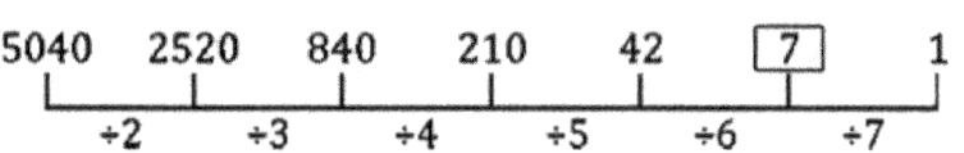

52. (b)

53. (d)

54. (a)

55. (c)

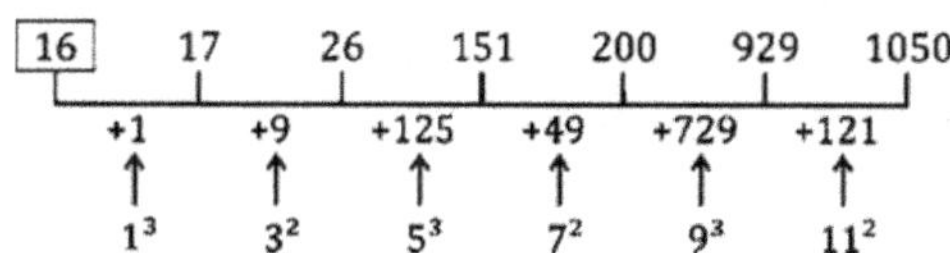

Solution (56-60): Let total employees in company be 100x

ATQ,

$$\frac{25}{100} \times 100x = 90$$

⇒ Total employees in company = $100x$ = 360

Employees working in HR department

$= \frac{2}{9} \times 360 = 80$

Employees working in Sales department

$= \frac{125}{100} \times 80 = 100$

Remaining employees = $360 - 90 - 80 - 100 = 90$

Employees working in Security department

$= \frac{4}{9} \times 90 = 40$

Employees working in Housing department

$= \frac{5}{9} \times 90 = 50$

Sales	Finance	HR	Security	Housing	Total
100	90	80	40	50	360

56. (d) Required % $= \frac{80-40}{40} \times 100 = \frac{40}{40} \times 100 = 100\%$

57. (c) Required average $= \frac{100+90+50}{3} = \frac{240}{3} = 80$

58. (a) Required difference $= 50 - 40 = 10$

59. (e) Total number of male employees working in Security department $= \frac{60}{100} \times 40 = 24$

60. (b) Total number of female employees working in HR department $= \frac{3}{5} \times 80 = 48$

61. (b) $?^2 = 4^2 + 8^2 - 31$

$?^2 = 16 + 64 - 31 = 80 - 31 = 49$

$? = 7$

62. (d) $13 \times 6 + ? \times 4 = 18 \times 7$

$78 + ? \times 4 = 126$

$? = \frac{126 - 78}{4} = 12$

63. (a) $40\%\ of\ ? = 25\%\ of\ 320 + 75\%\ of\ 160$

$\frac{2}{5} \times ? = \frac{25}{100} \times 320 + \frac{75}{100} \times 160$

$\frac{2}{5} \times ? = 80 + 120$

$? = 200 \times \frac{5}{2} = 500$

64. (c) $11^2 + 6^2 = ? + 37$

$121 + 36 - 37 = ?$

$? = 120$

65. (e) $\frac{360}{?} = 12 \times 6 - 3^3$

$\frac{360}{?} = 72 - 27$

$? = \frac{360}{45} = 8$

66. (d) $\sqrt{225} + \sqrt{441} = ?^2$

$15 + 21 = ?^2$

$?^2 = 36$

$? = 6$

67. (a) $16 \times 8 - ? = 2^6$

$128 - 64 = ? \Rightarrow ? = 64$

68. (b) $16 \times 54 \div 36 + 6 = ?$

$? = 16 \times \dfrac{54}{36} + 6 = 30$

69. (e) $? = \sqrt{6 \times 3 \times 5 + 50\% \ of \ 620}$

$? = \sqrt{90 + 310} = \sqrt{400} = 20$

70. (c) $6^2 = \dfrac{18 \times 8 - ? \times 2}{3}$

$36 \times 3 = 144 - ? \times 2$

$? \times 2 = 144 - 108$

$? = \dfrac{36}{2} = 18$

71. (c) Marks scored by Sandy in English and Maths together = $60 + 60 = 120$

Marks scored by Aditya and Neeraj in English together = $75 + 85 = 160$

Required % = $\dfrac{120}{160} \times 100 = 75\%$

72. (a) Required ratio = $\dfrac{60+75+55+60}{80+60+95+65} = \dfrac{250}{300} = \dfrac{5}{6}$

73. (d) Total marks scored by Paul = $65 + 60 + 80 + 65 = 270$

Total marks scored by Neeraj = $85 + 55 + 95 + 85 = 320$

Required difference = $320 - 270 = 50$

74. (e) Required average = $\dfrac{75+75+60}{3} = 70$

75. (b) $Required \ \% = \dfrac{60+60+65+60}{400} \times 100 = 61.25\%$

76. (b) MP of article = $\dfrac{1020}{80} \times 100 = $ Rs. 1275

Selling price = $1275 - 199 = $ Rs. 1076

77. (c) Sum of present age of A, B and C

$= 98 - 4 \times 3$

$= 98 - 12 = 86$ yr.

Present age of C = $86 - (32 + 23) = 31$ yr.

Age of C four years hence = $31 + 4 = 35$ yr.

78. (b) Profit share ratio of

$$A \qquad\qquad B$$
$$12000 \times x \qquad 16000 \times 9$$
$$x \qquad : \qquad 12$$

ATQ,

$$\dfrac{x}{12} = \dfrac{9000}{12000}$$

$\Rightarrow x = 9$ months.

79. (e) Let, total quantity = 100ℓ

Quantity of milk = $60\ \ell$

And quantity of water = $40\ \ell$

ATQ,

$$\dfrac{40}{100} = \dfrac{60}{100+x}$$

$2(100 + x) = 5 \times 60$

$200 + 2x = 300$

$2x = 100$

$x = 50\ \ell$

$Water \ added \ in \ \% = \dfrac{50}{100} \times 100 = 50\%$

80. (e) $Let \ the \ sum \ be \ Rs.\ P.$

$$P\left[\dfrac{11}{10} \times \dfrac{11}{10} - 1\right] - \dfrac{P \times 2 \times 8}{100} = 225$$

$$\Rightarrow P\left[\dfrac{21}{100}\right] - \dfrac{16P}{100} = 225$$

$$\Rightarrow P = \dfrac{225 \times 100}{5} \Rightarrow P = Rs.\ 4500$$

REASONING ABILITY

Directions (1-5): In each of the questions, relationships between some elements are shown in the statements(s). These statements are followed by conclusions numbered I and II. Read the statements carefully and give the answer.
(a) If only conclusion I follows.
(b) If only conclusion II follows.
(c) If either conclusion I or II follows.
(d) If neither conclusion I nor II follows.
(e) If both conclusions I and II follow.

1. **Statements:** $A < B > N = M, B \le V, M > R$
   Conclusions: I. $B > R$ II. $V > A$
2. **Statements:** $D < E > F = G > H = I \le J$
   Conclusions: I. $F > I$ II. $J \ge E$
3. **Statements:** $M < N < O > P, N < E$
   Conclusions: I. $E < M$ II. $E > O$
4. **Statements:** $C \ge D < E = F \ge G, C < W$
   Conclusions: I. $E = G$ II. $G < E$
5. **Statements:** $R < T < S < P > Q, R > X$
   Conclusions: I. $S < Q$ II. $X < S$

Direction (6-10): Study the following information carefully and answer the questions given below:

Eight people viz. G, H, I, J, K, L, M and N live in a building on different floors from top to bottom (such that the ground floor is numbered as 1 and the topmost floor is numbered as 8), but not necessarily in the same order.

There is a gap of three floors between J and L and both of them live on an odd-numbered floor. N lives just above H, who lives on an even-numbered floor. I lives on floor number 6. Only one person lives between L and M. J lives above I. Three persons live between K and H.

6. Who among the following lives on the ground floor?
   (a) N (b) J
   (c) K (d) M
   (e) None of these
7. Who among the following lives immediately below L?
   (a) K (b) I
   (c) G (d) H
   (e) None of these
8. How many persons live between I and H?
   (a) one (b) three
   (c) fives (d) two
   (e) None of these
9. Who among the following lives on the topmost floor?
   (a) N (b) J
   (c) K (d) M
   (e) None of these
10. Which of the following combination is false?
    (a) J-7 (b) L-3 (c) G-2
    (d) H-4 (e) N-1
11. In a row of children facing north, Rajan is twelfth from the right end and is fifth to the right of Satyarthi who is tenth from the left end. What is the total number of children in the row?
    (a) 29 (b) 28
    (c) 26 (d) 27
    (e) None of these
12. Raj leaves his home and goes 20 meters straight, then turns right and goes 10 meters. He turns left and goes 30 meters and finally turns right and starts walking. If he is now moving in the north direction, then in which direction did he start his walking?
    (a) east (b) west
    (c) north (d) south
    (e) None of these

Directions (13-17): In each of the questions given below, a group of digits/letters is given followed by four combinations of symbols numbered (a), (b), (c) and (d). You have to find out which of the four combinations correctly represents the group of digits/letters based on the symbol codes and the conditions given below. If none of the four combinations represents the group of digits correctly, give (e)'None of these' as the answer.

Digit	Z	L	F	1	I	5	7	A	E	B	2	X	6	W
Symbol	@	!	$	^	µ	Δ	Å	&	>	≠	<	®	£	∞

Condition for coding the group elements:
(i) If the first letter is a vowel and the last digit is divisible by 2, then both are to be coded as +.
(ii) If the first as well as the last digit is odd, then both are to be coded by the code of the first digit.
(iii) If the first letter is a consonant and the last digit is an odd number, then the code of the first and last elements are to be interchanged.

13. WX6ZF1
    (a) ^®$@£∞ (b) ^@$∞<!
    (c) ^®£@$∞ (d) ∞®@>!<
    (e) None of these

14. FE1XI6
    (a) ∞^@<!£   (b) $<^^£@
    (c) $>^®µ£   (d) $<^@^£
    (e) None of these

15. 5L2IA1
    (a) Δ!<µ&Δ   (b) Δ!&^<µ
    (c) Δ!<µ^&   (d) µ&Δ!<^
    (e) None of these

16. E2ZA6
    (a) &>!^@   (b) @<@&!
    (c) @&<@&   (d) +<@&+
    (e) None of these

17. IZ2W2
    (a) @≠^$&   (b) +@<∞+
    (c) <∞µ@≠   (d) @≠>!^
    (e) None of these

Directions (18-22): Read the following information carefully and answer the questions given below.

A, B, C, D, E, F, G and H are eight members standing in a row (not necessarily in the same order) facing north.

C and B have as many members between them as G and C have between them. D, who is 4th from the extreme left end, is 2nd to the left of E. G is 3rd place away from one of the extreme ends. Neither B nor C sits at any extreme end. F sits at the immediate right of A.

18. How many persons sit between G and B?
    (a) one   (b) three
    (c) two   (d) four
    (e) None of these

19. Who among the following persons sits at the extreme ends?
    (a) A, G   (b) B, C
    (c) F, H   (d) H, A
    (e) None of these

20. Who sits second to the right of E?
    (a) B   (b) H
    (c) G   (d) C
    (e) None of these

21. Who sits third to the left of G?
    (a) A   (b) None
    (c) F   (d) E
    (e) B

22. Who sits to the immediate left of C?
    (a) A   (b) H
    (c) C   (d) D
    (e) None of these

23. Find the odd one out.
    (a) ACB   (b) DFE
    (c) GIH   (d) JLK
    (e) MNO

Directions (24-28): Study the following number sequence and answer the questions following it.

9 3 2 4 5 7 9 5 8 1 5 0 6 4 2 9 8 2 6 3 5 9 8 2 1 5 4 3 2 1

24. How many odd numbers are there in the numeric series which are immediately preceded by a number, which is a whole square?

    (a) one
    (b) two
    (c) three
    (d) More than three
    (e) None of these

25. If all the odd numbers are dropped from the series, which number will be eighth to the left of the eleventh number from the left end?
    (a) 2   (b) 8
    (c) 6   (d) 4
    (e) None of these

26. If 1 is subtracted from all odd numbers and 2 is subtracted from all even numbers in the given number series, then which number will be sixteenth from the right end?
    (a) 0   (b) 2   (c) 3
    (d) 8   (e) 6

27. If the position of the 1st and the 16th numbers, the 2nd and the 17th numbers, and so on up to the 15th and the 30th numbers, are interchanged, which number will be 7th to the right of the 19th number from the right end?
    (a) 5   (b) 9
    (c) 8   (d) 4
    (e) None of these

28. How many even numbers are there in the above sequence that are immediately preceded by a 'whole cube' or 'immediately preceded by a whole square'?
    (a) four   (b) five
    (c) three   (d) six
    (e) None of these

Directions (29–33): In each question below are given some statements followed by two conclusions numbered I and II. You have to take the given statements to be true even if they seem to be at variance with commonly known facts. Read all the conclusions and then decide which of the given conclusions logically follow from the given statements, disregarding commonly known facts. Give answer

(a) If only conclusion I follows.
(b) If only conclusion II follows.
(c) If either conclusion I or II follows.
(d) If neither conclusion I nor II follows.
(e) If both conclusions I and II follow.

29. Statements: All shirts are skirts.
No skirt is top. All tops are kurta.
    Conclusions: I. All shirts are kurta
        II. Some kurta are skirts.

30. Statements: Some chocolate are chips.
Some chips are jelly.
All jelly are whoppers.
    Conclusions: I. Some jelly are chips.
        II. All chocolate being whoppers is a possibility

31. Statements: Some frooti are Maaza.
No Maaza is slice.
All slice are fanta.

Conclusions: I. Some Frooti are definitely not Slice.

II. Some Fanta are definitely not Maaza.

32. Statements: All carbon are oxygen.

All Nitrogen are carbon.

Some oxygen are Sulphur.

Conclusions I. All Nitrogen being Sulphur is a possibility.

II. All Nitrogen are not oxygen.

33. Statements: All September are October.

No October is November.

No November is December.

Conclusions: I. Some September are not Novembers.

II. No October is December.

Directions (34-38): The following questions are based on the five words given below. Study the following words and answer the following questions.

NOW   SAD   WAF   RAT   CAT

(The new words formed after performing the mentioned operations may not necessarily be a meaningful English word.)

34. If the given words are arranged in the order as they appear in a dictionary from left to right, which of the following will be the fourth from the left end?

(a) WAF   (b) NOW   (c) SAD

(d) CAT   (e) RAT

35. How many letters are there in the English alphabetical series between the second letter of the word which is second from the right end and the third letter of the word which is second from the left end?

(a) two   (b) three

(c) four   (d) five

(e) None of these

36. If the third alphabet in each of the words is changed to the previous alphabet in the English alphabetical order, how many words thus formed will be without any vowels?

(a) none   (b) one

(c) two   (d) three

(e) More than three

37. If the position of the first and the third alphabet of each of the words are interchanged, which of the following will form a meaningful word in the new arrangement?

(a) NOW   (b) SAD

(c) RAT   (d) WAF

(e) Both (a) and (c)

38. If in each of the given words, each of the consonants is changed to its previous letter and each vowel is changed to its next letter in the English alphabetical series, then in how many words thus formed will at least one vowel appear?

(a) none   (b) one

(c) two   (d) three

(e) None of these

39. If in the number 9737132710, positions of the first and the second digits are interchanged, positions of the third and fourth digits are interchanged and so on till the positions of the 9th and 10th digits are interchanged, then which digit will be the 6th from the left end?

(a) 7   (b) 1

(c) 3   (d) 9

(e) None of these

40. How many pairs of letters are there in the word "WORSHIP" which have as many letters between them in the word as in alphabetical series, backwards or forwards?

(a) none   (b) one   (c) two

(d) three   (e) four

QUANTITATIVE APTITUDE

41. The retail price of a water geyser is Rs. 1265. If the manufacturer gains 10%, the wholesale dealer gains 15% and the retailer gains 25%, then the cost of the product is:

(a) Rs. 800   (b) Rs. 900

(c) Rs. 700   (d) Rs. 600

(e) None of these

42. A pipe can fill a cistern in six hours. Due to a leak in its bottom, it is filled in seven hours. When the cistern is full, in how much time will it be emptied by the leak?

(a) 42 hrs   (b) 40 hrs

(c) 43 hrs   (d) 45 hrs

(e) None of these

43. Ram travels a certain distance at 3 km/h. and reaches 15 minutes late. If he travels at 4 km/h., he reaches 15 minutes earlier. The distance he has to travel is:

(a) 4.5 km.   (b) 6 km.

(c) 7.2 km.   (d) 12 km.

(e) None of these

44. In a mixture of 45 litres, the ratio of milk and water is 3:2. How much water must be added to make the ratio 9:11?

(a) 10 litres   (b) 15 litres
(c) 17 litres   (d) 20 litres
(e) None of these

45. A person can row with the stream at 8 Km per hour and against the stream at 6 Km an hour. The speed of the current is:
(a) 1 $Km/h.$ (b) 2 $Km/h.$
(c) 4 $Km/h.$ (d) 5 $Km/h.$
(e) None of these

46. A father's age is three times the sum of the ages of his two children, but 20 years hence his age will be equal to the sum of their ages. Then, the father's age is:
(a) 30 years   (b) 40 years
(c) 35 years   (d) 45 years
(e) None of these

47. A sum was put at simple interest at a certain rate for three years. Had it been put at 1% higher rate, it would have fetched Rs. 5100 more. The sum is:
(a) Rs. 170000   (b) Rs. 150000
(c) Rs. 125000   (d) Rs. 120000

(e) None of these

48. From among 36 teachers in a school, one principal and one vice-principal are to be appointed. In how many ways can this be done?
(a) 1260   (b) 1250
(c) 1240   (d) 1800
(e) None of these

49. A card is drawn at random from a well-shuffled pack of 52 cards. What is the probability of getting a two of hearts or a two of diamonds?
(a) $\frac{3}{26}$ (b) $\frac{2}{17}$
(c) $\frac{1}{26}$ (d) $\frac{4}{13}$
(e) None of these

50. A sum is invested for three years at compound interest at 5%, 10% and 20% respectively. In three years, if the sum amounts to Rs. 16632, then find the sum invested.
(a) Rs. 11000   (b) Rs. 12000
(c) Rs. 13000   (d) Rs. 14000
(e) None of these

Directions (51-55): The table below shows the mobile phones sold on different days by different sellers. Read the table carefully and answer the questions.

Mobiles Phones Sellers/Days→	Monday	Tuesday	Wednesday	Thursday	Friday	Saturday	Sunday
P	40	45	48	28	50	24	20
Q	90	92	27	12	16	98	26
R	80	36	30	13	28	62	47
S	60	46	12	64	52	34	76
T	48	18	58	69	70	10	15

51. Find the difference in the number of mobile phones sold by P and R together on Monday and the mobile phones sold by S and T on Wednesday?
(a) 60   (b) 50
(c) 80   (d) 20
(e) None of these

52. Find the ratio of mobile phones sold by Q on Tuesday and Saturday together to the mobile phones sold by R on Thursday and Sunday together?
(a) 7:19   (b) 19:5
(c) 19:6   (d) 2:5
(e) None of these

53. Mobile phones sold by P and S together on Wednesday is what percent of the number of mobile phones sold by T on Sunday?
(a) 400%   (b) 200%
(c) 100%   (d) 50%
(e) None of these

54. What is the average number of mobile phones sold by Q on Wednesday, T on Sunday and S on Monday?
(a) 24   (b) 36
(c) 30   (d) 28
(e) None of these

55. The mobiles sold by P on Thursday are of two types i.e. Windows phones and Android phones in the ratio 3:4. Find the number of Windows phones sold by P on Thursday.
(a) 14   (b) 24
(c) 16   (d) 12
(e) None of these

Directions (Q.56-65): What should come in place of the question mark (?) in the following simplification problems?

56. 45% of $600 + ?\%$ of $480 = 390$
(a) 20   (b) 25
(c) 30   (d) 40
(e) None of these

57. $4\frac{2}{3} + 7\frac{1}{6} - 5\frac{2}{9} = ?$

(a) $6\frac{2}{3}$ (b) $6\frac{2}{9}$

(c) $6\frac{11}{18}$ (d) $6\frac{7}{18}$

(e) None of these

58. $65\% \ of \ 240 + ?\% \ of \ 150 = 210$

(a) 45   (b) 46

(c) 32   (d) 36

(e) None of these

59. $\frac{2}{3} \ of \ 1\frac{2}{5} \ of \ 75\% \ of \ 540 = ?$

(a) 378   (b) 756

(c) 252   (d) 332

(e) None of these

60. $555.05 + 55.50 + 5.55 + 5 + 0.55 = ?$

(a) 621.65   (b) 655.75

(c) 634.85   (d) 647.35

(e) None of these

61. $1425 + 8560 + 1680 \div 200 = ?$

(a) 58.325   (b) 9973.4

(c) 56.425   (d) 9939.4

(e) None of these

62. $?\% \ of \ 800 = 293 - 22\% \ of \ 750$

(a) 14   (b) 18

(c) 12   (d) 16

(e) 20

63. $25.6\% \ of \ 250 + \sqrt{?} = 119$

(a) 4225   (b) 3025

(c) 2025   (d) 5625

(e) None of these

64. $4\frac{5}{6} \quad 5\frac{5}{9} = ? \ -2\frac{1}{3} + \frac{11}{18}$

(a) $\frac{3}{4}$ (b) $2\frac{1}{18}$

(c) $1\frac{7}{9}$ (d) $1\frac{11}{18}$

(e) None of these

65. $[30\% \ of \ \{(80\% \ of \ 850) \div 34\}] = ?$

(a) 5   (b) 4   (c) 6

(d) 8   (e) 9

66. The sides of a triangle are in the ratio of $\frac{1}{2} : \frac{1}{3} : \frac{1}{4}$. If the perimeter is 52 cm., then the length of the smallest side is:

(a) 9 cm.   (b) 10 cm.

(c) 11 cm.   (d) 12 cm.

(e) None of these

67. If A's salary is 25% higher than B's salary, then by what per cent is B's salary lower than A's?

(a) 15%   (b) 20%

(c) 25%   (d) $33\frac{1}{3}\%$

(e) None of these

68. Ravi sells an article at a gain of $12\frac{1}{2}\%$. If he had sold it at Rs. 22.50 more, he would have gained 25%. The cost price of the article is:

(a) Rs. 162   (b) Rs. 140

(c) Rs. 196   (d) Rs. 180

(e) None of these

69. A certain job assigned to a group of men was to be completed in 20 days. But 12 men did not turn up for the job and the remaining men did the job in 32 days. The original number of men in the group was:

(a) 32   (b) 34

(c) 36   (d) 40

(e) None of these

70. A vessel contains liquid P and Q in the ratio 5:3. If 16 litres of the mixture are removed and the same quantity of liquid Q is added, the ratio will become 3:5. What quantity does the vessel hold?

(a) 35 litres

(b) 45 litres

(c) 40 litres

(d) 50 litres

(e) None of these

Directions (Q.71-75): What should come in place of the question mark (?) in the following simplification problems?

71. $50\% \ of \ 250 + \sqrt{?} = 165$

(a) 1700   (b) 1600

(c) 1800   (d) 2000

(e) None of these

72. $140\% \ of \ 56 + 56\% \ of \ 140 = ?$

(a) 78.4   (b) 158.6

(c) 156.6   (d) 87.4

(e) None of these

73. $1\frac{1}{4} + 1\frac{5}{9} \times 1\frac{5}{8} \div 6\frac{1}{2} = ?$

(a) 17   (b) 27

(c) 42   (d) 18

(e) None of these

74. $999.09 + 99.90 + 9.99 + 9 + 0.99 = ?$

(a) 1118.97

(b) 1128.97

(c) 1218.97

(d) 1139.97

(e) None of these

75. $20\% \ of \ [\{(220\% \ of \ 40) - 10\}]\% \ of \ 500 = ?$

(a) 58   (b) 68

(c) 98   (d) 78

(e) None of these

Directions (Q.76-80): What should come in place of the question mark (?) in the following number series?

76. 5,   8,   12,   18,   27,   ?

(a) 39   (b) 40   (c) 41

(d) 42   (e) 43

77. 2,   10,   30,   68,   130,   ?

(a) 210   (b) 215   (c) 222

(d) 228   (e) 235

78. 142,   133,   115,   88,   ?

(a) 50   (b) 53   (c) 55

(d) 51   (e) 52

79. 3,   8,   18,   38,   78,   ?

(a) 158   (b) 154   (c) 150
(d) 162   (e) 166
80. 6,   3,   3,   6,   24,   ?

(a) 184   (b) 186   (c) 188
(d) 190   (e) 192

Solutions

REASONING ABILITY

1. **(e)** I. B > R (True)   **II.** V > A (True)
2. **(a)** I. F > I (True)   **II.** J ≥ E (False)
3. **(d)** I. E < M (False)   **II.** E>O (False)
4. **(c)** I. E =G (False)   **II.** G< E (False)
5. **(b)** I. S < Q (False)   **II.** X < S (True)

Direction (6-10):

Floors	Persons
8	K
7	J
6	I
5	N
4	H
3	L
2	G
1	M

6. **(d)**   7. **(c)**   8. **(a)**
9. **(c)**   10. **(e)**
11. **(c)** Sathyarthi's position from left end = 10th
    Sathyarthi's position from right end = 17th
    Total number of children in the row
    = 10 + 17 – 1 = 26
12. **(b)** Raj started walking towards west.
13. **(c)** By using condition (iii) the code of WX6ZF1 will be ^®£@$∞.
14. **(c)** The code of FE1XI6 will be $>^®μ£.
15. **(a)** By using condition (ii) the code of 5L2IA1 will be Δ!<μ&Δ.
16. **(d)** By using condition (i) the code ofE2ZA6 will be +<@&+.
17. **(b)** By using condition (i) the code of IZ2W2 will be +@<∞+.

Directions (18-22):

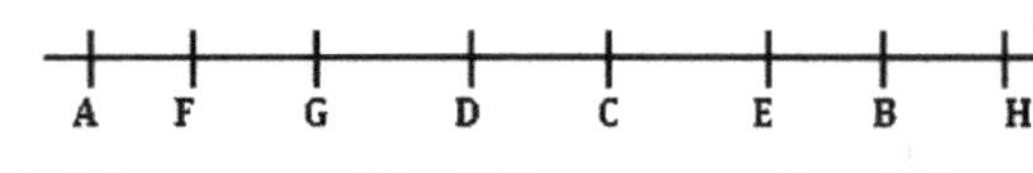

18. **(b)**   19. **(d)**   20. **(b)**
21. **(b)**   22. **(d)**

23. **(e)**

   1 3 2   4 6 5   7 9 8   10 12 11   13 14 15
   A C B   **D F E**   **G I H**   **J L K**   **M N O**

    So, the odd one out will be MNO.

24. **(d)** More than three
25. **(b)** 8
26. **(a)** 0
27. **(d)** 4
28. **(b)** Five
29. **(d)**

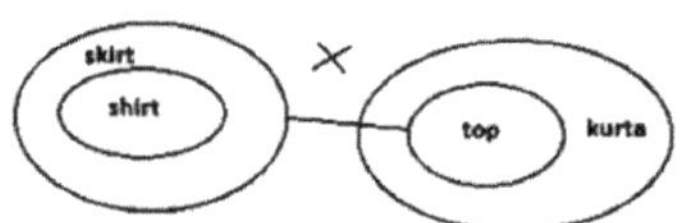

30. **(e)**

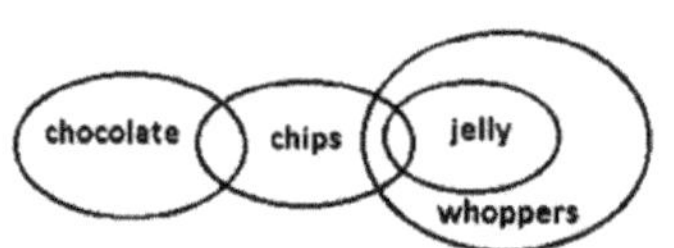

31. **(e)**

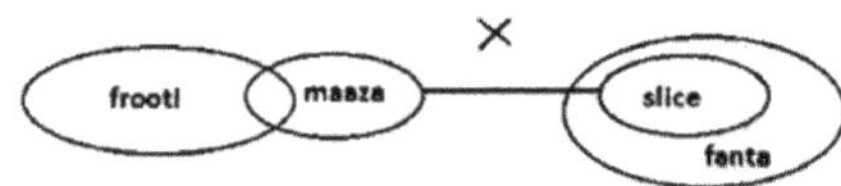

32. **(a)**

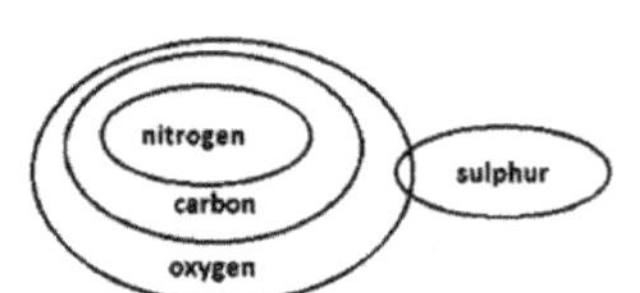

33. **(a)**

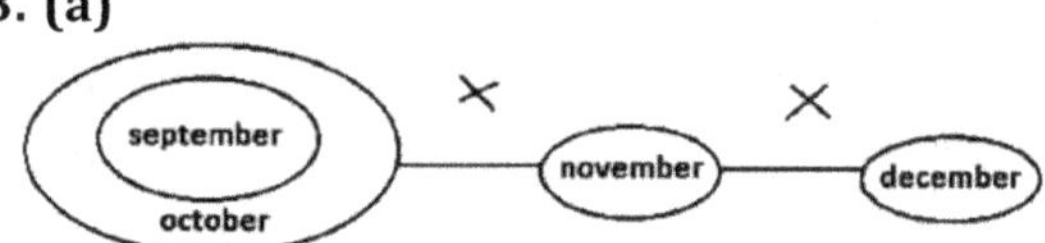

34. **(c)** SAD
35. **(a)** TWO
36. **(a)** None
37. **(e)** WON, TAR
38. **(b)** One
39. **(b)** 1
40. **(d)** Three- RS, HI, and PS

41. (a) Cost price $= \frac{100}{110} \times \frac{100}{115} \times \frac{100}{125} \times 1265 =$ Rs. 800

42. (a) In one hour, $\frac{1}{6}$ of the cistern can be filled

In one hour, only $\frac{1}{7}$ of the cistern can be filled due to leak in its bottom

∴ In one hour $\frac{1}{6} - \frac{1}{7} = \frac{1}{42}$ of the cistern is empty

∴ The whole cistern will be emptied in 42 hrs

43. (b) Let D be the required distance

So, $\frac{D}{3} - \frac{D}{4} = \frac{15+15}{60}$

Or, D = 6 km

44. (b) Let, M = 3K, W = 2K

∴ 3K + 2K = 45 ⇒ K = 9

⇒ Milk = 27 litres and water = 18 litres

Now suppose x litres of water is added to the mixture such that

$\frac{27}{18+x} = \frac{9}{11} \Rightarrow 162 + 9x = 297$

$\Rightarrow 9x = 135 \Rightarrow x = 15$

45. (a) Let the speed of the current be x Km/h and speed of the person in still water be y km/h.

∴ y + x = 8

y − x = 6

⇒ y = 7, x = 1

∴ Speed of the current = 1 Km/h.

46. (a) Let the father's age be x years and age of his children be a and b years

∴$(a + b) = \frac{x}{3}$

And $(a + b) + 20 + 20 = x + 20$

$\Rightarrow \frac{x}{3} + 20 = x$

$\Rightarrow x = 30$ years

47. (a) Simple interest for 1 year $= \frac{5100}{3} = Rs\ 1700$

1% of sum = 1700

∴ sum $= \frac{1700 \times 100}{1} = Rs\ 170000$

48. (a) One principal can be appointed in 36 days

One vice-principal appointed in remaining 35 ways

∴ Total no. of ways = 36 × 35 = 1260.

49. (b) ∴ Required probability

$= \frac{^{13}C_2 + \ ^{13}C_2}{^{52}C_2}$

$= \frac{78 + 78}{1326} = \frac{156}{1326} = \frac{2}{17}$

Alternately,

Required probability

$= \frac{13}{52} \times \frac{12}{51} + \frac{13}{52} \times \frac{12}{51}$

$= 2 \times \frac{13}{52} \times \frac{12}{51} = \frac{2}{17}$

50. (b) Let, P be the sum.

$\therefore 16632 = P\left(1 + \frac{5}{100}\right)\left(1 + \frac{10}{100}\right)\left(1 + \frac{20}{100}\right)$

Or, $16632 = P \times \frac{21}{20} \times \frac{11}{10} \times \frac{6}{5}$

Or, P = Rs.12,000

51. (b) Required difference = (40 + 80) − (12 + 58)

= 120 − 70 = 50

52. (c) *Required ratio* $= \frac{92+98}{13+47} = \frac{190}{60} = 19 : 6.$

53. (a) *Required percentage* $= \frac{48+12}{15} \times 100 = \frac{60}{15} \times 100 = 400\%$

54. (e) *Average* $= \frac{27+15+60}{3} = \frac{102}{3} = 34.$

55. (d) Windows phones sold by P on Thursday $= \frac{3}{7} \times 28 = 12$

56. (b) $\frac{45}{100}$ *of* $600 + \frac{?}{100}$ *of* $480 = 390$

⇒ 270 + 4.8 ×? = 390

∴? $= \frac{390 - 270}{4.8} = 25$

57. (c) ? $= \frac{14}{3} + \frac{43}{6} - \frac{47}{9} = \frac{84+129-94}{18} = \frac{119}{18} = 6\frac{11}{18}$

58. (d) $\frac{65}{100}$ *of* $240 + \frac{?}{100}$ *of* $150 = 210$

⇒ 156 + 1.5 ×? = 210

∴ ? $= \frac{210 - 156}{1.5} = 36$

59. (a) ? $= \frac{2}{3}$ *of* $\frac{7}{5}$ *of* $\frac{75}{100}$ *of* $540 = 7 \times 54 = 378$

60. (a) ? = 555.05 + 55.50 + 5.55 + 5 + 0.55

= 621.65

61. (e) ? = 1425 + 8560 + 1680 ÷ 200

$= 1425 + 8560 + \frac{1680}{200}$

= 9985 + 8.4 = 9993.4

62. (d) $\frac{800 \times ?}{100} = 293 - \frac{750 \times 22}{100}$

⇒ 8 × ? = 293 − 165 = 128

$\Rightarrow ? = \frac{128}{8} = 16$

63. (b) $250 \times \frac{25.6}{100} + \sqrt{?} = 119$

$\Rightarrow 64 + \sqrt{?} = 119$

$\Rightarrow \sqrt{?} = 119 - 64 = 55$

$\Rightarrow ? = 55 \times 55 = 3025$

64. (e) $4 + \frac{5}{6} - 5 - \frac{5}{9} = ? - 2 - \frac{1}{3} + \frac{11}{18}$

$\Rightarrow ? = 4 - 5 + 2 + \left(\frac{5}{6} - \frac{5}{9} + \frac{1}{3} - \frac{11}{18}\right)$

$\Rightarrow 1 + \left(\frac{15-10+6-11}{18}\right) = 1 + 0 = 1$

65. (c) $? = \left[\frac{30}{100} \times \left\{\left(\frac{80}{100} \times 850\right) \div 34\right\}\right]$

$= \left[\frac{30}{100} \times \{680 \div 34\}\right]$

$= \left[\frac{30}{100} \times 20\right] = 6$

66. (d) Sides of a triangle are in ratio $\frac{1}{2} : \frac{1}{3} : \frac{1}{4}$, i.e.,

6 : 4 : 3.

Let the sides be 6K, 4K and 3K, respectively.

∴ 13K = 52 ⇒ K = 4

∴ Sides of the triangle are 24 cm, 16 cm and 12 cm, respectively.

67. (b) A = B + 25% of B

$$\Rightarrow A = B + \frac{B}{4} = \frac{5B}{4}$$

$$\Rightarrow B = \frac{4}{5}A = A - \frac{1}{5}A$$

$$= A - 20\% \ of \ A$$

68. (d) $12\frac{1}{2}\% = Rs \ 22.50$

⇒C.P. = Rs 180.

69. (a) Suppose x = original number of men in the group

∴ (x- 12) men did the job in 32 days

∴ 20x = 32(x – 12)

i.e., x = 32

70. (c) Let, the quantity of liquid P and Q be 5x and 3x litres respectively.

Quantity of P removed $= \frac{5}{5+3} \times 16 = 10$ litres

Quantity of Q removed $= \frac{3}{5+3} \times 16 = 6$ litres

Now, $\frac{5x-10}{3x-6+16} = \frac{3}{5}$

$\Rightarrow 25x - 50 = 9x + 30$

$\Rightarrow 16x = 80 \Rightarrow x = 5$

∴ Quantity that the vessel holds = 8 ×5 = 40 litres

71. (b) $\frac{50}{100} of \ 250 + \sqrt{?} = 165$

$$\Rightarrow 125 + \sqrt{?} = 165$$

$$\Rightarrow \sqrt{?} = 40$$

$$\therefore ? = (40)^2 = 1600$$

72. (e) $\frac{140}{100} of \ 56 + \frac{56}{100} of \ 140$

$$= 78.4 + 78.4 = 156.8$$

73. (e) $? = 1\frac{1}{4} + 1\frac{5}{9} \times 1\frac{5}{8} \div 6\frac{1}{2} = \frac{5}{4} + \frac{14}{9} \times \frac{13}{8} \div \frac{13}{2}$

$$= \frac{5}{4} + \frac{14}{9} \times \frac{13}{8} \times \frac{2}{13}$$

$$= \frac{5}{4} + \frac{7}{18} = \frac{45 + 14}{36} = \frac{59}{36} = 1\frac{23}{36}$$

74. (a) 999.09 + 99.90 + 9.99 + 9 + 0.99

$$= 1118.97$$

75. (d) $\frac{20}{100} \times \left[\left\{ \left(\frac{220}{100} \times 40 \right) - 10 \right\} \right] \% \ of \ 500 = ?$

$$\frac{1}{5} \times [\{88 - 10\}]\% \ of \ 500 = ?$$

$$\frac{1}{5} \times \frac{78}{100} \times 500 = ?$$

$$? = 78$$

76. (b)

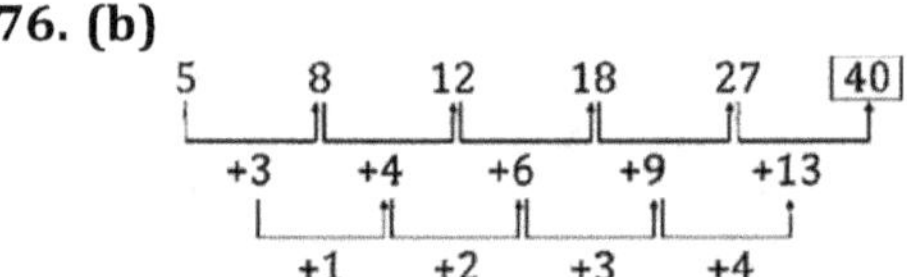

77. (c)

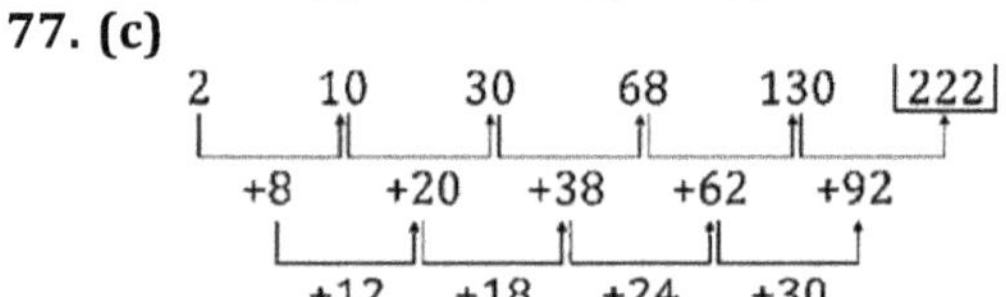

78. (e)

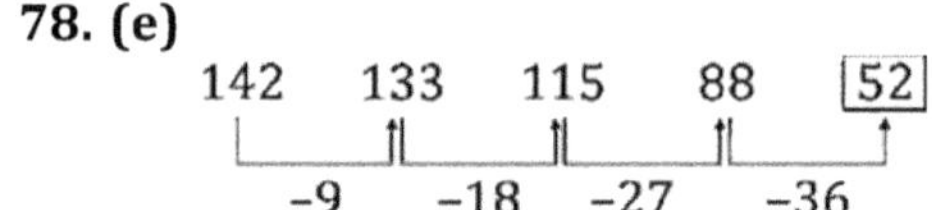

79. (a)

3   8   18   38   78   [158]

+5   +10   +20   +40   +80

80. (e)

6   3   3   6   24   [192]

×0.5   ×1   ×2   ×4   ×8

REASONING ABILITY

Directions (1-5): Study the following information carefully to answer the questions below:

Eight friends A, B, C, D E, F G and H are sitting around a circle facing the centre. A sits third to the left of B, while second to the right of F. D does not sit next to A or B. C and G always sit next to each other. H never sits next to D and C does not sit next to B.

1. Which of the following pairs sits between H and E?
   (a) F, D   (b) H, B
   (c) C, G   (d) E, G
   (e) None of these

2. Starting from A's position, if all the eight were arranged in an alphabetical order in clockwise direction, the seating position of how many members (excluding A) will not change?
   (a) none   (b) one
   (c) two   (d) three
   (e) None of these

3. Which of the following pairs has only one person sitting between them, if the counting is done in a clockwise direction?
   (a) A, B   (b) C, D
   (c) F, E   (d) G, H
   (e) None of these

4. Who sits to the immediate right of E?
   (a) A   (b) D
   (c) F   (d) H
   (e) None of these

5. What is the position of B with respect to C?
   (a) Second to the left   (b) Third to the right
   (c) Third to the left   (d) Can't be determined
   (e) None of these

Directions (6–10): Study the following information carefully and answer the questions given below.
Give answer:
(a) If only conclusion I is true
(b) If only conclusion II is true
(c) If either conclusion I or conclusion II is true
(d) If neither conclusion I nor conclusion II is true
(e) If both conclusions I and II are true

6. **Statements;** $H = W \leq R > F$
   Conclusions; I. $R = H$ II. $R > H$

7. **Statements;** $M < T > K = D$
   Conclusions; I. $D < T$ II. $K < M$

8. **Statements** $R \leq N \geq F > B$
   Conclusions; I. $F = R$ II. $B < N$

9. **Statements** $H > W < M \geq K$
   Conclusions I. $K < W$ II. $H > M$

10. **Statements** $R \geq T = M > D$
    Conclusions I. $D < T$ II. $R \geq M$

Directions (11-15): In each of the following questions below, a group of letters is followed by four combinations of digits/symbols. You have to find out which of the four combinations provided, correctly represents the group of letters based on the following coding system and mark the number of that combination as the answer. If none of the four combinations correctly represents the group of letters, mark (e), i.e. 'None of these', as the answer.

Letter	T	G	E	L	P	I	C	B	R	A	Q	M	U	H	J
Digit/Symbol	©	#	%	9	7	3	★	$	1	8	2	6	4	@	5

Conditions:
(i) If both the first and the last letter of the group are vowels, their codes are to be interchanged.
(ii) If the first letter is a consonant and the last letter is a vowel, both are to be coded as the code for the consonant.

11. ERHBMT
    (a) %1@$6©   (b) %1$@6©
    (c) ©1$@6©   (d) @%1$6©
    (e) None of these

12. PQGALE
    (a) 72#89%   (b) 72#897
    (c) 72%#97   (d) 27#892
    (e) None of these

13. EMTAHA
    (a) 8©68@8   (b) 36©#83
    (c) 86©8@3   (d) 86©8@%
    (e) None of these

14. BQRLHA
    (a) 8219@$ (b) $219@8
    (c) $219@$ (d) 82198@
    (e) None of these

15. RGMALB
    (a) 1#6891   (b) $#6891
    (c) 16#89$ (d) $#689$
    (e) None of these

Directions (16-20): In each question below are two/three statements followed by two conclusions, I and II. You have to take the two/three given statements to be true even if they seem to be at variance with commonly known facts. Read all the conclusions and then decide which of the given conclusions logically follows from the given statements disregarding commonly known facts.

Give answer:
(a) If only Conclusion I follows
(b) If only Conclusion II follows
(c) If either Conclusion I or II follows
(d) If neither Conclusion I nor II follows
(e)If both Conclusions I and II follow

16. **Statements:** No tea is coffee.
    No sweet is tea.
    Conclusions: I. No coffee is sweet.
    II. All sweets are coffee.

17. **Statements:** All medals are awards
    All rewards are medals
    Conclusions: I. All rewards are awards.
    II. All awards are medals.

18. **Statements:** Some leaves are plants.
    All bushes are plants.
    Conclusions: I. At least some leaves are bushes.
    II. Some leaves are definitely not bushes.

19. **Statements:** All bottles are mugs.
    No cup is a mug.
    Conclusions: I. No bottle is a cup.
    II. At least some mugs are bottles.

20. **Statements:** All windows are doors.
    All entrances are windows.
    No gate is a door.
    Conclusions: I. At least some windows are gates
    II. No gate is an entrance

Directions (21-25): Study the following information carefully and answer the questions given below:

A, B, C, D, E, F and G are sitting in a straight line facing north, but not necessarily in the same order. There is only one person between F and C. E sits between A and D. There are only two persons between E and G. F sits on the immediate left of A, who sits in the middle of the row.

21. How many persons are there between E and F?
    (a) one
    (b) two
    (c) three
    (d) Can't be determined
    (e) None of these

22. Who among the following sit at the extreme ends of the row?
    (a) D, F
    (b) G, C
    (c) B, C
    (d) Can't be determined
    (e) None of these

23. Who among the following sits on the immediate right of D?
    (a) G   (b) E
    (c) F   (d) B

(e) None of these

24. Who among the following sits third to the right of A?
    (a) C   (b) G
    (c) B   (d) E
    (e) None of these

25. Which of the following statements is true with regard to B?
    (a) B is second to the right of A.
    (b) B is fourth to the left of G.
    (c) B sits at the extreme right end of the row.
    (d) B sits at the extreme left end of the row.
    (e) None of these

26. The positions of how many digits in the number 59164823 will remain unchanged after the digits are rearranged in a descending order within the number?
    (a) none   (b) one
    (c) two   (d) three
    (e) More than three

27. What should come next in the following letter series based on the English alphabet?
    CEA   IKG   OQM   ?
    (a) STW   (b) WUS
    (c) SWU   (d) UWS
    (e) None of these

28. In a row of 40 children facing North, E is eighth to the right of V. If V is 18th from the right end of the row, how far is E from the left end of the row?
    (a) 32nd   (b) 10th
    (c) 31st   (d) 29th
    (e) None of these

Direction (29-33): The following questions are based on the five three-digit numbers given below:
853 581 747 474 398

29. If all the digits in each of the numbers are arranged in a descending order, which of the following will form the lowest in the new arrangement of numbers?
    (a) 853   (b) 581   (c) 747
    (d) 398   (e) 474

30. If all the numbers are arranged in an ascending order from left to right, which of the following will be the sum of all the three digits of the number which is exactly in the middle of the new arrangement?
    (a) 17   (b) 15   (c) 14
    (d) 13   (e) 19

31. What will be the result when the third digit of the lowest number is multiplied with the second digit of the highest number?
    (a) 27   (b) 40   (c) 20
    (d) 45   (e) 19

32. If the positions of the second and the third digits of each of the numbers are interchanged, how many even numbers will be formed?

(a) none   (b) one   (c) two
(d) three   (e) four

33. If one is added to the first digit of each of the numbers, how many numbers thus formed will be divisible by three?

(a) none   (b) one   (c) two
(d) three   (e) four

34. In a certain code language JANUARY is written as ZSBTOBK. How is OCTOBER written in that code language?

(a) SFCPUDP   (b) SFCNUDP
(c) SCFNDUP   (d) FSCNUDP
(e) None of these

Directions (35-37): Study the following information carefully to answer the given questions:

B is the sister of A. A is the father of G. H is the only son of F. F is the only son-in-law of A. G is the mother of H.

35. If C is the husband of B, then how is A related to C?

(a) father   (b) brother-in-law
(c) mother   (d) brother
(e) None of these

36. How is G related to B?

(a) brother   (b) niece   (c) sister
(d) nephew   (e) None of these

37. How is A related to H?

(a) uncle
(b) father
(c) paternal grandfather
(d) maternal grandfather
(e) None of these

Directions (38-39): Study the following information carefully to answer the questions.

A vehicle starts from point P and runs 10 km. towards the North. It takes a right turn and runs 15 km. Now it runs 6 km. after taking a left turn. Finally, it takes another left turn, runs 15 km. and stops at point Q.

38. How far is point Q with respect to point P?

(a) 16 km.   (b) 25 km.
(c) 4 km.   (d) 10 km.
(e) None of these

39. Towards which direction was the vehicle moving before it stopped at point Q?

(a) north   (b) east   (c) south
(d) west   (e) north-west

40. In a row of 34 students, W is fifth after X from the front and X is 20th from the back. What is the position of W from the front?

(a) 20   (b) 25
(c) 30   (d) 22
(e) None of these

QUANTITATIVE APTITUDE

Directions (41-45): What will come in place of the question mark (?) in the following questions?

41. 12 , 13 , 17 , 26 , 42 , ?

(a) 67   (b) 58
(c) 59   (d) 75
(e) None of these

42. 1, 2, 8, 48, 384 ?

(a) 3440   (b) 3840
(c) 3820   (d) 3550
(e) None of these

43. 157, 150, 136 ,115, 87 , ?

(a) 50   (b) 51
(c) 52   (d) 54
(e) None of these

44. 41472, 5184 , 576, 72, 8, ?

(a) 0   (b) 9
(c) 1   (d) 8
(e) None of these

45. 8 ,4, 4 ,6 ,12, ?

(a) 30   (b) 34
(c) 38   (d) 42
(e) None of these

Directions (46-60): What will come in place of the question mark (?) in the following questions?

46. $\frac{3}{9} \times 2286 + \frac{2}{11} \times 1397 = ?$

(a) 916   (b) 1016   (c) 1216
(d) 1026   (e) 1256

47. $7802 + 132 - 8963 + 1326 = ? \times 33$

(a) 6   (b) 12   (c) 21
(d) 9   (e) 14

48. 21.9% of $650 = ? + 23.12$

(a) 121.23   (b) 109.23   (c) 119.32
(d) 129.23   (e) 119.23

49. $6666 \div 66 \div 0.25 = ?$

(a) 101   (b) 404
(c) 304   (d) 40.4
(e) None of these

50. $\sqrt{?} + 18 = \sqrt{2704}$

(a) 1256   (b) 1156   (c) 1296
(d) 1024   (e) 1466

51. $2\frac{1}{7} + 4\frac{3}{5} - 3\frac{1}{7} + 5\frac{1}{10} = ?$

(a) $9\frac{7}{10}$ (b) $7\frac{7}{10}$
(c) $8\frac{7}{10}$ (d) $8\frac{4}{70}$

(e) None of these
52. $164 \times 43 - 6070 = ?$
    (a) 682   (b) 792   (c) 882
    (d) 1082   (e) 982
53. 14.5% of 740 – ?% of 320 = 87.3
    (a) 6.75   (b) 6.25   (c) 12.5
    (d) 14.75   (e) 8.25
54. $(27)^3 \times 3^4 \div (81)^2 = 3^?$
    (a) 2   (b) 5
    (c) 4   (d) 3
    (e) None of these
55. $\frac{3}{7} of\ 329 + \frac{4}{11} of\ 2530 = \sqrt{?} + 894$
    (a) 28899   (b) 29899
    (c) 27789   (d) 27889
    (e) None of these
56. $4376 + 3209 - 1784 + 97 = 3125 + ?$
    (a) 2713   (b) 2743   (c) 2773
    (d) 2793   (e) 2737
57. $\sqrt{?} + 14 = \sqrt{2601}$
    (a) 1521   (b) 1369   (c) 1225
    (d) 961   (e) 1296
58. 85% of 420 + ?% of 1080 = 735
    (a) 25   (b) 30   (c) 35
    (d) 40   (e) 45
59. $\frac{7}{3} of\ \frac{5}{4} of\ \frac{1}{9} of\ 3024 = ?$
    (a) 920   (b) 940   (c) 960
    (d) 980   (e) 840
60. 30% of 1225 – 64% of 555 = ?
    (a) 10.7   (b) 12.3
    (c) 13.4   (d) 17.5
    (e) None of these

Directions (61-65): Study the following table and answer the questions below. Given: the number of tourists who visited different cities by using different modes of transport.

Cities	Vehicle				
	Car	Train	Bus	Bike	By Air
Delhi	192	188	172	191	174
Mumbai	180	166	178	187	182
Chandigarh	156	194	163	181	148
Dehradun	132	185	142	170	148
Mussoorie	149	159	155	149	183
Jaipur	168	163	158	142	174

61. What was the average number of tourists who came by train?
    (a) 190.5   (b) 188·5
    (c) 175.83   (d) 137·5
    (e) None of these

62. What is the difference between the total number of tourists who went to Mumbai and Mussoorie by using all modes of transport?
    (a) 78   (b) 98
    (c) 88   (d) 83
    (e) None of these
63. What is the percent of tourists who went to Dehradun by train to the tourists who went to Chandigarh by air?
    (a) 125   (b) 145
    (c) 137   (d)160
    (e) None of these
64. What is the difference between the average number of tourists who travelled by air to the average number of tourists who went by bus?
    (a) 7.58   (b) 9.97
    (c) 6.83   (d) 2.30
    (e) None of these
65. What is the respective ratio of the number of tourists who went to Delhi by car and who went to Mumbai by air?
    (a) 35:83   (b) 45:71
    (c) 96:91   (d) 32:7
    (e) None of these
66. If the wheel of a bicycle makes 560 revolutions in travelling 1.1 km., what is its radius? (use $\pi = 22/7$)
    (a) 31.25 cm.   (b) 37.75 cm.
    (c) 35.15 cm.   (d) 11.25 cm.
    (e) None of these
67. Elena's age after 15 years will be five times her age five years back. What is Elena's present age?
    (a) 10   (b) 37
    (c) 35   (d) 11
    (e) None of these
68. A man purchased a cow for Rs. 3000 and sold it the same day for Rs. 3600, allowing the buyer a credit of two years. If the rate of interest is 10% per annum, then the man has a gain of:
    (a) 5%   (b) 0%
    (c) 20%   (d) 10%
    (e) none of these
69. A man takes 3 hours 45 minutes to row a boat 15 kms. downstream on a river and 2 hours 30 minutes to cover a distance of 5 kms upstream. Find the speed of the current.
    (a) 1 kmph.   (b) 3 kmph.
    (c) 5 kmph.   (d) 2 kmph.
    (e) None of these
70. A cistern 6m. long and 4m. wide contains water up to a height of 1m. 25 cms. Find the total area of the wet surface.
    (a) 42 m.sqaure   (b) 49 m. sqaure

(c) 52 m. sqaure   (d) 64 m. square
(e) none of these

71. In terms of percentage profit, which among following is the best transaction?
(a) C.P. 36, Profit 17
(b) C.P. 50, Profit 24
(c) C.P. 40, Profit 19
(d) C.P. 60, Profit 29
(e) C.P. 30, Profit 11

72. The mixture of milk and water in two vessels—A and B—is in the ratio 4:3 and 2:3 respectively. In what ratio must the liquids in both the vessels be mixed to obtain a new mixture in vessel C consisting half milk and half water?
(a) 8:3   (b) 7:5
(c) 4:3   (d) 2:3
(e) None of these

73. The average price of 10 books is Rs.12 while the average price of 8 of these books is Rs.11.75. Of the remaining two books, if the price of one book is 60% more than the price of the other, what is the price of each of these two books?
(a) Rs. 5, Rs.7.50   (b) Rs. 8, Rs. 12
(c) Rs. 10, Rs. 16   (d) Rs. 12, Rs. 14
(e) None of these

74. A fort has provisions for 60 days. If after 15 days, 500 men join them and the food lasts 40 days longer, how many men are there in the fort?
(a) 3500   (b) 4000
(c) 6000   (d) 8000
(e) None of these

75. If a commission of 10% is given by a truck dealer to a person on the marked price of the truck, then the dealer gains 20%. If the commission is increased to 15%, what will be the percentage gain of the dealer?
(a) 40/3   (b) 10

(c) 20   (d) 15
(e) None of these

76. If a carton containing a dozen mirrors is dropped, which of the following cannot be the ratio of broken mirrors to unbroken mirrors.
(a) 7:5   (b) 3:1
(c) 3:2   (d) 2:1
(e) Can't be determined

77. A bag contains Rs. 216 in the form of 1 Rs., 50 paisa and 25 paisa coins in the ratio of 2:3:4. How many 50 paisa coins are there in the bag?
(a) 140   (b) 175
(c) 184   (d) 160
(e) 144

78. A is twice as fast as B and B is thrice as fast as C. The journey covered by C in 42 minutes can be covered by B in how much time?
(a) 14 min   (b) 4 min
(c) 5 min   (d) 8 min
(e) 6 min

79. The CP of two dozen mangoes is Rs. 32. After selling 18 mangoes at Rs.12 per dozen, the shopkeeper reduced the rate to Rs. 4 per dozen. Find the loss percentage.
(a) 15   (b) 20
(c) 25   (d) 37.5
(e) None of these

80. How many kilograms of sugar costing Rs. 9 per kg. must be mixed with 27kgs. of sugar costing Rs.7 per kg. so that there may be a gain of 10% by selling the mixture at Rs.9.24 per kg.?
(a) 60 kg.   (b) 63 kg.
(c) 50 kg.   (d) 77 kg.
(e) None of these

Solutions

REASONING ABILITY

Directions (1–5):

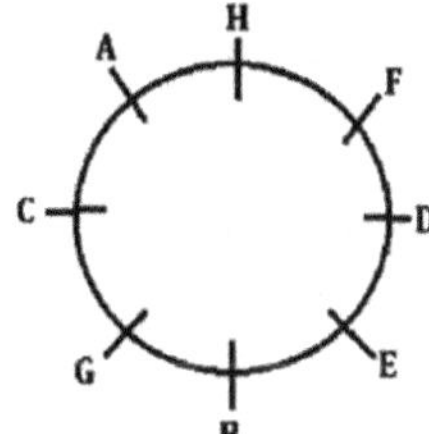

1. (a)   **2.** (d)   **3.** (c)
4. (b)   **5.** (e)

Directions (6–10):

6. (c). R $\geq$ W = H(False)   II. R $\geq$ W = (False)
7. (a) I. D = K < T(True)   II. K < T > M(False)
8. (b) I. F $\leq$ N $\geq$ R(False)   II. B < F $\leq$ N(True)
9. (d) I. K $\leq$ M > W(False)   II. H > Q < M(False)
10. (e) I. D < M = T(True)   II. R $\geq$ T = M(True)

Direction (11-15):
11. (a) %1@$6©
12. (b) 72#897
13. (d) 86©8@%
14. (c) $219@$
15. (e) 1#689$
Directions (16-20):

16. (d)

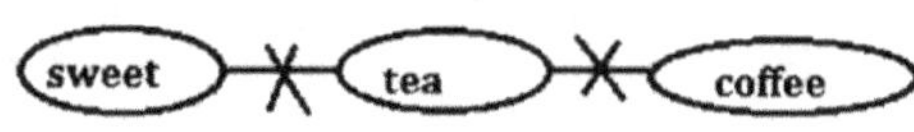

17. (a)

18. (c)

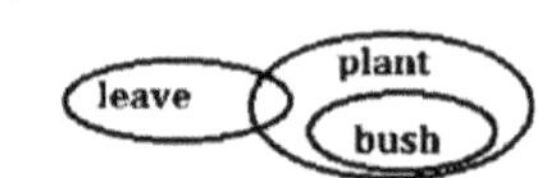

19. (e)

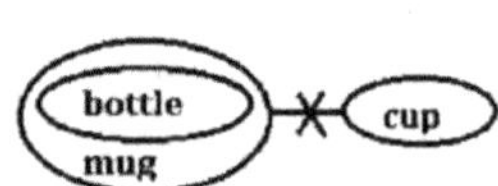

20. (b)

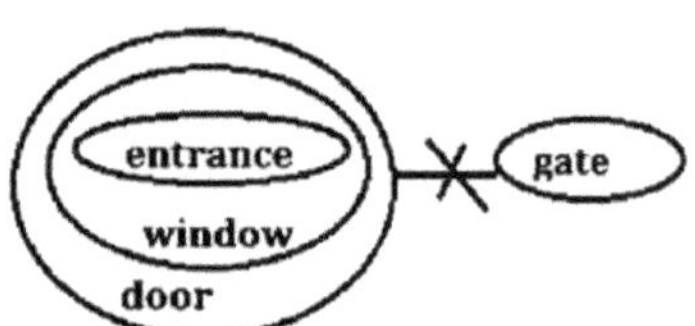

Directions (21-25):

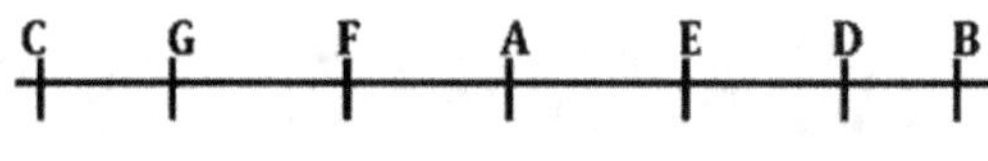

21. (a)   22. (c)   23. (d)
24. (c) 25.   (c)
26. (c)

59164823
98654321

27. (d) UWS
28. (c) V is 18th from the left and E is 8th to the right of V so E is 30+1=31ˢᵗ from the left.
Direction (29-33):

29. (e) 474
30. (c) (5+8+1) = 14

31. (b) 8*5=40
32. (c) Two
33. (c) Two
34. (b)

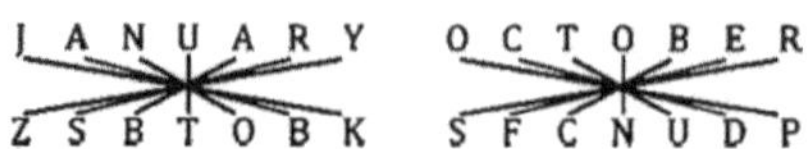

Direction (35-37):
35. (b)

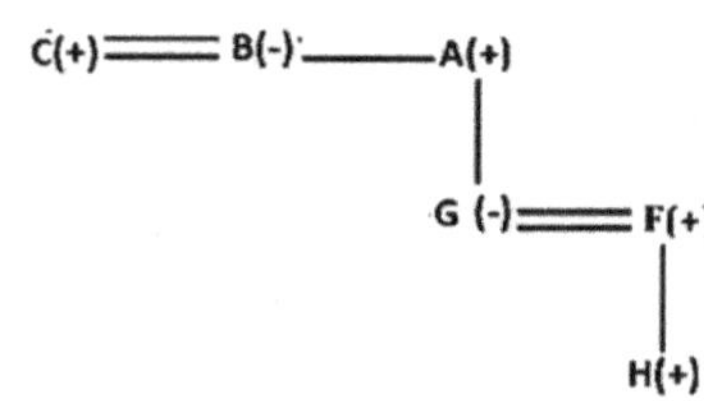

36. (b)

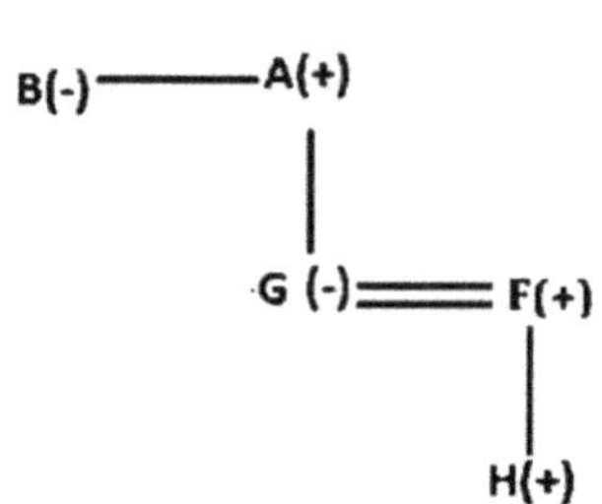

37. (d)

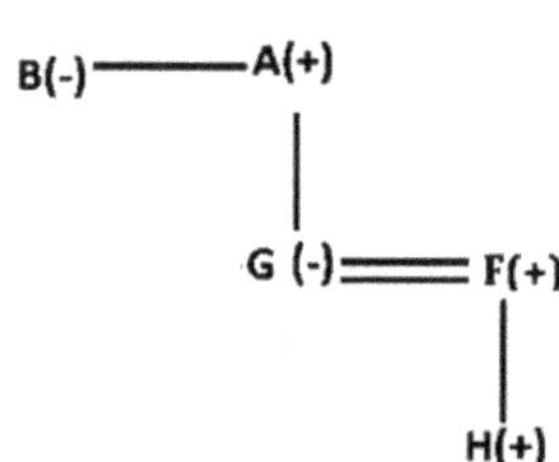

Directions (38-39):

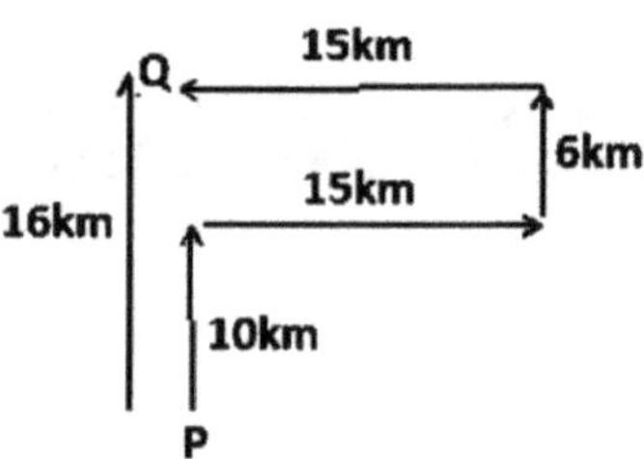

38. (a)
39. (d)
40. (a) X is 20th from the back.
The position of w from the back is (20-5) = 15th
Hence the position of W from the front is (34-15+1) = 20th

41. (a) The pattern is $+1^2, +2^2 +3^2 ... 42 + 25 = 67$

42. (b) The pattern is $\times 2, \times 4, \times 6, \times 8$ ......$384 \times 10 = 3840$

43. (c) The pattern is $-7, -14, -21, -28 ... 87 - 35 = 52$

44. (c)

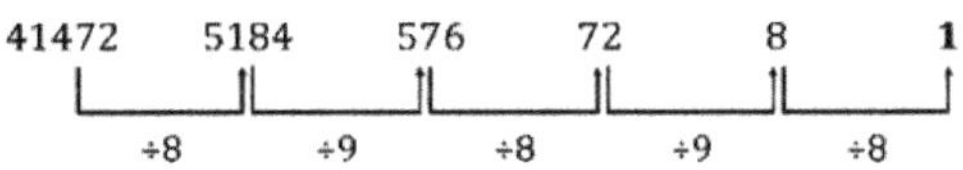

45. (a) The pattern is $\times 0.5, \times 1, \times 1.5, \times 2$ ... ... $12 \times 2.5 = 30$

46. (b) $762 + 254 = 1016$

47. (d) $9260 - 8963 = ? \times 33 \Rightarrow ? = \frac{297}{33} = 9$

48. (e) $142.35 = ? + 23.12 \Rightarrow ? = 119.23$

49. (b) $6666 \times \frac{1}{66} \times \frac{1}{0.25} = ?? = 404$

50. (b) $\sqrt{?} = 52 - 18$
$? = 1156$

51. (c) $(2 + 4 + 5 - 3) + \left(\frac{1}{7} + \frac{3}{5} + \frac{1}{10} - \frac{1}{7}\right)$
$= 8 + \frac{10+42+7-10}{70} = 8 + \frac{49}{70} = 8\frac{49}{70} = 8\frac{7}{10}$

52. (e) $7052 - 6070 = ?$
$? = 982$

53. (b) $107.3 - 87.3 = \frac{?}{100} \times 320$
$? = \frac{20 \times 100}{320} = 6.25$

54. (b) $\frac{(3^3)^3 \times 3^4}{(3^4)^2} = 3^?$
$? = 9 + 4 - 8 = 5$

55. (d) $141 + 920 = \sqrt{?} + 894$
$\sqrt{?} = 167 \Rightarrow ? = 27889$

56. (c) $? = 7682 - 4909 = 2773$

57. (b) $\sqrt{?} = \sqrt{2601} - 14 = 51 - 14 - 37$
$? = 1369$

58. (c) $\frac{85}{100} \times 420 + \frac{?}{100} \times 1080 = 735$
$\Rightarrow ? = 35$

59. (d) 980

60. (b) $? = 367.5 - 355.2 = 12.3$

61. (c) Average number of tourists which go by train
$= \frac{188+166+194+185+159+163}{6} = 175.83$

62. (b) Total tourists to Mumbai = 893
Total tourists to Mussoorie = 795
Difference = 98

63. (a) Required percentage $= \frac{185}{148} \times 100 = 125\%$

64. (c) Average of tourists who go by air = 168.16
Average of tourists who go by bus = 161.33
Required difference = 6.83

65. (c) Required ratio = $192 : 182 = 96 : 91$

66. (a) Perimeter $= \frac{1.1 \times 1000}{560} m$
$2 \times \frac{22}{7} \times r = \frac{1.1 \times 100}{56}$
$r = \frac{110 \times 7}{56 \times 22 \times 2} = \frac{5}{16} m = 31.25$ cm

67. (a) Let Elena's age = x
$x + 15 = 5 (x - 5)$
$x = 10$ years

68. (b) Man's interest for 2 years $= \frac{3000 \times 2 \times 10}{100} = 600$
$\therefore$ After two years, the man will pay = 3000 + 600 = 3600 Rs.
So then is 0% gain

69. (a) Let downstream speed = x
Upstream speed = y
$\frac{15}{x} = 3\frac{45}{60} \Rightarrow \frac{15}{x} = \frac{15}{4} \Rightarrow x = 4$
$\frac{5}{y} = 2\frac{30}{60} \Rightarrow \frac{5}{y} = \frac{5}{2} \Rightarrow y = 2$
$\therefore$ Speed of current = 1 kmph

70. (b) Total Surface Area of wet surface
$= 2 (l + b) \times h + lb$
$= 2 (6 + 4) 1.25 + 6 \times 4$
$= 20 \times 1.25 + 24$
$= 25 + 24 = 49$ m square

71. (d) Clearly from the options
Ans- option (d)

72. (b)

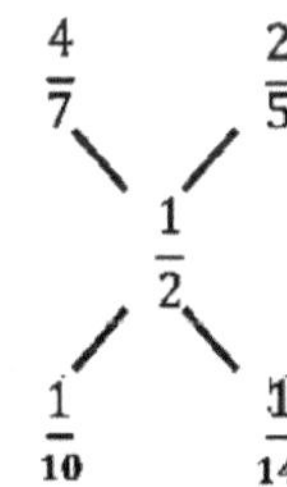

$\therefore$ Required Ratio $= \frac{14}{10} = 7 : 5$

73. (c) Sum of price of the remaining two
Books = $12 \times 10 - 11.75 \times 8 = 26$
$\therefore$ Let cost of First book be x
$\therefore x + \frac{160x}{100} = 26$
$\frac{260x}{100} = 26$
$x = 10$
$\therefore$ Price of second book = 10 + 6 = 16

74. (b) Let No. of soldiers = x
$60 \times x = 15x + 40 (x + 500)$
$60x = 15x + 40x + 20000$
$5x = 20000$

$x = 4000$

75. (a) Let S.P. $= 100$

∴ After commission, price $= 90$

∴ CP $= \frac{100}{120} \times 90 = 75$

Now, commission $= 15\%$

∴ gain $\% = \frac{85-75}{75} \times 100 = \frac{4}{3} \times 10 \Rightarrow \frac{40}{3}\%$

76. (c) Mirrors are multiple of 12

So expect 3:2. All the other ratios can be divided by 12

77. (e) $2x + \frac{3x}{2} + \frac{4x}{4} = 216$

$\frac{8x+6x+4x}{4} = 216$

$\frac{18x}{4} = 216 \Rightarrow x = 48$

∴ No of 50 paise coin $= 48 \times 3 = 144$

78. (a)
$$A \quad B \quad C$$
$$6 \quad x \quad 3 \quad x \quad x$$

Ratio of their speeds $= 6 : 3 : 1$

Ratio of their time $= \frac{1}{6} : \frac{1}{3} : \frac{1}{1} = 1 : 2 : 6$

∴Time taken by B $= \frac{42}{6} \times 2 = 14$ min

79. (d) Total CP $= 32$

Total SP $= 12 + 6 + 2 = 20$

∴ Loss percentage $= \frac{12}{32} \times 100 = 37.5\%$

80. (b) Mean price $= \frac{10}{110} \times 9.24$

$= 10 \times 0.84 = 8.4$

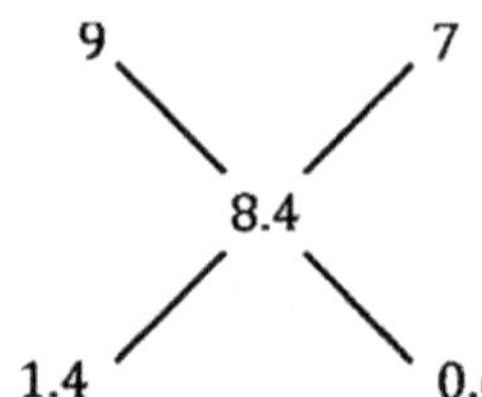

Ratio $= \frac{1.4}{0.6} = \frac{7}{3}$

∴ Required quantity $= \frac{27}{3} \times 7$

$= 63$ kg

REASONING ABILITY

1. How many such numerals are there in the number '4185476429' which will remain at the same position when arranged in ascending order from left to right?
   (a) none
   (b) three
   (c) More than three
   (d) two
   (e) None of these

Directions (2-5): In each of the questions below are given some statements followed by some conclusions. You have to take the given statements to be true even if they seem to be at variance with commonly known facts. Read all the conclusions and then decide which of the given conclusions logically follows from the given statements disregarding commonly known facts.
(a) If only conclusion I follows.
(b) If only conclusion II follows.
(c) If either conclusion I or II follows.
(d) If neither conclusion I nor II follows.
(e) If both conclusions I and II follow.

2. **Statements:** Only a few Bubbles are Soap. All Soap are Margo. Some Neem are not Margo.
   Conclusions:
   I. Some Bubbles are not Neem.
   II. Some Soap are not Bubbles.

3. **Statements:** All Ship are Jeep. All Jeep are Bike. Some Car are Bike.
   Conclusions:
   I. Some Ship can be Car.
   II. All Car are Bike.

4. **Statements:** Some Egg are Roll. Some Roll are not Paratha.
   Conclusions:
   I. All Egg can never be Paratha.
   II. Some Paratha are not Roll.

5. **Statements:** All Noun are Pronoun. Some Pronoun are Verb. Some Verb are Tense.
   Conclusions:
   I. Some Noun can be Verb.
   II. Some Tense being Pronoun is a possibility.

6. In a family with five members, A is the Father of B's sister. E is the paternal grandmother of

D. B is the only son of C. Find the relation of D with respect to A.
   (a) sister
   (b) daughter
   (c) daughter-in-law
   (d) mother
   (e) None of these

Directions (7-11): Study the following information carefully and answer the questions given below:

Six persons are sitting in a row. Some of them are facing north while the rest are facing south. P sits 3rd to the left of B and neither of them sit at the extreme ends. The persons who sit at the extreme ends are facing opposite directions. There are two persons who sit between X and T. X does not sit near B. R sits 3rd to the right of Y, who is an immediate neighbour of B. R faces north. Y faces the opposite direction with respect to R. Both P and T are facing the same direction as R.

7. How many persons are facing north?
   (a) two   (b) three   (c) one
   (d) four   (e) five

8. Four of the following five are alike in a certain way and hence they form a group. Which one of the following does not belong to that group?
   (a) P   (b) T   (c) Y
   (d) B   (e) R

9. What is the position of X with respect to R?
   (a) 3rd to the left
   (b) 2nd to the right
   (c) Immediate to the left
   (d) 2nd to the left
   (e) None of these

10. How many persons are sitting on the right from T?
    (a) two   (b) one
    (c) three   (d) four
    (e) None of these

11. Who among the following persons are sitting at the extreme end?
    (a) P-X   (b) X-Y   (c) P-T
    (d) B-X   (e) R-Y

Directions (12-15): Study the following information carefully and answer the questions given below:

Point G is in 5kms. north of Point E. Point B is in 8kms. east of Point G. Point C is 8kms. west of Point H. Point B is 14kms. north of Point H. Point D is 6kms. west of Point F. Point A is 5kms. north of Point D. Point E is 12kms. east of Point A.

12. What is the total distance between Point A and Point B?
    (a) 22 kms.   (b) 2500m.
    (c) 25kms.   (d) 20kms.
    (e) None of these

13. What is the direction of Point D with respect to Point G?
    (a) south-west   (b) south-east   (c) north
    (d) south   (e) north-west

14. What is the shortest distance between Point A and Point G?
    (a) 11km.   (b) 13km.
    (c) 14km.   (d) 18km.
    (e) None of these

15. What is the direction of Point D with respect to Point C?
    (a) south-east   (b) north-west
    (c) south-west   (d) south
    (e) north

Directions (16-20): Study the following information carefully and answer the questions given below:

In a certain code language:

"Indian cricket players famous" is coded as "blue white green red"

"Indian players from foreign" is coded as "green pink purple blue"

"Win by Indian cricket" is coded as "yellow violet white blue"

"Players are famous" is coded as "red magenta green"

16. What is the code for "players" in the given code language?
    (a) green   (b) red
    (c) white   (d) pink
    (e) None of these

17. The code "purple" is coded as which of the following words?
    (a) from   (b) famous
    (c) foreign   (d) Indian
    (e) Either (a) or (c)

18. What is the code for "Indian" in the given code language?
    (a) white   (b) blue
    (c) green   (d) red
    (e) None of these

19. If "near cricket" is coded as "black white" then what is the possible code for "near around" in the given code language?
    (a) hazel black
    (b) blue white
    (c) red hazel
    (d) pink black
    (e) purple white

20. What is the code for "Indian win by" in the given code language?
    (a) white red pink
    (b) yellow purple blue
    (c) green red pink
    (d) violet blue yellow
    (e) None of these

Directions (21-25): Study the following information carefully and answer the questions given below:

Eight persons A, B, C, Q, R, S, T and W were born on different months in the same year—January, February, March, June, July, October, November and December—but not necessarily in the same order.

A was born in the month which has less than 30 days. C was born in the month which has 30 days. There were three persons born between C and S. No one was born between S and R. The number of persons born between Q and T is the same as between W and T. B was born just after W.

21. How many persons were born after W?
    (a) four   (b) three
    (c) one   (d) five
    (e) More than five

22. Who among the following persons was born in the month of November?
    (a) Q   (b) W
    (c) T   (d) R
    (e) None of these

23. The number of persons born before T is the same as the persons born after which of the following persons?
    (a) B   (b) Q
    (c) C   (d) R
    (e) None of these

24. How many persons were born between B and T?
    (a) none   (b) one
    (c) two   (d) three
    (e) More than Three

25. Which of the following statements is true, as per the given information?
    (a) There were two persons born between B and S.
    (b) C was born just before T.
    (c) W was born in July.

(d) No one was born after R.
(e) None is true.

Directions (26-30): Study the following alphanumeric series carefully and answer the questions given below:

F H % 9 M 6 # A 3 4 & @ E * 8 B ^ % 5 4 S D

26. How many numbers are present in the above series which are immediately followed by a symbol and preceded by an alphabet?
    (a) none   (b) one
    (c) two   (d) three
    (e) More than three

27. Which element is exactly between the elements which are 7th from the left and 6th from the right end?
    (a) 4   (b) &
    (c) @   (d) E
    (e) None of these

28. How many symbols are present in the above series which are immediately followed by a vowel and preceded by a number?
    (a) three   (b) one
    (c) two   (d) none
    (e) More than three

29. How many vowels are between the elements which are 7th from the right and 4th from the left end?
    (a) none   (b) one
    (c) two   (d) three
    (e) More than three

30. If all the numbers are removed from the above series, then which element is 13th from the right end?
    (a) F   (b) %
    (c) H   (d) #
    (e) None of these

Direction (31-35): Study the following information carefully and answer the questions given below:

Eight persons i.e. S, T, U, V, W, X, Y and Z are sitting around a square table but not necessarily in the same order. Four of them sit at the corners and the remaining sit at the middle of the side of the square table. All are facing towards the centre.

S sits 3rd to the right of T, who is an immediate neighbour of U. Three persons sit between U and V. W faces X. X and Y are not immediate neighbours of S. Z sits at a corner.

31. Who among the following persons sits to the immediate right of S?

(a) W   (b) X
(c) Y   (d) Z
(e) None of these

32. Who among the following persons face Y?
    (a) S   (b) T
    (c) U   (d) V
    (e) None of these

33. How many persons are sitting between T and Z?
    (a) one   (b) two
    (c) three   (d) four
    (e) Either (b) or (d)

34. Who among the following persons are immediate neighbours of V?
    (a) X-Y   (b) Y-Z
    (c) X-Z   (d) X-S
    (e) None of these

35. Four of the following five are alike in a certain way and form a group. Find the one which does not belong to that group?
    (a) S   (b) T   (c) U
    (d) V   (e) Y

Direction (36-40): Study the following information carefully and answer the questions given below:

Five boxes i.e. D, E, F, G and H of different colours i.e. Red, Green, Pink, Blue and Black are arranged one above the other but not necessarily in the same order. Three boxes are placed between D and the Red coloured box. There are as many boxes above E as below F, which is Blue coloured. The Green coloured box is placed just above G and just below H. D is placed above the black coloured box.

36. Which among the following boxes is Pink coloured?
    (a) D   (b) E
    (c) G   (d) H
    (e) None of these

37. How many boxes are in the gap between D and F?
    (a) none   (b) one
    (c) two   (d) three
    (e) None of these

38. Which of the following colours is box H?
    (a) Green   (b) Black
    (c) Pink   (d) Red
    (e) None of these

39. Which of the following boxes is in the topmost position?
    (a) Green coloured box
    (b) Red coloured box
    (c) Pink coloured box

(d) Black coloured box
(e) None of these

40. Four of the following five are alike in a certain way and form a group. Find the one which does not belong to that group?

(a) D-Blue   (b) E-Black   (c) F-Red
(d) G-Green   (e) H-Blue

QUANTITATIVE APTITUDE

Directions (41-45): The given pie chart shows the percentage distribution of various expenses of a family in a given month.

Study the graph carefully and answer the following questions.

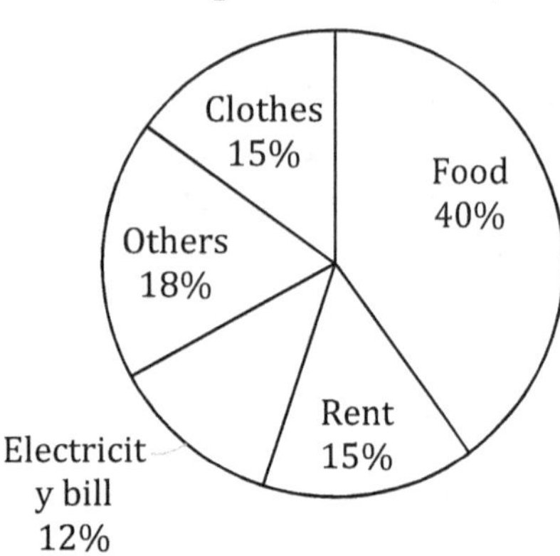

Total expense = Rs 25,000

Note: Monthly Income = Expense + Savings

41. What is the average expense on Rent, Electricity bill and Others?

(a) Rs 5000   (b) Rs 3000   (c) Rs 3750
(d) Rs 2750   (e) Rs 3250

42. If the expense on Food is $\frac{125}{4}$% of the monthly family income, then find the total monthly income of the family.

(a) Rs. 28000
(b) Rs. 42000
(c) Rs. 35000
(d) Rs. 38000
(e) Rs. 32000

43. If expense on Others consists of telephone bill, entertainment and commuting expenses in the ratio 4: 6 : 5, then the monthly expense on the electricity bill is what percent more or less than that on telephone bill?

(a) 100%   (b) 150%   (c) $\frac{200}{3}$%
(d) 125%   (e) 75%

44. If the monthly saving of the family is 30% of the monthly income, then find the ratio of the expenses on clothes to savings of the family.

(a) $\frac{3}{20}$ (b) $\frac{7}{20}$ (c) $\frac{11}{20}$
(d) $\frac{9}{20}$ (e) $\frac{1}{4}$

45. Find the central angle (in degrees) of the monthly expense of the family on electricity bill.

(a) 76.4   (b) 68.6   (c) 32.8
(d) 54.6   (e) 43.2

Directions (46-55): What should come in place of question mark (?) in the following questions?

46. $\sqrt{484} \div \frac{11^2}{8} +? = \frac{38}{11}$

(a) 22   (b) 2   (c) 1
(d) 11   (e) 4

47. ?% of $2800 \div \frac{3}{7} of 49 = 420$

(a) 315   (b) 305   (c) 560
(d) 460   (e) 360

48. 20% of $360 \div 15\%$ of $240 \times (12)^2 = ? \times 6^2$

(a) 4   (b) 6   (c) 8
(d) 12   (e) 9

49. $0.06 \times 0.84 = ? \times 1.2 \times 0.015$

(a) 8.2   (b) 6.4   (c) 2.6
(d) 3.8   (e) 2.8

50. $8.41 + 6.25 + 0.79 = ? - 0.55$

(a) 17   (b) 14.9   (c) 13.9
(d) 16   (e) 14.7

51. $\frac{(12+44)}{8} \times 28 =?^2$

(a) 13   (b) 16   (c) 17
(d) 14   (e) 19

52. $616 + 472 - 811 + 317 = ? + 576$

(a) 28   (b) 16   (c) 24
(d) 18   (e) 14

53. $12.5 \times 80 + 37.5 \times 16 - 6.25 \times 112 = ?$

(a) 1000   (b) 900   (c) 2300
(d) 600   (e) 1300

54. $23 \div 48 \times 576 = ? \times \frac{3}{2}$

(a) 148   (b) 194   (c) 176
(d) 154   (e) 184

55. $(1.2)^2 + (1.5)^2 + (2.1)^2 - (1.9)^2 = ?$

(a) 4.99   (b) 5.69   (c) 3.69
(d) 6.79   (e) 4.49

Directions (56-60): Find the wrong number in the given series.

56. 5, 9, 25, 59, 125, 225, 369

(a) 59   (b) 5   (c) 25
(d) 225   (e) 369

57. 540, 550, 575, 585, 615, 620, 645

(a) 540   (b) 585   (c) 615

(d) 645   (e) 575

58. 4, 11, 30, 67, 128, 221, 346
(a) 346   (b) 221   (c) 128
(d) 4   (e) 11

59. 16, 4, 2, 1.5, 1.75, 1.875, 2.8125
(a) 16   (b) 1.875   (c) 2.8125
(d) 1.75   (e) 2

60. 18, 30, 52, 79, 116, 148, 210
(a) 148   (b) 18   (c) 116
(d) 52   (e) 79

Directions (61 – 65): Two equations (I) and (II) are given. You have to solve both the equations and answer the following questions.
(a) x > y
(b) x < y
(c) x ≥ y
(d) x ≤ y
(e) x = y or no relation.

61. I. $2x^2 - 17x + 36 = 0$ II. $2y^2 - 19y + 45 = 0$

62. I. $x^2 - 25x + 154 = 0$ II. $y^2 - 28y + 195 = 0$

63. I. $\dfrac{10}{x} - \dfrac{24}{x^2} = 1$ II. $\dfrac{5}{y} - \dfrac{6}{y^2} = 1$

64. I. $3x^2 - 10x - 8 = 0$ II. $2y^2 - 23y + 60 = 0$

65. I. $12x - 16y = -16$ II. $17y - 13x = 12$

66. If an amount of Rs. 12,120 is distributed amongst three persons such that the share of C is half of A and B together and the share of B is one-third of A and C together, then find the share of B and C together.
(a) Rs. 5050   (b) Rs. 7070   (c) Rs. 4040
(d) Rs. 8080   (e) Rs. 9090

67. What would be the compound interest obtained on an amount of Rs. 4500 at the rate of 15% p.a. compounding annually in 2 yrs?
(a) Rs. 1451.25
(b) Rs. 1144.8
(c) Rs. 1482.25
(d) Rs. 7750.50
(e) None of these

68. If the M.R.P. of an article is marked 50% above cost price and profit earned on the article is equal to half the discount given on article, then find the S.P., if M.R.P. is Rs. 2250.
(a) Rs. 2000   (b) Rs. 1750
(c) Rs. 1850   (d) Rs. 1650
(e) None of these

69. Two trains are moving in opposite directions with a speed of 50km/hr. and 80 km/hr. respectively. They cross each other in 1 second and the ratio between the length of the faster train to that of the slower train is 7:6. Find the length of another train whose length is 20% more than length of slower train.
(a) 0.1 km.
(b) 1.167 km.
(c) 1.200 km.
(d) 0.1800 km.

(e) None of these

70. If a certain sum becomes double in three years at a certain rate at SI, then find the simple interest earned on Rs. 1500 after 4 years at the same rate of interest.
(a) Rs. 1500   (b) Rs. 2000   (c) Rs. 2250
(d) Rs. 1550   (e) Rs. 1750

71. Simple interest will be how many times the principal amount of Rs. 2500 after 8 years at the rate of 22.5% per annum SI?
(a) 1.2 times
(b) 1.8 times
(c) 1.5 times
(d) 2.2 times
(e) None of these

72. Ten years ago, a father's age was 12 times his son's age and the present age of father is 7 times his son's age. Find the present age of son.
(a) 20 yrs   (b) 22 yrs   (c) 32 yrs
(d) 40 yrs   (e) 18 yrs

73. A and B invested into a partnership for $\frac{2}{3}rd$ and $\frac{2}{5}th$ of the investment time respectively. If A and B invested Rs.2000 and Rs. 5000 respectively, find the profit share of A as a percentage more/less than profit share of B.
(a) 16.33%   (b) 14.28%   (c) 7.14%
(d) 33.33%   (e) 33.67%

74. The population of a city increases by 15% and $4\frac{8}{23}\%$ in two successive years respectively. If the population of the city after two years becomes 24024, then find initial population of the city.
(a) 20020   (b) 20002   (c) 20120
(d) 20802   (e) None of these

75. Find the total number of results that can be obtained when two coins are tossed and two dice are rolled simultaneously.
(a) 124   (b) 24   (c) 180
(d) 144   (e) 120

Directions (76-80): - Deepak, Dharam and Shivam invested in a partnership for one year. The ratio of investment of Deepak, Dharam and Shivam for the first six months, next four months and for the remaining time was 3:2:3, 2:5:3 and 4:3:3 respectively. The amount invested by Deepak in the first six months, Dharam in the next four months and by Shivam in the remaining time is Rs.1500, Rs. 2000 and Rs. 900 respectively. The total difference between the profit share of Dharam and Shivam together and Deepak and Dharam together is Rs. 450.

76. The total investment of Deepak is approximately what percent of the total investment of Shivam in one year?
(a) 96%   (b) 95%   (c) 97%

(d) 92%   (e) 99%

77. What is the profit share of Dharam after one year?
(a) Rs.7110   (b) Rs. 6570   (c) Rs. 7020
(d) Rs. 6560   (e) Rs. 7220

78. What is the ratio of investment made by Deepak for four months to investment made by Shivam for two months?
(a) 5:7   (b) 6:7   (c) 4:5
(d) 8:9   (e) 3:2

79. What is the difference between investment made by Dharam for six months and four months together and total investment made by Shivam?
(a) Rs. 900   (b) Rs. 600   (c) Rs. 800
(d) Rs. 400   (e) Rs. 500

80. Investment made by Deepak for two months is how much percent more or less than the investment made by Shivam for six months?
(a) 20% more
(b) 25% less
(c) 25% more
(d) 20% less
(e) None of these

Solutions

REASONING ABILITY

1. (b)

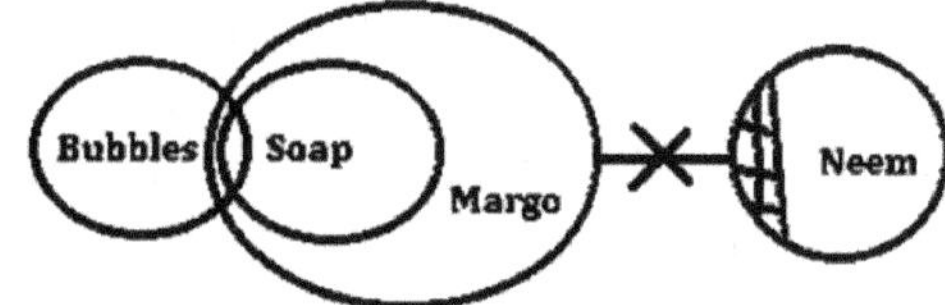

Solutions (2-5):

2. (d)

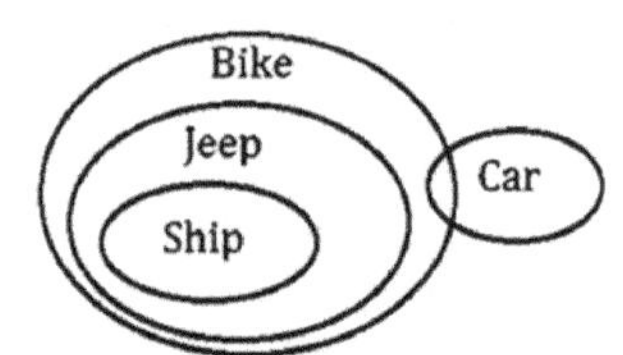

3. (a)

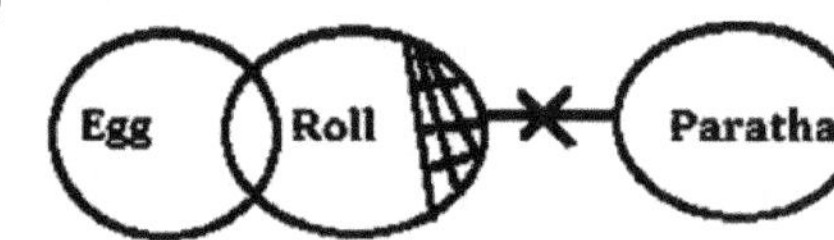

4. (d)

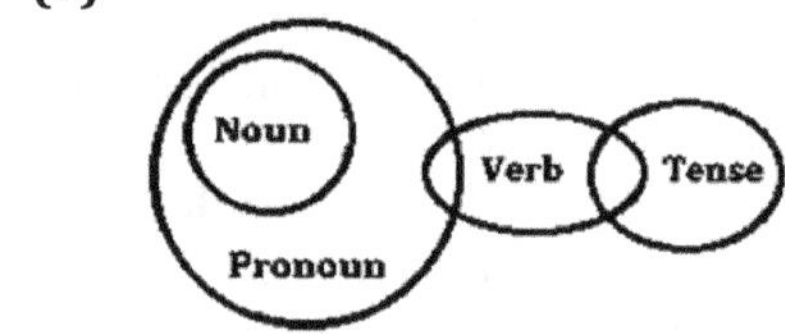

5. (e)

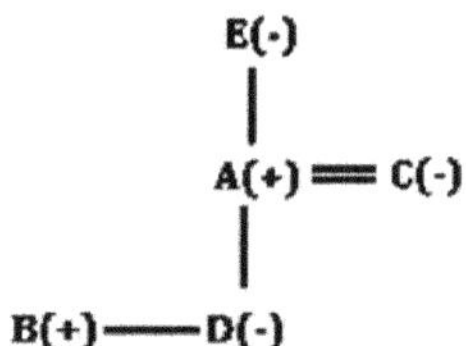

6. (b)

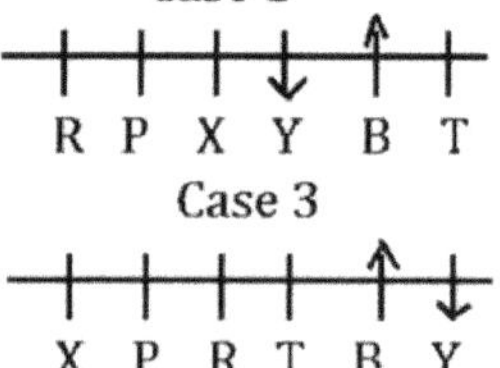

Solutions (7-11):

Step – 1 P sits 3rd to the left of B and both are not sitting at the extreme ends. There are two persons who sit between X and T. X does not sit near B. R sits 3rd to the right of Y, who is an immediate neighbour of B. Here we have four possibilities i.e. Case 1, Case 2, Case 3 and Case 4.

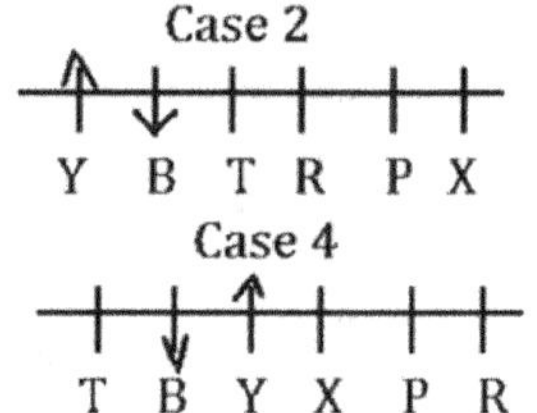

Step – 2 R faces north. Y faces in the opposite direction with respect to R. Here, Case 2 and Case 4 are ruled out. The persons who sit at the extreme ends facing opposite direction.

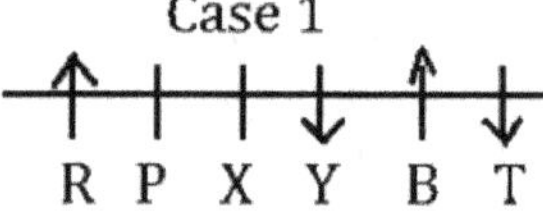

Step – 3 Both P and T are facing the same direction as R. Here, Case 1 is ruled out.

So, the final arrangement -

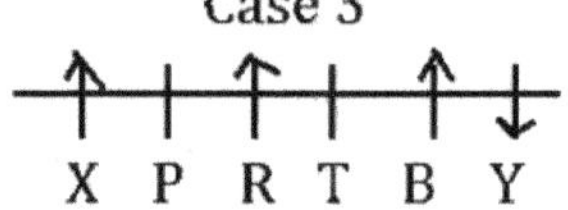

7. (e)   **8. (c)**   **9. (d)**
10. (a)   **11. (b)**
12. (c)
13. (a)

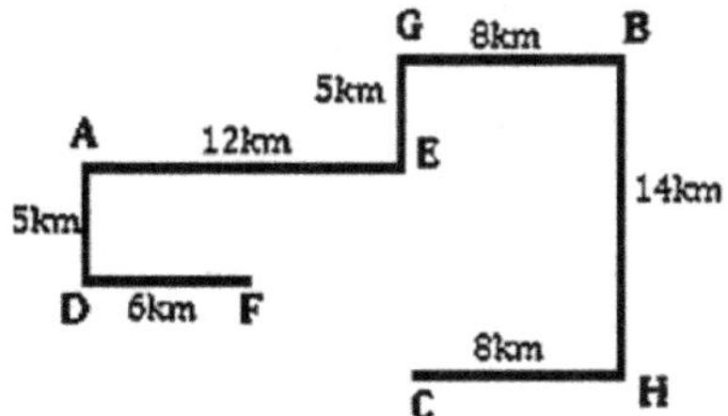

14. (b)

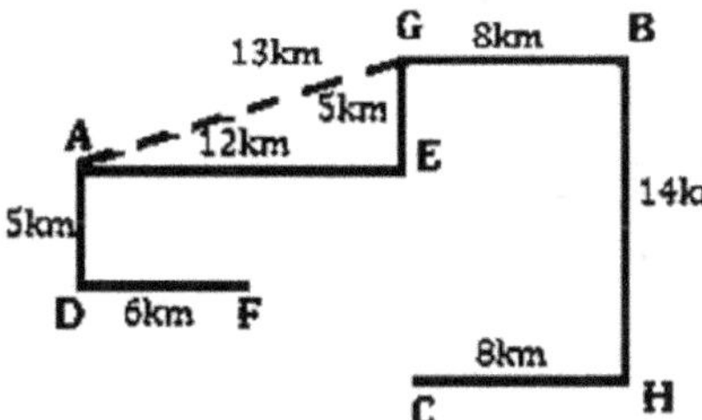

15. (b)

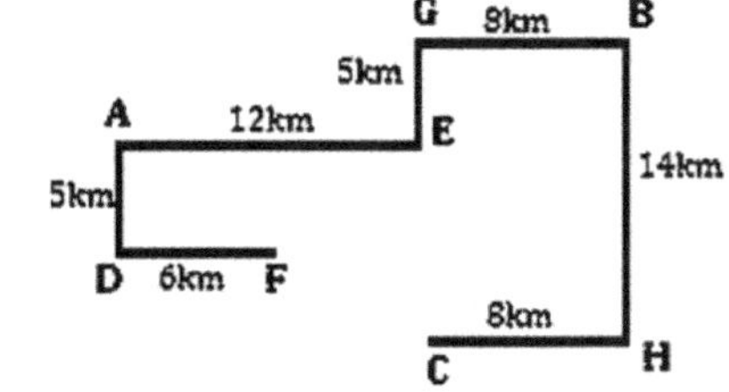

Solutions (16-20):

Words	Codes
Indian	Blue
Cricket	White
Players	Green
Famous	Red
From/Foreign	Purple/pink
Win/by	Violet/Yellow
Are	Magenta

16. (a)   **17.(e)**   **18. (b)**
19. (a)   **20. (d)**

Solutions (21-25): A was born in the month which has less than 30 days. C was born in the month which has 30 days. **Here we get two possibilities i.e. Case 1 and Case 2.** There were three persons born between C and S. No one was born between S and R.

Months	Case 1 Persons	Case 2 Persons
January		
February	A	A
March		S
June	C	R
July		
October		
November	R	C
December	S	

The number of persons born between Q and T is same as W and T. **Hence, case 2 is ruled out.** B was born just after W.

So, the final arrangement is -

Months	Persons
January	Q
February	A
March	T
June	C
July	W
October	B
November	R
December	S

21. (b)   **22.(d)**   **23. (a)**
24. (c)   **25.(c)**
26. (b) M6#
27. (c)
28. (b)   6#A
29. (c)   **30.(b)**

Solutions (31-35):
From the given statements, S sits 3rd to the right of T, who is an immediate neighbour of U. Three persons sit between U and V. Here, we get two possibilities i.e. Case 1 and Case 2.

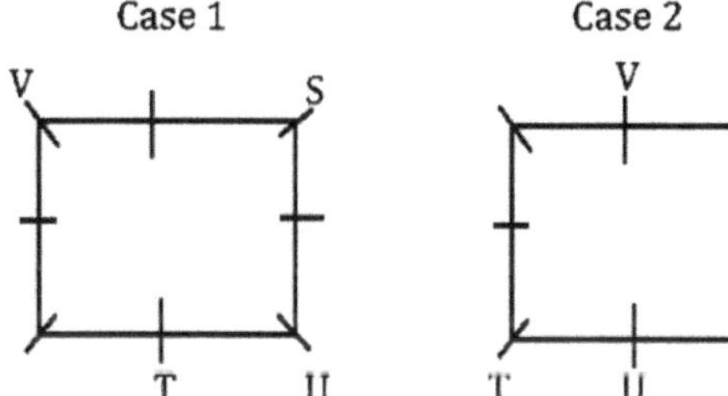

From the given statements, W faces X. X and Y are not an immediate neighbour of S. Z sits at a corner. Here, Case 1 is ruled out.
So, the final arrangement will be: -

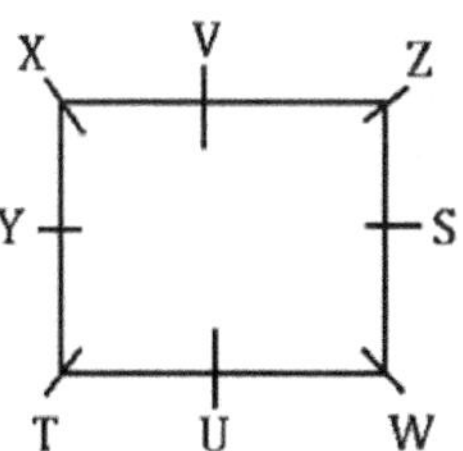

31. (d)   **32. (a)**   **33.(c)**
34. I   **35.(b)**

Solutions (36-40):
From the given statements, three boxes are placed between D and the Red coloured box. D is placed above the black coloured box. Here, we get two possibilities i.e. Case 1 and Case 2. Green coloured box is placed just above G and just below H.

Case 1 Box	Case 1 Colour	Case 2 Box	Case 2 Colour
D		D	
H	Black/		Black/
	Green	H	Black/

199

G	Black/		Green
	Red	G	Red

From the given statements, there are as many boxes above E as below F, which is Blue coloured. Here, Case 1 is ruled out.

So, the final arrangement will be:

Box	Colour
D	Pink
F	Blue
H	Black
E	Green
G	Red

36. (a)   **37. (a)**   **38.(b)**
39. (c)   **40. (c)**

QUANTITATIVE APTITUDE

41. (c) required average $= \frac{15+12+18}{3} = 15\%$

$= \frac{15}{100} \times 25000 = $ Rs 3750

42. (e) required income $= 40 \times \frac{4}{125} \times 25000$

$= $ Rs 32000

43. (b) expense on Telephone bill

$= \frac{18}{100} \times 25000 \times \frac{4}{15} = $ Rs 1200

$\therefore$ Required percentage

$= \frac{25000 \times \frac{12}{100} - 1200}{1200} \times 100 = \frac{1800}{1200} \times 100$

$= 150\%$

44. (b) monthly savings

$= 25000 \times \frac{30}{100-30} = $ Rs $\frac{75000}{7}$

Required ratio $= \frac{\frac{15}{100} \times 25000}{\frac{75000}{7}} = \frac{3750 \times 7}{75000} = \frac{7}{20}$

45. (e) Required angle $= \frac{12}{100} \times 360 = 43.2$

46. (b) $22 \times \frac{8}{121} + ? = \frac{38}{11}$

$? = \frac{38}{11} - \frac{16}{11}$

$? = \frac{22}{11} = 2$

47. (a) $? \times 28 \div 21 = 420$

$? = \frac{420 \times 21}{28}$

$? = 315$

48. (c) $72 \div 36 \times 144 = ? \times 36$

$? = \frac{2 \times 144}{36}$

$? = 8$

49. (e) $? = \frac{0.06 \times 0.84}{1.2 \times 0.015}$

$? = 2.8$

50. (d) $? = 15.45 + 0.55$

$? = 16$

51. (d) $?^2 = \frac{56}{8} \times 28$

$?^2 = 196$

$? = 14$

52. (d) $? = 1405 - 811 - 576$

$? = 18$

53. (b) $\frac{100}{8} \times 80 + \frac{300}{8} \times 16 - \frac{100}{16} \times 112 = ?$

$? = 1000 + 600 - 700$

$? = 900$

54. (e) $? = 23 \times \frac{1}{48} \times 576 \times \frac{2}{3}$

$? = 23 \times 4 \times 2$

$? = 184$

55. (e) $? = 1.44 + 2.25 + 4.41 - 3.61$

$? = 4.49$

56. (a) Wrong no. is 59

$5 + (2)^2 = 9$

$9 + (4)^2 = 25$

$25 + (6)^2 = \boxed{61}$

$61 + (8)^2 = 125$

$125 + (10)^2 = 225$

$225 + (12)^2 = 369$

So, there should be 61 in place of 59.

57. (c) Wrong no. is 615

540		550		575		585		$\boxed{610}$		620		645

+10   +25   +10   +25   +10   +25

So, there should be 610 in place of 615

58. (b) Wrong no. is 221

$(1)^3 + 3 = 4$

$(2)^3 + 3 = 11$

$(3)^3 + 3 = 30$

$(4)^3 + 3 = 67$

$(5)^3 + 3 = 128$

$(6)^3 + 3 = \boxed{219}$

$(7)^3 + 3 = 346$

So, there should be 219 in place of 221

59. (d) Wrong no. is 1.75

16		4		2		1.5		$\boxed{1.5}$		1.875		2.8125

$\times 0.25$ $\times 0.50$ $\times 0.75$ $\times 1$ $\times 1.25$ $\times 1.50$

So, there should be 1.5 in place of 1.75

60. (a) Wrong no. is 148

18		30		52		79		116		$\boxed{158}$		210

+12   +22   +27   +37   +42   +52

+10   +5   +10   +5   +10

So, there should be 158 in place of 148.

61. (d) I. $2x^2 - 17x + 36 = 0$

$2x^2 - 8x - 9x + 36 = 0$

$2x(x - 4) - 9(x - 4) = 0$

$(2x - 9)(x- 4) = 0$

$x = \frac{9}{2}, 4$

II. $2y^2 - 19y + 45 = 0$

$2y^2 - 10y - 9y + 45 = 0$

$2y(y- 5) - 9(y- 5) = 0$

$(2y- 9)(y- 5) = 0$

$y = \frac{9}{2}, 5$

$\therefore y \geq x$

62. (e) I. $x^2 - 25x + 154 = 0$

$x^2 - 14x - 11x + 154 = 0$

$x(x - 14) - 11(x- 14) = 0$

$(x - 11)(x- 14) = 0$

$x = 11, 14$

II. $y^2 - 28y + 195 = 0$

$y^2 - 13y - 15y + 195 = 0$

$y(y- 13) - 15(y -13) = 0$

$(y- 13)(y - 15) = 0$

$y = 13, 15$

$\therefore$ no relation

63. (a) I. $\frac{10}{x} - \frac{24}{x^2} = 1$

Multiplying by x^2 on both side

$10x - 24 = x^2$

$x^2 - 10x + 24 = 0$

$x^2 - 6x - 4x + 24 = 0$

$x(x - 6) - 4(x- 6) = 0$

$(x - 4)(x- 6) = 0$

$x = 4, 6$

II. $\frac{5}{y} - \frac{6}{y^2} = 1$

Multiplying by y^2 on both side

$5y - 6 = y^2$

$y^2 - 5y + 6 = 0$

$y^2 - 3y - 2y + 6 = 0$

$y(y- 3) - 2(y- 3) = 0$

$(y - 2)(y- 3) = 0$

$y = 2, 3$

$\therefore x > y$

64. (d) I. $3x^2 - 10x - 8 = 0$

$3x^2 - 12x + 2x - 8 = 0$

$3x(x - 4) + 2(x- 4) = 0$

$(3x+ 2)(x- 4) = 0$

$x = -\frac{2}{3}, 4$

II. $2y^2 - 23y + 60 = 0$

$2y^2 - 8y - 15y + 60 = 0$

$2y(y- 4) - 15(y-4) = 0$

$(y- 4)(2y- 15) = 0$

$y = 4, \frac{15}{2}$

$\therefore y \geq x$

65. (a) I. $12x - 16y + 16 = 0$

$3x - 4y + 4 = 0 \qquad \dots(i)$

II. $17y - 13x = 12 \qquad \dots(ii)$

By multiplying equation (i) by 13 & equation (ii) by 3

$39x - 52y = -52$

$-39x + 51y = 36$

$y = 16 \ \& \ x = 20$

$\therefore x > y$

66. (b) Let share of A, B and C are Rs. a, b and c respectively

ATQ

$\frac{a+b}{c} = \frac{2}{1}$

$a + b = 2c \ \dots(i)$

And $\frac{a+c}{b} = \frac{3}{1}$

$a + c = 3b \ \dots\dots\dots (ii)$

On solving (i) and (ii)

$a : b : c = 5 : 3 : 4$

Let a, b and c are 5x, 3x and 4x respectively share of B and C together

$= \frac{12120}{5x+3x+4x} \times (3x + 4x)$

$= \frac{12120}{12x} \times 7x = $ Rs. 7070

67. (a) Required interest $= P\left[\left(1 + \frac{R}{100}\right)^2 - 1\right]$

$= 4500 \left[\left(1 + \frac{15}{100}\right)^2 - 1\right]$

$= 4500 \times \frac{129}{400} = $ Rs 1451.25

68. (b) C.P. of article $= \frac{2250}{150} \times 100 = $ Rs. 1500

Let discount given be $=$ Rs. 2y

ATQ;

$2250 - 2y = 1500 + y$

$750 = 3y \Rightarrow y = 250$

S.P. of article $= 1500 + 250 = $ Rs. 1750

69. (c) Total length of both trains

$= (50 + 80) \times \frac{1000}{60} = 130 \times \frac{1000}{60}$

$= \frac{13000}{6}$ metre

Required length of train

$= \frac{13000}{6} \times \frac{6}{13} \times \frac{120}{100} = 1.200$ km

70. (b) Let principal be Rs.P.

ATQ,

Rate of interest $= \frac{P \times 100}{P \times 3} = \frac{100}{3}\%$

Required interest $= \frac{1500 \times 100 \times 4}{100 \times 3} = $ Rs. 2000

71. (b) Simple interest $= \frac{2500 \times 225 \times 8}{100 \times 10} = $ Rs 4500

Simple interest becomes $= \frac{4500}{2500} = 1.8$ times

72. (b) Let father and son's present age be 'F' and 'S' yrs. respectively.

ATQ,

$(F - 10) = 12(S - 10)$

$F - 10 = 12S - 120 \qquad \dots(i)$

And,

$F = 7S \qquad \dots(ii)$

Put (ii) in (i)

$7S - 10 = 12S - 120$

$5S = 110$

$S = 22$ yrs

73. (d) let total time of investment be 15x months

Ratio of profit share of A to B

$= 2000 \times 15x \times \frac{2}{3} : 5000 \times 15x \times \frac{2}{5}$

$= 2 : 3$

Required percentage

$= \frac{3-2}{3} \times 100 = 33.33\%$

74. (a) let population of city initially = 100a

ATQ

$100a \times \frac{115}{100} \times \frac{2400}{2300} = 24024$

$120a = 24024$

So, $100a = \frac{24024}{120} \times 100 = 20020$

75. (d) Required number of results $= 4 \times 36 = 144$

Solutions (76-80): Investment of Deepak for first 6 months = Rs. 1500

Investment of Dharam for first 6 months

$= 1500 \times \frac{2}{3} = $ Rs. 1000

Investment of Shivam for first 6 months

$= 1500 \times \frac{3}{3} = $ Rs. 1500

Investment of Dharam for next 4 months = Rs. 2000

Investment of Deepak for next 4 months

$= 2000 \times \frac{2}{5} = $ Rs. 800

Investment of Shivam for next 4 months

$= 2000 \times \frac{3}{5} = $ Rs. 1200

Investment of Shivam for remaining time = Rs. 900

Investment of Deepak for remaining time

$= 900 \times \frac{4}{3} = $ Rs. 1200

Investment of Dharam for remaining time

$= 900 \times \frac{3}{3} = $ Rs. 900

Profit share of Deepak, Dharam and Shivam

$(1500 \times 6 + 800 \times 4 + 1200 \times 2) : (1000 \times 6 + 2000 \times 4 + 900 \times 2) : (1500 \times 6 + 1200 \times 4 + 900 \times 2)$

$\Rightarrow 73 : 79 : 78$

Let profit of Deepak, Dharam and Shivam be Rs.73x, Rs. 79x and Rs.78x respectively.

ATQ;

$(79x + 78x - 79x - 73x) = 5x = $ Rs. 450

$x = 90$

Profit share of Deepak = Rs. 6570

Profit share of Dharam = Rs. 7110

Profit share of Shivam = Rs. 7020

76. (c) Total investment of Deepak

$= (1500 + 800 + 1200) = $ Rs. 3500

Total investment of Shivam

$= (1500 + 1200 + 900) = $ Rs. 3600

Required percentage $= \frac{3500}{3600} \times 100 \approx 97\%$

77. (a) Profit of Dharam after one year

$= 79 \times 90 = $ Rs. 7110

78. (d) Required ratio $= 800 : 900 = 8 : 9$

79. (b) required difference $= (1500 + 1200 + 900) - (1000 + 2000) = $ Rs.600

80. (d) Required percentage $= \frac{1500-1200}{1500} \times 100$

$= 20\%$ less

REASONING ABILITY

Directions (1-5): Study the following information carefully and answer the questions given below:

Eight persons i.e. P, Q, R, S, T, U, V and W are sitting around a circular table, but not necessarily in the same order. All are facing towards the centre. P sits 2nd to the right of Q, who is an immediate neighbour of R. Three persons sit between R and T, who is not an immediate neighbour of P. W sits 2nd to the left of V, who is not an immediate neighbour of S.

1. Who among the following persons sits to the immediate right of S?
   (a) P   (b) R
   (c) T   (d) Q
   (e) None of these

2. Who among the following persons faces U?
   (a) Q   (b) R
   (c) S   (d) T
   (e) None of these

3. How many persons are sitting between W and Q?
   (a) two   (b) three
   (c) one   (d) four
   (e) Either (a) or (d)

4. Who among the following persons are immediate neighbours of V?
   (a) T and Q   (b) T and U
   (c) P and R   (d) P and S
   (e) None of these

5. Four of the following five are alike in certain ways based on a certain pattern. Find the one which does not belong to that group.
   (a) P-V   (b) P-U   (c) Q-W
   (d) R-T   (e) S-U

6. In the word 'MANAGER', how many pairs of the letters have the same number of letters (backwards or forwards) between them in the word as in the alphabet.
   (a) four   (b) two
   (c) one   (d) three
   (e) More than four

7. How many such numerals are there in the number '452316897' which will remain at the same position when arranged in ascending order from left to right?
   (a) one   (b) two
   (c) three   (d) none
   (e) More than Three

Directions (8-10): Study the following information carefully and answer the questions given below:
There are two couples in a family with six members. A is the sister-in-law of B, who is the father of C. D is grandmother of E, who is the son of C. F is the daughter-in-law of B.

8. How is B related to E?
   (a) father
   (b) grandfather
   (c) grandson
   (d) son
   (e) Can't be determined

9. How many male members are in the family?
   (a) two
   (b) three
   (c) four
   (d) Either (b) or (c)
   (e) None of these

10. How is A related to C?
   (a) aunt   (b) uncle
   (c) niece   (d) daughter
   (e) Can't be determined

Directions (11-15): Study the following information carefully and answer the questions given below:
Eight persons are sitting in two rows. In row 1, A, B, C and D are sitting and all of them face North. In row 2, P, Q, R and S are sitting and all of them face South. Each person of row 1 is facing another person of row 2, but not necessarily in the same order.

A sits 2nd to the left of the person who faces S. B faces the person who sits to the immediate left of P. Two persons sit between Q and R. C neither faces P nor R.

11. Who among the following persons faces D?
   (a) P   (b) Q
   (c) R   (d) S
   (e) None of these

12. Who among the following persons sits 3rd to the left of the person who faces A?

(a) Q   (b) P
(c) R   (d) S
(e) None of these

13. Who among the following persons faces the person who sits to the immediate left of R?
(a) B   (b) A
(c) D   (d) C
(e) None of these

14. Who among the following persons sits to the immediate right of C?
(a) No one   (b) A
(c) B   (d) D
(e) None of these

15. Four of the following five are alike in certain ways based on a certain pattern. Find the one which does not belong to that group.
(a) R   (b) P   (c) Q
(d) A   (e) C

Directions (16-20): The following five questions are based on the three-digit numbers given below.

123 320 287 424 521

16. If all the digits in each of the numbers are arranged in ascending order within the number, then which of the following numbers will become the highest in the new arrangement of numbers?
(a) 123   (b) 320   (c) 287
(d) 424   (e) 521

17. If all the numbers are arranged in descending order from left to right, then which of the following will be the product of the 3rd digit of the 2nd number from the left and the 3rd digit of the 2nd number from right in the new arrangement?
(a) 26   (b) 24   (c) 28
(d) 20   (e) 30

18. What will be the result when the 3rd digit of the highest number is multiplied with the 2nd digit of the lowest number?
(a) 2   (b) 6   (c) 8
(d) 16   (e) 12

19. If the positions of the second and the third digits of each of the numbers are interchanged, then how many odd numbers will be formed?
(a) none   (b) one   (c) two
(d) three   (e) four

20. If one is subtracted from each of the numbers, then how many numbers thus formed will be divisible by three?
(a) none   (b) one   (c) two
(d) three   (e) four

Directions (21-25): In each of the questions below are given some statements followed by two conclusions. You have to assume that the given statements are true even if they seem to be at variance with commonly known facts. Read all the conclusions and then decide which of the given conclusions logically follows from the given statements, disregarding commonly known facts.
(a) If only conclusion I follows.
(b) If only conclusion II follows.
(c) If either conclusion I or II follows.
(d) If neither conclusion I nor II follows.
(e) If both conclusions I and II follow.

21. Statements: Some America is USA. All England is Europe. No England is America.
Conclusion
I: Some USA is Europe.
II: No USA is Europe.

22. Statements: All Assistant is Clerk. Some Clerk is PO. All PO is Manager.
Conclusion
I: Some Clerk is Manager.
II: All Clerk is Manager.

23. Statements: All Home is House. All Office is Home. All House is Building.
Conclusion
I: Some Home is Building.
II: No Home is Building.

24. Statements: No Problem is Solution. All Solution is Question. Some Question is Answers.
Conclusion
I: Some Solution being Answers is a possibility.
II: No Solution being Answers is a possibility.

25. Statements: Only Akash is Amar. Only a few Akash is Adarsh. Few Adarsh is Ashish.
Conclusion
I: Some Amar is Ashish.
II: Some Adarsh is Akash.

Directions (26-30): Study the following information carefully and answer the questions given below:

Eight persons i.e. A, B, C, D, P, Q, R and S are living in an eight-floored building, but not necessarily in the same order. First floor is numbered 1; just above is the floor numbered 2 and so on until the topmost floor, which is numbered 8.

B lives above C and below P. Three persons live between A and R, who lives at an odd numbered floor. S lives at an even-numbered floor but below floor number 5. There are as many persons living between S and C as between P and B. C lives at an even numbered floor. Q lives above D, who doesn't live at the bottommost floor. A lives above R. D lives below C.

26. Who among the following persons lives just above the floor on which Q lives?
(a) A   (b) B   (c) P
(d) R   (e) None of these

27. How many persons live above A?

(a) two (b) one
(c) four (d) three
(e) None of these

28. In which of the following floors does D live?
(a) Floor 2 (b) Floor 3
(c) Floor 4 (d) Floor 5
(e) None of these

29. Who among the following persons lives at the bottom-most floor?
(a) P (b) Q (c) R
(d) S (e) None of these

30. Four of the following five are alike in certain ways based on a certain pattern. Find the one which does not belong to that group?
(a) Q (b) R (c) A
(d) D (e) C

Directions (31-35): In each of the questions below are given some statements followed by two conclusions. You have to take the given statements to be true even if they seem to be at variance with commonly known facts. Read all the conclusions and then decide which of the given conclusions logically follows from the given statements disregarding commonly known facts.
(a) If only conclusion I follows.
(b) If only conclusion II follows.
(c) If either conclusion I or II follows.
(d) If neither conclusion I nor II follows.
(e) If both conclusions I and II follow.

31. Statements: $Z \leq X < C = V < B \leq N > M \leq K$
Conclusion: I: $Z < B$ II: $X > M$

32. Statements: $A = S \geq D \geq F > G < H \leq J$
Conclusion: I: $D \geq G$ II: $S > H$

33. Statements: $Q = W < E > R = T \geq Y \geq U$
Conclusion: I: $Q = Y$ II: $E > Y$

34. Statements: $U > J \geq I = K > O > L$
Conclusion: I: $J > L$ II: $K < U$

35. Statements: $M \leq N < J = K > L \leq H > G$
Conclusion I: $N > L$ II: $J > L$

Directions (36-40): Study the following information carefully and answer the questions given below:

Six persons i.e. A, B, C, D, E and G are working on different days i.e. Monday, Tuesday, Wednesday, Thursday, Friday and Saturday starting from Monday of the same week, but not necessarily in the same order.

A works before B but not just before. Three persons work in between C and D. E doesn't work on Tuesday and Wednesday. G works after Thursday. There are as many persons working before E as after B. C works before D.

36. Who among the following persons is working on Friday?
(a) C (b) D
(c) E (d) G
(e) None of these

37. How many persons are working between B and G?
(a) none (b) one
(c) two (d) three
(e) More than three

38. On which of the following days does C work?
(a) Monday
(b) Tuesday
(c) Wednesday
(d) Thursday
(e) None of these

39. Who among the following persons works on Monday?
(a) A (b) C
(c) B (d) D
(e) None of these

40. Four of the following five are alike in a certain way based on a certain pattern. Find the one which does not belong to that group?
(a) B-Monday
(b) C-Thursday
(c) D-Wednesday
(d) G-Friday
(e) E-Tuesday

QUANTITATIVE APTITUDE

Directions (41-50): What should come in place of the question mark (?) in the following questions?

41. $\left(\frac{71.94 - 44.79}{719.4 - 447.9}\right) \div \left(\frac{7.194 - 4.479}{719.4 - 447.9}\right) = ?$
(a) 1 (b) 0.1 (c) 100
(d) 10 (e) 0.01

42. $747 + 22\%$ of $? - 472 = 759$
(a) 2000 (b) 2200 (c) 1800
(d) 2400 (e) 2100

43. $(P)^{a(b+c)} \div (P)^{b(c-a)} \times (P)^{c(a+b)} = (P)^?$
(a) 2bc + 2ac (b) ac + ab (c) 2ab+2ac
(d) 2ab + 2bc (e) 2ab – 2bc

44. $\frac{4}{5}$th of $160 \div 20 - \frac{3}{7}$th of $154 \div 11 = ?$
(a) 0.6 (b) 0.4 (c) 4
(d) 6 (e) 0.8

45. 64% of $850 \div 16 - ? = \sqrt{784}$
(a) 7 (b) 5 (c) 4
(d) 8 (e) 6

46. $1217 + 841 - 724 + 819 = ? + 1843$
(a) 210 (b) 310 (c) 360
(d) 270 (e) 410

47. $(43)^2 - (31)^2 = ? + (23)^2$

(a) 339   (b) 539   (c) 459
(d) 359   (e) 121

48. $\frac{3}{8}$ of $\frac{2}{5}$ of $\frac{1}{4}$ of 280 = ?

(a) 10.5   (b) 12.5   (c) 13.5
(d) 9.5   (e) 10

49. $11\frac{1}{4} + 7\frac{2}{5} - 8\frac{3}{5} = ? + 9\frac{1}{12}$

(a) $1\frac{2}{15}$ (b) $\frac{29}{30}$ (c) $1\frac{1}{30}$
(d) $\frac{23}{30}$ (e) $\frac{9}{10}$

50. 75% of $(40)^2 \div \frac{3}{5}$ of 80 = $?^2$

(a) 5   (b) 6   (c) 4
(d) 25   (e) 12

Directions (51-55): Study the given table carefully and answer the following questions.

The table given below shows the amount invested by four persons for different durations and at different rates at SI and the amount returned. Some data is missing in this table and you have to calculate the missing data according to the question.

Persons	Principal (Rs)	Rate of interest	Time (Years)	Amount (Rs)
Sanjay	-	20%	4	11700
Praveen	5000	-	3	-
Deepak	7500	15%	-	10312.5
Harish	8000	-	2	9000

51. Interest earned by Sanjay is how much more/less than that earned by Harish?
(a) Rs. 3500   (b) Rs. 4900   (c) Rs. 4200
(d) Rs. 3800   (e) Rs. 4500

52. What was the duration for which Deepak invested?
(a) 3 years   (b) 2.5 years
(c) 3.5 years   (d) 1.5 years
(e) 2 years

53. Amount invested by Sanjay is how much percent more than the amount invested by Praveen?
(a) 30%   (b) 24%   (c) $23\frac{1}{13}\%$
(d) 35%   (e) $23\frac{3}{13}\%$

54. If the ratio of rate of interest for Deepak and Praveen is 3:5 then, find the ratio between the amounts returned to Praveen and Deepak.
(a) 31 : 33   (b) 14 : 11   (c) 29 : 22
(d) 28 : 33   (e) 26 : 33

55. If Harish and Praveen invested at the same rate of interest, then find the interest amount earned by Praveen.
(a) Rs. 937.5   (b) Rs. 945.5
(c) Rs. 935.5   (d) Rs. 957.5
(e) Rs. 927.5

56. Amit started doing a work and after fifteen days of continuous work, he completed 62.5% of the total work. If the remaining work is completed by Amit with the help of Hemant in

six days, find the ratio between the efficiency of Amit and Hemant.
(a) 1 : 2   (b) 1 : 3   (c) 2 : 3
(d) 2 : 1   (e) 3 : 1

57. A person invests his money in two schemes. He invested Rs. (X+20,000) in scheme A at 10% SI for three years and Rs. X in scheme B at 15% SI for three years. After three years he receives a total of Rs. 36000 with interest. Find the value of X.
(a) Rs. 25000   (b) Rs. 35000
(c) Rs. 50000   (d) Rs. 45000
(e) Rs. 40000

58. A person marks his goods 40% above the cost price. He sold half of his goods at a discount of 20%, one-fourth of the goods at marked price and the remaining at cost price. Find the profit percentage.
(a) 16%   (b) 24%   (c) 12%
(d) 32%   (e) 26%

59. How many words can be formed using the word MISSISSIPPI, using factorial function.
(a) 54300   (b) 34650   (c) 12640
(d) 33640   (e) 13600

60. Two boats X and Y start from point A and point B respectively towards each other in a straight path. Speed of the current is 15kmph. and speed of boat in still water for boat X and boat Y are 25kmph. and 20kmph. respectively. If distance between A and B is 80 km. and boat X moves in downstream, find after how much time they will meet.
(a) $\frac{14}{9}$ hours   (b) $\frac{16}{9}$ hours   (c) 2 hours
(d) 3 hours   (e) $\frac{13}{9}$ hours

Directions (61-65): What will come in place of the question mark (?) in the following number series:

61. 15, 30, 10, 40, 8, ?
(a) 50   (b) 36   (c) 42
(d) 48   (e) 40

62. −4, −9, −2, −11, ?, −13, 2
(a) 0   (b) −6   (c) −2
(d) 1   (e) −8

63. 1, 10, 28, 55, 91, 136, ?
(a) 180   (b) 195   (c) 176
(d) 190   (e) 200

64. 4, 6, 12, 30, 90, 315, ?
(a) 1240   (b) 1280   (c) 1260
(d) 1340   (e) 1380

65. 17, ?, 25, 33, 58, 91, 149
(a) 22   (b) 16   (c) 20
(d) 24   (e) 8

Directions (66-70): What approximate value should come in place of the question mark '?' in the following questions? (You are not expected to calculate the exact value.)

66. $18.09 \div 27.02 \times 8.999 + (17.979)^2 = ?$
(a) 310   (b) 330   (c) 318

(d) 350   (e) 343

67. 121% of 854.8 + 179% of 555.4 = ?^{2}
(a) 55   (b) 40   (c) 45
(d) 50   (e) 35

68. $(4.04)^3 + (15.96)^{\frac{1}{4}} + (8.08)^2 = ? + 117.89$
(a) 12   (b) 18   (c) 21
(d) 15   (e) 13

69. $\frac{4}{7}$% of 67199 $- \frac{2}{5}$ of 644.96 = ?
(a) 132   (b) 140   (c) 144
(d) 126   (e) 120

70. $(14.96)^2 - \sqrt{1155} + \sqrt[3]{126} = ?^2$
(a) 9   (b) 14   (c) 20
(d) 18   (e) 7

71. The average age of a group of nine persons is 42. Two persons leave the group due to which the average age of the group decreases by 2. If the ratio of age between two persons is 3 : 4, find the age of the older person.
(a) 42 years   (b) 56 years   (c) 52 years
(d) 48 years   (e) 36 years

72. A copper billet of length, breadth and height of 80 cm., 40 cm. and 22 cm. respectively is made into a cylindrical wire of length 89,600 cm. What is the diameter of the wire?
(a) 1 cm.   (b) 0.25 cm.   (c) 0.5 cm.
(d) 2 cm.   (e) 1.5 cm.

73. Ratio between expenditure and savings of a person is 5 : 4. If his income is increased by 15% and expenditure increased by 20%, then by what percentage have his savings increased?
(a) 7.5%   (b) 8.75%   (c) 6.25%
(d) 7.75%   (e) 8.25%

74. Rs. 840 is divided among A, B and C. A get as much as half of B and C together and B gets as much as one fifth of A and C together. Find the share of B.
(a) Rs. 480   (b) Rs. 360   (c) Rs. 240
(d) Rs. 120   (e) Rs. 140

75. Two friends A and B enter into a partnership. B and A invest Rs. 45,000 and Rs. 60,000 respectively. B and A withdraw Rs. P and Rs. 12000 after four months and eight months respectively. If profit ratio of A and B at the end of the year is 168 : 125, find the value of P(in Rs.).
(a) 4500   (b) 6000   (c) 9000
(d) 7500   (e) 5000

Directions (76-80): The given bar graph shows the total no. of students of five different schools and the number of boys from each school.
Study the graph carefully and answer the following questions.

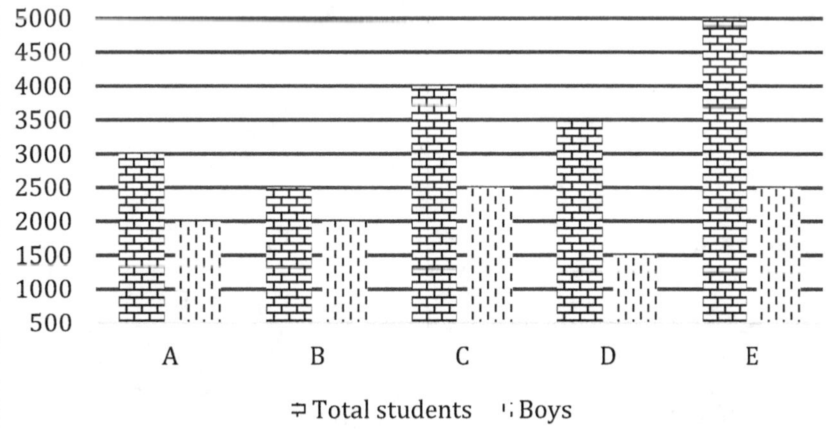

76. What is the ratio between no. of boys of school B and no. of girls of school C?
(a) 4 : 3   (b) 1 : 1   (c) 5 : 4
(d) 3 : 4   (e) 4 : 5

77. No. of girls of school B and C together is what percent of total students of school A?
(a) 150%   (b) 125%   (c) 100%
(d) 66.67%   (e) 75%

78. What is the average no. of boys in school A, B, C and E?
(a) 1800   (b) 2250   (c) 2300
(d) 1950   (e) 2875

79. Girls in school A and B together are what percent more/less than girls of school B and D together?
(a) 60%   (b) 50%   (c) 40%
(d) 70%   (e) 80%

80. No. of boys in school B and E together are how much more/less than girls in schools A, C and D together?
(a) 500   (b) 1000   (c) 1500
(d) 2000   (e) 0

REASONING ABILITY

Solutions (1-5): From the given statements, P sits 2nd to the right of Q, who is an immediate neighbour of R. Here, we get two possibilities i.e. Case 1 and Case 2. Three persons sit between R and T.

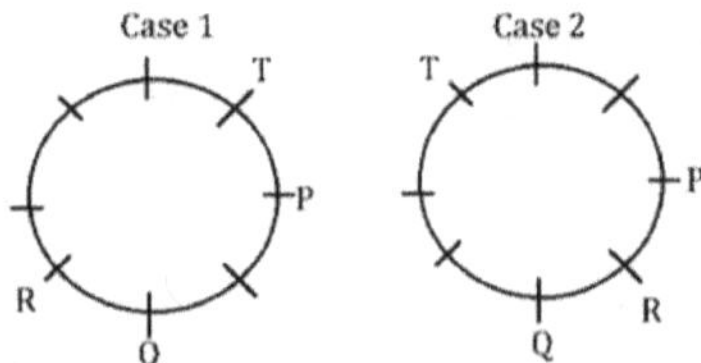

From the given statements, T is not an immediate neighbour of P. Here, Case 1 is ruled out. W sits 2nd to the left of V, who is not an immediate neighbour of S.

So, the final arrangement will be: -

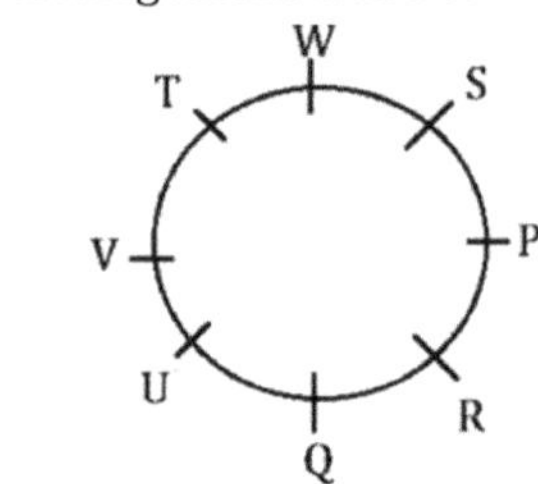

1. (e)   2. (c)   3. (b)
4. (b)   5. (b)
6. (b)

7. (a)

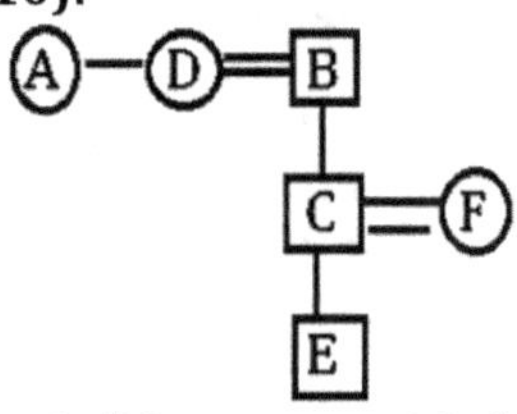

Direction (8-10):

8. (b)   9. (b)   10. (a)

Direction (11-15): From the given statements, two persons sit between Q and R. Here, we get two possibilities i.e. Case 1 and Case 2. A sits 2nd to the left of the person who faces S. B faces the person who sits immediate left of P.

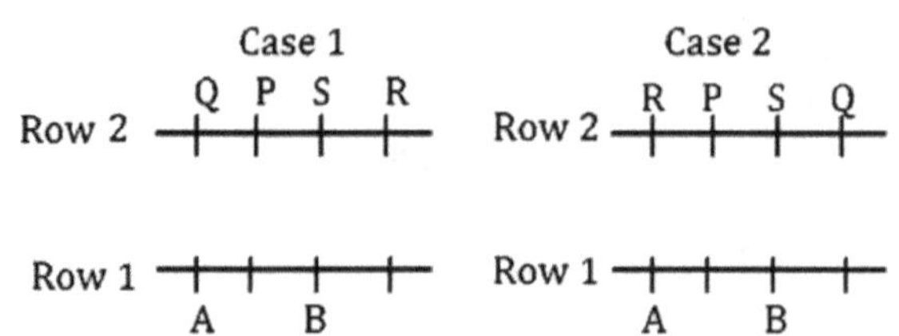

From the given statements, C neither faces P nor faces R. Here, Case 1 is ruled out.
So, the final arrangement will be: -

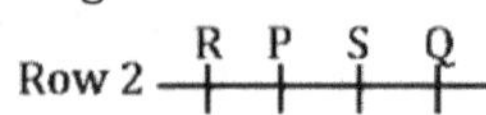

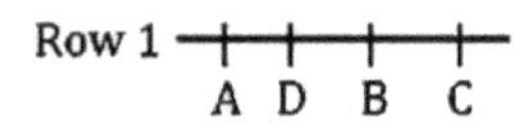

11. (a)   12. (a) 13. (c)
14. (a)   15. (b)
16. (c)   17. (c) 18. (a)
19. (a)   20. (b)
21. (c)

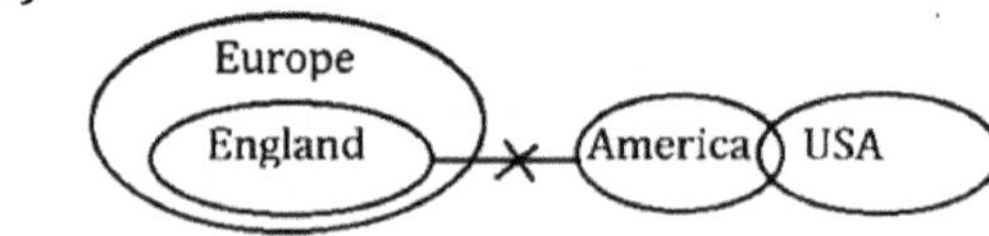

22. (a)

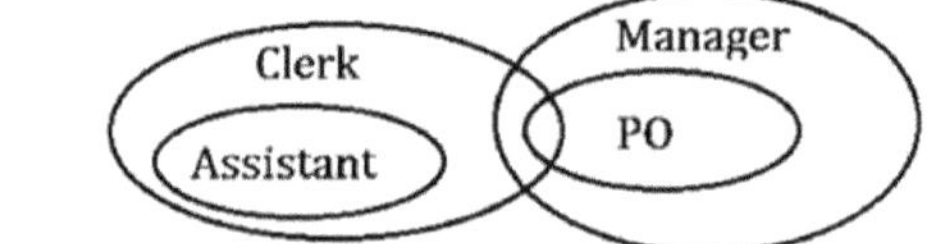

23. (a)

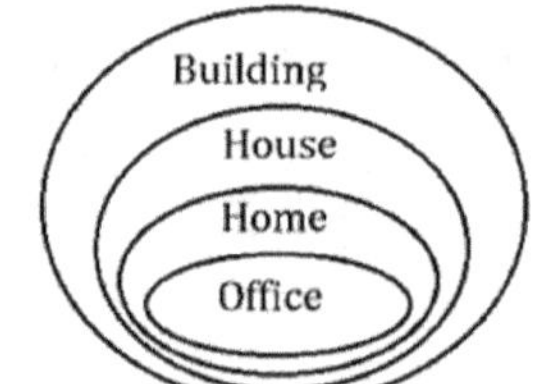

24. (e)

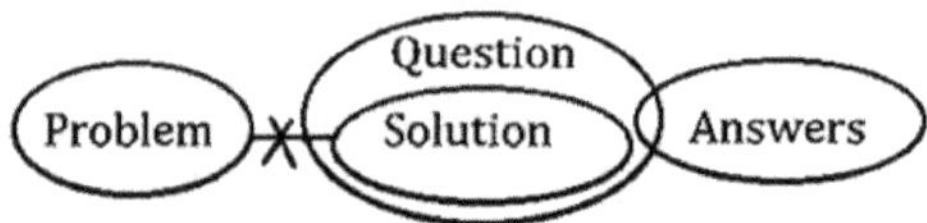

25. (b)

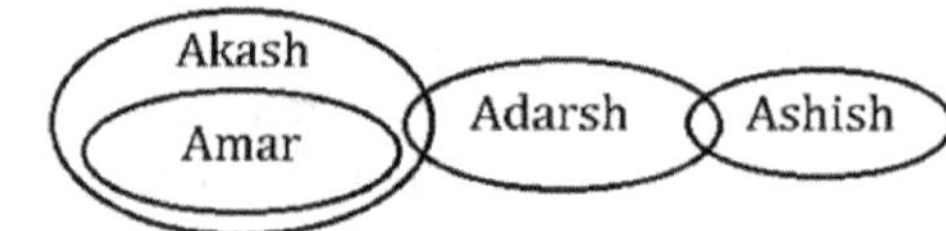

Direction (26-30): From the given statements, three persons live between A and R, who lives on an odd numbered floor. A lives above R. B lives above C and below P. C lives at an even numbered floor. S lives at an even numbered floor but below floor number 5. There are as many persons living between S and C as between P and B. Here, we get four possibilities i.e.

Case 1, Case 2, Case 3 and Case 4.

Floors	Case 1	Case 2	Case 3	Case 4
8	P	P	P	P
7	A			A
6	B	B	B	B
5		A		A
4	C	C	S	S
3	R		R	
2	S	S	C	C
1		R		R

From the given statements, Q lives above D, who doesn't live at the bottom-most floor. Here, Case 1 and Case 3 are ruled out.

Floors	Case 2	Case 4
8	P	P
7	Q	Q
6	B	B
5	A	A
4	C	S
3	D	D
2	S	C
1	R	R

From the given statements, D lives below C. Here, Case 4 is ruled out.

So, the final arrangement will be:

Floors	Persons
8	P
7	Q
6	B
5	A
4	C
3	D
2	S
1	R

26. (c)   **27. (d)**   **28. (b)**

29. (c)   **30.(e)**

Direction (31-35):

31. (a) I: Z < B (True)   II: X > M (False)

32. (d) I: D ≥ G (False)   II: S > H (False)

33. (b) I: Q = Y (False)   II: E > Y (True)

34. (e) I: J > L (True)   II: K < U (True)

35. (b) I: N > L (False)   II: J > L (True)

Direction (36-40): From the given statements, three persons work in between C and D. C works before D. G works after Thursday. E doesn't work on Tuesday and Wednesday.

Days	Case 1	Case 2
Monday	C	E/
Tuesday		C
Wednesday		
Thursday	E	E/
Friday	D	G
Saturday	G	D

From the given statements, there are as many persons who work before E as after B. A works before B but not just before. Here, Case 1 is ruled out.

So, the final arrangement will be: -

Days	Persons
Monday	A
Tuesday	C
Wednesday	B
Thursday	E
Friday	G
Saturday	D

36. (d)   **37. (b) 38. (b)**

39. (a)   **40. (d)**

QUANTITATIVE APTITUDE

41. (d) $? = \dfrac{27.15}{271.5} \div \dfrac{2.715}{271.5}$

$? = \dfrac{27.15}{271.5} \times \dfrac{271.5}{2.715}$

$? = 10$

42. (b) $\dfrac{22}{100} \times ? = 759 - 747 + 472$

$? = \dfrac{484 \times 100}{22}$

$? = 2200$

43. (c) $(P)^{ab+ac} \times \dfrac{1}{(P)^{bc-ab}} \times (P)^{ca+bc} = (P)^?$

$(P)^{ab+ac-bc+ab+ac+bc} = (P)^?$

$(P)^{2ab+2ac} = (P)^?$

$? = 2ab + 2ac$

44. (b) $128 \times \dfrac{1}{20} - \dfrac{66}{11} = ?$

$? = 6.4 - 6$

$? = 0.4$

45. (e) $\dfrac{64}{100} \times 850 \times \dfrac{1}{16} - ? = 28$

$? = 34 - 28 \Rightarrow ? = 6$

46. (b) $? = 1217 + 841 + 819 - 724 - 1843$

$= 2877 - 2567$

$? = 310$

47. (d) $? = 1849 - 961 - 529$

$? = 359$

48. (a) $\dfrac{3}{8} \times \dfrac{2}{5} \times \dfrac{1}{4} \times 280 = ?$

$? = 10.5$

49. (b) $? = \dfrac{45}{4} + \dfrac{37}{5} - \dfrac{43}{5} - \dfrac{109}{12}$

$? = \frac{135-109}{12} - \frac{6}{5}$

$? = \frac{130-72}{60} = \frac{58}{60}$

$? = \frac{29}{30}$

50. (a) $\frac{75}{100} \times 1600 \div \frac{3}{5} \text{ of } 80 = ?^2$

$\frac{1200}{48} = ?^2$

$?^2 = 25$

$? = 5$

S(51-55)

51. (c) let Sanjay earned Rs S as interest.

So, $S = \frac{(11700-S)\times20\times4}{100}$

$\frac{5S}{4} = 11700 - S$

$\frac{9S}{4} = 11700$

$S = 5200$

$\therefore$ Required difference

$= 5200 - (9000 - 8000) = 5200 - 1000$

$= Rs\ 4200$

52. (b) required time $= \frac{(10312.5-7500)\times100}{7500\times15} = \frac{2812.5}{75\times15}$

$= 2.5$ years

53. (a) Let Sanjay earn Rs S as interest.

So, $S = \frac{(11700-S)\times20\times4}{100}$

$\frac{5S}{4} = 11700 - S$

$\frac{9S}{4} = 11700$

$S = 5200$

So, principle $= 11700 - 5200 = Rs\ 6500$

$\therefore$ required percentage $= \frac{6500-5000}{5000} \times 100$

$= 30\%$

54. (d) Interest earned by Praveen

$= \frac{5000\times15\times\frac{5}{3}\times3}{100} = Rs\ 3750$

So, Required ratio

$= \frac{5000+3750}{10312.5} = \frac{8750}{10312.5} = \frac{28}{33}$

55. (a) Rate of interest $= \frac{1000\times100}{8000\times2} = 6.25\%$

So, required interest

$= \frac{5000\times6.25\times3}{100} = Rs\ 937.5$

56. (d) let total work be 240 units.

Amount of work completed by Amit

$= \frac{62.5}{100} \times 240 = 150$ units

So, efficiency of Amit $= \frac{150}{15} = $ 10 units/day

Remaining work = 240 – 150 = 90 units

Amount of work completed by Hemant

$= 90 - 10 \times 6 = 30$ units

So, efficiency of Hemant

$= \frac{30}{6} = 5$ units/day

$\therefore$ Required ratio = 10 : 5 = 2 : 1

57. (e) ATQ;

$\frac{(X+20000)\times10\times3}{100} + \frac{X\times15\times3}{100} = 36000$

$30X + 600000 + 45X = 3600000$

$75X = 3000000 \Rightarrow X = 40000$

58. (a) Let cost price of an article be Rs x and total article are 4 units.

So, marked price = Rs 1.4x

And, total cost price = Rs 4x

ATQ

Total selling price

$= 2 \times 1.4x \times \frac{80}{100} + 1 \times 1.4x + 1 \times x$

$= 2.24x + 1.4x + x = Rs\ 4.64x$

So, required profit % $= \frac{4.64x-4x}{4x} \times 100 = $ 16%

59. (b) Required no. of words $= \frac{11!}{4!\times4!\times2!} = 34650$

60. (b) Speed of boat X in downstream

$= 15 + 25 = 40$ kmph

As boat Y moves in the opposite direction of boat X, so boat Y moves in Upstream.

So, speed of boat Y in upstream

$= 20 - 15 = 5$ kmph

$\therefore$ Required time $= \frac{80}{40+5} = \frac{80}{45} = \frac{16}{9}$ hours

61. (d) The series is $\times2, \div 3, \times4, \div 5, \times6$

So $8 \times 6 = 48$

62. (a)

-4	-9	-2	-11	$\boxed{0}$	-13	2
-5	+7	-9	+11	-13	+15	

63. (d)

1	10	28	55	91	136	$\boxed{190}$
+9	+18	+27	+36	+45	+54	
+9	+9	+9	+9	+9		

64. (c) The Series is

$\times1.5, \times2, \times2.5, \times3, \times3.5, \times4$

So, $315 \times 4 = 1260$

65. (e) $17 + 8 = 25$

$8 + 25 = 33$

$25 + 33 = 58$

$33 + 58 = 91$

$58 + 91 = 149$

So, ?=8

66. (b) $18 \times \frac{1}{27} \times 9 + 324 \approx ?$

$? \approx 6 + 324$

$? \approx 330$

67. (c) $\frac{120}{100} \times 855 + \frac{180}{100} \times 555 \approx ?^2$

$1026 + 999 \approx ?^2$

$?^2 \approx 2025$

$? \approx 45$

68. (a) $64 + 2 + 64 \approx ? + 118$

$? \approx 130 - 118$

$? \approx 12$

69. (d) $\frac{4}{700} \times 67200 - \frac{2}{5} \times 645 \approx ?$

$384 - 258 \approx ?$

$? \approx 126$

70. (b) $(15)^2 - \sqrt{1156} + \sqrt[3]{125} \approx ?^2$

$225 - 34 + 5 \approx ?^2$

$?^2 \approx 196$

$? \approx 14$

71. (b) sum of age of 9 persons

$= 9 \times 42 = 378$ years

sum of age of group after two person leaves $7 \times 40 = 280$ years

sum of age of two persons

$= 378 - 280 = 98$ years

so, age of older person

$= \dfrac{4}{7} \times 98 = 56$ years

72. (a) volume of billet = volume of the wire

$80 \times 40 \times 22 = \pi r^2 \times 89600$

$r^2 = \dfrac{70400 \times 7}{22 \times 89600} = 0.25$

$r = 0.5$ cm

So, diameter of the wire $= 0.5 \times 2 = 1$ cm

73. (b) let his expenditure and savings be Rs 5x and Rs 4x respectively.

ATQ

Increased income

$= (5x + 4x) \times \dfrac{115}{100} = $ Rs $10.35x$

And increased expenditure

$= 5x \times \dfrac{120}{100} = 6x$

So, new savings $= 10.35x - 6x = $ Rs $4.35x$

Required percentage

$= \dfrac{4.35x - 4x}{4x} \times 100 = \dfrac{35}{4}\% = 8.75\%$

74. (e) Let A, B and C got a, b and c Rs respectively.

ATQ

$\dfrac{a}{b+c} = \dfrac{1}{2}$ and $\dfrac{b}{a+c} = \dfrac{1}{5}$

Let a = x and b+c = 2x

So, $\dfrac{2x - c}{x + c} = \dfrac{1}{5}$

$9x = 6c$

$\Rightarrow c = \dfrac{3}{2}x$

$\Rightarrow b = 2x - \dfrac{3}{2}x = \dfrac{1}{2}x$

So, $x + \dfrac{1}{2}x + \dfrac{3}{2}x = 840$

$x = 280$

$\therefore$ share of B $= \dfrac{1}{2}x = $ Rs 140

75. (e) Ratio of profit share of A and B

$= \dfrac{60000 \times 8 + 48000 \times 4}{45000 \times 4 + (45000 - P) \times 8} = \dfrac{168}{125}$

$= \dfrac{168000}{135000 - 2P} = \dfrac{168}{125}$

$= 125000 = 135000 - 2P$

$= P = 5000$

76. (a) Required ratio $= \dfrac{2000}{(4000 - 2500)} = \dfrac{2000}{1500} = \dfrac{4}{3}$

77. (d) Required %

$= \dfrac{(2500 - 2000) + (4000 - 2500)}{3000} \times 100$

$= \dfrac{2000}{3000} \times 100 = 66.67\%$

78. (b) Required average

$= \dfrac{2000 + 2000 + 2500 + 2500}{4} = \dfrac{9000}{4} = 2250$

79. (c) Total girls in school A and B

$= (3000 - 2000) + (2500 - 2000)$

$= 1000 + 500 = 1500$

Total girls in school B and D

$= (2500 - 2000) + (3500 - 1500)$

$= 500 + 2000 = 2500$

So, required percentage $= \dfrac{2500 - 1500}{2500} \times 100$

$= \dfrac{1000}{2500} \times 100 = 40\%$

80. (e) Total no. of girls in school A, C and D

$= (3000 - 2000) + (4000 - 2500) + (3500 - 1500)$

$= 1000 + 1500 + 2000 = 4500$

Required difference

$= (2000 + 2500) - (4500) = 0$

REASONING ABILITY

Directions (1-5): Study the following information carefully and answer the questions given below:

Nine persons L, M, N, O, P, Q, R, S and T are sitting in a row facing north but not necessarily in the same order.

L sits 3rd to the left of N and one of them sits at the extreme end. The number of persons who sit to the right of L is same as to the left of T. S sits 3rd to the left of Q. Both Q and T are immediate neighbours. O sits 2nd to the left of P. R sits 3rd from one of the ends.

1. How many persons are sitting between S and L?
   (a) none   (b) one
   (c) two   (d) three
   (e) More than three

2. What is the position of Q with respect to M?
   (a) immediate left
   (b) 3rd to the left
   (c) 4th to the right
   (d) 2nd to the right
   (e) None of these

3. Who among the following persons sits at the extreme end?
   (a) P   (b) Q   (c) L
   (d) O   (e) R

4. Four of the following five are alike in a certain way and hence they form a group. Which one of the following does not belong to that group?
   (a) S-T   (b) P-Q   (c) N-O
   (d) L-M   (e) R-N

5. Who among the following persons sits in the middle of the row?
   (a) P   (b) Q   (c) T
   (d) R   (e) L

Directions (6-8): Study the following information carefully and answer the questions given below:

Point D is 15m. south of Point A. Point D is 10m. west of Point B. Point E is 15m. south of Point B. Point F is 18m. west of Point E. Point C is 8m. north of Point F.

6. Point C is in which direction with respect to B?
   (a) north-east   (b) south-west
   (c) north   (d) south
   (e) None of these

7. What is the total distance between Point D and Point F?
   (a) 33m.   (b) 13m.   (c) 27m.
   (d) 43m.   (e) 30m.

8. How far and in which direction is Point E with respect to Point C?
   (a) 26m., south-east
   (b) 20m., north-west
   (c) 32m., south-west
   (d) 28m., south
   (e) None of these

Directions (9-13): Study the following information carefully and answer the questions given below:

Eight persons T, U, V, W, X, Y, Z and M are sit around a square table and face the centre, but not necessarily in the same order. Four of them sit at the corners of the table while the rest sit at the middle of the table.

V sits to the immediate left of M. There are two persons who sit between M and W, who doesn't sit at the corner. Y sits to the immediate right of T and is an immediate neighbour of W. Z sits 2nd to the right of U.

9. Who among the following persons faces Y?
   (a) U   (b) M   (c) V
   (d) Z   (e) X

10. How many persons sit between U and V, when counted in the anti-clockwise direction from U?
    (a) four   (b) two
    (c) three   (d) one
    (e) Either (a) or (b)

11. What is the position of T with respect to U?
    (a) 2nd to the right
    (b) 3rd to the left
    (c) 2nd to the left
    (d) 3rd to the right
    (e) Immediate to the right

12. Four of the following five are alike in a certain way and hence they form a group. Which one of the following does not belong to that group?
    (a) V   (b) U   (c) Z
    (d) Y   (e) M

13. Which of the following is not true, as per the given information?
    (a) U sits immediate left of X
    (b) M faces U
    (c) W sits 2nd to the right of T
    (d) V does not face Y
    (e) All are true

Directions (14-18): Study the following information carefully and answer the given questions.

Eight friends A, B, C, D, W, X, Y and Z are living on eight different floors of a building, but not necessarily in the same order. The ground floor is numbered as 1 and the floor above it is numbered 2 and so on till the topmost floor, that is numbered 8.

There are four friends living between B and Y, who lives below B. Y does not live on the ground floor. C lives on an odd-numbered floor, but not on the 3rd floor. Z lives below A, but not on the floor just below. C lives above A, but not on the floor just above. More than one friend lives between A and W. C lives between X and Y.

14. Who among the following lives on the 3rd floor?
    (a) W   (b) A
    (c) Z   (d) Y
    (e) None of these

15. On which of the following floors does D live?
    (a) 2nd   (b) 5th
    (c) 4th   (d) 8th
    (e) None of these

16. Who among the following lives just above C?
    (a) X   (b) B
    (c) D   (d) W
    (e) None of these

17. How many friends live between B and A?
    (a) three   (b) one   (c) none
    (d) four   (e) two

18. Four of the following five belong to a group in a certain way. Find out which one does not belong to that group?
    (a) W   (b) Z   (c) X
    (d) D   (e) Y

Direction (19-23): The following questions are based on the five three-digit numbers given below:

544   241   425   712   323

19. What is the sum of the 2nd digit of the 2nd number from the left and the 1st digit of the 2nd number from right?
    (a) 9   (b) 11
    (c) 13   (d) 17
    (e) None of these

20. If 1 is added to the second digit of each of the numbers and then all the digits are added, then how many numbers thus formed will be divisible by two?
    (a) none   (b) one
    (c) two   (d) three
    (e) None of these

21. If all the digits in each of the numbers are arranged in a descending order within the number, which of the following will be the highest number in the new arrangement of numbers?
    (a) 241   (b) 425   (c) 712

22. If in each number, the first and the third digits are interchanged, then which will be the highest number?
    (a) 323   (b) 425   (c) 712
    (d) 241   (e) 544

23. If in each number, the first and the second digits are interchanged then which will be the 2nd highest number?
    (a) 712   (b) 425   (c) 323
    (d) 241   (e) 544

Directions (24-28): Study the following information carefully and answer the questions given below.

Eight persons A, B, C, D, E, F, G and H are sitting around a circular table, but not necessarily in the same order. Four of them are facing outside of the table and four of them are facing the centre of the table.

A sits third to the right of the one who sits to the immediate left of G. Only one person sits between A and D, who sits opposite E. H sits third to the left of D. H is not an immediate neighbour of G. D does not face the centre. C sits second to the left of B. F sits second to the left of C. Immediate neighbours of D face the opposite direction. F does not face the same direction as A.

24. Who among the following sits opposite H?
    (a) F   (b) B   (c) C
    (d) G   (e) None of these

25. What is the position of A with respect to B?
    (a) Second to the right
    (b) Third to the right
    (c) Third to the left
    (d) Immediate left
    (e) None of these

26. Who among the following sits to the immediate right of C?
    (a) G   (b) D
    (c) E   (d) A
    (e) None of these

27. How many persons sit between G and E, when counted from the right of E?
    (a) one   (b) No one
    (c) three   (d) two
    (e) More than three

28. Four of the following five belong to a group in a certain way. Find out which one of the following does not belong to that group?
    (a) E   (b) H   (c) F
    (d) B   (e) G

Directions (29-31): In these questions, relationship between different elements is shown in the statements. The statements are followed by two conclusions. Study the conclusions based on the given statements and select the appropriate answer:
(a) If only conclusion I follows.
(b) If only conclusion II follows.
(c) If either conclusion I or II follows.
(d) If neither conclusion I nor II follows.
(e) If both conclusions I and II follow.

29. **Statements:** W = T ≥ O > H ≥ F ≤ D < A
    Conclusions: I. W > F   II. O > D
30. **Statements:** S = T ≥ W ≤ G ≤ L = O
    Conclusions: I. L > W   II. O = W
31. **Statements:** K > M ≤ V < C = X > S ≥ Q
    Conclusions: I. M < S   II. C > Q

Directions (32-35): In each of the questions below are given some statements followed by two conclusions. You have to take the given statements to be true even if they seem to be at variance with commonly known facts. Read all the conclusions and then decide which of the given conclusions logically follows from the given statements, disregarding commonly known facts.
(a) If only conclusion I follows.
(b) If only conclusion II follows.
(c) If either conclusion I or II follows.
(d) If neither conclusion I nor II follows.
(e) If both conclusions I and II follow.

32. **Statements:** Some Clock are Time. Only a few Time is Watch. No Watch is Clock.
    Conclusions:
    I. All Watch being Time is a possibility.
    II. All Time are Watch is a possibility.
33. **Statements:** Some Song are Tone. Some Tone are Lyrics. All Lyrics are Music.
    Conclusions:
    I. Some Song can be Lyrics.
    II. Some Music are not Tone.
34. **Statements:** All Reebok are Raymond. Some Raymond are Puma. Only a few Puma are Titan.
    Conclusions:
    I. Some Titan can never be Reebok.
    II. Some Titan can be Reebok.
35. **Statements:** Some Drink are Water. All Water are Tea. All Drink are Coffee.

Conclusions:
    I. Some Coffee can never be Tea.
    II. Some Water can never be Coffee.

Direction (36-40): Study the following information carefully and answer the questions given below:
In a certain code language:
"human are intelligent person" is coded as "fg wq dl kp"
"person are emotionally here" is coded as "kp wq nm bg"
"intelligent student becomes today" is coded as "dl fv ut py"
"you are today here" is coded as "ft wq py bg"

36. What is the code for "intelligent person" in the given code language?
    (a) dl fg   (b) dl kp
    (c) py ft   (d) nm fg
    (e) None of these
37. What is the code for "human" in the given code language?
    (a) fg   (b) bg   (c) fv
    (d) ft   (e) nm
38. Which of the following word is coded as "ut" in the given code language?
    (a) becomes   (b) person
    (c) student   (d) human
    (e) Either (a) or (c)
39. What is the code for "today" in the given code language?
    (a) py   (b) wq   (c) dl
    (d) nm   (e) fg
40. If "today market" is coded as "ju py", then what will "around market" becoded as?
    (a) ju mn   (b) dl wq
    (c) ju mx   (d) fg py
    (e) None of these

QUANTITATIVE APTITUDE

Directions (41-50): What will come in place of the question mark (?) in the following questions?

41. 87.5% of $888 + 8\frac{1}{3}\% \ of \ 600 = ? + (28)^2$
    (a) 41   (b) 47   (c) 43
    (d) 62   (e) 53
42. $12\frac{3}{4} \times 7\frac{1}{3} \div 8\frac{1}{2} \times 1\frac{1}{11} = ?$
    (a) $\frac{121}{12}$ (b) 12   (c) $\frac{119}{12}$
    (d) 9   (e) 11
43. $(1.32 + 1.18)^2 + ? \times 0.5 = (4.6 - 1.4)^2$
    (a) 3.99   (b) 1.995   (c) 7.98
    (d) 4.68   (e) 8.98
44. $(256)^{\frac{1}{4}} \times (512)^{-\frac{1}{3}} \times 6^2 = ?$

    (a) 18   (b) 12   (c) 16
    (d) 13   (e) 24
45. $\dfrac{?-7^2}{40\% \ of \ 35} \times 15 \div 0.3 = \dfrac{150}{7}$
    (a) 45   (b) 65   (c) 55
    (d) 75   (e) 35
46. $784 + 1297 - 613 = ? + 429 + 811$
    (a) 228   (b) 342   (c) 1454
    (d) 1086   (e) 338
47. $[(40)^2 \times 8] \div 50 \div 16 = (5)^2 - ?$
    (a) 3   (b) 9   (c) 6
    (d) 12   (e) 15
48. 76% of $340 - 152\%$ of $170 = ?$
    (a) 27   (b) 0   (c) 12.8

214

(d) 9.4 (e) 14.2

49. $\frac{4}{5}$ of $\sqrt{1225} \div \frac{1}{3}$ of $(729)^{\frac{1}{3}} = ? + \frac{1}{3}$

(a) 10 (b) 18 (c) 15
(d) 9 (e) 3

50. $\frac{5}{8}$ th of 160% of ?= $\sqrt{225} \times 4$

(a) 70 (b) 80 (c) 60
(d) 40 (e) 50

Directions (51-56): Study the line graph carefully and answer the following questions.
The line graph shows the runs scored by two different teams in a series of five cricket matches.

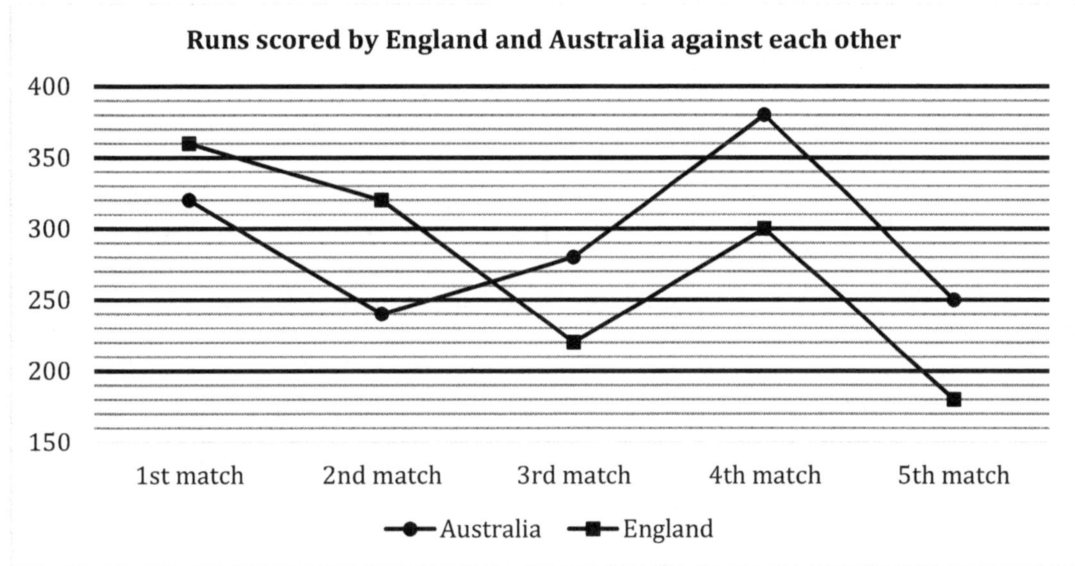

51. Runs scored by Australia in the first and third match together is what percent of the runs scored by England in the second and fifth match together?

(a) 100% (b) 125% (c) $83\frac{1}{3}$%
(d) 120% (e) 75%

52. Find the difference between maximum runs scored by England and minimum runs scored by Australia.

(a) 120 runs (b) 80 runs (c) 150 runs
(d) 200 runs (e) 180 runs

53. What is the ratio between total runs scored by Australia to that of England in all matches?

(a) 25 : 23 (b) 46 : 47 (c) 43 : 46
(d) 49 : 46 (e) 23 : 43

54. Runs scored by Australia in the second match is what percent more or less than the runs scored by England in the fourth match?

(a) 25% (b) 20% (c) 35%
(d) 10% (e) 50%

55. How many matches did Australia win out of all the five matches?

(a) 1 (b) 4 (c) 3
(d) 5 (e) 2

56. What was the average runs scored by England in the first four matches?

(a) 250 (b) 280 (c) 345
(d) 320 (e) 300

57. A alone can complete a piece of work in four days working nine hours a day, while B alone can complete the same piece of work in nine days working five hours a day. If they work on alternate days (starting with A), then how much time will they take to complete the same work, working five hours a day?

(a) 4 days (b) 8 days (c) 9 days
(d) 2 days (e) 6 days

58. The monthly income of Kunal is $66\frac{2}{3}$% of e the monthly income of Hemant. If Hemant's total monthly expenditure is Rs. 18,000 and he saves 20% of his salary, find the monthly income of Kunal.

(a) Rs. 22,500
(b) Rs. 17,500
(c) Rs. 13,000
(d) Rs. 15,000
(e) Rs. 33,750

59. If a man rides from his home at a speed of 36 kmph., then he will reach his office late by two min and if he rides at a speed of 45kmph. then he will reach two min early. Find the distance between his home and office.

(a) 12 km. (b) 18 km. (c) 21 km.
(d) 15 km. (e) 10 km.

60. Pipe A alone and pipe B alone can fill a tank in 15 min and 20 min respectively. There is a pipe C at the bottom of the tank which can empty the tank in 30 min. If all the three pipes are opened together, find how much time they will take to fill the empty tank.
    (a) 15 min   (b) 18 min   (c) 9 min
    (d) 30 min   (e) 12 min

Directions (61-65): What will come in place of the question mark (?) in the following number series:

61. 6, 18, 33, 57, 108, ?, 615
    (a) 220   (b) 324   (c) 308
    (d) 240   (e) 460

62. ?, 8, 32, 72, 128, 200
    (a) 0   (b) 4   (c) 2
    (d) 6   (e) -2

63. 6, 6, 12, 36, 144, 720, ?
    (a) 3600   (b) 2880   (c) 4320
    (d) 1440   (e) 4230

64. 8, 21, 47, 86, 138, 203, ?
    (a) 287   (b) 281   (c) 372
    (d) 278   (e) 268

65. 30, 60, 20, 80, ?, 96
    (a) 90   (b) 40   (c) 48
    (d) 26   (e) 16

Directions (Q66-70): In the following questions, calculate quantity I and quantity II. Then, compare them and answer
(a) If quantity I > quantity II
(b) If quantity I < quantity II
(c) If quantity I ≥ quantity II
(d) if quantity I ≤ quantity II
(e) if quantity I = quantity II or no relation can be established

66. **Quantity I, cost price of book (in Rs.):** If the book is sold at a profit of 5% instead of a loss of 5%, the shopkeeper gets Rs. 18 more.
    Quantity II, selling price of bottle (in Rs.): A shopkeeper marked up the price of the bottle by 50% and gave a discount of $16\frac{2}{3}$%. The cost price of the bottle is Rs. 160.

67. **Quantity I, x:** $35x^2 - 41x + 12 = 0$
    Quantity II, y: $9y^2 - 18y + 8 = 0$

68. **Quantity I, time taken by a leak to empty a filled tank (in min):** Pipe A alone and pipe B alone can fill a tank in 20 minutes and 30 minutes respectively. But it is found that there is a leak in the tank, due to which the pipes take 3 minutes extra to fill the tank when both pipes are opened together.
    Quantity II: 55 minutes

69. **Quantity I, x:** $x^2 + 7x + 10 = 0$
    Quantity II, y: $y^2 + 13y + 40 = 0$

70. **Quantity I, distance travelled by man (in km):** A man covers half the distance at a speed of 20kmph. and the remaining half at a speed of 30kmph. Total time taken by the man to cover the whole distance was8 hours.
    Quantity II, total distance travelled by boat in upstream and in downstream together (in km): A boat takes 10 hours to cover a distance in upstream and 5 hours to cover the same distance in downstream. The speed of the boat in still water is 15kmph. and the speed of stream is 5kmph.

71. A shopkeeper marked up the price of an article by 40%. He gained a profit of Rs. 304 on selling the article. If he gave a discount of 15%, find the selling price of the article?
    (a) Rs. 1600   (b) Rs. 2240   (c) Rs. 1904
    (d) Rs. 1604   (e) Rs. 1900

72. Four years ago, the ratio of the age of Deepak and Sanjay was 3 : 4. Average of the present age of Deepak, Sanjay and Harish is 26 years. Harish is 11 years younger than Sanjay. What is the present age of Sanjay?
    (a) 25 years   (b) 21 years   (c) 22 years
    (d) 32 years   (e) 26 years

73. In how many different ways can the letters of the word CRICKET be arranged so that vowels occupy only the extreme ends?
    (a) 720   (b) 360   (c) 260
    (d) 120   (e) 240

74. 700 grams of sugar solution has 60% sugar. How much sugar should be added in the solution to make this solution contain 80% sugar.
    (a) 700 gram
    (b) 300 gram
    (c) 450 gram
    (d) 600 gram
    (e) 200 gram

Directions (75-80): The table given below shows the no. of students enrolled in four different colleges over the years.
Study the data carefully and answer the following questions.

College / Year	A	B	C	D
2015	600	450	500	350
2016	550	400	650	450
2017	700	500	600	550
2018	300	350	400	500

75. What is the average no. of students who enrolled in college B over the given years?
    (a) 450   (b) 400   (c) 425
    (d) 475   (e) 500

76. If in year 2016, 20% students of college B enrolled in B.SC, 30% students enrolled in

B.COM and remaining students enrolled in BCA, then find the difference between the numbers of BCA students and B.SC students.
(a) 200 (b) 80 (c) 100
(d) 120 (e) 140

77. Students enrolled in college A in year 2015 and 2016 together is what percent more or less than students enrolled in college C in year 2017 and 2018 together?
(a) 15% (b) 25% (c) 30%
(d) 12% (e) 20%

78. If the ratio between girls and boys in college B in 2016 was 3 : 5 and the ratio between girls and boys in college C in 2017 was 7 : 5, then find the ratio between girls of college B in 2016 to boys of college C in 2017.
(a) 2 : 5 (b) 3 : 5 (c) 1 : 3
(d) 2 : 3 (e) 5 : 3

79. Students enrolled in college A in 2017 is what percent of students enrolled in college B in the same year?
(a) 120% (b) 40% (c) 28%
(d) 71% (e) 140%

80. The total students enrolled in year 2015 in all the colleges together is how much more/less than the total students enrolled in 2018 in all the colleges together?
(a) 250 (b) 450 (c) 150
(d) 350 (e) 550

Solutions

REASONING ABILITY

Direction (1-5): From the given statements, L sits 3rd to the left of N and one of them sits at an extreme end. **Here we get two possibilities i.e. Case 1 and Case 2.** The number of persons who sit right to L is same as to the left of T.

S sits 3rd to the left of Q. Both Q and T are immediate neighbours.

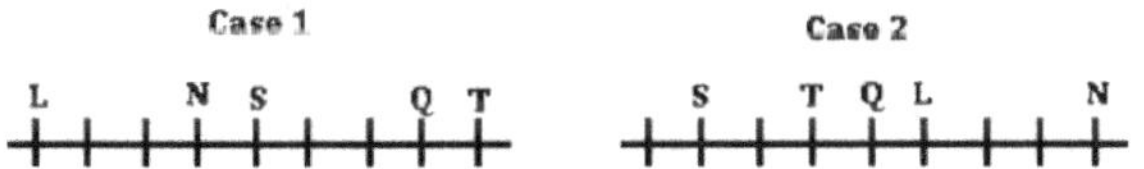

From the given statements, O sits 2nd to the left of P. **Here Case 1 is ruled out.** R sits 3rd from one of the end.

So, the final arrangement is-

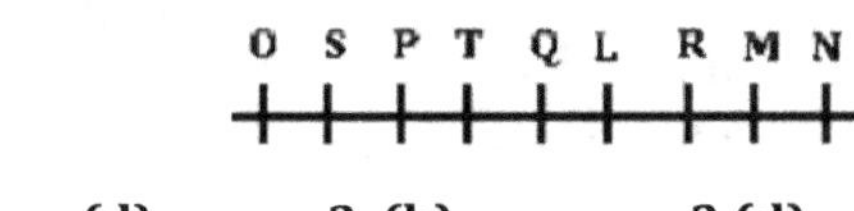

1. (d)   2. (b)   3. (d)
4. (c)   5. (b)

Directions (6-8):

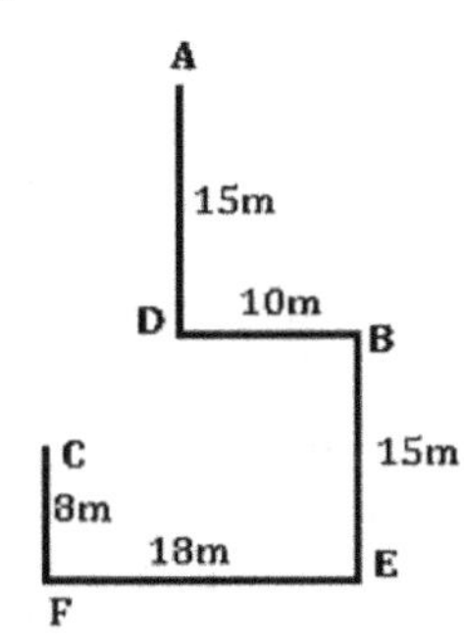

6. (b)   7. (d)   8. (a)

Directions (9-13): From the given statements, V sits immediate left of M. There are two persons sitting between M and W, who doesn't sit at the corner. **Here we get two possibilities i.e. Case 1 and Case 2.** Y sits to the immediate right of T and is an immediate neighbour of W.

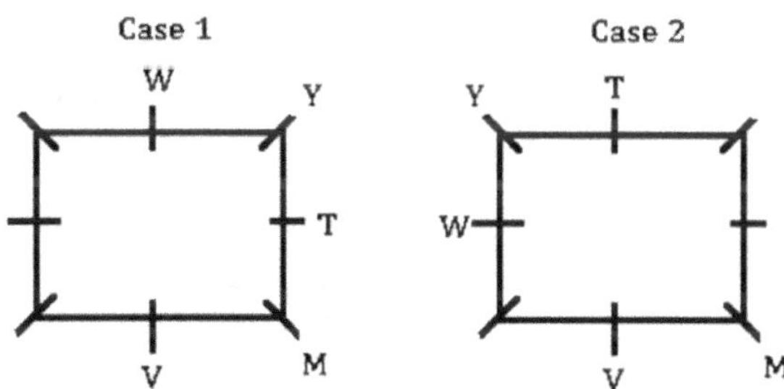

From the given statements, Z sits 2nd to the right of U. **Here Case 2 is ruled out.**

So, the final arrangement is-

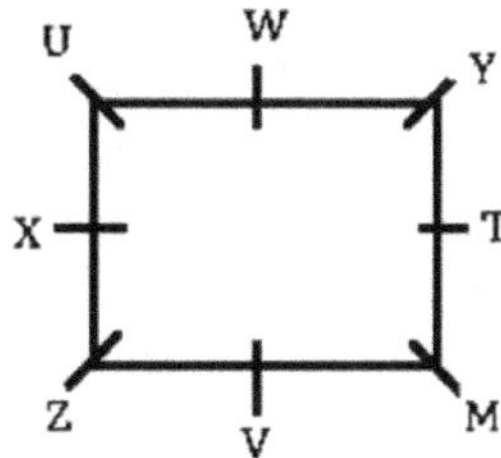

9. (d)   10. (b)   11. (b)
12. (a)   13. (e)

Directions (14-18): There are four friends living between B and Y, who lives below B. Y does not live on the ground floor. From these conditions we have two possible cases. C lives on an odd numbered floor, but not on the 3rd floor. C lives between X and Y. So, arrangement will be-

Floor	Case- 1	Case- 2
	Friend	Friend
8	X	B
7	B	X
6		
5	C	C
4		
3		Y
2	Y	
1		

Z lives below A, but not on the floor just below. C lives above A, but not on the floor just above. By these conditions Case-2 is cancelled. So new arrangement will be:

Floor	Case- 1
	Friend
8	X
7	B
6	
5	C
4	
3	A
2	Y
1	Z

There is more than one friend living between A and W. It means D lives on the 4th floor. So final arrangement will be:

Floor	Friend
8	X
7	B
6	W
5	C
4	D
3	A
2	Y
1	Z

14. (b)   **15. (c)**   **16. (d)**
17. (a)   **18. (b)**
19. (b) 2nd digit of 2nd number from left = 4,
1st digit of 2nd number from right = 7,
4+7=11

20. (d)

544	241	425	712	323
554	251	435	722	333

21. (c)

544 241 425 |712| 323
544 421 542 |721| 332

22. (b)

544 241 |425| 712 323
445 142 |524| 217 323

23. (d)

544 |241| 425 712 323
454 |421| 245 172 233

Directions (24-28): A sits third to the right of the one who sits immediate left of G. From this condition we have four possible cases-

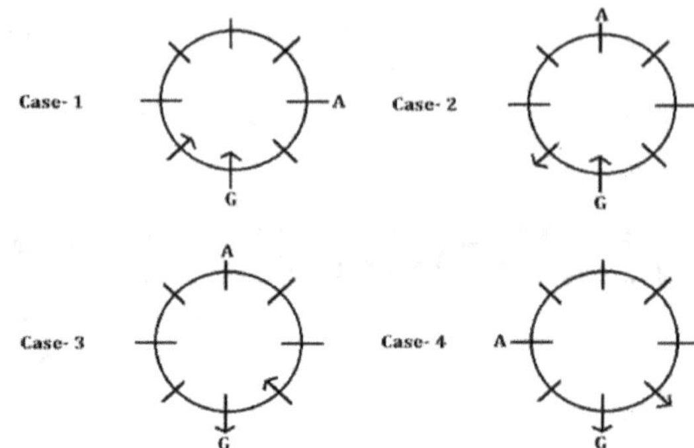

Only one person sits between A and D, who sits opposite E. By this condition, Case- 1 and Case-4 are cancelled. H sits third to the left of D. H is not an immediate neighbour of G. D does not face the centre. So new arrangement will be-

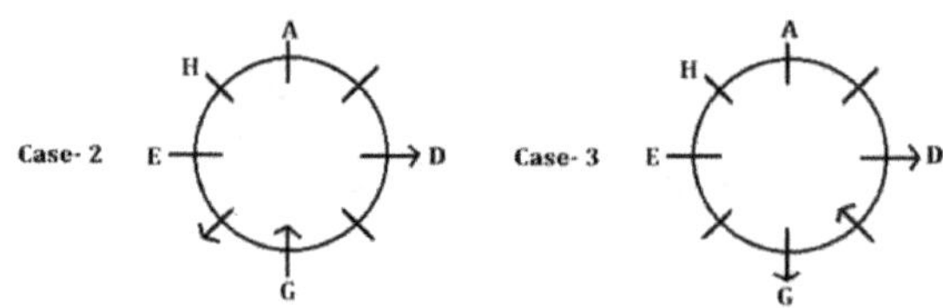

C sits second to the left of B. F sits second to the left of C. By these conditions Case-3 is cancelled. Immediate neighbours of D face opposite direction. F does not face the same direction as A. So new arrangement will be-

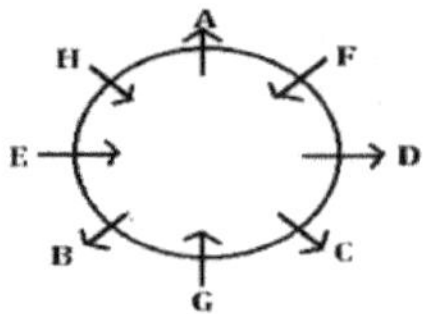

24. (c)   **25. (b)**   **26. (a)**
27. (a)   **28. (d)**
29. (a) I. W > F (True)   II. O > D (False)
30. (c) I. L > W (False)   II. O = W (False)
31. (b) I. M < S (False)   II. C > Q (True)
32. (a)

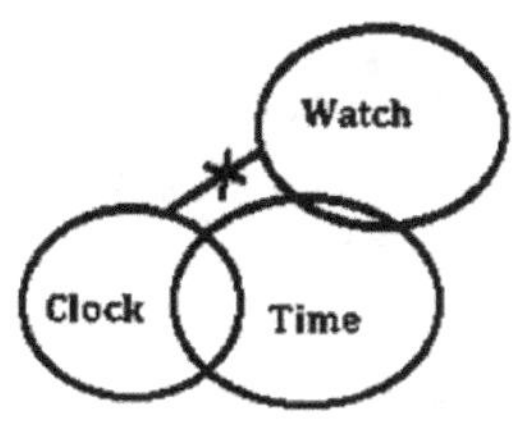

33. (a)

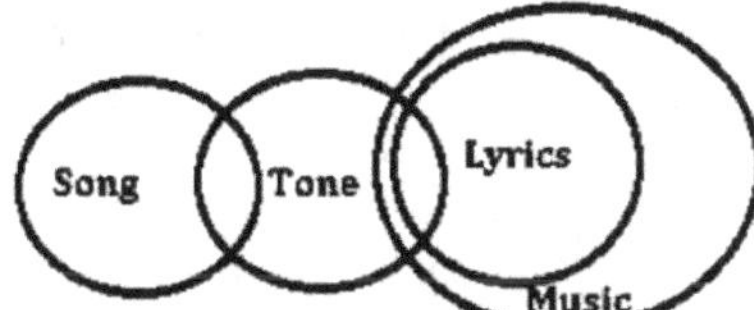

34. (b)

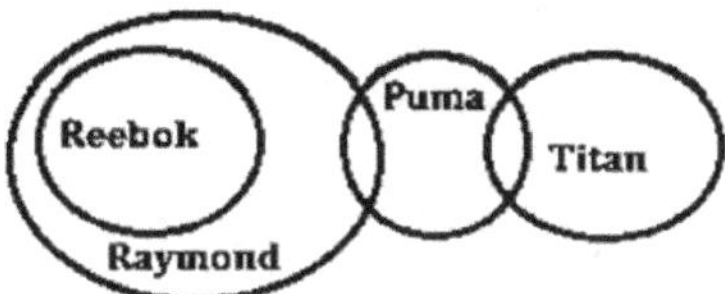

35. (d)

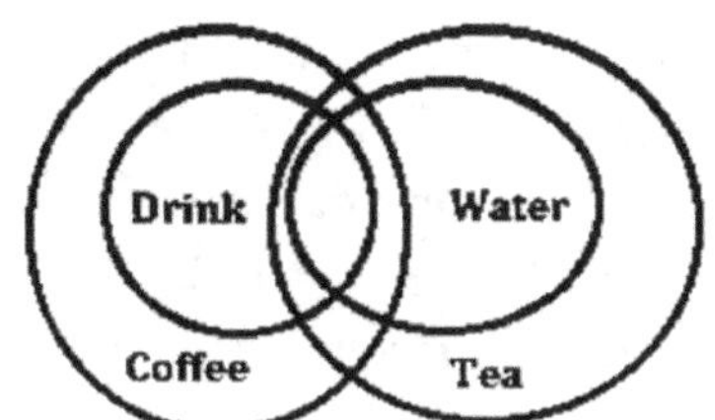

Direction (36-40):

Words	Codes
Human	fg
Are	wq
Intelligent	dl
Person	kp
Emotionally	nm
Here	bg
Student/becomes	fv/ut
Today	py
You	ft

36. (b) **37.(a)** **38.(e)**

39. (a) **40.(c)**

QUANTITATIVE APTITUDE

41. (c) $\frac{7}{8} \times 888 + \frac{25}{3} \times 6 = ? + 784$

$777 + 50 = ? + 784$

$? = 43$

42. (b) $\frac{51}{4} \times \frac{22}{3} \times \frac{2}{17} \times \frac{12}{11} = ?$

$? = 12$

43. (c) $(2.5)^2 + ? \times 0.5 = (3.2)^2$

$? = \frac{10.24 - 6.25}{0.5}$

$? = \frac{3.99}{0.5} = 7.98$

44. (a) $\frac{4}{8} \times 36 = ?$

$? = 18$

45. (c) $\frac{?-49}{14} \times 50 = \frac{150}{7}$

$? - 49 = 6$

$? = 55$

46. (a) $? = 2081 - 1853$

$? = 228$

47. (b) $\frac{1600 \times 8}{50 \times 16} = 25 - ?$

$? = 25 - 16$

$? = 9$

48. (b) $\frac{76}{100} \times 340 - \frac{152}{100} \times 170 = ?$

$? = 258.4 - 258.4$

$? = 0$

49. (d) $\frac{4}{5} \times 35 \div \left(\frac{1}{3} \times 9\right) = ? + \frac{1}{3}$

$\frac{28}{3} = ? + \frac{1}{3}$

$? = 9$

50. (c) $\frac{5}{8} \times \frac{160}{100} \times ? = 15 \times 4$

$? = 60$

51. (d) Required percentage $= \frac{320 + 280}{320 + 180} \times 100$

$= \frac{600}{500} \times 100 = 120\%$

52. (a) Required difference

$= 360 - 240 = 120 \, runs$

53. (d) Required ratio

$= \frac{320 + 240 + 280 + 380 + 250}{360 + 320 + 220 + 300 + 180} = \frac{1470}{1380} = \frac{49}{46}$

54. (b) Required percentage $= \frac{300 - 240}{300} \times 100$

$= 20\%$

55. (c) From graph, it is clearly visible that Australia won 3 matches i.e. third, fourth and fifth match.

56. (e) Required average

$= \frac{360 + 320 + 220 + 300}{4} = \frac{1200}{4} = 300$ runs

57. (b) Time taken by A to complete the work alone $= 4 \times 9 = 36$ hours

Time taken by B to complete the work alone $= 9 \times 5 = 45$ hours

Let total work be 180 units (LCM)

So, efficiency of A and B are 5 units/hour and 4 units/hour respectively.

ATQ

Two day work of A and B working 5 hours a day $= (5 + 4) \times 5 = 45$ units

So, total time taken by them to complete the work $= \frac{180}{45} \times 2 = 8$ days

58. (d) Monthly income of Hemant
$= 18000 \times \frac{100}{100-20} = $ Rs 22500
So, monthly income of Kunal
$= 22500 \times \frac{200}{300} = $ Rs 15000

59. (a) Let distance be D km
ATQ
$\frac{4}{60} = \frac{D}{36} - \frac{D}{45}$
$\Rightarrow \frac{1}{15} = \frac{5D-4D}{180} \Rightarrow D = 12$ km

60. (e) Let the capacity of the tank be 60 units (LCM)
So, the efficiency of the pipe A, pipe B and pipe C be 4 units/min, 3 units/min and 2 units/min respectively.
So, required time $= \frac{60}{(4+3-2)} = \frac{60}{5} = 12$ min

61. (d)

6	18	33	57	108	[240]	615

$+12 \quad +15 \quad +24 \quad +51 \quad +132 \quad +375$

$+3 \quad +9 \quad +27 \quad +81 \quad +243$

62. (a) The pattern is
$\boxed{0} + 8 \times 1 = 8$
$8 + 8 \times 3 = 32$
$32 + 8 \times 5 = 72$
$72 + 8 \times 7 = 128$
$128 + 8 \times 9 = 200$

63. (c) The pattern is $\times 1, \times 2, \times 3, \times 4, \times 5 \ldots\ldots$
So, $? = 720 \times 6 = 4320$

64. (b)

8	21	47	86	138	203	[281]

$+13 \quad +26 \quad +39 \quad +52 \quad +65 \quad +78$

$+13 \quad +13 \quad +13 \quad +13 \quad +13$

65. (e) The pattern is $\times 2, \div 3, \times 4, \div 5, \times 6$
So, the no. is $80 \div 5 = \boxed{16}$

66. (b) From quantity I,
Let cost price of the book be Rs 100x.
ATQ
$105x - 95x = 18$
$x = 1.8$
So, cost price of book $= 100x = $ Rs 180
From quantity II,
Selling price of bottle
$= 160 \times \frac{150}{100} \times \frac{5}{6} = $ Rs 200
$\therefore$ quantity II > quantity I

67. (b) From quantity I,
$35x^2 - 41x + 12 = 0$
$35x^2 - 20x - 21x + 12 = 0$
$5x(7x - 4) - 3(7x - 4) = 0$
$(5x - 3)(7x - 4) = 0$
$x = \frac{3}{5}, \frac{4}{7}$
From quantity II,

$9y^2 - 18y + 8 = 0$
$9y^2 - 12y - 6y + 8 = 0$
$3y(3y - 4) - 2(3y - 4) = 0$
$(3y - 4)(3y - 2) = 0$
$y = \frac{2}{3}, \frac{4}{3}$
$\therefore$ quantity II > quantity I

68. (a) From quantity I,
Let leakage takes T minutes to empty the tank alone.
ATQ
Let pipe A and pipe B together takes x minutes to fill the tank
Time taken by pipe A and B together to fill the tank
$\Rightarrow x \left[\frac{1}{20} + \frac{1}{30}\right] = 1 \Rightarrow x = 12$ minutes
Now,
$\Rightarrow (12 + 3) \left[\frac{1}{20} + \frac{1}{30} - \frac{1}{T}\right] = 1$
$\Rightarrow \frac{1}{12} - \frac{1}{T} = \frac{1}{15} \Rightarrow \frac{1}{T} = \frac{1}{60}$
$T = 60$ minutes
$\therefore$ quantity I > quantity II

69. (c) From quantity I,
$x^2 + 5x + 2x + 10 = 0$
$x(x + 5) + 2(x + 5) = 0$
$(x + 5)(x + 2) = 0$
$x = -5, -2$
From quantity II,
$y^2 + 8y + 5y + 40 = 0$
$y(y + 8) + 5(y + 8) = 0$
$(y + 8)(y + 5) = 0$
$y = -8, -5$
$\therefore$ quantity I $\geq$ quantity II

70. (b) From quantity I,
Let total distance covered by man is D km.
ATQ
$8 = \frac{\frac{D}{2}}{20} + \frac{\frac{D}{2}}{30} \Rightarrow 8 = \frac{D}{40} + \frac{D}{60}$
$D = \frac{120 \times 8}{5} = 192$ km
From quantity II,
Distance covered by boat
$= 10 \times (15 - 5) + 5 \times (15 + 5)$
$= 100 + 100 = 200$ km
$\therefore$ quantity II > quantity I

71. (c) Let cost price of the article be Rs 100x.
ATQ
$100x \times \frac{140}{100} \times \frac{85}{100} - 100x = 304$
$19x = 304 \Rightarrow x = 16$
So, selling price of the article $= 100x \times \frac{140}{100} \times \frac{85}{100} = 119x = $ Rs 1904

72. (d) Let present age of Deepak, Sanjay and Harish be x, y and z years respectively.
ATQ,
$\Rightarrow \frac{x-4}{y-4} = \frac{3}{4}$
$4x - 3y = 4 \ \ldots\ldots. \text{(i)}$
$\Rightarrow x + y + z = 26 \times 3 = 78 \ \ldots.. \text{(ii)}$

$\Rightarrow z = y - 11$ ..... (iii)

From (i), (ii) and (iii)

$x = 25, y = 32, z = 21$

So, present age of Sanjay = $y = 32$ years

73. (d) Required no. $= \frac{5! \times 2!}{2!} = 5! = 120$

74. (a) Quantity of sugar in mixture initially

$= 700 \times \frac{60}{100} = 420$ gram

Let sugar added in the solution be x gram.

ATQ

$\frac{420 + x}{700 + x} = \frac{80}{100}$

$2100 + 5x = 2800 + 4x \Rightarrow x = 700$ gram

75. (c) Required average

$= \frac{450 + 400 + 500 + 350}{4} = \frac{1700}{4} = 425$

76. (d) Students enrolled in B.SC

$= \frac{20}{100} \times 400 = 80$

Students enrolled in BCA

$= \frac{(100 - 20 - 30)}{100} \times 400 = 200$

Required difference $= 200 - 80 = 120$

77. (a) Required percentage

$= \frac{(600 + 550) - (600 + 400)}{(600 + 400)} \times 100$

$= \frac{150}{1000} \times 100 = 15\%$

78. (b) No. of girls in college B in 2016

$= \frac{3}{8} \times 400 = 150$

And no. of boys in college C in 2017

$= \frac{5}{12} \times 600 = 250$

Required ratio $= \frac{150}{250} = \frac{3}{5}$

79. (e) Required percentage $= \frac{700}{500} \times 100 = 140\%$

80. (d) Required difference $= (600 + 450 + 500 + 350) - (300 + 350 + 400 + 500)$

$= 1900 - 1550 = 350$

REASONING ABILITY

Directions (1-5): Study the following information carefully and answer the questions given below:

Eight persons i.e. P, Q, R, S, T, U, V and W are sitting around a rectangular table with four of them sitting at the corners of the table, facing inside. The rest are sitting at the middle of the sides of this rectangular table and they are facing outside.

P sits third to the right of T. S sits to the immediate left of T. Q sits to the immediate right of V. V sits at the middle of the table. U sits opposite W. W does not sit next to S. T does not face Q.

1. Who among the following sits to the immediate left of Q?
   (a) U (b) P
   (c) T (d) R
   (e) None of these

2. Who among the following sits to the immediate right of P?
   (a) S (b) W
   (c) Q (d) R
   (e) None of these

3. Who among the following sits to the immediate right of R?
   (a) P (b) Q
   (c) T (d) S
   (e) None of these

4. Who among the following sits second to the right of V?
   (a) P (b) Q
   (c) R (d) U
   (e) None of these

5. Who among the following sits second to the left of R?
   (a) U (b) Q
   (c) V (d) S
   (e) None of these

Directions (6-10): Study the following information carefully and answer the questions given below:

J $ 3 # @ 4 K * 4 P ^ $ 4 # L & 3 * M 2 % * N 2 B & 1 % I * 6 O # 7 @ 9 8 P

6. How many numbers are there which are immediately followed by letters and are immediately preceded by symbols?
   (a) one (b) two
   (c) three (d) four
   (e) None of these

7. How many symbols are there which are immediately followed by letters and are immediately preceded by numbers?
   (a) one (b) two
   (c) three (d) four
   (e) None of these

8. How many numbers are there which are immediately followed by symbols and are immediately preceded by letters?
   (a) one (b) two
   (c) three (d) four
   (e) None of these

9. Which element is sixth from the right end of the series?
   (a) $ (b) #
   (c) 4 (d) P
   (e) None of these

10. Which element is third to the right of the one which is ninth from the right end of the series?
    (a) 4 (b) @
    (c) # (d) %
    (e) None of the above

Direction (11-12): Study the following information carefully and answer the questions given below:

In a family, there are eight members and only 3 generations. A is the husband of B. D is the brother-in-law of B. P is the father of only two girls. P is the father of B. E is the niece of D. F is the cousin of E. C is the daughter of Q. Q is not the wife of D. D is not the brother of A.

11. How is F related with respect to C?
    (a) daughter (b) son
    (c) brother (d) mother
    (e) Cannot be determined

12. How is Q related with respect to F?
    (a) grandfather
    (b) grandmother
    (c) brother
    (d) sister
    (e) None of these

Direction (13-15): Study the following information carefully and answer the questions given below:

Kapil starts his journey from point O. From there he moves 10m.tothe east, then he turns to his right and walks 10m. Then again he turns to his right and walks for 10m. to reach point P. From point P he moves 10m. in the South direction and finally he turns to his left and walks 10m. to reach point X.

13. What is the total distance covered by Kapil from point O to point X?

(a) 50m.   (b) 80m.
(c) 70m.   (d) 60m.
(e) None of these

14. In which direction is point X with respect to point O?
(a) east   (b) north
(c) north-west   (d) south-east
(e) None of these

15. In which direction is point O with respect to point P?
(a) north   (b) north-east
(c) south-west   (d) south
(e) None of these

Direction (16-20): Study the following information carefully and answer the questions given below:

Eight persons i.e. J, K, L, M, N, O, P and Q are sitting in two parallel rows i.e. row 1 and row 2. Four persons are sitting in row 1 and they are facing the south direction. Rest are sitting in row 2 and are facing north.

J faces the one who sits third to the left of Q. One person sits between J and K. P sits to the immediate left of O. O and P do not face J. L faces the one who sits third to the right of N. N does not face Q. L does not sit in row 2.

16. Who among the following sits to the immediate left of Q?
(a) J   (b) K
(c) L   (d) N
(e) None of these

17. Who among the following sits to the immediate right of L?
(a) J   (b) L
(c) M   (d) K
(e) No one

18. Who among the following sits to the immediate right of K?
(a) J   (b) K
(c) M   (d) L
(e) None of these

19. Who among the following sits second to the left of O?
(a) K   (b) N
(c) J   (d) L
(e) None of these

20. Who among the following sits second to the left of M?
(a) L   (b) J
(c) K   (d) Q
(e) None of these

Direction (21-23): In each of the questions below are given some statements followed by two conclusions. You have to assume that the given statements are true, even if they seem to be at variance with commonly known facts. Read all the conclusions and then decide which of the given conclusions logically follows from the given statements disregarding commonly known facts.
(a) If only conclusion I follows.
(b) If only conclusion II follows.
(c) If either conclusion I or II follows.
(d) If neither conclusion I nor II follows.
(e) If both conclusions I and II follow.

21. Statements: All Laptop are HP.
                No Laptop is Dell.
Conclusion: I. All HP can never be Dell.
            II. Some HP are Dell.

22. Statements: Only a few Book are Paper.
                No Paper are Pen.
Conclusion: I. Some Book are Pen.
            II. All Book can never be Pen.

23. Statements: Only Book are Pencil.
                No Book are Cat.
Conclusion: I. Some Book are Cat.
            II. Some Pencil can be Cat

24. How many pairs of letters are there in the word **'HELICOPTER'**, if each of which have as many letters between then in the word as they have between them in the English alphabet backwards or forwards?
(a) one   (b) two
(c) three   (d) Four
(e) More than four

25. If the number "981245367" is arranged in a descending order, then how many numbers are there which remained unchanged?
(a) one   (b) two
(c) three   (d) four
(e) More than four

Directions (26-30): Study the following information carefully and answer the questions given below:

Six persons i.e. P, Q, R, S, T and U were born in six different months i.e. January, February, March, April, May and June of the same year. Each of them likes a different colour i.e. Cyan, Purple, Magenta, Blue, Pink and Grey. No two persons like the same colour. No two persons were born in same month. The year in which they were born is not a leap year.

Two persons were born between the one who likes Purple and U. The one who likes Blue was born after the one who likes Cyan, but before the one who likes Grey. Three persons were born between R and the one who likes Pink. R was born before the one who likes Pink Colour. Two persons were born between the one who likes Pink colour and the one who likes Magenta. One person was born between the one who likes Magenta and Q. P was born just before S. S was born in a month that has odd number of days.

26. Who among the following was born just before the one who likes Blue colour?
    (a) S   (b) P
    (c) Q   (d) R
    (e) None of these

27. Who among the following was born in the month of May?
    (a) T   (b) P
    (c) Q   (d) R
    (e) None of these

28. Who among the following was born in the month of June?
    (a) P   (b) Q
    (c) U   (d) R
    (e) None of these

29. Who among the following was born just after the one who likes Cyan colour?
    (a) R   (b) Q
    (c) S   (d) P
    (e) None of these

30. Who among the following likes the colour Pink?
    (a) U   (b) Q
    (c) T   (d) S
    (e) None of these

Directions (31-35): In each of the questions below are given some statements followed by two conclusions. You have to take the given statements to be true even if they seem to be at variance with commonly known facts. Read all the conclusions and then decide which of the given conclusions logically follows from the given statements disregarding commonly known facts.
(a) If only conclusion I follows.
(b) If only conclusion II follows.
(c) If either conclusion I or II follows.
(d) If neither conclusion I nor II follows.
(e) If both conclusions I and II follow.

31. **Statements:** J>K<L; L<M≤N; N>O
    Conclusion: I. J>N   **II.** O>M

32. **Statements:** P>Q>R; R<J<K; K=Z
    Conclusion: I. P>K   **II.** Z>P

33. **Statements:** J>K>L; L<P=Q; Q<N
    Conclusion I. J>L   **II.** N>J

34. **Statements:** P<Q<R; R>F>G; G>H
    Conclusion I. G>R   **II.** R>H

35. **Statements:** J<D<S; S=N>B; B>M
    Conclusion **I.** M>N   **II.**B>J

Directions (36-40): Study the following information carefully and answer the questions given below:

Eight boxes i.e. P, Q, R, S, T, U, V and W are kept one above the other. Box V is kept just above Box U. Box Q is not kept immediately below Box P. Five boxes are kept between Box P and Box U. There are as many boxes kept above P as there are below W. Box P is kept above box U. Box Q was kept just above the Box S and Box T was placed just below Box S.

36. Which among the following boxes is kept immediately below the Box P?
    (a) S   (b) R
    (c) Q   (d) T
    (e) None of these

37. Which among the following boxes is kept at the top?
    (a) T   (b) R
    (c) Q   (d) P
    (e) None of these

38. Which among the following boxes is kept at the bottom?
    (a) P   (b) Q
    (c) W   (d) R
    (e) None of these

39. Which among the following boxes is kept just below Box U?
    (a) R   (b) Q
    (c) S   (d) W
    (e) None of these

40. Which among the following boxes is kept just above Box V?
    (a) U   (b) Q
    (c) P   (d) T
    (e) None of these

Quantitative Aptitude

Directions (41-45): What approximate value should come in place of question mark (?) in the following questions.

41. 17.97% of 649.9 – 8.02% of 1149.99 = $?^2$
    (a) 4   (b) 5   (c) 3
    (d) 6   (e) 7

42. $\frac{?-7.97}{12.04+8.02} \times (5.997)^2 = 72$
    (a) 48   (b) 36   (c) 54
    (d) 32   (e) 40

43. 30.08% of $\frac{4}{7}th$ of $\frac{1}{8}th$ of 419.91 = ?
    (a) 6   (b) 18   (c) 15
    (d) 12   (e) 9

44. $719.97 \div 80.02 \div 60.07 \times 119.97$
(a) 14 (b) 20 (c) 18
(d) 10 (e) 24

45. $899.9 \times 25.02 \div 36 = (? + 17)^2$
(a) 10 (b) 5 (c) 18
(d) 12 (e) 8

Directions (46-50): The table given below shows the no. of books published by four different publishers in four months. Study the data and answer the following questions.

Publisher/Month	February	March	April	May
A	2000	2400	1800	2500
B	1500	1850	2000	2100
C	1750	2000	2250	2400
D	1200	1350	800	1250

46. What is the average no. of books published by A in all the given months?
(a) 1740 (b) 2275 (c) 2050
(d) 2175 (e) 2250

47. Books published by B in February and March together is what percent more/less than that by C in March and April? (approximate)
(a) 21% (b) 24% (c) 16%
(d)12% (e) 27%

48. Find the ratio between books published by C to D in all the given months.
(a) 23:45 (b) 24:43 (c) 42:23
(d) 41:25 (e) 23:42

49. Find the revenue obtained by B in March and how much more/less is it than D's revenue in the same month, if selling price of the book is Rs. 120 and all the books are sold. (Note: cost price and selling price of each book is same for all publishers)
(a) Rs. 50,000 (b) Rs. 40,000 (c) Rs. 55,000
(d) Rs. 70,000 (e) Rs. 60,000

50. Books published by A in April is what percent of books published by C in March?
(a) $\frac{1000}{9}$% (b) 90% (c) 10%
(d) $\frac{100}{9}$% (e) 75%

51. A train travelling at 54 kmph. crosses another train, which is its length and was movingin opposite direction at 36 kmph. in 48 seconds. It also passed a railway platform in 100 seconds. Find the length of the platform.
(a) 400 m. (b) 600 m. (c) 700 m.
(d) 900 m. (e) 500 m.

52. By selling an article at Rs. 900, a shopkeeper suffers a loss of 25%. Find, to make a profit of 20% he should sell the article at how much price?
(a) Rs. 1200 (b) Rs. 1320 (c) Rs. 1180
(d)Rs. 1440 (e) Rs. 1560

53. Find the difference between interest earned on the amount of Rs. 20000 at CI and SI at the same rate of interest of 15% per annum and forthe same time of 2 years.
(a) Rs. 450 (b) Rs. 540 (c) Rs. 620
(d)Rs. 480 (e) Rs. 520

54. P, Q and R can do a piece of work in 8 days, 12 days and 20 days respectively. If the total wage earned by them is Rs. 3720, then how much more/less is Q's wage than R.
(a) Rs. 520 (b) Rs. 480 (c) Rs. 660
(d)Rs. 620 (e) Rs. 450

55. In a series of 11 matches of Cricket, average runs scored by Rohit Sharma was85. In the first four matches his average run rate was 72 and in the next six matches his average run rate was 90. How many runs were scored by Rohit Sharma in the last match?
(a) 115 (b) 120 (c) 107
(d) 97 (e) 112

Direction (56-60) Replace the question mark (?) with missing no. in the following series?

56. 64, 32, 32, 48, 96, 240, ?
(a) 360 (b) 324 (c) 720
(d) 576 (e) 600

57. 5, 16, 38, 71, 115, ?, 236
(a) 140 (b) 159 (c) 181
(d) 170 (e) 178

58. 1, ?, 17, 53, 161, 485, 1457
(a) 3 (b) 5 (c) 7
(d)9 (e) 12

59. 7.1, 7.7, 8.9, 10.7, 13.1, 16.1, ?
(a) 19.7 (b) 19.3 (c) 18.7
(d) 18.3 (e) 20.1

60. 3, 5, 10, 20, 37, 63, ?
(a) 90 (b) 115 (c) 95
(d) 80 (e) 100

Directions (61-65): The line graph shows the no. of consumers of alcohol and cigarettes in a state in five different years. Study the graph carefully and answer the following questions.

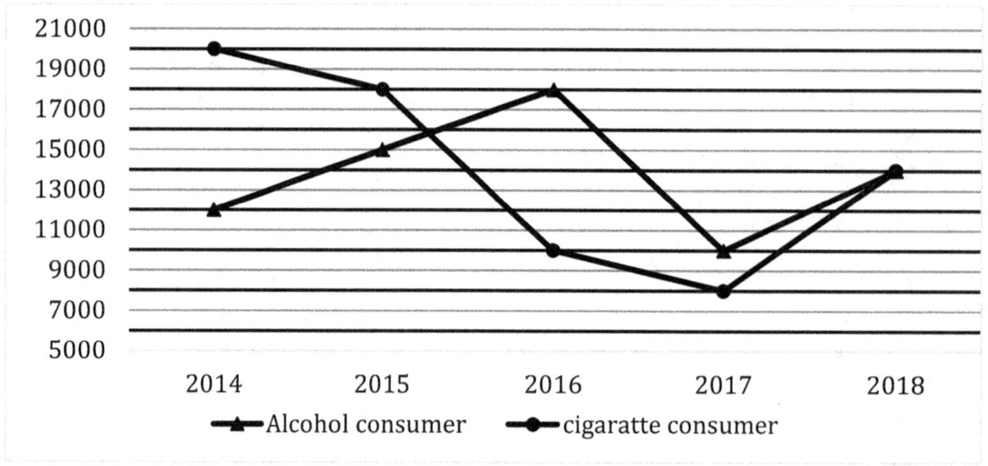

61. Find the ratio between alcohol consumers in 2014 and 2016 together to the cigarette consumers in 2016 and 2017 together.
(a) 5:6   (b) 5:3   (c) 10:9
(d) 5:4   (e) 7:6

62. Find the no. of alcohol consumers that increased or decreased in 2018 over 2014.
(a) 4000   (b) 3000   (c) 2000
(d) 5000   (e) 6000

63. What is the average no. of cigarette consumers over all the years?
(a) 12000   (b) 15000   (c) 13000
(d) 14000   (e) 16000

64. Cigarette consumers is what percent of alcohol consumers in 2015?
(a) 120%   (b) 83.33%   (c) 125%
(d) 150%   (e) 78%

65. Alcohol consumers in 2015 and 2017 together is what percent more/less than cigarette consumers in 2014 and 2016 together?
(a) 16.67%   (b) 23.25%   (c) 17.25%
(d) 20%   (e) 12.5%

Directions (66-70): What value should come in place of (?) in the following questions?

66. $2\frac{3}{5} + 3\frac{4}{5} - 2\frac{3}{4} - 7\frac{1}{4} = ? -4\frac{3}{5}$
(a) 5   (b) 1   (c) 2
(d) 10   (e) 4

67. $0.016 \times 2.16 \div 0.6 \div 0.18 = ?$
(a) 32   (b) 0.32   (c) 3.2
(d) 0.032   (e) 320

68. $(17)^2 - 676 + \frac{200}{3}\%$ of $600 = ?$
(a) 17   (b) 21   (c) 13
(d) 15   (e) 9

69. ?% of $20 - 450\%$ of $50 = \sqrt{784}$
(a) 1565   (b) 1625   (c) 1265
(d) 1345   (e) 1525

70. $\frac{(0.5)^2 - (0.3)^2}{0.5 + 0.3} = ?$
(a) 0.5   (b) 0.02   (c) 2

(d) 5   (e) 0.2

Directions (71-75): Study the following paragraph and answer the questions below:

Four friends A, B, C and D have a total of Rs 54,000 and they invest this amount in four different schemes. A invests Rs 12,000 for four years at SI at 15% per annum. C invests Rs 20,000 for three years at 10% compounded annually. B invests Rs 15,000 at the rate of 12.5% per annum at SI and he earned interest of Rs 9,375. D invested the remaining amount for 1.5 years compounded half yearly and received a total amount of Rs 9317.

71. What was the duration of B's investment?
(a) 3 years   (b) 2 years   (c) 5 years
(d) 4 years   (e) 6 years

72. What is total amount received by A after 4 years?
(a) Rs 9200   (b) Rs 15200   (c) Rs 7200
(d) Rs 19200   (e) Rs 16200

73. What is the rate of interest per year at which D invests?
(a) 15%   (b) 20%   (c) 5%
(d) 25%   (e) 10%

74. Interest earned by C is how much more/less than that of A?
(a) Rs 580   (b) Rs 460   (c) Rs 520
(d) Rs 560   (e) Rs 640

75. Interest earned by B is approximately what percent of interest earned by A?
(a) 120%   (b) 110%   (c) 75%
(d) 150%   (e) 130%

Directions (76-80): In the following questions, calculate quantity I and quantity II, compare them and answer,
(a) If quantity I > quantity II
(b) If quantity I < quantity II
(c) If quantity I ≥ quantity II
(d) if quantity I ≤ quantity II

(e) if quantity I = quantity II or no relation can be established

76. A shopkeeper marked up the price of an article 50% above cost price.

Quantity I, profit (in Rs.): The shopkeeper gave two successive discounts of 10% and 15% on the article. The selling price of article was Rs. 229.5.

Quantity II, discount (in Rs.): Shopkeeper sold the article for Rs 253 and made a profit of 15%.

77. Quantity I, interest earned: A person invests Rs. 15,000 at SI for 4 years at rate of 12.5% per annum.

Quantity II, interest earned: A person invests Rs. 12,500 at CI for 3 years at rate of 20%.

78. Quantity I, x: $7x^2 - 23x + 18 = 0$

Quantity II, y: $3y^2 - 16y + 21 = 0$

79. A boat takes 10 hours to cover a distance of 800 kms. in downstream and 20 hours to cover the same distance in upstream.

Quantity I: Distance covered by the boat in downstream in 7 hours.

Quantity II: Distance covered by the boat in upstream in 13 hours.

80. Two persons A and C together can complete a piece of work in 10 days while B alone can complete the same piece of work in 24 days. A is twice as efficient as C.

Quantity I: Time taken by B and C together to complete the work.

Quantity II: Time taken by A and B together to complete the work

Solutions

REASONING ABILITY

Direction (1-5): From the given condition P sits third to the right of T. S sits to the immediate left of T. Q sits to the immediate right of V. V sits at the middle side of table. U sits opposite to W. W does not sit next to S.

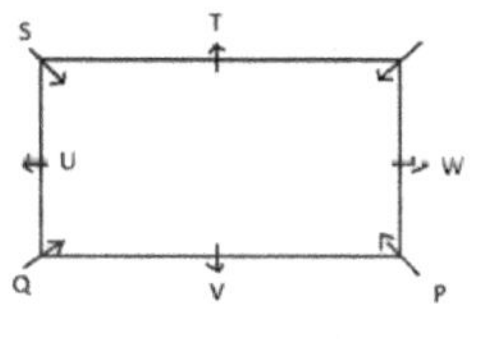

Case 1

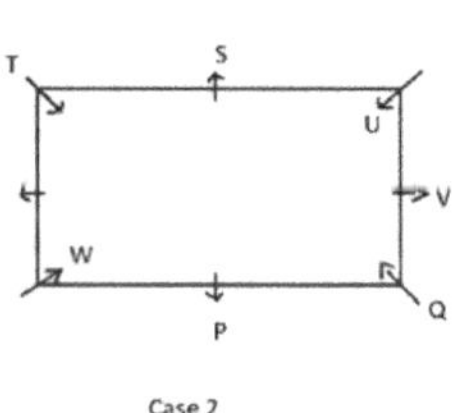

Case 2

T does not face Q. Hence, Case 2 gets cancelled.

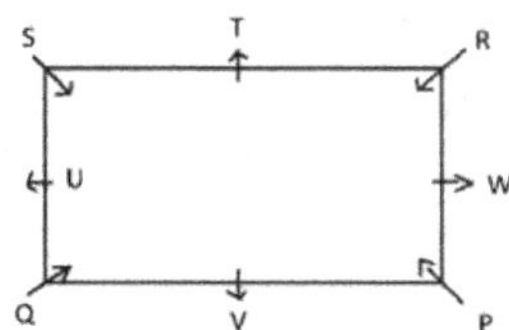

1. (a) 2. (b) 3. (c)
4. (d) 5. (e)

Directions (6-10):
6. (c) (@4K), (*4P) and (*6O)
7. (c) (4#L), (3*M) and (1%I)
8. (a) (M2%)
9. (b)
10. (c)

Directions (11-12):

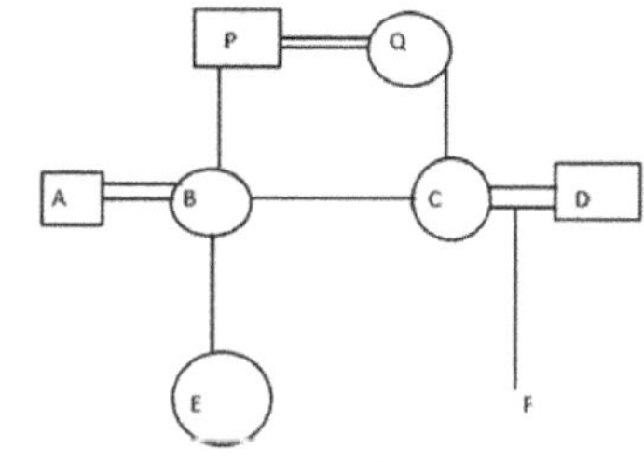

11. (e) 12. (b)

Direction (13-15):

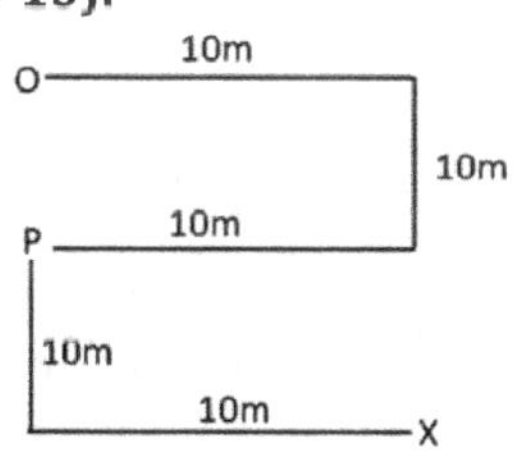

13. (a) 14. (d) 15. (a)

Direction (16-20): From the given conditions, J faces the one who sits third to the left of Q. One person sits between J and K. P sits to the immediate left of O. O and P does not face J. L faces the one who sits third to the right of N. N does not face Q.

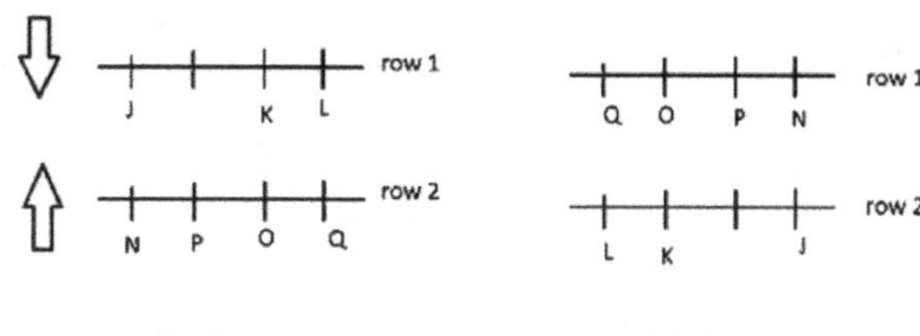

Case 1 Case 2

L does not sit in row 2. Hence, case 2 gets eliminated.

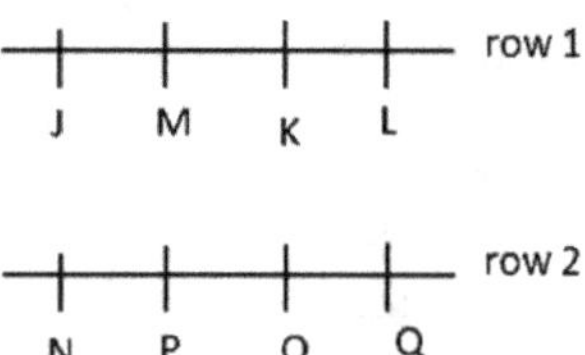

16. (e)   **17. (d)**   **18. (c)**
19. (b)   **20. (a)**

Direction (21-23):

21. (a)

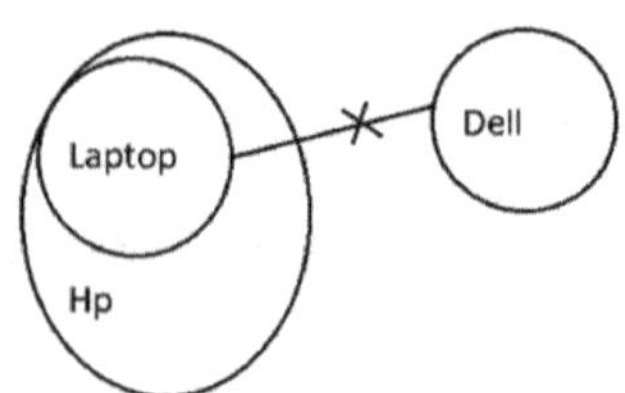

22. (b)

23. (d)

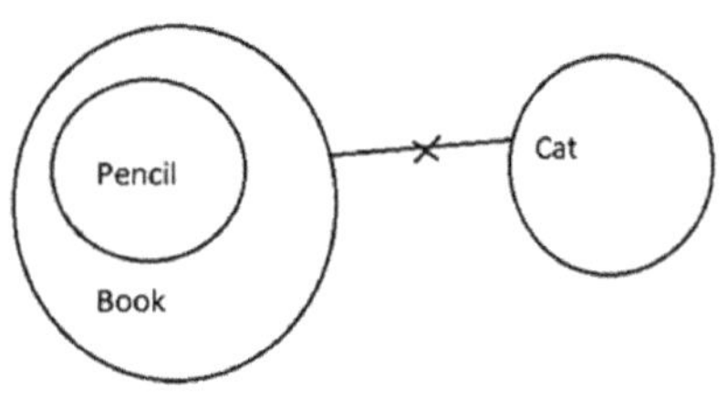

24. (d)
25. (c)

Direction (26-30): From the given conditions:

Three persons were born between R and the one who likes Pink. R was born before the one who likes Pink Colour. Two persons were born between the one who likes Pink colour and the one who likes Magenta. One person was born between the one who likes Magenta and Q. P was born just before S. S was born in a month that has an odd number of days.

Months	Case 1 Person	Case 1 Colours	Case 2 Persons	Case 2 Colours
January	R		Q	
February	P	Magenta	R	
March	S			Magenta
April	Q		P	
May		Pink	S	
June				Pink

Two persons were born between the one who likes Purple and U. Here, case 2 gets eliminated. The one who likes Blue was born after the one who likes Cyan but before the one who likes Grey.

Months	Persons	Colours
January	R	Cyan
February	P	Magenta
March	S	Purple
April	Q	Blue
May	T	Pink
June	U	Grey

26. (a)   **27. (a)**   **28. (c)**
29. (d)   **30. (c)**

Direction (31-35):
31. (d) I. J>N (False)   II. O>M (False)
32. (d) I. P>K (False)   II. Z>P (False)
33. (a) I. J>L (True)   II. N>J (False)
34. (b) I. G>R (False)   II. R>H (True)
35. (d) I. M>N (False)   II. B>J (False)

Direction (36-40): From the given conditions: Five boxes are kept between the Box P and Box U. As many boxes are kept above P as there are below W. Box P is kept above Box U. Here, there are two cases possible i.e. case 1 and case 2.

Case 1	Case 2
P	
	P
U	W
W	U

Box V is kept just above box U. Hence, case 2 gets eliminated. Box Q is not kept immediately below Box P. Box Q is kept just above Box S and Box T is placed just below Box S.

Boxes
P
R
Q
S
T
V
U
W

36. (b)   **37. (d)**   **38. (c)**
39. (d)   **40. (d)**

41. (b) $\frac{18}{100} \times 650 - \frac{8}{100} \times 1150 \approx ?^2$

$117 - 92 \approx ?^2$

$?^2 \approx 25$

$? \approx 5$

42. (a) $\frac{?-8}{20} \times 36 \approx 72$

$? - 8 \approx \frac{72 \times 20}{36}$

$? \approx 40 + 8$

$? \approx 48$

43. (e) $\frac{30}{100} \times \frac{4}{7} \times \frac{1}{8} \times 420 \approx ?$

$? \approx 9$

44. (c) $720 \times \frac{1}{80} \times \frac{1}{60} \times 120 \approx ?$

$? \approx 18$

45. (e) $\frac{900 \times 25}{36} \approx (?+17)^2$

$(?+17)^2 \approx 625$

$? + 17 \approx 25$

$? \approx 8$

46. (d) Required average $= \frac{2000+2400+1800+2500}{4} =$

$\frac{8700}{4}$

$= 2175$

47. (a) Required percentage

$= \frac{(2000+2250)-(1500+1850)}{(2000+2250)} \times 100$

$= \frac{4250-3350}{4250} \times 100 = \frac{900}{4250} \times 100$

$= \frac{360}{17} = 21.176 \simeq 21\%$

48. (c) Required ratio $= \frac{1750+2000+2250+2400}{1200+1350+800+1250} = \frac{8400}{4600}$

$= 42 : 23$

49. (e) Difference in revenue $= (1850 - 1350) \times$

$120 = 500 \times 120$

$= $ Rs 60,000

50. (b) Required percentage $= \frac{1800}{2000} \times 100 = 90\%$

51. (c) Let length of the train be 2x meter.

ATQ

$48 = \frac{2x+x}{(54+36)\times\frac{5}{18}}$

$48 = \frac{3x}{25}$

$x = 400$ m

So, length of train $= 2x = 800$ m

Now, let length of the platform be L meter.

$100 = \frac{L+800}{54\times\frac{5}{18}}$

$L + 800 = 1500$

$L = 700$ meter

52. (d) Let cost price of the article be Rs. x.

ATQ

$x \times \frac{75}{100} = 900$

$x = $ Rs 1200

So, required selling price

$= 1200 \times \frac{120}{100} = $ Rs 1440

53. (a) Interest earned at CI

$= 20000\left[\left(1 + \frac{15}{100}\right)^2 - 1\right]$

$= 20000\left(\frac{529-400}{400}\right) = $ Rs 6450

Interest earned at SI

$= \frac{20000\times15\times2}{100} = $ Rs 6000

So, required difference

$= 6450 - 6000 = $ Rs 450

Alternate,

Let P be the amount, R be the rate of interest and D be the difference between interest earned at SI and CI after two years.

ATQ

$D = \frac{PR^2}{100^2} = \frac{20000\times225}{10000} = $ Rs 450

54. (b) Let total work be 120 units (LCM)

So, efficiency of P, Q and R be 15, 10 and 6 units/day respectively.

So, required difference in wages

$= \left(\frac{10}{31} - \frac{6}{31}\right) \times 3720$

$= \frac{4}{31} \times 3720 = $ Rs 480

55. (c) Total score of Rohit Sharma in 11 matches

$= 11 \times 85 = 935$

Total score in first four matches

$= 4 \times 72 = 288$

Total score in next six matches

$= 6 \times 90 = 540$

So, required runs

$= 935 - 288 - 540 = 107$

56. (c) $64 \times 0.5 = 32$

$32 \times 1 = 32$

$32 \times 1.5 = 48$

$48 \times 2 = 96$

$96 \times 2.5 = 240$

$? = 240 \times 3 = 720$

57. (d)

$5 \quad 16 \quad 38 \quad 71 \quad 115 \quad 170 \quad 236$

$\quad +11 \quad +22 \quad +33 \quad +44 \quad +55 \quad +66$

So, missing no. is 170

58. (b) $? = 1 \times 3 + 2 = 5$

$5 \times 3 + 2 = 17$

$17 \times 3 + 2 = 53$

$53 \times 3 + 2 = 161$

$161 \times 3 + 2 = 485$

$485 \times 3 + 2 = 1457$

59. (a)

$$7.1 \;,\; 7.7 \;,\; 8.9 \;,\; 10.7 \;,\; 13.1 \;,\; 16.1 \;,\; 19.7$$
$$+0.6 \quad +1.2 \quad +1.8 \quad +2.4 \quad +3.0 \quad +3.6$$
$$+0.6 \quad +0.6 \quad +0.6 \quad +0.6 \quad +0.6$$

So, missing no. is 19.7

60. (e) $3 + (1^2 + 1) = 5$

$5 + (2^2 + 1) = 10$

$10 + (3^2 + 1) = 20$

$20 + (4^2 + 1) = 37$

$37 + (5^2 + 1) = 63$

$? = 63 + (6^2 + 1) = 100$

61. (b) Required ratio $= \dfrac{12000+18000}{10000+8000} = \dfrac{30}{18}$

$= 5:3$

62. (c) Required difference $= 14000 - 12000$

$= 2000$

63. (d) Required average

$= \dfrac{20000+18000+10000+8000+14000}{5} = \dfrac{70000}{5}$

$= 14000$

64. (a) Required percentage $= \dfrac{18000}{15000} \times 100$

$= 120\%$

65. (a) Required percentage

$= \dfrac{(20000+10000)-(15000+10000)}{20000+10000} \times 100$

$= \dfrac{30000-25000}{30000} \times 100$

$= \dfrac{5000}{30000} \times 100 = \dfrac{50}{3}\% = 16.67\%$

66. (b) $\dfrac{13}{5} + \dfrac{19}{5} - \dfrac{11}{4} - \dfrac{29}{4} + \dfrac{23}{5} = ?$

$? = \dfrac{55}{5} - \dfrac{40}{4}$

$? = 11 - 10 = 1$

67. (b) $\dfrac{16}{1000} \times \dfrac{216}{100} \times \dfrac{10}{6} \times \dfrac{100}{18} = ?$

$? = \dfrac{32}{100}$

$? = 0.32$

68. (c) $289 - 676 + \dfrac{200}{300} \times 600 = ?$

$? = 289 - 676 + 400$

$? = 689 - 676$

$? = 13$

69. (c) $\dfrac{?}{100} \times 20 - \dfrac{450}{100} \times 50 = 28$

$\dfrac{?}{5} - 225 = 28$

$? = 253 \times 5$

$? = 1265$

70. (e) $\dfrac{(0.5+0.3)(0.5-0.3)}{0.5+0.3} = ?$

$? = 0.2$

Directions (71-75) Interest earned by A

$$= \dfrac{12000 \times 15 \times 4}{100} = \text{Rs } 7200$$

Interest earned by C $= 20000\left[\left(1 + \dfrac{10}{100}\right)^3\right] - 20000$

$$= 20000\left[\dfrac{1331-1000}{1000}\right] = 20 \times 331$$
$$= \text{Rs } 6620$$

71. (c) Let B invest for T years.

So, $9375 = \dfrac{15000 \times 12.5 \times T}{100}$

$T = \dfrac{9375}{150 \times 12.5} = 5$ years

72. (d) Total amount received by A after 4 years = principal + interest

So, required sum

$= 12000 + 7200 = \text{Rs } 19200$

73. (b) Investment of D$= 54000 - (12000 + 20000 + 15000)$

$= 54000 - 47000 = \text{Rs } 7000$

Let rate of interest for D be R% per annum

So, $9317 = 7000\left(1 + \dfrac{R}{200}\right)^3$

$\dfrac{9317}{7000} = \left(1 + \dfrac{R}{200}\right)^3$

$\dfrac{1331}{1000} = \left(1 + \dfrac{R}{200}\right)^3$

$\dfrac{11}{10} = 1 + \dfrac{R}{200}$

$R = 20\%$

74. (a) Required difference $= 7200 - 6620$

$= \text{Rs } 580$

75. (e) Required percentage $= \dfrac{9375}{7200} \times 100$

$= \dfrac{3215}{24}\% = 130.21\% \approx 130\%$

76. (b) from quantity I,

Let cost price of article be Rs 100x. So marked price of article is Rs 150x.

ATQ

$150x \times \dfrac{90}{100} \times \dfrac{85}{100} = 229.5$

$\dfrac{459}{4}x = 229.5$

$x = 2$

So, profit $= 229.5 - 200 = \text{Rs } 29.5$

From quantity II,

Cost price of article $= 253 \times \dfrac{100}{115} = \text{Rs } 220$

So, discount $= 220 \times \dfrac{150}{100} - 253 = 330 - 253$

$= \text{Rs } 77$

$\therefore$ quantity II > quantity I

77. (b) from quantity I,

Interest earned $= \frac{15000 \times 12.5 \times 4}{100} = $ Rs 7500

From quantity II,

Interests earned $= 12500 \left[\left(1 + \frac{20}{100}\right)^3 - 1 \right]$

$= 12500 \left(\frac{216-125}{125}\right)$

$= $ Rs 9100

$\therefore$ quantity II > quantity I

78. (b) from I,

$7x^2 - 23x + 18 = 0$

$7x^2 - 14x - 9x + 18 = 0$

$7x(x - 2) - 9(x - 2) = 0$

$(7x - 9)(x - 2) = 0$

$x = \frac{9}{7}, 2$

From II,

$3y^2 - 16y + 21 = 0$

$3y^2 - 9y - 7y + 21 = 0$

$3y(y - 3) - 7(y - 3) = 0$

$(3y - 7)(y - 3) = 0$

$y = \frac{7}{3}, 3$

$\therefore$ quantity II > quantity I

79. (a) let x kmph be the speed of boat in downstream and y kmph be the speed of boat in upstream.

ATQ

$x = \frac{800}{10} = 80$ kmph

$y = \frac{800}{20} = 40$ kmph

from I,

required distance $= 7 \times 80 = 560$ km

from II,

required distance $= 13 \times 40 = 520$ km

$\therefore$ quantity I > quantity II

80. (a) Let total work be 120 units (LCM)

So, efficiency of A + C = 12 units/day

And, efficiency of B = 5 units/day

As, A = 2C

3C = 12

C = 4 units/day , A = 8 units/day

From I,

Required time $= \frac{120}{5+4} = \frac{40}{3}$ days

From II,

Required time $= \frac{120}{8+5} = \frac{120}{13}$ days

$\therefore$ quantity I > quantity II

REASONING ABILITY

Directions (1-5): Study the following information carefully and answer the questions given below:

Eight persons i.e. A, B, C, D, E, F, G and H are sitting around a circular table, but not necessarily in the same order. All are facing towards centre.

A sits 3rd to the right of B, who is an immediate neighbour of C. Two persons are sitting between C and D. E sits 2nd to the left of H, who is not an immediate neighbour of A and D. F faces G, who is an immediate neighbour of B.

1. Who among the following persons is facing A?
   (a) C
   (b) D
   (c) E
   (d) F
   (e) None of these

2. Who among the following persons sits to the immediate left of F?
   (a) C
   (b) D
   (c) E
   (d) H
   (e) None of these

3. How many persons sit between B and H when counted from left of B?
   (a) none
   (b) one
   (c) two
   (d) three
   (e) More than three

4. Who among the following persons sits to the immediate right of E?
   (a) A
   (b) B
   (c) C
   (d) D
   (e) None of these

5. If B is related to D and C is related to G, then in the same pattern, who is related to A?
   (a) D
   (b) E
   (c) F
   (d) G
   (e) None of these

Directions (6-10): In each of the questions below are given some statements followed by two conclusions. You have to assume that the given statements are true, even if they seem to be at variance with commonly known facts. Read all the conclusions and then decide which of the given conclusions logically follow from the given statements disregarding commonly known facts.

(a) If only conclusion I follows.
(b) If only conclusion II follows.
(c) If either conclusion I or II follows.
(d) If neither conclusion I nor II follows.
(e) If both conclusions I and II follow.

6. **Statements:** All Sumit is Adarsh.
   No Aman is Dinesh.
   Only a few Dinesh is Adarsh.
   Conclusion I. Some Sumit is Dinesh.
   II. No Sumit is Dinesh.

7. **Statements:** Only a few Paper is Tree.
   No Tree is Plant.
   All Plant is Grass.
   Conclusion I. No Paper is Plant.
   II. All Tree is Grass.

8. **Statements:** All Motor is Car.
   Some Car is Bike.
   No Bike is Aircraft.
   Conclusion I. Some Motor being Aircraft is a possibility.
   II. Some Car is Aircraft.

9. **Statements:** Only a few Pizza is Burger.
   All Aloo chat is Noodles.
   Some Noodles is Pizza.
   Conclusion I. Some Burger is Aloo chat.
   II. No Burger is Aloo chat.

10. **Statements:** Only Cat is Dog.
    All Eagle is Cat.
    Some Cat is Cow.
    Conclusion: I. Some Dog is Cow.
    II. Some Eagle is Cow.

Direction (11-15): Study the following information carefully and answer the questions given below:

Eight persons are sitting in a row. Some of them are facing North and some are facing South. P sits 2nd to the right of Q, who sits 3rd from an extreme end. R sits 3rd to the left of P. R does not sit next to Q. U sits to the immediate right of R. S sits immediately left of T, who faces North. V sits 2nd to the left of W, who is not an immediate neighbour of U. Immediate neighbours of V face the opposite direction with respect to V. S faces North. Persons sitting at extreme ends face the opposite direction with respect to each other.

11. Who among the following persons sits 5th to the left of V?
    (a) P
    (b) Q
    (c) R
    (d) S
    (e) None of these

12. How many persons are facing South?
    (a) two
    (b) three
    (c) four
    (d) five
    (e) None of these

13. Who among the following persons are sitting at an extreme end?

(a) P-Q   (b) Q-R   (c) R-S
(d) S-T   (e) T-U

14. Who among the following persons sits 4th from left end?

(a) S   (b) T   (c) U
(d) V   (e) W

15. Four of the following five are alike in certain ways and so form a group. Find the one which does not belong to that group.

(a) S   (b) T   (c) R
(d) Q   (e) V

Direction (16-20): Study the following information carefully and answer the questions given below:

In a certain code language:

"two one three five" is written as 'kesi li na'

"one three four six" is written as 'nasituky'

"one six five two" is written as 'keky li si'

16. "three" will be coded as?

(a) si   (b) na
(c) li   (d) ke
(e) None of these

17. If "six seven" is coded as "zxky", then find the code for "two seven".

(a) li zx
(b) kezx
(c) tu zx
(d) None of these
(e) Either (a) or (b)

18. What is the code for "four six"?

(a) na tu
(b) tu ky
(c) kysi
(d) Either (a) or (b)
(e) None of these

19. What may be the code for "one six eight"?

(a) tu ki na   (b) si na tu   (c) si kyze
(d) ky na si   (e) si ke li

20. What is the code for "two"?

(a) li
(b) si
(c) ke
(d) Either (a) or (c)
(e) None of these

Directions (21-25): The following questions are based on the five three-digit numbers given below.

113 215 512 423 261

21. If all the digits in each of the numbers are arranged in an ascending order within the number, then which of the following numbers will become the highest in the new arrangement of numbers?

(a) 113   (b) 215   (c) 512
(d) 423   (e) 261

22. If all the numbers are arranged in descending order from left to right, then which of the following will be the sum of all the three digits of the number which is 2nd from the right of the new arrangement?

(a) 7   (b) 5   (c) 11
(d) 8   (e) 6

23. What will be the result when the 2nd digit of the highest number is multiplied with the 3rd digit of the lowest number?

(a) 3   (b) 2   (c) 1
(d) 10   (e) 5

24. If the positions of the second and the third digits of each of the numbers are interchanged, then how many odd numbers will be formed?

(a) none   (b) one   (c) two
(d) three   (e) four

25. If one is subtracted to the third digit of each of the numbers, then how many numbers thus formed will be divisible by four?

(a) none   (b) one   (c) two
(d) three   (e) four

Directions (26-30): Study the following information carefully and answer the given questions.

Seven friends A, B, C, G, J, K and L play different sports viz. Cricket, Hockey, Golf, Football, Tennis, Squash and Baseball, but not necessarily in the same order. Each of them likes different sport brands viz. Puma, Reebok, Nike, Fila, Adidas, HRX and Lotto, but not necessarily in the same order.

K likes Puma and plays neither Golf nor Football. The one who plays Cricket likes Reebok. A plays Hockey and likes neither Fila nor Adidas. The one who plays Baseball likes Lotto. B likes HRX and does not play Football. The one who plays Football does not like Adidas. G plays Tennis. L does not like Reebok and does not play Football. J does not play Football.

26. Which of the following sports does C play?

(a) Squash   (b) Football
(c) Golf   (d) Baseball
(e) None of these

27. Who among the following plays Cricket?

(a) B   (b) J
(c) L   (d) K
(e) None of these

28. Who among the following likes Adidas?

(a) G   (b) A
(c) J   (d) C
(e) None of these

29. Which of the following brands does L like?

(a) Fila   (b) Nike
(c) HRX   (d) Lotto
(e) None of these

30. Which of the following sports is played by the one who likes Nike?

(a) Golf   (b) Squash
(c) Tennis   (d) Hockey
(e) None of these

Direction (31-35): In each of the questions below are given some statements followed by two conclusions. You have to take the given statements to be true even if they seem to be at variance with commonly known facts. Read all the conclusions and then decide which of the given conclusions logically follows from the given statements disregarding commonly known facts.

(a) If only conclusion I follows.
(b) If only conclusion II follows.
(c) If either conclusion I or II follows.
(d) If neither conclusion I nor II follows.
(e) If both conclusions I and II follow.

31. Statements: $M < N \leq O < P \leq Q < R < S = T$
    Conclusion I. $M < R$ II. $M < N$

32. Statements: $A = B < C > = D = E \leq F < G \leq H$
    Conclusion I. $A \geq G$ II. $E < H$

33. Statements: $S < T = U \geq V = W \leq X; W > Y \leq Z$
    Conclusion I. $U > S$ II. $U \geq Y$

34. Statements: $P = Q \leq R > S \leq T < U < V < W < X < Y > Z$
    Conclusion I. $P < U$ II. $X < Z$

35. Statements: $P < X < R < S < T < U = V < W > Q \leq Y \leq Z$
    Conclusion I. $Z \geq Q$ II. $P < W$

Direction (36-40): Study the following information carefully and answer the questions given below.

Nine persons i.e. P, Q, R, S, T, U, V, W and X are sitting in a linear row facing the North direction. V does not sit next to S. Two persons sit between P and S. One person sits between U and W. There are as many persons to the left of P as there are to the right of X. Three persons sit between S and W. U and V sit together. X sits second to the right of V. S sits to the right of Q. Q sits to the immediate next to P. T sits second to the right of R.

36. Who among the following sits to the immediate left of W?
(a) V   (b) R
(c) Q   (d) P
(e) None of the above

37. Who among the following sits at the second right of U?
(a) P   (b) W
(c) R   (d) T
(e) None of these

38. Which among the following is true regarding T?
(a) T sits in the middle of U and V
(b) T sits in the middle of R and P
(c) T sits in the middle of S and U
(d) T sits next to W
(e) None is true

39. Who among the following sits second to the left of T?
(a) V   (b) P   (c) W
(d) R   (e) S

40. Which pair sits at the extreme ends of the row?
(a) T and V   (b) T and P   (c) U and V
(d) R and Q   (e) P and X

Quantitative Aptitude

Directions (41-45): The given pie chart shows the distribution (in degrees) of total monthly income of a person into 6 different categories. Study the graph carefully and answer the following questions.

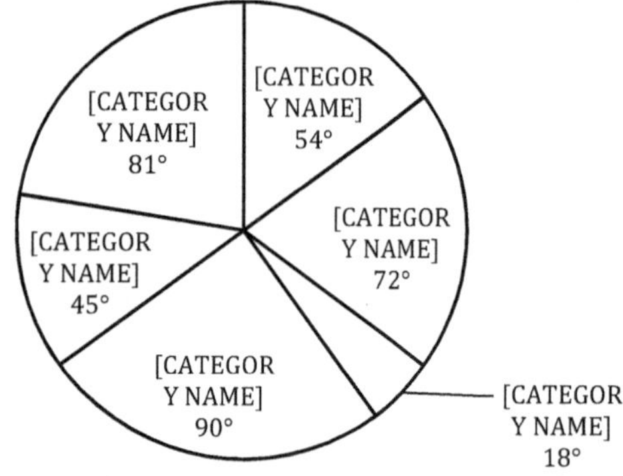

Note: Consider all categories as monthly expenditure of the person except savings.

41. If monthly salary is Rs. 18000, find monthly expenditure on food.
(a) Rs. 7200   (b) Rs. 5400   (c) Rs. 4500
(d) Rs. 6300   (e) Rs. 6800

42. If difference between monthly expenditure on House rent and Clothes is Rs. 2800, then find the monthly income of the person.
(a) Rs. 48000   (b) Rs. 56000   (c) Rs. 54000
(d) Rs. 42000   (e) Rs. 62000

43. Find the average of monthly expenditure on Food, Clothes and House rent, if monthly expenditure on Loan is Rs. 3600.
(a) Rs. 5760   (b) Rs. 4670   (c) Rs. 6370
(d) Rs. 5670   (e) Rs. 5360

44. If monthly income of a person is Rs. 84000, what is his total monthly expenditure?
(a) Rs. 65000   (b) Rs. 64900   (c) Rs. 65900
(d) Rs. 65100   (e) Rs. 64100

45. Monthly expenditure on Clothes is what percent of monthly expenditure on House rent?
(a) 90%   (b) 75%   (c) 50%
(d) 66.67%   (e) 133.33%

46. Simple interest on a certain sum at the rate of $16\frac{2}{3}\%$ per annum for three years is Rs. 1250. Find the sum.
(a) Rs. 3,000 (b) Rs. 2,500 (c) Rs. 2,400
(d) Rs. 4,000 (e) Rs. 5,000

47. A fraction becomes $\frac{5}{3}$ when 20% of numerator is added to the numerator and 30% of denominator is subtracted from the denominator. Find the fraction.
(a) $\frac{35}{36}$ (b) $\frac{36}{25}$ (c) $\frac{33}{35}$
(d) $\frac{27}{35}$ (e) $\frac{35}{33}$

48. Rajjo borrows Rs. 6300 from PNB on compound interest at the rate of $33\frac{1}{3}\%$ p.a. for two years. Find the total interest given by Rajjo to the bank after 2 years.
(a) Rs.4,100 (b) Rs.3,900 (c) Rs.4,900
(d) Rs.4,600 (e) Rs. 4,500

49. Raheem spends 36% of his monthly income on daily spending, 40% on house rent and children fees together and rest of the amount he saves for future needs. If his total monthly savings is Rs. 14,400, then find his total monthly income.
(a) Rs.45,000 (b) Rs. 40,000 (c) Rs. 48,000
(d) Rs. 60,000 (e) Rs. 55,000

50. The population of a city after three years will be 21,600. If the rate of increase of the population per year is 20%, then find the present population of the city.
(a) 12,500 (b) 16,500 (c) 14,500
(d) 10,500 (e) 11,600

Directions (51-55): Find the missing number in the following series.

51. 4, 12, 48, 240, 1440, ?
(a) 9080 (b) 10280 (c) 10080
(d) 12080 (e) 11080

52. ?, 12.7, 14.9, 18.2, 22.6, 28.1, 34.7
(a) 12.8 (b) 12.2 (c) 11.5
(d) 11.6 (e) 11.1

53. 13, 17, 19, 23, 29, 31, ?
(a) 37 (b) 33 (c) 35
(d) 39 (e) 41

54. 16, 8, 24, 6, 30, ?, 35
(a) 4 (b) 5 (c) 6
(d) 7 (e) 3

55. 7, 15, 24, ? 45, 57, 70
(a) 33 (b) 37 (c) 39
(d) 36 (e) 34

Directions (56-60): In each of the following questions, two equations (I) and (II) are given. You have to solve both the equations and give the answer.
(a) if x < y
(b) if x ≤ y
(c) if x > y
(d) if x ≥ y
(e) if x = y or no relationship can be obtained between x and y.

56. I. $x^2 - 14x + 48 = 0$ II. $y^2 - 18y + 80 = 0$
57. I. $x^3 + 328 = 2525$ II. $y^3 + 349 = 1680$
58. I. $x^2 - 19x + 88 = 0$ II. $y^2 - 21y + 108 = 0$
59. I. $x^3 = 1728$ II. $y^2 = 144$
60. I. $2x^2 + 25x + 75 = 0$ II. $3y^2 + 26y + 56 = 0$

Directions (61–65): Simplify the following questions and find the value of (?)

61. 24 × 18 + 560 ÷ 14 = 600 – ?
(a) 132 (b) 128 (c) 140
(d) 146 (e) 152

62. $2685 - 1460 + 737 = 1793 + (?)^2$
(a) 12 (b) 14
(c) 13 (d) 11
(e) None of these

63. 780 ÷ 12 × 14 + 220 = ?
(a) 1130 (b) 1140 (c) 1155
(d) 1170 (e) 1148

64. $840 ÷ 14 + 28 × 14 + (?)^2 = 533$
(a) 10 (b) 8
(c) 11 (d) 9
(e) None of these

65. 3120 ÷ 24 + 1650 + ? = 2180
(a) 420 (b) 430 (c) 440
(d) 450 (e) 400

Directions (66-70): What approximate value should come in place of the question mark (?) in the following questions.

66. 3599 ÷ 20 + 110 × 24.9 + 418 = ?
(a) 3400 (b) 3350 (c) 3200
(d) 3300 (e) 3250

67. $25 × 12.9 + \sqrt{399} + 1145 = ?$
(a) 1550 (b) 1600 (c) 1490
(d) 1400 (e) 1300

68. 3453.9 + 6119.8 + 1729.9 = ?
(a) 11360 (b) 11310 (c) 11500
(d) 11250 (e) None of these

69. 140 × 12.9 – 442 ÷ 22 + 979 = ?
(a) 2830 (b) 2710 (c) 2850
(d) 2680 (e) 2780

70. $\sqrt[3]{2746} + 2449 - 7358 ÷ 23 = ?$
(a) 2150 (b) 2200 (c) 2100
(d) 2300 (e) 2250

71. Tap 'A' can alone fill a cistern in 12 hours, while another tap 'B' alone can empty the tank in 18 hours. If both pipes are opened together and after 3 hours tap 'B' is closed, then in how much time will the tank be filled?
(a) 14 hours (b) 16 hours (c) 10 hours
(d) 12 hours (e) 20 hours

72. Three friends running around a circular track can complete a single loop in 24 min, 32 min and 56 min respectively. If they started running

from the same initial point, then after how much time will they meet together for the first time?
(a) 8.4 hours (b) 9.6 hours (c) 11.2 hours
(d) 6.4 hours (e) 10 hours

73. A man covers half the total distance at12 km/h and another half distance at24km/h. Find his average speed.
(a) 12 km/h (b) 16 km/h (c) 10 km/h
(d) 18 km/h (e) 6 km/h

74. I bought 16 pencils at the rate of Rs. 9 per dozen and sold all of them at the rate of Rs. 12 per dozen. What is the overall profit percentage in this transaction?
(a) $66\frac{2}{3}\%$ (b) $22\frac{1}{7}\%$ (c) 22%
(d) $33\frac{1}{3}\%$ (e) 44%

75. In a zoo, there are 480 deer and ostriches together. If the total number of legs are 1040 then find the number of deer and ostriches respectively.
(a) 80, 400 (b) 60, 420 (c) 40, 440
(d) 120, 360 (e) 100, 380

Directions (76–80): The following table shows the total no. of senior citizens of different age groups in Japan. The table also shows the ratio of male to female in them. Study the table carefully to answer the following questions.

Age group (in year)	Total no. of senior citizen	Ratio of male to female
50–60	2400	5:3
61–70	3200	3:1
71–80	4800	7:5
81–90	6000	2:1

76. The total no. of female senior citizens of age group 50–60 years are how much percent more or less than female senior citizens of age group 61–70years?
(a) 12.5% more
(b) 12.5% less
(c) 10.5% more
(d) 10.5% less
(e) 8.5% more

77. What is the average no. of male senior citizens of age group 61–70 years and 81–90 years?
(a) 3600 (b) 2600 (c) 3200
(d) 2800 (e) 2300

78. If $33\frac{1}{3}\%$ senior citizens of age group 81–90 died due to bad health, then senior citizens who are alive of age group 81-90 are what percent of total senior citizens of age group 61–70 years and 71–80 years together?
(a) 50% (b) 60% (c) 54%
(d) 64% (e) 45%

79. If 20% male senior citizens of age group 7 – 80yrs are pensioners, then how many male senior citizens are non-pensioners in the same age group?
(a) 2140 (b) 2440 (c) 2240
(d) 2420 (e) 2040

80. What is the difference between total male and total female senior citizens of age group 50 –60 and 61 –70 yrs together?
(a) 2300 (b) 2100 (c) 2400
(d) 2200 (e) 1850

Solutions

REASONING ABILITY

Directions (1-5): From the given statements, A sits 3rd to the right of B, who is an immediate neighbour of C. Two persons are sitting between C and D. E sits 2nd to the left of H, who is not an immediate neighbour of A and D. Here, we get two possibilities i.e. Case 1 and Case 2.

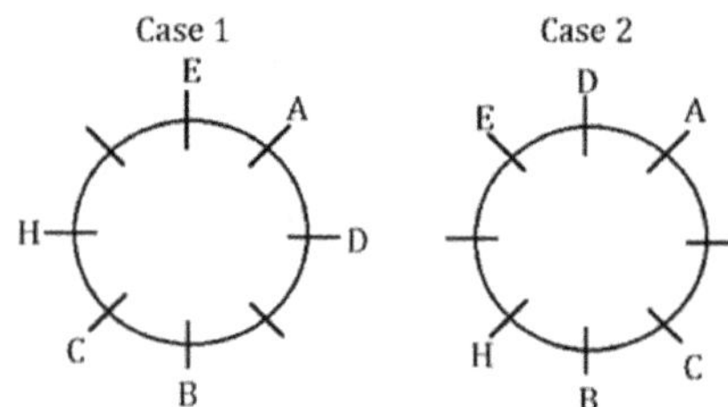

From the given statements, F faces G, who is an immediate neighbour of B. Here, Case 2 is ruled out.

So, the final arrangement will be:

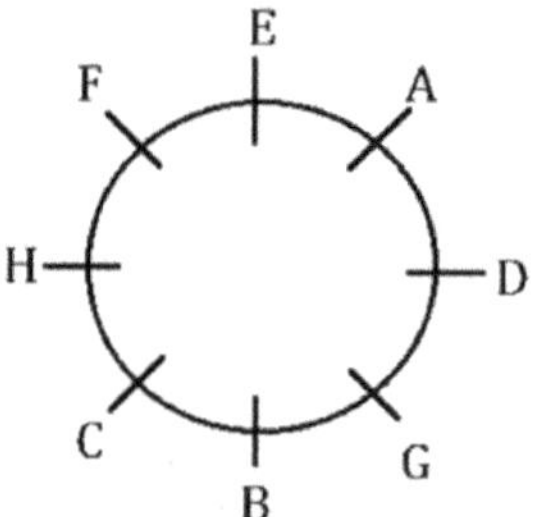

1. (a)   2. (c)   3. (b)
4. (e)   5. (d)

6. (c)

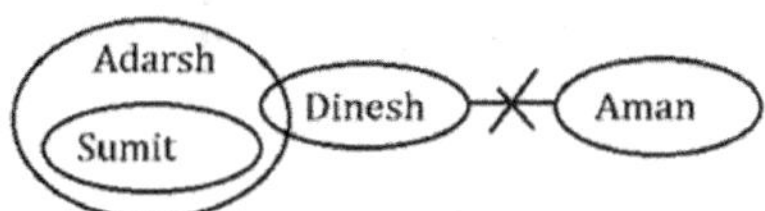

7. (d)

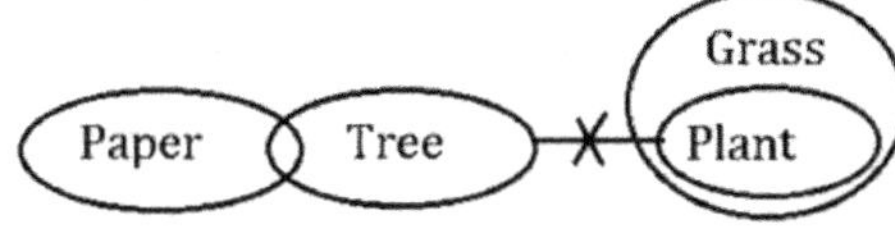

8. (a)

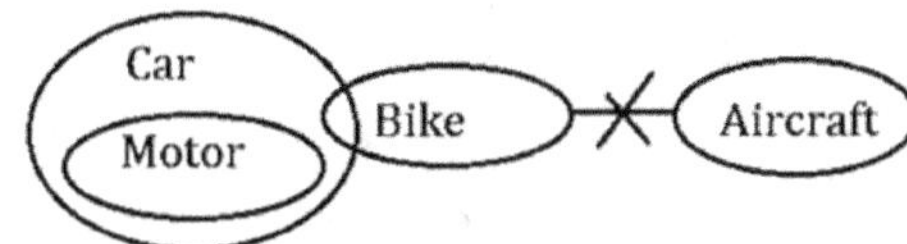

9. (c)

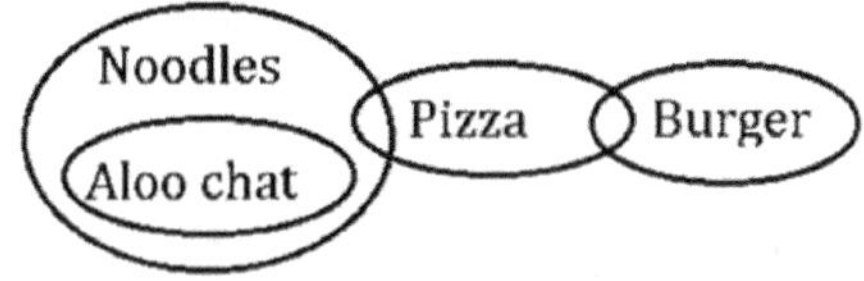

10. (d)

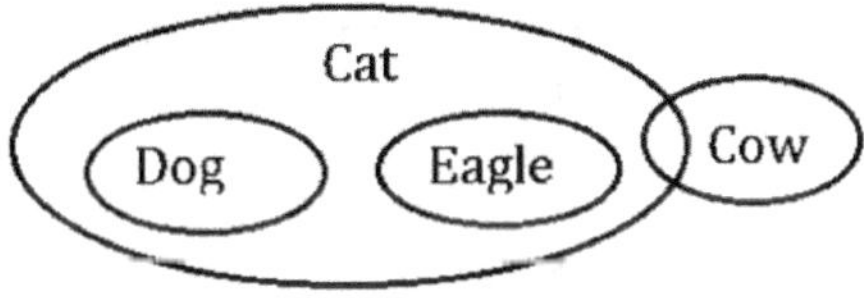

Direction (11-15): From the given statements, P sits 2nd to the right of Q, who is 3rd from extreme end. R sits 3rd to the left of P. R doesn't sit next to Q. U sits immediate right of R. S sits immediate left of T, who faces North. Here, we get two possibilities i.e. Case 1, Case 2.

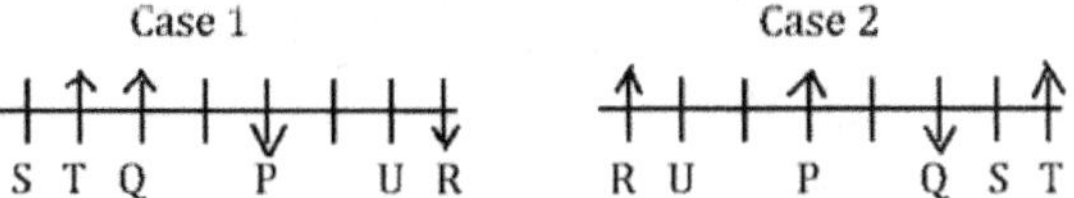

From the given statements, V sits 2nd to the left of W, who is not an immediate neighbour of U. Immediate neighbours of V face opposite directions with respect to V. S faces North. Persons sitting at extreme ends face opposite directions with respect to each other. Hence, Case 2 is ruled out.

So, the final arrangement will be: -

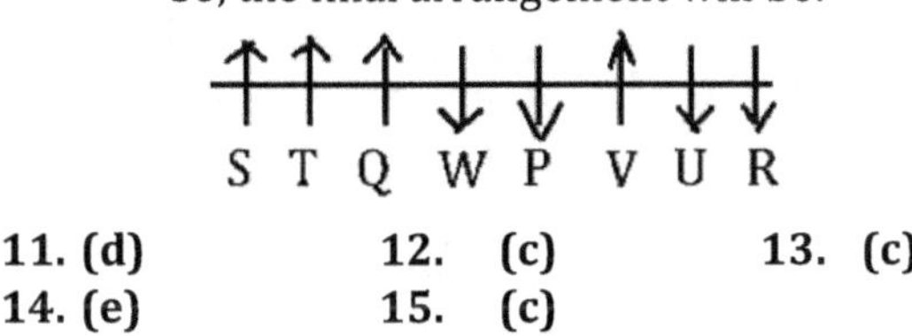

11. (d) **12. (c)** **13. (c)**
14. (e) **15. (c)**

Direction (16-20):

Word	Code
Two/five	li/ke
One	si
Three	na
Four	tu
Six	ky

16. (b) **17. (e)** **18. (b)**
19. (c) **20. (d)**

Direction (21-25):

21. (d) **22. (d)** **23. (a)**
24. (d) **25. (c)**

Directions (26-30): K likes Puma and plays neither Golf nor Football. A plays Hockey and likes neither Fila nor Adidas. B likes HRX and does not play Football. G plays Tennis. L does not like Reebok and does not play Football. J does not play Football. From these conditions' arrangement will be:

Friend	Brand	Sport
A	~~Fila/Adidas~~	Hockey
B	HRX	~~Football~~
C		
G		Tennis
J		~~Football~~
K	Puma	~~Golf/Football~~
L	~~Reebok~~	~~Football~~

From above conditions it is clear that C plays Football. The one who plays Cricket likes Reebok. So, the only one possibility left is that J plays Cricket and likes Reebok. The one who plays Baseball likes Lotto. There is one possibility left that L plays Baseball and likes Lotto. The one who plays Football does not like Adidas. So, G likes Adidas. C likes Fila. A likes Nike. So final arrangement will be-

Friend	Brand	Sport
A	Nike	Hockey
B	HRX	Golf
C	Fila	Football
G	Adidas	Tennis
J	Reebok	Cricket
K	Puma	Squash
L	Lotto	Baseball

26. (b) **27. (b)** **28. (a)**
29. (d) **30. (d)**

Direction (31-35):

31. (e) I. $M < R$ (True) II. $M < N$ (True)
32. (b) I. $A \geq G$ (False) II. $E < H$ (True)
33. (a) I. $U > S$ (True) II. $U \geq Y$ (False)
34. (d) I. $P < U$ (False) II. $X < Z$ (false)
35. (e) I. $Z \geq Q$ (True) II. $P < W$ (True)

Q sits immediately next to P. Two persons are sitting between P and S. S sits to the right of Q.

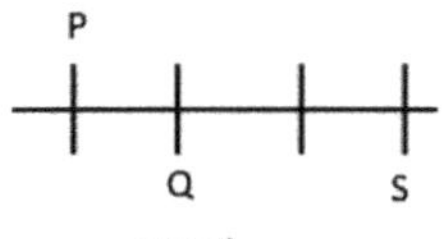
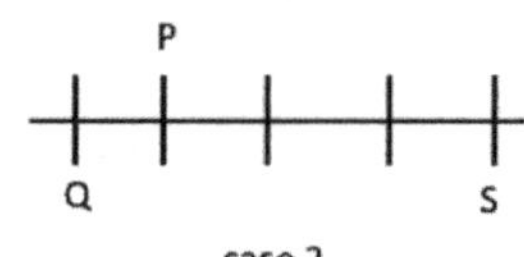

Three persons sit between S and W. One person sits between U and W. U and V sits together. V does not sit next to S.

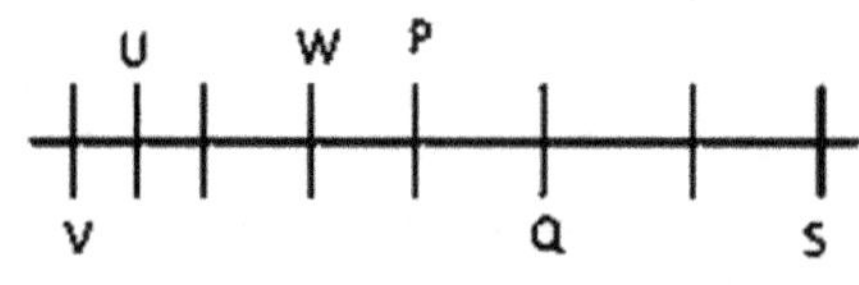

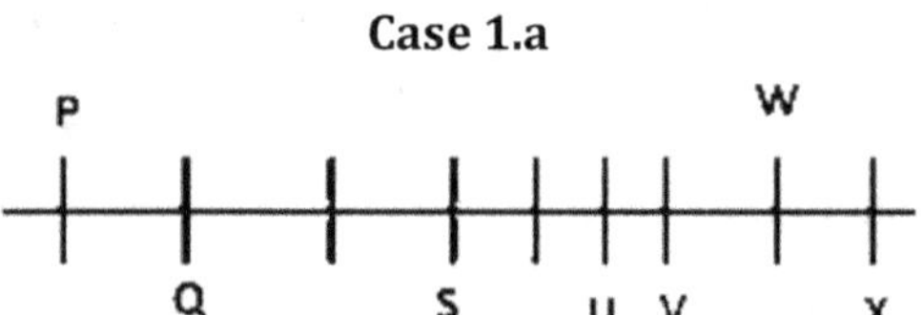

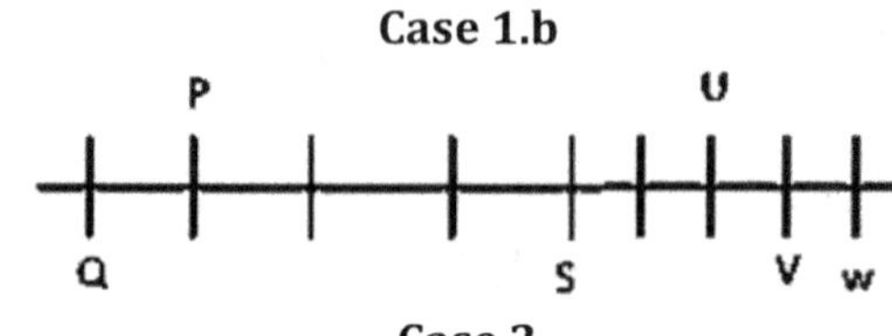

Case 2

As many persons sit to the left of P as to the right of X. (Hence case 1.a gets cancelled). X sits second to the right of V. (Hence, case 2 gets eliminated). T sits second to the right of R.

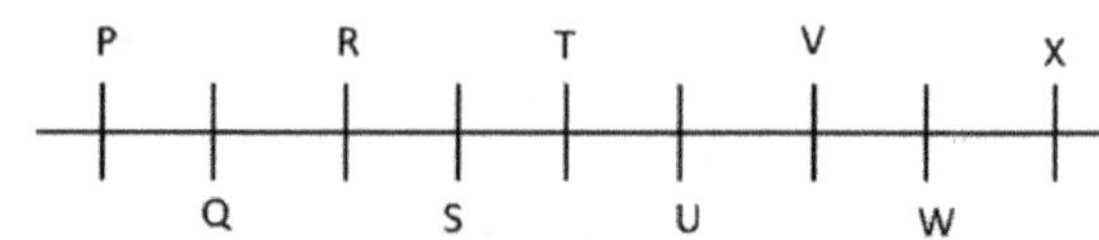

36. (a)   37. (b)   38. (c)
39. (d)   40. (e)

Quantitative Aptitude

41. (c) Required expenditure

$$= \frac{90}{360} \times 18000 = Rs\ 4500$$

42. (b) Required income

$$= 2800 \times \frac{360}{72-54} = Rs\ 56000$$

43. (a) Required average expenditure

$$= \frac{1}{3}[90 + 54 + 72] \times \frac{3600}{45} = Rs\ 5760$$

44. (d) Required expenditure

$$= 84000 - \frac{81}{360} \times 84000$$
$$= 84000 - 18900 = Rs\ 65100$$

45. (b) Required percent $= \frac{54}{72} \times 100 = 75\%$

46. (b) Let sum = Rs. P

$$\because 16\frac{2}{3}\% = \frac{50}{3}\%$$
$$\therefore 1250 = \frac{P \times 3 \times 50}{100 \times 3}$$
$$\therefore P = Rs.2,500$$

47. (a) Let fraction $= \frac{p}{q}$

$$ATQ, \frac{p + \frac{20}{100} \times p}{q - \frac{30}{100} \times q} = \frac{5}{3}$$

$$\Rightarrow \frac{\frac{6p}{5}}{\frac{7q}{10}} = \frac{5}{3} \Rightarrow \frac{12p}{7q} = \frac{5}{3} \Rightarrow \frac{p}{q} = \frac{35}{36}$$

48. (c) Required C.I. paid by Rajjo to PNB

$$= 6300 \left[\left(1 + \frac{100}{300}\right)^2 - 1\right]$$
$$= 6300 \times \frac{7}{9} = Rs.4900$$

49. (d) Savings of Raheem = 100 − (36 + 40)
$$= 24\%$$
$$ATQ, 24\% \to 14,400$$
$$\Rightarrow 100\% \to \frac{14400}{24} \times 100 = Rs.\ 60,000$$

50. (a) Let present population = P

$$\therefore 21,600 = P \left(1 + \frac{20}{100}\right)^3$$
$$\Rightarrow P = \frac{21,600 \times 125}{216}$$
$$\Rightarrow P = 12,500$$

51. (c) The series is ×3, ×4, ×5, ×6, ×7,

So, ? = 1440 × 7 = 10080

52. (d)

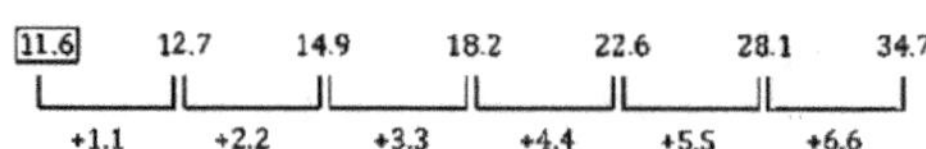

53. (a) The series is successive prime no.

So, 13, 17, 19, 23, 29, 31, 37

54. (b) The series is

16 ÷ 2 = 8
8 × 3 = 24
24 ÷ 4 = 6
6 × 5 = 30
30 ÷ 6 = 5
5 × 7 = 35

55. (e)

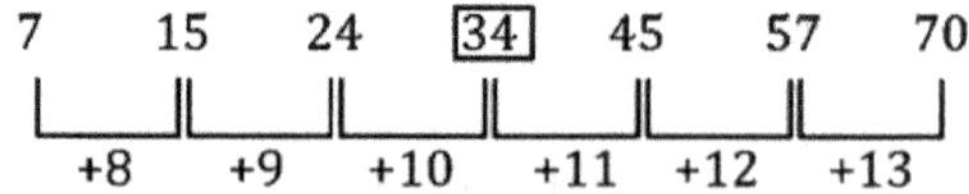

56. (b) I. $x^2 - 14x + 48 = 0$

$$\therefore x^2 - 8x - 6x + 48 = 0$$
$$x(x - 8) - 6(x - 8) = 0$$
$$(x - 8)(x - 6) = 0$$
$$\therefore x = 8, 6$$

II. $y^2 - 18y + 80 = 0$

$\therefore y^2 - 8y - 10y + 80 = 0$

$\therefore y(y-8) - 10(y-8) = 0$

$\therefore (y-8)(y-10) = 0$

$\therefore y = 8, 10$

$\therefore x \leq y$

57. (c) I. $x^3 + 328 = 2525$

$\therefore x^3 = 2525 - 328$

$\therefore x^3 = 2197$

$\therefore x = 13$

II. $y^3 + 349 = 1680$

$\therefore y^3 = 1680 - 349$

$\therefore y^3 = 1331$

$\therefore y = 11$

$\therefore x > y$

58. (e) I. $x^2 - 19x + 88 = 0$

$\therefore x^2 - 8x - 11x + 88 = 0$

$\therefore x(x-8) - 11(x-8) = 0$

$\therefore (x-8)(x-11) = 0$

$\therefore x = 8, 11$

II. $y^2 - 21y + 108 = 0$

$\therefore y^2 - 9y - 12y + 108 = 0$

$\therefore y(y-9) - 12(y-9) = 0$

$\therefore (y-12)(y-9) = 0$

$\therefore y = 9, 12$

So, no relation

59. (d) I. $x^3 = 1728$

$\therefore x = \sqrt[3]{1728}$

$\therefore x = 12$

II. $y^2 = 144$

$\therefore y = \sqrt{144}$

$y = \pm 12$

$\therefore x \geq y$

60. (a) I. $2x^2 + 25x + 75 = 0$

$2x^2 + 10x + 15x + 75 = 0$

$2x(x+5) + 15(x+5) = 0$

$\therefore (2x+15)(x+5) = 0$

$x = -5, \dfrac{-15}{2}$

II. $3y^2 + 26y + 56 = 0$

$\therefore 3y^2 + 12y + 14y + 56 = 0$

$\therefore 3y(y+4) + 14(y+4) = 0$

$\therefore (y+4)(3y+14) = 0$

$\therefore y = -4, \dfrac{-14}{3}$

So, $y > x$

61. (b) $24 \times 18 + 560 \div 14 = 600 - ?$

$\therefore 432 + 40 = 600 - ?$

$\therefore 472 = 600 - ?$

$\therefore ? = 600 - 472 = 128$

62. (c) $2685 - 1460 + 737 = 1793 + (?)^2$

$\therefore 1225 + 737 = 1793 + (?)^2$

$\therefore 1962 = 1793 + (?)^2$

$\therefore (?)^2 = 1962 - 1793 = 169$

$? = (13)$

63. (a) $780 \div 12 \times 14 + 220 = ?$

$? = 65 \times 14 + 220$

$? = 910 + 220$

$? = 1130$

64. (d) $840 \div 14 + 28 \times 14 + (?)^2 = 533$

$\therefore 60 + 392 + (?)^2 = 533$

$\therefore 452 + (?)^2 = 533$

$\therefore (?)^2 = 533 - 452$

$(?)^2 = 81$

$? = 9$

65. (e) $3120 \div 24 + 1650 + (?) = 2180$

$\therefore 130 + 1650 + (?) = 2180$

$\therefore 1780 + (?) = 2180$

$\therefore ? = 2180 - 1780 = 400$

66. (b) $\therefore 3599 \div 20 + 110 \times 24.9 + 418 = ?$

$3600 \div 20 + 110 \times 25 + 418 = ?$

$? \cong 180 + 2750 + 418$

$? = 3348$

$? \cong 3350$

67. (c) $25 \times 12.9 + \sqrt{399} + 1145 = ?$

$25 \times 13 + \sqrt{400} + 1145 = ?$

$? = 325 + 20 + 1145$

$? = 345 + 1145$

$? \cong 1490$

68. (b) $3453.9 + 6119.8 + 1729.9 = ?$

$? = 3454 + 6120 + 1730$

$? = 11304$

$? \cong 11310$

69. (e) $140 \times 12.9 - 442 \div 22 + 979 = ?$

$140 \times 13 - 440 \div 22 + 979 = ?$

$? = 1820 - 20 + 979$

$? = 1800 + 979$

$? = 2779$

$? \cong 2780$

70. (a) $\sqrt[3]{2746} + 2449 - 7358 \div 23 = ?$

$\sqrt[3]{2744} + 2450 - 7360 \div 23 = ?$

$? = 14 + 2450 - 320$

$? = 2464 - 320$

$? = 2144$

$? \cong 2150$

71. (a) Let total work = 36 units

One hour's work of A $= \dfrac{36}{12} = 3$ units

One hour's work of B $= \dfrac{-36}{18} = -2$ units

($\because$ B is emptying pipe)

$\therefore$ Remaining work after 3 hours

$= 36 - (3 \times 3 - 2 \times 3)$

$= 33$ units

$\therefore$ Total time required to fill the tank

$= 3 + \dfrac{33}{3} = 14$ hours

72. (c) Required time = LCM of $(24, 32, 56)$

$= 672$ min $= 11.2$ hours

73. (b) Let total distance = d

$\therefore$ Average speed $= \dfrac{d}{\frac{d}{24} + \frac{d}{48}}$

$= 16$ km/h

74. (d) CP of 16 pencils $= \frac{9}{12} \times 16 = Rs.\ 12$

SP of 16 pencils $= \frac{12}{12} \times 16 = Rs\ 16$

$\therefore$ Required profit percentage $= \frac{16-12}{12} \times 100 = 33\frac{1}{3}\%$

75. (c) Let total number of deer and ostriches be x and y respectively.

$\therefore$ x + y = 480   ...(i)

And,

4x + 2y = 1040

$\Rightarrow$ 2x + y = 520   ...(ii)

Solving equation (i) and (ii) respectively.

x = 40 and y = 440

76. (a) Female Senior citizens of age group (50 – 60) yrs

$= \frac{3}{8} \times 2400 = 900$

Female senior citizens of age group (61 – 70) yrs

$= \frac{1}{4} \times 3200 = 800$

Required percentage $= \frac{900-800}{800} \times 100$

$= 12.5\%$ more

77. (c) Required average $= \frac{1}{2} \times (\frac{3}{4} \times 3200 + \frac{2}{3} \times 6000)$

$= \frac{1}{2} \times 6400 = 3200$

78. (a) Remaining senior citizens

$= \left(100 - \frac{100}{3}\right)\% \ of\ 6000 = 4000$

$\therefore$ Required percentage $= \frac{4000}{3200+4800} \times 100$

$= \frac{1}{2} \times 100 = 50\%$

79. (c) Non–pensioner males

$= (100 - 20)\% \ of\ \frac{7}{12} \ of\ 4800$

$= \frac{80}{100} \times \frac{7}{12} \times 4800 = 2240$

80. (d) Required difference $= \left(\frac{5}{8} \times 2400 + \frac{3}{4} \times 3200\right) - \left(\frac{3}{8} \times 2400 + \frac{1}{4} \times 3200\right)$

$= 1500 + 2400 - 900 - 800$

$= 2200$

REASONING ABILITY

Directions (1-5): In each of the questions below, relationships between some elements are shown in the statements. These statements are followed by conclusions numbered I and II. Read the statements and give the answer.

(a) If only conclusion I follows.
(b) If only conclusion II follows.
(c) If either conclusion I or II follows.
(d) If neither conclusion I nor II follows.
(e) If both conclusions I and II follow.

1. **Statements:** $J < F \leq S > L \geq O = P \geq M$
   Conclusions: I. $L < J$ II. $S > M$
2. **Statements:** $D \geq F \geq O = G < E \leq A \leq B$
   Conclusions: I. $G \geq D$ II. $B < O$
3. **Statements:** $F \leq P = O \leq I \leq N > K \geq E$
   Conclusions: I. $N \geq F$ II. $E > N$
4. **Statements:** $Y > Z \geq W = X \geq V \geq U < T$
   Conclusions: I. $U < Z$ II. $Z = U$
5. **Statements:** $O \geq P = E > D < M \leq R < G$
   Conclusions: I. $D < O$ II. $G > M$

Directions (6-10): The following questions are based on the five words given below. Study the words and answer the following questions.

HUB INK WIN BUT POT

(The new words formed after performing the operations mentioned below may not necessarily be a meaningful English word.)

6. If the given words are arranged in the descending order as they appear in a dictionary from left to right, which of the following will be fourth from the right end?
   (a) HUB   (b) INK   (c) WIN
   (d) BUT   (e) POT

7. How many letters are there in the English alphabetical series between the first letter of the word which is fourth from the right end and the third letter of the word which is third from the left end?
   (a) two   (b) three
   (c) four   (d) five
   (e) None of these

8. If the positions of the first and the third alphabet in each of the given words is interchanged, then how many meaningful words will be formed?

(a) none   (b) one   (c) two
(d) three   (e) four

9. If in each of the given words, the third alphabet is replaced by its previous alphabet and the first alphabet is replaced by its following alphabet as per the English alphabetical order, then how many words thus formed will have more than two vowels?
   (a) none   (b) one   (c) two
   (d) three   (e) four

10. If in each of the given words, every consonant is changed to its next letter and every vowel is changed to its previous letter according to the English alphabetical series, then in how many words, thus formed, at least one vowel will appear?
    (a) none   (b) two
    (c) three   (d) four
    (e) None of these

Directions (11-15): In each of the questions below are given some statements followed by two conclusions. You have to take the given statements to be true even if they seem to be at variance with commonly known facts. Read all the conclusions and then decide which of the given conclusions logically follows from the given statements, disregarding commonly known facts. Give the answer accordingly.

11. **Statements:** Some ice is cube
    No cube is water
    All water are glass
    Conclusions: I. Some glass are not cube
    II. Some ice being water is a possibility.
    (a) Both I and II follow.
    (b) Either I or II follows.
    (c) Only II follows.
    (d) Only I follows.
    (e) Neither I nor II follows.

12. **Statements:** Some circle are radius
    Some radius are diagonal
    All diagonal are square
    Conclusions: I. Some square are circle
    II. Some radius being square is a possibility
    (a) Both I and II follow.
    (b) Either I or II follows.

(c) Only II follows.
(d) Only I follows.
(e) Neither I nor II follows.

13. **Statements:** All time is money
    All money is status
    No status is permanent
    Conclusions: I. All status is time
    II. Some money is not permanent
    (a) Both I and II follow.
    (b) Either I or II follows.
    (c) Only II follows.
    (d) Only I follows.
    (e) Neither I nor II follows.

14. **Statements:** Some exams are tough
    No tough is easy
    Some easy are scoring
    Conclusions: I. Some exams being easy is a possibility
    II. All tough are not scoring
    (a) Both I and II follow.
    (b) Either I or II follows.
    (c) Only II follows.
    (d) Only I follows.
    (e) Neither I nor II follows.

15. **Statements** No word is sheet
    Some sheet are point
    No point is table
    Conclusions: I. All word are not table
    II. Some sheet are not table
    (a) Both I and II follow.
    (b) Either I or II follows.
    (c) Only II follows.
    (d) Only I follows.
    (e) Neither I nor II follows.

Directions (16-20): Study the information provided and answer the following questions:

Eight persons A, B, C, D, E, F, G and H are sitting in a row with some facing north and others facing south (but not necessarily in the same manner).
(**Note:** Facing the same direction means if one is facing north then the other also faces north and vice versa. Facing opposite directions means if one is facing north then the other faces south and vice versa).

A sits fourth to the right of C and one of them sits at the extreme end of the row. Both A and C face the same direction. H sits to the immediate left of A and faces south. C faces the opposite direction of H. Three persons sit between H and F. D sits to the immediate right of F.B is an immediate neighbour of H. Three persons sit between E and G. G is not at an extreme end of the row. E and G face the same direction as F. B and D face the same direction as C. Neither E nor G is an immediate neighbour of A.

16. Who among the following sits to the immediate left of E?

17. How many persons sit between A and E?
    (a) none
    (b) one
    (c) two
    (d) three
    (e) More than three

18. What is the position of H with respect to G?
    (a) Second to the right
    (b) Second to the left
    (c) Immediate right
    (d) Immediate left
    (e) None of these

19. Who among the following pairs sit at the extreme ends of the row?
    (a) C, F
    (b) D, A
    (c) E, C
    (d) A, E
    (e) None of these

20. How many persons face south?
    (a) one
    (b) two
    (c) three
    (d) four
    (e) Cannot be determined

Directions (21-23): Study the following sequence and answer the given questions:

Point D is 6m. to the west of Point A. Point B is 10m. to the south of Point D. Point C is 4m. to the east of Point B. Point F is 5m. to the north of Point C. Point G is exactly between Point D and Point B.

21. What is the direction of Point G with respect to Point A?
    (a) northeast
    (b) north
    (c) southeast
    (d) southwest
    (e) Cannot be determined

22. How far is Point F from Point G?
    (a) 5m.
    (b) 6m.
    (c) 4m.
    (d) 10m.
    (e) Cannot be determined

23. What is the shortest distance between Point F and Point A?
    (a) 4m.
    (b) 5m.
    (c) $\sqrt{27}$m.
    (d) $\sqrt{29}$m
    (e) Cannot be determined

Directions (24-26): Study the following information and answer the given questions:

In a family of seven members, P is the father of Q, who is the grandchild of R. T is married to P. G is the grandmother of D, who is the brother of Q. S is the sister-in-law of T.

24. How is S related to D?
    (a) mother
    (b) aunt
    (c) sister
    (d) cousin
    (e) Cannot be determined

25. How is Q related to G?
    (a) son
    (b) daughter

(a) B
(b) C
(c) D
(d) A
(e) None of these

(c) grandson
(d) grand-daughter
(e) Cannot be determined

26. How many single members are there among the given family members?
(a) one
(b) two
(c) three
(d) More than three
(e) Cannot be determined

27. Raghu, a male person, points towards a picture and says," She is the daughter of the wife of my father's only grandson". How is Raghu related to that person?
(a) father
(b) uncle
(c) brother
(d) grandfather
(e) grandson

28. In a row of 32 students, Neel is 24th from the left end. Eight persons sit between Neel and Nitin. All of them are facing north. What is the position of Nitin from the right end?
(a) 15th
(b) 16th
(c) 17th
(d) 18th
(e) Cannot be determined

29. If F means '–', H means '×', G means '÷ ' and E means '+' then
25 G 5 H 8 F 15 E 4 = ?
(a) 5
(b) 29
(c) 43
(d) 21
(e) None of these

30. How many pairs of letters are there in the word "GLOBAL" which have as many letters between them (backwards or forwards) in the word as in the alphabetical series?
(a) none
(b) one
(c) two
(d) three
(e) four

Directions (31-35): Study the following information and answer the given questions:

Seven students A, B, C, D, E, F and G participate in three different sports viz. Cricket, Football and Hockey. At least two students participate in one sport. All of them like different subjects viz. English Hindi, Geography, History, Chemistry, Biology and Computer (but not necessarily in the same order).

C likes Geography and participates in Cricket. The one who likes English participates in Football only with the one who likes Hindi. D likes History but does not participate in Cricket. E who likes Chemistry participates with the one who likes Biology. Neither A nor G likes Biology. B likes Computer and does not participate with C. A does not like English.

31. Who among the following participates in Cricket?

(a) A
(b) D
(c) E
(d) G
(e) None of these

32. Who among the following participates in Football?
(a) G
(b) D
(c) The one who likes Computer
(d) F
(e) None of these

33. Who among the following pairs participates in Hockey?
(a) A, B
(b) A, G
(c) B, F
(d) B, D
(e) None of these

34. Which statement is true?
(a) F likes English
(b) G likes Hindi
(c) The one who likes Computer participates in Cricket
(d) G participates in Hockey
(e) A participates in Football

35. Who among the following likes Hindi?
(a) A
(b) G
(c) F
(d) The one who participates in Cricket
(e) The one who participates in Hockey

Directions (36-40): Study the information provided and answer the following questions:

Eight persons A, B, C, D, E, F, G and H are sitting around a circular table. Some are facing inside and some are facing outside (not necessarily in the same order).

(**Note:** Facing the same direction means if one is facing inside, then the other also faces inside and vice versa. Facing the opposite direction means if one is facing inside, then the other faces outside and vice versa).

C sits fourth to the left of F. G sits second to the right of F. Two persons sit between A and G. H sits third to the right of G. D sits to the immediate left of H. E sits second to the right of B. E is not an immediate neighbour of F. Immediate neighbours of C face the same direction as G. D faces the opposite direction of F. F faces inside.

36. Who among the following sits third to the left of E?
(a) F
(b) D
(c) A
(d) B
(e) None of these

37. What is the position of H with respect to C?
(a) Third to the left

(b) Third to the right
(c) Immediate left
(d) Immediate right
(e) Cannot be determined
38. Who sits opposite A?
(a) B (b) E
(c) D (d) H
(e) None of these
39. How many persons face outside?

(a) two (b) three
(c) four (d) five
(e) Cannot be determined

40. Four of the following five are alike in a certain way and hence form a group. Who among the following does not belong to that group?
(a) A (b) D (c) G
(d) B (e) E

QUANTITATIVE APTITUDE

41. A milkman buys some milk. If he sells it at Rs. 5 per litre, he loses Rs. 300, but when he sells it at Rs. 6 per litre, he gains Rs. 250. How much milk did he purchase?
(a) 550 lt (b) 300 lt (c) 250 lt
(d) 800 lt (e) 650 lt

42. In an election 8% of the voters did not cast their votes. In this election, there were only two candidates. The winner got 48% of the total votes and defeated his opponent by 1200 votes. What was the total number of voters in the election?
(a) 20000 (b) 30000 (c) 35000
(d) 25000 (e) 36000

43. Bhavya have ₹10,000. He invested some amount in Scheme 'A' which offers 15% p.a. at SI and rest in Scheme 'B' which offers 20% p.a. at CI. Interest earned form scheme 'A' after two years is ₹780 more than interest earned form scheme 'B' after two years. Find the amount invested in Scheme 'B'.
(a) ₹8000 (b) ₹7000 (c) ₹3000
(d) ₹2000 (e) ₹5000

44. A train travels 60% faster than a car. Both start from point A at the same time and reach point B, which is 160 km. away, at the same time. If on the way the train stops for 20 minutes at a station, then find the speed (in km/hr.) of the train.
(a) 144 (b) 168 (c) 198
(d) 288 (e) 248

45. A takes three times as long as B and C together take to do a job. If all the three work together and complete the job in 24 days, then find in how many days A will complete the job alone.
(a) 100 (b) 96 (c) 84
(d) 90 (e) 104

46. Find the ratio of area of a circle to the area of square if perimeter of circle and square is equal.
(a) 11 : 14 (b) 11 : 4 (c) 8 : 11
(d) 14 : 11 (e) 2 : 4

47. The average score of a cricketer in 8 innings is 44. He had scored 60, 24, x, 50, 73, y, z, 13 respectively in those innings. Find the average of x, y and z.
(a) 40 (b) 44 (c) 48
(d) 52 (e) 42

48. A librarian purchased 50 story books for his library. But he saw that he could get 12 more books, if he spent ₹128 more and the average price per book would be reduced by Rs.2. Find the average price (in Rs.) of each book he bought.
(a) 15 (b) 25 (c) 20
(d) 21 (e) 23

49. A jar contains water and milk in the ratio of 2:3. Some amount of milk is added to the jar that is equal to 30% of water present in the jar. After this, some water is added whose amount is equal to 10% of the quantity of milk present in the jar presently. What is the new ratio of water and milk in the jar?
(a) 59:90 (b) 11:18 (c) 90:59
(d) 18:11 (e) 57:67

50. Marks scored by Sumit is 12.5% more than Sahil's marks. Ajay got $6\frac{2}{3}$% more marks than Sumit. If the difference between marks scored by Ajay and Sahil is 40, then find the total marks scored by all three.
(a) 665 (b) 450 (c) 555
(d) 745 (e) 625

Directions (51-55): The given bar graph shows the number of phones (Samsung, Micromax and MI) sold by Store 'A' in five different years. Study the graph and answer the following questions:

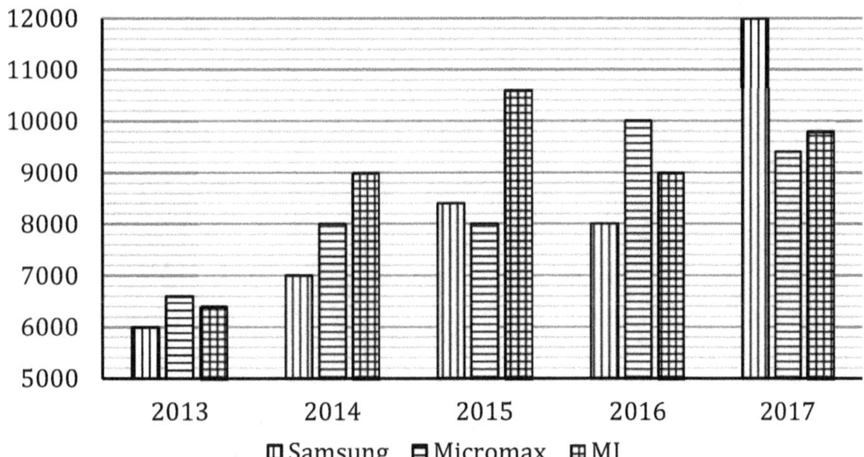

51. Samsung phones sold in 2014 and MI phones sold in 2016 together is what percent more/less then Samsung phones sold in 2016.
(a) 137.5% (b) 75% (c) 100%
(d) 84% (e) 80%

52. Find the difference between average number of Samsung phones sold to average number of Micromax mobile sold in given five years by store A.
(a) 120 (b) 82 (c) 98
(d) 136 (e) 125

53. If Samsung, Micromax and MI phones sold in 2013 is 20%, 10% and 0% respectively more than these mobiles sold in 2012, then, find the average number of phones sold in 2012 of all three companies by store A.
(a) 4000 (b) 6275 (c) 5600
(d) 5800 (e) 5000

54. In 2015, Samsung phones sold to male customers and female customers is in the ratio 7:5. In 2017, Samsung phones sold to male customers and female customers is in the ratio 13:11. Find the ratio of male customers to female customers who bought Samsung phones in 2015 and 2017 together.
(a) 17:13 (b) 19:15 (c) 31:19
(d) 11:15 (e) 11:17

55. If in 2015, $44\frac{4}{9}\%$ customers of store 'A' are female and the ratio of male customers to female customers of Samsung and Micromax in 2015 is 7:5 and 7:9 respectively, then find the number of female customers who bought MI phones in 2015.
(a) 4000 (b) 3500 (c) 6000
(d) 5400 (e) 4800

56. There are four Red, two Green and two Blue ball in a bag. If one ball is drawn at random from the bag, then find the probability of the ball drawn out not being blue.
(a) $\frac{1}{4}$ (b) $\frac{3}{8}$ (c) $\frac{3}{6}$
(d) $\frac{5}{8}$ (e) $\frac{3}{4}$

57. The sum of 30% of x and 45% of y is equal to zero and the difference between 60% of x and 20% of y is equal to 22, then find the sum of x and y.
(a) 25 (b) 15 (c) 10
(d) 30 (e) 20

58. The ratio of the speeds of Ajay and Ramesh is 2:5. If Ajay covers 240 km in 8hrs then in how much time will Ramesh cover a distance of 780 km?
(a) 10hrs 24minutes
(b) 5 hrs 48 minutes
(c) 8 hrs40minutes
(d) 12 hrs20 minutes
(e) 10 hrs and 36 minutes

59. If 6 women or 8 boys can do a piece of work in 12 days then in how many days 3 women and 5 boys can do the same piece of work?
(a) $7\frac{1}{3}$ days (b) $6\frac{1}{3}$ days
(c) $10\frac{2}{3}$ days (d) $12\frac{4}{5}$ days
(e) $14\frac{2}{3}$ days

60. A father has three children with at least one boy. What will be the probability that he has two boys and one girl?
(a) $\frac{1}{4}$ (b) $\frac{1}{3}$ (d) $\frac{2}{3}$
(d) $\frac{3}{8}$ (e) $\frac{5}{8}$

Directions (61-65): Find the wrong number in the following number series:

61. 256, 384, 576, 864, 1296, 1944 , 2924

    (a) 1944   (b) 864   (c) 1296

    (d) 2924   (e) 384

62. 175, 900, 1143, 1224, 1251, 1260, 1263

    (a) 175   (b) 900   (c) 1143

    (d) 1260   (e) 1263

63. 20, 32, 60, 150, 450, 1575, 6300

    (a) 60   (b) 20   (c) 1575

    (d) 6300   (e) 32

64. 824, 568, 440, 376, 344, 330, 320

    (a) 824   (b) 330   (c) 568

    (d) 344   (e) 320

65. 90, 177, 268, 373, 499, 653, 842

    (a) 653   (b) 177   (c) 90

    (d) 842   (e) 499

Directions (66–75): Simplify the following problems and find the value of (?)

66. $\dfrac{750 \div 25 \times 2.5}{384 \div 32 + 0.5} \times 2 = ?$

    (a) 6   (b) 12   (c) 18

    (d) 3   (e) 7

67. 80% 170 + 75% 216 − 10 = ? × 6

    (a) 36   (b) 12   (c) 63

    (d) 54   (e) 48

68. $\sqrt{289} + \sqrt{338 \times 32} = ? + \sqrt{121}$

    (a) 112   (b) 102   (c) 104

    (d) 108   (e) 110

69. $\dfrac{15^2 + 31^2 + 15 \times 62}{11^2 + 12^2 + 11 \times 24} = (?)^2$

    (a) 7   (b) 4   (c) 2

    (d) 8   (e) 10

70. $28\frac{4}{7} \times 16\frac{5}{8} - ? = 36 \times 12 - 8\frac{4}{7} \times 2\frac{1}{3}$

    (a) 43   (b) 63   (c) 73

    (d) 83   (e) 93

71. $62\% \text{ of } \dfrac{1600}{31} + 36\% \text{ of } 1300 = ? \times 4 - 92$

    (a) 296   (b) 148   (c) 152

72. $37\frac{1}{2}\%$ of 600 + $14.\frac{2}{7}\%$ of 210 = ?

    (a) 250   (b) 260   (c) 255

    (d) 265   (e) 280

73. $5\frac{1}{4} + 7\frac{1}{8} + 9\frac{1}{6} = 3\frac{1}{2} + ? + 7\frac{1}{6}$

    (a) $10\frac{7}{8}$ (b) $12\frac{3}{4}$ (c) $17\frac{2}{3}$

    (d) $7\frac{6}{7}$ (e) $7\frac{3}{4}$

74. $3^5 \times 2^6 + 81 \times 2^{(?)} = 16200$

    (a) 2   (b) 3   (c) 4

    (d) 5   (e) 6

75. $9^7 \times 3^{12} = 729 \div 81 \times 3^? \times 3^7$

    (a) 12   (b) 15   (c) 17

    (d) 19   (e) 21

Direction (76–80): What approximate value should come in the place of the question (?) marks in the given questions:

76. 540.05% of 9.99 + 14.89 × 4.02 = ? × 2

    (a) 51   (b) 53   (c) 57

    (d) 60   (e) 62

77. $\sqrt[3]{215.99 \times 8.07} + \sqrt{16.11 \times 24.82} = \sqrt{? \times 4}$

    (a) 16   (b) 256   (c) 4

    (d) 512   (e) 216

78. $3.89 \times \sqrt[3]{1727.99} - \dfrac{11.92 \times 14.11}{6.91 \times 2.01} = \sqrt{?} + \sqrt{168.87}$

    (a) 676   (b) 324   (c) 529

    (d) 729   (e) 1024

79. ?% of 1399.87 + (49.88)² = 269.99 + 19.99% of 11850.11

    (a) 7   (b) 8   (c) 5

    (d) 10   (e) 12

80. $\dfrac{728.87}{(2.99)^{3.99}} + ? = \dfrac{624.92 \times 4.88}{(4.89)^2}$

    (a) 112   (b) 116   (c) 119

    (d) 121   (e) 123

Solutions

REASONING ABILITY

Directions (1-5):

1. **(b)** I. L < J (False)   II. S > M (True)
2. **(d)** I. G ≥ D (False)   II. B < O (False)
3. **(a)** I. N ≥ F (True)   II. E > N (False)
4. **(c)** I. U < Z (False)   II. Z = U (False)
5. **(e)** I. D < O (True)   II. G > M (True)

Directions (6-10):

6. **(e)** POT
7. **(c)** FOUR letters between I and N i.e. J, K, L, M
8. **(c)** TWO i.e. TUB and TOP
9. **(b)** One i.e. IUA
10. **(e)** All words will have at least one vowel. i.e. ITC, HOL, XHO, CTU, QNU

Directions (11-15):

11. **(a)**

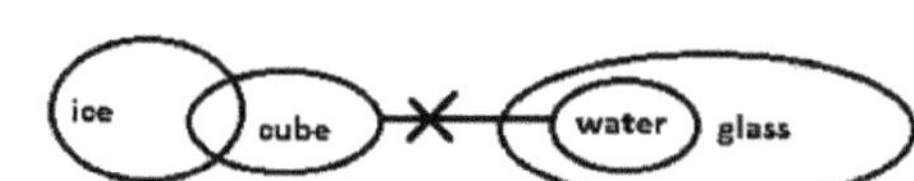

For I – As all water is glass and no water is cube, therefore some glass are not cube will hold true. Hence, Conclusion I can be concluded.

For II – As there is no direct relation between ice and water therefore possibility case will hold true. Hence, Conclusion II can be concluded.

12. (e)

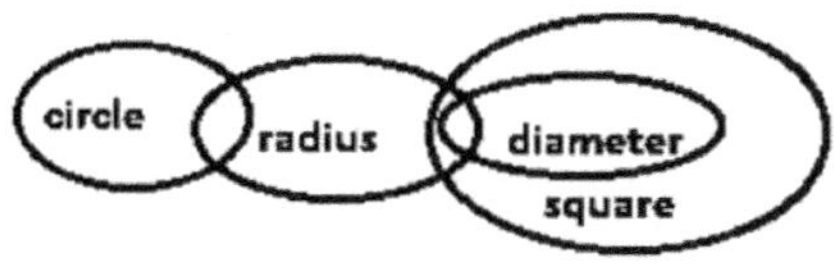

For I – There is no direct relation between circle and square. Hence, Conclusion I cannot be concluded.

For II – From Venn diagram it is clear that some radius are square. So the possibility case will not hold true. Hence, Conclusion II cannot be concluded.

13. (c)

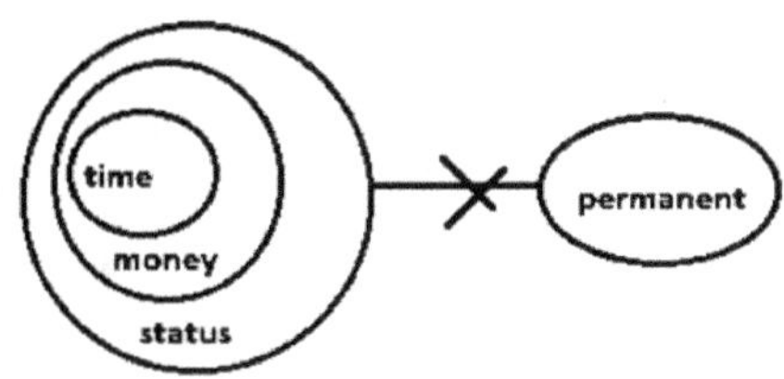

For I –Since all time is status but it cannot be said that all status will be time. Hence, Conclusion I cannot be concluded.

For II – Since all money is status and no status is permanent therefore some money is not permanent will hold true. Hence, Conclusion II can be concluded.

14. (d)

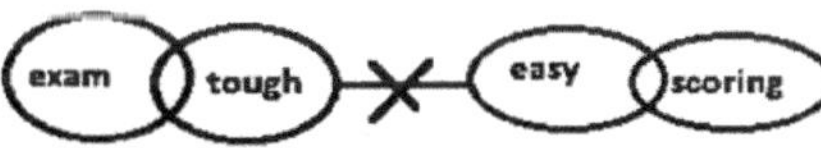

For I – Since, there is no direct relation between the elements exam and easy, therefore possibility case will hold true. Hence, Conclusion I can be concluded.

For II – As there is a no direct relation between tough and scoring, therefore Conclusion II will not hold true. Hence, Conclusion II cannot be concluded.

15. (c)

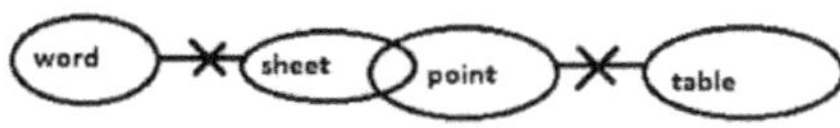

For I – No conclusion can be drawn from two negative statements. Hence, Conclusion I cannot be concluded.

For II – As some sheet are point and no point is table, therefore some sheet which are point cannot be table. Hence, Conclusion II can be concluded.

Directions (16-20):

C faces opposite direction of H. H faces south. A sits fourth to the right of C and one of them sits at the extreme end of the row. Both A and C face same direction (i.e. both faces north).Three persons sit between H and F. D sits to the immediate right of F.B is an immediate neighbour of H. There are two possible cases

Case I

Case II

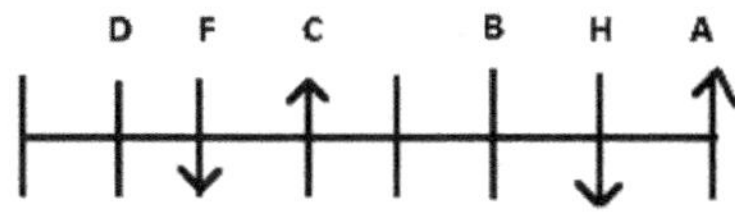

Neither E nor G is an immediate neighbour of A. This will eliminate Case I.

Three persons sit between E and G. G is not at an extreme end of the row. E and G face the same direction as F. B and D face the same direction as C. So final arrangement will be

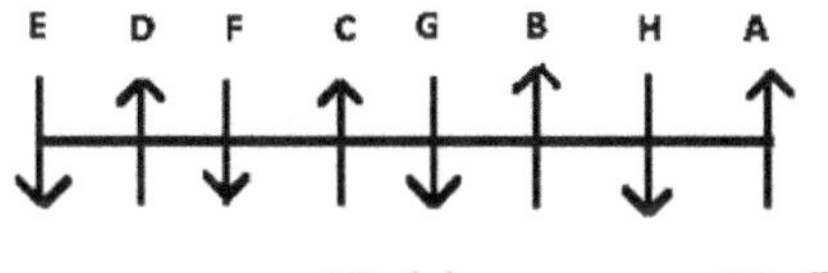

16. (c)	**17. (e)**	**18. (b)**
19. (d)	**20. (d)**	

Directions (21-23):

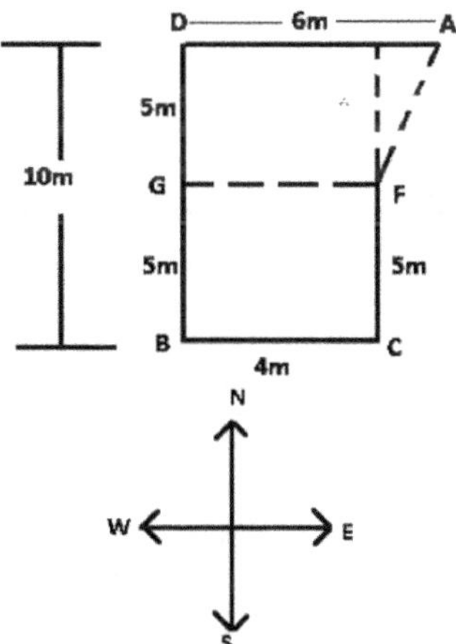

21. (d) Southwest

22. (c) 4m

23. (d) $\sqrt{5^2 + 2^2} = \sqrt{29}$ m

Directions (24-26):

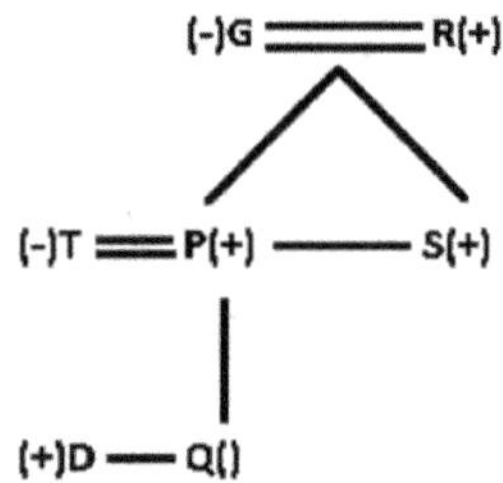

24. (b)   **25. (e)**   **26. (c)**
27. (d) Grandfather
28. (d)

Neel's position from right end = (33-24)
=9th from right end
Eight persons sit between Neel and Nitin so Nitin's position from right hand = (9+9) = 18th from right end. As there are only eight persons to the right of Neel, Nitin cannot sit on the right side of Neel.

29. (b) $(25 \div 5 \times 8 - 15 + 4) = 29$
30. (d) Three

Directions (31-35):
C likes Geography and participates in Cricket. D likes History but does not participate in Cricket, i.e. D participates in Hockey (Since only the one who likes English and Hindi participates in Football). E likes Chemistry. B likes Computer and does not participate with C, i.e., B participates in Hockey.

Sports	Students	Subjects
	A	
Hockey	B	Computer
Cricket	C	Geography
Hockey	D	History
	E	Chemistry
	F	
	G	

Now, neither A nor G likes Biology, i.e. F likes Biology. E participates with the one who likes Biology, so E participates in Cricket. A does not like

English so G likes English and A likes Hindi. So the final arrangement is:

Sports	Students	Subjects
Football	A	Hindi
Hockey	B	Computer
Cricket	C	Geography
Hockey	D	History
Cricket	E	Chemistry
Cricket	F	Biology
Football	G	English

31. (c)   **32. (a)**   **33. (d)**
34. (e)   **35. (a)**

Directions (36-40):
C sits fourth to the left of F.F faces inside. G sits second to the right of F. Two persons sit between A and G. H sits third to the right of G. D sits to the immediate left of H. We get two possibilities:

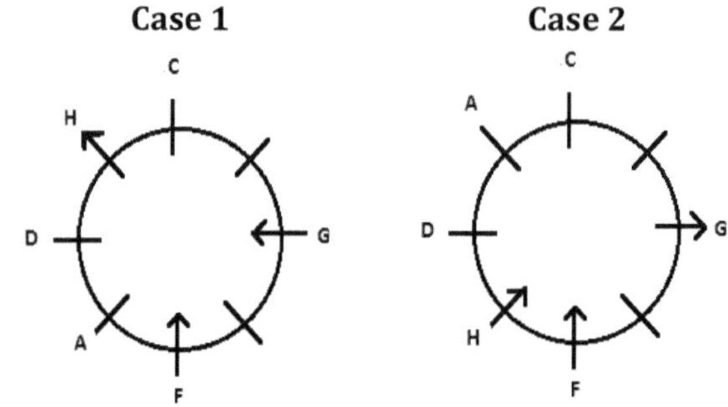

Immediate neighbours of C face the same direction as G. This will eliminate Case 1 as both are stated to be facing opposite direction. E sits second to the right of B. E is not an immediate neighbour of F. D faces opposite direction of F. Direction of C is not known. So, the final arrangement will be:

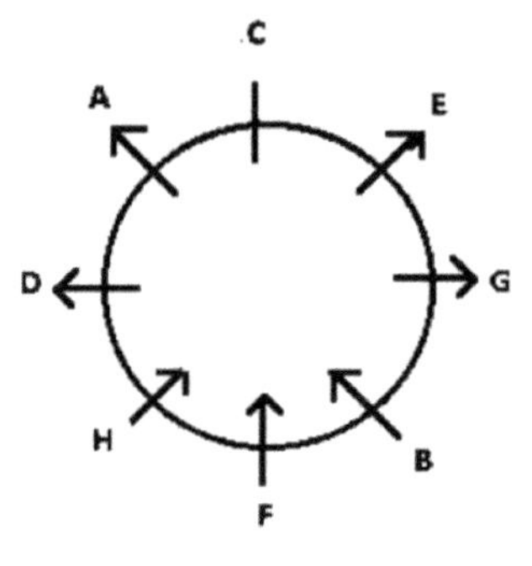

36. (b)   **37. (e)**   **38. (a)**
39. (e)   **40. (d)**

41. (a) Let the milkman buy = y litre of milk.
At the rate of = x Rs./litre
$xy - 5y = 300$ ... (i)
$6y - xy = 250$ ... (ii)
from solving equation (i) & (ii)
$y = 550$ litre

42. (b) Let the Total No. of voters= 100 x
Total No. of voters who cast vote=100x – 8x = 92x
Winner has received = 48x
Votes another candidate received = 92x – 48x = 44x
Given, 48x – 44x = 1200
x = 300
Total no. of voters = 300 × 100 = 30000

43. (c) Let Amount invested by Bhavya in Scheme 'B' = Rs x
Amount invested by Bhavya in Scheme 'A'= Rs (10000 – x)
ATQ,
$$\frac{(10000-x)\times 2\times 15}{100} - x\left[\left(1+\frac{20}{100}\right)^2 - 1\right] = 780$$
$$\frac{(10000-x)\times 3}{10} - x\left[\left(\frac{144}{100}-1\right)\right] = 780$$
$$\frac{30000}{10} - \frac{3x}{10} - \frac{44x}{100} = 780$$
On Solving x = 3000 Rs.

44. (d) let the speed of train = 160x km/hr
Let the speed of car = 100x km/hr
$$\frac{160}{160x} + \frac{20}{60} = \frac{160}{100x}$$
$$\frac{1}{x} + \frac{1}{3} = \frac{8}{5x}$$
$$\frac{1}{3} = \frac{8-5}{5x} \Rightarrow x = \frac{9}{5}$$
Speed of the train = $160 \times \frac{9}{5}$= 32 × 9= 288 km/hr

45. (b) $\frac{3}{A} = \frac{1}{B} + \frac{1}{C}$ ...(i)
$\frac{4}{B} = \frac{1}{A} + \frac{1}{C}$ ...(ii)
$\frac{1}{A} + \frac{1}{B} + \frac{1}{C} = \frac{1}{24}$ ...(iii)
From eqn (i) and (iii)
$\frac{4}{A} = \frac{1}{24}$
A= 96 Days

46. (d) Let radius of circle and side of square be 'r' and 'a' respectively
Perimeter of Circle and square is equal
$\Rightarrow 2\pi r = 4a$
$a = \frac{\pi r}{2}$
Required Ratio = Area of circle : Area of square
$= \pi r^2 : a^2 = \pi r^2 : \left(\frac{\pi}{2}r\right)^2 = 14 : 11$

47. (b) $\frac{60+24+50+73+13+x+y+z}{8} = 44$
$x + y + z = 352 - 220$

$x + y + z = 132$
Average of (x, y & z) = $\frac{x+y+z}{3} = \frac{132}{3} = 44$

48. (d) Let the average = x Rs.
50x + 128 = 62 (x – 2)
50x + 128 = 62x – 124
12x = 252 ⇒x = 21 Rs.

49. (a) Let quantity of water and milk present in jar be 200x and 300x
1. Milk added 30% of quantity of water
$\rightarrow \frac{30}{100} \times 200x = 60$
Now, milk quantity $\rightarrow$ 360x
2. water added milk present 10% of quantity of $= \frac{10}{100} \times 360x = 36x$
Water quantity become = 236x
New ratio of water : Milk = 236x : 360x= 59:90

50. (a) Let Sahil's marks = 80x
So, Sumit's marks $= \frac{80x \times 112.5}{100} = 90x$
So, Ajay's marks $= \frac{90x \times 106\frac{2}{3}}{100} = 96x$
ATQ,
Ajay's marks is 40 more than the Sahil's marks
$\Rightarrow 96x - 80x = 40$
$\Rightarrow x = 2.5$
Total marks scored by all three = (80 + 90 + 96) × 2.5 =266× 2.5 =665

51. (c) Samsung phones sold in 2014 = 7000
MI phones sold in 2016 = 9000
Samsung phones sold in 2016 = 8000
Required % $= \frac{(7000+9000)-8000}{8000} \times 100\% =$ 100%

52. (a) Average of Samsung phones sold
$= \frac{6000+7000+8400+8000+12000}{5} = 8280$
Average of Micromax phones sold
$= \frac{6600+8000+8000+10000+9400}{5} = 8400$
Required difference = 8400 – 8280 = 120

53. (d) Samsung phones sold in 2012 $= \frac{6000\times 100}{120} = 5000$
Micromax phones sold in 2012 $= \frac{6600\times 100}{100} = 6000$
MI phones sold in 2012 = 6400
So, Average number of phones sold in 2012
$= \frac{5000+6000+6400}{3} = \frac{17400}{3} = 5800$

54. (b) Total customers who bought Samsung phones in 2015 = 8400
Male customers who bought Samsung phones in 2015 $= \frac{7}{12} \times 8400 = 4900$

Females customers who bought Samsung phones in 2015 = 8400 – 4900 = 3500

Total customers who bought Samsung phones in 2017 = 12000

Male customers who bought Samsung phones in 2017 = $12000 \times \frac{13}{24}$ = 6500

Female customers who bought Samsung phones in 2017 = 12000 – 6500 = 5500

Required ratio = $\frac{4900+6500}{3500+5500} = \frac{11400}{9000}$ = 19 : 15

55. (a) Total customer in 2015 = 8400 + 8000 + 10600

= 27000

Total female customers in 2015

$= \frac{4}{9} \times 27000$

= 12000

Female customers who bought Samsung phones in 2015

$= \frac{5}{12} \times 8400 = 3500$

Female customers who bought Micromax phones in 2015

$= \frac{9}{16} \times 8000 = 4500$

So, female customers who bought MI phones

= 12000 – (3500 + 4500) = 4000

56. (e) Probability of drawn ball being blue $= \frac{2}{8} \Rightarrow \frac{1}{4}$

Probability of drawn ball being not blue

$= 1 - \frac{1}{4} = \frac{3}{4}$

57. (c) $30x + 45y = 0$

$6x + 9y = 0$

$2x = -3y$ ...(i)

$\frac{60x}{100} - \frac{20y}{100} = 22$

$6x - 2y = 220$ ...(ii)

From equation (1) & (2)

$-9y - 2y = 220$

$-11y = 220$

$y = -20$

$x = 30$

Hence, $x + y = 10$

58. (a) Speed of Ajay $= \frac{240}{8}$ km/hr = 30 km/hr

Speed of Ramesh $= \frac{30}{2} \times 5$ = 75 km/hr

Time required, travelling 780 km by Ramesh,

$= \frac{780}{75} = 10.4$

10.4 = 10 hrs 24 mins.

59. (c) Let the work done by each boy and a woman in a day be B and W units respectively.

$6W = 8B$

$\frac{W}{B} = \frac{4}{3}$

Efficiency of Women: Boys = 4:3

Total work if each woman does 4 units of work each day or each boy does 3 units each day $\Rightarrow$

$= 4 \times 6 \times 12$ or $= 3 \times 8 \times 12$

= 288 units = 288 units

Let 'D' Days be required to finish the entire work when 3women and 5 boys will work on it,

D × [3W + 5B] = 288

D [3 × 4 + 5 × 3] = 288

D [27] = 288

$d = \frac{288}{27} = 10\frac{2}{3}$days.

60. (b) Total no. of possible cases = 3

1) 1 boy 2 girl

2) 2 boy 1 girl

3) 3 boy 0 girl

Desired case = 2 boy, 1 girl

Probability $= \frac{1}{3}$

61. (d);

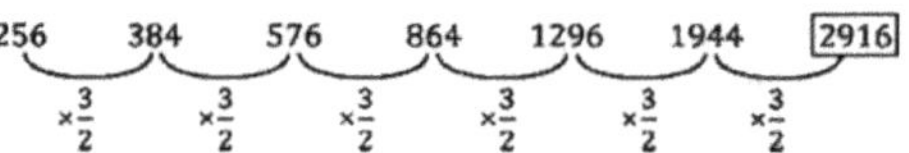

62. (a);

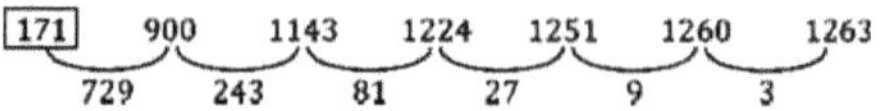

63. (e)

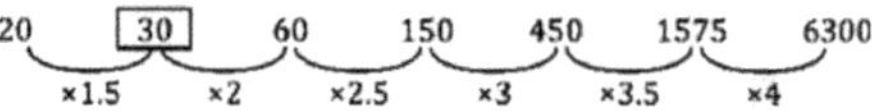

64. (b)

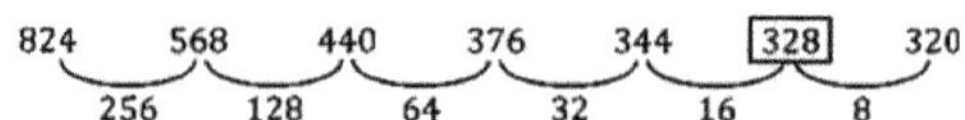

65. (c)

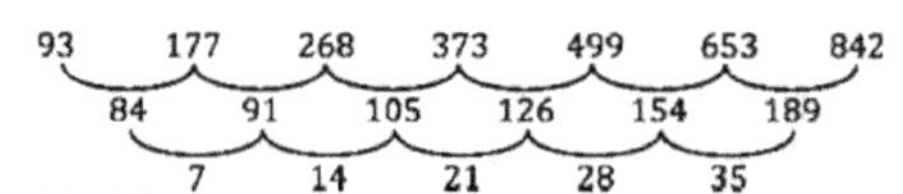

66. (b) $\frac{30 \times 2.5}{12 + 0.5} \times 2 = ?$

$\frac{75}{12.5} \times 2 = ?$

$12 = ?$

67. (e) $\frac{80 \times 170}{100} + \frac{3}{4} \times 216 - 10 = ? \times 6$

$136 + 162 - 10 = ? \times 6$

$\frac{288}{6} = ?$

$48 = ?$

68. (e) $17 + \sqrt{169 \times 2 \times 2 \times 16} = ? + 11$

$17 + 104 = ? + 11$

$110 = ?$

69. (c) $\frac{(15+31)^2}{(11+12)^2} = (?)^2$

$\left[\frac{46}{23}\right]^2 = (?)^2$

$4 = ?^2$

$? = 2$

70. (b) $\frac{200}{7} \times \frac{133}{8} - ? = 432 - \frac{60}{7} \times \frac{7}{3}$

$25 \times 19 - ? = 432 - 20$

$? = 63$

71. (b) $32 + 468 = ? \times 4 - 92$

$32 + 468 + 92 = ? \times 4$

$\frac{592}{4} = ?$

$? = 148$

72. (c) $\frac{3}{8} \times 600 + \frac{1}{7} \times 210 = 225 + 30 = 255$

73. (a) $21 + \frac{1}{4} + \frac{1}{8} + \frac{1}{6} = 10 + \frac{1}{2} + \frac{1}{6} + ?$

$21 + \frac{13}{24} = 10 + \frac{2}{3} + ?$

$11 + \frac{13}{24} - \frac{2}{3} = ?$

$11 - \frac{1}{8} = ?$

$\frac{87}{8} = ?$

$? = 10\frac{7}{8}$

74. (b) $15552 + 81 \times 2^{(?)} = 16200$

$81 \times 2^{(?)} = 648$

$2^? = \frac{648}{81}$

$2^? = 8$

$? = 3$

75. (c) $3^{14} \times 3^{12} = 9 \times 3^? \times 3^7$

$\frac{3^{14} \times 3^{12}}{3^2 \times 3^7} = 3^?$

$3^{17} = 3^?$

$? = 17$

76. (c) $\frac{10 \times 540}{100} + 15 \times 4 = ? \times 2$

$54 + 60 = ? \times 2$

$\frac{114}{2} = ?$

$57 = ?$

77. (b) $\sqrt[3]{216 \times 8} + \sqrt{16 \times 25} = \sqrt{? \times 4}$

$6 \times 2 + 4 \times 5 = \sqrt{? \times 4}$

$\frac{32}{2} = \sqrt{?}$

$? = 256$

78. (c) $4 \times 12 - \frac{12 \times 14}{7 \times 2} = \sqrt{?} + 13$

$48 - 6 \times 2 = \sqrt{?} + 13$

$36 - 13 = \sqrt{?}$

$23 = \sqrt{?}$

$? = 529$

79. (d) $?\% \text{ of } 1400 + (50)^2 = 270 + 20\% \text{ of } 11850$

$?\% \text{ of } 1400 + 2500 = 270 + \frac{11850}{5}$

$?\% \text{ of } 1400 = 2640 - 2500$

$?\% \text{ of } 1400 = 140$

$? = 10$

80. (b) $\frac{729}{3^4} + ? = \frac{625 \times 5}{5^2}$

$\frac{729}{81} + ? = 125$

$? = 116$

REASONING ABILITY

Directions (1-5): In each of the following questions, relationships between some elements are shown in the statements. These statements are followed by conclusions numbered I and II. Read the statements and give the answer.
(a) If only conclusion I follows.
(b) If only conclusion II follows.
(c) If either conclusion I or II follows.
(d) If neither conclusion I nor II follows.
(e) If both conclusions I and II follow.

1. **Statements:** $Z \leq X \leq T > U = V$; $A \geq B = T < R$
   Conclusions: I. $A > Z$ II. $Z = A$
2. **Statements:** $J > P > E = G \leq M$; $D > O \geq C = E$
   Conclusions: I. $D < J$ II. $G < D$
3. **Statements:** $D \leq O \leq N = S < R$; $T \geq F > M > R$
   Conclusions: I. $T > D$ II. $N < F$
4. **Statements:** $G < I \leq F = M \leq E > N \geq O$
   Conclusions: I. $N < G$ II. $F < O$
5. **Statements:** $T = R \leq O < Y = W \geq I > N$
   Conclusions: I. $W > T$ II. $N \leq Y$

Directions (6-10): Study the following information carefully and answer the questions given below.

In a certain code language 'mango is very tasty' is written as 'la ja ta sa'; 'mango is a fruit' is written as 'ja sa op nm' and 'apple is tasty' is written as 'sa ty ta'.

6. Which of the following represents the code for 'apple'?
   (a) sa (b) ty
   (c) ta (d) ja
   (e) None of these
7. How is 'fruit' coded in the given language?
   (a) ja (b) sa
   (c) op (d) nm
   (e) Cannot be determined
8. How is 'tasty' coded in the given language?
   (a) la (b) ja
   (c) sa (d) ta
   (e) Cannot be determined
9. What can be the code for 'apple is a fruit'?
   (a) op ja nm sa
   (b) sa ta la ty
   (c) sa ty nm op
   (d) sa ta op nm
   (e) Cannot be determined
10. Which of the following is coded as 'op'?
    (a) very (b) a
    (c) tasty (d) fruit
    (e) Either (b) or (d)

Directions (11-15): Study the information and answer the following questions:

Nine persons A, B, C, D, E, F, G, H and I are sitting in a row. Some are facing north and some are facing south (but not necessarily in the same order).
(**Note:** Facing the same direction means if one is facing north then the other also faces north and vice versa. Facing opposite direction means if one is facing north then the other faces south and vice versa).

D sits third to the right of A and one of them sits at the extreme end of the line. Both D and A face north. Three persons sit between A and E, who faces south. C sits to the immediate left of D. Four persons sit between C and H and both face the same direction as A. G sits second to the left of E. B sits to the immediate right of A. I sits at one of the extreme ends. Immediate neighbours of H face the same direction as E. H does not sit to the immediate left of E. B and F face the same direction. B and E face opposite directions.

11. Who among the following sits to the immediate right to E?
    (a) D (b) H
    (c) F (d) I
    (e) None of these
12. How many persons sit between B and G?
    (a) none (b) one
    (c) two (d) three
    (e) More than three
13. Four of the following five are alike in a certain way and form a group. Who among the following does not belong to that group?
    (a) B (b) I
    (c) F (d) H
    (e) A
14. Which pair among the following sits at the extreme ends of the row?
    (a) A, F (b) D, I
    (c) A, I (d) A, D
    (e) None of these
15. How many persons face south?
    (a) one (b) two
    (c) three (d) four
    (e) Cannot be determined

Directions (16-17): Study the following sequence and answer the given questions:

Suresh leaves his house and starts walking in the north direction. After 10m. he turns left. Then he walks for 5m. and turns to his right. He walks for 4m. and then takes three consecutive left turns and walks 9m., 14m. and 10 m. respectively. Finally, he stops at point T.

16. How far is Suresh from his starting point?
    (a) 5m.   (b) 9m.
    (c) 4m.   (d) 14m.
    (e) Cannot be determined

17. In which direction is point T with respect to the starting point?
    (a) west   (b) south-east
    (c) south   (d) north-west
    (e) Cannot be determined

Directions (18-20): Study the following information and answer the given questions.

In a family of eight members there are two married couples. A is the mother of B, who is married to D. E is the son of B. D has two children. F is the mother-in-law of E. B is grandmother of G, who is niece of C. K is the daughter of F.

18. How is A related to C?
    (a) granddaughter
    (b) grandmother
    (c) grandson
    (d) grandfather
    (e) Cannot be determined

19. How is C related to B?
    (a) son   (b) daughter
    (c) grandson   (d) uncle
    (e) Cannot be determined

20. How many male members are there in the family?
    (a) one   (b) three
    (c) two   (d) four
    (e) either (b) or (c)

Directions (21-25): Study the following sequence and answer the given questions.
A @ 3 4 % E N M $ 8 6 & L D S # 9 8 6 Q Y Z 1 7 % R O G @ 2 I B 2 U &

21. Which of the following elements is eighth to the left of the nineteenth from the left end of the given arrangement?
    (a) 6   (b) %
    (c) $ (d) 8
    (e) None of these

22. If all the symbols are dropped from the series, which element will be fourth to the right of the one which is twelfth from the right end?
    (a) 9   (b) O
    (c) R   (d) 7
    (e) None of these

23. How many such symbols are there in the given series, which are immediately preceded by a consonant and followed by a digit?

    (a) none   (b) one   (c) two
    (d) three   (e) four

24. How many consonants are there in the given series, which are immediately preceded by a consonant but not immediately followed by a consonant?
    (a) one
    (b) two
    (c) three
    (d) More than three
    (e) None of these

25. What should come in place of the question mark (?) in the following series based on the above arrangement?
    @%4 N8$ &SD 9Q6 ?
    (a) Y71   (b) Z7%
    (c) Z%R   (d) ZR%
    (e) Z%7

26. Find the odd one out.
    (a) BDG   (b) HJM
    (c) NPS   (d) TVX
    (e) OQT

27. In a row of 25 students Mahesh is 18th from the right end. Nine students sit between Vijay and Mahesh. All of them are facing north. Find the position of Vijay from the right end?
    (a) 10th   (b) 9th
    (c) 8th   (d) 7th
    (e) Cannot be determined

28. If in the number 9182736405, positions of the 1st and the 2nd digits are interchanged, positions of the 3rd and 4th digits are interchanged and so on till the positions of 9th and 10th digits are interchanged, then which digit will be 8th from the right end?
    (a) 2   (b) 6
    (c) 5   (d) 9
    (e) None of these

29. How many pairs of letters are there in the word
    "PROPER" which have as many letters between them in the word as in alphabetical series (backwards or forwards)?
    (a) none   (b) one   (c) two
    (d) three   (e) four

30. If A means '–', B means '×', C means '÷' and D means '+' then
    4 D 80 C 4 B 2 A 1 = ?
    (a) 41   (b) 42   (c) 43
    (d) 13   (e) 14

Directions (31-35): In each of the questions below are given some statements followed by two conclusions. You have to take the given statements to be true even if they seem to be at variance with commonly known facts. Read all the conclusions and then decide which of the given conclusions logically follows from the given statements, disregarding commonly known facts. Give the answer accordingly:

31. **Statements:** Some cake is pastry
    No pastry is sugar
    All sugar are sweets
    Conclusions: I. Some cake are sweets.
    II. Some sweets are pastry
    (a) Both I and II follow.
    (b) Either I or II follows.
    (c) Only II follows.
    (d) Only I follows.
    (e) Neither I nor II follows.

32. **Statements:** All radio are printer
    Some printer are drives
    All ink are drives
    Conclusions: I. Some printer are ink
    II. Some radio are drives
    (a) Both I and II follow.
    (b) Either I or II follows.
    (c) Only II follows.
    (d) Only I follows.
    (e) Neither I nor II follows.

33. **Statements:** No hero is villain
    Some heroine are hero
    No villain is comedian
    Conclusions: I. No hero is comedian
    II. Some heroine are not villain
    (a) Both I and II follow.
    (b) Either I or II follows.
    (c) Only II follows.
    (d) Only I follows.
    (e) Neither I nor II follows.

34. **Statements:** All space is fire
    All fire is water
    Some water is ice
    Conclusions: I. Some ice being space is a possibility
    II. Some space is water
    (a) Both I and II follow.
    (b) Either I or II follows.
    (c) Only II follows.
    (d) Only I follows.
    (e) Neither I nor II follows.

35. **Statements** Some apple are red

All red are mango
Some mango are green
Conclusions: I. Some apple are green
II. No apple is green.
(a) Both I and II follow.
(b) Either I or II follows.
(c) Only II follows.
(d) Only I follows.
(e) Neither I nor II follows.

Directions (36-40): Study the following information carefully and answer the given questions.

Eight people i.e. A ,B ,C ,D ,E ,F ,G and H are sitting around a circular table, facing towards the centre (not necessarily in the same order). C sits fourth to the right of G, who is not an immediate neighbour of B. B who faces F, is an immediate neighbour of A. E sits third to the left of H who is not an immediate neighbour of D.

36. Who among the following sits to the immediate left of A?
    (a) B
    (b) D
    (c) E
    (d) Cannot be determined
    (e) None of these

37. What is the position of E with respect to B?
    (a) Third to the right
    (b) Fourth to the right
    (c) Third to the left
    (d) Second to the left
    (e) None of these

38. How many people sit between A and E?
    (a) one   (b) two
    (c) three   (d) none
    (e) Cannot be determined

39. What is the position of H with respect to C?
    (a) Immediate left
    (b) Immediate right
    (c) Third to the right
    (d) Third to the left
    (e) Second to the left

40. Who sits opposite D?
    (a) B   (b) C   (c) H
    (d) A   (e) G

QUANTITATIVE APTITUDE

41. The length of a rectangular field is thrice its breadth. If Rs. 480 is required to paint the floor at the rate Rs. 2.5 per sq m., then what would be the difference between the length and breadth of the field?
    (a) 16 m.   (b) 8 m.   (c) 12 m.
    (d) 24 m.   (e) 20 m.

42. A trader sells two articles for Rs. 4,800 each, neither losing nor gaining in total. If he sold one of the articles at a gain of 20%, the other is sold at a loss of what percent?

(a) 20%   (b) $18\frac{2}{9}\%$ (c) $14\frac{2}{7}\%$

(d) 21%   (e) None of these

43. If the manufacturer gains 10%, the whole-sale dealer 15% and the retailer 25%, then what would be the cost of production of a table (in Rs.), the retail price of which is Rs. 1265?

(a) Rs. 1400   (b) Rs. 800   (c) Rs. 1000

(d) Rs. 1200   (e) Rs. 900

44. 12 men can complete a project in 15 days and 10 women can complete the same project in 24 days. 9 men start working and after 6 days they are replaced by 12 women. In how many days will 12 women complete the remaining work?

(a) 20   (b) 10   (c) 16

(d) 18   (e) 14

45. Arjun and Suman together can complete an assignment of data entry in 6 days. Suman's speed in key depression is 60% of Arjun's speed and the total number of key depressions during the completion of an assignment of data entry was 5,76,000. What is Arjun's speed in key depressions per hour if each works for 12 hours a day?

(a) 4800   (b) 6400   (c) 5000

(d) 7200   (e) 8400

Directions (46-50): What will come in place of the question mark (?) in the following questions?

46. $\sqrt{360 - 225 \times 2 + 379} = ?$

(a) 17   (b) 19   (c) 27

(d) 13   (e) 23

47. $9^3 \times 81^2 \div 27^3 = (3)^?$

(a) 3   (b) 4   (c) 5

(d) 6   (e) 8

48. $572 \div 26 \times 12 - 200 = (2)^?$

(a) 5   (b) 6   (c) 7

(d) 8   (e) 10

49. $4\frac{1}{2} - 2\frac{5}{6} = ? -1\frac{7}{12}$

(a) $3\frac{1}{4}$ (b) $3\frac{5}{12}$ (c) $2\frac{7}{12}$

(d) $3\frac{3}{4}$ (e) $5\frac{2}{3}$

50. 36% of 245 – 40% of 210 = 10 –?

(a) 4.2   (b) 6.8   (c) 4.9

(d) 5.6   (e) 5.8

Directions (51-55): The table shown below shows the population of five different cities. Some data is given in percent while some data is given in numbers. Study the table carefully and solve the following questions.

City	Male	Female	Transgender
X	45%	30%	2000
Y	50%	3000	35%
Z	8000	35%	15%
A	45%	3600	25%
B	38%	32%	4200

Note: Total population = Male + Female + Transgender

51. The total Population in city Z is what percent less than the total population in city Y.

(a) 30%   (b) 25%   (c) 20%

(d) 15%   (e) 17.5%

52. The ratio of number of literate males to number of illiterate males in city A is 11:7. What is the difference between the number of literate males and number of Illiterate males in city A?

(a) 900   (b) 1050   (c) 1400

(d) 800   (e) 1200

53. Number of Female population in city Z is how much percent less than the total number of male and transgender population in city A.

(a) 25%   (b) $33\frac{1}{3}\%$ (c) 50%

(d) $66\frac{2}{3}\%$ (e) 75%

54. The number of male population in city B is how much more than the number of female population in city X?

(a) 2900   (b) 2840   (c) 2760

(d) 2920   (e) 2980

55. Find the ratio of number of transgender population in city Z to the number of transgender population in city A.

(a) 4 : 5   (b) 5 : 4   (c) 3 : 5

(d) 5 : 3   (e) 2 : 5

56. A man sees a train passing over a bridge of length 1 km. The length of the train is half the length of the bridge. If the train passes the bridge in 2 minutes, then find the speed of the train.

(a) 30 kmph.   (b) 45 kmph.

(c) 50 kmph.   (d) 60 kmph

(e) 54 kmph.

57. A man can swim 48 m/min in still water. He swims 200 m against the current and 200 m with the current. If the difference between the time taken in both the cases is 10 min, then what is the speed of the current?

(a) 30 m/min   (b) 31 m/min   (c) 29 m/min

(d) 32 m/min   (e) 26 m/min

58. A booster pump can be used for filling as well as for emptying a tank. The capacity of the tank is 2400 m³. The emptying capacity of the pump is 10 m³ per minute more than its filling capacity and the pump needs 8 minutes less to empty the tank than it needs to fill it. What is the filling capacity of the pump (in m³ per minute)?

(a) 54   (b) 60   (c) 50

(d) 45   (e) 65

59. Find the number of ways in which the letters of the word ARRANGE can be arranged such that both Rs do not come together.
   (a) 950   (b) 800   (c) 900
   (d) 750   (e) 920

60. Shikha's age is one-sixth of her father's age. After 10 years, Shikha's father's age will be twice of Vignesh's age at that time. If Vignesh's eighth birthday was celebrated 2 years ago, then what is Shikha's present age?
   (a) 7 years   (b) 4 years   (c) 6 years
   (d) 4.5 years   (e) 5 years

Directions (61 – 65): In the following questions two quantities are given for each question. Compare the numeric value of both the quantities and answer accordingly.

(a)   Quantity I > Quantity II
(b)   Quantity II > Quantity I
(c)   Quantity I ≥ Quantity II
(d)   Quantity II ≥ Quantity I
(e)   Quantity I = Quantity II or relation can't be established.

61. **Quantity I:** Sum of the first and second number is $\frac{2}{3}$rd of the first number, equal to the cube of the second number and the second number is equal to 12% of 100.
   Quantity II: 2352

62. **Quantity I:** Time taken by the police to catch the thief. A thief robbed a shop and got away in a car going at a speed of 60 km/h. at 11:00 am. The Police located the position of the thief and chased him at 11:15 a.m. from the shop in a car. Maximum speed of the police car is 65 km/h.
   Quantity II: 3hr

63. **Quantity I:** 4
   Quantity II: Value of 'x' A, B and C started a business together with Rs. 12,000, Rs. 12,000 and Rs. 8,000 respectively. B worked only for 'x' months while C left the business 'x' months before the completion of the year. Out of the annual profit of Rs. 3,200, 'A' got Rs. 1,800.

64. **Quantity I: Value of 'X'** The time taken by a boat for covering 'X – 18' km. upstream is equal to the time taken by it for covering 'X' km. downstream, if the upstream speed is 6 km/hr. less than the downstream speed and the speed of boat in still water is 15 kmph.
   Quantity II: 50

65. **Quantity I:** Price at which P sold watch to Q.'P' sells his watch at 20% profit to Q while Q sells it to R at a loss of 10%. R pays Rs.2160.
   Quantity II: 1600

Directions (66-70): What will come in the place of the question mark (?) in the following number series?

66. 2, 4, 11, 37, ? , 771
   (a) 148   (b) 147   (c) 151
   (d) 153   (e) 155

67. 24, 12, 12, 24, ? , 408
   (a) 96   (b) 84   (c) 88
   (d) 92   (e) 100

68. 2, 12, 30, 56, 90, ?
   (a) 122   (b) 127   (c) 135
   (d) 125   (e) 132

69. 3, 8, 15, 24, ? , 48
   (a) 34   (b) 35   (c) 36
   (d) 37   (e) 38

70. 18, 18, 27, 54, ? , 405
   (a) 120   (b) 125   (c) 130
   (d) 135   (e) 140

71. Two groups of students, whose average ages are 15 years and 25 years, combine to form a third group, whose average age is 22 years. What is the ratio of the number of students in the first group to that in the second group?
   (a) 5 : 2   (b) 2 : 5   (c) 3 : 7
   (d) 5 : 3   (e) 4 : 5

72. Ram's age is (3x+2y) years and his only son's age is 'x' years, while his only daughter's age is 'y' years. Ram's son is 3 years older than his sister. Find the average age of the family if the age of Ram's wife, who is 5 years younger than her husband, is 29 years.
   (a) 14.5   (b) 19.0   (c) 16.5
   (d) 22.5   (e) 20.5

73. The average temperature from Monday to Thursday is 48°C and from Tuesday to Friday it is 52° C. If the temperature on Monday is 42° C, what was it on Friday?
   (a) 55° C   (b) 52° C   (c) 58° C
   (d) 51° C   (e) 56° C

74. How many kgs. of tea worth Rs. 25 per kg must be blended with 30 kgs. of tea worth Rs. 30 per kg, so that by selling the blended variety at Rs. 30 per kg there would be a gain of 10%?
   (a) 30 kg   (b) 32 kg   (c) 36 kg
   (d) 42 kg   (e) 34 kg

75. An alloy contains aluminium and zinc in the ratio of 5:3 and another alloy contains aluminium and copper in the ratio of 8:5. If equal weights of both the alloys are mixed together, then the weight of copper in the resulting alloy per kg will be
   (a) $\frac{26}{5}$ (b) $\frac{5}{26}$ (c) $\frac{7}{31}$
   (d) $\frac{31}{7}$ (e) None of these

Directions (76-80): Simplify the following questions.

76. $\sqrt{?} \times \sqrt{3025} = 2695$
   (a) 2401   (b) 2209   (c) 2601

(d) 2304   (e) 2400

77. $(98)^2 + (?) = (150)^2 - (80)^2 - 737$
     (a) 6084   (b) 5759   (c) 5777
     (d) 6724   (e) 5658

78. $48 + 8 \times 0.75 - 5 = ?$
     (a) 22   (b) 36   (c) 49
     (d) 56   (e) 46

79. $18.657 - 7.549 - 4.111 - 1.630 = ?$
     (a) 4.673   (b) 6.893   (c) 6.562
     (d) 5.367   (e) 6.367

80. $2950 \div 12.5 + 160 = ?$
     (a) 392   (b) 390   (c) 396
     (d) 394   (e) 400

Solutions

REASONING ABILITY

Direction (1-5):
1. **(c)** I. A > Z (False)   II. Z = A (False)
2. **(b)** I. D < J (False)   II. G < D (True)
3. **(e)** I. T > D (True)   II. N < F (True)
4. **(d)** I. N < G (False)   II. F < O (False)
5. **(a)** I. W > T (True)   II. N ≤ Y (False)

Direction (6-10):

Word	Code
mango	ja
is	sa
tasty	ta
apple	ty
very	la
a/fruit	op/nm

6. **(b)**   7. **(e)**   8. **(d)**
9. **(c)**   10. **(e)**

Direction (11-15):
D sits third to the right of A and one of them sits at the extreme end of the line. Both face north. Three persons sit between A and E, who faces south. G sits second to the left of E. B sits to the immediate right of A. I sits at one of the extreme ends. There are two cases:

Case I

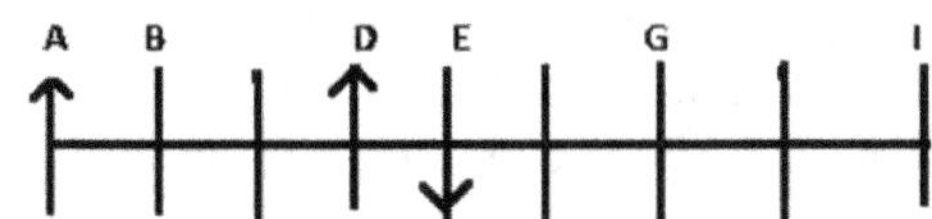

Case II

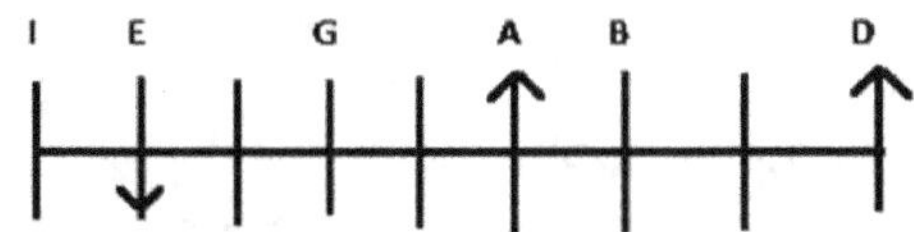

C sits to the immediate left of D. Four persons sit between C and H and both faces the same direction as A. H does not sit to the immediate left of E. This will eliminate Case II.

Now immediate neighbours of H face the same direction as E. B and F face the same direction. B and E face opposite directions. So final arrangement will be

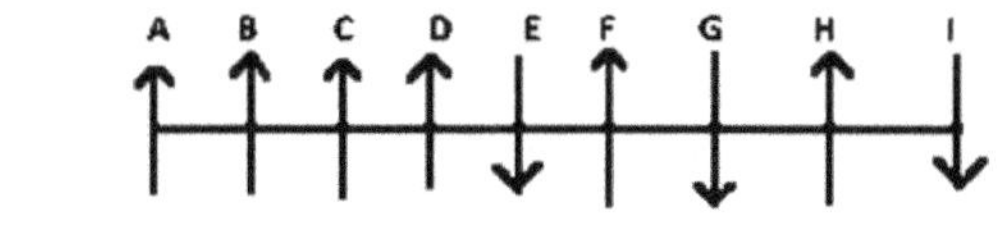

11. **(a)**   12. **(e)**   13. **(b)**
14. **(c)**   15. **(c)**

Direction (16-17):

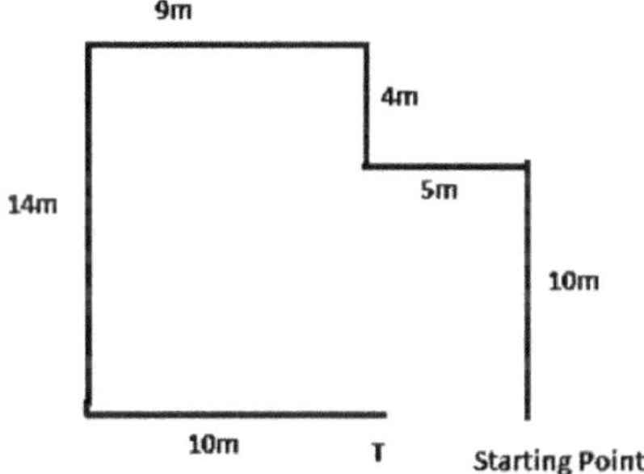

16. **(c)** $((9+5) - 10) = 4m$
17. **(a)** West

Direction (18-20):

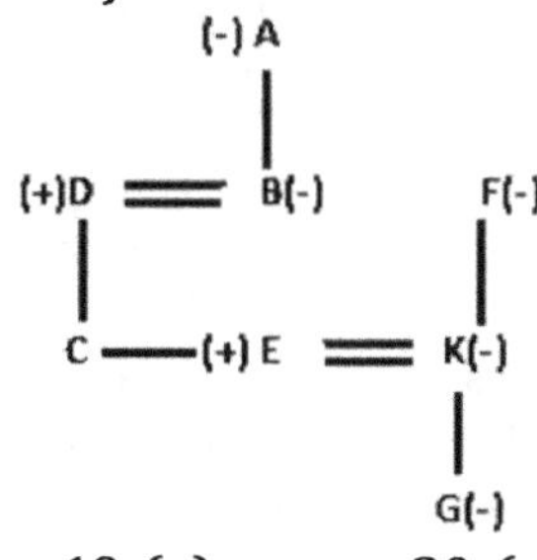

18. **(b)**   19. **(e)**   20. **(e)**

Direction (21-25):
21. **(a)** 6
22. **(c)** R
23. **(d)** Three – M$8, S#9, G@2
24. **(c)** Three – NM$, DS#, YZ1
25. **(e)** Z%7
26. **(d)**
27. **(c)**

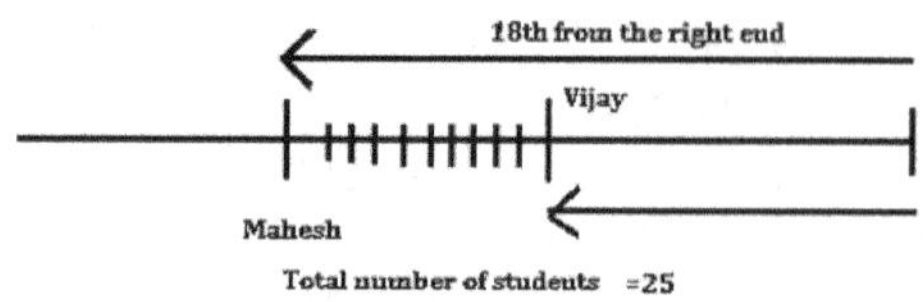

Mahesh's position from right end is 18th
So Vijay's position from the right end is
(18 – 10) = 8th from the right end.

28. (a)

9 1 8 2 7 3 6 4 0 5

1 9 2 8 3 7 4 6 5 0 (New Arrangement)

29. (e) Four

30. (c) $4 + 80 \div 4 \times 2 - 1 = 43$

31. (e);

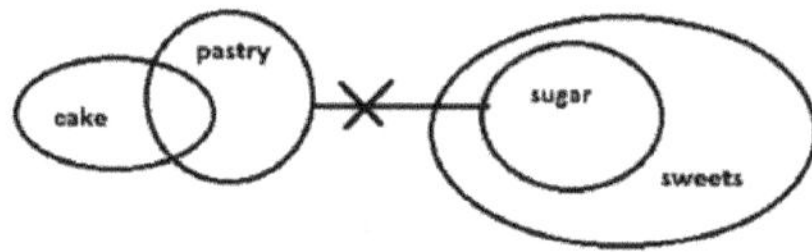

For I – There is no direct relation between the elements cake and sweets. Hence, Conclusion I cannot be concluded.

For II – There is no direct relation between the elements sweets and pastry. Hence, Conclusion II cannot be concluded.

32. (e)

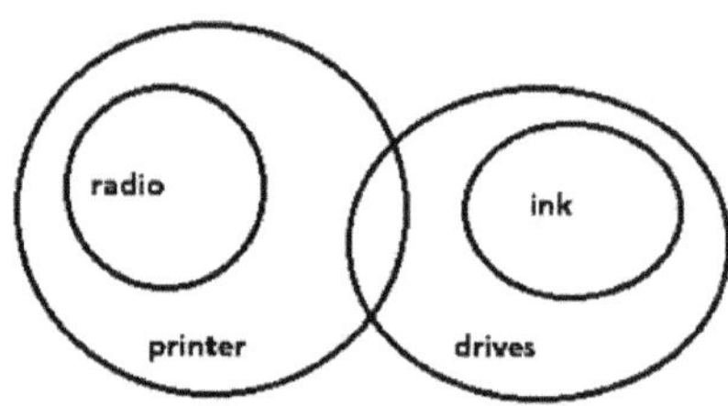

For I – There is no direct relation between the elements printer and ink. Hence, Conclusion I cannot be concluded.

For II – There is no direct relation between element radio and drives. Hence, Conclusion II cannot be concluded.

33. (c)

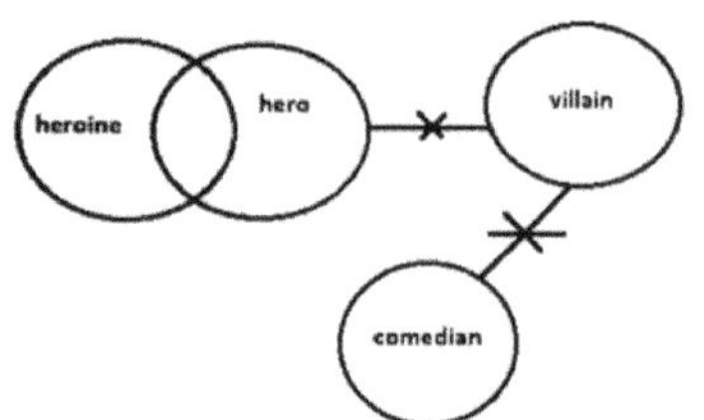

For I – Since, there is no relation between the elements hero and comedi Hence, Conclusion I cannot be concluded.

For II – From Venn diagram it is clear that some heroine are hero and no hero is villain, therefore, some heroine are not villain. Hence, Conclusion II can be concluded.

34. (a)

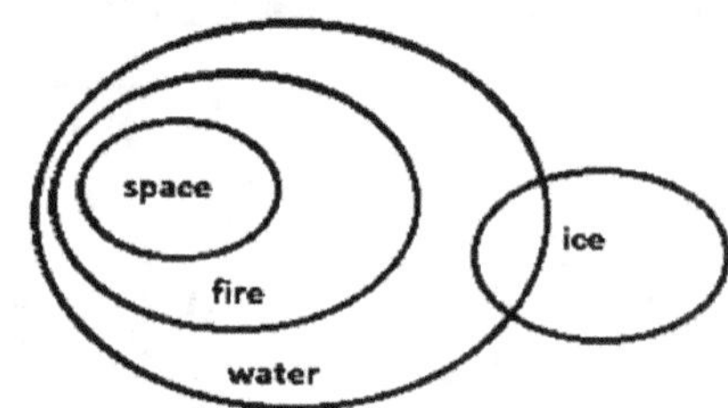

For I – Since, there is no direct relation between the elements ice and space, therefore possibility case will hold true. Hence, Conclusion I can be concluded.

For II – As all space is fire and all fire is water, therefore some space are water is definitely true. Hence, Conclusion II can be concluded.

35. (b)

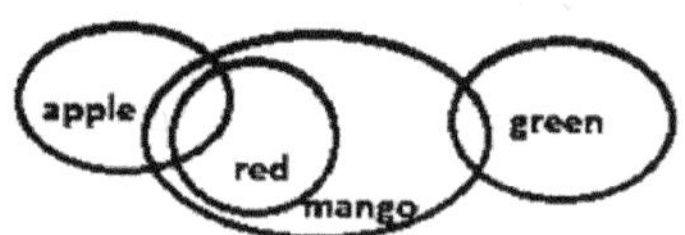

For I – There is no direct relation between elements apple and green. Hence, Conclusion I cannot be concluded.

For II – There is no direct relation between elements apple and green. Hence, Conclusion II cannot be concluded. As the elements are the same. Therefore, "Either –Or" case will be concluded.

Direction (36-40):

C sits fourth to the right of G who is not an immediate neighbour of B. B who faces F is an immediate neighbour of A. We get four possibilities

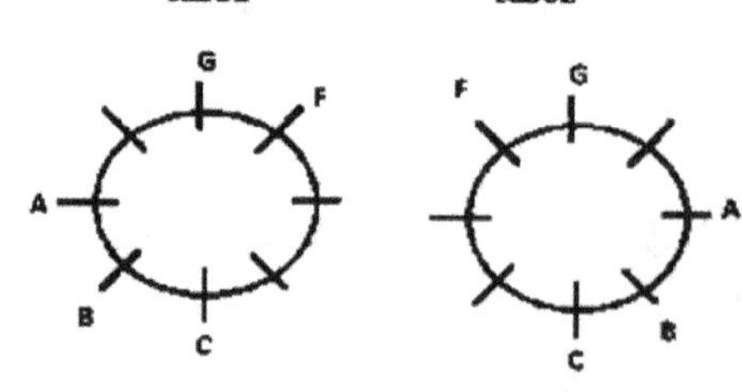

258

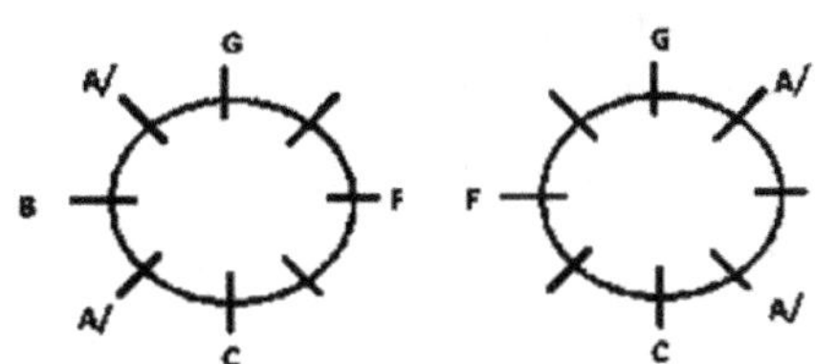

E sits third to the left of H, So cases 3 and 4 get eliminated. H is not an immediate neighbour of D. So, Case 2 will be eliminated.

So, the final arrangement will be:

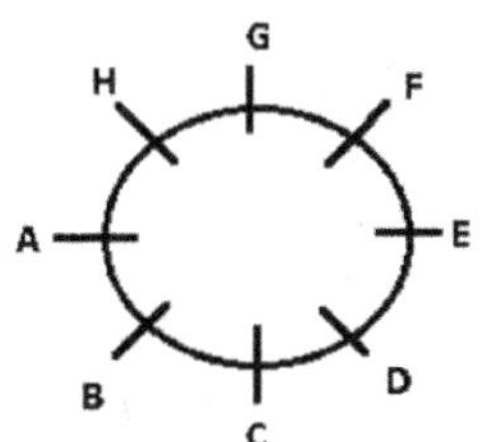

36. (e)   37. (a)   38. (c)
39. (d)   40. (c)

QUANTITATIVE APTITUDE

41. (a) Let the breadth of field be x m and that of length will be 3x m.

Area $= 3x^2$ m²

$\therefore 3x^2 \times 2.5 = 480$

$x^2 = 64$

$x = 8$

$\therefore$ Required difference $= 2 \times 8 = 16$ m

42. (c) S.P. of two articles $= 4800 + 4800 = $ Rs 9600

CP of first article $= \frac{100}{120} \times 4800 = 4000$

CP of second article $= 9600 - 4000 = 5600$

Required % loss $= \frac{5600-4800}{5600} \times 100 = \frac{800}{5600} \times 100$

$= \frac{1}{7} \times 100 = 14\frac{2}{7}\%$

43. (b) Manufacturer $\xrightarrow{10\%}$ wholesaler $\xrightarrow{15\%}$ retailer $\xrightarrow{25\%}$ Rs. 1265

Let cost price be x. Then,

$\therefore$ Final price of the table $= \frac{110}{100} \times \frac{115}{100} \times \frac{125}{100} \times$ x

$= 1265$

$\therefore$ Cost of production of the table

$= \frac{1265 \times 100 \times 100 \times 100}{110 \times 115 \times 125} = $ Rs. 800

44. (e) One day's work of 1 man $= \frac{1}{12 \times 15}$

$\therefore$ One day's work of 9 men $= \frac{9}{12 \times 15} = \frac{1}{20}$

and one day's work of 12 women

$= \frac{12}{10 \times 24} = \frac{1}{20}$

Let the time required by 12 women to complete the remaining work be x days.

$\therefore \frac{6}{20} + \frac{x}{20} = 1 \Rightarrow x = 14$ days

45. (c) Let Arjun's speed = x depressions per hr.

$\therefore$ Suman's speed = 0.6x depressions per hr.

ATQ,

$(x + 0.6x) \times 12 \times 6 = 5,76,000$

$\Rightarrow x = 5000$ depressions per hour

46. (a) $\sqrt{360 - 450 + 379} = \sqrt{289} = 17$

47. (c) $3^? = (3^2)^3 \times (3^4)^2 = 3^6 \times 3^8 \div 3^9 = 3^5$

Or, ? = 5

48. (b) $2^? = 572 \div 26 = 22 \times 12 = 264 - 200 = 64 = 2^6$

Or, ? = 6

49. (a) $? = (4 + 1 - 2) + \left(\frac{1}{2} + \frac{7}{12} - \frac{5}{6}\right)$

$= 3 + \left(\frac{6+7-10}{12}\right) = 3\frac{1}{4}$

50. (e) 36% of 245 = (40 − 4) % of 245

$= \frac{2}{5} \times 245 - \frac{4 \times 245}{100} = 98 - 9.8 = 88.2$

40% of 210 $= \frac{2}{5} \times 210 = 84$

Difference = 88.2 − 84 = 4.2

? = 10 − 4.2 = 5.8

51. (c) Population of city Y $= \frac{3000}{0.15} = 20,000$

Population city of Z $= \frac{8000}{0.5} = 16,000$

Required percentage $= \frac{20,000 - 16,000}{20,000} \times 100$

$= \frac{4000}{20,000} \times 100 = 20\%$

52. (e) Required difference $= \frac{(11-7)}{18} \times 0.45 \times \frac{3600}{0.3}$

$= 1200$

53. (b) Female population is city Z $= \frac{8000}{0.5} \times 0.35 = 5600$

Male & transgender population in city A $= \frac{3600}{0.3} \times [0.7] = 8400$

Required percentage $= \frac{8400 - 5600}{8400} \times 100$

$= \frac{2800}{84}\% = \frac{100}{3}\% = 33\frac{1}{3}\%$

54. (d) Male population in city B $= \frac{4200}{0.3} \times 0.38 = 5320$

Female population in city X $= \frac{2000}{0.25} \times 0.3 = 2400$

Required difference = 5320 − 2400 = 2920

55. (a) Required ratio $= \frac{\frac{8000}{0.5} \times 0.15}{\frac{3600}{0.3} \times 0.25} = \frac{2400}{3000} = \frac{4}{5}$

56. (b) Speed = $\frac{\text{Distance}}{\text{Time}}$
Total Distance = Length of bridge + Length of train
$= 1 + \frac{1}{2} = \frac{3}{2}$ km
Speed = $\frac{\frac{3}{2}}{2\times\frac{1}{60}} = \frac{3}{4} \times 60 = 45$ kmph

57. (d) Let the speed of current be V m/min.
$\frac{200}{48-V} - \frac{200}{48+V} = 10$
Or, $20(48 + V) - 20(48 - V) = 48^2 - V^2$
Or, $V^2 + 40V - 2304 = 0$
Or, V = 32 m/min.

58. (c) Let the filling capacity of the pump be x m^3 per minute
Then, emptying capacity of the pump = (x + 10) m^3 per minute
So, $\frac{2400}{x} - \frac{2400}{(x+10)} = 8 \Rightarrow x^2 + 10x - 3000 = 0$
$\Rightarrow (x - 50)(x + 60) = 0$
$\Rightarrow x = 50\ m^3$ per minute

59. (c) Total Letters = 7. Total A = 2, Total R = 2
Total number of words = $\frac{7!}{2!2!} = 1260$
Now, taking both RR together, we consider them as one unit RR, that can be arranged in $\frac{2!}{2!}$ ways and
The words having both Rs together
$= \frac{6\times5\times4\times3\times2!}{2!} \times \frac{2!}{2!} = 360$
Number of words not having both R together
= 1260 – 360 = 900

60. (e) Let the present age of Vignesh be V years.
Then, V – 2 = 8
∴ V = 10 years
ATQ, F + 10 = 2(V + 10),
F = 2 (10 + 10) – 10 = 30 years.
$S = \frac{F}{6}$
So, Shikha's present age = 5 years.

61. (a) **Quantity I.**
Second no. = $\frac{100\times12}{100} = 12$
∴ first no. = $12^3 \times \frac{3}{2} = 1728 \times \frac{3}{2} = 2592$
∴ Required sum = 12 + 2592 = 2604
Quantity I > Quantity II

62. (c) **Quantity I.**
Distance travelled by thief in 15 min = $60 \times \frac{15}{60}$
= 15 km
Time taken by police to catch thief after 11:15 pm $\geq \frac{15}{65-60} \geq 3$ hr
Quantity I ≥ Quantity II

63. (e) **Quantity II.**
Ratio of profit ⇒

A	:	B	:	C
12×12	:	12×x	:	8×(12–x)
36	:	3x	:	2(12–x)

ATQ,
$\frac{36}{60+x} = \frac{1800}{3200} \Rightarrow 60 + x = 64 \Rightarrow x = 4$
Quantity I = Quantity II

64. (a) **Quantity I.**
Let speed of stream = y km/hr.
ATQ,
$\frac{x-18}{15-y} = \frac{x}{15+y}$ ... (i)
Also, 15 + y – (15 – y) = 6
2y = 6
y = 3. ...(ii)
From (i) and (ii)
$\frac{x-18}{12} = \frac{x}{18} \Rightarrow$ x = 54 km
Quantity I > Quantity II

65. (a) **Quantity I:**
Let C.P. of watch for P be Rs. 100
Amount paid by R = $120 \times \frac{90}{100}$ = Rs. 108
ATQ, 108 → 2160
1 → 20
100 → 2000
C.P. of watch for P = Rs. 2000
Required price at which P sold to Q
$= 2000 \times \frac{120}{100}$ = Rs. 2400
Quantity I > Quantity II

66. (d)
2   4   11   37   [153]   771
×1+2   ×2+3   ×3+4   ×4+5   ×5+6

67. (b)
24   12   12   24   [84]   408
×1–12   ×2–12   ×3–12   ×4–12   ×5–12

68. (e)
2   12   30   56   90   [132]
10   18   26   34   42
8   8   8   8
Or
2   12   30   56   90   [132]
↑   ↑   ↑   ↑   ↑   ↑
1×2   3×4   5×6   7×8   9×10   11×12

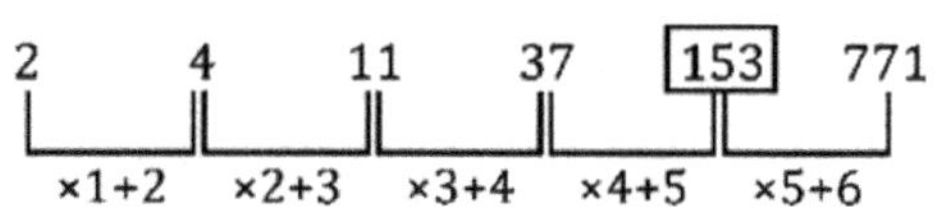

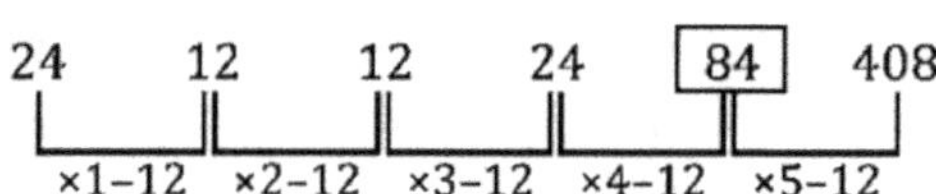

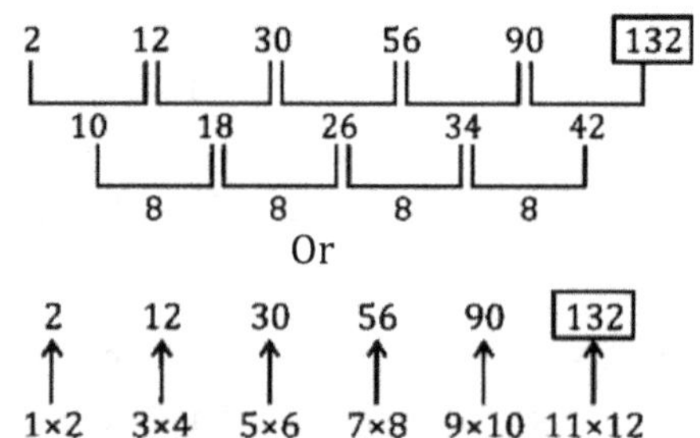

69. (b)

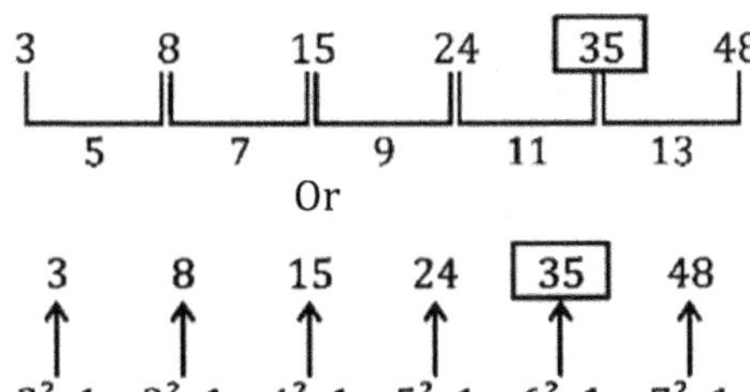

Or

$$3 \quad 8 \quad 15 \quad 24 \quad \boxed{35} \quad 48$$
$$2^2-1 \quad 3^2-1 \quad 4^2-1 \quad 5^2-1 \quad 6^2-1 \quad 7^2-1$$

70. (d)

$$18 \quad 18 \quad 27 \quad 54 \quad \boxed{135} \quad 405$$
$$\times 1 \quad \times 1.5 \quad \times 2 \quad \times 2.5 \quad \times 3$$

71. (c) Let the number of students in two groups
be x & y
$\therefore 15x + 25y = 22(x + y)$
$\Rightarrow (25 - 22)y = (22 - 15)x$
$\Rightarrow 3y = 7x$
$\Rightarrow x : y = 3 : 7$

72. (b) ATQ,
Ram's age = 29 + 5 = 34 years
$\Rightarrow 3x + 2y = 34$ ... (i)
Also, $x - y = 3$ ... (ii)
Solving (i) & (ii),
$x = 8$, $y = 5$
required average age $= \frac{34+29+8+5}{4} = 19$

73. (c) Given
$\frac{Mon+Tue+Wed+Thu}{4} = 48°$
$\therefore 42° + Tue + Wed + Thu = 192°$
$\Rightarrow Tue + Wed + Thu = 150°$ ...(i)
And, $\frac{Tue+Wed+Thu+Fri}{4} = 52°$

$\Rightarrow 150° + Fri = 208°$ [from Eq. (i)]
$\Rightarrow Fri = 58°$

74. (c) C.P. of mixture of tea$= 30 \times \frac{100}{110}$
$= \frac{300}{11}$ rupee/kg
According to law of allegation

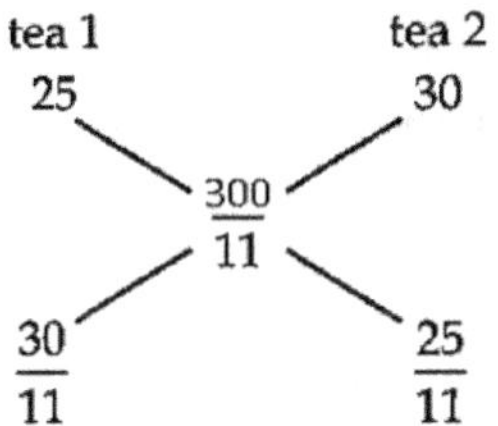

$\therefore \frac{tea1}{tea2} = \frac{30}{25} = \frac{6}{5}$
$\therefore$ Quantity of tea1 $= \frac{6}{5} \times 30 = 36$ kg

75. (b) Let quantity of alloy of alluminium and
zinc
= 8 kg
And that of alluminium and copper = 13
kg
Let 1 kg of each was mixed
$\therefore$ weight of copper in this mixture of 2 kg
$= 1 \times \frac{5}{13} = \frac{5}{13}$ kg
$\therefore$ Weight of copper per kg $= \frac{5}{26}$ kg

76. (a) $\sqrt{?} = \frac{2695}{55} = 49 \Rightarrow ? = 2401$

77. (b) $(?) = 15363 - 9604$
$? = 5759$

78. (c) $? = 49$

79. (d) $? = 5.367$

80. (c) $? = 236 + 160 = 396$

REASONING ABILITY

Directions (1-5): In each of the questions below, relationships between some elements are shown in the statements. These statements are followed by conclusions numbered I and II. Read the statements and give the answer.

(a) If only conclusion I follows.
(b) If only conclusion II follows.
(c) If either conclusion I or II follows.
(d) If neither conclusion I nor II follows.
(e) If both conclusions I and II follow.

1. **Statements:** $P < R \leq M = O > S \leq V > Y$
   Conclusions: I. $O > P$　　II. $S > R$
2. **Statements:** $A \geq B > D = F < E \leq C$
   Conclusions: I. $B > E$　　II. $D < C$
3. **Statements:** $V = W \geq X \geq Y < Z \leq U$
   Conclusions: I. $Y < V$　　II. $V = Y$
4. **Statements:** $M \geq N = O > P \leq R > T$
   Conclusions: I. $R < M$　　II. $N < R$
5. **Statements:** $F < G \leq I < J > H = K \geq L$
   Conclusions: I. $G < J$　　II. $L < J$

Directions (6-10): In each of the questions given below, a group of digits/letter is given followed by four combinations of symbols numbered (a), (b), (c) and (d). You have to find out which of the four combinations correctly represents the group of digits/letters based on the symbol codes and the conditions given below. If none of the four combinations represents the group of digits correctly, give (e) i.e. 'None of these' as the answer.

Digit	W	U	2	0	J	M	7	D	L	P	9	X	4	S
Symbol	®	£	µ	∞	≠	©	@	#	$	&	^	*	%	+

Condition for coding the group elements:
(i)　If the first letter is a consonant and the last digit is a perfect square, then both are to be coded as ^.
(ii)　If the first digit is an odd number and the last letter is a consonant, then both are to be coded by the code of the last element.
(iii)　If the first letter is a vowel and the last element is a number, then the code of the first and the last elements is to be interchanged.
(iv)　If the first digit and the last digit are even numbers, then the obtained code will be reversed.

6. D9UPS4
   (a) #^£&+%　　(b) ^#£&+^
   (c) ^^£&+%　　(d) ^^£&+^

7. 9W0JX7
   (a) @®∞≠*@　　(b) ^®∞≠*@
   (c) ^@∞≠*@　　(d) ^®∞≠*®
   (e) None of these

8. U47LJ0
   (a) £%@$≠∞　　(b) ∞%$@≠£
   (c) ∞%@$≠£　　(d) ∞%≠$@£
   (e) None of these

9. 4MD0W2
   (a) %©#∞®µ　　(b) µ©#∞®%
   (c) µ©#∞®@　　(d) µ®∞#©%
   (e) None of these

10. 7PU49M
    (a) ©&£%^©　　(b) @&£%^@
    (c) ©&%£^@　　(d) ©&£^%©
    (e) None of these

Directions (11-15): Study the information and answer the following questions:

Eight persons A, B, C, D, E, F, G, and H are sitting in a row facing north. No two persons are sitting adjacent to each other according to the English alphabet (i.e. A is not next to B, B is not next to A and C and so on). A sits at one of the ends. Three persons sit between A and C, who is at the immediate left of F. Four persons sit between E and D and none of them sits at any end. No one sits between B and G.

11. Who among the following sits at the immediate right of G?
    (a) A　　(b) F
    (c) C　　(d) B
    (e) None of these

12. How many persons sit between A and E?
    (a) none　　(b) one
    (c) two　　(d) three
    (e) More than three

13. Four of the following five are alike and form a group. Who among the following does not belong to that group?
    (a) H　　(b) F　　(c) C
    (d) B　　(e) G

14. Who among the following sits 3rd right to the one who is 2nd from the left end?
    (a) A　　(b) F　　(c) C
    (d) B　　(e) G

15. If in a certain way B is related to A, D is related to C, then who among the following is H related to?

(a) A   (b) F   (c) C

(d) B   (e) G

Directions (16-20): In each of the questions below are given some statements followed by two conclusions. You have to take the given statements to be true even if they seem to be at variance with commonly known facts. Read all the conclusions and then decide which of the given conclusions logically follows from the given statements, disregarding commonly known facts. Give the answer accordingly.

16. **Statements:** Some rice is sugar

                 Some sugar is milk

                 No milk is water

       Conclusions: I. Some sugar is not water.

                  II. All rice being water is a possibility.

(a) Both I and II follow.

(b) Either I or II follows.

(c) Only II follows.

(d) Only I follows.

(e) Neither I nor II follows.

17. **Statements:** All laptop are camera.

                 All camera are mobile.

                 No laptop is charger.

       Conclusions: I. Some camera being laptop is a Possibility.

                  II. Some mobile is not charger.

(a) Both I and II follow.

(b) Either I or II follows.

(c) Only II follows.

(d) Only I follows.

(e) Neither I nor II follows.

18. **Statements:** No mouse is keyboard.

                 Some keyboard is pointer

                 All pointer is monitor.

       Conclusions: **I.** No keyboard is monitor.

                  II. Some mouse can never be Pointer.

(a) Both I and II follow.

(b) Either I or II follows.

(c) Only II follows.

(d) Only I follows.

(e) Neither I nor II follows.

19. **Statements:** All truck is car.

                 Some truck is road

                 All road is cycle.

       Conclusions: **I.** Some road being car is a possibility.

                  II. Some cycle is car.

(a) Both I and II follow.

(b) Either I or II follows.

(c) Only II follows.

(d) Only I follows.

(e) Neither I nor II follows.

20. **Statements:** All white are red.

                 All red are blue.

                 Some black are red.

       Conclusions: **I.** Some black is blue.

                  II. Some red are not white.

(a) Both I and II follow.

(b) Either I or II follows.

(c) Only II follows.

(d) Only I follows.

(e) Neither I nor II follows.

Directions (21-25): Study the following number sequence and answer the following questions.

4 5 2 7 8 2 9 7 2 1 5 6 8 1 3 2 5 4 7 6 8 9 6 1 3 5 2 8 4 4

21. How many even numbers are there in the numeric series which are immediately preceded by a number, which is a whole square?

(a) one

(b) two

(c) three

(d) More than three

(e) None of these

22. If all the odd numbers are dropped from the series, which number will be fifth to the right of the seventh number from the left end?

(a) 2   (b) 8

(c) 6   (d) 4

(e) None of these

23. If 1 is replaced by 2 and 4 is replaced by 5 in the given number series, then which number will be fourth to the left of the seventeenth number from the right end?

(a) 1   (b) 2   (c) 3

(d) 5   (e) 6

24. If the position of the 1st and the 16th number, the 2nd and the 17th number, and so on up to the 15th and the 30th number are interchanged, then which number will be 8th to the right of the 17th number from the right end?

(a) 5   (b) 6

(c) 8   (d) 9

(e) None of these

25. How many total odd number/s which is/are immediately preceded by a 'perfect square' are there in the above sequence?

(a) four   (b) five   (c) three

(d) seven   (e) None of these

Direction (26-30): Study the following information carefully and answer the questions given below:

Seven people viz. A, B, C, D, E, F and G live in a building on eight different floors, such that ground floor is numbered one, the floor just above is numbered 2 and so on till the top floor which is numbered as eight, but not necessarily in the same order. One of the floors is vacant.

There is a gap of more than three floors between D and B. D lives above B, but not on the top floor. C lives immediately above B. E lives on floor number 4. F lives immediately below E. A lives above G, who lives on an even-numbered floor.

26. Who among the following lives on the ground floor?
    (a) B   (b) G   (c) F
    (d) A   (e) None of these

27. Who among the following lives immediately below the vacant floor?
    (a) G   (b) A   (c) E
    (d) D   (e) None of these

28. How many persons live between D and C?
    (a) one   (b) three   (c) four
    (d) two   (e) None of these

29. Who among the following lives on the top floor?
    (a) A   (b) D   (c) F
    (d) G   (e) None of these

30. Which of the following floors is vacant?
    (a) 8th   (b) 6th   (c) 2nd
    (d) 1st   (e) 5th

31. In a row of students facing south, Ravi is fifteenth from the left end and fourth to the left of Shiva, who is sixth from the right end. How many students are there in the row?
    (a) 25   (b) 26   (c) 24
    (d) 28   (e) 27

32. Jay leaves his home and goes straight 30 meters, then turns left and goes 10 meters. He again turns left and goes 20 meters and finally turns right and starts walking. If he is now moving in the East direction, then in which direction did he start to walk?
    (a) east   (b) west
    (c) north   (d) south
    (e) None of these

33. Find the odd one out.
    (a) ZXY   (b) WUV   (c) TRS
    (d) QOP   (e) LNM

Directions (34-38): The following questions are based on the five words given below. Study the following words and answer the following questions.

CUTBETTUBOWLSIT

(The new words formed after performing the operations as mentioned may not necessarily be a meaningful English word.)

34. If the given words are arranged in the order as they appear in a dictionary from left to right, which of the following will be the fourth from the left end?
    (a) CUT   (b) BET   (c) TUB
    (d) OWL   (e) SIT

35. How many letters are there in the English alphabetical series between the second letter of the word, which is second from the right end and the second letter of the word which is third from the left end?
    (a) one   (b) two   (c) three
    (d) four   (e) None of these

36. If the second alphabet in each of the words is changed to the previous alphabet in the English alphabetical order, then how many words thus formed will be without any vowels?
    (a) none   (b) one   (c) two
    (d) three   (e) four

37. If the position of the first and the third alphabet of each of the words are interchanged, then how many meaningful words will be formed in the new arrangement?
    (a) one   (b) two   (c) three
    (d) four   (e) five

38. If in each of the given words, every consonant is changed to its previous letter and every vowel is changed to its next letter according to the English alphabetical series, then in how many words, thus formed, at least one vowel will appear?
    (a) none   (b) one   (c) two
    (d) three   (e) None of these

39. If in the number 9876534567, position of the first and the last digit is interchanged, position of the second and the ninth digit is interchanged and so on till the position of the fifth and the sixth digit is interchanged, then which digit will be sixth to the left of the one which is fourth from the right end?
    (a) 7   (b) 9   (c) 5
    (d) 4   (e) 8

40. How many pairs of letters are there in the word "GURUGRAM" which have as many letters between them in the word as in alphabetical series (backwards or forwards)?
    (a) one   (b) two   (c) three
    (d) four   (e) none

41. The price of a product after getting 10% discount is Rs.9,450 which includes 5% tax on selling price. Find the marked price of the product (in Rs).
(a) 8500   (b) 9000   (c) 10000
(d) 9500   (e) 10500

42. A's income is 75% of B's income and A's expenditure is 60% of B's expenditure. If A's income is 80% of B's expenditure, then find the ratio of A's savings to B's savings.
(a) 1 : 2   (b) 2 : 1   (c) 5 : 2
(d) 3 : 1   (e) 5 : 3

43. A takes three times longer than the time taken by B and C to do a work. B takes four times as long as A and C together to do the same work. If all the three working together can complete the same work in 24 days, then 'A' alone can complete the work in how many days?
(a) 84   (b) 96   (c) 48
(d) 192   (e) 144

44. Two men A and B are 60 km. apart and walk towards each other at a speed of 10 kmph. and 5 kmph. respectively. A dog moving at a speed of 12 kmph. runs from man A to man B and then again towards man A and so on, until A meets B. Find the distance travelled by the dog.
(a) 60 km.   (b) 36 km.   (c) 24 km.
(d) 48 km.   (e) 72 km.

45. Population of a city X is 1,60,000. In the next three years, there will be a total increase of 8% in the male population and increase of 20% in the female population, which will result in a male to female ratio of 3:2. Find the original male and female population of the city.
(a) 84000, 96000   (b) 100000, 60000
(c) 120000, 40000   (d) 90000, 70000
(e) 85000, 75000

46. A pyramid with a square base of side 3 cm. and height 7 cm. is carved out of a rectangular block of wood 7 cm. × 3 cm. × 3 cm. Find the percentage of wood wasted in the process.
(a) $33\frac{1}{3}\%$ (b) $62\frac{2}{3}\%$ (c) $57\frac{1}{7}\%$
(d) $54\frac{2}{7}\%$ (e) $66\frac{2}{3}\%$

47. A man can row 12 kmph. in still water and it takes him 90 minutes to reach a place and return. If the speed of the current is 4 kmph. then how far is the place?
(a) 8 km.   (b) 6 km.   (c) 10 km.
(d) 12 km.   (e) 16 km.

48. Population of two cities A and B is in the ratio of 5:6. If 40% and $66\frac{2}{3}\%$ of the population of city A and city B respectively is literate and the difference between the number of illiterate people of these cities is 600, then find the total population of city A.
(a) 3300   (b) 3000   (c) 6600
(d) 3600   (e) 2500

49. An urn contains 3 Red, 6 Blue and 2 Green marbles. Find the probability of choosing a Blue marble.
(a) $\frac{6}{13}$ (b) $\frac{3}{13}$ (c) $\frac{6}{11}$
(d) $\frac{3}{11}$ (e) $\frac{2}{11}$

50. A container carries a wine and water solution in the ratio of 7:5. 58 litres of water has been added to dilute the solution further and the ratio of the wine and water was reversed. Find the original volume of the solution.
(a) 130 litre   (b) 244 litre   (c) 248 litre
(d) 145 litre   (e) 184 litre

Directions (51-55): What should come in place of the question mark (?) in the following questions?

51. 7, 7, 23, 87, 231, ?
(a) 485   (b) 487   (c) 489
(d) 491   (e) 493

52. 27, 29, 26, 31, 24, ?
(a) 33   (b) 34   (c) 35
(d) 36   (e) 37

53. 170, 173, 178, 185, 196, ?
(a) 209   (b) 205   (c) 207
(d) 211   (e) 213

54. 2880, 480, 96, 24, 8, ?
(a) 12   (b) 4   (c) 2
(d) 6   (e) 8

55. 8, 9, 21, 68, 279, ?
(a) 1404   (b) 1395   (c) 1405
(d) 1415   (e) 1495

Direction (56– 60): What approximate value should come in the place of the question (?) mark in the given questions?

56. $8399.99 \times 14.996 \div 374.982 + \sqrt{16.011} = ?$
(a) 564   (b) 340   (c) 320
(d) 324   (e) 384

57. $\sqrt{2499.99} + 14.97\% \ of \ 14 = ?$
(a) 40   (b) 45   (c) 52
(d) 58   (e) 64

58. $24.987\% \times 639.97 + 45.21\% \ of \ 359 = ?$
(a) 358   (b) 378   (c) 322
(d) 302   (e) 288

59. $33.30003\% \ of \ 509.99 = ?$
(a) 140   (b) 185   (c) 155

(d) 170   (e) 100

60. 74.79% of 1344.11 + 12.48% of 128.20 = ?

(a) 1048   (b) 1024   (c) 1072
(d) 1096   (e) 1120

Directions (61-65): The bar chart given below shows the total number of admissions that took place in two different schools, A and B, from year 2012 to year 2016. Based on this bar chart, solve the following questions.

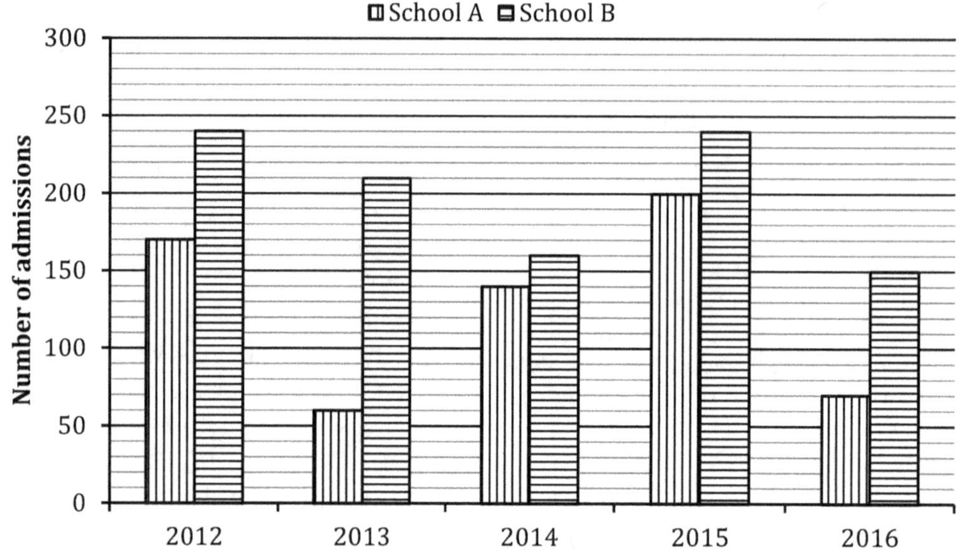

61. If in another school C, the total students who took admission in year 2013 is $33\frac{1}{3}$% more than the difference of admissions that took place in school A and B in the same year, then find the average of admission in school C in year 2013 and school B in year 2015 together.
(a) 225   (b) 220   (c) 210
(d) 205   (e) 200

62. Ratio of boys to girls who take admission in school A in 2012 is 9:8 and the number of boys taking admission in school A in 2015 is $11\frac{1}{9}$% more than the boys taking admission in school A in 2012. Find the sum of girls who take admission in school A in 2012 and in school A in 2015 together.
(a) 180   (b) 220   (c) 195
(d) 150   (e) 240

63. If in the year 2017 there was a 60% increase in the total number of admissions in both schools from the previous year, then find the total number of admissions in 2017.
(a) 312   (b) 322   (c) 332
(d) 342   (e) 352

64. Total admissions in year 2014 in both schools together is what percent more or less than total admissions in both schools in year 2016.
(a) $35\frac{2}{11}$%   (b) $36\frac{4}{11}$%   (c) $44\frac{2}{9}$%
(d) $38\frac{1}{11}$%   (e) $39\frac{5}{11}$%

65. Find the ratio of total admission in both schools in year 2013 to total admission in both schools in year 2016.
(a) 29:22   (b) 13:11   (c) 14:11
(d) 27:22   (e) 25:22

Directions (66-75): What should come in place of the question mark (?) in the following questions?

66. $\sqrt[3]{729} + 37\frac{1}{2}\%$ of $5\frac{1}{3} = ? +2$
(a) 9   (b) $8\frac{1}{3}$ (c) 7
(d) $9\frac{1}{3}$ (e) 8

67. $? \times 65 \div 72 = 195 \times 352 \div 192$
(a) 369   (b) 396   (c) 594
(d) 297   (e) 376

68. $(444 \div 4) + (625 \div 25) + (2991 \div 3) = ?$
(a) 1153   (b) 1143   (c) 1113
(d) 1123   (e) 1133

69. $\sqrt{6.25} + 5\frac{1}{5} \times 7\frac{4}{13} + ? = 72$
(a) 30.5   (b) 32.5   (c) 31.5
(d) 29.5   (e) 25

70. $(\sqrt{7921} - \sqrt[3]{2197}) \times \frac{1}{4} = ?$
(a) 20   (b) 19   (c) 18
(d) 17   (e) 16

71. $266\frac{2}{3}\%$ of $153 + 58\frac{1}{3}\%$ $300 = ?$
(a) 583   (b) 493   (c) 575
(d) 543   (e) 549

72. $77077 \div 7007 \times 125 \div 5 \times 2 = ?$
(a) 275   (b) 550   (c) 1100
(d) 2200   (e) 1650

73. 25% of 124 + 35% of 60 = ?
    (a) 52   (b) 57   (c) 62
    (d) 67   (e) 72
74. 8557 + 1723 – 1231 – 7321 = (?)³
    (a) 11   (b) 12   (c) 13
    (d) 14   (e) 15
75. $(?)^2 = 39 \times 1323 \times \dfrac{1}{117}$
    (a) 19   (b) 21   (c) 24
    (d) 27   (e) 18
76. Radha's age, four years ago, was twice her age10 yrs ago. Also, the respective ratio between Raju's present age and Radha's present age is 3:4. Find Raju's age 3 years hence.
    (a) 15 years (b) 12 years (c) 13 years
    (d) 18 years (e) 21 years
77. How many different words can be formed with the letters of the word "REGRESSIVE"
    (a) 16800   (b) 30240   (c) 151200
    (d) 90720   (e) 15120
78. Average weight of A, B and C is 93 kg. If another man D joins the group whose weight is 81 kg. then the new average of the four people will be equal to:
    (a) 65 kg.   (b) 67 kg.   (c) 86 kg.
    (d) 90 kg.   (e) 96 kg.
79. A person covered 9 km. at 3 km/hr., 15 km. at 5 km/hr. and 30 km. at 10 km/hr. Find the average speed of the person in covering the entire distance.
    (a) 5 km/hr.   (b) 6 km/hr.
    (c) 7 km/hr.   (d) 8 km/hr.
    (e) 7.5 km/hr.
80. Two pipes A and B fill a tank in 30 min and 60 min respectively. Initially both the pipes are opened, but after 10 minutes, pipe A was closed. In how much time did the tank get filled?
    (a) 30 minutes
    (b) 45 minutes
    (c) 40 minutes
    (d) 35 minutes
    (e) 25 minutes

Solutions

REASONING ABILITY

Direction (1-5):

1. **(a)** I. O > P (True)   II. S > R (False)
2. **(b)** I. B > E (False)   II. D < C (True)
3. **(c)** I. Y < V (False)   II. V = Y (False)
4. **(d)** I. R < M (False)   II. N < R (False)
5. **(e)** I. G < J (True)   II. L < J (True)

Directions (6-10):

6. **(d)** By using condition (i) the code of D9UPS4 will be ^^£&+^.
7. **(b)** The code of 9W0JX7 will be ^®∞≠*@ .
8. **(c)** By using condition (iii) the code of U47LJ0will be ∞%@$≠£
9. **(d)** By using condition (iv) the code of 4MD0W2 will be μ®∞#©%
10. **(a)** By using condition (ii) the code of 7PU49Mwill be ©&£%^© .

Direction (11-15):

A sits at one of the ends. Three persons sit between A and C, who is immediate left to F. Four persons sit between E and D, none of them sits at any end.

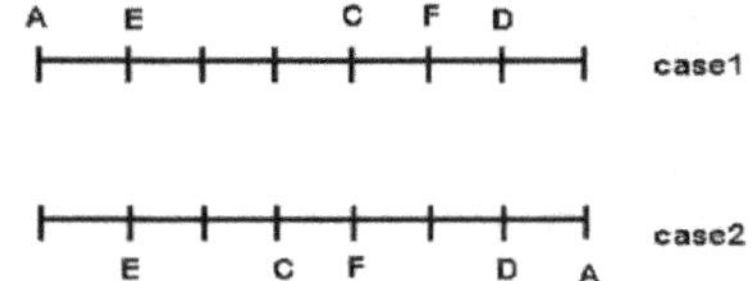

No one sits between B and G, So case2 gets eliminated as there is no place for G and B. No two persons are sitting adjacent to each other according to the English alphabet. Therefore, B cannot sit next to C. The final arrangement is:

11. **(c)**   12. **(a)**   13. **(a)**
14. **(c)**   15. **(b)**

Directions (16-20):

16. **(a)**

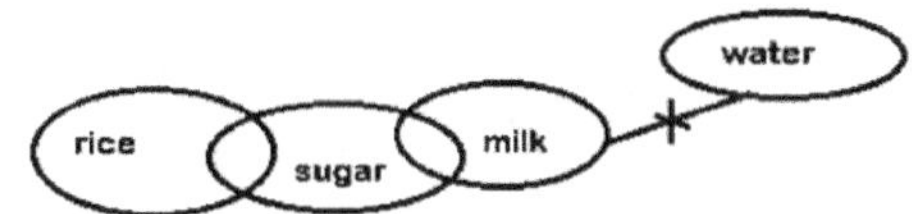

For I- From the venn diagram it is clear that some sugar is milk and no milk is water. So, some sugar which is milk will not be water. Hence, conclusion I can be concluded.

For II- There is no direct relation between the elements rice and water. So, possibility case will hold true. Therefore, we can conclude that some rice being water is a possibility.

17. (c)

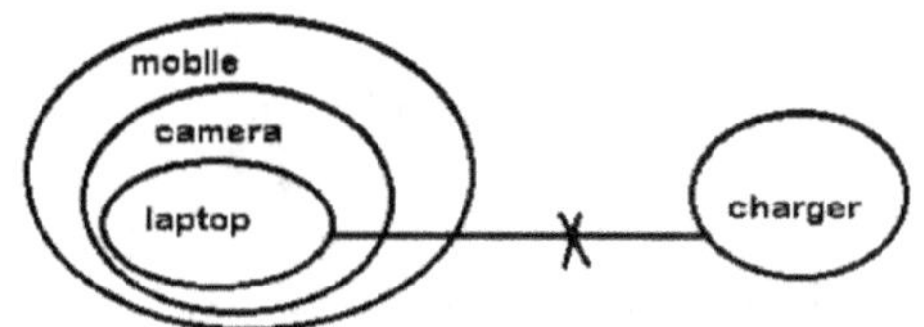

For I- From the venn diagram it is clear that some camera is laptop, So, possibility case will not hold true. Therefore, we cannot conclude that some camera being laptop is a possibility.

For II- From the venn diagram some mobile is laptop and no laptop is charger. Therefore, some mobile is not charger can be concluded.

18. (e)

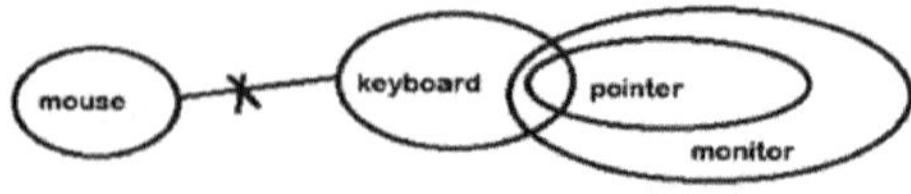

For I- From the venn diagram it is clear that some keyboard is definitely monitor. Therefore, we cannot conclude that no keyboard is Monitor.

For II- There is no direct relation between the elements mouse and pointer. Therefore, we cannot conclude that some mouse can never be pointer.

19. (c)

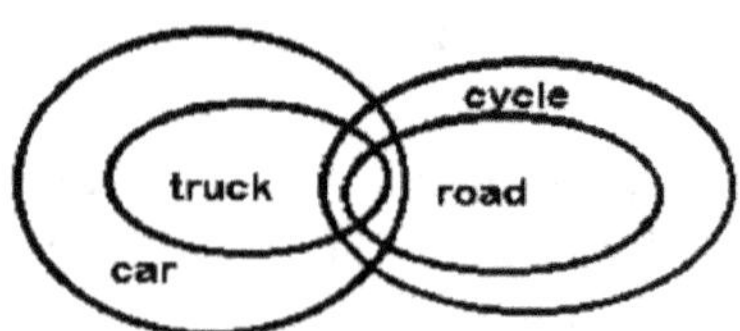

For I- From the venn diagram it is clear that some road is car. So, possibility case will not hold true. Therefore, we cannot reach conclusion I.

For II-From the venn diagram it is clear that some cycle is definitely car. Hence, conclusion II follows.

20. (d)

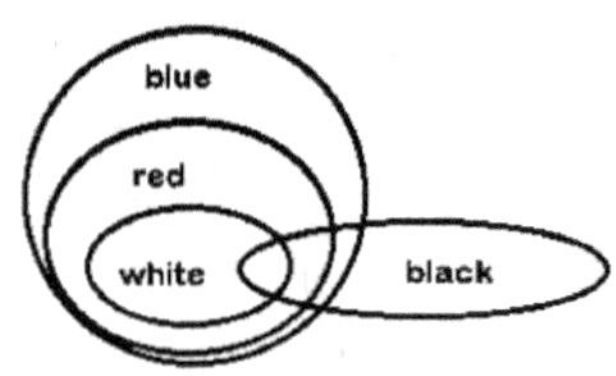

For I- From the venn diagram it is clear that some blue is black. Therefore, we can go with conclusion I.

For II-From the venn diagram it is clear that some red is definitely white. Hence, conclusion II does not follow.

Directions (21-25):

21. (b) 96,44

22. (c) 6

23. (b) 2

24. (d) 9

25. (e) Six- 45,97,15,13,13,47

Directions (26-30):

E lives on floor number 4. F lives immediately below E. There is a gap of more than three floors between D and B. D lives above B but not on the top floor. C lives immediately above B.

Case1		Case2	
Floor	Person	Floor	Person
8		8	
7	D	7	
6		6	D
5		5	
4	E	4	E
3	F	3	F
2	C	2	C
1	B	1	B

A lives above G, who lives on an even numbered floor. So case 2 will be eliminated.

8	A
7	D
6	G
5	Vacant
4	E
3	F
2	C
1	B

26. (a)   **27. (c)**   **28. (b)**

29. (a)   **30. (e)**

31. (c) Shiva's position from left end = 19th

Shiva's position from right end = 6th

Total number of students in the row=19+6-1=24

32. (d)

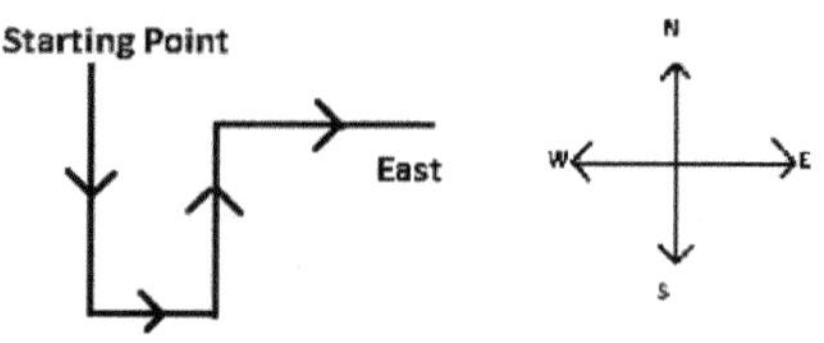

Jay started walking towards south.

33. (e)

ZXY	WUV	TRS	QOP	LNM
26 24 25	23 21 22	20 18 19	17 15 16	12 14 13

Directions (34-38):

34. (e) SIT

35. (a) One letter between U and W i.e. V

36. (e) CTT, BDT, TTB, SHT

37. (a) BUT

38. (c) AFS, SVA

39. (a) 9876534567
7654356789
So, the digit is 7.

40. (b) 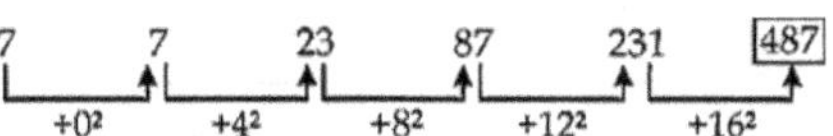

QUANTITATIVE APTITUDE

41. (c) If MP is x Rs then after 10% discount, selling price of the product will be equal to 0.9x

But there is 5% tax on selling price which is also included in the price of the product.

5% of 0.9x $\Rightarrow$ 0.045x

Net value of the product= 0.9x+0.045x=0.945x

ATQ,

$0.945x = 9450 \Rightarrow x = \frac{9450}{0.945}$

$\Rightarrow x = 10000$

42. (d)

	A	B
Income	0.75x	x
Expenditure	0.6y	y

A's saving= (0.75x−0.6y)

B's saving = (x−y)

Given, 0.75x = 0.8y

Or, 15x = 16y

$\Rightarrow \dfrac{A's\ Savings}{B's\ savings} = \dfrac{0.8y - 0.6y}{\frac{16y}{15} - y} = \dfrac{0.2y}{\frac{1}{15}y} = \dfrac{3}{1}$

43. (b) ATQ,

$\frac{3}{A} = \frac{1}{B} + \frac{1}{C}$ ...(i)

$\frac{4}{B} = \frac{1}{A} + \frac{1}{C}$ ...(ii)

$\frac{1}{A} + \frac{1}{B} + \frac{1}{C} = \frac{1}{24}$ ...(iii)

From equation (i) and (iii)

$\frac{4}{A} = \frac{1}{24}$

A = 96 Days

44. (d) Total time of travel required for A & B to meet

$= \frac{60}{10+5} = 4\ hr$

And dog will travel only for 4 hr (until A & B meet)

= 12 × 4 = 48 km

45. (b) Let the population of males and females in city X be x and y respectively.

Population of males after 3 years = $x + \frac{8}{100}x$

= 1.08x

Population of females after 3 years = $y + \frac{20}{100}y = 1.2y$

ATQ,

$\Rightarrow \frac{1.08x}{1.2y} = \frac{3}{2} \Rightarrow \frac{x}{y} = \frac{5}{3}$

$\Rightarrow$ Male and Female population is 1,00,000 and 60,000 respectively

46. (e) Vol. of wooden block =7 × 3 × 3= 63 cm^2

Vol. of pyramid = $\frac{1}{3} \times 3^2 \times 7$ = 21 cm^3

Wood wasted = 63 – 21 = 42 cm^3

$\therefore$ % of wood wasted = $\frac{42}{63} \times 100 = 66\frac{2}{3}$%

47. (a) Let the total distance = x km

$\frac{x}{12-4} + \frac{x}{12+4} = \frac{90}{60}$

$\frac{x}{8} + \frac{x}{16} = 1.5$

3x = 1.5 × 16

x = 8km

48. (b) Let the total population of city A and B be 5x and 6x respectively.

A

Total	literate people	Illiterate people
5x	$\xrightarrow{40\%}$ 2x	3x
6x	$\xrightarrow{66\frac{2}{3}\%}$ 4x	2x

Given 3x – 2x = 600

x = 600

hence, total population of city A = 5x= 5 × 600= 3000

49. (c) No. of desired outcome = 6

Total no. of outcomes = 11

Probability = $\frac{6}{11}$

50. (d) Let the quantity of wine and water be 7x and 5x.

ATQ,

$\frac{7x}{5x+58} = \frac{5}{7}$

49x = 25x + 290

24 x = 290

x= $\frac{290}{24}$ litre

Total volume of original solution

= (7 + 5)x=12× $\frac{290}{24}$ =145

51. (b) 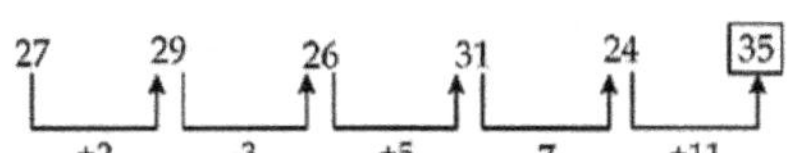

52. (c)

53. (a)

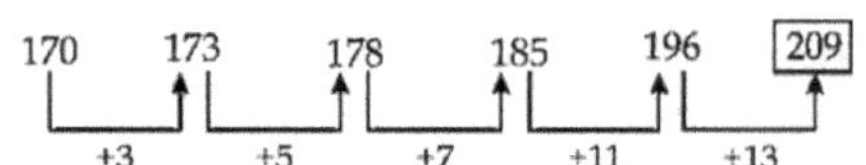

54. (b)

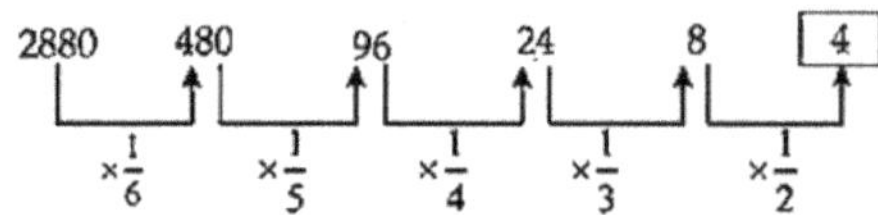

55. (a)

8 → 9 → 21 → 68 → 279 → [1404]

×1+1, ×2+3, ×3+5, ×4+7, ×5+9

56. (b) $\frac{8400\times15}{375} + \sqrt{16} \approx ?$

$\frac{84\times100}{25} + 4 \approx ?$

$336 + 4 \approx ?$

$340 \approx ?$

57. (c) $\sqrt{2500} + \frac{15}{100} \times 14 \approx ?$

$50 + 2.1 \approx ?$

$52 \approx ?$

58. (c) $? \approx 25\% \times 640 + 45\%$ of 360

$? \approx 160 + 162 \approx 322$

59. (d) 33.33% of $510 \approx ?$

$\frac{510}{3} \approx ?$

$? \approx 170$

60. (b) 75% of $1344 + 12.5\%$ of $128 \approx ?$

$\frac{3}{4} \times 1344 + \frac{1}{8} \times 128 \approx ?$

$1008 + 16 \approx ?$

$1024 \approx ?$

61. (b) Total admission in school 'C' in 2013

$= \frac{4}{3} \times (210 - 60) = \frac{4}{3} \times 150 = 200$

Required average $= \frac{200+240}{2} = \frac{440}{2} = 220$

62. (a) Boys who take admission in school A in

$2012 = \frac{9}{17} \times 170 = 90$

Girls who take admission in school A in

$2012 = \frac{8}{17} \times 170 = 80$

Boys who take admission in school A in 2015

$= 90 + 11\frac{1}{9}\%$ of $90 = 90 + 10 = 100$

Girls who take admission in school A in

$2015 = 200 - 100 = 100$

Required sum $= 100 + 80 = 180$

63. (e) Total number of admissions in 2017

$= \frac{160}{100} \times (70 + 150) = \frac{8}{5} \times 220 = 352$

64. (b) Total admissions in year 2014 = 140 + 160 = 300

Total admissions in year 2016 = 70 + 150 = 220

Required% $= \frac{300 - 220}{220} \times 100 = \frac{80}{220} \times 100$

$= 36\frac{4}{11}\%$

65. (d) Required ratio $= \frac{60+210}{70+150} = \frac{270}{220} = 27 : 22$

66. (a) $9 + \frac{3}{8} \times \frac{16}{3} = ? + 2$

$9 + 2 = ? + 2$

$? = 9$

67. (b) $? \times \frac{65}{72} = \frac{195\times352}{192}$

$? = \frac{195\times352\times72}{192\times65}$

$? = 396$

68. (e) $111 + 25 + 997 = ?$

$1133 = ?$

69. (c) $2.5 + \frac{26}{5} \times \frac{95}{13} + ? = 72$

$40.5 + ? = 72$

$? = 72 - 40.5$

$? = 31.5$

70. (b) $[89 - 13] \times \frac{1}{4} = ?$

$76 \times \frac{1}{4} = ?$

$? = 19$

71. (a)

$2[133.33\%]of\ 153 + \left(25 + 33\frac{1}{3}\right)\% \ 300 = ?$

$2\left[100 + 33\frac{1}{3}\right]\%\ of\ 153 + \frac{300}{4} + \frac{300}{3} = ?$

$2\left[153 + \frac{153}{3}\right] + 75 + 100 = ?$

$2 \times 204 + 175 = ?$

$408 + 175 = ?$

$583 = ?$

72. (b) $\frac{77077}{7007} \times \frac{125}{5} \times 2 = ?$

$11 \times 25 \times 2 = ?$

$550 = ?$

73. (a) $\frac{1}{4} \times 124 + 35\%\ of\ 60 = ?$

$31 + \frac{7}{20} \times 60 = ?$

$31 + 21 = ?$

$52 = ?$

74. (b) $8557 + 1723 - 1231 - 7321 = (?)^3$

$1236 + 492 = (?)^3$

$1728 = (?)^3$

$? = 12$

75. (b) $(?)^2 = \frac{39\times1323}{13\times9}$

$(?)^2 = 441$

$? = 21$

76. (a) Let Radha's present age = R

And Raju's present age = r

R – 4 = 2 (R - 10)

R – 4 = 2R – 20

R = 16

R : r = 4 : 3

r = 12 years

After 3 years Raju's age = r + 3

= 15 years

77. (c) REGRESSIVE

RREEEGSSIV

Total no. of ways $= \dfrac{\lfloor 10}{\lfloor 2 \lfloor 3 \lfloor 2}$

$= \dfrac{10 \times 9 \times 8 \times 7 \times 6 \times 5 \times 4 \times \lfloor 3}{2 \times \lfloor 3 \times 2} = 151200$

78. (d) $A + B + C = 93 \times 3$

$A + B + C = 279$

$A + B + C + D = 279 + 81 = 360$

Required average $= \dfrac{360}{4} = 90$ kg

79. (b) Average speed $= \dfrac{total\ distance}{total\ time} = \dfrac{9+15+30}{\frac{9}{3}+\frac{30}{10}+\frac{15}{5}} = \dfrac{54}{9}$

$= 6$ km/hr

80. (c) LCM(60,30)=60

let 60 units is the total work.

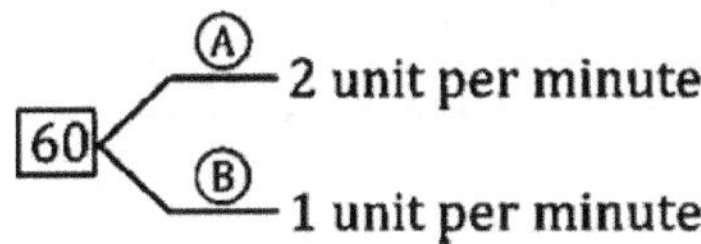

In 10 minutes A and B will do = (2 + 1) × 10 = 30 units

Remaining work will be done by B alone in

$= \dfrac{60-30}{1} = 30$ minutes.

Total time to fill the tank = 10 + 30 = 40 minutes

Mock
27   IBPS RRB Clerk Prelims

Directions (1-5): In each of the questions below, relationships between some elements are shown in the statements. These statements are followed by conclusions numbered I and II. Read the statements and give the answer.

(a) If only conclusion I follows.
(b) If only conclusion II follows.
(c) If either conclusion I or II follows.
(d) If neither conclusion I nor II follows.
(e) If both conclusions I and II follow.

1. **Statements:** $C \leq L = E \leq R \leq K = P \geq O$
   Conclusions: I. $P = C$ II. $C < P$

2. **Statements:** $W > A = S \geq H < I \leq N \leq G$
   Conclusions: I. $H < W$ II. $G > H$

3. **Statements:** $C < O \leq D = S > A \geq P \geq Q$
   Conclusions: I. $Q < D$ II. $C < A$

4. **Statements:** $F \leq B = I \leq C = A \geq S > E$
   Conclusions: I. $S \geq B$ II. $F > E$

5. **Statements:** $I \geq N = T \geq E > L \geq G > M$
   Conclusions: I. $G < N$ II. $I \geq L$

Directions (6-10): Study the following sequence and answer the given questions.

PR\$57#LO&1QA6@NM84©VE9®FU31SH4

6. Which of the following elements is 12ᵗʰ to the left of the one which is 19ᵗʰ from the left end of the given arrangement?
   (a) O   (b) L
   (c) #   (d) ®
   (e) None of these

7. If all the numbers are dropped from the series, which element will be sixth to the left of the one which is twelfth from the right end of the new arrangement?
   (a) R   (b) #
   (c) $ (d) E
   (e) None of these

8. How many symbols are there in the given series, which are immediately preceded or followed by a consonant?
   (a) two   (b) three
   (c) four   (d) five
   (e) None of these

9. How many such alphabets are there in the given series which are immediately preceded by or followed by a perfect cube?
   (a) one   (b) two
   (c) three   (d) four
   (e) None of these

10. What should come in place of the question mark (?) in the following series based on the above arrangement?
    P\$R#OLQ6AM48?
    (a) E9®   (b) E®9
    (c) V9E   (d) 9F®
    (e) None of these

Directions (11-15): Study the following information carefully and answer the questions given below:

Eight people viz. L, M, N, O, P, Q, R and S live in a building of ten different floors. Two floors are vacant. The ground floor is numbered as 1, the floor just above it is numbered as 2 and so on till the top floor which is numbered as 10 (but not necessarily in the same order).

More than three persons live between M and O. M lives on the floor number 9. R lives immediately above S. N lives on the floor number 5. L lives immediately below a vacant floor. There is a gap of two floors between P and O. No odd-numbered floor is vacant. S lives below P and O. Q does not live on the top floor.

11. Who among the following lives on the ground floor?
    (a) O   (b) R
    (c) S   (d) P
    (e) None of these

12. Who among the following lives on top floor?
    (a) M   (b) O   (c) P
    (d) L   (e) No one

13. How many persons live between N and M?
    (a) one   (b) two   (c) three
    (d) four   (e) None of these

14. Four of the following five are alike in a certain way and hence form a group. Who among the following does not belong to that group?
    (a) O   (b) N   (c) P
    (d) S   (e) L

15. Who among the following lives immediately below P?
    (a) M   (b) N
    (c) O   (d) L
    (e) None of these

Directions (16-20): Study the information and answer the following questions:

Eight persons P, Q, R, S, T, U, V and W are sitting in a row. Some are facing north and some are facing south.

(**Note:** Facing the same direction means if one is facing north then the other also faces north and vice versa. Facing the opposite direction means if one is facing north then the other faces south and vice versa).

P sits fifth to the right of W and both of them do not sit at either end of the row. Two persons sit between R and W. V sits second to the left of R. One person sits between U and V. T is not an immediate neighbour of R. Q sits second to the right of T. S sits to the immediate left of V. Immediate neighbours of V face opposite directions. U and Q face south. Immediate neighbour of Q faces the opposite direction. Not more than four people face south.

16. Who among the following sits to the immediate right of T?
    (a) P
    (b) Q
    (c) U
    (d) V
    (e) None of these
17. How many persons sit between Q and V?
    (a) None
    (b) One
    (c) Two
    (d) Three
    (e) More than three
18. What is the position of W with respect to U?
    (a) Second to the right
    (b) Second to the left
    (c) Immediate right
    (d) Immediate left
    (e) None of these
19. Who among the following sits at the extreme end of the row?
    (a) S
    (b) R
    (c) V
    (d) T
    (e) None of these
20. How many persons face north?
    (a) one
    (b) two
    (c) three
    (d) four
    (e) More than four

Directions (21-23): Study the following information carefully and answer the questions given below.

Six friends P, Q, R, S, T and U have different numbers of coins. The person who has the second highest number of coins has 36 coins. P has more coins than Q, but not the highest. S has more coins than R and U, but not more than Q. R has more coins than only one person.

21. How many coins does T possibly have?
    (a) 33
    (b) 27
    (c) 38
    (d) 19
    (e) 30
22. Who among the following has the third lowest number of coins?
    (a) S
    (b) R
    (c) U
    (d) Q

(e) None of the above
23. If P and R together have 59 coins, then how many coins does R have?
    (a) 15
    (b) 23
    (c) 12
    (d) 29
    (e) None of the above

Directions (24-26): Study the following information carefully and answer the questions given below.

Rohan started walking 2km. in the North direction and then took three consecutive right turns and walked distances—3km., 6km.,5km.—respectively and reached point O.

24. What is the direction of Rohan's initial point (position) with respect to point O?
    (a) north-west
    (b) north-east
    (c) south-west
    (d) southeast
    (e) None of these
25. If Rohan walks a distance of 4 km. towards north from O, then what is the shortest distance from his new position to his initial position?
    (a) 2 km.
    (b) 3 km.
    (c) 4 km.
    (d) 1 km.
    (e) None of these
26. If Karan starts walking from point O for 1 km., then what is the direction of Karan's final position with respect to Rohan's initial position?
    (a) south
    (b) north
    (c) north-east
    (d) south-west
    (e) Cannot be determined

Directions (27-28): Study the information and answer the following questions:

N is the grandfather of L, who is son of E. N has two children i.e. one son and one daughter. J is the sister-in-law of E and T is the brother-in-law of S, who is the sibling of E.T and J has no siblings.

27. How is J related to N?
    (a) daughter-in-law
    (b) son
    (c) daughter
    (d) son-in-law
    (e) None of these
28. How is T related to L?
    (a) uncle
    (b) grandfather
    (c) brother
    (d) father
    (e) Cannot be determined

Directions (29-33): Study the information and answer the following questions:

In a certain code language
"No person is good" is coded as "lo mojasa"
"god is present everywhere" is coded as "jamkka la"
"good person no present " is coded as "la mosa lo"
"No one god" is coded as "karo lo"

29. What is the code for "No"?
    (a) ja   (b) sa
    (c) lo   (d) ka
    (e) None of these
30. Which of the following is denoted as "ja"?
    (a) good   (b) present
    (c) everywhere   (d) person
    (e) is
31. What is the code for "good person"?
    (a) roja   (b) sa ka
    (c) loja   (d) samo
    (e) None of these
32. Which of the following is denoted as "kamk"?
    (a) god everywhere
    (b) good present
    (c) No one
    (d) person is
    (e) None of these
33. What can be the code of "some one"?
    (a) ac sa   (b) la ka   (c) roac
    (d) jaro   (e) mo ac
34. How many pairs of letters are there in the word "SCHEDULE" which have as many letters between them in the word as in the alphabetical series (backwards or forwards)?
    (a) none   (b) one   (c) two
    (d) three   (e) four
35. If in the number 7921456238, positions of the first and the last digits are interchanged, positions of the second and ninth digits are interchanged and so on till the positions of fifth and sixth digits are interchanged, then which digit will be 4th from the right end?
    (a) 2   (b) 1
    (c) 4   (d) 6
    (e) None of these
36. Find the odd one out?
    (a) BDE   (b) GIJ   (c) VYX
    (d) QST   (e) LNO

Directions (37-40): Each of the questions below consists of a question and two statements, numbered I and II. You have to decide whether the data provided in these statements is sufficient to answer the question. Read both the two statements and give the answer:
(a) If the data in Statement I is sufficient to answer the question while the data in Statement II is not required to answer the question
(b) If the data in Statement II is sufficient to answer the question, while the data in Statement I is not required to answer the question
(c) If the data in either Statement I alone or Statement II alone is sufficient to answer the question
(d) If the data neither in Statement I nor in Statement II together are sufficient to answer the question
(e) If the data in the Statement I and II together are necessary to answer the question

37. In which month of the year did Abhay go abroad for a meeting?
    I.   Abhay correctly remembers that he went for a meeting in the first quarter of the year.
    II. Abhay's father correctly remembers that he went for a meeting after 31st January, but before 1st March.
38. Among six friends A, B, C, D, E and F, who is the second heaviest?
    I.   C is heavier than only two friends. D is heavier than C but lighter than B. F is the heaviest.
    II. A is lighter than only two friends. B is heavier than C, but lighter than F. D is heavier than only E.
39. How many marks did Sumit score in the fifty marks exam?
    I.   Sumit scored two-digit marks and his score was a perfect square.
    II. Sumit scored more than 25 but less than 45 marks.
40. Who among A, B, C, D and E is the tallest?
    I.   A is taller than B. E is not the tallest.
    II. C is taller than A. D is not the tallest.

QUANTITATIVE APTITUDE

Directions (41-45): What value should come in place of (?) in the following questions?

41. $\frac{510}{?} = \sqrt{324} + \sqrt{256}$
    (a) 20   (b) 5   (c) 10
    (d) 15   (e) 25
42. $2^{?+2} = 32 \div 1024 \times 128 \div 8 \times 128$
    (a) 6   (b) 5   (c) 4
    (d) 8   (e) 3
43. $?^2 = 55\%$ of $440 - 80\%$ of $345 + 2 \times 7^2$
    (a) 6   (b) 2   (c) 4
    (d) 16   (e) 8
44. $\frac{209}{399} \times 21^2 - (11)^2 = ?$
    (a) 110   (b) 320   (c) 100
    (d) 120   (e) 80
45. $86 \times 5 + 26 \times 11 - 22 \times 13 = ?$
    (a) 1002   (b) 716   (c) 430
    (d) 144   (e) 380

Directions (46–50): Read the data carefully and answer the questions below.

There are 900 students in school 'X' and they like two Indian cricket players, i.e. either **Virat Kohli** or **M.S. Dhoni**.

The ratio of boys to girls who like **M.S. Dhoni** is 13:7 and the total number of boys who like **Virat Kohli** is 30 less than the total number of girls who like **M.S. Dhoni**. The total number of girls who like **Virat Kohli** is 60 less than the number of boys who like **Virat Kohli**.

46. Find difference between the total number of boys who like M.S. Dhoni and the total number of boys who like Virat Kohli?
(a) 210 (b) 220 (c) 225
(d) 230 (e) 250

47. Find the ratio between the total number of girls who like M.S. Dhoni to the total number of girls who Like Virat Kohli?
(a) 8:5 (b) 7:4 (c) 7:3
(d) 7:2 (e) 7:9

48. Total number of boys who like M.S. Dhoni and Virat Kohli together is what percent more than total number of girls who like M.S. Dhoni and Virat Kohli together?
(a) $63\frac{8}{11}\%$
(b) $65\frac{8}{11}\%$
(c) $71\frac{8}{11}\%$
(d) $72\frac{8}{11}\%$
(e) $75\frac{8}{11}\%$

49. In school 'Y' number of boys who like M.S. Dhoni and Virat Kolhi is $133\frac{1}{3}\%$ and 175% more than the total number of girls who like M.S. Dhoni and Virat Kolhi in school 'X' respectively. Find the difference between the total number of boys who like M.S. Dhoni and Virat Kohli together in school 'X' to the total number of boys who like M.S. Dhoni and Virat Kohli together in school 'Y'?
(a) 225 (b) 220 (c) 230
(d) 250 (e) 260

50. Find average number of boys and girls who like M. S. Dhoni?
(a) 300 (b) 275 (c) 320
(d) 360 (e) 250

Directions (51-55): The data given in the pie chart shows the number of girls in six different schools. Some data has been given in absolute value, while others in percentage. Study the data carefully and answer the following questions.

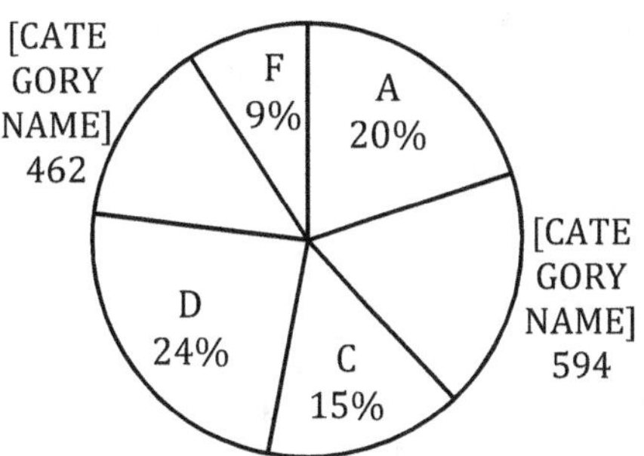

51. Find the central angle of girls in school B.
(a) 57.6° (b) 64.8° (c) 72°
(d) 79.2° (e) 86.4°

52. The total number of girls in school 'D' is how much more than the total number of girls in school 'E'?
(a) 264 (b) 297 (c) 330
(d) 363 (e) 396

53. Find the total number of girls in school 'A' and 'D' together?
(a) 1364 (b) 1386 (c) 1408
(d) 1430 (e) 1452

54. If the ratio between the number of girls and number of boys in school 'F' is 9:8, then find the total number of students in school 'F'.
(a) 561 (b) 550 (c) 528
(d) 539 (e) 572

55. The total number of girls in school 'C' is what percent less than the total number of girls in school 'A'?
(a) $33\frac{1}{3}\%$ (b) 25% (c) $66\frac{2}{3}\%$
(d) 75% (e) 50%

Directions (56-60): What approximate value should come in place of (?) in the following questions?

56. 39.89% of 240.01 + 21.01 × 9.01 = 19.05 × ?
(a) 5 (b) 15 (c) 25
(d) 35 (e) 20

57. ? × 24.9 = $\sqrt{899.89}$ + 120.01
(a) 40 (b) 20 (c) 10
(d) 8 (e) 6

58. ? = $\frac{249.99}{165.01} \times \frac{180.01}{74.99} \times \frac{121.01}{19.99}$
(a) 22 (b) 11 (c) 15
(d) 33 (e) 44

59. $5^? = 124.99 \times 499.9 \div 99.99 \div 24.99$
(a) 5 (b) 4 (c) 3
(d) 2 (e) 1

60. 60.01% of 719.89 + 44.98% of 960.01 = 89.99% of ?
(a) 690 (b) 780 (c) 870
(d) 960 (e) 1050

Directions (61-65): What should come in place of the question mark (?) in the following number series?

61. 15, 35, 45, 55, 70, ?
    (a) 95   (b) 90   (c) 80
    (d) 100   (e) 110

62. ?, 12.7, 4.6, 1.9, 1,0.7
    (a) 35   (b) 37   (c) 28.9
    (d) 85.6   (e) 25.4

63. 497, 466, 437, 414, ?, 378
    (a) 395   (b) 397   (c) 399
    (d) 401   (e) 393

64. 16, 7, 5, 7, 24, ?
    (a) 191   (b) 189   (c) 187
    (d) 185   (e) 183

65. ?, 60, 39, 66, 33, 72
    (a) 45   (b) 42   (c) 39
    (d) 48   (e) 36

Directions (66-70): What value should come in place of (?) in the following questions?

66. $(15)^2 + (?)^2 = 24 \times 22 + 23 \times 6$
    (a) 23   (b) 22   (c) 11
    (d) 9   (e) 21

67. $? + 312 + (2)^5 = (4)^5 - 17 \times 5$
    (a) 575   (b) 585   (c) 595
    (d) 605   (e) 615

68. 55% of 320 + 88% of 400 = ?
    (a) 496   (b) 480   (c) 512
    (d) 528   (e) 544

69. $\sqrt{?} = \sqrt{12^2 - 18 \times 9 + 26}$
    (a) 4   (b) 8   (c) 64
    (d) 16   (e) 2

70. $? \div 27 \times 48 = 288 \div 18 \times 9$
    (a) 1   (b) 9   (c) 27
    (d) 81   (e) 729

71. B's age 8 years ago is 60% more than A's age 8 years ago. If ratio between present age of A and B is 3:4, then find B's age, four years hence.
    (a) 22 years   (b) 24 years   (c) 26 years
    (d) 28 years   (e) 32 years

72. If the ratio between the volume of a cylinder and the volume of sphere is 3:1, then find the ratio between the total surface area of the cylinder to the total surface area of the sphere (Radius of sphere = Radius of cylinder).
    (a) 2:1   (b) 5:2   (c) 4:1
    (d) 3:2   (e) 7:2

73. 'X' men can complete a work in (X–2) days while (X–10) men can complete the same work in 2X days. Find in how many days (X–6) men can complete half the work.
    (a) 8 days   (b) 12 days   (c) 16 days
    (d) 20 days   (e) 24 days

74. A container contains 60 l. milk and 40 l. water. How much quantity of water should be added in the container so that if the shopkeeper sells the mixture in the container at the cost price of the milk, he will earn a profit of 150%?
    (a) 80 l.   (b) 100 l.   (c) 30 l.
    (d) 40 l.   (e) 50 l.

75. A box contains 12 red, 6 green and 'x' yellow balls. If the probability of choosing one green ball out of the box is $\frac{2}{9}$, then find the probability of choosing one ball which can be either red or yellow.
    (a) $\frac{4}{9}$ (b) $\frac{5}{9}$ (c) $\frac{2}{3}$
    (d) $\frac{7}{9}$ (e) $\frac{8}{9}$

76. A train of length 180 meters crosses a platform in 15 seconds with a speed of 60 km/h. If a man crosses the same platform in 4 minutes, find the speed of the man.
    (a) 1.05 km/h.   (b) 3 km/h.
    (c) 2.05 km/h.   (d) 2.1 km/h.
    (e) 2 km/h.

77. What is 80% of a number, whose $\frac{3}{7}$th is 60?
    (a) 98   (b) 112   (c) 48
    (d) 126   (e) 80

78. Find the no. of ways to arrange the letters of the word "EDUCATION" using factorial function.
    (a) $\frac{8!}{2}$ (b) $\frac{10!}{2}$ (c) $\frac{6!}{2}$
    (d) $\frac{7!}{2}$ (e) 9!

79. What is the probability of finding a red card or a queen from a well-shuffled pack of 52 cards.
    (a) $\frac{15}{26}$ (b) $\frac{7}{12}$ (c) $\frac{7}{13}$
    (d) $\frac{5}{13}$ (e) $\frac{8}{13}$

80. If Bhavya's income is Rs. 20,000, then he saves Rsx . If his salary is Rs 35,000, then at what percent will his savings increase such that the saving percent will neither increase or nor decrease.
    (a) 75%   (b) 80%   (c) 90%
    (d) 50%   (e) 60%

REASONING ABILITY

Direction (1-5):
1. **(c)** I. P = C (False) II. C < P (False)
2. **(e)** I. H < W (True) II. G > H (True)
3. **(a)** I. Q < D (True) II. C < A (False)
4. **(d)** I. S ≥ B (False) II. F > E (False)
5. **(a)** I. G < N (True) II. I ≥ L (False)

Direction (6-10):
6. **(b)** L
7. **(c)** $
8. **(d)** Five – R$, #L, @N, ©V, ®F
9. **(c)** Three – 1Q, M8, 1S
10. **(b)** E®9

Directions (11-15):
More than three persons live between M and O. M lives on floor number 9. N lives on floor number 5. There is a gap of two floors between P and O. S lives below P and O. R lives immediately above S. We have three possibilities:

Case1		Case2		Case 3	
Floor	Person	Floor	Person	Floor	Person
10		10		10	
9	M	9	M	9	M
8		8		8	
7	P	7		7	P
6		6	P	6	
5	N	5	N	5	N
4	O	4		4	O
3	R	3	O	3	
2	S	2	R	2	R
1		1	S	1	S

Now, L lives immediately below the vacant floor. This will eliminate Case 1 and Case 3. No odd numbered floor is vacant. Q does not live on the top floor. So the final arrangement will be:

Floor	Person
10	Vacant
9	M
8	Vacant
7	L
6	P
5	N
4	Q
3	O
2	R
1	S

11. **(c)** 12. **(e)** 13. **(b)**
14. **(c)** 15. **(b)**

Directions (16-20): P sits fifth to the right of W and both of them do not sit at any end of the row. Two persons sit between R and W. V sits second to the left of R. One person sits between U and V. T is not an immediate neighbour of R. Q sits second to the right of T. S sits to the immediate left of V. Immediate neighbours of V face opposite directions. U and Q faces south. There are two possible cases:

Case I

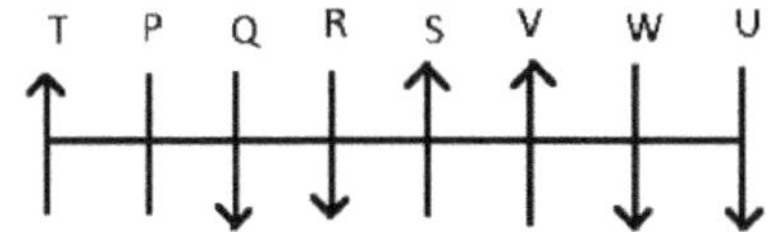

Case II

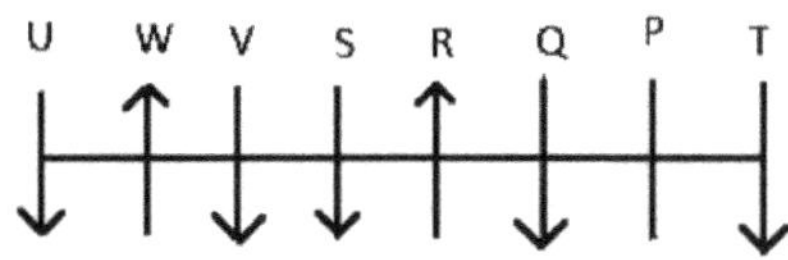

Now, immediate neighbour of Q faces opposite direction. Not more than four people face south. This will eliminate Case II. So final arrangement will be

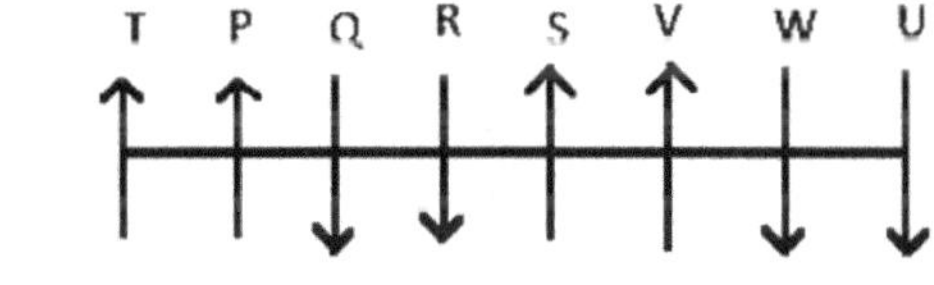

16. **(a)** 17. **(c)** 18. **(c)**
19. **(d)** 20. **(d)**

Directions (21-23):
T > P(36 coins) > Q > S > R > U
21. **(c)** 22. **(a)**
23. **(b)** Coins of R = (59 – P) = (59 – 36) = 23 coins

Directions (24-26):
24. **(b)**

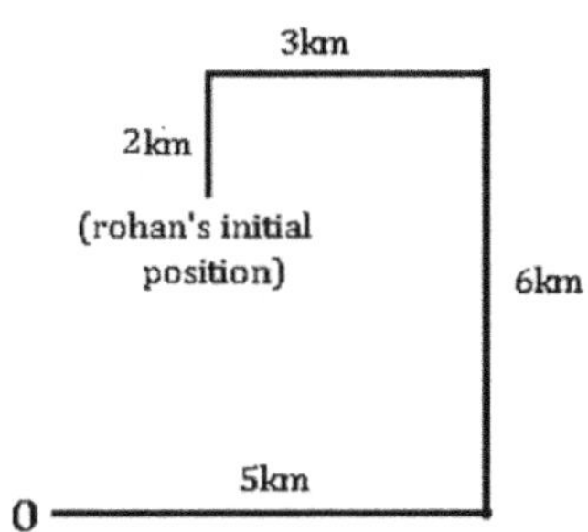

25. (a)

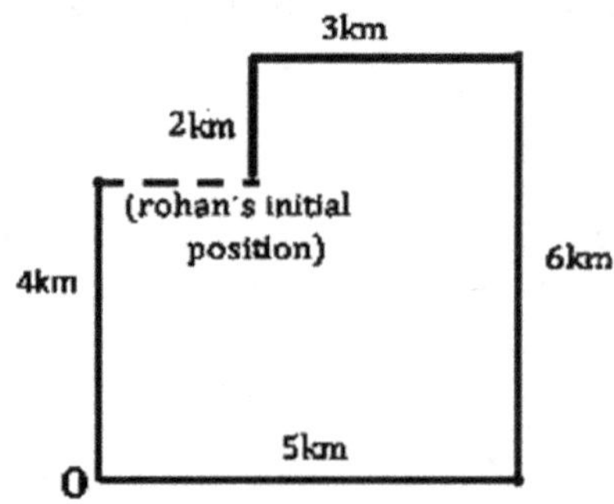

26. (d) Karan can walk in any direction still he will be in South-west direction from initial position of Rohan.

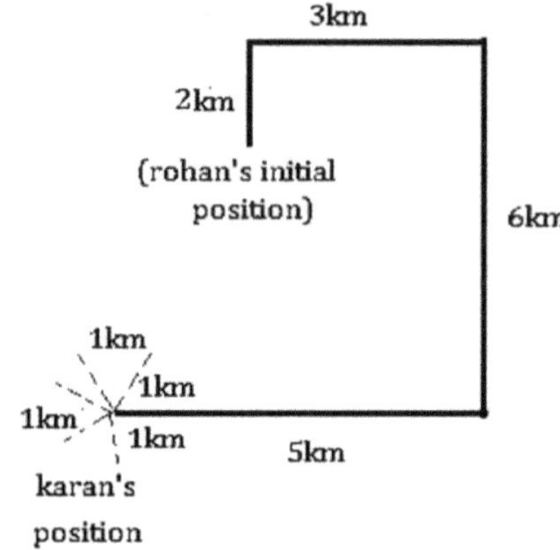

Directions (27-28):

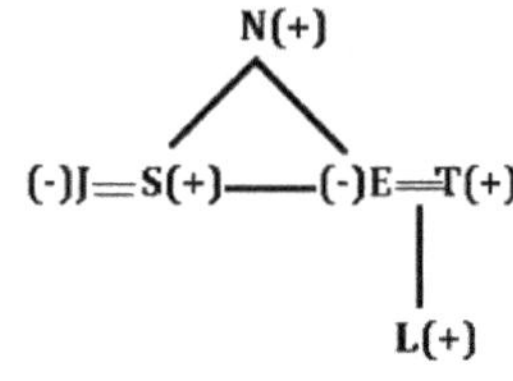

27. (a)   **28. (d)**

Directions (29-33):

Element	Code
person/good	mo/sa
no	lo
is	ja
god	ka
present	la
everywhere	mk
one	ro

29. (c)   **30. (e)**   **31. (d)**

32. (a)   **33. (c)**

34. (d) Three

35. (b)   **36. (c)**

Directions (37-40):

37. (b) From I, First quarter of the year i.e. Jan, Feb, March. Hence I alone is not sufficient. From II, It is clear that Abhay went for meeting in Feb. Hence II alone is sufficient.

38. (c) From I, F > B > D > C > E/A > A/E
Hence B is second heaviest
From II, F > B > A > C > D > E
Hence B is the second heaviest

39. (e) From I, Sumit scores 16, 25, 36, 49
From II, Sumit scores 26 to 44
So From I and II Sumit scores 36 marks.

40. (e) From I, A >B,E is not the tallest
From II, C >A,D is not the tallest
From I and II C > A > B and neither E & D is tallest. So C is the tallest.

QUANTITATIVE APTITUDE

41. (d) $\frac{510}{?} = \sqrt{324} + \sqrt{256}$

$\Rightarrow \frac{510}{?} = 18 + 16 \Rightarrow ? = \frac{510}{34} = 15$

42. (c) $2^{?+2} = \frac{32}{1024} \times \frac{128}{8} \times 128 = 64 = 2^6$

$\Rightarrow ? + 2 = 6 \Rightarrow ? = 4$

43. (e) $?^2 = \frac{55}{100} \times 440 - \frac{80}{100} \times 345 + 2 \times 7^2$

$?^2 = 242 - 276 + 98 = 64$

$\Rightarrow ? = 8$

44. (a) $? = \frac{209}{399} \times 21^2 - (11)^2$

$? = \frac{19 \times 11}{19 \times 21} \times 21^2 - 11^2$

$? = 231 - 121 = 110$

45. (c) $? = 86 \times 5 + 26 \times 11 - 22 \times 13$

$? = 430 + 286 - 286$

$? = 430$

Direction (46 − 50):

Let the total number of boys and girls who like M.S. Dhoni be 13x and 7x respectively

And total number of boys who like Virat Kohli = 7x − 30

While total number of girls who like Virat Kohli = 7x −30 − 60 = 7x − 90

ATQ −

$13x + 7x + (7x−30) + (7x − 90) = 900$

$34x = 1020$

$x = 30$

Boys like M.S. Dhoni	Girls Like M.S. Dhoni	Boys Like Virat Kohli	Girls like Virat Kohli
13×30 = 390	7×30 = 210	7×30 − 30 = 180	7×30 − 90 = 120

46. (a) Required difference = 390 – 180 = 210

47. (b) Required ratio = $\frac{210}{120}$ = 7 : 4

48. (d) Total number of boys who like M.S. Dhoni and Virat Kohli = 390 + 180 = 570
Total number of girls who like M.S. Dhoni and Virat Kohli = 210 + 120 = 330
Required percentage = $\frac{570-330}{330} \times 100$
= $\frac{240}{330} \times 100 = 72\frac{8}{11}$ %

49. (d) Total number of boys who like M.S. Dhoni and Virat Kohli together in school 'Y'
= $210 \times \frac{7}{3} + 120 \times \frac{275}{100}$ = 490 + 330 = 820
Required difference = 820 – (390 + 180) = 250

50. (a) Required average = $\frac{390+210}{2}$ = 300

Solution (51-55)
Total number of girls in school B and E together
→ $[100-20-15-24-9]$ % = 462 + 594
⇒ 32% = 1056
⇒ 100% = 3300
Total number of girls in six schools together = 3300

51. (b) Required central angle = $\frac{594}{3300} \times 360$ = 64.8°

52. (c) Total number of girls in school D – $\frac{24}{100} \times$ 3300
= 792
Required difference = 792 – 462 = 330

53. (e) Total number of girls in school A and D together
= $\frac{(20+24)}{100} \times 3300$ = 44 × 33 = 1452

54. (a) Total number of students in school F
= $\frac{9}{9} \times \frac{17}{100} \times 3300$ = 561

55. (b) Required % = $\frac{20-15}{20} \times 100 = \frac{5}{20} \times 100$ = 25%

56. (b) ? ≈ $\frac{96+189}{19} = \frac{285}{19} = 15$

57. (e) ? × 25 ≈ $\sqrt{900} + 120$ ⇒ ? ≈ $\frac{30+120}{25} = 6$

58. (a) ? ≈ $\frac{250}{165} \times \frac{180}{75} \times \frac{121}{20} = 22$

59. (d) $5^?$ ≈ $\frac{125 \times 500}{100 \times 25} = 25$
? = 2

60. (d) $\frac{60}{100} \times 720 + \frac{45}{100} \times 960 \approx \frac{90}{100} \times ?$
⇒ ? = $\frac{(432+432)}{9} \times 10$ ⇒ ? = $\frac{864}{9} \times 10 =$ 960

61. (d)

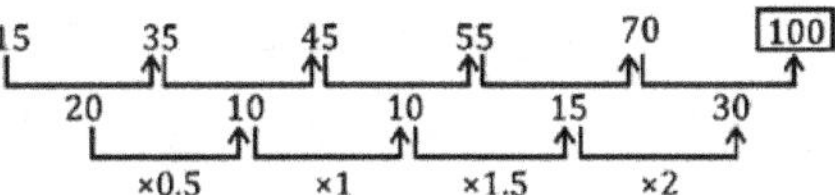

62. (b)

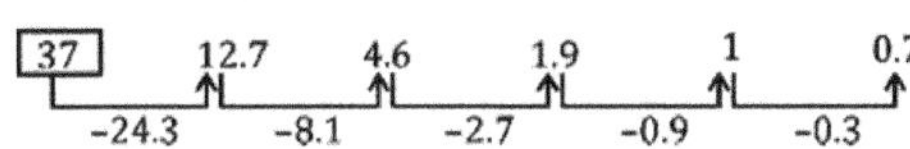

63. (a)

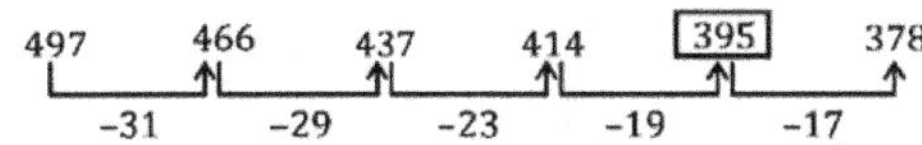

64. (c)

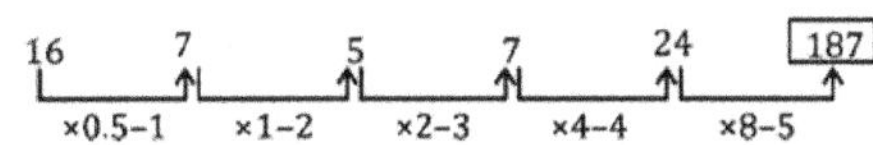

65. (a)

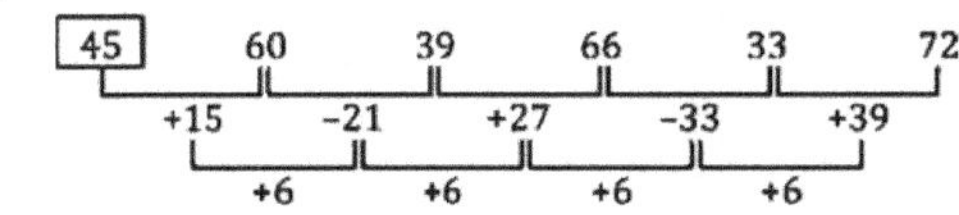

66. (e) $(15)^2 + (?)^2 = 24 \times 22 + 23 \times 6$
⇒ $?^2 = 528 + 138 - 225$
⇒ $?^2 = 441 \Rightarrow ? = 21$

67. (c) $? + 312 + 2^5 = 4^5 - 17 \times 5$
⇒ ? = 1024 - 85 - 312 - 32
⇒ ? = 595

68. (d) ? = $\frac{55}{100} \times 320 + \frac{88}{100} \times 400$
? = 176 + 352
⇒ ? = 528

69. (b) $\sqrt{?} = \sqrt{144 - 162 + 26}$
$\sqrt{?} = \sqrt{8}$ ⇒ ? = 8

70. (d) $\frac{? \times 48}{27} = \frac{288}{18} \times 9 \Rightarrow ? = 81$

71. (d) Let present age of A and B be a and b respectively
ATQ,
b – 8 = 1.6 (a–8)
5b – 40 = 8a – 64
⇒ 8a – 5b = 24   ...(i)
while $\frac{a}{b} = \frac{3}{4}$ ...(ii)
On solving (i) & (ii)
a = 18, b = 24
B's age four years hence = 24 + 4 = 28 years

72. (b) Volume of cylinder = $\pi r^2 h$ (r-radius , h – height)
Volume of sphere = $\frac{4}{3}\pi r^3$
ATQ
$\frac{\pi r^2 h}{\frac{4}{3}\pi r^3} = \frac{3}{1} \Rightarrow \frac{h}{r} = \frac{4}{1} \Rightarrow h = 4r$
T.S.A of cylinder = $2\pi r (r+h)$
T.S.A of sphere = $4\pi r^2$

Required Ratio $= \frac{2\pi r (r+h)}{4\pi r^2} = \frac{4r+r}{2r} = \frac{5}{2}$

73. (b) Total work $= (X) (X-2) = (X-10) (2X)$

$\Rightarrow X - 2 = 2X - 20 \Rightarrow X = 18$

Let $(X-6)$ men complete half of the work in 'y' days

ATQ,

$(X-6) \times y = \frac{X(X-2)}{2}$

$\Rightarrow y = \frac{18 \times 16}{2 \times 12} = 12$ days

74. (e) On selling mixture, retailer earns 150% profit

$\Rightarrow$ If container contains 5 l of mixture then quantity of milk is 2 l.

Let x l of water be added into container

ATQ

$\frac{60}{40+x} = \frac{2}{3}$

$\Rightarrow 180 = 80 + 2x \Rightarrow \boxed{x = 50\ l}$

75. (d) ATQ,

$\frac{6}{12+6+x} = \frac{2}{9} \Rightarrow x = \frac{18}{2} = 9$

Required probability $= \frac{9+12}{12+6+9} = \frac{21}{27} = \frac{7}{9}$

Alternate, Required Probability $= 1 -$ Probability of choosing one green ball $= 1 - \frac{2}{9} = \frac{7}{9}$

76. (a) Speed of train in m/s $= \frac{60 \times 505}{18} = \frac{50}{3}$ m/s

Distance covered by train in 15 seconds

$= \frac{50}{3} \times 15 = 250$ meter

Length of platform $= 250 - 180 = 70$ meter

Speed of man $= \frac{70}{4} \times \frac{60}{1000} = 1.05$ km/hr

77. (b) Let number is 'x'

$So \Rightarrow \frac{3}{7}x = 60$

x= 140

80% $of\ x = \frac{80}{100} \times 140 = 112$

78. (e) Number of ways = 9!

79. (c) Total cards = 52

Red cards = 26

Queen cards = 4

Required Probability $\Rightarrow \frac{26+4-2}{52} = \frac{7}{13}$

80. (a) Total income = 20000 Rs

Saving = x Rs

Saving % $= \frac{x}{20000} \times 100 = \frac{x}{200}$ %

New, salary = 35000

New saving $= \frac{35000 \times x}{200 \times 100} = \frac{7}{4}x\ Rs$

percentage increase in saving

$= \frac{\frac{7}{4}x - x}{x} \times 100$

$= 75\%$

REASONING ABILITY

Directions (1-5): In each of the questions below, relationships between some elements are shown in the statements. These statements are followed by conclusions numbered I and II. Read the statements and give the answer.
(a) If only conclusion I follows.
(b) If only conclusion II follows.
(c) If either conclusion I or II follows.
(d) If neither conclusion I nor II follows.
(e) If both conclusions I and II follow.

1. **Statements:** $E \geq J = O \geq T \geq Y < M > C$
   Conclusions: I. $J > C$ II. $M < E$
2. **Statements:** $W > O \leq R < T \leq V = U > Q$
   Conclusions: I. $U > O$ II. $V < W$
3. **Statements:** $P > U < C \geq Z = X \geq S > F$
   Conclusions: I. $Z \geq P$ II. $S \leq C$
4. **Statements:** $A \leq B \leq D = E \leq C = H > G$
   Conclusions: I. $B < C$ II. $C = B$
5. **Statements:** $I = N > K \geq P < O \leq T \leq S$
   Conclusions: I. $P < I$ II. $S \geq O$

Directions (6-10): In each of the questions given below, a group of digits/letters is given followed by four combinations of symbols numbered (a),(b),(c) and(d). You have to find out which one of the four combinations correctly represents the group of digits/letters based on the symbol codes and the conditions given below. If none of the four combinations represents the group of digits correctly, give(e) i.e. 'None of these' as the answer.

Digit	I	G	4	8	E	N	9	P	K	W	3	U	1	R	B
Symbol	?	<	μ	>	=	©	$	@	#	&	^	*	%	+	~

Condition for coding the group elements:
(i) If the first element is a vowel and the last element is a perfect cube, then both are to be coded as %.
(ii) If the first element is a consonant and the last element is an even number, then both are to be coded by the code of the first element.
(iii) If the first element is an odd number and the last element is an alphabet, then both are to be coded by the code of the last element.
(iv) If the first element is an odd number and the last element is an even number, then the obtained code will be reversed.

6. G8NEI4
   (a) <>©=?μ   (b) ><©=?>
   (c) <>©=?>   (d) <>©=?<
   (e) None of these
7. 1PK9W8
   (a) %@#$&>   (b) <&$#@%
   (c) >&#$@%   (d) >&$#@%
   (e) None of these
8. 39K4RB
   (a) ^$#μ+~   (b) ~$μ#+~
   (c)~$#μ+~   (d) ~$#μ+^
   (e)None of these
9. 1UG8B9
   (a) $*<>~$ (b) %*<>~$
   (c) %*><~$ (d) %>*<~$
   (e) None of these
10. U4RN91
   (a) %μ+©$%   (b) *μ+©$%
   (c) %μ+©$*   (d) %μ+$©%
   (e) None of these

Directions (11-15): In each of the questions below are given some statements followed by two conclusions. You have to take the given statements to be true even if they seem to be at variance with commonly known facts. Read all the conclusions and then decide which of the given conclusions logically follows from the given statements, disregarding commonly known facts, to give the answer.

11. **Statements:** All fruits are flowers.
    Some flowers are vegetables.
    No vegetables is grain.
    Conclusions: I. Some grain are not flowers.
    II. Some fruits are vegetables.
    (a) Both I and II follow.
    (b) Either I or II follows.
    (c) Only II follows.
    (d) Only I follows.
    (e) Neither I nor II follows.
12. **Statements:** Some rice are wheat.
    Some wheat are pulses.
    All pulses are diet.
    Conclusions: I. Some diet being rice is a Possibility.
    II. All pulses are rice.
    (a) Both I and II follow.

(b) Either I or II follows.
(c) Only II follows.
(d) Only I follows.
(e) Neither I nor II follows.

13. **Statements:** All film is movie.
    All movie is Netflix.
    Some Netflix is Prime.
    Conclusions: I. Some film being Prime is a Possibility.
    II. All film is Netflix
(a) Both I and II follow.
(b) Either I or II follows.
(c) Only II follows.
(d) Only I follows.
(e) Neither I nor II follows.

14. **Statements:** Some cup are glass.
    Some glass are plate.
    No plate is vessel.
    Conclusions: I. Some cup are not vessel.
    II. All cup are vessel.
(a) Both I and II follow.
(b) Either I or II follows.
(c) Only II follows.
(d) Only I follows.
(e) Neither I nor II follows.

15. **Statements** Some red are white.
    Some white are pink.
    All red are blue.
    Conclusions: I. Some blue are white.
    II. Some pink are blue.
(a) Both I and II follow.
(b) Either I or II follows.
(c) Only II follows.
(d) Only I follows.
(e) Neither I nor II follows.

Directions (16-20): Study the following information carefully and answer the given questions:

Eight friends A, B, C, D, E, F, G and H are sitting around a square table in such a way that four of them sit at four corners of the square while the other four sit in the middle of each sides. The ones who sit at the four corners face towards the centre while those who sit in the middle of the sides face outside.

E sits third to the left of B. Two persons sit between F and B. D sits to the immediate right of F. G sits second to the left of H. H is an immediate neighbour of C. C faces outside. A is not an immediate neighbour of D.

16. Who sits exactly between G and H?
    (a) E   (b) B
    (c) C   (d) D
    (e) None of these

17. What is the position of A with respect to B?
    (a) Immediate right

(b) Second to the right
(c) Third to the right
(d) Fourth to the left
(e) None of these

18. Four of the following five are alike in a certain way and so form a group. Who among the following does not belong to that group?
    (a) E   (b) F   (c) H
    (d) D   (e) G

19. Who sits opposite B?
    (a) G   (b) H
    (c) A   (d) D
    (e) None of these

20. Who among the following pairs sits at the corner?
    (a) A, C   (b) E, B
    (c) D, H   (d) F, G
    (e) None of these

Directions (21-25): Study the following information carefully to answer the given questions.

P, Q, R, S, T and U are six faculties. All faculties take lectures on different days of the week starting from Monday to Sunday (but not necessarily in the same order). One day in the week is a holiday.

S takes a lecture on Saturday. Not more than two persons take a lecture between S and R. P takes his lecture immediately before R. T takes his lecture before U, but not on Thursday. No one takes lecture after Q. Neither Monday nor Friday is a holiday. T does not take his lecture on Monday.

21. On which of the following days of the week does P takes his lecture?
    (a) Friday   (b) Tuesday   (c) Thursday
    (d) Wednesday   (e) Monday

22. How many persons take lectures between S and P?
    (a) none   (b) one
    (c) two   (d) three
    (e) More than three

23. Which among the following days is a holiday?
    (a) Tuesday
    (b) Wednesday
    (c) Thursday
    (d) Sunday
    (e) None of these

24. Which of the following statements is not true?
    (a) R takes his lecture on Tuesday
    (b) U takes his lecture before S
    (c) T takes his lecture after R
    (d) P takes his lecture on Wednesday
    (e) None of these

25. U takes his lecture on which day?
    (a) Saturday   (b) Friday   (c) Tuesday
    (d) Thursday   (e) Monday

26. If "SHIP" is coded as "4721", "PLUS" is coded as "1854", then "HILL" will be coded as?
    (a) 1847 (b) 5421
    (c) 7288 (d) 1788
    (e) None of these

27. How many meaningful words can be formed from the second, third, fifth and seventh letter of the word "**BEAUTIFUL**" without repeating the letters?
    (a) one
    (b) two
    (c) three
    (d) More than three
    (e) None of the above

28. If all the digits are rearranged in ascending order in the number **89436521**, then which of the following will be fifth from the right end?
    (a) 3 (b) 5 (c) 4
    (d) 6 (e) None of these

29. If all the vowels are dropped from the word "**INCREDIBLE**", then which among the following will be fourth from the left end?
    (a) R (b) D (c) B
    (d) L (e) None of these

30. How many pairs of letters are there in the word "**FISCAL**" which have as many letters between them in the word as in alphabetical series (backwards or forwards)?
    (a) none (b) one (c) two
    (d) three (e) four

Directions (31-35): These questions are based on the following set of numbers.
428527139814729

31. If all the digits in each number are arranged in a descending order within the number, then which of the following will form the second highest in the new arrangement?
    (a) 428 (b) 527 (c) 139
    (d) 814 (e) 729

32. If all the digits in each number are arranged in an ascending order within the number, then which of the following will form the third lowest in the new arrangement?
    (a) 428 (b) 527 (c) 139
    (d) 814 (e) 729

33. What will be the difference between the third digit of the lowest number and second digit of the highest number?
    (a) 6 (b) 3 (c) 5
    (d) 8 (e) 7

34. If '1' is added to all the given numbers, then the resultant of how many numbers will not be divisible by 3?
    (a) one (b) two
    (c) three (d) four
    (e) More than four

35. Which of the following will be the sum of the second digit of the highest number and the third digit of the second lowest number?
    (a) 10 (b) 9
    (c) 8 (d) 6
    (e) None of these

Directions (36-40): Study the information and answer the following questions:

Twelve persons are sitting in two parallel rows facing each other. A, B, C, D, E and F are sitting in row 1 facing north and P, Q, R, S, T and U are sitting in row 2 facing south (not necessarily in the same order).

E sits third to the right of B and one of them sits at an extreme end of the row. R faces B. R sits to the immediate right of S. Three persons sit between P and Q and one of them sits at an extreme end of the row. P does not face E or F. D sits to the immediate left of F and neither of them sits at any extreme end. U faces C. R is not an immediate neighbour of U.

36. Who among the following sits fourth to the right of T?
    (a) P (b) U
    (c) R (d) Q
    (e) None of these

37. What is the position of C with respect to D?
    (a) Third to the left
    (b) Third to the right
    (c) Second to the left
    (d) Immediate right
    (e) Cannot be determined

38. Who faces E?
    (a) U (b) P
    (c) R (d) Q
    (e) None of these

39. Who faces the immediate neighbour of U?
    (a) B (b) A
    (c) C (d) D
    (e) Cannot be determined

40. Four of the following five are alike in a certain way and hence form a group. Who among the following does not belong to that group?
    (a) E (b) Q (c) U
    (d) B (e) C

Directions (41-45): Find the approximate value of question marks (?) in the following questions?

41. $64.98\%\ of\ 360.01 - ?\%\ of\ 249.99 = 138.923$
 (a) 45   (b) 38   (c) 52
 (d) 32   (e) 25

42. $\sqrt{911.95 \div 24.11 + 184.01 - 52.937} = ?$
 (a) 13   (b) 17   (c) 15
 (d) $(17)^2$ (e) 169

43. $(14.9)^2 - (5.01)^3 + \sqrt{1520.98} + 8.933 \times 13.011 = (?)^2$
 (a) 12   (b) 14   (c) 16
 (d) 18   (e) 26

44. $(3749.98 - ?) \div 55.012 = 22.991$
 (a) 2465   (b) 2445   (c) 2495
 (d) 2475   (e) 2485

45. $(3416.023 \div 55.991) - (1133.96 \div ?) = 18.989$
 (a) 13   (b) 17   (c) 23
 (d) 27   (e) 37

Directions (46-50): The given table shows data related to five students and the total number of movies watched by them during a period of ten years.

Total number of movies = Number of Hollywood movies + Number of Bollywood movies.

Students	Total number of movies watched	Ratio of Hollywood to Bollywood movies
A	350	4:3
B	400	11:9
C	250	3:7
D	200	13:12
E	375	16 : 9

46. What is the average number of Bollywood movies watched by students A, B and D together?
 (a) 132   (b) 138   (c) 142
 (d) 144   (e) 146

47. The total number of Hollywood movies watched by student E is what percent more/less than the total number of movies watched by student B?
 (a) 40%   (b) 45%   (c) 35%
 (d) 30%   (e) 50%

48. The total number of Hollywood movies watched by students C and B together is how much more/less than the total number of Bollywood movies watched by students D and E together?
 (a) 54   (b) 74   (c) 60
 (d) 64   (e) 70

49. Find the ratio of the total number of movies watched by students C and D together to the number of Bollywood movies watched by B, C and E together.
 (a) 49:45   (b) 45:49   (c) 90:97
 (d) 10:11   (e) 9:11

50. The average of the total number of movies watched by B and D is what percent of the average of total number of movies watched by A and C.
 (a) 125%   (b) 75%   (c) 80%
 (d) 120%   (e) 100%

51. If the present population of a city is 55,566, which was 35,000, two years ago, then find the rate of increase of population per year.
 (a) 24%   (b) 25%   (c) 23%
 (d) 26%   (e) 22%

52. Roni purchased a cycle for Rs. 12,000 and sold it at a loss of 20%. With that amount he purchased another cycle and sold it at 30% profit. What was his overall gain/loss?
 (a) 720 loss   (b) 480 loss
 (c) 480 profit   (d) 720 profit
 (e) No profit and no loss

53. On a sum, Sima earns an interest of Rs. 1,519 at S.I. in 7 years at 7% p.a. Find the sum.
 (a) 3100 Rs.   (b) 3000 Rs.   (c) 2800 Rs.
 (d) 3200 Rs.   (e) 3500 Rs.

54. A certain amount was to be distributed between X, Y and Z in the ratio of 1:2:3 respectively. At the time of distribution, the amount was distributed wrongly in the ratio of 5:4:6 due to which X got Rs.305 more. Find the actual amount that Z got.
 (a) 915 Rs.   (b) 477 Rs.   (c) 610 Rs.
 (d) 183 Rs.   (e) 732 Rs.

55. Mahendra is 12 years younger than Niraj. Niraj's age 3 years ago was three times the present age of Bhavya. At present Mahendra's age is twice the age of Bhavya. What is the present age of Niraj.
 (a) 18   (b) 30   (c) 27
 (d) 9   (e) 15

Directions (56–65): Simplify and find the value of the question marks (?) in the following questions.

56. $\frac{2}{3}\ of\ \frac{4}{5}\ of\ \frac{3}{7}\ of\ 2205 = ?$

(a) 494   (b) 504   (c) 484
(d) 514   (e) 524

57. $2\frac{3}{7} - 3\frac{1}{4} + 4\frac{3}{8} - 1\frac{1}{56} = ?$

(a) $2\frac{15}{28}$ (b) $2\frac{31}{56}$ (c) $2\frac{1}{2}$
(d) $2\frac{25}{56}$ (e) $2\frac{4}{7}$

58. $-119 + 34 - 67 + 259 - ? = 88$

(a) 15   (b) 9   (c) 39
(d) 29   (e) 19

59. $\sqrt{12^2 \times 32 \div 48 + 174 + 9 \times 6} = (?)^2$

(a) $2\sqrt{3}$ (b) $3\sqrt{2}$ (c) 3
(d) 6   (e) 9

60. $53 \times 48 - ? = 29 \times 70$

(a) 504   (b) 524   (c) 514
(d) 512   (e) 518

61. 85% of ? of 6755 = 3281

(a) $\frac{4}{7}$ (b) $\frac{2}{7}$ (c) $1\frac{1}{7}$
(d) $\frac{6}{7}$ (e) $1\frac{3}{7}$

62. $\sqrt[3]{?} \times \sqrt[3]{2197} = \sqrt[4]{(8281)^2}$

(a) 512   (b) 216   (c) 125
(d) 343   (e) 729

63. $\sqrt{9409} - \sqrt{1156} = 3339 \div ?$

(a) 43   (b) 63   (c) 53
(d) 47   (e) 57

64. $(320\% \text{ of } 825) \div ? = 48$

(a) 55   (b) 45   (c) 65
(d) 58   (e) 75

65. $\frac{2}{21} \text{ of } 2268 \div 12 + ? = \sqrt{3025}$

(a) 47   (b) 37   (c) 27
(d) 57   (e) 45

66. To dilute a 100 litres solution of acid to 40% from 50%, how much water must be added?
(a) 50 litre   (b) 75 litre   (c) 15 litre
(d) 10 litre   (e) 25 litre

67. 5 men can do a work in 16 days and 8 women can do the same work in 15 days. In how many days 2 men and 3 women can do the work together?
(a) 22 days   (b) 20 days   (c) 21 days
(d) 18 days   (e) 24 days

68. A car can cover a distance in 9 hours at the speed of 70 km/hr. At what percent should the speed of the car increase so that the distance can be covered in 6 hr?
(a) 25%   (b) 40%   (c) 35%
(d) 50%   (e) 60%

69. The number obtained by interchanging the two digits of a two-digit number is lesser than the original number by 54. If the sum of the two digits of number is 12, then what is the original number?
(a) 28   (b) 39   (c) 82
(d) 89   (e) 93

70. What is the speed of a car (in km/hr.), which overtakes a running train in 20 seconds? Length of the train is 180 meters and its speed is 33⅓% less than the speed of the car. (Car's length is negligible)
(a) 100 km/hr.
(b) 81 km/hr.
(c) 105 km/hr.
(d) 90 km/hr.
(e) 97.2 km/hr.

Direction (71–75): What will come in the place of the question (?) mark in the following number series.

71. ?, 46, 71, 87, 96, 100
(a) 8   (b) 12   (c) 9
(d) 10   (e) 11

72. 218, 231, 253, 293, 369, ?
(a) 507   (b) 517   (c) 515
(d) 516   (e) 519

73. 1308, ?, 324, 160, 78, 37
(a) 652   (b) 762   (c) 682
(d) 672   (e) 632

74. 64, 71, 81, 96, ?, 149
(a) 116   (b) 112   (c) 118
(d) 122   (e) 120

75. 18, 57, 174, 525, 1578, ?
(a) 4737   (b) 4677   (c) 4697
(d) 4717   (e) 4767

76. A man has two dice. If he rolled both dice, what will be the probability of the sum of the digits being either 5 or 7?
(a) $\frac{1}{18}$ (b) $\frac{1}{12}$ (c) $\frac{5}{9}$
(d) $\frac{5}{18}$ (e) $\frac{7}{18}$

Directions (77–80): Each of the following questions below consists of a question and two statements numbered I and II. You have to decide whether the data provided in the statements is sufficient to answer the questions. Give answer

(a) if the data given in statement I alone is sufficient to answer the question while the data in statement II alone is not sufficient to answer the question.

(b) if the data given in statement II alone is sufficient to answer the question while the data in statement I alone is not sufficient to answer the question.

(c) if the data either in statement I alone or in statement II alone is sufficient to answer the question.

(d) If the data in neither statement I nor II is sufficient to answer the question.

(e) If the data in both statements I and II together is necessary to answer the question.

77. Find the cost price of an article for the shopkeeper when he sells the article at Rs. 240.

(I) If the article is sold at 25% more, the profit earned will be Rs. 40.

(II) Marked price of article is Rs. 400 and profit% is equal to discount% and profit% is 40%.

78. Find the volume of the right circular cone.

(I) Height of cone is 100% more than radius of cone.

(II) Area of base of cone is 154 cm².

79. Find the value of $2^x \times 3^y$. x and y are natural numbers and x is greater than y.

(a) Sum of value of x and y is 8.

(b) Product of value of x and y is 12.

80. Find the speed of a boat in still water.

(I) Time taken by the boat to cover 64 km. in downstream is half the time taken by the same boat to cover the same distance in still water.

(II) Speed of the stream is 5 km/hr.

Solutions

REASONING ABILITY

Direction (1-5):

1. **(d)** I. J > C (False) II. M < E (False)
2. **(a)** I. U > O (True)   II. V < W (False)
3. **(b)** I. Z ≥ P (False)   II. S ≤ C (True)
4. **(c)** I. B < C (False)   II. C = B (False)
5. **(e)** I. P < I (True) II. S ≥ O (True)

Directions (6-10):

6. **(d)** By using condition (ii) the code for 'G8NEI4' will be <>©=?<
7. **(d)** By using condition (iv) the code for '1PK9W8' will be >&$#@%
8. **(c)** By using condition (iii) the code for '39K4RB' will be ~$#μ+~
9. **(b)** The code for '1UG8B9' will be %*<>~$
10. **(a)** By using condition (i) the code for 'U4RN91' will be %μ+©$%

Directions (11-15):

11. **(e)**

For I – There is no direct relation between the elements flowers and grain. Hence, Conclusion I cannot follow.

For II – There is no direct relation between the elements fruits and vegetables. Hence, Conclusion II cannot be concluded.

12. **(d)**

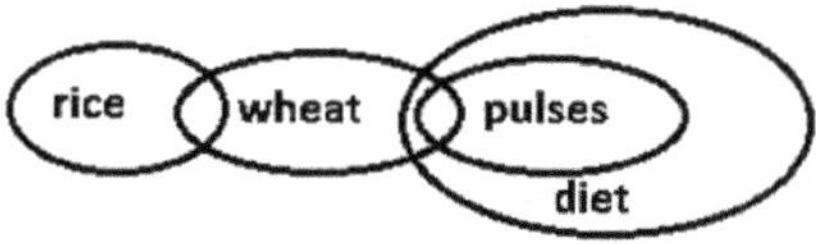

For I – As there is no direct relation between elements rice and diet, therefore

possibility case will hold true. Hence, Conclusion I can be concluded.

For II – As there is no direct relation between element rice and pulses, Conclusion II cannot be concluded.

13. **(a)**

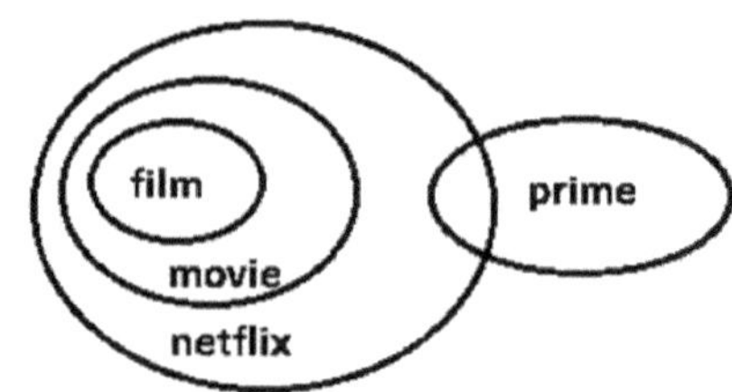

For I –As there is no direct relation between the elements film and prime, therefore possibility case will hold true. Hence, Conclusion I can be concluded.

For II – As all film is movie and all movie is netflix therefore all film is netflix will hold true. Hence, Conclusion II can be concluded.

14. **(b)**

For I –There is no direct relation between the elements cup and vessel. Hence, Conclusion I cannot be concluded.

For II – There is a no direct relation between the elements cup and vessel. Hence, Conclusion II cannot be concluded. Since the elements are same and 'all' and 'some not' case is mentioned, therefore, "Either –Or" case will be concluded.

15. (d)

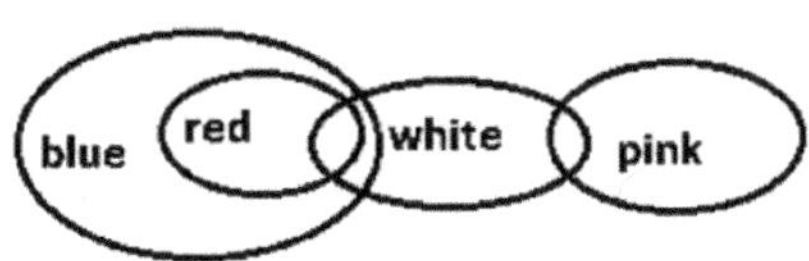

For I – Some red is white and all red is blue, therefore some blue is white will hold true. Hence, Conclusion I can be concluded.

For II – There is no direct relation between pink and blue. Hence, Conclusion II cannot be concluded.

Directions (16-20) E sits third to the left of B. Two persons sit between F and B. D sits to the immediate right of F. We got two possibilities:

Case I   Case II

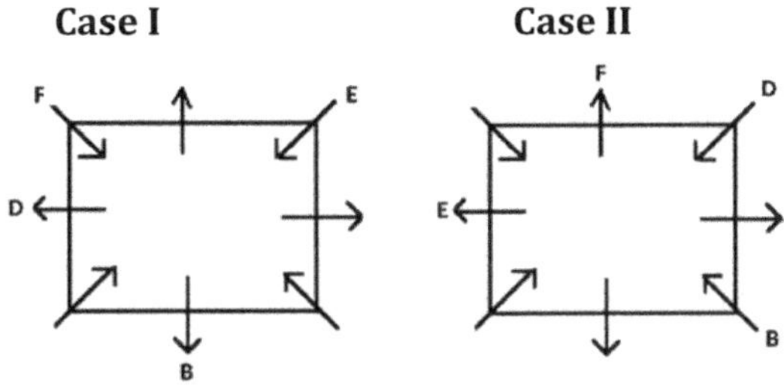

Now, C faces outside. H is an immediate neighbour of C. G sits second to the left of H.

Case I   Case II

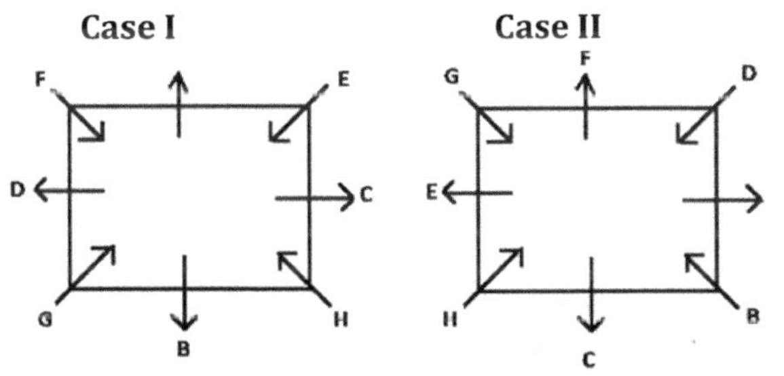

Now, A is not an immediate neighbour of D. This will eliminate Case II. The final arrangement will be

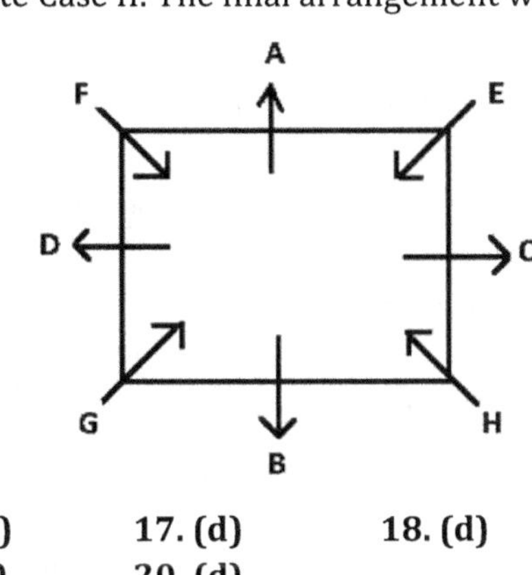

16. (b)   **17. (d)**   **18. (d)**
19. (c)   **20. (d)**

Directions (21-25): S takes a lecture on Saturday. No one takes a lecture after Q i.e. Q takes his lecture on Sunday. Not more than two persons take their lecture between S and R. P takes his lecture immediately before R. We will have four possibilities:

Case 1   Case 2

Days	Person	Days	Person
Monday		Monday	
Tuesday		Tuesday	
Wednesday		Wednesday	P
Thursday	P	Thursday	R
Friday	R	Friday	
Saturday	S	Saturday	S
Sunday	Q	Sunday	Q

Case 3   Case 4

Days	Person	Days	Person
Monday		Monday	P
Tuesday	P	Tuesday	R
Wednesday	R	Wednesday	
Thursday		Thursday	
Friday		Friday	
Saturday	S	Saturday	S
Sunday	Q	Sunday	Q

Now, T takes his lecture before U but not on Thursday. Neither Monday nor Friday is a holiday. T does not take his lecture on Monday. This will eliminate Case 1, Case 2 and Case 3. The final arrangement will be:

Days	Person
Monday	P
Tuesday	R
Wednesday	T
Thursday	Holiday
Friday	U
Saturday	S
Sunday	Q

21. (e)   **22. (d)**   **23. (c)**
24. (d)   **25 .(b)**
26. (c)

H	I	L	L
7	2	8	8

27. (c) FATE, FEAT, FETA

28. (c) 4

29. (b) D

30. (b)

Directions (31-35):

31. (c) **32. (a)** **33. (d)**

34. (c) **35. (b)**

Directions (36-40): E sits third to the right of B and one of them sits at an extreme end of the row. R faces B. R sits to the immediate right of S. D sits to the immediate left of F and neither of them sits at any extreme end. We get two possibilities –

Case 1

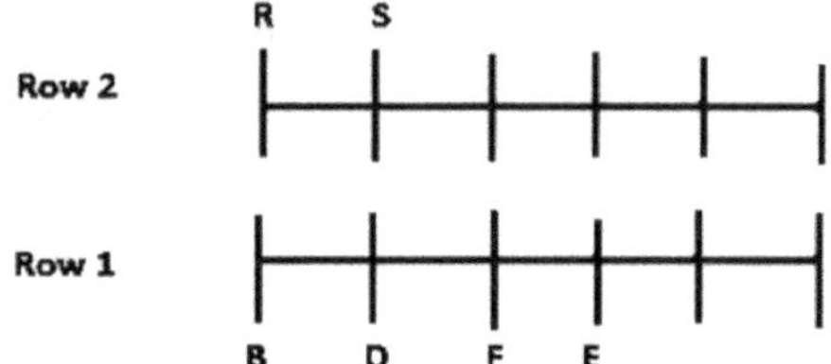

Case 2

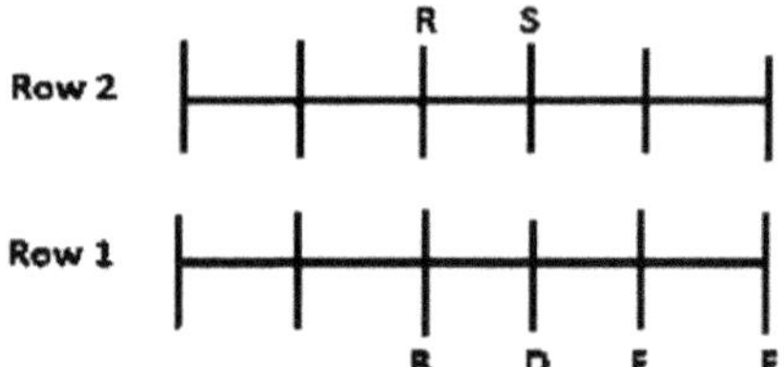

Now, three persons sit between P and Q and one of them sits at an extreme end of the row. This will eliminate Case 1. P does not face E or F. U faces C. Now we will have two possibilities in Case 2 –

Case 2(a)

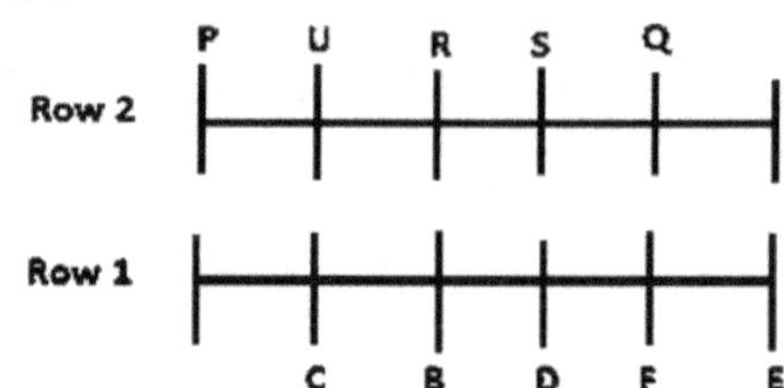

Case 2(b)

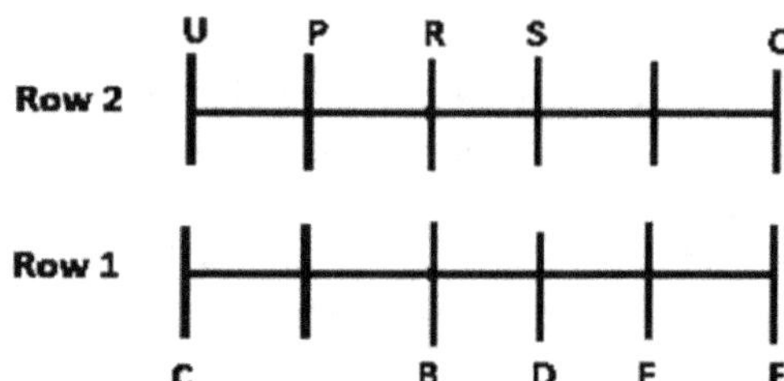

Now, R is not an immediate neighbour of U. This will eliminate Case 2(a). So the final arrangement will be:

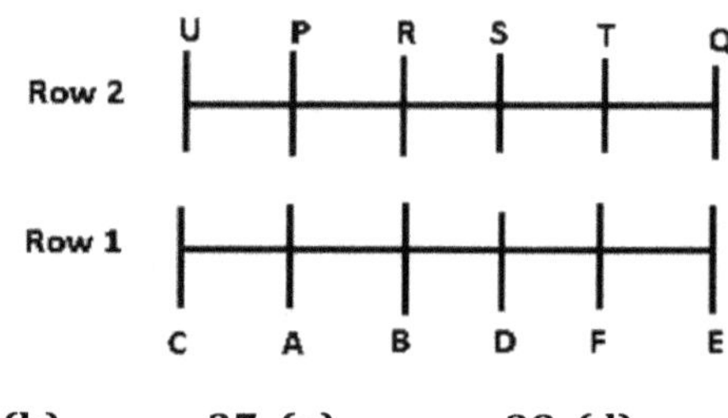

36. (b) **37. (a)** **38. (d)**

39. (b) **40. (d)**

QUANTITATIVE APTITUDE

41. (b) $\frac{65 \times 360}{100} - \frac{?}{100} \times 250 \approx 139$

$\Rightarrow 234 - \frac{25 \times ?}{10} = 139 \quad \Rightarrow ? = \frac{95 \times 10}{25} = 38$

42. (a) $\sqrt{912 \div 24 + 184 - 53} \approx ?$

$\Rightarrow ? = \sqrt{169} = 13$

43. (c) $(15)^2 - (5)^3 + \sqrt{1521} + 9 \times 13 \approx (?)^2$

$\Rightarrow 225 - 125 + 39 + 117 = (?)^2$

$\Rightarrow ? = \sqrt{256} = 16$

44. (e) $(3750 - ?) \div 55 \approx 23$

$\Rightarrow ? = 3750 - 55 \times 23$

$? = 2485$

45. (d) $(3416 \div 56) - (1134 \div ?) \approx 19$

$\Rightarrow 61 - \frac{1134}{?} = 19 \Rightarrow 42 = \frac{1134}{?} \Rightarrow ? = 27$

46. (c) Required average $= \dfrac{350 \times \frac{3}{7} + 400 \times \frac{9}{20} + 200 \times \frac{12}{25}}{3}$

$= \frac{150 + 180 + 96}{3} = 142$

47. (a) Total number of Hollywood movies watched by student

$E = 375 \times \frac{16}{25} = 240$

Required percentage $= \frac{(400 - 240)}{400} \times 100$

$= \frac{160}{400} \times 100 = 40\%$

48. (d) Total number of Hollywood movies watched by students C and B together

$= 250 \times \frac{3}{10} + 400 \times \frac{11}{20}$

$= 75 + 220 = 295$

Total number of Bollywood movies watched by students D and E together

$$= \frac{200 \times 12}{25} + \frac{375 \times 9}{25}$$
$$= 96 + 135 = 231$$
Required difference = 295 – 231 = 64

49. (b) Required ratio $= \frac{250+200}{\frac{400 \times 9}{20} + \frac{250 \times 7}{10} + \frac{375 \times 9}{25}} = \frac{450}{490} =$ 45:49

50. (e) Required percentage $= \frac{(400+200)}{(350+250)} \times 100 = $ 100%

51. (d) Let increase per year is $x\%$
So,
$$35000 \times \frac{(100+x)}{100} \times \frac{(100+x)}{100} = 55566$$
$x = 26\%$

52. (c) 1st C.P. $\rightarrow$ 12000 Rs.
1st S.P. $\rightarrow \frac{12000 \times 80}{100}$ = 9600 Rs.
Now,
2nd C.P. $\rightarrow$ 9600 Rs.
2nd S.P. $\rightarrow \frac{9600 \times 130}{100}$ = 12480 Rs.
Profit $\Rightarrow$ 480 Rs.

53. (a) Let sum = P
Now,
$$\frac{P \times 7 \times 7}{100} = 1519$$
$$P = \frac{1519 \times 7 \times 7}{100}$$
P = 3100 Rs.

54. (e) Let amount = 30x
So,
X, Y and Z was to get $\Rightarrow$ 5x, 10x, 15x respectively
But
X, Y and Z actually get $\Rightarrow$ 10x, 8x, 12x respectively
X got $\Rightarrow$ 10x – 5x = 305 $\Rightarrow$ x = 61
o Z get $\Rightarrow$ 61 × 12 = 732 Rs.

55. (b) Let age of Mahendra = x
So age of Niraj = x + 12
Present age of Bhavya $= \frac{(x+12-3)}{3} = \frac{x+9}{3}$
Now,
$$\frac{x}{\frac{x+9}{3}} = \frac{2}{1}$$
$x = 18$
Niraj's age $\Rightarrow$ 18 + 12 = 30

56. (b) $\frac{2}{3} \times \frac{4}{5} \times \frac{3}{7} \times 2205 = ? \Rightarrow ? = 504$

57. (a) $? = 2 - 3 + 4 - 1 + \left(\frac{3}{7} - \frac{1}{4} + \frac{3}{8} - \frac{1}{56}\right)$
$? = 2 + \left(\frac{24-14+21-1}{56}\right) = 2\frac{30}{56} = 2\frac{15}{28}$

58. (e) $-119 + 34 - 67 + 259 - ? = 88 \Rightarrow ? = 19$

59. (b) $\sqrt{144 \times 32 \div 48 + 174 + 54} = (?)^2$
$\Rightarrow (?)^2 = \sqrt{324} \Rightarrow (?)^2 = 18 \Rightarrow ? = 3\sqrt{2}$

60. (c) $53 \times 48 - ? = 29 \times 70$
$\Rightarrow ? = 53 \times 48 - 29 \times 70$
$? = 514$

61. (a) $\frac{85}{100} \times ? \times 6755 = 3281 \Rightarrow ? = \frac{3281 \times 100}{85 \times 6755} = \frac{4}{7}$

62. (d) $\sqrt[3]{?} \times 13 = 91 \Rightarrow ? = (7)^3 = 343$

63. (c) $\sqrt{9409} - \sqrt{1156} = 3339 \div ?$
$\Rightarrow 3339 \div ? = 97 - 34 = 63$
$\Rightarrow ? = \frac{3339}{63} = 53$

64. (a) $\left(\frac{320}{100} \times 825\right) \div ? = 48$
$\Rightarrow \frac{2640}{48} = ? \Rightarrow ? = 55$

65. (b) $216 \div 12 + ? = 55$
$\Rightarrow ? = 37$

66. (e) Present acid = 50 × 100 = 50 litres
Amount of water in final solution $= \frac{50}{40} \times 60$
= 75 litres
Extra water to be added $\Rightarrow$ 75 – 50 = 25 litres

67. (b) Let efficiency of 1 man and 1 woman be m and w respectively.
So, total work
5m × 16 = 8w × 15
$\frac{m}{w} = \frac{3}{2}$
Work done in $= \frac{3 \times 5 \times 16}{6+6} = 20$ days

68. (d) Total distance = 9 × 70 = 630
New speed $= \frac{630}{6} = 105$ km/hr
Increase in speed $= \frac{105-70}{70} \times 100 = 50\%$

69. (e) Let the two digits be $x \& y$ with x on tens place.
ATQ, $10x + y - (10y + x) = 54$
or, $9x - 9y = 54$ or $x - y = 6$
and, $x + y = 12$
$\therefore x = 9$ and $y = 3$
So number is 93

70. (e) Distance = 180 meters
Time = 20 second
Relative speed of train and car $= \frac{180}{20} = 9$ m/s
Let speed of car = x m/s
o speed of train $= \frac{2}{3}x$ m/s
$x - \frac{2}{3}x = 9$ m/s
$x = 27$ m/speed of car in km/hr $= \frac{27 \times 18}{5} = $ 97.2 km/hr

71. (d)

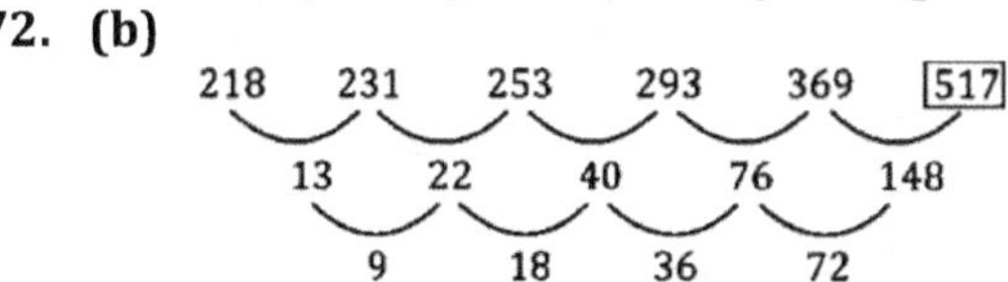

72. (b)

73. (a)

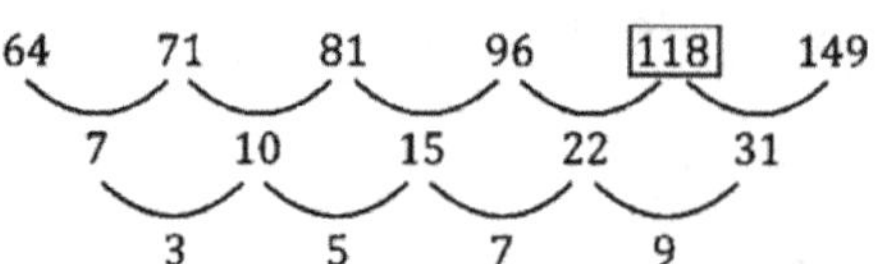

74. (c);

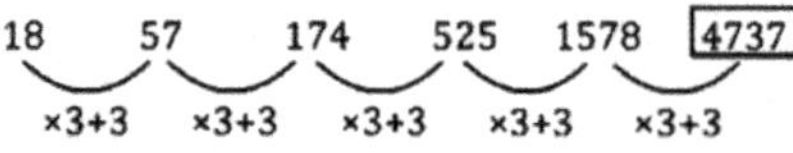

75. (a)

$$18 \xrightarrow{\times 3+3} 57 \xrightarrow{\times 3+3} 174 \xrightarrow{\times 3+3} 525 \xrightarrow{\times 3+3} 1578 \xrightarrow{\times 3+3} \boxed{4737}$$

76. (d) Total cases → 36

Favourable cases → (1, 4), (4, 1), (1, 6), (6, 1), (2, 3), (3, 2), (2, 5), (5, 2), (3, 4), (4, 3)

Required probability $= \dfrac{10}{36} = \dfrac{5}{18}$

77. (c) From I

Let C.P. of article be Rs. x.

$\dfrac{125}{100} \times 240 - x = 40$

$x = 300 - 40 = Rs\ 260$

<u>From II</u>

Since profit% & discount% is given and S.P. & marked price is given.

∴ cost price can be determined.

∴ Either from I or II.

78. (e) From I & II

Area of base of cone $(\pi r^2) = 154$

∴ $\pi r^2 = 154$

$r^2 = 49$

∴ $r = 7$ cm

∴ height (h) $= 7 \times 2 = 14$ cm.

Volume $= \dfrac{1}{3}\pi r^2 h$

$= \dfrac{1}{3} \times \dfrac{22}{7} \times 7 \times 7 \times 14 = \dfrac{2156}{3}$ cm^3

79. (e) From I & II

$x + y = 8 \qquad\qquad …(i)$

$xy = 12$

$(x - y)^2 = (x + y)^2 - 4xy$

$(x - y)^2 = (8)^2 - 4 \times 12$

$(x - y)^2 = 16$

$x - y = 4 \qquad\qquad …(ii)$

∴ $x = 6$ & $y = 2$

80. (e) From I & II

Let speed of boat in still water be x km/hr and speed of stream be y km/hr.

$\dfrac{64}{x+y} = \dfrac{1}{2}\dfrac{64}{x}$

$x = y = 5$ km/hr

IBPS RRB PO & CLERK PRELIMS
(MEMORY BASED PAPERS 2020)

REASONING ABILITY

1. If 2 is subtracted from each even digit and 1 is added to each odd digit in the given number '2145673', then how many digits will appear more than one in the new number thus formed?
   (a) None
   (b) One
   (c) Two
   (d) Three
   (e) None of these

Directions (2-6): Study the following information carefully and answer the question given below-
Eight persons live in a building of four floors such that ground floor is numbered 1 and floor above it is 2 and so on up to 4th floor. Each of the floor consist of 2 flats as flat-P, which is in west of flat Q. Flat-P of floor-2 is immediately above flat-P of floor-1 and immediately below flat-P of floor-3 and in the same way flat-Q of each floor follow same pattern.

A lives on an even numbered floor. A lives just above the flat of E. B lives to the west of E. One floor gap between D and C. H lives in the east of D. G lives on the 3rd floor. Both F and C live in the different flats.

2. Who among the following lives just below the flat in which G lives?
   (a) B
   (b) C
   (c) A
   (d) Both (b) and (c)
   (e) None of these

3. How many floors gap between B and H?
   (a) None
   (b) Two
   (c) One
   (d) Either (a) or (c)
   (e) Either (b) or (c)

4. What is the direction of G with respect to E?
   (a) South
   (b) North-east
   (c) North
   (d) East
   (e) North-west

5. Which of the following floor does C lives?
   (a) Floor-1
   (b) Floor-4
   (c) Floor-3
   (d) Floor-2
   (e) None of these

6. Which of the following is true regarding H?
   (a) Floor 4 – Flat P
   (b) Floor3- Flat Q
   (c) Floor 2- Flat P
   (d) Floor4- Flat Q
   (e) Floor1- Flat Q

Direction (7-11): Study the following information carefully and answer the questions given below:
In a certain code language

'plan to go exam' is coded as 'oj kr mn pc'
'exam today easy' is coded as 'si oj ly'
'plan your exam today' is coded as 'zm oj si mn'
'make your plan today' is coded as 'zm si mn rk'

7. What is the code of 'make' as per the given code language?
   (a) zm
   (b) mn
   (c) rk
   (d) pc
   (e) None of these

8. What is the code of 'exam' as per the given code language?
   (a) rk
   (b) pc
   (c) kr
   (d) oj
   (e) None of these

9. What is the code of 'go' as per the given code language?
   (a) pc
   (b) si
   (c) kr
   (d) either 'pc' or 'kr'
   (e) None of these

10. What is the code of 'exam today' as per the given code language?
    (a) si oj
    (b) mn kr
    (c) lv si
    (d) zm oj
    (e) None of these

11. If 'easy to plan' is coded as 'mn ly pc' then what is the code of 'go' as per the given code language?
    (a) pc
    (b) zm
    (c) kr
    (d) mn
    (e) None of these

12. How many pairs of letters are there in the word "GRANDUAL" each of which have as many letters between them in the word as they have between them in the English alphabetical series??
    (a) Three
    (b) Four
    (c) Two
    (d) One
    (e) Five

Directions (13-15): Study the information carefully and answer the questions given below.

Point P is 26m west of point S. Point G is 52m north of point P. Point M is 39m east of point G and point K is 13m south of point G. Point H is 39m north of point S.

13. In which direction point P with respect to point M?
    (a) South
    (b) South-east

(c) North-east   (d) East
(e) None of these

14. What is the shortest distance between point K and point H?
(a) 13m   (b) 26m
(c) 39m   (d) 25m
(e) None of these

15. If Point Z is 13m north of point H, then what is the distance between point M and point Z?
(a) 13m   (b) 26m
(c) 39m   (d) 25m
(e) None of these

Directions (16-20): Study the following information carefully and answer the question given below:

Seven persons D, G, P, L, J, U and Q are sitting in a row facing to the north. They all have of different ages. D sits 3rd from one of the extreme ends of the row. Q sits 2nd to the right of D. The number of persons sit to the left of Q is same as the number of persons sit to the right of G, who is 20 years old. P sits 4th to the left of the one who is 35 years old. Q is not 35 years old. Total age of immediate neighbours of D is 75 years. J is 30 years old. P is 20 year older than one of his immediate neighbours. U sits to the right of L, who sits immediate to the left of the one who is 25 years old. Q is 5 year younger than P.

16. The number of persons sit between L and Q is same as the number of persons sit between P and ___?
(a) D   (b) G
(c) U   (d) Q
(e) None of these

17. What is the position of J with respect to Q?
(a) 2nd to the left
(b) Immediate left
(c) Immediate right
(d) 4th to the left
(e) 3rd to the right

18. Four of the following five are alike in a certain way and so form a group. Find the one who does not belong to that group?
(a) P   (b) G   (c) J
(d) L   (e) U

19. Who among the following is 40 years old?
(a) L   (b) P
(c) D   (d) U
(e) None of these

20. Which of the following statement is true?
(a) J sits to the right of L
(b) D sits 3rd to the right of G
(c) P sits at one of the extreme ends
(d) None is true
(e) Q sits immediate right of the one who is 35 years old

21. Study the following information carefully and answer the given questions.

Six persons i.e. P, Q, R, S, T and U was born on different days of the same week starting from Monday to Saturday, but not necessarily in the same order. P was born on Friday. Two persons were born between U and P. One person was born between R and S. If T was born immediate before S, then who among the following person was born on Wednesday?
(a) U   (b) R
(c) S   (d) T
(e) None of these

Directions (22-26): Study the following information carefully and answer the question given below:

Ten boxes are placed one above the other. Four boxes are placed between J and M. Two boxes are placed between J and k, which placed above of the J. L is placed just below K. The number of boxes between L and M is same the number of boxes between M and Q. T is placed just above Q. Y is placed just above O. X is adjacent to M. P is placed below X.

22. How many boxes are placed between O and L?
(a) One   (b) More than Five
(c) Four   (d) Three
(e) Two

23. Four of the following five are alike in a certain way and so form a group. Find the one who does not belong to that group?
(a) T-Y   (b) X-L
(c) K-P   (d) Q-O
(e) M-Q

24. Which of the following statement is true?
(a) L is 3rd from the topmost position
(b) Two boxes placed between K and M
(c) Q is above P
(d) T is placed at bottommost position
(e) Three boxes placed between Y and M

25. What is the position of Y from the bottommost?
(a) Seven   (b) Eight
(c) Six   (d) Five
(e) Three

26. If T and O interchange their positions then which among the following box is placed just below O?
(a) Y   (b) X
(c) K   (d) Q
(e) None of these

Directions (27-31): Study the following information carefully and answer the question given below:

A certain number of persons sit in a row facing to the north direction. L sits 3rd to the left of M. Five persons sit between M and N. J sits immediate to the right of M. Three persons sit between Q and J. Q does not sit next to N. N is 7th from one of the ends. The number of persons sit to the right of Q is four more than the persons who sit to the left of N. K sits 2nd from one of the ends and sit to the right of M.

27. How many persons sit in the above arrangement?
(a) 25   (b) 26
(c) 28   (d) 24
(e) None of these

28. If two persons sit between X and N, then what is the position of X with respect to L?
(a) 4th to the left
(b) 6th to the left
(c) 5th to the right
(d) 3rd to the left
(e) 7th to the left

29. How many persons sit between L and J?
(a) Five   (b) None of these
(c) Seven   (d) Four
(e) Three

30. What is the position of L with respect to Q?
(a) 8th to the right
(b) 8th to the left
(c) 6th to the right
(d) 5th to the left
(e) None of these

31. How many persons sit to the right of the one, who sits immediate left of J?
(a) Ten   (b) Seven
(c) None of these   (d) Eight
(e) Eleven

Directions (32-35): In these questions, relationships between different elements are shown in the statements. These statements are followed by two conclusions. Give answer
(a) If only conclusion I follows.
(b) If only conclusion II follows.
(c) If either conclusion I or II follows
(d) If neither conclusion I nor II follows.
(e) If both conclusions I and II follow.

32. Statements: $Z > 0 = G < I \leq S > P$
    Conclusions: I. $S > 0$ **II.** $P > G$

33. Statements: $K \geq M > W \geq T \leq Y < Q$
    Conclusions: I. $T < Q$ **II.** $T < K$

34. Statement: $J \leq V < R > M, L > M = I \geq H$

Conclusions: I. $V \geq H$ **II.** $H \leq M$

35. Statement: $I = H \geq B \geq N < D > L$
    Conclusions: I. $B < N$ **II.** $L > H$

Directions (36-40): Study the following information carefully and answer the question given below:

Nine persons sit around a circular table. Some of them are facing to the centre while some are facing outside the centre. C sits 2nd to the right of A, who faces inside. Two persons sit between C and G. J sits 3rd to the left of G. L sits 2nd to the left of J, who does not sit next to C. B sits 3rd to the right of L and is an immediate neighbour of P. K sits 4th to the right of H, who does not sit near J. Both B and P face same direction as A. C and G face opposite direction to each other. K does not face outside.

36. What is the position of P with respect to K?
(a) 3rd to the right
(b) 2nd to the left
(c) Immediate left
(d) 3rd to the left
(e) 5th to the right

37. How many persons sit between J and H, when counted from the left of H?
(a) Five   (b) Six (c) Four
(d) One   (e) Three

38. Four of the following five are alike in a certain way and so form a group. Find the one who does not belong to that group?
(a) C-H   (b) L-K (c) B-J
(d) H-L   (e) B-P

39. How many persons sit between G and H, when counted from the left of G?
(a) Three   (b) Five (c) Two
(d) Four   (e) None of these

40. How many persons face outside from the centre?
(a) Three   (b) Four
(c) None of these   (d) Six
(e) Five

Directions (41-46): Pie chart shows the percentage distribution of total students appeared in six different shifts of an exam. Study the pie chart given below and answer the following questions.

Total students appeared in exam - 5500

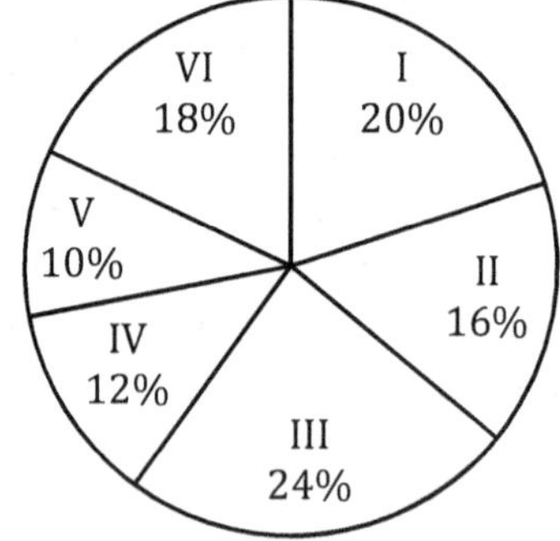

41. Find average number of students appeared in shift I, II & IV of the exam.
    (a) 1040 (b) 900 (c) 720
    (d) 1140 (e) 880
42. Find the central angle for students appeared in shift II of the examination.
    (a) 64.2° (b) 48° (c) 57.6°
    (d) 43.6° (e) 52.8°
43. Find total number of students appeared in shift V & VI together of the examination.
    (a) 1740 (b) 1600 (c) 1820
    (d) 1960 (e) 1540
44. Students appeared in shift III & IV together of the examination are what percent more or less than students appeared in shift I of the examination?
    (a) 90% (b) 80% (c) 70%
    (d) 50% (e) 60%
45. Find ratio of students appeared in shift IV & VI together of the examination to students appeared in shift II & III together of the examination.
    (a) 3:4 (b) 5:7 (c) 4:3
    (d) 7:5 (e) None of the above.
46. Students appeared in shift I & VI together of the examination are how much more or less than students appeared in shift III & V together of the examination?
    (a) 330 (b) 150 (c) 360
    (d) 280 (e) 220
47. A vessel contains mixture of milk and water in the ratio of 7:1 respectively. 24 liters mixture is removed from the vessel and if the quantity of remaining milk in the vessel is 56 liters, then find quantity of water in the vessel initially.

    (a) 11 liters (b) 15 liters (c) 12 liters
    (d) 9 liters (e) 8 liters
48. A & B together can complete a piece of work in 9 days. Time taken by A alone to complete the same work is 7.5 days less than time taken by B alone to complete the same work. In how many days B alone will complete $\frac{2}{9}$ of the work?
    (a) 8 days (b) 6 days (c) 7 days
    (d) 5 days (e) 4 days
49. Ratio of ages of A and B, 4 years later is 8:9 respectively. If average of present ages of A & B is 47 years, then find difference in present ages of A & B.
    (a) 5 years (b) 6 years (c) 3 years
    (d) 2 years (e) 4 years
50. There are 75% boys out of total students (boys + girls) in a school and 39% of the total students of the school went on a picnic. If 32% of the total boys went on a picnic, then find what percent of total girls went on a picnic?
    (a) 60% (b) 90% (c) 75%
    (d) 80% (e) 50%
51. Number of passed students in an exam in section A & B are 240 & 210 respectively. If in section A 40% of the total students got failed and in section B 30% of the total students got failed, then find difference between total number of students in section A & B.
    (a) 40 (b) 80 (c) 150
    (d) 120 (e) 100
Directions (52-56): In the given questions, two equations (I) & (II) are given. You have to solve both the equations and mark the answer accordingly.
52. I. $x^2 + 9x + 20 = 0$
    II. $8y^2 - 15y + 7 = 0$
    (a) $x < y$ (b) $x > y$ (c) $x \leq y$
    (d) $x \geq y$ (e) $x = y$ or no relation.
53. I. $x^2 - 11x + 30 = 0$
    II. $y^2 + 12y + 36 = 0$
    (a) $x < y$ (b) $x > y$
    (c) $x \leq y$ (d) $x \geq y$
    (e) $x = y$ or no relation.
54. I. $x^2 + 13x + 40 = 0$
    II. $y^2 + 7y + 10 = 0$
    (a) $x < y$ (b) $x > y$
    (c) $x \leq y$ (d) $x \geq y$
    (e) $x = y$ or no relation.
55. I. $x^2 - 20x + 91 = 0$
    II. $y^2 + 16y + 63 = 0$
    (a) $x < y$ (b) $x > y$ (c) $x \leq y$

(d) x ≥ y   (e) x = y or no relation.

56. I. $x^2 - x - 12 = 0$

II. $y^2 + 5y + 6 = 0$

(a) x < y

(b) x > y

(c) x ≤ y

(d) x ≥ y

(e) x = y or no relation.

Directions (57-62): Study the table given below and answer the following questions.

Table gives information about total number of students in 3 different schools in 1999 & 2000 and also gives information about total number of girls in these 3 schools in 1999 & 2000.

School	Year			
	1999		2000	
	Total students	Total Girls	Total students	Total girls
A	720	360	900	450
B	360	180	600	180
C	450	270	400	120

Note: Total students in any school in any year = Total (Boys + Girls) in that school in that year.

57. If average number of students in school A in 1999, 2000 & 2001 are 700, then find total number of students in school A in 2001.

(a) 540   (b) 480   (c) 420

(d) 600   (e) 360

58. Number of girls in school – A & B together in 2000 are what percent more or less than total number of students in school – B & C together in 2000?

(a) 27%   (b) 42%   (c) 37%

(d) 30%   (e) 45%

59. Find total number of boys in school – A, B & C together in 1999.

(a) 720   (b) 640   (c) 680

(d) 760   (e) 800

60. Average number of students in school – A, B & C in 1999 are what percent of total students in school – B in 2000?

(a) 95%   (b) 85%   (c) 75%

(d) 55%   (e) 65%

61. Find ratio of number of boys in school – B in 2000 to number of boys in school – C in 2000.

(a) 5:4   (b) 4:5

(c) 2:3   (d) 3:2

(e) None of the above.

62. Total number of girls in school – A, B & C together in 1999 are how much more or less than total number of girls in school – A, B & C together in 2000?

(a) 140   (b) 60   (c) 180

(d) 90   (e) 100

Directions (63-67): In the following questions, calculate quantity I and quantity II, compare them and answer according to the following options.

(a) If Quantity I > Quantity II

(b) If Quantity I < Quantity II

(c) If Quantity I ≥ Quantity II

(d) if Quantity I ≤ Quantity II

(e) if Quantity I = Quantity II or no relation can be established

63. Quantity I. Profit earned on selling an article at Rs. 450 at 20% profit

Quantity II. Cost price of the article which is sold at Rs.84 on 20% profit

64. In a village there are 60% males and rest are females. 30% of total male are illiterate and 25% of total female are illiterate. Number of illiterate males is 1152.

Quantity I. Literate females in the village.

Quantity II. 1940

65. A man invested Rs. P at 12% p.a. on simple interest for two years.

Quantity I. If at the end of second year he gets Rs.1200 as interest, then find Rs.P.

Quantity II. Rs.6000

66. Ploughing cost of a rectangular field is Rs.288 at the rate of Rs.3 per square meter. Length of the field is 4 meters more than the width of field.

Quantity I. Length of rectangular field.

Quantity II. 12 meters.

67. Quantity I. Sum of present ages of Shivam and Prashant is 32 years and Shivam is 8 years older than Prashant. Find present age of Prashant.

Quantity II. 15 years.

68. 'A' invested Rs.4000 and 'B' invested Rs.1000 more than A. After eight months 'C' invested Rs.3000. If at the end of the year 'C' gets profit of Rs.700, then find the total profit.

(a) Rs.7000   (b) Rs.8400   (c) Rs.5600

(d) Rs.8800   (e) Rs.6400

69. 440 meters long train passes a platform in 80 seconds. If speed of train is increased by 3 m/sec, then it crosses a pole in 22 seconds. Find the length of platform.

(a) 720m   (b) 840m   (c) 700m

(d) 920m   (e) 900m

70. Selling price of an article becomes Rs.2160 after giving two successive discounts of x% and 25% and marked price of article is Rs.3600. Find the cost price of article if there is a profit of x% on selling the article after giving two successive discounts.

(a) Rs. 1720   (b) Rs.1500   (c) Rs.1600

(d) Rs.1800   (e) Rs.1900

71. Three are 5 green balls, 7 blue balls and 3 red balls in a bag. If 2 balls are chosen randomly from the bag, then find the probability that at least one ball is green ball.

(a) $\frac{1}{9}$ (b) $\frac{2}{7}$ (c) $\frac{3}{8}$

(d) $\frac{3}{5}$ (e) $\frac{4}{7}$

72. Speed of boat in still water is six times of speed of stream. If boat covers 210 km in upstream in 7 hours, then find the downstream speed of boat?

(a) 42 km/hr.   (b) 36 km/hr.
(c) 30 km/hr.   (d) 32 km/hr.
(e) 24 km/hr.

73. Length of rectangle 'A' is 125% of its breadth and area of rectangle 'A' is 1280 cm². If width of rectangle 'A' is half of the side of a square, then find perimeter of square.

(a) 72m   (b) 64m   (c) 84m
(d) 96m   (e) 60m

74. The average weight of a class of 45 girls is 53 kg. It was later found that weight of two girls was read as 49 kg and 57 kg instead of 45 kg and 52 kg. Find the actual average weight of the class.

(a) 54 kg   (b) 53.40 kg   (c) 50.6 kg
(d) 52.80 kg   (e) 51.5 kg

Directions (75-80): Find the value of (?) in the following number series.

75. 1.5, 3, 12, 72, 576, ?

(a) 5480   (b) 5620   (c) 5580
(d) 5340   (e) 5760

76. 80, 66, 85, 61, 90, ?

(a) 50   (b) 56   (c) 64
(d) 60   (e) 63

77. 163, ?, 43, 23, 13, 8

(a) 92   (b) 83   (c) 78
(d) 54   (e) 69

78. 150, 152, 157, 167, 184, ?

(a) 229   (b) 245   (c) 232
(d) 210   (e) 206

79. 3.5, 2.5, 3, 6, 20, ?

(a) 95   (b) 80   (c) 65
(d) 75   (e) 90

80. 6300, ?, 525, 105, 17.5, 2.5

(a) 2400   (b) 2100   (c) 4200
(d) 5200   (e) 3600

Solutions

REASONING ABILITY

1. (c)   2 1 4 5 6 7 3
        0 2 2 6 4 8 4

Solutions (2-6)

Floors	Flat-P	Flat-Q
4	D	H
3	G	F
2	C	A
1	B	E

2. (b)   **3. (b)**   **4. (e)**
5. (d)   **6. (d)**

Solutions (7-11)

Words	Codes
Plan	mn
To	kr/pc
Go	pc/kr
Exam	oj
Easy	ly
Today	si
Your	zm
Make	rk

7. (c)   **8. (d)**   **9. (d)**
10. (a)   **11. (c)**
12. (c)

Solutions (13-15)

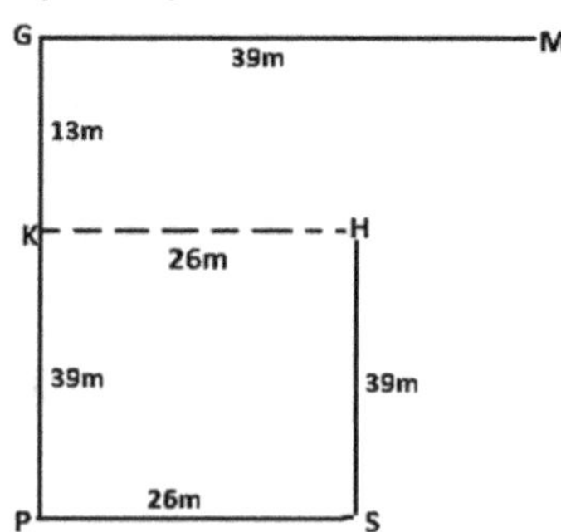

13. (e)
14. (b)
15. (a)

Solutions (16-20)

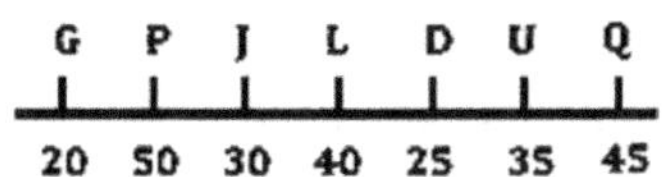

16. (a)   **17. (d)**   **18. (e)**

19. (a)   **20. (e)**

21. (d)

Days	Persons
Monday	Q
Tuesday	U
Wednesday	T
Thursday	S
Friday	P
Saturday	R

Solutions (22-26)

Boxes
T
Q
Y
O
M
X
K
L
P

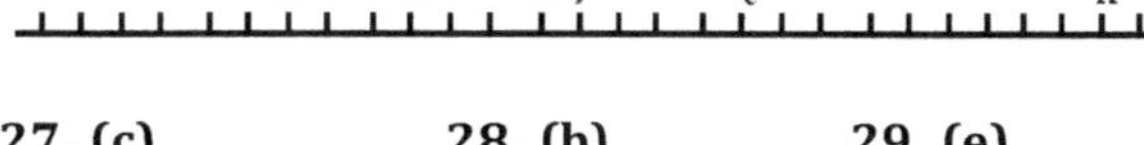

22. (d)   **23. (e)**   **24. (c)**

25. (b)   **26. (d)**

Solutions (27-31)

27. (c)   **28. (b)**   **29. (e)**

30. (b)   **31. (c)**

32. (a) I. S > O (True)   II. P > G(False)

33. (e) I. T < Q (True)   II. T < K (True)

34. (b) I. V ≥ H(False)   II. H ≤ M (True)

35. (d) I. B < N (False)   II. L > H (False)

Solutions (36-40)

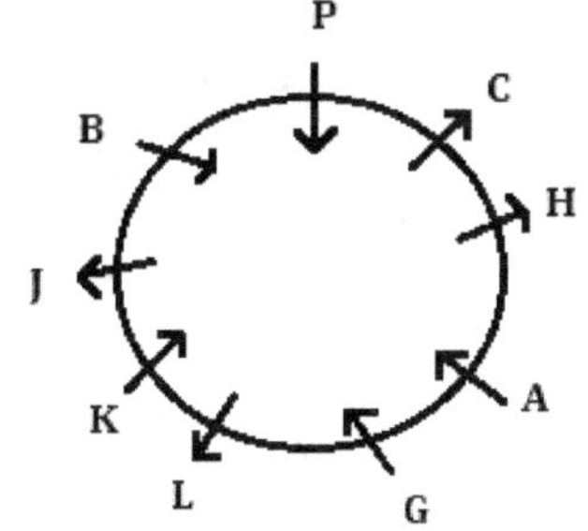

36. (d)   **37. (e)**   **38. (d)**

39. (e)   **40. (b)**

Quantitative Aptitude

41. (e) Required average $= \frac{1}{3} \times \left(5,500 \times \frac{20+16+12}{100}\right)$

$= 880$

42. (c) Required angle $= \frac{16}{100} \times 360° = 57.6°$

43. (e) Required number of students $=$

$5,500 \times \frac{10+18}{100} = 1,540$

44. (b) Students appeared in shift III & IV together

of the examination $= 5,500 \times \frac{(24+12)}{100} = 1,980$

Students appeared in shift I of the examination $= 5,500 \times \frac{20}{100} = 1,100$

Required percentage $= \frac{1980-1100}{1100} \times 100 = 80\%$

Or, required percentage $= \frac{(24+12)-20}{20} \times 100 = 80\%$

45. (a) Students appeared in shift IV & VI together

of the examination $= 5,500 \times \frac{12+18}{100} = 1,650$

Students appeared in shift II & III together

of the examination $= 5,500 \times \frac{16+24}{100} = 2,200$

Required ratio $= \frac{1650}{2200} = 3:4$

Or required ratio $= \frac{(12+18)}{(16+24)} = 3:4$

46. (e) Students appeared in shift I & VI together

of the examination $= 5,500 \times \frac{20+18}{100} = 2,090$

Students appeared in shift III & V together

of the examination $= 5,500 \times \frac{10+24}{100} = 1,870$

Required difference $= 2090 - 1870 = 220$

47. (a) ATQ,

Let quantity of milk and water in the vessel initially be 7x liters & x liters respectively.

ATQ,

$\left(7x - 24 \times \frac{7x}{8x}\right) = 56$

$x = 11$

48. (d) Let time taken by B alone to complete the work be x days.

So, time taken by A alone to complete the same work $= (x - 7.5)$ days

ATQ,

$\frac{1}{x-7.5} + \frac{1}{x} = \frac{1}{9}$

$x = 3, \frac{45}{2}$

x cannot be 3 as time taken by A alone cannot be negative.

Required time = $\dfrac{1 \times \frac{2}{9}}{\frac{1}{\frac{45}{2}}}$

= 5 days

49. (b) Let ages of A & B, 4 years later be 8x years & 9x years respectively.

ATQ,

$(8x - 4) + (9x - 4) = 47 \times 2$

$17x = 102$

$x = 6$ years

Required difference = $9x - 8x = 6$ years

50. (a) Let total students in the school be 100x.

So, number of students went on the picnic = 39x

And, number of boys went on the picnic = $75x \times \dfrac{32}{100} = 24x$

So, number of girls went on the picnic = $39x - 24x = 15x$

Required percentage = $\dfrac{15x}{25x} \times 100 = 60\%$

51. (e) Total number of students in section A = $\left(240 \times \dfrac{100}{60}\right) = 400$

Total number of students in section B = $\left(210 \times \dfrac{100}{70}\right) = 300$

Required difference = $400 - 300 = 100$

52. (a) I. $x^2 + 9x + 20 = 0$

$x^2 + 5x + 4x + 20 = 0$

$x(x + 5) + 4(x + 5) = 0$

$(x + 5)(x + 4) = 0$

$x = -4, -5$

II. $8y^2 - 15y + 7 = 0$

$8y^2 - 8y - 7y + 7 = 0$

$8y(y - 1) - 7(y - 1) = 0$

$(y - 1)(8y - 7) = 0$

$y = 1, \dfrac{7}{8}$

So, $x < y$.

53. (b) I. $x^2 - 11x + 30 = 0$

$x^2 - 6x - 5x + 30 = 0$

$x(x - 6) - 5(x - 6) = 0$

$(x - 6)(x - 5) = 0$

$x = 5, 6$

II. $y^2 + 12y + 36 = 0$

$y^2 + 6y + 6y + 36 = 0$

$y(y + 6) + 6(y + 6) = 0$

$(y + 6)(y + 6) = 0$

$y = -6$

So, $x > y$.

54. (c) I. $x^2 + 13x + 40 = 0$

$x^2 + 8x + 5x + 40 = 0$

$x(x + 8) + 5(x + 8) = 0$

$(x + 8)(x + 5) = 0$

$x = -8, -5$

II. $y^2 + 7y + 10 = 0$

$y^2 + 5y + 2y + 10 = 0$

$y(y + 5) + 2(y + 5) = 0$

$(y + 5)(y + 2) = 0$

$y = -2, -5$

So, $x \le y$.

55. (b) I. $x^2 - 20x + 91 = 0$

$x^2 - 13x - 7x + 91 = 0$

$x(x - 13) - 7(x - 13) = 0$

$(x - 13)(x - 7) = 0$

$x = 7, 13$

II. $y^2 + 16y + 63 = 0$

$y^2 + 9y + 7y + 63 = 0$

$y(y + 9) + 7(y + 9) = 0$

$(y + 9)(y + 7) = 0$

$y = -7, -9$

So, $x > y$.

56. (e) I. $x^2 - x - 12 = 0$

$x^2 - 4x + 3x - 12 = 0$

$x(x - 4) + 3(x - 4) = 0$

$(x - 4)(x + 3) = 0$

$x = 4, -3$

II. $y^2 + 5y + 6 = 0$

$y^2 + 3y + 2y + 6 = 0$

$y(y + 3) + 2(y + 3) = 0$

$(y + 3)(y + 2) = 0$

$y = -2, -3$

So, *no relation.*

57. (b) Required number of students = $(700 \times 3) - (720 + 900) = 480$

58. (c) Number of girls in school – A & B together in 2000 = $450 + 180 = 630$

Total number of students in school – B & C together in 2000 = $600 + 400 = 1000$

Required percentage = $\dfrac{1000 - 630}{1000} \times 100 = 37\%$

59. (a) Required number of boys = $(720 - 360) + (360 - 180) + (450 - 270)$

$= 360 + 180 + 180$

$= 720$

60. (b) Average number of students in school – A, B & C in 1999 = $\dfrac{1}{3} \times (720 + 360 + 450) = 510$

Required percentage = $\dfrac{510}{600} \times 100 = 85\%$

61. (d) Required ratio = $\dfrac{600 - 180}{400 - 120}$

$= \dfrac{420}{280} = 3:2$

62. (b) Total number of girls in school – A, B & C together in 1999 = $(360 + 180 + 270) = 810$

Total number of girls in school – A, B & C together in 2000 = $(450 + 180 + 120) = 750$

Required difference = $810 - 750 = 60$

63. (a) Quantity I:

Required profit = $450 \times \frac{20}{120}$ = Rs.75

Quantity II:

Required cost price = $84 \times \frac{100}{120}$ = Rs.70

So, Quantity I > Quantity II.

64. (b) Quantity I:

Required female = $1152 \times \frac{100}{30} \times \frac{40}{60} \times \frac{100-25}{100}$

= 1920

Quantity II:

1940

So, Quantity I < Quantity II.

65. (b) Quantity I:

ATQ,

$\frac{P \times 12 \times 2}{100} = 1200$

$P = 5{,}000$ Rs.

Quantity II:

Rs.6,000

So, Quantity I < Quantity II.

66. (e) Let breadth of the field be x m.

So, length of the field = $(x + 4)$ m

Area of a rectangular field = $\frac{288}{3}$ = 96 m^2

ATQ, $x(x + 4)$ = 96

$x^2 + 4x - 96 = 0$

$x^2 + 12x - 8x - 96 = 0$

$x(x + 12) - 8(x + 12) = 0$

$(x + 12)(x - 8) = 0$

$x = 8, -12$

Quantity I:

Length of rectangular field = 12m

Quantity II: 12 m

So, Quantity I = Quantity II.

67. (b) Quantity I:

Let present age of Prashant be x years.

So, present age of Shivam = $(x + 8)$ years

$x + 8 + x = 32$

$x = 12$ years

Quantity II:

15 years

So, Quantity I < Quantity II.

68. (a) Profit sharing ratio of A, B & C = (4000 × 12) : (4000 +1000) × 12 : (3000 × 4)

= 48000 : 60000 : 12000

= 4 : 5 : 1

Let total profit be Rs. P

ATQ,

$\frac{1}{(4 + 5 + 1)} \times P = 700$

P = Rs. 7000

69. (d) Let speed of train be 'V' m/sec'

And let length of platform be 'l meters.

ATQ, $\frac{l + 440}{80}$ = V ... (i)

And,

$\frac{440}{22}$ = V + 3

$\Rightarrow$ V = 17 ... (ii)

Put value of (ii) in (i),

$\frac{l + 440}{80}$ = 17

l = 1360 – 440

l = 920 m

70. (d) ATQ,

$2160 = 3600 \times \frac{75}{100} \times \frac{(100 - x)}{100}$

2160 = 2700 – 27x

27x = 540

x = 20

So, required amount = $2160 \times \frac{100}{120}$ = Rs. 1800

71. (e) Possible cases = 1 green ball or 2 green balls

Required probability = $\frac{5_{C_1} \times 10_{C_1}}{15_{C_2}} + \frac{5_{C_2}}{15_{C_2}}$

$= \frac{5 \times 10}{15_{C_2}} + \frac{10}{15_{C_2}} = \frac{50}{105} + \frac{10}{105}$

$= \frac{60}{105} = \frac{4}{7}$

72. (a) Let speed of stream be x km/hr.

So, speed of boat in still water = 6x km/hr.

ATQ,

$\frac{210}{7}$ = (6x - x)

$\Rightarrow$ 5x = 30

x = 6 km/hr

So, required downstream speed of boat = (6x + x) = 7x = 42 km/hr

73. (b) Let width of rectangle A be '4x meters'

So, length of rectangle A = $4x \times \frac{125}{100}$ = 5x meters

ATQ,

4x × 5x = 1280

$20x^2 = 1280$

$x^2 = 64$

x = 8

Hence, side of square = 2 × 8 = 16 cm

Required perimeter = 4 × 16 = 64 cm

74. (d) Required average = $53 - \frac{[(49+57)-(45+52)]}{45}$

$= 53 - \frac{9}{45}$

= 52.80 kg

75. (e) Missing number = 5760

Pattern of series –

1.5 × 2 = 3

3 × 4 = 12

12 × 6 = 72

72 × 8 = 576

576 × 10 = 5760

76. (b) Missing number = 56

Pattern of series –

80 − 14 = 66

66 + 19 = 85

85 − 24 = 61

61 + 29 = 90

$90 - 34 = 56$

77. (b) Missing number = 83
Pattern of series –
$163 - 80 = 83$
$83 - 40 = 43$
$43 - 20 = 23$
$23 - 10 = 13$
$13 - 5 = 8$

78. (d) Missing number = 210
Pattern of series –

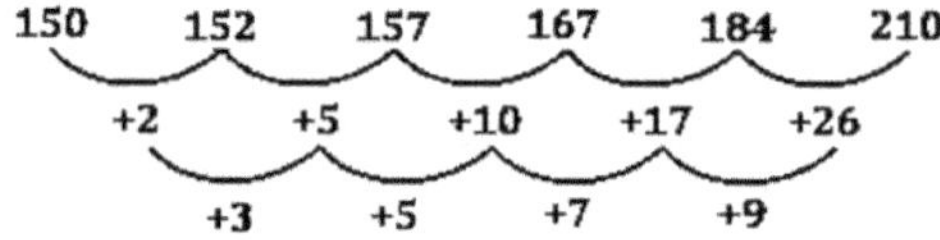

79. (a) Missing number = 95
Pattern of series –
$3.5 \times 1 - 1 = 2.5$
$2.5 \times 2 - 2 = 3$
$3 \times 3 - 3 = 6$
$6 \times 4 - 4 = 20$
$20 \times 5 - 5 = 95$

80. (b) Missing number = 2100
Pattern of series –
$? = 6300 \div 3 = 2100$
$2100 \div 4 = 525$
$525 \div 5 = 105$
$105 \div 6 = 17.5$
$17.5 \div 7 = 2.5$

REASONING ABILITY

Directions (1-5) Study the following information carefully and answer the questions given below:
Eight persons i.e. D, Q, G, H, K, S, E and W are sitting around a square table in such a way that four persons sit at the corner side of the table and other four persons sit in the middle side of the table. The persons who sit at the corner side are facing away from the center and the persons who sit in the middle side are facing towards the center. D sits at the corner side of the table. One person sits between D and G. Q sits third to the right of G. Three persons sit between Q and E. W sits second to the right of E. W is not an immediate neighbour of D. H sits second to the right of K.

1. Who among the following sits second to the right of S?
  (a) Q   (b) E
  (c) D   (d) W   (e) None of these

2. How many persons sit between D and W when counted from the right of D?
  (a) Three   (b) Four
  (c) One   (d) Two   (e) None of these

3. Who among the following sits second to the left of G?
  (a) D   (b) K
  (c) H   (d) S   (e) None of these

4. Who among the following are the immediate neighbours to each other?
  (a) K, E   (b) Q, D
  (c) G, H   (d) W, S   (e) None of these

5. Four of the following five are alike in a certain way and hence form a group. Find the one who does not belong to that group?
  (a) E   (b) D
  (c) G   (d) K   (e) H

Directions (6-9) Study the following sequence of numbers and alphabets and answer the given questions-
P 4 S A W 5 8 F 9 1 R E 7 2 O 3 7 5 1 B 6 K G N

6. How many numbers are there which are immediately preceded by a vowel?
  (a) One   (b) None
  (c) Two   (d) Three   (e) None of these

7. If all the numbers are removed from the given series, then which among the following element is seventh from the right end?

  (a) E   (b) O
  (c) F   (d) R   (e) None of these

8. If all the consonants are removed from the given series, then which among the following element is ninth from the left end?
  (a) 2   (b) O
  (c) 3   (d) 7   (e) None of these

9. Which among the following element is fifth to the left of twelfth element from the left end?
  (a) F   (b) 8
  (c) 9   (d) 1   (e) None of these

Directions (10-12) Study the following information carefully and answer the questions given below:
Five persons A, B, C, D and E have different heights. Less than two persons are shorter than D. As many persons are taller than D as shorter than C. A is taller than B but shorter than E. B is not the shortest person. The height of third tallest person is 86 cm.

10. If the height of shortest person is 68 cm, then what may be the height of B?
  (a) 69 cm
  (b) 81 cm
  (c) 78 cm
  (d) All the given heights
  (e) None of these

11. How many persons are taller than C?
  (a) None   (b) One
  (c) Two   (d) Three   (e) None of these

12. Who among the following is just shorter than E?
  (a) None   (b) C
  (c) A   (d) D   (e) None of these

Directions (13-16) In each of the questions below are given some statements followed by some conclusions. You have to take the given statements to be true even if they seem to be at variance with commonly known facts. Read all the conclusions and then decide which of the given conclusions logically follows from the given statements disregarding commonly known facts.

13. Statements: All Greens are Yellows. No Yellows are Black.
  Conclusions: I. No Greens are Black.
                II. Some Greens are Black.
  (a) If only conclusion I follows.
  (b) If only conclusion II follows.

(c) If either conclusion I or II follows.
(d) If neither conclusion I nor II follows.
(e) If both conclusions I and II follow.

14. Statements: All Chairs are Sofas. Only a few Sofas are Beds. No Beds are Curtains.

Conclusions: I. Some Sofas are not Beds.
II. Some Sofas are not Curtains.

(a) If only conclusion I follows.
(b) If only conclusion II follows.
(c) If either conclusion I or II follows.
(d) If neither conclusion I nor II follows.
(e) If both conclusions I and II follow.

15. Statements: Only a few Coffee are Tea. All Tea is Drinks. Only a few Drinks are Cold drinks.

Conclusions: I. Some Tea is not Cold drinks.
II. No Coffee are Drinks.

(a) If only conclusion I follows.
(b) If only conclusion II follows.
(c) If either conclusion I or II follows.
(d) If neither conclusion I nor II follows.
(e) If both conclusions I and II follow.

16. Statements: All Flowers are Trees. Only a few Trees are Gardens. No Gardens are Lawns.

Conclusions: I. All Lawns can never be Trees
II. Some Flowers can be Gardens

(a) If only conclusion I follows.
(b) If only conclusion II follows.
(c) If either conclusion I or II follows.
(d) If neither conclusion I nor II follows.
(e) If both conclusions I and II follow.

Directions (17-21) Study the following information carefully and answer the questions given below:

Seven persons A, B, C, D, E, F and G are sitting in row and all are facing towards north but not necessarily in the same order. B sits second from one of the extreme ends. Three persons sit between D and B. Two persons sit between D and A. C sits to the immediate left of A. F sits to left of C but is not an immediate neighbour of C. More than two persons sit between F and E.

17. How many persons sit to the left of F?
(a) Two   (b) None
(c) One   (d) Three   (e) None of these

18. Who among the following sits third to the right of G?
(a) E   (b) C
(c) B   (d) F   (e) None of these

19. Who among the following persons sit at the extreme ends?
(a) F, A   (b) A, E
(c) G, E   (d) F, E   (e) None of these

20. How many persons sit between D and E?
(a) Two   (b) Four
(c) Three   (d) One   (e) None of these

21. Who among the following sits to the immediate left of E?
(a) G   (b) A
(c) B   (d) D   (e) None of these

Directions (22-23) Study the following information carefully and answer the questions given below:

Point D is 10m north of point P. Point Y is 14m east of point D. Point Q is 8m north of point Y. Point S is 20m west of point Q. Point H is 8m south of point S.

22. What is the shortest distance between point H and point D?
(a) 8m   (b) 6m
(c) 4m   (d) 10m   (e) None of these

23. In which direction is point P with respect to point Q?
(a) South east
(b) North west
(c) South west
(d) North east
(e) None of these

Directions (24-27) Study the following information carefully and answer the questions given below:

There are certain number of persons sitting in a row facing towards north direction. A sits fifth to the right of B. Two persons sit between C and B. D sits fourth to the left of C. Four persons sit to the left of D. The number of persons sit between D and B is same as the number of persons sit between B and F. F sits at fourth position from one of the extreme ends.

24. How many persons sit between B and D?
(a) None   (b) Six
(c) Five   (d) Four   (e) None of these

25. How many persons sit in the row?
(a) Twenty
(b) Twenty-one
(c) Twenty-two
(d) Nineteen
(e) None of these

26. Who among the following sits second to the right of A?
(a) None   (b) C
(c) D   (d) F   (e) None of these

27. How many persons sit to the right of B?
(a) Nine   (b) Ten
(c) Eight   (d) Eleven   (e) None of these

28. How many such pairs of letters are there in the meaningful word 'MATCHES' each of which has as many letters between them in the word as in

the English alphabet (From both backward and forward)?
(a) Two
(b) One
(c) More than three
(d) Three
(e) None of these

Directions (29-33) Study the following sequence carefully and answer the given questions.

COT   IVY   PEA   FOX   MRU

29. If we add 'L' after first letter in every word, then how many meaningful words will be formed?
    (a) None   (b) Three
    (c) Two   (d) One   (e) None of these

30. If third letter of each word is replaced by its succeeding letter according to English alphabetical order, then in how many words vowels will appear more than once?
    (a) Two   (b) One
    (c) None   (d) Three   (e) None of these

31. If all the words are arranged according to English alphabetical order from left to right, then which word will appear fourth from the left end?
    (a) MRU   (b) FOX
    (c) PEA   (d) IVY   (e) None of these

32. If all the letters are arranged according to English alphabetical order within each word, then in how many words vowel will appear at second position?
    (a) One   (b) None
    (c) Two   (d) Three   (e) None of these

33. How many letters are there in English alphabetical series between the first letter of the second word from the left end and third letter of the third word from the right end?
    (a) Five   (b) Six
    (c) Seven   (d) Four   (e) None of these

34. If in the number '35982476', 1 is added to each even digit and 2 is subtracted from each odd digit, then which digits will not appear twice in the number thus obtained?
    (a) Only 1
    (b) Only 9
    (c) Both '1' and '9'
    (d) Only 5

(e) None of these

Directions (35-39) Study the following information carefully and answer the questions given below:

Six people P, Q, R, S, T and U have events on different dates 7th and 12th of different months i.e. January, February and March. D has event on even numbered date in the month having 31 days. The number of persons have event before D is same as the number of persons have event after A. One person has event between A and C. F has event before C. B has event just before E.

35. How many persons have event before B?
    (a) Two   (b) None
    (c) Three   (d) One   (e) None of these

36. Who among the following has event just after D?
    (a) C   (b) None
    (c) B   (d) F   (e) None of these

37. How many persons have event between F and D?
    (a) One   (b) Three
    (c) None   (d) Two   (e) None of these

38. E has event on which among the following date?
    (a) 12th February
    (b) 12th March
    (c) 7th March
    (d) 7th January
    (e) None of these

39. Four of the following five are alike in a certain way and hence form a group. Which is the one that does not belong to that group?
    (a) A, F   (b) E, F
    (c) F, C   (d) E, B   (e) C, B

40. Four of the following five are alike in a certain way and hence form a group. Which is the one that does not belong to that group?
    (a) RUY   (b) SQO
    (c) OMK   (d) FDB   (e) YWU

Directions (41-45) Line graph given below shows number of passengers travelling in five (A, B, C, D & E) different compartment of a trains. Read the data carefully and answer the questions.

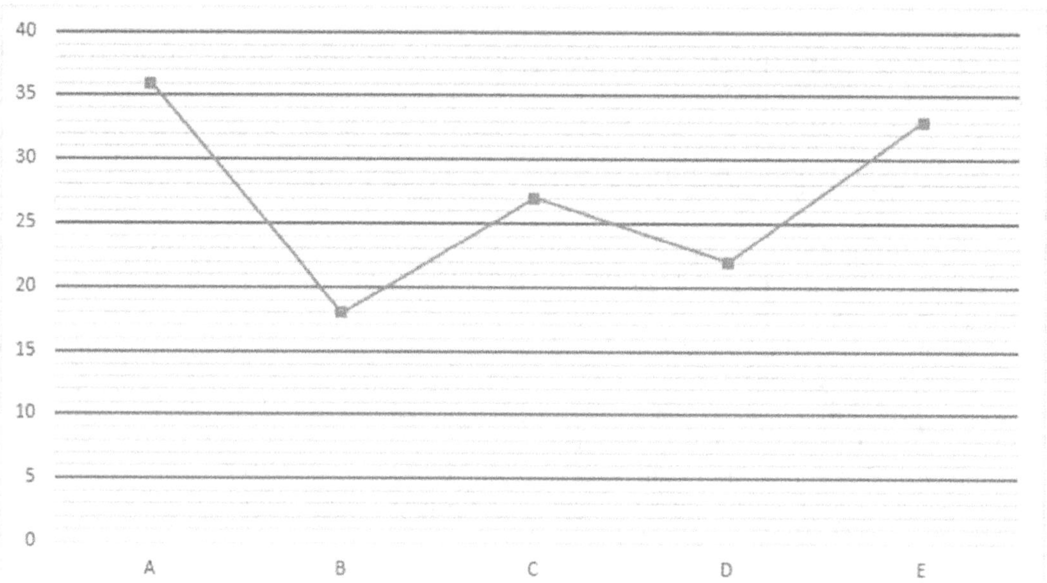

41. Total passengers in E are what percent less than total passengers in A?
    (a) 6 ¼ %   (b) 8 ⅓%
    (c) 6 ⅓%   (d) 6 ⅔%   (e) 5%

42. Find average number of passengers in A, C & E?
    (a) 32   (b) 30
    (c) 36   (d) 33   (e) 27

43. Find the ratio of total passenger in B to that of in D?
    (a) 7 : 9   (b) 9 : 10
    (c) 11 : 9   (d) 9 : 13   (e) 9 : 11

44. Total passenger in C and E together are what percent more than total passenger in A?
    (a) 33 ⅓%   (b) 66 ⅔%
    (c) 66 ⅓%   (d) 50%   (e) 60%

45. Find total number of passengers traveling in B, C & D together?
    (a) 69   (b) 65
    (c) 67   (d) 63   (e) 71

Directions (46-50) What will come in the place of question (?) mark in following questions.

46. 12, 12, 24, 72, ?, 1440
    (a) 256   (b) 288
    (c) 284   (d) 296   (e) 316

47. 16, 17.8, 21.4, 28.6, 43, ?
    (a) 69.8   (b) 72.8
    (c) 73.8   (d) 70.8   (e) 71.8

48. 12, 7, 8, 13, ?, 68.5
    (a) 28   (b) 27
    (c) 26   (d) 27.5   (e) 26.5

49. 72, 79, 65, 93, ?, 149
    (a) 36   (b) 31
    (c) 33   (d) 37   (e) 35

50. 8, 9, 19, 58, 233, ?
    (a) 1164   (b) 1166
    (c) 1156   (d) 1152   (e) 1158

51. If the difference between the present age of P and Q is three years and the ratio between the age of P and Q after two years will be 5 : 4, then find the age of P after two years (in years)?
    (a) 15   (b) 13
    (c) 18   (d) 16   (e) 14

52. A and B both spend 30% of their income together which is equal to Rs. 26400. If income of A is 20% more than that of B, then find the income of B (in Rs.)?
    (a) 52000   (b) 48000
    (c) 40000   (d) 36000   (e) 30000

53. If a man invests equal sum at the same rate of interest on simple interest for T and T+4 years and the respective ratio of interest gets by man is 1:2 respectively, then find 'T'?
    (a) 6   (b) 2
    (c) 5   (d) 3   (e) 4

54. 12 women can complete a work in 64 day, then find how many women will be required to complete 2/3 rd of the same work in 16 days?
    (a) 28   (b) 24
    (c) 36   (d) 32   (e) 48

55. A train running at the speed of 72 kmph crosses a pole in 30 seconds. Find the time taken by the same train to cross the pole with the speed of 54 kmph (in sec)?
(a) 42   (b) 48
(c) 54   (d) 45   (e) 40

56. The upstream speed and downstream speed of a boat is 10 kmph and 14 kmph respectively and boat travelled for T hours & 6 hours in upstream and downstream respectively. If the distance travelled in downstream is 44 km more than upstream, then find the value of 'T'
(a) 4   (b) 3
(c) 6   (d) 5   (e) 8

57. An article was marked up by 50% above cost price and allowed Rs 50 discount on marked price. If shopkeeper still made a profit of Rs. 50, then find the selling price of the article (in Rs.)?
(a) 350 Rs.   (b) 300 Rs.
(c) 250 Rs.   (d) 200 Rs.   (e) 150 Rs.

58. A & B invested Rs. X and Rs. (X + 800) for same period of time in a business. If A gets Rs. 3200 as profit share out of total profit of Rs. 6800, then find 'X'?
(a) 7800   (b) 6000
(c) 8400   (d) 7200   (e) 6400

59. A vessel contains mixture of milk and water in the ration of 3 : 1 respectively. If 20 liters mixture taken out from the vessel and now the difference between milk and water in the remaining mixture is 70 liters, then find initial mixture in vessel (in liters)?
(a) 240   (b) 160
(c) 120   (d) 80   (e) 180

60. Perimeter of a rectangle is 2 cm more than circumference of a circle and area of circle is 616 cm². If breath of rectangle is equal to radius of circle, then find length of rectangle (in cm)?
(a) 35   (b) 33
(c) 31   (d) 21   (e) 27

Directions (61-65) Table given below shows number of orders received by three (P, Q & R) companies of their three (A, B & C) items. Read the data carefully and answer the questions.

Companies	A	B	C
P	80	60	50
Q	40	70	90
R	80	100	30

61. Total orders of item A & B received by R is how much more than total orders of item B & C received by Q?
(a) 50   (b) 10
(c) 40   (d) 20   (e) 30

62. Find total orders (all three items) received by R is what percent more than that of total orders (all three items) received by Q?

(a) 5%   (b) 12.5%
(c) 10%   (d) 15%   (e) 20%

63. Find ratio of total orders of item A & B received by P to total orders of item B & C received by Q?
(a) 7 : 9   (b) 8 : 7
(c) 4 : 7   (d) 5 : 6   (e) 7 : 8

64. Find average number of orders of item B received by Q & R is what percent of total orders of item A received by P?
(a) 104 ¼ %   (b) 106 ¼ %
(c) 108 ¼ %   (d) 102 ¼ %   (e) 110 ¼ %

65. Find total orders of item A, B & C received by P?
(a) 210   (b) 220
(c) 190   (d) 180   (e) 200

Directions (66-80) What should come in place of question mark (?) in following questions?

66. (48% of 625) ÷ 0.75 = ?
(a) 800
(b) None of these
(c) 40
(d) 4000
(e) 400

67. $\dfrac{(4)^6 + (18)^2}{7^2 + 121 - 73} = ?$
(a) 1   (b) 2
(c) 4   (d) 5   (e) 3

68. $(4)^7 \times 2 = \dfrac{(16)^2}{\sqrt[4]{16}}$
(a) 2   (b) 3
(c) 4   (d) 1   (e) None of these

69. 4× (? + 120 = (8)³
(a) 6   (b) 12
(c) 8   (d) 4   (e) 16

70. ? + 432 – 205 = 550
(a) 384   (b) 244
(c) 224   (d) 276   (e) 324

71. 12×8+(?)² = (14)²
(a) 10   (b) 12
(c) 8   (d) 6   (e) 9

72. 40% of 400 + ? % of 300 = 250
(a) 40   (b) 36
(c) 25   (d) 30   (e) 20

73. $\sqrt{441} \div 7 = ? - 180$
(a) 185   (b) 183
(c) 187   (d) 184   (e) 182

74. $\sqrt{576} - \sqrt{144} + \sqrt{729} = 36 + ?$
(a) 1   (b) 4
(c) 5   (d) 2   (e) 3

75. 119 + 41 + 9 = ?²
(a) 10   (b) 13
(c) 17   (d) 8   (e) 16

76. 12% (? + 100) = 18
(a) 40   (b) 50
(c) 30   (d) 100   (e) 60

77. $\dfrac{\sqrt[3]{1331}}{11} + \sqrt{81} + ? = 27$
(a) 19   (b) 18

(c) 17   (d) 16   (e) 15

78. $?^2 + \sqrt{400} = 6^2$

(a) 3   (b) 4

(c) 2   (d) 1   (e) 5

79. $9\frac{1}{3} + 7\frac{1}{2} = ? + 5\frac{1}{6} + 6\frac{1}{3}$

(a) 4   (b) 4 ½

(c) 5   (d) 5⅙   (e) 6

80. $(3^4 \times 9^7) \div 27^6 = 3?$

(a) 2   (b) 3

(c) 0   (d) 6   (e) 7

Solutions

REASONING ABILITY

Directions (1-5)

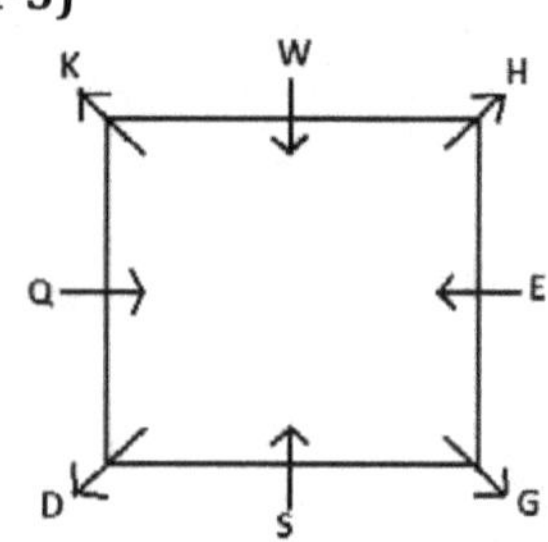

1. (b)   2. (d)   3. (c)
4. (b)   5. (a)   6. (c)
7. (d)   8. (a)   9. (b)

Directions (10-12)

$C > E > A (86) > B > D$

10. (d)
11. (a)
12. (c)

Directions (13-16)

13. (a)

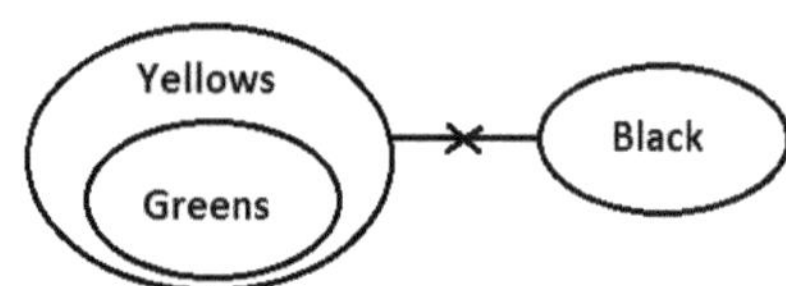

S14. (e)

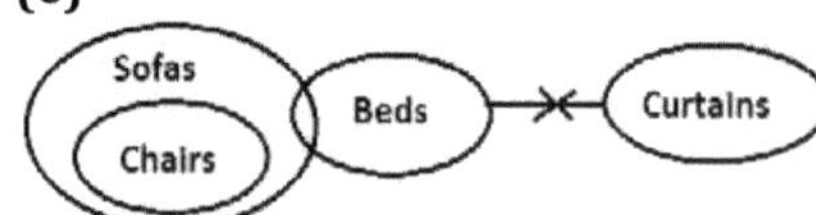

15. (d)

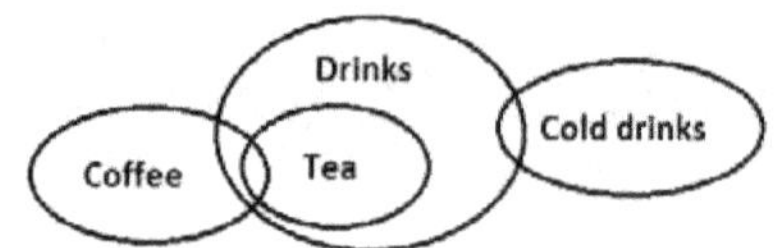

16. (b)

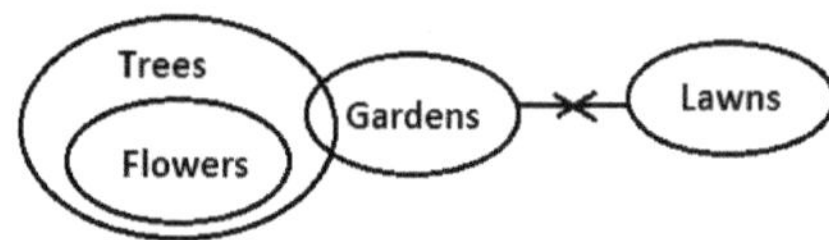

Directions (17-21)

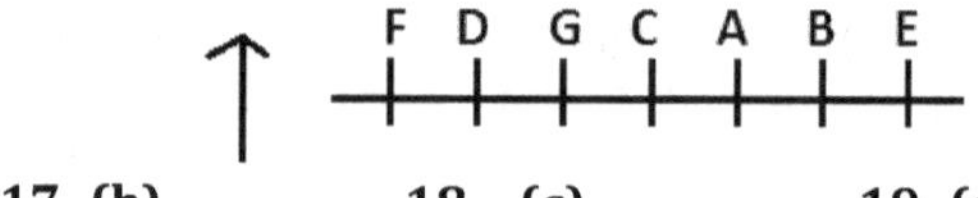

17. (b)   18. (c)   19. (d)
20. (b)   21. (c)

Directions (22-23)

22. (b)

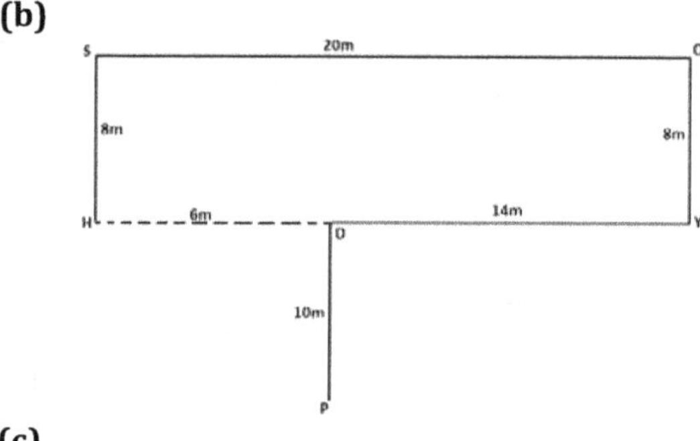

23. (c)

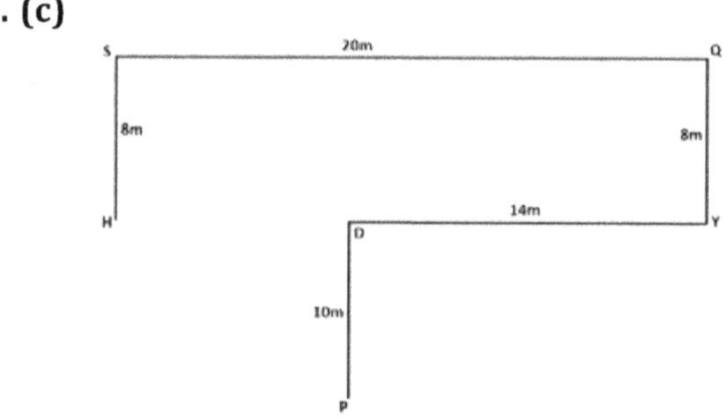

Directions (24-27)

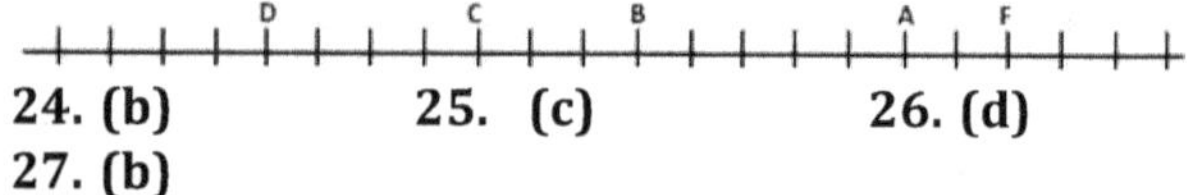

24. (b)   25. (c)   26. (d)
27. (b)
28. (c)

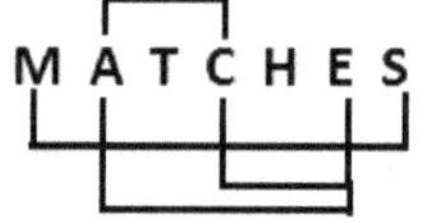

Directions (29-33)

29. (c)   30. (b)   31. (a)
32. (d)   33. (c)
34. (c)   3 5 9 8 2 4 7 6
        1 3 7 9 3 5 5 7

Months	7th	12th
January	A	F
February	C	B
March	E	D

Quantitative Aptitude

41. (b) Required percentage $= \frac{36-33}{36} \times 100$

$= \frac{3}{36} \times 100 = 8\frac{1}{3}\%$

42. (a) Required average $= \frac{36+27+33}{3} = 32$

43. (e) Required ratio $= 18 : 22 = 9 : 11$

44. (b) Total passenger in C and E $= 27 + 33 = 60$

Required percentage $= \frac{60-36}{36} \times 100$

$= \frac{24}{36} \times 100 = 66\frac{2}{3}\%$

45. (c) Required number of passengers $= 18 + 27 + 22 = 67$

46. (b) Pattern of series –

$12 \times 1 = 12$

$12 \times 2 = 24$

$24 \times 3 = 72$

$? = 72 \times 4 = 288$

$288 \times 5 = 1440$

47. (e) Pattern of series –

$16 + 1.8 = 17.8$

$17.8 + 3.6 = 21.4$

$21.4 + 7.2 = 28.6$

$28.6 + 14.4 = 43$

$? = 43 + 28.8 = 71.8$

48. (b) Pattern of series –

$12 \times 0.5 + 1 = 7$

$7 \times 1 + 1 = 8$

$8 \times 1.5 + 1 = 13$

$? = 13 \times 2 + 1 = 27$

$27 \times 2.5 + 1 = 68.5$

49. (d) Pattern of series –

$72 + 7 = 79$

$79 - 14 = 65$

$65 + 28 = 93$

$? = 93 - 56 = 37$

$37 + 112 = 149$

50. (b) Pattern of series –

$8 \times 1 + 1 = 9$

$9 \times 2 + 1 = 19$

$19 \times 3 + 1 = 58$

$58 \times 4 + 1 = 233$

$233 \times 5 + 1 = 1166$

51. (a) Let present age of Q = t years

So, present age of P = (t + 3) years

ATQ –

$\frac{t+2}{(t+3)+2} = \frac{4}{5}$

t = 10 years

So, Age of P after two years $= (10 + 3) + 2 = 15$ year

52. (c) Let total income of B = 100x Rs.

So, total income of A $= 100x \times \left(1 + \frac{20}{100}\right) = 120x$ Rs.

ATQ –

$(100x + 120x) \times \frac{30}{100} = 26400$

$66x = 26400$

x = 400 Rs.

So, income of B $= 400 \times 100 = 40000$ Rs.

53. (e) Let sum invested by man = Rs. X

And, rate of interest = r%

ATQ-

$\frac{X \times r \times T}{X \times r \times (T+4)} = \frac{1}{2}$

$\frac{T}{(T+4)} = \frac{1}{2} \Rightarrow T = 4$

54. (d) Let total work $= 12 \times 64 = 768$ units

Required women $= 768 \times \frac{2}{3} \times \frac{1}{16} = 32$

55. (e) Let length of train be 'l' meters

ATQ –

$72 \times \frac{5}{18} = \frac{l}{30}$

l = 600 meters

Required time $= \frac{600}{54 \times \frac{5}{18}} = 40$ sec

56. (a) ATQ –

$14 \times 6 - 10 \times T = 44$

$10T = 40$

$T = 4$

57. (c) Let cost price of article = 100x Rs.

So, marked price of article $= 100x \times \left(1 + \frac{50}{100}\right) = 150x$ Rs.

And, selling price of article = (150x – 50) Rs.

ATQ –

$(150x - 50) - 100x = 50$

$50x = 100$

x = 2 Rs.

So, selling price of article $= (150 \times 2 - 50) = 250$ Rs.

58. (e) ATQ –

$\frac{X}{(X+800)} = \frac{3200}{(6800-3200)}$

$X = 6400$

59. (b) Let total initial mixture in vessel = 4x

So, milk in vessel = 3x

And water in vessel = x

ATQ –

$(3x - 20 \times \frac{3x}{4x}) - (x - 20 \times \frac{x}{4x}) = 70$

$(3x - 15) - (x - 5) = 70$

$2x = 80$

$x = 40$

So, initial mixture in vessel = 4x = 4 × 40 = 160 liters

60. (c) Let radius of circle be 'r' cm

ATQ –

$\frac{22}{7} \times r \times r = 616$

r = 14 cm = breath of rectangle

Let length of rectangle be 'l' cm

Perimeter of rectangle = circumference of a circle + 2

$2(14 + l) = 2 \times \frac{22}{7} \times 14 + 2$

$2(14 + l) = 90$

l = 31 cm

61. (d) Required difference = (80 + 100) – (70 + 90) = 20

62. (a) Total orders (all three items) received by R = (80 + 100 + 30) = 210

Total orders (all three items) received by Q = (40 + 70 + 90) = 200

Required percentage = $\frac{210-200}{200} \times 100 = 5\%$

63. (e) Total orders of item A & B received by P = 80 + 60 = 140

Total orders of item B & C received by Q = 70 + 90 = 160

Required ratio = 140 : 160 = 7 : 8

64. (b) Average number of orders of item B received by Q & R = $\frac{70+100}{2} = 85$

Required percentage = $\frac{85}{80} \times 100 = 106\frac{1}{4}\%$

65. (c) Required sum = 80 + 60 + 50 = 190

66. (e) $\frac{48}{100} \times 625 \times \frac{4}{3} = ? \Rightarrow ? = 400$

67. (c) $\frac{64+324}{97} = ?$

$? = 4$

68. (b) $4^? \times 2 = \frac{256}{2}$

$4^? = 64$

$4^? = (4)^3$

$? = 3$

69. (c) $4 \times ? = 512 - 480$

$? = \frac{32}{4}$

$? = 8$

70. (e) $? + 432 - 206 = 550$

$? = 550 - 226$

$? = 324$

71. (a) $(?)^2 = 196 - 96$

$?^2 = 100 \Rightarrow ? = 10$

72. (d) $\frac{40}{100} \times 400 + \frac{300}{100} \times ? = 250$

$160 + 3 \times ? = 250$

$? = \frac{90}{3} = 30$

73. (b) $\div 7 = ? -180$

$? = 183$

74. (e) $24 - 12 + 27 = 36 + ?$

$? = 3$

75. (b) $119 + 41 + 9 = ?^2$

$? = 13$

76. (b) $\frac{12}{100} \times (? +100) = 18$

$? = 150 - 100$

$? = 50$

77. (c) $\frac{11}{11} + 9 + ? = 27$

$1 + 9 + ? = 27$

$? = 17$

78. (b) $?^2 + 20 = 36$

$?^2 = 16 \Rightarrow ? = 4$

79. (d) $? = 9\frac{1}{3} + 7\frac{1}{2} - 5\frac{1}{6} - 6\frac{1}{3}$

$? = 9 + 7 - 5 - 6 \left(\frac{1}{3} + \frac{1}{2} - \frac{1}{6} - \frac{1}{3}\right)$

$? = 5\frac{1}{6}$

80. (c) $\frac{3^4 \times 3^{7\times2}}{3^{6\times3}} = 3^?$

$3^? = 3^{4+14-18}$

$3^? = 3^0$

$? = 0$